W9-BCF-896

THE CASH BOX CHARTS
FOR
THE POST-MODERN AGE
1978–1988

by
FRANK HOFFMANN
and
GEORGE ALBERT

The Scarecrow Press, Inc.
Metuchen, N.J., & London
1994

British Library Cataloguing-in-Publication data available

Library of Congress Cataloging-in-Publication Data

Hoffmann, Frank W., 1949–
    The Cash box charts for the post-modern age 1978–1988 / by Frank
Hoffman[n] and George Albert.
      p.   cm.
    Includes bibliographical references and index.
    ISBN 0-8108-2850-2 (alk. paper)
    1. Popular music—United States—1971–1980—Discography.   2. Popular
music—United States—1981–1990—Discography.   I. Albert, George.   II.
Cash box.   III. Title.
ML 156.4.P6H5895   1994
016.78164'0266—dc20

                                               93-51246

TABLE OF CONTENTS

Table of Contents

INTRODUCTION

This volume represents a notable departure from the seven previous titles in Scarecrow's *Cash Box* chart compilation series in that (1) it is devoted to one dozen different charts rather than one particular listing, (2) many of the genres/media formats have been covered for a comparatively short period of time, and (3) combined, these various charts provide a fascinating glimpse at the sociocultural changes affecting the United States—and the world at large—during the past decade. Many of the media formats included in this volume were not a force within the home consumer market prior to the 1980s; now some of them (*e.g.,* compact discs, videocassettes) seem likely to dominate the entertainment business well into the twenty-first century.

The primary purpose of *The Cash Box Charts for the Post-Modern Age* is to make available to the widest possible public the wealth of data contained in these various charts over roughly a ten-year period (late 1978 through 1988). This information, previously available only through a search of the weekly charts themselves, has been completely integrated and accessed via artist and format-title entries. The compilation contains features not presently available in any other reference tool of its type. In addition to its wide time span of coverage, most notable is the week-by-week listing of chart positions. Given the date of chart entry for each item, it becomes possible to determine its exact position for any particular date.

Cash Box has been a leader in reflecting and analyzing the developments within the entertainment industry for almost fifty years. This authorized compilation should represent an invaluable source for students, scholars, educators, librarians, retailers, radio and television programmers, and record and video collectors and hobbyists.

An introduction has been provided to each chart in order to define the role of the genre or medium within the greater context of the entertainment business. The end of 1988 was determined to be a logical cut-off date in that *Cash Box* adopted an entirely new line-up of charts beginning in January 1989.

ORGANIZATION OF THIS WORK

The American Library Association's filing rules were generally followed in organizing the raw data in the various artist and title sections, the rationale being that these procedures are both workable and widely employed by librarians and educators. A few exceptions were adopted in order to enhance the utility of the work while taking into account certain idiosyncrasies of the music industry.

—Any group of letters that spell a word (and are not acronyms) are filed under the word spelled. For example, "L-O-V-E" is filed as "love."

—All contracted forms of personal pronouns—I, you, they, we, he, and she—are alphabetized together.

A few general rules should be noted in order to optimize use of this reference tool:

—An alphabetical arrangement is employed in all artist and title indexes. Artist indexes are subdivided alphabetically by format title for each artist.

—Artists, both solo and group, are entered under the last name (if one exists). Otherwise, the first word dictates point of entry.

—If a record, video clip, etc., has been performed by two or more artists, the artist listed first functions as the main entry. "See also" references have been provided for all additional artists.

—Complete titles have been provided for all of the artist and title indexes.

—"See also" references in caps (within parentheses) have been provided in the artist indexes to denote (1) group affiliations of solo performers, and (2) members of a group possessed of hit recordings as a solo artist. Members of a group who have not enjoyed hits as soloists are not cited unless they have had hits with another group. The most comprehensive listing of group affiliations for those soloists possessed of more than one such affiliation can be found under the artist's solo recording name. Those affiliations which have not resulted in a hit have not been noted. The designation has also not been employed in cases where the same name appears in two successive entries; *e.g.,* Gladys Knight (solo artist) and Gladys Knight & The Pips (group artist).

—"Featuring," "and," and "with" are all treated as the same word with respect to the alphabetizing of duos, trios, etc.

—Parentheses have been employed within the chart-position data in the artist sections to designate the number of weeks off the chart prior to reentry; *e.g.,* "60,(2),56,40,20,60" indicates that the item was on the chart at #60, fell off for two weeks, and re-entered at #56, #40, etc. Titles falling off the charts for a period of time of more than three months have been treated as another title (*i.e.,* entry).

COMPACT DISCS

A. INTRODUCTION

It could be argued that the compact disc charts were doomed to a comparatively short lifespan. From its introduction by U.S. labels in late 1983, the medium represented, as had the various audiotape formats (*e.g.,* cassettes, 8-tracks), another version of the longplaying (33 1/3 r.p.m.) vinyl record. As was the case with the midline-priced album, CD's merited the special recognition accorded by a separate chart in view of the following factors:

(1) The early consumers of the compact disc were substantially different from the at-large record-buying public. Given the high cost (generally over twice the retail cost of record albums) and inherent snob appeal of the CD, its initial supporters tended to be intellectually sophisticated and well-heeled, financially speaking. These consumers also tended to be somewhat more conservative—and less trendy—than other record buyers.

(2) The medium's promise of enhanced acoustic returns helped dictate which genres received the earliest emphasis—*e.g.,* pop classics, progressive AOR rock. Classical music in general, spurred both by far-sighted industry leadership and a devoted hardcore audience willing to pay the price for top quality sound reproduction, began implementing the digital recording process almost a full decade prior to the widespread availability of the CD, the medium best suited to displaying such technological advancements to the consumer.

(3) The early CD catalog—abroad as well as stateside—was not representative of the large number and diversity of titles

1

available in print in the comparable formats (as evidenced in the monthly listings of the record industry's leading commercial discography, *The Schwann Catalog*).

Market considerations aside, the idiosyncrasies of record label executives as well as problems in negotiating royalty rates (witness the protracted efforts behind the release of the back catalogs of artists such as the Beatles, the Beach Boys, and the Phil Spector stable of artists) assured that during the 1984–1987 period the CD listings bore only a passing resemblance to the mainstream album charts. However, the increasing attention given the contemporary catalog by record executives—a key development at this time consisted of the simultaneous release of new titles in the record album, cassette, and CD formats—combined with the changeover of a significant percentage of record buyers to the newer medium (by 1988 CD's were reported to be running ahead of vinyl three-to-one in total unit sales) far more quickly than even the most optimistic industry insiders had foreseen, led to a gradual diminishing of the differences between the compact disc and album charts. Accordingly, with the deletion of its CD charts beginning the week of June 25, 1988, *Cash Box* (as it had done previously with the cassette and the 8-track tape) simply incorporated the sales action associated with this medium into its longrunning album listing.

Initial chart title/title changes: "Top 30 Compact Discs"/"Top 40 Compact Discs" (June 1, 1985–June 18, 1988)

Beginning date/termination date (last week chart included): September 15, 1984/June 18, 1988

Initial number of positions/changes in number of positions: 30/40 (June 1, 1985–June 18, 1988)

B. ARTIST INDEX

AC/DC

3-12-88　*Blow Up Your Video*　(Atl. 2-81828)　14, 12, 16, 20, 23, 21, 21, 24,
24, 27, 36　(11)

ACADEMY OF ST. MARTIN-IN-THE-FIELDS/NEVILLE MARRINER

9-15-84　*Brandenburg Concertos, Vol. 1*　(Philips 400 076-2)　22　(1)

9-15-84　*Brandenburg Concertos, Vol. 2*　(Philips 400 077-2)　23　(1)

12-29-84　*Tchaikovsky: Nutcracker Suite, Serenade For Strings*　(Philips 411 471-
2)　29, 29, 27, 29　(4)

ADAMS, BRYAN

4-18-87　*Into The Fire*　(A&M CD 3907)　35, 28, 24, 20, 18, 13, 10, 11, 17,
17, 20, 27, 28, 28, 31, 31, 35, 34, 35, 38　(20)

2-02-85　*Reckless*　(A&M CD 5013)　24, 19, 15, 13, 13, 12, 16, 19, 21, 21, 19,
18, 17, 17, 17, 17, 16, 16, 15, 15, 19, 21, 21, 19, 17, 15, 13, 9, 9, 9, 8,
8, 10, 10, 8, 8, 8, 8, 8, 9, 12, 12, 11, 10, 14, 13, 13, 13, 12, 12, 16, 19,
26, 25, 31, 29, 30, 27, 25, 26, 26, 25, 23, 23, 25, 26, 26, 32, 31, 33,
35　(71)

AEROSMITH

9-19-87　*Permanent Vacation*　(Geffen 24162-2)　29, 26, 26, 21, 18, 15, 15,
22, 27, 23, 25, 24, 24, 25, 23, 23, 23, 26, 24, 27, 27, 27, 28, 29, 33,
34, 36, 36, 35, 36, 35, 36, 35, 36, 36, 33, 33, 33, 37, 37　(40)

A-HA

11-16-85　*Hunting High And Low*　(WB 25300)　28, 25, 21, 18, 16, 22, 22, 30,
30, 37, 34, 32, 35, 37, 40　(15)

ALABAMA

5-10-86　*Greatest Hits*　(RCA PCD1-7170)　37, 36, 32　(3)

AMADEUS

2-02-85   *{Original Film Soundtrack}*   (Fantasy FCD-900-1791-2)   25, 22, 21, 21, 26, 28, 27, 27, 26, 26, 28   (11)

ASIA

2-01-86   *Astra*   (Geffen 24072)   33, 32, 33, 38, 39, 38, 39, 40   (8)

ASTLEY, RICK

3-12-88   *Whenever You Need Somebody*   (RCA 6822-2-R)   16, 11, 13, 16, 20, 25, 27, 28, 29, 39   (10)

ATLANTA SYMPHONY ORCHESTRA/LANE

10-27-84   *Copland: Appalachian Spring, Rodeo, Fanfare For The Common Man*   (Telarc CD-80040)   27, 26, 25, 30, 30   (5)

ATLANTA SYMPHONY ORCHESTRA/ROBERT SHAW

12-08-84   *The Many Moods Of Christmas*   (Telarc CD-80087)   28, 27, 28, 28, 28, 29   (6)

BACK TO THE FUTURE

10-19-85   *{Original Film Soundtrack}*   (MCA MCAD 6144)   24, 20, 16, 13, 13, 16, 28, 29, 34, 37, 37, 40, 40   (13)

BAKER, ANITA

6-21-86   *Rapture*   (Elektra 60444-2)   37, 35, 37   (3)

8-23-86   *Rapture*   (Elektra 60444-2)   30, 29, 22, 21, 29, 29, 29, 31, 32, 32, 36, 39   (12)

1-31-87   *Rapture*   (Elektra 60444-2)   25, 19, 15, 16, 14, 9, 18, 13, 15, 15, 17, 19, 10, 16, 15, 26, 20, 18, 18, 15, 15, 16, 18, 24, 19, 20, 20, 21, 20, 29, 32, 24, 19, 19, 20, 28, 35, 37, 39, 38, 40   (41)

BANANARAMA

10-11-86   *True Confessions*   (London/PolyGram 828 013-2)   25, 23, 24, 34, 40   (5)

THE BANGLES

4-05-86 *Different Light* (Col. CK 40039) 37, 34, 29, 27, 24, 24, 24, 26, 37, 39, 40 (11)

2-21-87 *Different Light* (Col. CK 40039) 23, 16, 10, 14, 14, 17, 23, 36 (8)

THE BEASTIE BOYS

3-21-87 *Licensed To Ill* (Def Jam/Col. CK 40238) 36, 23, 20, 31, 32, 34, 27, 22, 34, 29, 29, 32, 35, 35, 38, 40 (16)

THE BEATLES *(See also:* GEORGE HARRISON; JOHN LENNON; PAUL McCARTNEY)

11-07-87 *Abbey Road* (Cap. CDP7 46446 2) 3, 2, 1, 2, 3, 6, 7, 11, 11, 11, 11, 11, 12, 16, 19, 23, 23, 29, 35, 37, 37, 40, 40 (23)

3-14-87 *Beatles For Sale* (Cap. CDP7 46439 2) 4, 4, 4, 6, 11, 13, 20, 28, 39, 39 (10)

3-14-87 *A Hard Day's Night* (Cap. CDP7 46437 2) 1, 1, 1, 5, 8, 11, 18, 13, 32 (9)

5-16-87 *Help!* (Cap. CDP7 46439 2) 3, 3, 2, 4, 4, 4, 6, 7, 15, 30, 30, 30, 31, 32, 32, 36, 39, 40 (18)

11-07-87 *Let It Be* (Cap. CDP7 46447 2) 10, 8, 8, 8, 14, 20, 26, 27, 27, 27, 32, 37, 38, 37, 38, 39 (16)

10-17-87 *Magical Mystery Tour* (Cap. CDP7 48062) 11, 4, 8, 13, 18, 20, 28, 32, 35, 38 (10)

3-26-88 *Past Masters, Volume I* (Cap. CDP7 90043 2) 12, 4, 4, 5, 8, 10, 12, 17, 23, 30, 39 (11)

3-26-88 *Past Masters, Volume II* (Cap. CDP7 90044 2) 8, 1, 1, 2, 4, 9, 11, 14, 16, 18, 25, 31, 38 (13)

5-16-87 *Revolver* (Cap. CDP7 46441) 2, 1, 1, 1, 3, 3, 4, 5, 12, 12, 24, 24, 26, 29, 31, 35, 38, 38, 40 (18)

5-16-87 *Rubber Soul* (Cap. CDP7 46440 2) 1, 2, 3, 2, 2, 2, 3, 4, 9, 11, 12, 12, 14, 18, 21, 23, 23, 15, 27, 39 (20)

6-06-87   *Sgt. Pepper's Lonely Hearts Club Band*   (Cap. CDP7 46442 2)   31, 12, 12, 1, 1, 2, 2, 2, 2, 3, 3, 3, 7, 9, 11, 10, 10, 20, 20, 23, 24, 24, 27, 31, 33, 36, 39   (27)

9-12-87   *White Album*   (Cap. CDP7 46443 2/CDP7 46444 2)   25, 14, 3, 1, 3, 5, 7, 6, 9, 13, 14, 22, 27, 32, 33, 33, 33, 33, 33, 32, 34, 33, 35, 36   (24)

3-14-87   *With The Beatles*   (Cap. CDP7 46436 2)   3, 3, 3, 3, 5, 7, 8, 11, 40, 40   (10)

BECK, JEFF

10-05-85   *Flash*   (Epic EK 39483)   23, 20, 18, 22, 26, 37   (6)

BENATAR, PAT

1-25-86   *Seven The Hard Way*   (Chrysalis VK 41507)   29, 27, 26, 27, 33, 34, 36, 37, 38   (9)

12-15-84   *Tropico*   (Chrysalis VK 41471)   21, 17, 16, 16, 15, 14, 15, 14, 14, 19, 26, 28   (12)

BENSON, GEORGE, AND EARL KLUGH

7-18-87   *Collaboration*   (WB 2-25580)   27, 22, 22, 15, 12, 14, 14, 15, 29, 28, 27, 31, 31, 31, 31, 32, 35, 37, 40   (19)

BERNSTEIN, LEONARD

6-15-85   *West Side Story*   (Deutsche Grammophon 415 253-2)   30, 26, 26, 26, 30, 29, 35, 39   (8)

BEVERLY HILLS COP

5-04-85   *{Original Film Soundtrack}*   (MCA MCAD 5553)   23, 21, 20, 19, 18, 17, 16, 15, 13, 14, 14, 13, 13, 12, 14, 14, 15, 15, 16, 15, 17, 17, 20, 21, 21, 33   (26)

BON JOVI

11-29-86   *Slippery When Wet*   (Mer./PolyGram 830 264-2)   31, 18, 6, 7, 4, 4, 4, 4, 6, 3, 2, 2, 3, 3, 5, 6, 5, 5, 5, 10, 10, 4, 3, 5, 7, 8, 11, 9, 8, 7, 7, 12, 12, 10, 22, 23, 23, 24, 26, 30, 29, 34, 35, 38   (43)

BOSTON

11-22-86 *Boston* (Epic EK 34188) 28, 16, 10, 4, 5, 7, 7, 7, 7, 10, 11, 13, 16, 15, 20, 19, 26, 23, 28 (19)

11-15-86 *Third Stage* (MCA MCAD 6188) 24, 14, 1, 2, 2, 3, 2, 2, 2, 2, 3, 7, 11, 10, 9, 10, 14, 21, 17, 16, 19, 27, 29, 30, 38 (25)

BOWIE, DAVID

5-23-87 *Never Let Me Down* (EMI America 46677) 17, 15, 12, 19, 19, 24, 23, 27, 25, 28, 28, 33, 39, 39 (13)

BROWNE, JACKSON

7-05-86 *Lives In The Balance* (Asylum 9 60457-2) 25, 24, 23, 20, 23, 21, 23, 29, 33, 36, 38, 39, 39 (13)

BUFFETT, JIMMY

9-13-86 *Songs You Know By Heart* (MCA MCAD 5633) 24, 23, 23, 36, 40, 40, 40 (7)

BUSH, KATE

11-02-85 *Hounds Of Love* (EMI America CDP7 46164 2) 30, 28, 26, 21, 20, 20, 24, 24, 24, 26, 26, 27, 37 (13)

2-07-87 *The Whole Story* (EMI America CDP7 46414 2) 31, 24, 30, 32, 39 (5)

CAMEO

1-31-87 *Word Up* (A.A. 830 265-2) 28, 26, 26, 24, 24, 30, 36, 37, 38, 30 (10)

CARLISLE, BELINDA

8-16-86 *Belinda Carlisle* (I.R.S. 5741) 24, 21, 21, 20, 19, 25, 25, 32, 39, 39, 39, 40 (12)

THE CARS

9-19-87 *Door To Door* (Elektra 9 60747-2) 24, 21, 16, 24, 33 (5)

1-18-86   *Greatest Hits*   (Elektra 9 60464-2)   28, 21, 20, 23, 26, 27, 27, 29, 27, 24, 21, 18, 16, 12, 11, 11, 11, 11, 11, 12, 16, 17, 20, 20, 23, 25, 31, 37, 38   (29)

9-15-84   *Heartbeat City*   (Elektra 9 60296-2)   9, 8, 7, 6, 5, 4, 3, 3, 4, 4, 4, 4, 4, 5, 6, 7, 7, 8, 8, 9, 9, 7, 7, 8, 14, 13, 13, 14, 13, 14, 17, 17, 15, 16, 27, 26, 29, 31, 36, 37   (40)

CHAPMAN, TRACY

6-04-88   *Tracy Chapman*   (Elektra 60774-2)   34, 28, 14———   (3)

CHEAP TRICK

6-04-88   *Lap Of Luxury*   (Epic EK 40922)   30, 26, 26———   (3)

CHER

3-19-88   *Cher*   (Geffen 24164-2)   34, 29, 30, 33, 36, 39   (6)

CHICAGO

11-10-84   *Chicago 17*   (WB 25060-2)   26, 21, 19, 15, 14, 13, 10, 8, 8, 7, 7, 6, 5, 5, 5, 4, 3, 6, 6, 6, 5, 6, 6, 8, 7, 6, 5, 5, 4, 5, 7, 6, 6, 8, 11, 12, 16, 20, 30, 33, 36, 39, 39   (43)

11-29-86   *Greatest Hits*   (Col. CK 33900)   34, 34, 34, 35, 36, 36, 36, 36, 38   (9)

THE CHURCH

6-11-88   *Starfish*   (Arista ARCD 8521)   32, 29———   (2)

CINCINNATI POPS ORCHESTRA/KUNZEL

9-15-84   *Star Tracks*   (Telarc CD-80094)   15, 13, 15, 17, 19, 20, 26, 27, 27, 28, 27   (11)

11-10-84   *Tchaikovsky: Capriccio Italien—Op. 45, Cossack Dance From Mazeppa, "1812" Overture—Op. 49*   (Telarc CDE-80041)   28, 27, 26, 28, 29, 28, 30   (7)

1-26-85   *Time Warp*   (Telarc CD-80106)   27, 26, 24, 24, 24, 21, 22, 25, 25, 27, 28   (11)

Compact Discs

CINDERELLA

  1-31-87 *Night Songs* (Mer. 830 076-2) 30, 27, 27, 27, 28, 38 (6)

CLAPTON, ERIC

  4-25-87 *August* (WB 25476-2) 29, 25, 18, 31, 26, 27, 23, 24, 24, 29, 31, 33, 33, 34, 34, 37, 36, 36, 40 (18)

  5-25-85 *Behind The Sun* (WB 25166-2) 25, 20, 18, 17, 17, 17, 17, 17, 20, 19, 19, 25, 30, 30, 35, 38, 39, 40 (18)

  5-07-88 *Crossroads* (Polydor 835 261-2) 32, 7, 3, 1, 2, 7, 8———— (7)

CLEVELAND SYMPHONY ORCHESTRA/LOREN MAAZEL

  9-15-84 *Beethoven: Symphony No. 9* (CBS Masterworks MK 38868) 26, 30 (2)

CLUB NOUVEAU

  4-11-87 *Life, Love And Pain* (WB 25531-2) 26, 23, 26, 30, 26, 36, 33, 31, 35, 40, 40 (11)

COLLINS, PHIL *(See also:* GENESIS)

  3-30-85 *Face Value* (Atl. 16029-2) 25, 23, 21, 22, 23 (5)

  5-11-85 *No Jacket Required* (Atl. 81240-2) 22, 12, 6, 3, 2, 1, 1, 1, 1, 1, 2, 2, 5, 3, 2, 1, 2, 2, 2, 3, 2, 2, 3, 3, 3, 3, 3, 2, 2, 2, 2, 2, 2, 22, 2, 2, 2, 5, 5, 4, 5, 5, 6, 6, 6, 5, 4, 4, 4, 5, 6, 5, 5, 5, 6, 7, 7, 11, 13, 12, 10, 10, 9, 9, 8, 10, 11, 13, 14, 16, 14, 14, 22, 28, 27, 26, 19, 19, 20, 21, 21, 23, 21, 18, 15, 15, 15, 15, 15, 17, 18, 19, 21, 27, 33, 31, 38, 39, 40, 37, 38, 35 (103)

COOKE, SAM

  4-12-86 *The Man And His Music* (RCA PCD1-7127) 35, 32, 31, 30, 27, 27, 28 (7)

COSTELLO, ELVIS

  3-22-86 *The Best Of Elvis Costello* (Col. C2K 40121) 35, 30, 27, 27, 28, 28, 35, 39 (8)

  6-21-86 *King Of America* (Col. CK 40173) 35, 34, 36, 39 (4)

CRAY, ROBERT

2-21-87   *Strong Persuader*   (Mer./PolyGram 830 568-2)   29, 23, 20, 9, 7, 7, 9, 9, 9, 7, 6, 8, 12, 12, 7, 13, 11, 11, 13, 13, 16, 13, 15, 15, 19, 23, 24, 20, 30, 36, 36, 37, 39, 39, 39   (35)

CRAZY HORSE   *(See:* NEIL YOUNG)

CREEDENCE CLEARWATER REVIVAL   *(See also:* JOHN FOGERTY)

9-14-85   *Chronicles*   (Fantasy FCD 623-CCR2)   30, 25, 19, 17, 14, 12, 12, 14, 15, 15, 17, 17, 17, 17, 17, 17, 16, 16, 23, 23, 23, 34, 32, 28, 23, 21, 18, 18, 16, 19, 18, 16, 13, 12, 12, 12, 12, 17, 21, 25, 32, 30, 27, 29, 36, 39, 37, 32, 27, 25, 24, 25, 27, 26, 26, 25, 22, 22, 21, 23, 22, 21, 23, 23, 24, 23, 25, 25, 25, 25, 25, 24, 23, 28, 30, 40, 40   (77)

CROSBY, STILLS, NASH AND YOUNG   *(See also:* NEIL YOUNG)

12-07-85   *Deja Vu*   (Reprise 19118)   31, 29, 27, 27, 27, 27, 33, 32, 31, 31, 30, 31, 32, 30, 30, 28, 28, 31, 39   (19)

CROWDED HOUSE

5-02-87   *Crowded House*   (Cap. CDP7 46693 2)   29, 21, 19, 19, 16, 14, 9, 9, 11, 14, 18, 26, 26, 26, 34, 35, 37, 39   (18)

THE CURE

7-04-87   *Kiss Me, Kiss Me, Kiss Me*   (Elektra 2-60737)   24, 11, 9, 9, 9, 11, 14, 15, 28, 33, 33, 33, 35, 38   (14)

THE CUTTING CREW

6-13-87   *Broadcast*   (Virgin 2-90573)   33, 33, 37, 39   (4)

D'ARBY, TERENCE TRENT

3-12-88   *Introducing The Hardline According To Terence Trent D'Arby*   (Col. CK 40964)   32, 28, 25, 23, 14, 11, 9, 5, 4, 3, 4, 3, 8, 8, 10———   (15)

DAY, MORRIS

4-09-88   *Daydreaming*   (WB 25651-2)   32, 29, 32, 39   (4)

DEEP PURPLE

2-07-87   *The House Of Blue Light*   (Mer./PolyGram 831 318-2)   17, 14, 14, 13, 18, 38   (6)

4-06-85   *Perfect Strangers*   (Mer. 823 777-2)   27, 26, 27, 29   (4)

DEF LEPPARD

8-29-87   *Hysteria*   (Mer. 830 675-2)   24, 5, 2, 2, 1, 4, 8, 12, 16, 16, 17, 16, 16, 20, 20, 21, 20, 21, 21, 21, 23, 17, 15, 15, 12, 14, 16, 13, 13, 18, 23, 24, 24, 22, 25, 27, 27, 38, 40, 40, 40   (41)

DIAMOND, NEIL

7-26-86   *Headed For The Future*   (Col. CK 40368)   32, 30, 29, 35   (4)

3-23-85   *His 12 Greatest Hits*   (MCA MCAD 37252)   23, 20, 18, 16, 15, 16, 15, 15, 19, 20, 26, 26, 33, 40   (14)

DIO

8-22-87   *Dream Evil*   (WB 2-25612)   27, 21   (2)

DIRE STRAITS

6-01-85   *Brothers In Arms*   (WB 25264-2)   39, 30, 24, 16, 9, 4, 2, 1, 1, 1, 2, 3, 3, 5, 4, 4, 1, 1, 1, 1, 1, 1, 1, 1, 1, 1, 1, 1, 1, 1, 1, 1, 1, 1, 1, 1, 1, 1, 1, 1, 1, 1, 1, 1, 1, 2, 3, 3, 3, 2, 3, 3, 3, 2, 3, 3, 5, 5, 6, 6, 12, 12, 13, 13, 13, 12, 12, 12, 13, 12, 18, 19, 20, 25, 30, 33, 34, 32, 32, 32, 32, 34, 35, 35, 36, 35, 35, 40   (84)

10-19-85   *Dire Straits*   (WB 3266-2)   37, 36, 38, 38, 36, 35, 34   (7)

11-02-85   *Making Movies*   (WB 3480-2)   28, 25, 21, 19, 18, 27, 28, 31, 31, 34, 34, 34   (12)

DIRTY DANCING

10-03-87   [Original Film Soundtrack]   (RCA 6402-2-R) 35, 13, 10, 12, 13, 15, 15, 15, 10, 8, 7, 5, 5, 5, 5, 5, 5, 5, 7, 7, 7, 5, 4, 3, 1, 1, 1, 2, 5, 3, 3, 3, 2, 4, 5, 4, 4, 9, 9   (38)

DOKKEN

12-12-87   *Back For The Attack*   (Elektra 2-60735)   18, 16, 16, 16, 16, 20, 29, 29, 32, 36, 38   (11)

DOLBY, THOMAS

5-21-88   *Aliens Ate My Buick*   (EMI-Manhattan 48076)   32, 29, 27, 25, 22——— (5)

THE DOORS

9-05-87   *Best Of The Doors*   (Elektra 2-60345)   16, 12, 11, 11, 11, 15, 20, 22, 25, 37, 34, 37, 40, 40   (14)

DURAN DURAN

1-19-85   *Arena*   (Cap. CDP7 46048 2)   24, 22, 22, 23, 25   (5)

DYLAN, BOB

1-25-86   *Biograph*   (Col. CK 38830)   35, 29, 27, 25, 25, 25, 25, 28, 29, 33, 39   (11)

EMERSON, LAKE AND POWELL

7-26-86   *Emerson, Lake And Powell*   (Polydor 829 297-2)   16, 13, 12, 11, 16, 19, 21, 23, 31, 31, 30, 30, 29, 31, 29, 31, 29, 27, 32, 35, 34, 37, 38, 38, 38, 38, 40   (27)

ENO

12-07-85   *Thursday Afternoon*   (EG CD 64)   37, 35, 35, 35, 38, 38, 40   (7)

ESTEFAN, GLORIA, AND THE MIAMI SOUND MACHINE

4-30-88   *Let It Loose*   (Epic EK 40769)   33, 30, 30, 27, 24, 22, 23, 25   (8)

EUROPE

4-11-87   *The Final Countdown*   (Epic EK 40241)   32, 28, 31, 34, 30, 29, 37, 32, 34, 37, 37, 40   (12)

EURYTHMICS

7-27-85   *Be Yourself Tonight*   (RCA PCD1-5429)   29, 25, 10, 7, 7, 10, 12, 12, 12, 12, 11, 11, 10, 10, 12, 14, 14, 14, 13, 26, 26, 26, 26, 36, 36, 38, 38, 38, 37, 38   (29)

8-09-86 *Revenge* (RCA PCD1-5847) 22, 16, 12, 9, 8, 8, 9, 9, 14, 14, 13, 16, 15, 15, 30, 29, 33, 33, 36, 39, 40, 40, 40, 40 (24)

1-23-88 *Savage* (RCA 6794-2-R) 33, 30, 26, 24, 24, 24, 28, 36 (8)

9-22-84 *Touch* (RCA PCD1-4917) 26, 24, 26, 30 (4)

THE FABULOUS THUNDERBIRDS

7-05-86 *Tuff Enuff* (CBS Associated ZK 40304) 18, 13, 11, 11, 16, 15, 18, 14, 15, 18, 14, 12, 12, 15, 17, 16, 20, 21, 20, 27, 31, 37, 38 (23)

FAGEN, DONALD

9-29-84 *The Nightfly* (WB 23696-2) 23, 19, 17, 15, 14, 13, 12, 12, 14, 21, 24, 30, 29, 30, 30, 30 (16)

FALCO

6-28-86 *Falco 3* (A&M CD-5105) 36, 34, 32, 32, 30, 34, 39, 40 (8)

FERRY, BRYAN *(See also:* ROXY MUSIC)

12-05-87 *Bête Noire* (Reprise 2-25598) 33, 30, 27, 32, 32, 32, 38 (7)

7-06-85 *Boys And Girls* (WB 25082-2) 29, 27, 25, 24, 23, 23, 27, 27, 28, 32, 34, 38, 38 (13)

THE FIRM *(See also:* LED ZEPPELIN)

5-11-85 *The Firm* (Atl. 81239-2) 26, 24, 22, 22, 25, 26, 34, 38, 38, 38, 38, 39 (12)

5-07-86 *Mean Business* (Atl. 81628-2) 29, 27, 25, 23, 23, 23, 24, 30, 34, 40 (10)

FLEETWOOD MAC *(See also:* STEVIE NICKS)

9-15-84 *Rumours* (WB 3010-2) 30, 29, 28, 29, 29, 30 (6)

5-09-87 *Tango In The Night* (WB 25471-2) 4, 5, 5, 5, 5, 6, 6, 7, 8, 7, 7, 8, 8, 8, 8, 8, 9, 10, 9, 12, 16, 23, 22, 24, 28, 29, 30, 29, 31, 35, 36, 39 (32)

FLIM AND THE BB'S

2-22-86   *Big Notes*   (Digital Music Products CD 454)   37, 35, 33, 31, 30, 29,
28, 28, 27, 24, 23, 25, 34, 40   (14)

FOGERTY, JOHN   *(See also:* CREEDENCE CLEARWATER
REVIVAL)

2-23-85   *Centerfield*   (WB 25203-2)   12, 6, 5, 5, 7, 7, 7, 12, 13, 13, 13, 12,
11, 10, 10, 10, 10, 10, 12, 13, 13, 12, 12, 11, 15, 17, 18, 18, 17, 17,
16, 22, 25, 27, 40   (35)

FOOTLOOSE

9-15-84   [Original Film Soundtrack]   (Col. CK 39242)   12, 11, 10, 8, 9, 11,
11, 15, 19, 19, 25, 25, 25   (13)

FOREIGNER

2-16-85   *Agent Provocateur*   (Atl. 81999-2)   20, 14, 8, 4, 2, 2, 2, 2, 3, 6, 8, 8, 7,
6, 5, 7, 6, 7, 9, 10, 18, 20, 21, 21, 32, 35, 38, 40, 40   (29)

1-23-88   *Inside Information*   (Atl. 2-81808)   31, 28, 23, 18, 15, 14, 15, 19, 20,
26, 31, 37, 40, 40   (14)

FRANKLIN, ARETHA

10-05-85   *Who's Zoomin' Who*   (Arista ARCD-8286)   31, 29, 27, 32, 33   (5)

FRANKS, MICHAEL

9-05-87   *The Camera Never Lies*   (WB 2550-2)   28, 28, 31, 31, 33, 34, 36, 38,
39   (9)

GTR

6-21-86   *GTR*   (Arista JRCD 8400)   15, 12, 10, 8, 8, 7, 8, 10, 14, 13, 14, 16,
17, 24, 24, 31, 36, 34, 38, 39   (20)

GABRIEL, PETER   *(See also:* GENESIS)

6-28-86   *So*   (Geffen 24088)   17, 7, 4, 2, 1, 2, 2, 2, 1, 1, 1, 1, 1, 1, 1, 1, 1, 1,
1, 6, 8, 7, 8, 8, 9, 11, 11, 11, 11, 11, 12, 10, 8, 6, 6, 5, 4, 8, 9, 8, 12, 13,

12, 15, 9, 11, 14, 15, 19, 19, 22, 22, 25, 28, 32, 29, 27, 27, 29, 28, 28, 31, 29, 32, 37, 38, 37   (67)

GENESIS   *(See also:* PHIL COLLINS; PETER GABRIEL; MIKE AND THE MECHANICS)

9-29-84   *Genesis*   (Atl. 80116-2)   21, 23, 23, 25   (4)

7-12-86   *Invisible Touch*   (Atl. 81641-2)   28, 12, 4, 1, 1, 1, 2, 2, 2, 2, 4, 4, 10, 10, 9, 7, 3, 2, 3, 5, 4, 4, 7, 6, 5, 5, 5, 5, 5, 5, 4, 5, 6, 8, 11, 11, 13, 16, 15, 14, 17, 7, 9, 13, 14, 17, 15, 16, 16, 17, 19, 25, 21, 21, 21, 25, 27, 36, 30, 35, 37, 39   (60)

THE GEORGIA SATELLITES

3-07-87   *The Georgia Satellites*   (Elektra 60496-2)   25, 22, 19, 18, 26, 33, 37, 40   (8)

GIBSON, DEBBIE

3-05-88   *Out Of The Blue*   (Atl. 81780-2)   31, 27, 22, 21, 25, 28, 33, 33, 32, 35, 40   (11)

GOOD MORNING, VIETNAM

2-20-88   [Original Film Soundtrack]   (A&M CD 3913)   33, 25, 22, 18, 15, 17, 14, 13, 13, 17, 18, 21, 25, 26, 38   (16)

THE GRATEFUL DEAD

8-08-87   *Into The Dark*   (Arista ARCD 8452)   17, 6, 5, 2, 1, 3, 3, 4, 6, 10, 8, 11, 11, 16, 22, 24, 27, 29, 28, 28, 31, 31, 31, 34, 38, 37, 39, 39   (28)

GREAT WHITE

10-10-87   *Once Bitten*   (Cap. CDP7 46910 2)   29, 25, 25, 27, 33, 33, 34, 38   (8)

GRUSIN, DAVE, AND LEE RITENOUR

9-28-85   *Harlequin*   (GRP 1015)   32, 30, 28, 26, 25, 24, 36, 39, 39, 38, 36, 36, 34, 34, 35, 35, 36, 36, 39   (19)

GUNS N' ROSES

   3-05-88   *Appetite For Destruction* (Geffen 24148-2) 32, 29, 23, 19, 17, 16,
            15, 13, 11, 9, 12, 11, 12, 15, 17, 19 (16)

HAGAR, SAMMY *(See also:* **VAN HALEN)**

   7-11-86   *Sammy Hagar* (Geffen 24099-2) 23, 16, 14, 14, 12, 15 (6)

HALL, DARYL, AND JOHN OATES

   1-19-85   *Big Bam Boom* (RCA PCD1-5336) 17, 14, 11, 10, 10, 11, 11, 10,
            11, 12, 17, 19, 18, 19, 20, 22 (16)

   5-28-88   *Ooh Yeah!* (Arista ARCD 8539) 22, 17, 13, 16——— (4)

   9-15-84   *Rock 'N Soul, Part 1* (RCA PCD1-4858) 21, 16, 12, 13, 13, 14, 18,
            18, 17, 16, 17, 16, 19, 24, 24, 23, 23, 23, 25, 24, 28, 28, 29, 30,
            30 (25)

HANCOCK, HERBIE

   9-15-84   *Future Shock* (Col. CK 38814) 19, 25 (2)

HARRIS, EMMYLOU *(See:* **DOLLY PARTON)**

HARRISON, GEORGE *(See also:* **THE BEATLES)**

   11-28-87   *Cloud Nine* (Dark Horse/WB 2-25643) 9, 4, 3, 4, 3, 3, 3, 2, 1, 1, 1,
            3, 3, 5, 5, 6, 6, 5, 12, 17, 24, 28, 36, 38 (24)

HEART

   6-27-87   *Bad Animals* (Cap. CDP7 46676 2) 23, 17, 5, 5, 5, 5, 5, 5, 6, 4, 8,
            8, 9, 13, 22, 18, 22, 27, 26, 34, 35, 35, 39 (23)

   2-08-86   *Heart* (Cap. CDP7 46157 2) 28, 19, 15, 10, 7, 5, 5, 5, 7, 9, 7, 7, 9, 8,
            7, 8, 10, 11, 11, 11, 11, 11, 11, 13, 15, 14, 16, 25, 23, 25, 24, 28, 27,
            31, 34, 34, 34, 34, 36, 40 (52)

HENDRIX, JIMI, EXPERIENCE

   6-13-87   *Live At Winterland* (Rykodisc RCD 20038) 34, 34, 26, 20, 17, 14,
            11, 11, 10, 10, 10, 10, 18, 18, 26, 29, 32, 37, 38, 40, 40 (21)

HENLEY, DON

2-02-85   *Building The Perfect Beast*   (Geffen 24026-2)   21, 17, 12, 10, 9, 9, 9, 10, 11, 10, 8, 7, 6, 7, 8, 10, 14, 13, 12, 12, 12, 11, 10, 10, 11, 11, 10, 8, 8, 8, 9, 9, 8, 8, 11, 12, 12, 15, 14, 19, 19, 20, 20, 23, 28, 27, 33, 33, 37, 37   (50)

HIROSHIMA

8-29-87   *Go*   (Epic EK 40670)   26, 31, 34, 34, 34, 34, 38   (7)

THE HONEYDRIPPERS   *(See also:* LED ZEPPELIN; ROBERT PLANT)

6-15-85   *Volume One*   (Es Paranza 2-90220)   28, 24, 22, 22, 23, 28, 31, 36, 38   (9)

THE HOOTERS

10-19-85   *Nervous Night*   (Col. CK 39912)   30, 28, 34   (3)

HORNSBY, BRUCE, AND THE RANGE

5-28-88   *Scenes From The Southside*   (RCA 6686-2-R)   28, 6, 2, 2———   (4)

11-08-86   *The Way It Is*   (RCA PCD1-8058)   35, 26, 17, 19, 22, 20, 12, 9, 9, 9, 9, 1, 1, 1, 1, 2, 2, 3, 7, 6, 6, 11, 12, 5, 5, 4, 6, 11, 8, 14, 16, 14, 14, 15, 21, 26, 23, 25, 25, 27, 31   (41)

HOUSTON, WHITNEY

6-13-87   *Whitney*   (Arista ARCD-5732)   38, 38, 5, 2, 1, 1, 1, 1, 1, 1, 1, 1, 2, 4, 4, 5, 7, 9, 9, 9, 9, 11, 12, 13, 15, 22, 22, 23, 24, 24, 24, 24, 21, 17, 13, 15, 18, 19, 19, 23, 26, 27, 29, 29, 31, 31, 29, 31, 37, 39   (50)

9-28-85   *Whitney Houston*   (Arista JRCD-8221)   26, 24, 23, 23, 18, 11, 9, 7, 7, 11, 13, 14, 14, 14, 14, 14, 17, 18, 18, 19, 22, 20, 15, 10, 8, 7, 6, 5, 5, 3, 2, 2, 2, 1, 1, 1, 1, 1, 1, 1, 1, 1, 1, 2, 4, 3, 3, 3, 6, 7, 7, 7, 7, 7, 8, 10, 12, 11, 14, 14, 22, 28, 29, 28, 27, 30, 30, 30, 30, 31, 38, 34, 32, 25, 22, 22, 39, 24, 27, 35, 30, 33, 37, 40   (84)

INXS

11-28-87   *Kick*   (Atl. 81796-2)   21, 15, 14, 12, 13, 13, 13, 10, 7, 5, 4, 2, 2, 2, 1, 2, 3, 3, 6, 8, 7, 5, 4, 6, 6, 9, 9, 11, 11, 12———   (30)

3-15-86   *Listen Like Thieves*   (Atl. 81277-2)   35, 32, 36, 34, 33, 34, 34, 34, 34, 37, 37, 36, 37, 36, (2), 38, 37   (16)

IDOL, BILLY

11-24-84   *Rebel Yell*   (Chrysalis VK 41450)   24, 23, 20, 18, 15, 15, 15, 16, 16, 16, 18, 26   (12)

10-24-87   *Vital Idol*   (Chrysalis VK 41620)   35, 30, 25, 20, 18, 16, 21, 25, 30   (9)

IRON MAIDEN

5-14-88   *Seventh Son Of A Seventh Son*   (Cap. C2 48982)   24, 18, 14, 16, 16, 18———   (6)

JACKSON, JANET

6-07-86   *Control*   (A&M CD 3905)   38, 35, 33, 31, 22, 19, 13, 12, 12, 11, 15, 15, 17, 17, 20, 19, 19, 23, 21, 25, 28, 35, 38, 40, 40   (25)

2-21-87   *Control*   (A&M CD 3905)   31, 29, 21, 27, 26, 29, 29, 35, 34, 38, (1), 25, 22, 23, 25, 27, 29, 29, 34, 36, 38, 38, 39, 39   (23)

JACKSON, JOE

5-17-86   *Big World*   (A&M CD 6021)   21, 18, 14, 13, 15, 14, 15, 20, 22, 18, 19, 18, 23, 25, 33, 36, 38, 39, 40, 40   (20)

6-11-88   *Joe Jackson Live 1980/86*   (A&M CD 6706)   34, 30———   (2)

JACKSON, MICHAEL

9-26-87   *Bad*   (Epic EK 40600)   25, 2, 1, 2, 3, 3, 4, 4, 4, 6, 9, 12, 17, 15, 15, 15, 13, 10, 9, 9, 9, 10, 12, 11, 10, 10, 14, 10, 6, 6, 10, 8, 8, 9, 10, 10, 10, 10, 11———   (39)

9-15-84   *Thriller*   (Epic EK 38112)   3, 4, 4, 7, 7, 6, 6, 8, 8, 10, 11, 11, 12, 15, 22, 22, 22, 21, 21, 23, 29   (21)

JAGGER, MICK   *(See also: ROLLING STONES)*

10-03-87   *Primitive Cool*   (Col. CK 40919)   30, 19, 17, 20, 22, 31, 38, 39   (8)

3-09-85   *She's The Boss*   (Col. CK 39940)   16, 12, 8, 6, 5, 5, 4, 4, 5, 6, 7, 12, 15, 16, 18, 23, 27, 34, 35, 35, 38   (21)

JAMES, BOB, AND DAVID SANBORN

7-05-86   *Double Vision*   (WB 25393-2)   21, 18, 14, 13, 11, 14, 13, 17, 16, 15, 12, 10, 10, 18, 18, 21, 22, 32, 30, 37, 38   (21)

JARREAU, AL

11-08-86   *L Is For Lover*   (WB 25477-2)   33, 32, 32, 27, 31, 35, 38, 39, 39, 39, 39, (6)31, 25, 34, 36, 38   (16)

JETHRO TULL

10-31-87   *Crest Of A Knave*   (Chrysalis VK 41590)   35, 24, 21, 21, 17, 17, 15, 15, 12, 12, 12, 18, 20, 23, 30, 29, 29, 30, 36, 39   (20)

10-26-85   *Thick As A Brick*   (Chrysalis VK 41003)   31, 29, 29, 38   (4)

JOEL, BILLY

9-20-86   *The Bridge*   (Col. CK 40402)   17, 17, 9, 6, 5, 4, 8, 5, 6, 9, 14, 17, 17, 21, 17, 17, 17, 17, 14, 14, 14, 20, 18, 18, 15, 20, 16, 12, 18, 28, 30, 33, 36, 36   (33)

9-07-85   *Greatest Hits Volume I & Volume II*   (Col. G2K 40121)   25, 13, 11, 10, 7, 6, 6, 6, 7, 8, 10, 9, 8, 8, 9, 9, 8, 8, 10, 11, 11, 11, 16, 18, 22, 23, 24, 25, 25, 26, 36, 37, 38   (24)

9-15-84   *An Innocent Man*   (Col. CK 38837)   13, 14, 13, 14, 14, 12, 15, 17, 16, 18, 18, 22, 21, 20, 20, 21, 21, 20, 28, 30   (20)

11-21-87   *KOHUEPT (Live In Leningrad)*   (Col. CK 40996)   22, 18, 19, 19, 22, 25, 25, 25, 31, 39   (10)

JOHN, ELTON

10-20-84   *Breaking Hearts*   (Geffen 24031-2)   24, 22, 21, 21, 22, 29, 29   (7)

8-08-87   *Elton John Live In Australia With The Melbourne Symphony Orchestra*   (MCA MCAD 8022)   28, 22, 23, 19, 20, 20, 25, 32, 40   (9)

1-30-88   *Elton John Live In Australia With The Melbourne Symphony Orchestra*   (MCA MCAD 8022)   35, 19, 13, 11, 11, 17, 21, 25, 33   (9)

10-20-84   *Goodbye Yellow Brick Road*   (MCA MCAD2 6894)   26, 17, 12, 10, 9, 8, 8, 15, 19, 19, 17, 17, 17, 18, 20, 20, 25, 28   (18)

12-15-84   *Greatest Hits, Volume I*   (MCA MCAD 37215)   23, 21, 19, 19, 18, 19, 21, 27, 29   (9)

2-01-86   *Ice On Fire*   (Geffen 24077)   30, 29, 29, 35, 37, 37, 38   (7)

JONES, HOWARD

6-29-85   *Dream Into Action*   (Elektra 9 60390-2)   33, 28, 26, 23, 23, 21, 21, 21, 21, 21, 20, 25, 26, 29, 29, 34, 35, 34   (18)

JONES, RICKIE LEE

11-17-84   *The Magazine*   (WB 25117-2)   24, 22, 19, 18, 16, 18, 20, 20, 22, 30   (10)

JOURNEY

5-17-86   *Raised On Radio*   (Col. CK 39936)   23, 19, 11, 5, 4, 5, 4, 5, 7, 7, 14, 19, 24, 29, 36, 38, 40   (17)

JUDAS PRIEST

6-18-88   *Ram It Down*   (Col. CK 44244)   34——— (1)

6-14-86   *Turbo*   (Col. CK 40158)   39, 36, 32, 31, 31, 30, 33, 39   (8)

KENNY G

4-04-87   *Duotones*   (Arista ARCD 8427)   21, 18, 17, 16, 17, 16, 15, 24, 24, 28, 30, 30, 21, 10, 4, 4, 4, 4, 4, 4, 4, 6, 7, 7, 8, 8, 10, 12, 15, 18, 21, 26, 26, 29, 33, 35, 37, 39, 38, 38, 38, 37, 36, 40, 38, 37, 37, 38, 40, 40, 40, 39   (52)

KHAN, CHAKA

12-01-84   *I Feel For You*   (WB 25162-2)   24, 22, 22, 23, 24, 24, 25, 26, 26   (9)

KING, CAROLE

4-19-86   *Tapestry*   (Epic EK 34946)   35, 32, 28, 38, 40, 38, 38   (7)

KINGDOM COME

4-02-88   *Kingdom Come*   (Polydor 835 362-2)   26, 22, 18, 14, 13, 13, 13, 13, 17, 24, 27, 33————   (12)

KLUGH, EARL   (*See:* GEORGE BENSON)

KNIGHT, GLADYS, & THE PIPS

2-06-88   *All Our Love*   (MCA MCAD 42004)   35, 32, 31, 28, 25, 30, 30, 34, 37, 39, 39   (11)

LA BAMBA

8-15-87   [Original Film Soundtrack]   (WB/Slash 25605-2)   19   (1)

LaBELLE, PATTI

8-02-86   *The Winner In You*   (MCA MCAD 5737)   15, 13, 12, 18, 20, 19, 18, 22, 22, 24, 38, 36, 37, 33, 37, 39   (16)

LAUPER, CYNDI

9-22-84   *She's So Unusual*   (Portrait RK 38930)   18, 16, 12, 10, 8, 7, 6, 5, 6, 7, 7, 6, 7, 5, 5, 5, 5, 5, 5, 5, 6, 6, 6, 6, 10, 15, 23, 24, 23, 25, 30, 29, 27, 27, (3), 40, 39, 38, 39   (37)

11-08-86   *True Colors*   (Epic EK 40313)   29, 17, 16, 12, 14, 16, 16, 13, 13, 13, 13, 20, 18, 15, 23, 37, 36   (17)

LED ZEPPELIN   (*See also:* THE FIRM; THE HONEYDRIPPERS; ROBERT PLANT)

6-22-85   *Houses Of The Holy*   (Atl. 19130-2)   35, 29, 27, 25, 24, 26, 33, 36, 37, 37, 36, 40   (12)

6-14-86   *In Through The Out Door*   (Atl. 16002-2)   37, 34, 33, 33, 40   (5)

12-13-86   *Led Zeppelin*   (Atl. SD 19128-2)   32, 24, 20, 20, 20, 20, 22, 26, 25, 28, 26, 30, 35, 31, 35, 31   (16)

1-24-87   *Led Zeppelin II*   (Atl. 19127-2)   33, 31, 29, 33, 36, 34, 27, 37   (8)

5-02-87   *Physical Graffiti*   (Swan Song SS 200-2)   31, 28, 28, 35, 38, 40, 39, 39   (8)

3-22-86   *Zoso*   (Atl. 19129-2)   33, 31, 33, 32, 36, 37, 39   (7)

LENNON, JULIAN

5-17-86   *The Secret Value Of Daydreaming*   (Atl. 81640-2)   26, 24, 24, 24, 24, 24, 25   (7)

2-16-85   *Valotte*   (Atl. 80184-2)   23, 19, 18, 21, 21, 21, 22, 22, 22, 20, 22, (4), 32, 29, 29, 28, 30, 36, 36, 37, 37   (20)

LESS THAN ZERO

12-19-87   [Original Film Soundtrack]   (Def Jam/CBS CK 44042)   32, 29, 29, 29, 28, 26, 24, 28, 31, 32, 34, 37   (12)

LEVEL 42

6-14-86   *World Machine*   (Polydor 827 487-2)   22, 19, 22, 24, 23, 22, 22, 26, 33, 32, 32, 32, 33, 33, 37, 37, 39   (17)

LEWIS, HUEY, AND THE NEWS

10-25-86   *Fore!*   (Chrysalis VK41534)   —, 25, 7, 2, 1, 6, 6, 10, 10, 18, 18, 18, 18, 16, 16, 16, 22, 19, 19, 17, 24, 21, 26, 24, 38, 39   (26)

2-09-85   *Sports*   (Chrysalis VK 41412)   21, 14, 9, 4, 3, 3, 4, 8, 15, 20, 28, (8), 33, 28, 23, 21, 19, 16, 15, 11, 10, 11, 11, 10, 9, 9, 9, 10, 10, 9, 9, 8, 10, 10, 13, 14, 16, 25, 25, 25, 24, 24   (41)

LOS LOBOS

4-04-87   *By The Light Of The Moon*   (Slash/WB 25523-2)   32, 24, 24, 24, 22, 33, 37   (7)

MADONNA

12-01-84   *Like A Virgin*   (Sire/WB 25157-2)   20, 11, 4, 3, 2, 2, 2, 2, 1, 1, 1, 1, 1, 1, 1, 1, 1, 1, 1, 1, 3, 3, 3, 2, 1, 1, 1, 1, 2, 2, 5, 5, 6, 6, 7, 7, 6, 12, 12, 13, 13, 14, 14, 14, 14, 13, 14, 15, 15, 16, 18, 18, 19, 19, 18, 20, 20, 25, 25, 31, 31, 36, 40   (63)

9-22-84   *Madonna*   (Sire/WB 23867-2)   20, 19, 15, 18, 18, 16, 14, 14, 13, 12, 10, 8, 8, 9, 11, 11, 10, 10, 11, 19, 27, 27, 29   (23)

8-30-86 *True Blue* (Sire/WB 25442-2) 8, 5, 3, 2, 2, 2, 3, 3, 5, 4, 10, 13, 12, 18, 20, 22, 19, 16, 16, 16, 16, 13, 12, 10, 9, 12, 12, 16, 23, 33, 33, 36, 39, 40 (34)

12-12-87 *You Can Dance* (Sire/WB 25535-2) 26, 19, 18, 18, 18, 15, 15, 19, 25, 30, 34 (11)

MALMSTEEN, YNGWIE J.

5-14-88 *Odyssey* (Polydor 835 451-2) 33, 31, 31, 36 (4)

MANHATTAN TRANSFER

11-09-85 *Vocalese* (Atl. 81266-2) 26, 24, 24, 32, 39, 40 (6)

MANNHEIM STEAMROLLER

12-07-85 *Fresh Aire Christmas* (American Gramaphone AGCD-1984) 35, 33, 30, 30 (4)

12-13-86 *Fresh Aire Christmas* (American Gramaphone AGCD-1984) 30, 23, 22, 22, 22, 22, 25, 27, 37, 37 (10)

5-25-85 *Fresh Aire V* (American Gramaphone AGCD-385) 27, 24, 23, 22, 22, 25, 25, 29, 30, 32, 31, 32, 34, 33, 32, 31, 33, 33, 34, 39, 38, 38, 39 (23)

10-05-85 *Fresh Aire III* (American Gramaphone AGCD-365) 37, 35, 29, 29, 27, 27, 34, 36, 36, 32, 32, 32, 32, 32, 32, 35 (16)

MARLEY, ZIGGY, AND THE MELODY MAKERS

5-14-88 *Conscious Party* (Virgin 2-90878) 32, 28, 25, 23, 22, 21 (6)

MARSALIS, WYNTON

2-15-86 *Black Codes (From The Underground)* (Col. CK 40009) 35, 36, 38, 40 (4)

MARSALIS, WYNTON, AND THE NATIONAL PHILHARMONIC ORCHESTRA

9-15-84 *Haydn/Hummel/L. Mozart: Trumpet Concertos* (CBS Masterworks MK 37846) 17, 24, 30, 30 (4)

McCARTNEY, PAUL   (*See also:* THE BEATLES)

12-26-87   *All The Best*   (Cap. CDP7 48227 2)   26, 26, 26, 19, 19, 20, 22, 23,
20, 18, 20, 25, 35   (13)

10-04-86   *Press To Play*   (Cap. CDP7 12475 2)   16, 11, 11, 10, 18, 26, 34, 34,
38   (9)

McFERRIN, BOBBY

5-07-88   *Simple Pleasures*   (EMI-Manhattan 48059-2)   34, 31, 29, 32, 35, 40,
40   (7)

MELLENCAMP, JOHN COUGAR

9-19-87   *Lonesome Jubilee*   (Riva 832 465-2)   17, 12, 8, 5, 3, 5, 5, 6, 5, 9, 13,
11, 10, 10, 7, 7, 7, 6, 6, 6, 6, 6, 6, 6, 7, 8, 9, 11, 15, 18, 19, 20, 22, 23,
29, 30, 30, 37   (37)

10-26-85   *Scarecrow*   (Riva 824 865-2)   21, 13, 6, 5, 4, 4, 4, 4, 5, 5, 6, 6, 8, 13,
13, 12, 10, 7, 6, 5, 4, 4, 4, 6, 6, 6, 6, 7, 9, 10, 9, 9, 10, 13, 12, 11, 17,
20, 24, 31, 29, 35, 31, 31, 30, 35, 37   (47)

METHENY, PAT, GROUP

8-22-87   *Still Life (Talking)*   (Geffen 2-24145)   20, 15, 17, 17, 18, 19, 19, 16,
16, 17, 17, 20, 23, 28, 31, 30, 31, 31, 35, 35, 35, 36, 35, 39, 40, 40,
40   (27)

MIAMI VICE

11-23-85   [Original Television Soundtrack]   (MCA MCAD 6150)   22, 16, 9,
7, 6, 6, 5, 5, 3, 3, 3, 4, 5, 4, 4, 4, 7, 9, 12, 15, 22, 22, 22, 22, 21, 20, 22,
39, 40   (29)

MICHAEL, GEORGE   (*See also:* WHAM!)

11-28-87   *Faith*   (Col. CK 40867)   30, 6, 4, 3, 4, 4, 4, 4, 4, 4, 2, 1, 1, 1, 2, 3, 2,
2, 7, 7, 8, 6, 7, 7, 8, 7, 5, 3, 3, 4———   (30)

MIDNIGHT OIL

4-30-88   *Diesel And Dust*   (Col. CK 40967)   30, 25, 20, 17, 13, 13, 15,
13———   (8)

MIKE AND THE MECHANICS

5-10-86   *Mike And The Mechanics*   (Atl. 81287-2)   28, 25, 23, 21, 18, 16, 17, 18, 15, 17, 17, 18, 17, 16, 19, 20, 25, 30, 32, 30, 30, 28, 27, 30, 30, 37, 32, 38, 39   (29)

MILLER, GLENN, ORCHESTRA

9-15-84   *In The Digital Mood*   (GRP GRPD 9502)   16, 15, 14, 16, 16, 19, 20, 19, 20, 29, 28, 26, 26, 25, 26, 25, 25, 26, 27, 29, 30, 30, 30   (23)

MINNELLI, LIZA

10-17-87   *Liza Minnelli At Carnegie Hall*   (Telarc CD 85502)   34, 36   (2)

MR. MISTER

1-25-86   *Welcome To The Real World*   (RCA PCD1-8045)   25, 24, 24, 20, 16, 13, 11, 9, 8, 8, 7, 8, 8, 15, 15, 13, 14, 13, 13, 12, 14, 13, 16, 32, 35, 37, 40   (27)

MITCHELL, JONI

4-16-88   *Chalk Mark In A Rain Storm*   (Geffen 2-24172)   32, 22, 12, 10, 10, 12, 16, 21, 20, 20——   (10)

2-22-86   *Dog Eat Dog*   (Geffen 2-24074)   34, 31, 31, 33, 37, 37, 40   (7)

THE MONKEES

10-11-86   *Then And Now . . . The Best Of The Monkees*   (Arista JRCD 8432)   29, 26, 23, 27, 24, 31, 30, 36, 37   (9)

THE MOODY BLUES

6-21-86   *Days Of Future Past*   (Threshold 826 006-2)   18, 14, 13, 14, 19, 26, 27, 34, 37, 39, 40   (11)

5-31-86   *The Other Side Of Life*   (Polydor 829 179-2)   23, 15, 10, 10, 10, 8, 6, 5, 6, 3, 4, 4, 5, 5, 6, 9, 8, 8, 6, 7, 6, 9, 5, 11, 16, 19, 20, 26, 31, 33, 35, 35, 35, 35, 37   (32)

3-02-85   *Voices In The Sky—The Best Of The Moody Blues*   (Threshold 820 155-2)   23, 19, 17, 17, 16, 16, 15, 14, 14, 14, 14, 21, 21, 27, 27, 32, 32, 32, 32, 31, 31, 30, 29, 29, 31, 32, 31, 35, 37, 36, 39, 40, 39, 39   (34)

MORE DIRTY DANCING

4-02-88   [Original Film Soundtrack]   (RCA 6965-2-R)   22, 10, 9, 7, 6, 5, 5, 6, 8, 14, 18, 23   (12)

MORRISSEY   (See also: THE SMITHS)

4-23-88   *Viva Hate*   (Sire/WB 2-24699)   30, 25, 22, 23, 20, 26, 38   (7)

MOTLEY CRUE

6-27-87   *Girls, Girls, Girls*   (ELektra 60752-2)   22, 16, 19, 18, 18, 18, 16, 21, 22, 27, 32, 39   (12)

THE NATIONAL PHILHARMONIC ORCHESTRA   (See: WYNTON MARSALIS)

NEW ORDER

10-10-87   *Substance 1987*   (Qwest/WB 25621-2)   —, 26, 21, 19, 18, 17, 17, 24, 28, 29, 29, 28, 28, 28, 29, 28, 32, 31, 28, 25, 26, 30, 33, 39   (24)

NICKS, STEVIE   (See also: FLEETWOOD MAC)

2-01-86   *Rock A Little*   (Modern/Atl. 90479-2)   28, 21, 15, 14, 16, 14, 17, 21, 23, 24, 21, 19, 18, 21, 22, 33, 39   (17)

NIGHT RANGER

10-27-84   *Midnight Madness*   (MCA MCAD 5456)   25, 24, 23, 26   (4)

9-21-85   *7 Wishes*   (MCA MCAD 5593)   24, 21, 19, 17, 16, 16, 17, 17, 19, 37   (10)

THE NYLONS

11-02-85   *One Size Fits All*   (Open Air/Windham Hill OAO 301)   32, 30, 27, 30, 37, 38, 38, 38, 39, 39, 39   (12)

OCEAN, BILLY

6-21-86   *Love Zone*   (Arista JRCD 8409)   22, 19, 16, 15, 15, 15, 14, 20, 21, 28, 31, 34, 36, 36, 38, 40   (16)

5-04-85   *Suddenly*   (Arista JRCD 8213)   24, 23, 23, 24, 28, 33, 35   (7)

4-09-88   *Tear Down These Walls*   (Jive/Arista ARCD 8495)   27, 20, 15, 15, 15, 15, 14, 20, 29, 35, 39   (11)

O'CONNOR, SINEAD

4-02-88   *The Lion And The Cobra*   (Ensign/Chrysalis 2-41612)   33, 30, 27, 23, 20, 17, 18, 25, 34   (9)

O'HEARN, PATRICK

12-07-85   *Ancient Dreams*   (Private Music CD 1201)   33, 30, 29, 29, 28, 28, 30, 39   (8)

O'NEAL, ALEXANDER

9-12-87   *Hearsay*   (Tabu/CBS EK 40320)   22, 16, 14, 14, 27, 40   (6)

OSBOURNE, OZZY

4-26-86   *The Ultimate Sin*   (CBS Associated ZS4 05810)   26, 31, 31, 30, 30, 30, 31, 39, 39, 38   (10)

THE OUTFIELD

7-25-87   *Bangin'*   (Col. CK 40619)   29, 29, 32, 37, 37   (5)

5-24-86   *Play Deep*   (Col. CK 40027)   33, 31, 28, 27, 30, 37, 35, 33, 25, 23, 24, 18, 20, 23, 27, 31, 34, 35, 35, 37, 37, 37   (22)

PALMER, ROBERT

2-08-86   *Riptide*   (Island 2-90471)   30, 28, 30, 33, 35, 36, 36, 39, 36, 31, 31, 30, 29, 30, 39, 34, 34, 34, 32, (3), 36, 35, 34, 33, 31, 26, 27, 28, 28, 28, 27, 27, 26, 26, 28, 25, 20, 27, 35, 36, 39, 39, 39, 36, 37, 37, 37, 37, 39, 37, 33, 35, 33, 33, 37   (52)

PAPA DOO RUN RUN

8-03-85   *California Project*   (Telarc CD-70501)   24, 22, 23, 23, 26, 27, 32, 32, 36   (9)

PARSONS, ALAN, PROJECT

9-15-84   *The Best Of The Alan Parsons Project*   (Arista ARCD 8193)   29, 28   (2)

2-14-87   *Gaudi*   (Arista ARCD 8448)   18, 17, 15, 12, 15, 15, 10, 14, 14, 15, 14, 19, 24, 35, 25, 30, 30   (17)

2-22-86   *Stereotomy*   (Arista ARCD 8384)   24, 20, 17, 14, 11, 9, 13, 13, 17, 21, 37   (11)

3-09-85   *Vulture Culture*   (Arista ARCD 8263)   24, 20, 18, 15, 12, 10, 11, 12, 12, 13, 18, 17, 17, 19, 19, 29, 34, 37, 37, 39, 40   (21)

PARTON, DOLLY/LINDA RONSTADT/EMMYLOU HARRIS

3-28-87   *Trio*   (WB 2-25491)   22, 2, 4, 8, 9, 14, 2, 6, 6, 8, 6, 13, 13, 14, 15, 20, 32, 33, 33, 36, 38, 38   (22)

THE PET SHOP BOYS

10-17-87   *Actually*   (EMI-Manhattan CDP 46972)   32, 32, 34, 38   (4)

8-23-86   *Please*   (EMI America CDP 46271)   24, 22, 23, 26, 33, 33, 33, 34, 35   (9)

PETTY, TOM, AND THE HEARTBREAKERS

6-06-87   *Let Me Up (I've Had Enough)*   (MCA 27429-2)   33, 23, 23, 27, 29, 30, 31, 32, 32, 30, 30, 26, 34, 37   (14)

4-05-86   *Pack Up The Plantation—Live*   (MCA MCAD2 8021)   38, 37, 38, 35, 38, 40   (6)

6-29-85   *Southern Accents*   (MCA MCAD 5486)   35, 30, 28, 27, 25, 26, 30, 32, 35, 33, 37, 40   (12)

PHANTOM OF THE OPERA

3-05-88   *{Original London Cast}*   *(Polydor 831 272-2)*   *23, 17, 13, 15, 18, 21, 30, 34, 34, 37*   *(10)*

PINK FLOYD   (*See also:* ROGER WATERS)

9-15-84   *The Dark Side Of The Moon*   (Cap. CDP7 46001 2)   5, 3, 3, 3, 3, 5, 5, 4, 3, 3, 3, 3, 3, 3, 4, 4, 4, 4, 4, 4, 4, 4, 2, 2, 2, 2, 4, 3, 3, 3, 2, 1, 1, 2, 3,

2, 3, 4, 4, 4, 3, 2, 2, 3, 3, 5, 4, 5, 5, 6, 6, 7, 6, 6, 7, 6, 5, 5, 5, 5, 4, 4, 5, 5, 6, 6, 7, 7, 7, 7, 9, 10, 12, 13, 12, 12, 11, 15, 13, 14, 13, 12, 10, 9, 8, 9, 8, 6, 6, 5, 6, 6, 7, 8, 11, 12, 20, 21, 25, 25, 28, 26, 26, 27, 29, 28, 28, 27, 24, 18, 17, 13, 17, 12, 11, 11, 16, 19, 22, 21, 21, 21, 21, 17, 19, 20, 17, 20, 25, 35, (4), 23, 21, 21, 21, 17, 20, 22, 33, 37, 36, 36, 39   (142)

9-15-84   *Meddle*   (Cap. CDP7 46034 2)   14, 17, 26, 28, 27, 27, 29, 30   (8)

9-26-87   *A Momentary Lapse Of Reason*   (Col. CK 40599)   28, 5, 2, 1, 2, 1, 1, 1, 2, 1, 1, 1, 2, 2, 2, 2, 3, 3, 2, 5, 5, 7, 8, 8, 9, 15, 18, 21, 25, 26, 29, 37, 39   (33)

6-01-85   *The Wall*   (Col. C2K 36183)   25, 22, 20, 18, 16, 15, 15, 14, 17, 18, 19, 19, 22, 22, 21, 21, 18, 23, 22, 24, 20, 19, 21, 24, 25, 38, 39   (27)

5-18-85   *Wish You Were Here*   (Col. CK 33453)   28, 28, 23, 21, 21, 21, 23, 24, 24, 26, 27, 35, 34, 35, 36, 34, 39, 38, 37, 37, 38, 37, 36, 35, 39   (25)

PLANT, ROBERT   (*See also:* THE HONEYDRIPPERS; LED ZEPPELIN)

3-19-88   *Now And Zen*   (Es Paranza/Atl. 7 90863-2)   16, 7, 3, 2, 1, 1, 1, 1, 1, 1, 2, 1, 6, 7———   (14)

6-22-85   *Shaken 'N Stirred*   (Es Paranza 7 90265-2)   27, 20, 16, 16, 15, 14, 14, 16, 18, 20, 20, 26, 31, 35   (14)

THE POINTER SISTERS/THE POINTERS

10-27-84   *Break Out*   (Planet PCD1-4705A)   24, 20, 18, 17, 16, 12, 10, 10, 12, 12, 12, 12, 11, 10, 10, 11, 11, 17, 16, 14, 14, 13, 12, 11, 11, 9, 9, 10, 10, 9, 9, 12, 13, 14, 14, 24, 31, 32, 33, 33, 38, 39, 40   (43)

9-07-85   *Contact*   (RCA PCD1-5487)   30, 23, 20, 18, 21, 22, 22, 26, 31, 40, 40   (11)

POISON

5-23-87   *Look What The Cat Dragged In*   (Enigma CDE-73202)   28, 20, 20, 25, 25, 30, 32, 34, 34, 35, 35, 38   (12)

5-21-88   *Open Up And Say . . . Ahh!*   (Enigma/Cap. C2-48493)   34, 11, 7, 4, 5———   (5)

POLICE   (*See also:* STING)

11-29-86   *Every Breath You Take; The Singles*   (A&M CD 3902)   29, 15, 5, 4, 6,
           6, 6, 6, 7, 8, 7, 7, 8, 8, 13, 16, 20, 19, 25, 34, 36, 39, 37, 37   (21)

9-15-84   *Synchronicity*   (A&M CD 3735)   4, 5, 8, 9, 8, 9, 9, 9, 13, 14, 13, 17,
          23, 26, 25   (15)

THE PRETENDERS

12-20-86   *Get Close*   (Sire/WB 2-25488)   32, 28, 28, 28, 28, 18, 15, 12, 12, 13,
           17, 24, 29, 35, 37   (12)

12-26-87   *The Singles*   (Sire/WB 2-25664)   30, 30, 30, 27, 30, 31, 36   (7)

PRETTY IN PINK

6-07-86   [Original Film Soundtrack]   (A&M CD 5113)   33, 30, 26, 21, 26,
          26, 34, 38, 36, 40   (10)

PRINCE (AND THE REVOLUTION)   (*See also:* THE TIME)

5-11-85   *Around The World In A Day*   (Paisley Park/WB 25286-2)   20, 13, 8,
          6, 5, 5, 5, 4, 7, 8, 8, 8, 8, 12, 16, 19, 19, 18, 18, 21, 24, 28, 33   (23)

6-04-88   *Lovesexy*   (Paisley Park/WB 25720-2)   5, 1, 3——— (3)

5-31-86   *Parade*   (Paisley Park/WB 25395-2)   18, 14, 11, 6, 5, 6, 11, 16, 17,
          21, 27, 34, 38, 39   (14)

9-15-84   *Purple Rain*   (WB 25110-2)   1, 1, 1, 1, 1, 1, 1, 1, 1, 1, 1, 1, 1, 1, 1,
          3, 3, 3, 3, 3, 3, 3, 3, 3, 7, 8, 7, 5, 4, 4, 9, 10, 11, 11, 11, 16, 18, 19, 20,
          23, 31, 37, 39, 40   (44)

4-18-87   *Sign "O" The Times*   (Paisley Park/WB 25577-2)   26, 19, 10, 10, 10,
          7, 13, 17, 21, 21, 26, 19   (12)

R.E.M.

5-30-87   *Dead Letter Office*   (I.R.S. CD 70054)   28, 21, 27, 27, 32, 34, 36, 36,
          37, 37, 40   (11)

9-26-87   *Document*   (I.R.S. IRSD-42059)   33, 12, 7, 6, 8, 7, 8, 9, 7, 5, 5, 5, 9,
          17, 17, 17, 22, 25, 21, 18, 17, 16, 15, 18, 28, 33, 38   (27)

9-07-85   *Fables Of The Reconstruction*   (I.R.S. IRDS-5592)   34, 22, 19, 16, 16, 19, 33   (7)

9-20-86   *Life's Rich Pageant*   (I.R.S. IRSD-5783)   21, 21, 17, 16, 17, 15, 22, 28, 36, 37, 40, 40, 40   (13)

RATT

3-07-87   *Dancing Undercover*   (Atl. 81683-2)   28, 33, 29, 31, 34   (5)

8-24-85   *Invasion Of Your Privacy*   (Atl. 81257-2)   28, 25, 24, 27, 31, 31, 36, 40   (8)

REED, LOU

7-05-86   *Mistrial*   (RCA PCD1-7190)   39, 38   (2)

REO SPEEDWAGON

2-23-85   *Wheels Are Turnin'*   (Epic EK 39593)   25, 24, 27, 26, 26, 29, 29, 27   (8)

RICHIE, LIONEL

9-15-84   *Can't Slow Down*   (Motown 6059 MD)   11, 9, 6, 4, 4, 3, 4, 5, 7, 7, 6, 6, 7, 9, 8, 6, 6, 6, 6, 7, 8, 9, 8, 7, 12, 11, 10, 11, 10, 9, 7, 5, 5, 4, 4, 4, 7, 11, 11, 11, 11, 15, 19, 18, 18, 18, 17, 20, 24, 24, 23, 22, 26, 29, 30, 32, 30, 28, 30   (59)

9-20-86   *Dancing On The Ceiling*   (Motown 6158 MD)   15, 15, 13, 15, 14, 11, 10, 9, 10, 10, 9, 12, 11, 9, 10, 10, 10, 10, 9, 9, 9, 11, 11, 11, 11, 17, 18, 20   (27)

RIDDLE, NELSON   *(See:* LINDA RONSTADT)

RITENOUR, LEE   *(See:* DAVE GRUSIN)

ROBERTSON, ROBBIE

11-21-87   *Robbie Robertson*   (Geffen 2-24160)   25, 23, 23, 23, 24, 22, 22, 22, 21, 23, 22, 21, 20, 21, 20, 24, 24, 27, 32, 38, 38, 38   (22)

ROGER

1-16-88   *Unlimited*   (Reprise 25496-2)   30, 27, 26, 24, 22, 27, 31, 34, 37   (9)

THE ROLLING STONES

4-12-86   *Dirty Work*   (Rolling Stones/CBS CK 40250)   17, 11, 7, 4, 3, 3, 2, 2, 2, 3, 4, 6, 4, 5, 6, 10, 20, 26, 33, 37, 37, 37, 35   (23)

1-24-87   *Hot Rocks* 1964–1971   (Abkco 6667-2)   35, 33, 39, 38, 38, 38   (6)

RONSTADT, LINDA   *(See also:* DOLLY PARTON)

1-30-88   *Canciones De Mi Padre*   (Elektra 60765-2)   33, 29, 26, 26, 27, 35, 38, 38, 40   (9)

RONSTADT, LINDA, WITH NELSON RIDDLE AND HIS ORCHESTRA

10-25-86   *For Sentimental Reasons*   (Asylum 9 60474-2)   35, 24, 21, 15, 15, 15, 19, 18, 17, 14, 14, 14, 14, 11, 13, 22, 29   (17)

3-09-85   *Lush Life*   (Asylum 9 60387-2)   25, 18, 16, 14, 13, 13, 16, 18, 20, 28, (2), 33, 32   (12)

9-15-84   *What's New*   (Asylum 9 60260-2)   2, 6, 9, 11, 12, 17, 23, 25, 24, 23, 23, 30, 30   (13)

ROTH, DAVID LEE

10-11-86   Eat Em And Smile   (WB 25470-2)   23, 20, 19, 14, 16, 18, 18, 17, 21, 24, 26, 27, 27, 27, 27, 29, 29, 38, 40   (19)

2-13-88   Skyscraper   (WB 25671-2)   33, 17, 9, 6, 5, 7, 9, 11, 11, 10, 11, 17, 16, 16, 15, 15, 20, 24, 28———   (19)

ROXY MUSIC   *(See also:* BRYAN FERRY)

9-15-84   *Avalon*   (WB 23686-2)   18, 19, 27, 27, 28, 29   (6)

RUN-D.M.C.

7-19-86   *Raising Hell*   (Profile PCD 1217)   38   (1)

11-11-86   *Raising Hell*   (Profile PCD 1217)   35, 35, 36, 38, 40   (5)

4-04-87   *Raising Hell*   (Profile PCD 1217)   8, 2, 2, 6, 8, 12, 21, 30, 36   (9)

RUSH

9-26-87   *Hold Your Fire*   (Mer. 832 464-2)   30, 15, 4, 4, 6, 4, 7, 7, 10, 14, 25, 36, 40   (13)

1-18-86   *Power Windows*   (Mer. 826 098-2)   20, 12, 10, 9, 9, 11, 17, 19, 22, 23, 24, 23, 30, 33, 39   (15)

SADE

5-04-85   *Diamond Life*   (Portrait RK 39581)   21, 19, 14, 11, 9, 8, 8, 7, 6, 8, 9, 9, 9, 16, 24, 28, 29, 29, 28, 28, 27, 27, 26, 25, 34, 37, 35, 31, 29, 26, 25, 22, 19, 16, 16, 15, 15, 15, 15, 15, 14, 14, 19, 19, 20, 21, 22, 20, 17, 19, 18, 17, 16, 17, 18, 25, 40   (56)

1-18-86   *Promise*   (Portrait RK 40263)   12, 7, 4, 3, 3, 3, 3, 3, 3, 2, 2, 2, 2, 2, 3, 3, 4, 4, 4, 4, 4, 5, 9, 9, 14, 16, 21, 29, 31, 37, 38, 40   (32)

6-04-88   *Stronger Than Pride*   (Epic EK 44210)   19, 12, 6———   (3)

SANBORN, DAVID   (*See also:* BOB JAMES)

3-21-87   *A Change Of Heart*   (WB 27479-2)   30, 25, 28, 19, 20, 12, 12, 13, 23, 36, 40, 38, 32, 32, 36, 37, 39, 39, 40, 40   (20)

SATRIANI, JOE

4-23-88   *Surfing With The Alien*   (Relativity/Important 8193-2)   35, 31, 28, 28, 24, 21, 18, 21, 15   (9)

THE SCORPIONS

5-14-88   *Savage Amusement*   (Mer. 832 963-2)   11, 8, 6, 9, 19, 24   (6)

11-02-85   *World Wide Live*   (Mer. 824 344-2)   37, 35, 35, 34, 33, 40, 39, 40, 40   (9)

SEGER, BOB(, AND THE SILVER BULLET BAND)

7-19-86   *Like A Rock*   (Cap. CDP7-46195 2)   28, 24, 10, 8, 10, 9, 7, 13, 15, 18, 18, 19, 19, 19, 18, 17, 36   (17)

5-31 86 Night Moves (Cap. CDP7-46128 2)   28, 22, 21, 29, 40 (5)

3-29-86 *Stranger In Town* (Cap. CDP7 46074)   32, 29, 26, 26, 33, 37, 36 (7)

SEVERINSEN, DOC *(See:* THE TONIGHT SHOW BAND)

SIMON, CARLY

5-23-87 *Coming Around Again* (Arista ARCD 8443)   32, 26, 26, 28, 28, 33, 35, 37, 37, 38, 38, (4), 27, 24, 20, 18, 18, 36 (17)

SIMON, PAUL *(See also:* SIMON AND GARFUNKEL)

10-04-86 *Graceland* (WB 25447-2)   8, 4, 4, 2, 7, 4, 5, 4, 3, 3, 3, 2, 3, 3, 3, 3, 2, 2, 3, 3, 1, 1, 1, 5, 8, 9, 7, 3, 3, 2, 2, 3, 7, 10, 11, 7, 8, 8, 8, 6, 6, 6, 6, 6, 6, 9, 13, 8, 13, 14, 15, 17, 24, 26, 28, 30, 31, 32, 30, 32, 34, 34, 34, 34, 34, 34, 34, 35, 34, 36, 34, 34, 35, 35, 38 (75)

SIMON AND GARFUNKEL *(See also:* PAUL SIMON)

3-02-85 *Greatest Hits* (Col. CK 31350)   25, 23, 22, 22, 24, 24, 23, 30, 30, 29, 30, 29, 30, 30, 35, 36, 37, 39 (18)

SIMPLE MINDS

1-04-86 *Once Upon A Time* (A&M/Virgin 5092)   33, 33, 22, 22, 22, 22, 24, 26, 26, 28, 29, 34, 38 (13)

SIMPLY RED

4-11-87 *Men And Women* (Elektra 60727-2)   20, 18, 11, 15, 14, 17, 16, 21, 25, 31, 31, 35, 38, 40, 40 (15)

7-19-86 *Picture Book* (Elektra 60452-2)   33, 27, 22, 17, 17, 19, 23, 29, 31, 36, 36, 35, 35, 38 (14)

THE SMITHS *(See also:* MORRISSEY)

5-09-87 *Louder Than Bombs* (Sire/WB 25569-2)   27, 25, 34, 36, 35, (3), 25, 22, 20, 16, 16, 22, 33, 34, 37, 40 (15)

10-10-87 *Strangeways, Here We Come* (Sire/WB 25649-2)   32, 29, 26, 23, 23, 25, 26, 26, 26, 27, 36 (11)

SPRINGSTEEN, BRUCE(, AND THE E STREET BAND)

9-15-84   *Born In The U.S.A.*   (Col. CK 38653)   6, 2, 2, 2, 2, 2, 2, 2, 2, 2, 2, 2, 2, 2, 2, 2, 1, 1, 1, 1, 2, 2, 2, 4, 5, 5, 5, 7, 8, 9, 9, 8, 4, 2, 2, 1, 1, 3, 2, 2, 3, 3, 4, 3, 3, 4, 5, 4, 2, 1, 1, 4, 3, 3, 3, 4, 3, 3, 2, 2, 2, 2, 2, 3, 3, 3, 3, 3, 4, 4, 4, 4, 7, 9, 9, 8, 7, 6, 7, 8, 10, 10, 11, 10, 12, 15, 16, 20, 19, 19, 17, 26, 29, 33, 40   (93)

12-06-86   *Bruce Springsteen And The E Street Band Live* 1975–1985   (Col. C3K 40558)   1, 1, 1, 1, 1, 1, 1, 1, 4, 4, 5, 8, 7, 7, 6, 19, 27, 30, 39, 40   (19)

6-01-85   *The River*   (Col. C2K 36854)   36, 34, 39, 38, 40, 40, 39, 40   (8)

10-24-87   *Tunnel Of Love*   (Col. CK 40999)   1, 2, 2, 3, 3, 4, 7, 8, 6, 9, 9, 9, 8, 8, 10, 12, 11, 8, 7, 9, 12, 17, 20, 19, 19, 17, 16, 16, 19, 22, 21, 23, 26, 30, 35   (35)

9-22-84   *The Wild, The Innocent And The E Street Shuffle*   (Col. CK 32432)   23, 25, 24, 26   (4)

SPYRO GYRA

11-02-85   *Alternating Currents*   (MCA MCAD 8606)   36, 31, 30, 29, 29, 30, 31, 36, 36   (9)

9-06-86   *Breakout*   (MCA MCAD 5753)   26, 25, 32, 32, 38   (5)

SQUEEZE

10-10-87   *Babylon And On*   (A&M CD 516)   —, 19, 19, 18, 19, 19, 19, 29, 38, 40, 37, 36, 36, 36, 40   (15)

THE STARSHIP   (Formerly: Jefferson Airplane/Jefferson Starship)

11-23-85   *Knee Deep In The Hoopla*   (Grunt/RCA 5488)   27, 22, 21, 20, 18, 18, 17, 17, 24, 33, 37, 36, 34, 32, 29, 26, 23, 20, 18, 14, 15, 20, 20, 19, 20, 17, 16, 15, 20, 20, 21, 27   (32)

8-08-87   *No Protection*   (Grunt/RCA G13-2-17)   20, 16, 16, 16, 19, 23, 35   (7)

STEELY DAN

10-13-84   *Aja*   (MCA MCAD 37214)   24, 16, 12, 10, 9, 8, 9, 9, 9, 11, 14, 14, 14, 14, 15, 17, 17, 20, 26   (19)

6-15-85   *A Decade Of Steely Dan*   (MCA MCAD 5570) 25, 20, 14, 9, 7, 7, 6, 6,
7, 11, 10, 14, 14, 16, 15, 15, 15, 18, 19, 23, 23, 33, 33, 32, 30, 24, 23,
23, 23, 21, 22, 21, 24, 40, (3), 36, 34, 32, 31, 34, 32, 29, 30, 36, 36,
33, 31, 29, 29, 27, 26, 25, 23, 19, 21, 29, 35, 35, 36, 36, 35, 34, 32,
30, 34, 34, 34, 32, 31, 29, 28, 23, 22, 24, 22, 27, 26, 30, 29, 29, 29,
29, 26, 24, 30, 31, 39, 39   (86)

STEWART, ROD

6-18-88   *Out Of Order*   (WB 25684-2)   32———   (1)

STING   *(See also:* THE POLICE)

8-03-85   *The Dream Of The Blue Turtles*   (A&M CD 3750)   22, 18, 6, 2, 1, 1, 1,
2, 5, 9, 9, 11, 11, 10, 11, 11, 12, 12, 10, 11, 12, 12, 11, 11, 6, 5, 6, 6,
6, 9, 9, 12, 12, 13, 15, 16, 14, 13, 12, 14, 18, 28, 36, 35, 36   (45)

10-31-87   *. . . Nothing Like The Sun*   (A&M CD 6402)   33, 21, 11, 6, 3, 2, 2, 1,
1, 1, 1, 1, 2, 3, 3, 4, 4, 3, 4, 4, 4, 4, 8, 9, 12, 12, 14, 14, 19, 19, 19, 28,
33, 36———   (34)

STREISAND, BARBRA

9-15-84   *Barbra Streisand's Greatest Hits, Vol. 2*   (Col. CK 35679)   28, 27,
29   (3)

1-04-86   *The Broadway Album*   (Col. CK 40092)   19, 19, 11, 4, 2, 2, 2, 2, 2, 2,
2, 3, 3, 3, 3, 5, 4, 5, 6, 7, 7, 8, 8, 12, 16, 26, 40   (27)

3-29-86   *Memories*   (Col. CK 37678)   35, 35, 38, 39, (2), 35, 35   (6)

5-23-87   *One Voice*   (Col. CK 40788)   21, 12, 9, 5, 5, 10, 11, 14, 15, 17, 17,
23, 25, 25, 33, 36   (16)

SUPERTRAMP

6-22-85   *Brother Where You Bound*   (A&M CD 5014)   25, 18, 12, 11, 10, 10, 9,
13, 13, 17, 17, 19, 20, 22, 25, 35, 36   (17)

SURE, AL B.

6-11-88   *In Effect Mode*   (Uptown/WB 9 25662-2)   36, 31———   (2)

SWEAT, KEITH

4-09-88 *Make It Last Forever* (Elektra 60763-2) 34, 28, 24, 21, 18, 21, 22, 27, 31, 38 (10)

SWING OUT SISTER

3-19-88 *It's Better To Travel* (Mer. 832 213-2) 32, 28, 34 (3)

TALKING HEADS

8-17-85 *Little Creatures* (Sire 9 25305-2) 22, 13, 7, 6, 5, 5, 4, 4, 7, 7, 4, 4, 8, 9, 8, 8, 7, 9, 10, 10, 13, 13, 14, 14, 14, 20, 23, 21, 21, 22, 20, 17, 14, 11, 11, 14, 14, 13, 14, 13, 14, 22, 26, 29, 38 (45)

10-25-86 *Little Creatures* (Sire 9 25305-2) —, 26, 13, 9, 8, 7, 7, 15, 20, 24, 24, 24, 24, 23, 20, 24, 25, 22, 21, 29, 12, 12, 14, 17, 21, 22, 25, 23, 35, 38, 38, 39, 39 (33)

4-02-88 *Naked* (Sire 9 25654-2) 5, 3, 4, 2, 2, 3, 2, 2, 7, 12, 14, 17——— (12)

11-17-84 *Stop Making Sense* (Sire 9 25186-2) 25, 21, 18, 16, 12, 11, 10, 10, 11, 13, 13, 12, 12, 18, 27 (15)

TAYLOR, JAMES

2-27-88 *Never Die Young* (Col. CK 40851) 32, 14, 7, 5, 6, 9, 15, 16, 19, 23, 33, 34, 38, 39 (14)

1-25-86 *That's Why I'm Here* (Col. CK 40052) 28, 19, 16, 18, 23, 28, 32, 34, 39, 40 (10)

TEARS FOR FEARS

4-20-85 *Songs From The Big Chair* (Mer. 824 300-2) 25, 24, 19, 16, 15, 13, 8, 9, 9, 8, 7, 6, 5, 4, 3, 3, 4, 4, 5, 4, 5, 7, 7, 6, 5, 4, 4, 7, 7, 5, 6, 6, 6, 11, 12, 11, 11, 9, 9, 5, 8, 8, 10, 11, 10, 12, 13, 15, 15, 17, 20, 24, 24, 29, 32, 32 (56)

10, 000 MANIACS

5-28-88 *In My Tribe* (Elektra 60738-2) 35, 32, 29, 27——— (4)

.38 SPECIAL

9-12-87   *Flashback*   (A&M CD 3910)   26, 23, 23, 25, 40   (5)

7-19-86   *Strength In Numbers*   (A&M CD 5115)   26, 25, 32, 38, 39   (5)

THE THOMPSON TWINS

5-02-87   *Close To The Bone*   (Arista ARCD 8449)   33, 29, 27, 31, 34, 29, 26, 26, 31, 33, 35, 35, 36, 36, 39, 40, 40   (17)

12-21-85   *Here's To Future Days*   (Arista JRCD 8276)   28, 28, 20, 20, 19, 20, 25, 33, 36, 39, 40, 39, 40   (13)

THOROGOOD, GEORGE, AND THE DESTROYERS

3-05-88   *Born To Be Bad*   (EMI-Manhattan 46973-2)   27, 26, 29, 30, 32, 35, 37, 38, 40   (9)

TIFFANY

1-16-88   *Tiffany*   (MCA MCAD 5793)   25, 22, 14, 11, 10, 13, 17, 16, 15, 19, 22, 27, 26, 23, 26, 26, 26, 35, 35, 36, 37, 39   (22)

'TIL TUESDAY

8-03-85   *Voices Carry*   (Epic RK 39458)   34, 26, 25, 25, 27, 33, 36, 39, 40   (9)

THE TIME   *(See also:* PRINCE)

5-04-85   *Ice Cream Castles*   (WB 25109-2)   26, 24, 27, (1), 35, 38   (5)

THE TONIGHT SHOW BAND/DOC SEVERINSEN

3-14-87   *The Tonight Show Band/Doc Severinsen*   (Amherst AMH 93311)   28, 22, 24, 22, 16, 16, 22, 20, 19, 24, 39, 37   (12)

4-04-87   *The Tonight Show Band II/Doc Severinsen*   (Amherst AMH 93312)   27, 25, 27, 27, 32   (5)

TOP GUN

8-09-86   [Original Film Soundtrack]   (Col. CK 40323)   19, 9, 4, 3, 4, 5, 5, 5, 4, 9, 8, 6, 9, 8, 7, 6, 10, 9, 14, 14, 12, 12, 12, 12, 19, 21, 36, 39   (25)

TOWNSHEND, PETE   *(See also:* THE WHO)

2-01-86   *White City—A Novel*   (Atco 90473-2)   21, 17, 13, 13, 14, 18, 19,
19, 22, 22, 20, 21, 19, 17, 15, 16, 20, 27, 32, 34   (20)

TURNER, TINA

11-01-86   *Break Every Rule*   (Cap. CDP7 46323 2)   31, 12, 11, 13, 13, 13, 13,
15, 23, 23, 23, 23, 27, 34, 40   (15)

10-06-84   *Private Dancer*   (Cap. CDP7 46041 2)   22, 15, 10, 8, 7, 6, 5, 5, 5, 5,
6, 7, 9, 9, 9, 9, 8, 7, 8, 9, 16, 17, 20, 19, 20, 18, 17, 14, 12, 10, 9, 9, 8,
15, 14, 14, 13, 13, 19, 20, 22, 22, 22, 27, 31, 33, 34, 37, 36, 35, 30,
28, 27, 26, 25, 24, 22, 18, 17, 15, 15, 15, 15, 15, 15, 21, 21, 25, 27,
34, 38, 39   (72)

U2

5-03-86   *Boy*   (Island 90040-2)   18, 16, 15, 15, 20, 25, 28   (7)

4-04-87   *The Joshua Tree*   (Island 90581-2)   1, 1, 1, 1, 1, 1, 4, 4, 4, 3, 1, 1, 2,
3, 3, 3, 3, 3, 2, 2, 2, 3, 4, 6, 6, 9, 13, 14, 14, 14, 12, 14, 14, 12, 12, 13,
13, 13, 14, 14, 14, 12, 9, 8, 8, 8, 9, 10, 10, 11, 8, 10, 13, 12, 14, 18,
19, 20, 26, 37   (60)

5-03-86   *Under A Blood Red Sky*   (Island 90127-2)   25, 23, 22, 21, 19, 19, 19,
28, 39   (9)

8-17-85   *The Unforgettable Fire*   (Island 90231-2)   20, 15, 12, 11, 11, 13, 13,
13, 16, 17, 17, 20, 22, 32, 40, 40   (16)

USA FOR AFRICA

8-03-85   *We Are The World*   (PolyGram 824 822-2)   20 17, 14, 16, 16, 15,
19, 28, 35   (9)

VAN HALEN

5-31-86   *5150*   (WB 25394-2)   16, 11, 8, 2, 2, 2, 3, 4, 5, 6, 6, 5, 7, 7, 9, 10,
16, 16, 21, 33, 33, 33, 30, 34, 25, 26, 30, 32, 29, 28, 31, 31, 31, 31,
32, 39   (33)

9-15-84   *1984*   (WB 23985-2)   8, 10, 11, 10, 11, 13, 13, 16, 15, 15, 15, 14,
17, 17, 16, 13, 13, 13, 12, 12, 13, 16, 22   (23)

6-11-88   *OU812*   (WB 25732-1)   5, 1——   (2)

VANDROSS, LUTHER

2-21-87   *Give Me The Reason*   (Epic EK 40415)   34, 26, 32, 30, 40   (5)

VANGELIS

9-15-84   *Chariots Of Fire—Original Film Soundtrack*   (Polydor 800 020-2)   25   (1)

VARIOUS ARTISTS

2-23-85   *Arista's Perfect 10*   (Arista ARCD 8268)   23, 22, 26, 28   (4)

10-26-85   *Atlantic Soul Classics*   (Warner Special Products 9 27601-2)   27, 25, 23, 22, 23, 35   (6)

12-29-84   *The Big Chill Soundtrack Plus Additional Classics*   (Motown 6120 MD)   27, 27, 24, 22, 19, 15, 13, 13, 18, 20, 30, 30, 29, 28, 30, 29, 26, 25   (18)

9-15-84   *Digital Domain*   (Elektra 60303-2)   20, 21, 17, 20, 21, 23, 28, 28, 29   (9)

9-29-84   *Hear The Light, Volume 1*   (PolyGram 816 054-2)   22, 21, 20, 22, 21, 23, 30   (7)

2-23-85   *Sampler III*   (American Gramaphone AGCD 366)   28, 27, 29, 29, 30, 30   (6)

5-24-86   *Windham Hill Records Sampler '86*   (Windham Hill/A&M CD 1048)   35, 32, 30, 31, 31, 29, 28, 27, 27, 28, 28, 28, 30, 34, 35, 39, 40   (17)

9-15-84   *Windham Hill Sampler; Vol. 1*   (Windham Hill/A&M WD 1015)   24   (1)

VAUGHN, STEVIE RAY, AND DOUBLE TROUBLE

3-07-87   *Live Alive*   (Epic EGK 40511)   26, 34, 25, 21, 33, 29, 31, 36, 39, 38   (10)

1-04-86   *Soul To Soul*   (Epic RK 40036)   31, 31, 29, 30, 35, 39, 40   (7)

VEGA, SUZANNE

5-16-87   *Solitude Standing*   (A&M CD 5136)   30, 27, 23, 24, 20, 20, 28, 30, 29, 24, 19, 19, 18, 13, 12, 18, 22, 21, 21, 24, 27, 28, 30, 33, 36, 36, 36, 36, 37, 37, 38   (31)

VISION QUEST

4-27-85   [Original Film Soundtrack]   (Geffen 24063-2)   28, 28, 29, 30, (1), 37, 40, 40   (7)

VOLLENWEIDER, ANDREAS

8-23-86   *Down To The Moon*   (CBS Masterworks MK 42255)   22, 18, 10, 6, 6, 6, 5, 5, 7, 8, 6, 3, 4, 3, 5, 11, 12, 13, 19, 19, 19, 19, 21, 22, 23, 21, 28, 31, 34, 32, 32, 32   (32)

4-13-85   *White Winds*   (CBS Masterworks MK 39963)   25, 21, 19, 18, 18, 22, 26, 29, 28, 34   (10)

WALSH, JOE

7-20-85   *The Confessor*   (WB 25281)   36, 34, 37, 37, 39, 38, 38   (7)

WATERS, ROGER   (*See also:* PINK FLOYD)

7-11-87   *Radio K.A.O.S.*   (Col. CKG 40795)   21, 17, 13, 13, 13, 17, 17, 25, 26, 31, 32, 36, 36, 33, 35, 37, 37, 39   (18)

WHAM!   (*See also:* GEORGE MICHAEL)

2-23-85   *Make It Big*   (Col. CK 39595)   21, 19, 17, 15, 15, 19, 20, 24, 24, 26, 25, 25, 25, 23, 21, 24, 27, 36, 36, 35, 34, 32, 28, 28, 27, 29, 31, 30, 29, 29, 34, 33, 33, 32, 32, 38, 40, 39, 37, 33, 27, 25, 22, 21, 21, 23, 23, 32, 40   (48)

9-06-86   *Music From The Edge Of Heaven*   (Col. CK 40285)   24, 22, 20, 20, 20, 20, 24, 27, 38   (9)

WHITESNAKE

4-25-87   *Whitesnake*   (Geffen 24099-2)   —, 26, 23, 16, 18, 22, 22, 18, 18, 18, 22, 13, 10, 7, 7, 7, 7, 7, 5, 6, 5, 5, 6, 9, 11, 13, 13, 14, 12, 10, 11, 11,

12, 11, 11, 19, 19, 19, 16, 14, 11, 10, 14, 12, 13, 12, 20, 21, 24, 28, 31, 34, 37, 38, 40   (54)

THE WHO   *(See also:* PETE TOWNSHEND)

6-01-85   *Quadrophenia*   (MCA MCAD2 6895)   34, 31, 31, 30, 31, 33, 33, 34, 36, 40, 40   (11)

6-01-85   *Who Are You*   (MCA MCAD 37003)   38, 37   (2)

1-26-85   *Who's Next*   (MCA MCAD 37217)   25, 23, 18, 16, 15, 15, 18, 24, 28, (3), 23, 21, 30   (12)

WHO'S THAT GIRL

8-29-87   [Original Film Soundtrack]   (Sire 25611-2)   22, 14, 10, 7, 7, 17, 17, 21, 34   (9)

WINSTON, GEORGE

9-15-84   *Autumn*   (Windham Hill/A&M WD 1012)   27, 22, 20, 25, 25, 28, 30, 29   (8)

11-09-85   *December*   (Windham Hill/A&M CD 1025)   34, 31, 28, 26, 23, 21, 19, 19, 18, 18, 18, 17, 17, 18, 21, 22, 24, 24, 26, 27, 27, 30, 40, 40, 40, 40   (27)

12-27-86   *December*   (Windham Hill/A&M CD 1025)   33, 33, 33, 33, 28, 36   (6)

WINWOOD, STEVE

11-15-86   *Arc Of A Diver*   (Island/WB 24576-2)   33, 33, 26, 25, 25, 29, 28, 28, 28, 28, 30, 32, 32, 34, 32, 37, 36, 40, 39, 40   (20)

8-09-86   *Back In The High Life*   (Island/WB 25448-2)   30, 22, 9, 4, 3, 4, 3, 3, 3, 2, 2, 3, 2, 1, 1, 2, 2, 5, 8, 8, 8, 8, 8, 8, 8, 6, 6, 5, 4, 4, 13, 13, 10, 11, 13, 6, 6, 4, 3, 5, 9, 9, 6, 10, 10, 10, 9, 9, 8, 8, 10, 10, 9, 11, 11, 12, 12, 13, 13, 15, 21, 25, 17, 29, 28, 29, 28, 30, 32, 31, 33, 35, 39, 39, 39, 39, 40   (77)

12-05-87   *Chronicles*   (Island/WB 25660-2)   16, 16, 18, 20, 20, 20, 17, 16, 13, 14, 16, 19, 21, 21, 22, 24, 31, 36   (18)

THE WOMAN IN RED (*See also:* STEVIE WONDER)

1-19-85 [Original Film Soundtrack] (Motown 6108 MD) 23, 18, 16, 15, 17, 20, 29 (7)

WONDER, STEVIE (*See also:* THE WOMAN IN RED)

12-19-87 *Characters* (Motown 6248 MD) 21, 10, 10, 10, 14, 18, 18, 17, 21, 22, 22, 26, 31, 31, 35, 39 (16)

11-09-85 *In Square Circle* (Tamla TAMD 06134) 21, 16, 9, 7, 5, 5, 8, 8, 10, 10, 13, 16, 16, 15, 17, 17, 18, 16, 16, 16, 19, 21, 25, 25, 23, 27, 29, 38 (28)

10-05-85 *Love Songs* (Tamla TAMD 6144) 34, 31, 31, 40 (4)

XTC

5-02-87 *Skylarking* (Geffen 24117-2) 35, 31, 32, 40 (4)

YES

10-24-87 *Big Generator* (Atl. 90522-2) 23, 10, 5, 6, 5, 7, 10, 9, 8, 6, 6, 6, 9, 13, 16, 20, 25, 30, 33, 39 (20)

9-15-84 *90125* (Atco 90125-2) 7, 12, 18, 18, 22, 21, 19, 22, 22, 20, 20, 27, 27, 29, 17, 26, 26, 28 (18)

YOUNG, NEIL, AND CRAZY HORSE

8-15-87 *Life* (Geffen 24154-2) 24, 19, 11, 11, 16, 30, 40 (7)

YOUNG, PAUL

8-10-85 *The Secret Of Association* (Col. CK 39957) 28, 26, 26, 24, 23, 24, 23, 20, 18, 15, 13, 13, 18, 20, 23, 31, 31, 34, 37, 39, 39 (21)

ZZ TOP

11-30-85 *Afterburner* (WB 25342-2) 24, 12, 10, 3, 3, 3, 3, 4, 6, 7, 7, 8, 8, 8, 9, 11, 12, 10, 8, 9, 10, 10, 10, 10, 9, 8, 7, 17, 18, 27, 28, 29, 30, 29, 36, 40 (36)

9-15-84 *Eliminator* (WB 23774-2) 10, 7, 5, 5, 6, 7, 10, 11, 11, 11, 10, 13, 13, 14, 13, 18, 18, 19, 20, 28 (20)

C. ALBUM-TITLE INDEX

Live 1975–1985 (Bruce Springsteen and The E Street Band)
Building The Perfect Beast (Don Henley)
By The Light Of The Moon (Los Lobos)

California Project (Papa Doo Run Run)
The Camera Never Lies (Michael Franks)
Canciones De Mi Padre (Linda Ronstadt)
Can't Slow Down (Lionel Richie)
Can't Wait Another Minute (Five Star)
Centerfield (John Fogerty)
Chalk Mark In A Rain Storm (Joni Mitchell)
Change Of Heart (Cyndi Lauper)
A Change Of Heart (David Sanborn)
Characters (Stevie Wonder)
Chariots Of Fire—Original Film Soundtrack (Vangelis)
Cher (Cher)
Chicago 17 (Chicago)
Chronicle (Creedence Clearwater Revival)
Chronicles (Steve Winwood)
Close To The Bone (Thompson Twins)
Cloud Nine (George Harrison)
Collaboration (George Benson and Earl Klugh)
Coming Around Again (Carly Simon)
The Confessor (Joe Walsh)
Conscious Party (Ziggy Marley and The Melody Makers)
Contact (The Pointer Sisters)
Control (Janet Jackson)
Copland: Appalachian Spring, Rodeo, Fanfare For The Common Man (Atlanta Symphony Orchestra/Lane)
Crest Of A Knave (Jethro Tull)
Crossroads (Eric Clapton)
Crowded House (Crowded House)

Dancing On The Ceiling (Lionel Richie)
Dancing Undercover (Ratt)

The Dark Side Of The Moon (Pink Floyd)
Daydreaming (Morris Day)
Days Of Future Past (The Moody Blues)
Dead Letter Office (R.E.M.)
A Decade Of Steely Dan (Steely Dan)
December (George Winston)
Déjà Vu (Crosby, Stills, Nash and Young)
Diamond Life (Sade)
Diesel And Dust (Midnight Oil)
Different Light (The Bangles)
Digital Domain (Various Artists)
Dire Straits (Dire Straits)
Dirty Dancing (under title)
Dirty Work (The Rolling Stones)
Document (R.E.M.)
Dog Eat Dog (Joni Mitchell)
Door to Door (The Cars)
Double Vision (Bob James and David Sanborn)
Down To The Moon (Andreas Vollenweider)
Dream Evil (Dio)
Dream Into Action (Howard Jones)
The Dream Of The Blue Turtles (String)
Duotones (Kenny G)

Earth Angel (New Edition)
Eat Em And Smile (David Lee Roth)
Eliminator (ZZ Top)
Elton John Live In Australia With The Melbourne Symphony Orchestra (Elton John)
Emerson, Lake And Powell (Emerson, Lake and Powell)
Every Breath You Take; The Singles (The Police)

Fables Of The Reconstruction (R.E.M.)
Face Value (Phil Collins)
Faith (George Michael)
Falco 3 (Falco)
5150 (Van Halen)
The Final Countdown (Europe)

The Firm   (The Firm)
Flash   (Jeff Beck)
Flashback   (.38 Special)
Footloose   (under title)
For Sentimental Reasons   (Linda Ronstadt)
Fore!   (Huey Lewis and The News)
Fresh Aire Christmas   (Mannheim Steamroller)
Fresh Aire V   (Mannheim Steamroller)
Fresh Aire III   (Mannheim Steamroller)
Future Shock   (Herbie Hancock)

GTR   (GTR)
Gaudi   (The Alan Parsons Project)
Genesis   (Genesis)
Georgia Satellites   (Georgia Satellites)
Get Close   (The Pretenders)
Girls, Girls, Girls   (Motley Crue)
Give Me The Reason   (Luther Vandross)
Go   (Hiroshima)
Good Morning, Vietnam   (under title)
Greatest Hits   (Simon and Garfunkel)
Greatest Hits, Volume 1   (Elton John)
Greatest Hits Volume I & Volume II   (Billy Joel)

A Hard Day's Night   (The Beatles)
Harlequin   (Dave Grusin and Lee Ritenour)
Haydn/Hummel/L. Mozart: Trumpet Concertos   (Wynton Marsalis and The National Philharmonic Orchestra)
Headed For The Future   (Neil Diamond)
Hear The Light, Volume 1   (Various Artists)
Hearsay   (Alexander O'Neal)
Heart   (Heart)
Heartbeat City   (Cars)
Help   (The Beatles)
Here's To Future Days   (The Thompson Twins)
His 12 Greatest Hits   (Neil Diamond)
Hold Your Fire   (Rush)
Hot Rocks 1964–1971   (The Rolling Stones)

Hounds Of Love   (Kate Bush)
The House Of Blue Light   (Deep Purple)
Houses Of The Holy   (Led Zeppelin)
Hunting High And Low   (A-Ha)
Hysteria   (Def Leppard)

I Feel For You   (Chaka Khan)
Ice Cream Castles   (The Time)
Ice On Fire   (Elton John)
In Effect Mode   (Al B. Sure)
In My Tribe   (10,000 Maniacs)
In Square Circle   (Stevie Wonder)

Introducing The Hardline According to Terence Trent D'Arby   (Terence Trent D'Arby)
Invasion of Your Privacy   (Ratt)
Invisible Touch   (Genesis)
It's Better To Travel   (Swing Out Sister)

Joe Jackson Live 1980/86   (Joe Jackson)
The Joshua Tree   (U2)
Jumpin' Jack Flash   (Aretha Franklin)

Kick   (INXS)
King Of America   (Elvis Costello)
Kingdom Come   (Kingdom Come)
Kiss Me, Kiss Me, Kiss Me   (The Cure)
Knee Deep In The Hoopla   (The Starship)
KOHUEPT (Live In Leningrad)   (Billy Joel)

L Is For Lover   (Al Jarreau)
La Bamba   (under title)
Lap Of Luxury   (Cheap Trick)
Led Zeppelin   (Led Zeppelin)
Led Zeppelin II   (Led Zeppelin)
Less Than Zero   (under title)
Let It Be   (The Beatles)
Let It Loose   (Gloria Estefan and The Miami Sound Machine)
Let Me Up (I've Had Enough)   (Tom Petty and The Heartbreakers)

Licensed To Ill (The Beastie Boys)
Life (Neil Young And Crazy Horse)
Life, Love And Pain (Club Nouveau)
Life's Rich Pageant (R.E.M.)
Like A Rock (Bob Seger and The Silver Bullet Band)
Like A Virgin (Madonna)
The Lion And The Cobra (Sinead O'Connor)
Listen Like Thieves (INXS)
Little Creatures (Talking Heads)
Live Alive (Stevie Ray Vaughn and Double Trouble)
Live At Winterland (The Jimi Hendrix Experience)
Live In Australia With The Melbourne Symphony Orchestra (See: Elton John Live . . .)
Lives In The Balance (Jackson Browne)
Liza Minnelli At Carnegie Hall (Liza Minnelli)
Lonesome Jubilee (John Cougar Mellencamp)
Look What The Cat Dragged In (Poison)
Louder Than Bombs (The Smiths)
Love Songs (Stevie Wonder)
Love Zone (Billy Ocean)
Lovesexy (Prince)
Lush Life (Linda Ronstadt with Nelson Riddle and His Orchestra)

Madonna (Madonna)
The Magazine (Rickie Lee Jones)
Magical Mystery Tour (The Beatles)
Make It Big (Wham!)
Make It Last Forever (Keith Sweat)
Making Music (Dire Straits)
The Man And His Music (Sam Cooke)
The Many Moods of Christmas (The Atlanta Symphony Orchestra/Robert Shaw)
Mean Business(The Firm)
Meddle (Pink Floyd)
Memories (Barbara Streisand)
Men And Women (Simply Red)
Miami Vice (under title)
The Midas Touch (Midnight Star)

Midnight Madness (Night Ranger)
Mike And The Mechanics (Mike and The Mechanics)
Mistrial (Lou Reed)
A Momentary Lapse Of Reason (Pink Floyd)
More Dirty Dancing (under title)
Music From The Edge Of Heaven (Wham!)

Nail It To The Wall (Stacy Lattisaw)
Naked (Talking Heads)
Nervous Night (The Hooters)
Never Die Young (James Taylor)
Never Let Me Down (David Bowie)
Night Moves (Bob Seger)
Night Songs (Cinderella)
The Nightfly (Donald Fagen)
1984 (Van Halen)
90125 (Yes)
No Jacket Required (Phil Collins)
No Protection (The Starship)
. . . Nothing Like The Sun (Sting)
Notorious (Duran Duran)
Now And Zen (Robert Plant)

OU812 (Van Halen)
Odyssey (Yngwie J. Malmsteen)
Once Bitten (Great White)
Once Upon A Time (Simple Minds)
One Size Fits All (The Nylons)
One Voice (Barbra Streisand)
Ooh Yeah! (Daryl Hall and John Oates)
Open Up And Say . . . Ahh! (Poison)
The Other Side Of Life (The Moody Blues)
Out Of Order (Rod Stewart)
Out Of The Blue (Debbie Gibson)

Pack Up The Plantation—Live (Tom Petty and The Heartbreakers)
Parade (Prince and The Revolution)
Past Masters, Volume I (The Beatles)
Past Masters, Volume II (The Beatles)
Perfect Strangers (Deep Purple)

Permanent Vacation   (Aerosmith)
Phantom Of The Opera   (under title)
Physical Graffiti   (Led Zeppelin)
Picture Book   (Simply Red)
Play Deep   (The Outfield)
Please   (The Pet Shop Boys)
Power Windows   (Rush)
Press To Play   (Paul McCartney)
Pretty In Pink   (under title)
Primitive Cool   (Mick Jagger)
Private Dancer   (Tina Turner)
Promise   (Sade)
Purple Rain   (Prince and The Revolution)

Quadrophenia   (The Who)

Radio K.A.O.S.   (Roger Waters)
Raised On Radio   (Journey)
Raising Hell   (Run-D.M.C.)
Ram It Down   (Judas Priest)
Rapture   (Anita Baker)
Rebel Yell   (Billy Idol)
Reckless   (Bryan Adams)
Revenge   (Eurythmics)
Revolver   (The Beatles)
Riptide   (Robert Palmer)
The River   (Bruce Springsteen)
Robbie Robertson   (Robbie Robertson)
Rock A Little   (Stevie Nicks)
Rock 'N Soul, Part 1   (Daryl Hall and John Oates)
Rubber Soul   (The Beatles)
Rumours   (Fleetwood Mac)

Sammy Hagar   (Sammy Hagar)
Sampler III   (Various Artists)
Savage   (Eurythmics)
Savage Amusement   (The Scorpions)
Scarecrow   (John Cougar Mellencamp)
Scenes From The Southside   (Bruce Hornsby and The Range)
The Secret Of Association   (Paul Young)
The Secret Value Of Daydreaming   (Julian Lennon)

Sgt. Pepper's Lonely Hearts Club Band   (The Beatles)
Seven The Hard Way   (Pat Benatar)
7 Wishes   (Night Ranger)
Seventh Son Of A Seventh Son   (Iron Maiden)
Shaken 'N Stirred   (Robert Plant)
She's So Unusual   (Cyndi Lauper)
She's The Boss   (Mick Jagger)
Sign "O" The Times   (Prince)
Simple Pleasures   (Bobby McFerrin)
The Singles   (The Pretenders)
Skylarking   (XTC)
Skyscraper   (David Lee Roth)
Slippery When Wet   (Bon Jovi)
So   (Peter Gabriel)
Solitude Standing   (Suzanne Vega)
Songs From The Big Chair   (Tears For Fears)
Songs You Know By Heart   (Jimmy Buffett)
Southern Accents   (Tom Petty and The Heartbreakers)
Sports   (Huey Lewis and The News)
Star Tracks   (The Cincinnati Pops Orchestra/Erich Kunzel)
Starfish   (The Church)
Stereotomy   (The Alan Parsons Project)
Still Life (Talking)   (Pat Metheny Group)
Stop Making Sense   (Talking Heads)
Stranger In Town   (Bob Seger)
Strangeways, Here We Come   (The Smiths)
Strength In Numbers   (.38 Special)
Strong Persuader   (Robert Cray)
Stronger Than Pride   (Sade)
Substance 1987   (New Order)
Suddenly   (Billy Ocean)
Surfing With The Alien   (Joe Satriani)
Synchronicity   (The Police)

Tango In The Night   (Fleetwood Mac)
Tapestry   (Carole King)
Tchaikovsky: Capriccio Italien—Op. 45, Cossack Dance From Mazeppa, "1812" Overture—Op. 49   (The Cincinnati Pops Orchestra/Erich Kunzel)

Tchaikovsky: Nutcracker Suite, Serenade For Strings (Academy Of St. Martin-In-The-Fields/Nevil Marriner)
Tear Down These Walls (Billy Ocean)
Temporary Love Thing (Full Force)
That's Why I'm Here (James Taylor)
Then & Now . . . The Best Of The Monkees (The Monkees)
Thick As A Brick (Jethro Tull)
Third Stage (Boston)
Thriller (Michael Jackson)
Thursday Afternoon (Brian Eno)
Tiffany (Tiffany)
Time Warp (The Cincinnati Pops Orchestra/Erich Kunzel)
The Tonight Show Band/Doc Severinsen (The Tonight Show Band/Doc Severinsen)
The Tonight Show Band II/Doc Severinsen (The Tonight Show Band/Doc Severinsen)
Top Gun (under title)
Touch (Eurythmics)
Tracy Chapman (Tracy Chapman)
Trio (Dolly Parton/Linda Ronstadt/Emmylou Harris)
Tropico (Pat Benatar)
True Blue (Modonna)
True Colors (Cyndi Lauper)
True Confessions (Bananarama)
Tuff Enuff (The Fabulous Thunderbirds)
Tunnel Of Love (Bruce Springsteen)
Turbo (Judas Priest)

The Ultimate Sin (Ozzy Osbourne)
Under A Blood Red Sky (U2)
The Unforgettable Fire (U2)
Unlimited (Roger)

Valotte (Julian Lennon)
Vision Quest (under title)
Vital Idol (Billy Idol)
Viva Hate (Morrissey)
Vocalese (Manhattan Transfer)

Voices Carry ('Til Tuesday)
Voices In The Sky—The Best Of The Moody Blues (The Moody Blues)
Volume One (The Honeydrippers)
Vulture Culture (The Alan Parsons Project)

The Wall (Pink Floyd)
The Way It Is (Bruce Hornsby and The Range)
We Are The World (USA For Africa)
Welcome To The Real World (Mr. Mister)
West Side Story (Leonard Bernstein)
What's New (Linda Ronstadt)
Wheels Are Turnin' (REO Speedwagon)
Whenever You Need Somebody (Rick Astley)
White Album (The Beatles)
White City—A Novel (Pete Townshend)
White Winds (Andreas Vollenweider)
Whitesnake (Whitesnake)
Whitney (Whitney Houston)
Whitney Houston (Whitney Houston)
Who Are You (The Who)
The Whole Story (Kate Bush)
Who's Next (The Who)
Who's That Girl (under title)
Who's Zoomin' Who (Aretha Franklin)
The Wild, The Innocent And The E Street Shuffle (Bruce Springsteen)
Windham Hill Records Sampler '86 (Various Artists)
Windham Hill Sampler, Vol. 1 (Various Artists)
The Winner In You (Patti LaBelle)
Wish You Were Here (Pink Floyd)
With The Beatles (The Beatles)
The Woman In Red (under title)
Word Up (Cameo)
World Machine (Level 42)
World Wide Live (The Scorpions)

You Can Dance (Madonna)

Zoso (Led Zeppelin)

D. APPENDIXES

[NUMBER 1 RECORDINGS—A CHRONOLOGICAL LISTING]

1984

9-15—12-22	*Purple Rain*—Prince (15)
12-29	*Born In The U.S.A.*—Bruce Springsteen (1)

1985

1-05— 1-19	*Born In The U.S.A.*—Bruce Springsteen (3; 4)
1-26— 4-13	*Like A Virgin*—Madonna (12)
4-20— 4-27	*The Dark Side Of The Moon*—Pink Floyd (2)
5-04— 5-11	*Born In The U.S.A.*—Bruce Springsteen (2; 6)
5-18— 6-08	*Like A Virgin*—Madonna (4; 16)
6-15— 7-13	*No Jacket Required*—Phil Collins (5)
7-20— 8-03	*Brothers In Arms*—Dire Straits (3)
8-10— 8-17	*Born In The U.S.A.*—Bruce Springsteen (2; 8)
8-24	*No Jacket Required*—Phil Collins (1; 6)
8-31— 9-14	*The Dream Of The Blue Turtles*—Sting (3)
9-21—12-28	*Brothers In Arms*—Dire Straits (15; 18)

1986

1-04— 5-10	*Brothers In Arms*—Dire Straits (19; 37)
5-17— 7-19	*Whitney Houston*—Whitney Houston (10)
7-26	*So*—Peter Gabriel (1)
8-02— 8-16	*Invisible Touch*—Genesis (3)
8-23—11-01	*So*—Peter Gabriel (11; 12)
11-08—11-15	*Back In The High Life*—Steve Winwood (2)
11-22	*Fore!*—Huey Lewis And The News (1)
11-29	*Third Stage*—Boston (1)
12-06—12-27	*Bruce Springsteen And The E Street Band Live 1975–1985*—Bruce Springsteen And The E Street Band (4)

1987

1-03— 1-17	*Bruce Springsteen And The E Street Band Live 1975–1985*—Bruce Springsteen And The E Street Band (3; 7)
1-24— 2-14	*The Way It Is*—Bruce Hornsby And The Range (4)
2-21— 3-07	*Graceland*—Paul Simon (3)
3-14— 3-28	*A Hard Day's Night*—The Beatles (3)

4-04— 5-09	*The Joshua Tree*—U2 (6)	
5-16	*Rubber Soul*—The Beatles (1)	
5-23— 6-06	*Revolver*—The Beatles (3)	
6-13— 6-20	*The Joshua Tree*—U2 (2; 8)	
6-27— 7-04	*Sgt. Pepper's Lonely Hearts Club Band*—The Beatles (2)	
7-11— 8-29	*Whitney*—Whitney Houston (8)	
9-05	*Into The Dark*—The Grateful Dead (1)	
9-12— 9-19	*La Bamba*—Original Film Soundtrack (2)	
9-26	*Hysteria*—Def Leppard (1)	
10-03	*White Album*—The Beatles (1)	
10-10	*Bad*—Michael Jackson (1)	
10-17	*A Momentary Lapse Of Reason*—Pink Floyd (1)	
10-24	*Tunnel Of Love*—Bruce Springsteen (1)	
10-31—11-14	*A Momentary Lapse Of Reason*—Pink Floyd (3; 4)	
11-21	*Abbey Road*—The Beatles (1)	
11-28—12-12	*A Momentary Lapse of Reason*—Pink Floyd (3; 7)	
12-19—12-26	*. . . Nothing Like The Sun*—Sting (2)	

1988

1-02— 1-16	*. . . Nothing Like The Sun*—Sting (3; 5)	
1-23— 2-06	*Cloud Nine*—George Harrison (3)	
2-13— 2-27	*Faith*—George Michael (3)	
3-05	*Kick*—INXS (1)	
3-12— 3-26	*Dirty Dancing*—Original Film Soundtrack (3)	
4-02— 4-09	*Past Masters, Volume II*—The Beatles (2)	
4-16— 5-21	*Now And Zen*—Robert Plant (6)	
5-28	*Crossroads*—Eric Clapton (1)	
6-04	*Now And Zen*—Robert Plant (1; 7)	
6-11	*Lovesexy*—Prince (1)	
6-18	*OU812*—Van Halen (1)	

[RECORDINGS WITH LONGEST RUN ON CHARTS]

1. *The Dark Side Of The Moon*—Pink Floyd.....142 (1984–1987)
2. *No Jacket Required*—Phil Collins.....103 (1985–1987)
3. *Born In The U.S.A.*—Bruce Springsteen.....93 (1984–1986)
4. *A Decade Of Steely Dan*—Steely Dan.....86 (1985–1987)
5. *Brothers In Arms*—Dire Straits.....84 (1985–1987)
5. *Whitney Houston*—Whitney Houston.....84 (1985–1987)
7. *Little Creatures*—Talking Heads.....78 (1985–1987)
8. *Back In The High Life*—Steve Winwood.....77 (1986–1988)
8. *Chronicles*—Creedence Clearwater Revival.....77 (1985–1987)
10. *Private Dancer*—Tina Turner.....72 (1984–1986)
11. *Reckless*—Bryan Adams.....71 (1985–1986)

12. *The Joshua Tree*—U2.....60   (1987–1988)
13. *Can't Slow Down*—Lionel Richie.....59   (1984–1985)
14. *Rapture*—Anita Baker.....56   (1986–1987)
14. *Diamond Life*—Sade.....56   (1985–1986)
14. *Songs From The Big Chair*—Tears For Fears.....56   (1985–1986)
17. *Duotones*—Kenny G.....52   (1987–1988)
17. *Heart*—Heart.....52   (1986–1987)
17. *Riptide*—Robert Palmer.....52   (1986–1987)
20. *Whitney*—Whitney Houston.....50   (1987–1988)
20. *Building The Perfect Beast*—Don Henley.....50   (1985–1986)

[MOST CHART HITS PER ARTIST*]

1. The Beatles.....13
2. Led Zeppelin.....6
3. Elton John.....5
3. Pink Floyd.....5
3. Prince (and The Revolution).....5
3. Linda Ronstadt.....5
3. Bruce Springsteen.....5
8. Eurythmics.....4
8. Billy Joel.....4
8. Madonna.....4
8. The Alan Parsons Project.....4
8. R.E.M......4
8. Barbra Streisand.....4
8. U2.....4

*Includes collaborations with other artists

[MOST NUMBER 1 RECORDINGS BY ARTIST]

1. The Beatles.....7
2. Bruce Springsteen.....3
3. Whitney Houston.....2
3. Pink Floyd.....2
3. Prince.....2
3. Sting.....2

[MOST WEEKS AT NUMBER 1 BY RECORDING]

1. *Brothers In Arms*—Dire Straits.....37
2. *Like A Virgin*—Madonna.....16

3. *Purple Rain*—Prince.....15
4. *So*—Peter Gabriel.....12
5. *Whitney Houston*—Whitney Houston.....10
6. *Born In The U.S.A.*—Bruce Springsteen.....8
6. *The Joshua Tree*—U2.....8
6. *Whitney*—Whitney Houston.....8
9. *Bruce Springsteen And The E Street Band Live 1975–1985*—Bruce Springsteen And The E Street Band.....7
9. *A Momentary Lapse Of Reason*—Pink Floyd.....7
9. *Now And Zen*—Robert Plant.....7
12. *No Jacket Required*—Phil Collins.....6
13. *. . . Nothing Like The Sun*—Sting.....5
14. *The Way It Is*—Bruce Hornsby and The Range.....4

[MOST WEEKS AT NUMBER 1 BY ARTIST]

1. Dire Straits.....37
2. Whitney Houston.....18
3. Madonna.....16
3. Prince.....16
5. Bruce Springsteen.....15
6. The Beatles.....13
7. Peter Gabriel.....12
8. Pink Floyd.....9
9. Sting.....8
9. U2.....8
10. Robert Plant.....7
11. Phil Collins.....6

THE JUKEBOX PROGRAMMER

A. INTRODUCTION

Cash Box has never completely lost sight of its original vision (circa 1943) to cover developments related to coin-operated machines, particularly jukeboxes and arcade games. Accordingly, the magazine briefly included a triparte listing—divided between the black contemporary, country, and pop music fields—based upon the relative popularity of recordings within the jukebox industry. Located on the inside portion of the back cover page of the magazine, the "Jukebox Programmer" attempted to minimize the degree of guesswork inherent in stocking the machine(s) on one's premises. However, given its similarity with the genre charts based upon sales activity and radio plays—*i.e.,* the "Cash Box Top 100 Singles," the "Top 100 Black Contemporary Singles," and the "Top 100 Country Singles"—the *raison d'être* for the "Jukebox Programmer" became moot and it was discontinued in the late 1980s. In the meantime, jukebox revenues have continued to comprise a substantial portion of the record industry's net receipts up to the present day.

Initial chart title/title changes: "Jukebox Programmer"
Beginning date/termination date: February 13, 1982/December 14, 1985
   (no chart issue between September 14, 1985–November 2, 1985)
Initial number of positions/changes in number of positions: 30 for each of
   three categories: popular music, black contemporary, and country

B. ARTIST INDEX—BLACK CONTEMPORARY

APOLLONIA 6 (*See also:* PRINCE AND THE REVOLUTION)

11-10-84   *Sex Shooter*   (WB 7-29182)   22, 16, 14, 14, 23   (5)

ARRINGTON, STEVE/STEVE ARRINGTON'S HALL OF FAME

8-03-85   *Dancin' In The Key Of Life*   (Atl. 7-89535)   29, 16, 11, 10, 6, 6   (6)

5-04-85   *Feel So Real*   (Atl. 7-89576)   30, 28, 25, 22, 20, 26   (6)

2-11-84   *Hump To The Bump*   (Atl. 7-89715)   30, 26, 21, 17, 24, 30, 30   (7)

4-09-83   *Nobody Can Be You*   (Atl. 7-89876)   29, 25, 22, 20, 27   (5)

6-25-83   *Weak At The Knees*   (Atl. 7-89831)   29, 23   (2)

ART OF NOISE

3-31-84   *Beat Box*   (Island 7-99782)   16, (2), 25, 20, 28   (4)

7-21-84   *Close (To The Edit)*   (Island 7-99754)   27, 24, 21, 20, 21, 28, 30   (7)

ASHFORD AND SIMPSON

8-13-83   *High-Rise*   (Cap. B-5250)   27, 20, 16, 15, 15, 15, 15, 21, 26, 26, 26, 26   (12)

12-03-83   *It's Much Deeper*   (Cap. B-5284)   29, 24, 22, 28, 28, 28, 28   (7)

8-28-82   *Love It Away*   (Cap.)   26, 21, 18, 15, 13, 12, 11, 10, 19, 29   (10)

2-16-85   *Outta The World*   (Cap. B-5435)   26, 20, 15, 13, 8, 6, 6, 8, 8, 18   (10)

10-31-84   *Solid*   (Cap. B-5399)   29, 25, 18, 18, 13, 9, 7, 3, 1, 1, 1, 2, 2, 2, 3, 5, 12, 14, 20   (19)

4-24-82   *Street Corner*   (Cap. B-5109)   28, 19, 14, 10, 7, 6, 4, 3, 5, 5, 4, 7, 7, 14, 19, 30   (16)

ATLANTIC STARR

3-13-82   *Circle*   (A&M AM 2392)   27, 13, 10, 9, 5, 3, 3, 1, 3, 4, 6, 12, 16, 21, 30   (15)

4-13-85   *Freak-A-Ristic*   (A&M AM 2718)   30, 25, 22, 20, 16, 11, 9, 8, 7, 5, 4, 6, 12, 12, 22, 22   (16)

6-19-82   *Love Me Down*   (A&M AM 2420)   28, 23, 19, 15, 12, 9, 7, 6, 6, 19, 29   (11)

3-03-84   *More, More, More*   (A&M AM 2619)   29, 25, 20, 20, 14, 29   (6)

11-09-85   *Silver Shadow*   (A&M AM 2766)   9, 9, 20, 30, 30   (5)

11-19-83   *Touch A Four Leaf Clover*   (A&M AM 2580)   25, 20, 16, 14, 12, 10, 10, 10, 10, 12, 18, 26   (12)

ATTITUDE

4-30-83   *We've Got The Juice*   (RFC 7-89879)   30, 30   (2)

AUSTIN, PATTI   *(See also:* JAMES INGRAM; NARADA MICHAEL WALDEN)

3-27-82   *Baby Come To Me*   (Qwest QUE 50036)   29, 25, 25, 23, 22   (5)

2-05-83   *Baby Come To Me*   (Qwest QUE 50036)   21, 16, 13, 18, 24, 30   (6)

3-17-84   *It's Gonna Be Special*   (Qwest 7-29373)   28, 28, 19, 14, 10, 15, 22   (7)

6-02084   *Rhythm Of The Street*   (Qwest 7-29305)   29, 25, 22, 29   (4)

BAILEY, PHILIP   *(See also:* EARTH, WIND AND FIRE)

9-17-83   *I Know*   (Col. 38-03968)   24, 24, 14, 11, 11, 11, 11, 18, 27   (9)

BAILEY, PHILIP, WITH PHIL COLLINS   *(See also:* EARTH, WIND AND FIRE)

1-26-85   *Easy Lover*   (Col. 38-04679)   24, 18, 10, 5, 3, 2, 3, 4, 7, 7, 9, 17, 28   (13)

BAKER, ANITA

11-05-83   *Angel*   (Beverly Glen BG-2010)   28, 23, 17, 13, 17, 19, 24   (7)

BANKS, RON

2-04-84   *Make It Easy On Yourself*   (CBS Associated ZS4 04242)   29, 23, 19, 23   (4)

THE BAR-KAYS

8-11-84   *Dirty Dancer*   (Mer. 880 045-7)   30, 24, 20, 21, 15, 14, 19, 25   (8)

11-06-82   *Do It*   (Mer. SR 76187)   28, 27, 24, 22, 20, 16, 13, 10, 10, 10, 7, 15, 22, 30   (14)

4-07-84   *Freakshow On The Dance Floor*   (Mer. 818 631-7)   30, 25, 19, 16, 10, 6, 5, 2, 2, 2, 1, 5, 7, 11, 16, 23   (16)

3-20-82   *Freaky Behavior*   (Mer. SR 76143)   26, 24, 20, 16, 13, 10, 9, 8, 8, 13, 19, 24   (12)

10-27-84   *Sexomatic*   (Mer. 880 255-7)   30, 30, 26, 19, 15, 9, 8, 18, 29   (9)

4-23-83   *She Talks To Me With Her Body*   (Mer. 810 435-7)   27, 24, 22, 21, 24, 23, 24, 30   (8)

8-31-85   *Your Place Or Mine*   (Mer. 880 966-7)   28, 28   (2)

BENSON, GEORGE

4-13-85   *I Just Wanna Hang Around*   (WB 7-29042)   28, 23, 21, 18, 17, 16, 15, 22, 29   (9)

6-04-83   *Inside Love*   (WB 7-29649)   25, 19, 15, 9, 5, 5, 3, 2, 1, 1, 11, 15, 22   (13)

9-17-83   *Lady Love Me*   (WB 7-29563)   29, 29, 25, 20, 20, 20, 20   (7)

1-26-85   *20/20*   (WB 7-29120)   30, 23, 18, 15, 11, 9, 14, 23, 24, 24   (10)

BLACKFOOT, J.

1-21-84   *Taxi*   (Sound Town ST-004)   25, 19, 13, 10, 9, 6, 4, 4, 3, 3, 7, 4, 8, 12, 18, 26   (16)

BLOODSTONE

9-18-82   *Go On And Cry*   (T-Neck)   26, 21, 19, 17, 17, 22   (6)

4-24-82   *We Go A Long Way Back*   (T-Neck ZS5-02825)   27, 21, 16, 14, 11, 9, 8, 6, 3, 3, 7, 9, 17, 21   (14)

BLOW, KURTIS

2-09-85   *Basketball*   (Polydor 880 529-7)   27, 25   (2)

10-13-84   *8 Million Stories*   (Mer. 880 170-7)   25, 23, 22, 22, 29   (5)

8-27-83   *Party Time*   (Mer. 812 687-7)   30, 26, 26, 27, 27   (5)

BOFILL, ANGELA

6-18-83   *Tonight I Give In*   (Arista AS 1060)   30, 22, 18, 15, 14, 14, 16, 28   (8)

2-12-83   *Too Tough*   (Arista AS 1031)   28, 24, 17, 12, 10, 8, 6, 5, 4, 5, 11, 18, 19   (13)

THE BOOGIE BOYS

8-10-85   *Fly Girl*   (Cap. B-5498)   21, 16, 12, 9, 9   (5)

BOWIE, DAVID

6-04-83   *Let's Dance*   (EMI America B-8158)   29, 24, 17, 14, 13, 20, 30   (7)

BRASS CONSTRUCTION

4-10-82   *Can You See The Light*   (Liberty PB-1453)   28, 26, 25, 23, 22, 20, 21, 29   (8)

6-04-83   *Walkin' The Line*   (Cap. B-5219)   27, 25, 20   (3)

THE BROTHERS JOHNSON

11-27-82   *Welcome To The Club*   (A&M AM 2506)   28, 18, 12, 8, 4, 4, 4, 3, 5, 10, 23   (11)

7-28-84   *You Keep Me Coming Back*   (A&M AM 2654)   27, 22, 16, 12, 10, 11, 10, 9, 12, 15, 21, 30   (12)

BROWN, JOCELYN

6-16-84   *Somebody Else's Guy*   (Vinyl Dreams VND D71)   14, 10, 4, 3, 2, 2, 4, 7, 22, 27, 30   (11)

BRUNSON, TYRONE

3-10-84   *Fresh*   (B.I.A.D. ZS4 04330)   29, 24, 24, 30   (4)

BRYSON, PEABO

9-18-82   *Give Me Your Love*   (Cap.)   29, 24, 17, 15, 14, 12, 11, 17, 28   (9)

6-30-84   *If Ever You're In My Arms Again*   (Elektra 76928)   27, 19, 15, 11, 10, 12, 15, 23, 26, 29   (10)

2-13-82   *Let The Feeling Flow*   (Cap.)   2   (1)

4-17-82   *There's No Guarantee*   (Cap. B-5098)   28, 24, 27   (3)

12-18-82   *We Don't Have To Talk (About Love)*   (Cap. B-5188)   30, 23, 23, 23, 20, 17, 17, 17, 17, 21, 27   (11)

BRYSON, PEABO, AND ROBERTA FLACK   *(See also:* **ROBERTA FLACK)**

7-3083   *Tonight I Celebrate My Love*   (Cap. B-5242)   27, 18, 14, 12, 10, 10, 10, 6, 6, 6, 7, 7, 7, 7, 14, 22, 28   (17)

BURCH, VERNON

2-13-82   *Do It To Me*   (Spector Records International)   12   (1)

4-17-82   *Playing Hard To Get*   (Spector Records International 00021)   30, 29, 29, 28   (4)

BURTON, JENNY

3-16-85   *Bad Habit*   (Atl. 7-89583)   26, 23, 23, 21, 18, 17, 25   (7)

2-04-84   *Remember What You Like*   (Atl. 7-89748)   30, 25, 22, 15, 16, 13, 12, 12, (1), 19, 24   (10)

CAMEO

6-22-85   *Attack Me With Your Love*   (A.A. 880 744-7)   30, 17, 13, 13, 9, 9, 7, 3, 3, 3, 13, 13   (12)

6-26-82   *Flirt*   (Chocolate City CC 3233)   26, 21, 16, 13, 11, 9, 8, 7, 10, 21, 29   (11)

3-27-82   *Just Be Yourself* (Chocolate City CC 3231)   27, 22, 14, 11, 9, 7, 5, 5, 10, 14, 18, 23, 29   (13)

2-25-84   *She's Strange* (A.A. 818 384-7)   30, 25, 22, 15, 15, 6, 5, 1, 1, 4, 4, 5, 7, 12, 15, 18   (16)

11-09-85   *Single Life* (A.A. 884 010-7)   15, 15, 25   (3)

5-15-83   *Style* (A.A. 812 054-7)   28, 23, 19, 17, 13, 13, 24   (7)

7-07-84   *Talkin' Out The Side Of Your Neck*   (A.A. 818 870-7)   28, 21, 18, 15, 16, 17, 25   (7)

CARA, IRENE

5-28-83   *Flashdance . . . What A Feeling*   (Casa. 811 440-7)   28, 22, 14, 3, 2, 2, 1, 1, 1, 5, 6, 6, 11, 23   (14)

CARLTON, CARL

9-18-82   *Baby I Need Your Loving* (RCA)   30, 26, 20, 19, 15, 13, 10, 10, 8, 18, 24   (11)

2-20-82   *I Think It's Gonna Be Alright* (20th C.)   30, 27, 26, 30   (4)

1-29-83   *Swing That Sexy Thang* (RCA PB-13406)   29, 24, 22, 22   (4)

CHAMPAIGN

10-20-84   *Off And On Love* (Col. 38-04600)   28, 25, 25, 20, 15, 12, 11, 14   (8)

3-19-83   *Try Again* (Col. 38-03563)   29, 24, 21, 19, 16, 12, 8, 4, 5, 7, 8, 9, 10, 21, 26, 30   (16)

CHANGE

5-19-84   *Change Of Heart* (RFC 7-89684)   28, 24, 21, 17, 15, 14, 26   (7)

5-08-82   *The Very Best In You* (RFC)   26, 22, 19, 16, 15, 13, 12, 12, 17, 28   (10)

CHARLENE AND STEVIE WONDER   (*See also:* STEVIE WONDER)

11-20-82   *Used To Be*   (Motown 1650 MF)   28, 25, 21, 17, 20, 26, 26, 26, 29   (9)

CHARLES, SONNY

12-04-82   *Put It In A Magazine*   (Highrise SHR-2001)   28, 25, 22, 15, 15, 15, 11, 8, 12, 22   (10)

CHERI

5-01-82   *Murphy's Law*   (Venture)   30, 9, 6, 5, 4, 7, 11, 19, 24, 30   (10)

CHERRELLE

9-22-84   *Fragile . . . Handle With Care*   (Tabu ZS4 04556)   29, 24, 20, 18, 18   (5)

6-16-84   *I Didn't Mean To Turn You On*   (Tabu ZS4 04406)   28, 20, 10, 6, 4, 3, 7, 8, 13, 19, 23, 18, 27   (13)

11-09-85   *You Look Good To Me*   (Tabu 34-5608)   19, 19, 14, 7, 7   (5)

CHIC

6-05-82   *Soup For One*   (Mirage WTG 4032)   25, 22, 20, 16, 12, 8, 14, 18, 29   (9)

2-13-82   *Stage Fright*   (Atl.)   7   (1)

THE CHI-LITES   (FEATURING EUGENE RECORD)

7-30-83   *Bad Motor Scooter*   (LARC LR 81023)   30, 25, 24   (3)

3-26-83   *Bottom's Up*   (LARC LR 81015)   25, 23, 20, 17, 13, 11, 9, 12, 11, 14, 16, 18   (12)

3-13-82   *Hot On A Thing (Called Love)*   (20th C,)   29, 23, 21, 21, 20, 19   (6)

CHOCOLATE MILK

2-13-82   *Let's Go All The Way*   (RCA)   22, 19, 17, 30   (4)

THE CLARK SISTERS

8-20-83   *You Brought The Sunshine*   (Westbound 7-69810)   27, 21, 20, 20, 19, 19, 17, 17, 17, 17, 17   (11)

CLINTON, GEORGE

2-19-83   *Atomic Dog*   (Cap. B-5201)   27, 19, 13, 9, 7, 5, 4, 3, 2, 2, 2, 2, 2, 3, 12, 12, 15, 26   (18)

7-06-85   *Double Oh-Oh*   (Cap. B-5473)   30, 30   (2)

4-07-84   *Last Dance*   (Cap. B-5332)   20, 17, 14, 12, 11, 20, 26, 28   (8)

11-13-82   *Loopzilla*   (Cap. B-5160)   29, 25, 16, 13, 11, 10, 17, 17, 17, 24, 29   (11)

12-03-83   *Nubian Nut*   (Cap. B-5296)   27, 22, 19, 16, 16, 16, 16, 13, 20, 28   (10)

COLE, NATALIE

5-25-85   *Dangerous*   (Modern 7-99648)   30, 25, 21, 20, 20, 29   (6)

COLLINS, PHIL   (*See also:* PHILIP BAILEY)

6-15-85   *Sussudio*   (Atl. 7-89560)   28, 21, 15, 11, 11, 11, 11, 17   (8)

COLLINS, WILLIAM "BOOTSY"

5-15-82   *Take A Lickin' And Keep On Kickin'*   (WB)   24, 24, 30   (3)

THE COMMODORES   (*See also:* LIONEL RICHIE)

2-09-85   *Nightshift*   (Motown 1773 MF)   30, 23, 14, 10, 2, 1, 1, 1, 2, 5, 5, 8, 9, 20   (14)

10-01-83   *Only You*   (Motown 1694 MF)   30, 25, 25, 25, 25, 15, 13, 10, 19, 22, 25, 30   (12)

12-04-82   *Painted Picture*   (Motown 1651 MF)   29, 24, 19, 13, 13, 13, 13, 12, 11, 11, 18, 25   (12)

2-13-82   *Why You Wanna Try Me*   (Motown 1604 MF)   26, 20, 15, 13, 12, 20   (6)

CON FUNK SHUN

11-12-83   *Baby, I'm Hooked*   (Mer. 814 581-7)   28, 22, 18, 15, 13, 11, 8, 8, 8, 8, 4, 4, 6, 8, 10, 14, 28   (17)

5-11-85   *Electric Lady*   (Mer. 880 636-7)   30, 22, 19, 11, 8, 6, 5, 9, 8, 8, 17, 17   (12)

8-10-85   *I'm Leaving Baby*   (Mer. 880 914-7)   27, 24, 21, 14, 14   (5)

2-26-83   *Ms. Got-The-Body*   (Mer. SR 76198)   26, 19, 15, 13, 9, 7, 7, 7, 8, 13, 20, 24, 25   (13)

THE CONTROLLERS

9-29-84   *Crushed*   (MCA 52450)   29, 25, 21, 20, 17, 17, 27   (7)

CRAWFORD, RANDY   (*See:* AL JARREAU)

THE CRUSADERS

4-14-84   *New Moves*   (MCA 52365)   30, 26, 29, (1), 17, 16, 14, 23, 28   (8)

CULTURE CLUB

4-02-83   *Do You Really Want To Hurt Me*   (Epic 34-03368)   27, 25, 30   (3)

3-03-84   *Karma Chameleon*   (Virgin 34-04221)   21, 16, 18, 18, 23, 21   (6)

4-21-84   *Miss Me Blind*   (Virgin 34-04388)   27, 21, 13   (3)

CYMONE, ANDRE   (*See also:* PRINCE)

8-10-85   *The Dance Electric*   (Col. 44-05249)   30, 27, 23, 19, 19   (5)

"D" TRAIN

6-12-82   *Keep On*   (Prelude PRL 8039)   27, 22, 18, 13, 10, 8, 8, 12, 23   (9)

2-04-84   *Something's On Your Mind*   (Prelude PRL 596)   20, 16, 13, 13, 18, 17, 23, 23   (8)

12-11-82   *Walk On By*   (Prelude PRL 8057)   27, 25, 30, 30, 30   (5)

2-13-82   *You're The One For Me*   (Prelude PRL 8043-A)   10   (1)

DAVIS, TYRONE

11-27-82   *Are You Serious*   (Highrise SHR-2005)   30, 26, 22, 18, 12, 12, 12, 10, 6, 4, 4, 10, 17, 23, 30   (15)

10-29-83   *I Found Myself When I Lost You*   (Ocean-Front OF 2001)   24, 20, 18, 16, 24, 28   (6)

DAWSON, CLIFF, AND RENEE DIGGS

4-02-83   *Never Say I Do*   (Boardwalk NB-12-173-1)   29, 26, 22, 19, 17, 16, 18, 20, 29   (9)

DAY, MORRIS   *(See also:* PRINCE; THE TIME)

11-09-85   *The Oak Tree*   (WB 7-28899)   1, 1, 4, 11, 11   (5)

DAYTON

7-24-82   *Hot Fun In The Summertime*   (Liberty PB-1469)   29, 25, 22, 19, 18, 17, 26   (7)

THE DAZZ BAND

3-09-85   *Heartbeat*   (Motown 1775 MF)   25, 18, 18, 15   (4)

8-31-85   *Hot Spot*   (Motown 1800 MF)   27, 27   (2)

1-21-84   *Joystick*   (Motown 1701 MF)   21, 15, 9, 6, 4, 3, 6, 9, 9, 9, 11, 27, 29   (13)

8-21-82   *Keep It Live*   (Motown)   29, 25, 22, 19, 16, 15, 18, 24, 30   (9)

10-27-84   *Let It All Blow*   (Motown 1760 MF)   29, 29, 19, 14, 9, 5, 3, 4, 6, 12, 12, 12, 23, 27   (14)

5-08-82   *Let It Whip*   (Motown 1609 MF)   29, 18, 15, 10, 9, 2, 1, 1, 1, 1, 2, 5, 10, 14, 26   (15)

2-05-83   *On The One For Fun*   (Motown 1659 MF)   29, 21, 16, 12, 8, 5, 4, 2, 2, 2, 4, 5, 7, 13, 19, 30   (16)

5-12-84   *Swoop*   (Motown 1725 MF)   26, 21, 18, 14, 12, 10, 9, 9, 17, 24, 28   (11)

DeBARGE (DeBARGE, EL, WITH DeBARGE)

5-07-83   *All This Love*   (Gordy 1660 GF)   29, 25, 16, 13, 8, 5, 5, 4, 4, 4, 7, 7, 11, 20, 29   (15)

2-12-83   *I Like It*   (Motown 1645 MF)   24, 18, 8, 4, 1, 1, 3, 3, 5, 8, 7, 16, 23, 30   (14)

4-07-84   *Love Me In A Special Way*   (Gordy 1723 GF)   28, 22, 18, 14, 20, 30   (6)

3-16-85   *Rhythm Of The Night*   (Gordy 1770 GF)   21, 17, 17, 13, 2, 1, 3, 2, 6, 6, 7, 13, 17, 24   (14)

11-12-83   *Time Will Reveal*   (Gordy 1705 GF)   24, 20, 7, 4, 2, 1, 1, 1, 1, 1, 2, 3, 4, 7, 12, 16, 24   (17)

6-29-85   *Who's Holding Donna Now*   (Gordy 1793 GF)   26, 21, 21, 14, 14, 10, 4, 4, 15, 26, 26   (11)

11-09-85   *You Wear It Well*   (Gordy 1804 GF)   7, 7, 15, 22, 22   (5)

THE DEELE

1-28-84   *Body Talk*   (Solar 7-69785)   26, 15, 12, 17, 19, 19, 28   (7)

6-01-85   *Material Thangz*   (Solar 7-69644)   28, 25, 21, 16, 11, 10, 10, 19, 19   (9)

DIGGS, RENEE   (*See:* CLIFF DAWSON)

DOZIER, LAMONT

2-27-82   *Shout About It*   (M&M)   29, 28, 28   (3)

DREAMBOY

3-03-84   *Don't Go* (Qwest 7-29389) 23, 20, 13, 13, 13, 15, 15, 22, 27 (9)

DUKE, GEORGE

2-13-82   *Shine On* (Epic) 9, 3, 1, 3, 6, 12, 11, 18 (8)

EARLAND, CHARLES

2-27-82   *The Only One* (Col.) 28, 27, 26, 25 (4)

EARTH, WIND AND FIRE   *(See also:* PHILIP BAILEY; MAURICE WHITE)

1-22-83   *Fall In Love With Me* (Col. 38-03375) 24, 20, 8, 5, 3, 3, 3, 8, 10, 14, 24, 28 (12)

11-19-83   *Magnetic* (Ccol. 38-04110) 27, 21, 18, 15, 13, 11, 11, 11, 11, 20, 25 (11)

4-30-83   *Side By Side* (Col. 38-03814) 28, 24, 23, 19, 17, 18, 22 (7)

3-03-84   *Touch* (Col. 38-04329) 26, 23, 22, 22, 18 (5)

2-13-82   *Wanna Be With You* (ARC/Col.) 11, 6, 10, 12, 19 (5)

EASTON, SHEENA

2-09-85   *Sugar Walls* (EMI America B-8253) 24, 18, 10, 7, 6, 6, 12, 12, 18 (9)

EDWARDS, DENNIS

7-07-84   *(You're My) Aphrodisiac* (Gordy 1737 GF) 25, 20, 19, 26 (4)

11-09-85   *Coolin' Out* (Gordy 1805 GF) 22, 22 (2)

3-17-84   *Don't Look Any Further* (Gordy 1715 GF) 26, 26, 15, 12, 6, 4, 2, 2, 2, 3, 5, 9, 13, 21, 26 (15)

FALTERMEYER, HAROLD

4-27-85   *Axel F* (MCA 52536) 29, 26, 22, 20, 18, 14, 10, 9, 13, 22, 27, 27 (12)

THE FAMILY

8-31-85   *The Screams Of Passion*   (Paisley Park 7-28953)   29, 29, 25, 25   (4)

THE FAT BOYS

8-17-85   *The Fat Boys Are Back*   (Sutra 034)   28, 19, 16, 16   (4)

12-08-84   *Jailhouse Rap*   (Sutra 027)   30, 19, 15, 11, 11, 11, 11, 19   (8)

FATBACK

4-09-83   *The Girl Is Fine*   (Spring SP 3030)   27, 24, 21, 19, 17, 17, 14, 16, 19, 27   (10)

7-17-82   *On The Floor*   (Spring SP 3025)   28, 23, 20, 17, 24   (5)

FELDER, WILTON, FEATURING BOBBY WOMACK AND INTRODUCING ALLTRINNA GRAYSON

2-23-85   *(No Matter How High I Get) I'll Still Be Lookin' Up To You*   (MCA 52462)   27, 20, 16, 11, 2, 2, 1, 1, 3, 5, 11, 23   (12)

FIELDS, RICHARD "DIMPLES"

3-20-82   *If It Ain't One Thing . . . It's Another*   (Boardwalk NB7-11-139)   16, 12, 8, 3, 2, 1, 5, 6, 12, 14, 17, 21, 28   (13)

8-04-84   *Your Wife Is Cheatin' On Us*   (RCA PB 13830)   29, 25, 20, 19, 20   (5)

FLACK, ROBERTA   *(See also: PEABO BRYSON)*

7-24-82   *I'm The One*   (Atl.)   26, 23, 19, 15, 11, 8, 6, 6, 5, 6, 6, 9, 16, 28   (14)

3-13-82   *Making Love*   (Atl.)   25, 21, 19, 15, 23, 25   (6)

THE FORCE MD'S

7-20-85   *Itchin' For A Scratch*   (Atl. 7-89557)   20, 20, 16   (3)

THE FOUR TOPS

7-20-85   *Sexy Ways*   (Motown 1790 MF)   27, 27, 25   (3)

2-13-82   *Tonight I'm Gonna Love You All Over*   (Casa.)   6, 5, 4, 4, 8, 27   (6)

FRANKLIN, ARETHA

11-05-83   *Every Girl*   (Arista AS1-9095)   11, 8, 8, 14, 19, 21, 26, 30, 30, 30, 30   (11)

7-06-85   *Freeway Of Love*   (Arista AS1-9354)   26, 26, 13, 13, 6, 1, 1, 2, 2, 2   (10)

7-16-83   *Get It Right*   (Arista AS1-9034)   29, 21, 17, 11, 5, 5, 4, 4, 4, 7, 7, 10, 12, 12, 12, 12   (16)

7-10-82   *Jump To It*   (Arista AS 0699)   29, 24, 20, 14, 9, 4, 2, 1, 1, 1, 2, 4, 10, 14, 22, 23   (16)

11-09-85   *Who's Zoomin' Who*   (Arista AS1-9410)   3, 3, 1, 2, 2   (5)

FREEEZ

9-17-83   *I.O.U.*   (Streetwise SWRL 2210)   28, 28, 23, 22, 22, 22, 22   (7)

FULL FORCE   *(See: LISA LISA . . .)*

GQ

2-20-82   *Sad Girl*   (Arista)   26   (1)

THE GAP BAND

12-22-84   *Beep A Freak*   (Total Experience TES1-2406)   28, 21, 21, 21, 18, 12, 8, 4, 2, 6, 12, 17, 27   (13)

5-01-82   *Early In The Morning*   (Total Experience TE 8201)   28, 19, 11, 9, 3, 2, 1, 2, 2, 2, 4, 3, 2, 3, 7, 14, 23, 27   (18)

4-20-85   *I Found My Baby*   (Total Experience TES1-2412)   27, 16, 14, 12, 9, 17, 24   (7)

12-17-83   *Jam The Motha*   (Total Experience TE 8210)   27, 23, 23, 23, 23, 16, 12, 17, 22, 27   (10)

12-04-82   *Outstanding*   (Total Experience TE 8205)   19, 14, 11, 8, 8, 8, 5, 2, 2, 1, 6, 8, 15, 21, 26, 30   (16)

8-20-83   *Party Train*   (Total Experience TE 8209)   26, 19, 18, 18, 12, 12, 9, 3, 3, 3, 3, 7, 7, 14, 22, 25, 30   (17)

8-21-82   *You Dropped A Bomb On Me*   (Total Experience)   27, 19, 12, 3, 1, 1, 2, 2, 5, 8, 17, 24   (12)

GAYE, MARVIN

5-11-85   *Sanctified Lady*   (Col. 38-04861)   27, 14, 8, 4, 2, 1, 2, 2, 2, 2, 5, 5, 8, 24   (14)

10-23-82   *Sexual Healing*   (Col. 38-03302)   26, 14, 2, 1, 1, 1, 1, 4, 4, 7, 7, 7, 8, 14, 21, 28   (16)

2-19-83   *'Til Tomorrow*   (Col. 38-03589)   29, 24, 17, 12, 12, 18, 26   (7)

GEILS, J., BAND

4-10-82   *Flamethrower*   (EMI America B-8108)   29, 24, 21, 20   (4)

GILL, JOHNNY   (*See also:* STACY LATTISAW)

3-09-85   *Half Crazy*   (Cot. 7-99671)   29, 24, 22, 22, 23, 27   (6)

GOODIE

8-14-82   *Do Something*   (Total Experience)   30, 26, 23, 19, 16, 13, 8, 8, 7, 6, 6, 13, 27   (13)

1-29-83   *You And I*   (Total Experience TE 8206)   27, 26, 23, 23, 22, 29   (6)

GRAHAM, LARRY

6-25-83   *I Never Forgot Your Eyes*   (WB 7-29620)   27, 26, 24, 20, 22   (5)

8-21-82   *Sooner Or Later*   (WB)   24, 16, 14, 23, 29   (5)

GRANDMASTER MELLE MEL AND THE FURIOUS FIVE

6-23-84   *Beat Street Breakdown*   (Atl. 7-89659)   30, 25, 20, 17, 14, 12, 10, 9, 13, 16, 19, 29   (12)

GRANT, EDDY

6-18-83   *Electric Avenue*   (Ice 37-03793)   27, 20, 14, 11, 10, 10, 10, 16, 18, 24   (10)

GRAYSON, ALLTRINNA   (*See:* WILTON FELDER)

GUTHRIE, GWEN

1-26-85   *Love In Moderation*   (Island 7-99685)   26, 20, 16, 14, 13, 19, 28   (7)

HALL, DARYL, AND JOHN OATES

2-13-82   *I Can't Go For That (No Can Do)*   (RCA PB-12357)   14   (1)

3-12-83   *One On One*   (RCA PB-13421)   25, 20, 16, 13, 12, 10, 9, 14, 14, 22   (10)

HALL, RANDY

9-01-84   *I've Been Watching You*   (MCA 52405)   27, 24, 22, 22, 30   (5)

HAMMER, JAN

11-09-85   *Miami Vice Theme*   (MCA 52666)   13, 13, 11, 19, 19   (5)

HANCOCK, HERBIE

8-25-84   *Hardrock*   (Col. 38-04565)   29   (1)

6-09-84   *Mega-Mix*   (Col. 38-04473)   30, 26, 25, 20, 21, 26   (6)

8-27-83   *Rockit*   (Col. 38-04054)   27, 23, 23, 9, 9, 2, 1, 1, 1, 1, 2, 6, 7, 11, 14, 16, 18, 24, 24, 24, 24, 30   (22)

HARDCASTLE, PAUL

6-29-85   *19*   (Chrysalis VS4-42860)   28, 24, 24, 10, 10, 9, 20   (7)

2-02-85   *Rain Forest*   (Profile PRO-7059)   25, 21   (2)

HAYWOOD, LEON

7-09-83   *I'm Out To Catch*   (Casa. 812 164-7)   26, 16, 17, 18, 29   (5)

10-20-84   *Tenderoni*   (Modern 7-99708)   26, 23, 23   (3)

HENDERSON, MICHAEL

5-21-83 *Fickle* (Buddah BDA-800) 27, 25 (2)

HENDRYX, NONA

5-21-83 *Keep It Confidential* (RCA) 26, 21, 21 (3)

HILL, Z.Z.

6-05-82 *Cheating In The Next Room* (Malaco) 30, 29, 27, 25, 24, 23, 29 (7)

HOLLIDAY, JENNIFER

7-03-82 *And I Am Telling You I'm Not Going* (Geffen 7-29983) 29, 19, 10, 4, 1, 1, 1, 3, 7, 15, 23 (11)

11-05-83 *I Am Love* (Geffen 7-29525) 5, 2, 2, 3, 5, 6, 8, 12, 12, 12, 12, 19, 24 (13)

HOUSTON, THELMA

11-24-84 *You Used To Hold Me So Tight* (MCA 52491) 30, 26, 25, 23, 18, 14, 14, 14, 13, 11, 10, 17 (12)

HOUSTON, WHITNEY *(See also:* TEDDY PENDERGRASS)

7-20-85 *Saving All My Love For You* (Arista AS1-9381) 23, 23, 12, 5, 2, 1, 1, 1 (8)

11-09-85 *Thinking About You* (Arista AS1-9412) 27, 27, 21, 13, 13 (5)

4-20-85 *You Give Good Love* (Arista AS1-9264) 26, 15, 13, 10, 5, 3, 2, 1, 3, 6, 7, 14, 14, 25, 25, 28 (16)

IMAGINATION

6-26-82 *Just An Illusion* (MCA 52067) 30, 28, 25, 21, 17, 16, 13, 12, 12, 24, 30 (11)

INDEEP

2-12-83 *Last Night A D.J. Saved My Life* (S.O.N.Y. 5102) 26, 20, 14, 10, 6, 5, 8, 10, 14, 18, 24 (11)

INGRAM, JAMES

4-21-84   *There's No Easy Way*   (Qwest 7-29316)   29, 24, 19, 14, 12, 10, 11, 15, 24   (9)

INGRAM, JAMES, AND PATTI AUSTIN

6-18-83   *How Do You Keep The Music Playing*   (Qwest 7-29618)   28, 21, 17, 14, 11, 9, 9, 9, 9, 9, 7, 9, 8, 8, 16, 16, 16, 21, 21, 21, 21   (20)

INGRAM, JAMES, WITH MICHAEL McDONALD

1-28-84   *Yah Mo B There*   (Qwest 7-29394)   17, 11, 9, 6, 8, 10, 10, 14, 14, 26   (10)

THE ISLEY BROTHERS   *(See also:* ISLEY, JASPER, ISLEY)

4-23-83   *Between The Sheets*   (T-Neck ZS4 03797)   26, 21, 15, 9, 5, 1, 1, 3, 4, 8, 8, 12, 15, 16, 21, 21   (16)

8-06-83   *Choosey Lover*   (T-Neck ZS4 03994)   24, 17, 14, 13, 13, 13, 14, 14, 19, 24, 24, 24   (12)

11-30-85   *Colder Are My Nights*   (WB 7-28860)   27, 27   (2)

6-26-82   *The Real Deal*   (T-Neck ZS5 02985)   27, 23, 18, 15, 13, 8, 5, 5, 9, 15, 20, 29   (12)

2-13-82   *Welcome Into My Heart*   (T-Neck)   28, 21, 23, 20, 18, 17, 20   (7)

ISLEY, JASPER, ISLEY   *(See also:* THE ISLEY BROTHERS)

11-09-85   *Caravan Of Love*   (CBS Associated ZS4 05611)   4, 4, 2, 5, 5   (5)

11-17-84   *Look The Other Way*   (Magic Sounds ZS4 04642)   26, 17, 15, 13, 10, 9, 7, 7, 7, 20, 29   (11)

JACKSON, FREDDIE

5-18-85   *Rock Me Tonight*   (Cap. B-5459)   21, 10, 6, 4, 2, 1, 1, 1, 1, 2, 2, 4, 14, 23, 29   (15)

8-24-85   *You Are My Lady*   (Cap. B-5459)   28, 24, 24, 5, 5, 9, 14, 14   (8)

JACKSON, JANET

3-05-83   *Come Give Your Love To Me*   (A&M AM 2522)   27, 21, 18, 15, 11, 9, 12, 23   (8)

9-08-84   *Don't Stand Another Chance*   (A&M AM 2660)   26, 23, 18, 14, 12, 11, 11, 10, 10, 11, 20, 26   (12)

6-04-83   *Say You Do*   (A&M AM 2545)   26, 21, 16, 11, 11, 13   (6)

10-23-82   *Young Love*   (A&M AM 2440)   30, 27, 21, 19, 17, 14, 11, 8, 6, 5, 5, 5, 14, 18, 26   (15)

JACKSON, JERMAINE   *(See also:* THE JACKSONS)

12-29-84   *Do What You Do*   (Arista AS1-9279)   28, 28, 28, 19, 21, 27   (6)

8-18-84   *Dynamite*   (Arista AS1-9190)   28, 22, 25, 17, 13, 11, 13, 16, 24   (9)

8-07-82   *Let Me Tickle Your Fancy*   (Motown 1628 MF)   29, 25, 17, 12, 10, 7, 4, 3, 3, 5, 8, 14, 22, 30   (14)

12-11-82   *Very Special Part*   (Motown 1649 MF)   29, 24, 18, 18, 18, 18, 26, 30   (8)

JACKSON, LA TOYA

6-09-84   *Heart Don't Lie*   (Private I ZS4 04439)   29, 25, 23, 22, 27   (5)

JACKSON, MICHAEL   *(See also:* THE JACKSONS; PAUL McCARTNEY)

3-26-83   *Beat It*   (Epic 34-03759)   29, 22, 21, 20, 16, 10, 3, 1, 2, 3, 3, 4, 9, 12, 21, 28   (16)

1-29-83   *Billie Jean*   (Epic 34-03509)   24, 10, 2, 1, 1, 2, 2, 2, 1, 1, 1, 1, 3, 6, 7, 11, 21, 22   (18)

6-09-84   *Farewell My Summer Love*   (Motown 1739 MF)   26, 23, 19, 19, 16, 13, 12, 19   (8)

9-03-83   *Human Nature*   (Epic 34-04026)   27, 27, 23, 23, 29   (5)

11-19-83   *P.Y.T. (Pretty Young Thing)*   (Epic 34-04165)   30, 25, 23, 29   (4)

2-18-84   *Thriller* (Epic 34-04364)   28, 24, 13, 5, 2, 2, 2, 2, 5, 8, 11, 17, 29   (13)

6-11-83   *Wanna Be Startin' Somethin'* (Epic 34-03914)   28, 11, 7, 7, 6, 4, 3, 3, 3, 3, 8, 11, 19, 19   (14)

JACKSON, MICHAEL, AND PAUL McCARTNEY   *(See also:* PAUL McCARTNEY)

11-13-82   *The Girl Is Mine* (Epic 34-03288)   26, 16, 8, 4, 2, 2, 1, 1, 1, 4, 10, 13, 20, 29   (14)

JACKSON, REBBIE

10-06-84   *Centipede* (Col. 38-04547)   27, 16, 12, 6, 6, 5, 3, 3, 4, 6, 9, 14, 27, 27, 27   (15)

THE JACKSONS   *(See also:* JERMAINE JACKSON; MICHAEL JACKSON)

7-14-84   *State Of Shock* (Epic 34-04503)   23, 15, 8, 5, 4, 3, 8, 3, 12, 24   (10)

9-15-84   *Torture* (Epic 34-04575)   25, (1), 28, 29   (3)

JAMES, RICK   *(See also:* THE TEMPTATIONS)

4-27-85   *Can't Stop* (Gordy 1776 GF)   27, 25, 21, 18, 16, 16, 22   (7)

8-06-83   *Cold Blooded* (Gordy 1687 GF)   22, 16, 10, 8, 7, 7, 1, 1, 1, 2, 2, 2, 2, 6, 9, 19, 26, 30   (18)

5-22-82   *Dance Wit' Me* (Gordy 1619 GF)   28, 18, 12, 10, 6, 4, 3, 3, 5, 12, 18, 28   (12)

7-20-85   *Glow* (Gordy 1796 GF)   21, 21, 14, 6, 5, 6, 17, 17, 17, 17   (10)

9-04-82   *Hard To Get* (Gordy)   27, 22, 20, 25, 30   (5)

7-21-84   *17* (Gordy 1730 GF)   30, 22, 17, 11, 10, 7, 7, 2, 1, 3, 6, 10, 19, 27   (14)

11-05-83   *U Bring The Freak Out* (Gordy 1703 GF)   19, 12, 6, 6, 6, 5, 6, 9, 9, 9, 9, 15, 22   (13)

JAMES, RICK, AND SMOKEY ROBINSON

12-24-83   *Ebony Eyes*   (Gordy 1714 GF)   29, 29, 29, 29, 18, 10, 7, 5, 8, 11, 30   (11)

JARREAU, AL

11-17-84   *After All*   (WB 7-29262)   27, 22, 20, 18, 15, 13, 22, 22, 22   (9)

6-25-83   *Boogie Down*   (WB 7-29624)   25, 20, 16, 13, 11, 8, 7, 15, 21, 29   (10)

3-12-83   *Mornin'*   (WB 7-29720)   29, 24, 20, 16, 13, 9, 6, 3, 5, 4, 6, 7, 7, 12, 18   (15)

JARREAU, AL, AND RANDY CRAWFORD

10-30-82   *Your Precious Love*   (WB 7-29908)   24, 19, 16, 12, 10, 8, 7, 14, 22, 22, 22   (11)

THE JETS

11-23-85   *Curiosity*   (MCA 52682)   24, 17, 17   (3)

JOHNSON, HOWARD

7-31-82   *So Fine*   (A&M AM 2415)   30, 24, 18, 15, 11, 7, 12, 12, 22, 27, 30   (11)

JOHNSON, JESSE/JESSE JOHNSON'S REVUE

2-23-85   *Be Your Man*   (A&M AM 2702)   29, 25, 20, 15, 9, 9, 5, 6, 9, 14, 19, 29   (12)

5-25-85   *Can You Help Me*   (A&M AM 2730)   26, 18, 14, 11, 8, 3, 4, 4, 8, 8, 15   (11)

8-10-85   *I Want My Girl*   (A&M AM 2749)   18, 13, 9, 4, 4   (5)

JONES, GLENN

5-04-85   *Bring Back Your Love*   (RCA PB-13999)   29, 26, 28, 27   (4)

10-20-84   *Show Me*   (RCA PB-13873)   29, 26, 26, 24, 21, 19, 13, 11, 3, 2, 3, 3, 3, 5, 13, 22   (16)

THE JONES GIRLS

2-20-82   *Nights Over Egypt*   (P.I.)   18, 11, 7, 5, 3, 3, 4, 18   (8)

THE JONZUN CREW

5-28-83   *Space Cowboy*   (Tommy Boy TB-833)   30, 30, 26, 22, 30, 29   (6)

JOSEPH, MARGIE

1-15-83   *Knockout*   (HCRC WS4 03337)   25, 20, 16, 16, 14, 12, 10, 9, 7, 9, 12, 19, 24   (13)

JUNIOR

7-16-83   *Communication Breakdown*   (Mer. 812 397-7)   26, 24, 29   (3)

2-13-82   *Mama Used To Say*   (Mer. SR 76132)   15, 10, 5, 2, 1, 1, 5, 10, 12, 12, 15, 17, 25   (13)

6-05-82   *Too Late*   (Mer. SR 76150)   29, 26, 23, 19, 15, 11, 9, 7, 11, 18, 28   (11)

KASHIF

10-27-84   *Are You The Woman*   (Arista AS1-9263)   28, 28, 28   (3)

7-14-84   *Baby Don't Break Your Baby's Heart*   (Arista AS1-9200)   27, 21, 16, 13, 8, 8, 12, 13, 13, 29   (10)

4-02-83   *I Just Gotta Have You*   (Arista AS 1042)   25, 23, 19, 15, 12, 10, 15, 29   (8)

7-02-83   *Stone Love*   (Arista AS1-9033)   28, 25, 21, 19, 15   (5)

KENNEDY, JOYCE

12-15-84   *Stronger Than Before*   (A&M AM 2685)   28, 27, 23, 23, 23   (5)

KENNEDY, JOYCE, AND JEFFREY OSBORNE

8-04-84   *The Last Time I Made Love*   (A&M AM 2656)   28, 18, 14, 11, 8, 4, 3, 1, 2, 4, 4, 14, 24, 24   (14)

KHAN, CHAKA   *(See also:* **RUFUS)**

11-20-82   *Got To Be There*   (WB 7-29881)   26, 20, 15, 9, 7, 6, 6, 6, 2, 1, 1, 9, 15, 19, 25   (15)

9-29-84   *I Feel For You*   (WB 7-29195)   23, 15, 8, 3, 2, 1, 1, 1, 2, 2, 4, 7, 12, 19, 19, 19, 26   (17)

11-09-85   *(Krush Groove) Can't Stop The Street*   (WB 7-28923)   14, 14, 13, 20, 20   (5)

2-16-85   *This Is My Night*   (WB 7-29097)   24, 18, 14, 12, 10, 10, 10, 16 25   (9)

5-25-85   *Through The Fire*   (WB 7-29025)   24, 21, 16, 13, 12, 19, 25, 25   (8)

KIDDO

4-16-83   *Try My Loving*   (A&M AM 2529)   29, 28, 25   (3)

KING, B.B.

4-13-85   *Into The Night*   (MCA 52530)   24, 16, 13, 12, 11, 26   (6)

KING, EVELYN "CHAMPAGNE"

1-28-84   *Action*   (RCA PB-13682)   21, 16, 13, 11, 9, 9, 21, 27, 27, (1), 25   (10)

12-18-82   *Betcha She Don't Love You*   (RCA PB-13380)   23, 16, 16, 16, 12, 9, 5, 3, 1, 4, 5, 7, 17, 23, 28   (15)

11-24-84   *Just For The Night*   (RCA PB-13914)   25, 23, 21, 21   (4)

8-14-82   *Love Come Down*   (RCA)   27, 21, 14, 9, 5, 3, 2, 1, 1, 1, 1, 3, 8, 11, 21, 29   (16)

4-07-84   *Shake Down*   (RCA PB-13748)   26, 21, 13, 10, 8, 13, 20, 23   (8)

2-13-82   *Spirit Of The Dancer*   (RCA)   27, 24, 22, 21   (4)

KLIQUE

1-21-84   *Flashback*   (MCA 52303)   27, 23, 21, 27, 30   (5)

9-03-83   *Stop Doggin' Me Around*   (MCA 52250)   28, 28, 21, 21, 18, 13, 13, 13, 13, 4, 3, 4, 5, 8, 9, 14, 17, 17, 17, 17, 26   (21)

6-22-85   *A Woman, A Lover, A Friend*   (MCA 52566)   26, 21, 18, 18   (4)

KLYMAXX

8-17-85   *I Miss You*   (Constellation 52606)   30, 25, 21, 21   (4)

4-27-85   *Meeting In The Ladies Room*   (Constellation 52545)   23, 21, 18, 13, 6, 10, 15, 14, 25   (9)

1-19-85   *The Men All Pause*   (MCA 52486)   22, 20, 14, 11, 7, 4, 3, 5, 7, 14, 14, 19,   (13)

KNIGHT, GLADYS, & THE PIPS

2-27-82   *A Friend Of Mine*   (Col.)   26, 23, 20, 18, 16, 14, 27   (7)

3-02-85   *My Time*   (Col. 38-04761)   28, 24, 18, 16, 16, 14, 13, 22, 30   (9)

4-16-83   *Save The Overtime*   (Col. 38-03761)   26, 20, 15, 12, 7, 4, 4, 2, 2, 2, 3, 9, 9, 12, 15   (15)

8-20-83   *You're Number One*   (Col. 38-04033)   29, 25, 21, 21, 11, 11, 7, 5, 5, 5, 5, 10, 11, 21, 28   (15)

KOOL & THE GANG

9-04-82   *Big Fun*   (De-Lite)   24, 11, 7, 5, 4, 3, 3, 4, 6, 12, 17   (11)

8-03-85   *Cherish*   (De-Lite 880 869-7)   26, 9, 7, 4, 3, 3   (6)

11-09-85   *Emergency*   (De-Lite 884 199-7)   30, 30, 30, 23, 23   (5)

4-06-85   *Fresh*   (De-Lite 880 623-7)   30, 19, 11, 9, 7, 5, 2, 1, 1, 3, 8, 10, 16, 23, 23   (15)

3-06-82   *Get Down On It*   (De-Lite DE 818)   29, 16, 9, 6, 3, 1, 1, 5, 8, 15, 19, 29   (12)   See: "Steppin' Out."

11-12-83   *Joanna*   (De-Lite DE 829)   26, 22, 16, 13, 11, 9, 3, 3, 3, 3, 1, 1, 3, 4, 5, 7, 8, 19, 29, 29   (20)

11-13-82   *Let's Go Dancin'*   (De-Lite DE 824)   24, 15, 12, 9, 5, 3, 2, 2, 2, 1, 3, 6, 19, 27   (14)

12-15-84 *Misled* (De-Lite 800 431-7) 30, 25, 20, 20, 20, 10, 6, 6, 3, 4, 9, 16, 23 (13)

2-13-82 *Steppin' Out* (De-Lite DE 818) 17, 12, 9, 14, 16, 9, 6, 3, 1, 1, 5, 8, 15, 19, 29 (15) Merged with "Get Down On It" as double-sided hit beginning March 13, 1982.

3-31-84 *Tonight* (De-Lite 818 226-7) 12, 13, 9, 6, 5, 3, 3, 8, 13, 19 (10)

L.T.D.

2-13-82 *April Love* (A&M) 25, 23, 18, 17, 14, 14, 13, 29 (8)

LaBELLE, PATTI *(See also:* GROVER WASHINGTON; BOBBY WOMACK)

11-26-83 *If Only You Knew* (P.I. ZS4 04176) 30, 26, 23, 21, 19, 19, 19, 19, 7, 2, 2, 1, 2, 2, 1, 2, 6, 6, 10, 10, 18, 24 (22)

4-28-84 *Love, Need And Want You* (P.I. ZS4 04399) 26, 22, 12, 9, 6, 3, 3, 5, 11, 18, 26 (11)

2-23-85 *New Attitude* (MCA 52517) 28, 24, 21, 17, 13, 13, 11, 11, 19, 28 (10)

7-20-85 *Stir It Up* (MCA 52517) 26, 26, 19, 8, 6, 5, 15, 15 (8)

LAID BACK

3-10-84 *White Horse* (Sire 7-29346) 26, 19, 19, 9, 8, 4, 3, 3, 7, 7, 10, 15, 25 (13)

LAKESIDE

2-13-82 *I Want To Hold Your Hand* (Solar) 24, 11, 30 (3)

7-14-84 *Outrageous* (Solar 7-69716) 29, 25, 21, 20, 29 (5)

4-30-83 *Raid* (Solar 7-69836) 27, 25, 20, 13, 6, 6, 9, 10, 19 (9)

5-22-82 *Something About That Woman* (Solar S-48009) 26, 23, 20, 17, 14, 14, 20, 30 (8)

LATTISAW, STACY

9-25-82   *Attack Of The Name Game*   (Cot.)   30, 26, 22, 19, 17, 15, 11, 9, 7, 7, 14, 20, 27   (13)

8-07-82   *Don't Throw It All Away*   (Cot.)   27, 23, 20, 18, 14, 10, 9, 14, 16, 21, 29   (11)

12-24-83   *Million Dollar Babe*   (Cot. 7-99819)   27, 27, 27, 27, 23, 29   (6)

8-06-83   *Miracles*   (Cot. 7-99855)   26, 22, 17, 14, 12, 12, 18, 18, 24, 30, 30, 30, 30   (13)

LATTISAW, STACY, AND JOHNNY GILL

5-26-84   *Baby It's You*   (Cot. 7-99750)   30, 24, 21, 18, 15, 15, 24   (7)

3-31-84   *Perfect Combination*   (Cot. 7-99785)   22, 18, 14, 10, 6, 5, 9, 14, 19, 27   (10)

LAVETTE, BETTYE

2-13-82   *Right In The Middle*   (Motown)   30, 28, 24   (3)

LAWS, RONNIE

7-30-83   *In The Groove*   (Cap. B-5241)   28, 23, 20, 19, 18, 17, 17   (7)

LISA LISA AND THE CULT JAM WITH FULL FORCE

6-15-85   *I Wonder If I Take You Home*   (Col. 38-04486)   30, 23, 18, 15, 15, 6, 6, 2, 2, 10, 20   (11)

LOOSE ENDS

6-08-85   *Hangin' On A String*   (MCA 52570)   30, 25, 17, 13, 7, 7, 4, 4, 1, 7, 14, 24   (12)

LOREN, BRYAN

5-05-84   *Lollipop Luv*   (Philly World 7-99760)   29, 21, 18, 17, 16, 20   (6)

LOVE, VIKKI   *(See:* NUANCE)

LUCAS, CARRIE

8-10-85   *Hello Stranger*   (Constellation 52602)   29, 25, 22, 18, 18   (5)

LYNN, CHERYL

3-09-85   *At Last You're Mine*   (Private I ZS4 04736)   30, 29   (2)

1-28-84   *Encore*   (Col. 38-04256)   30, 18, 15, 7, 4, 3, 3, 4, 4, 21, 6, 11, 20   (13)

7-20-85   *Fidelity*   (Col. 38-04832)   29, 29, 23   (3)

9-11-82   *If This World Were Mine*   (Col.)   28, 27, 10, 7, 6, 4, 3, 2, 9, 15, 23   (11)

7-31-82   *Instant Love*   (Col. 18-02905)   24, 21, 20, 28   (4)

MacDONALD, RALPH, WITH BILL WITHERS

9-15-84   *In The Name Of Love*   (Polydor 881 221-7)   28, 24, 18, 13, 12, 10, 9, 9, 9, 13, 23   (11)

MADONNA

12-22-84   *Like A Virgin*   (Sire 7-29210)   30, 24, 24, 24, 9, 8, 5, 5, 11, 19, 29   (11)

THE MANHATTANS

7-02-83   *Crazy*   (Col. 38-03939)   27, 21, 18, 13, 12, 8, 4, 3, 6, 9, 9, 17, 17, 22, 28, 28, 28, 28   (18)

2-13-82   *Honey, Honey*   (Col.)   21, 16, 12, 10, 9, 8, 25   (7)

3-23-85   *You Send Me*   (Col. 38-04754)   29, 29, 24, 16, 10, 7, 6, 7, 10, 20   (10)

MARIE, TEENA

11-05-83   *Fix It (Part 1)*   (Epic 34-04124)   23, 25, 29   (3)

12-15-84   *Lovergirl*   (Epic 34-04619)   26, 20, 13, 13, 13, 14, 23, 29   (8)

THE MARY JANE GIRLS

8-20-83   *All Night Long*   (Gordy 1690 GF)   30, 26, 22, 22   (4)

5-28-83   *Candy Man*   (Gordy 1670 GF)   26, 20, 16, 14, 10, 6, 8, 8, 12, 13, 27, 30   (12)

3-23-85   *In My House*   (Gordy 1741 GF)   20, 20, 17, 9, 6, 4, 3, 2, 4, 5, 5, 9, 16, 27, 30   (15)

8-03-85   *Wild And Crazy Love*   (Gordy 1789 GF)   24, 10, 9, 8, 7, 7   (6)

MAZE FEATURING FRANKIE BEVERLY

3-02-85   *Back In Stride*   (Cap. B-5431)   30, 27, 22, 15, 15, 12, 4, 2, 1, 4, 3, 8, 11, 17, 19, 27   (16)

5-14-83   *Love Is The Key*   (Cap. B-5221)   27, 22, 18, 14, 8, 8, 6, 3, 3, 5, 8, 6, 12, 21, 28   (15)

6-01-85   *Too Many Games*   (Cap. B-5474)   27, 23, 17, 15, 10, 9, 9, 7, 7, 13   (10)

2-13-82   *We Need Love To Live*   (Cap.)   18, 14   (2)

McCARTNEY, PAUL, AND MICHAEL JACKSON   *(See also:* MICHAEL JACKSON)

11-05-83   *Say, Say, Say*   (Col. 38-04168)   8, 5, 3, 2, 2, 4, 5, 7, 7, 7, 7, 10, 13, 19, 24, 29   (16)

McCARTNEY, PAUL, AND STEVIE WONDER   *(See also:* STEVIE WONDER)

5-15-82   *Ebony And Ivory*   (Col. 18-02860)   28, 25, 22, 19, 16, 15, 22, 27   (8)

McDONALD, MICHAEL   *(See also:* JAMES INGRAM)

10-16-82   *I Keep Forgettin'*   (WB)   27, 24, 20, 18, 23, 29   (6)

MENDES, SERGIO

7-02-83   *Never Gonna Let You Go*   (A&M)   24, 23, 23, 27   (4)

MIDNIGHT STAR

7-09-83   *Freak-A-Zoid*   (Solar 7-69828)   27, 24, 20, 14, 5, 2, 2, 2, 1, 1, 3, 3, 5, 8, 8, 8, 8, 24, 29   (19)

12-01-84   *Operator*   (Solar 7-69684)   28, 19, 11, 5, 1, 1, 1, 1, 1, 3, 9, 16, 22   (13)

11-05-83   *Wet My Whistle*   (Solar 7-6970)   21, 19, 18, 15, 12, 10, 7, 6, 6, 6, 6, 6, 9, 12, 17, 20, 27   (17)

THE MIGHTY CLOUDS OF JOY   *(See:* ROGER)

MILLS, STEPHANIE

11-26-83   *How Came U Don't Call Me Anymore*   (Casa. 814 747-7)   27, 24, 20, 17, 14, 14, 14, 14, 11, 16, 24, 29   (12)

10-09-82   *Keep Away Girls*   (Casa.)   27, 23, 20, 18, 15, 13, 13, 21   (8)

7-17-82   *Last Night*   (Casa. NB 2352)   30, 25, 21, 16, 11, 8, 5, 4, 4, 8, 17, 21, 26   (13)

9-22-84   *The Medicine Song*   (Casa. 880180-7)   25, 20, 17, 14, 9, 8, 11, 14, 22, 29   (10)

9-17-83   *Pilot Error*   (Casa. 814 142-7)   25, 25, 20, 16, 16, 16, 16, 30   (8)

MOORE, MELBA   *(See also:* LILLO THOMAS)

11-09-85   *I Can't Believe It*   (Cap. B-5520)   29, 29, 29, 26, 26   (5)

11-26-83   *Keepin' My Lover Satisfied*   (Cap. B-5288)   23, 20, 18, 16, 13, 13, 13, 13, 22, 27   (10)

2-13-82   *Let's Stand Together*   (EMI America)   20, 17   (2)

2-11-84   *Livin' For Your Love*   (Cap. B-5308)   26, 21, 17, 15, 14, 11, 11, 17, 16, 23, 30   (11)

5-05-84   *Love Me Right*   (Cap. B-5343)   30, 24, 19, 16, 12, 10, 9, 8, 12, 22, 28   (11)

9-18-82   *Love's Comin' At Ya*   (EMI America)   24, 18, 15, 13, 9, 7, 5, 4, 5, 6, 11, 16, 23   (13)

1-15-83   *Mind Up Tonight*   (Cap. B-5180)   22, 16, 14, 13, 11, 10, 16, 23, 28   (9)

4-13-85   *Read My Lips*   (Cap. B-5437)   26, 21, 18, 17, 13, 15, 25, 29   (8)

4-09-83   *Underlove*   (Cap. B-5208)   30, 28,   (2)

8-03-85   *When You Love Me Like This*   (Cap. B-5484)   21, 15, 12, 11, 20, 20   (6)

MTUME

11-17-84   *C.O.D. (I'll Deliver)*   (Epic 34-04567)   24, 20, 17, 15, 8, 7, 16, 16, 16, 24   (10)

5-07-83   *Juicy Fruit*   (Epic 34-03578)   28, 16, 12, 5, 4, 1, 1, 1, 1, 2, 2, 4, 4, 4, 8, 16, 17, 25, 25, 30, 30   (21)

11-05-83   *Would You Like To (Fool Around)*   (Epic 34-04087)   17, 16, 13, 12, 11, 17, 20, 26, 26, 26, 26   (11)

8-04-84   *You, Me And He*   (Epic 34-04504)   26, 21, 16, 21, 12, 9, 4, 2, 4, 5, 9, 13, 20, 20, 30   (15)

MURPHY, EDDIE

11-09-85   *Party All The Time*   (Col. 38-05609)   18, 18, 12, 10, 10   (5)

MUSICAL YOUTH

12-25-82   *Pass The Dutchie*   (MCA 52149)   28, 28, 28, 23, 19, 15, 12, 9, 6, 4, 6, 11, 17, 23, 30   (15)

·MYERS, ALICIA

9-01-84   *You Get The Best From Me*   (MCA 52425)   24, 21, 17, 13, 7, 6, 5, 5, 7, 7, 10, 17   (12)

THE NEW EDITION

4-30-83   *Candy Girl*   (Streetwise SWRL 2208)   26, 21, 14, 1, 2, 5, 6, 7, 13   (9)

9-15-84   *Cool It Now*   (MCA 52455)   30, 27, 21, 18, 13, 6, 5, 5, 3, 2, 1, 1, 2, 2, 3, 6, 6, 6, 17, 25, 30   (21)

11-09-85   *Count Me Out*   (MCA 52703)   26, 26, 19, 12, 12   (5)

8-06-83   *Is This The End*   (Streetwise SWRL 1111)   30, 25, 22, 20, 16, 16, 10, 10, 13, 18, 18, 18, 18, 26, 30   (15)

4-13-85   *Lost In Love*   (MCA 52553)   23, 15, 11, 10, 9, 12, 23, 26   (8)

12-29-84   *Mr. Telephone Man*   (MCA 52484)   25, 25, 25, 12, 9, 4, 1, 1, 2, 4, 11, 20, 26, 26, 28   (15)

9.9

8-10-85   *All Of Me For All Of You*   (RCA PB-14082)   23, 17, 16, 11, 11   (5)

NUANCE FEATURING VIKKI LOVE

2-09-85   *Loveride*   28, 27   (2)

NUNN, BOBBY

10-30-82   *She's Just A Groupie*   (Motown)   28, 26, 25, 22, 19, 25   (6)

O'BRYAN

8-18-84   *Breakin' Together*   (Cap. B-5376)   30, 25, 26, 22, 19, 17, 22, 26   (8)

2-27-82   *The Gigolo*   (Cap. PA-5067)   19, 16, 13, 10, 8, 6, 6, 8, 11, 13, 17, 25   (12)

2-26-83   *I'm Freaky*   (Cap. B-5203)   29, 22, 18, 15, 13, 12, 16, 21   (8)

4-28-84   *Lovelite*   (Cap. B-5329)   28, 23, 15, 13, 9, 6, 5, 4, 1, 2, 2, 3, 6, 11, 15, 19, 29   (17)

5-21-83   *You And I*   (Cap. B-5224)   28, 27, 28   (3)

OCEAN, BILLY

8-11-84   *Caribbean Queen*   (Jive JS1-9199)   28, 18, 14, 14, 11, 7, 4, 1, 1, 2, 2, 4, 4, 4, 6, 13, 21, 29   (18)

1-19-85   *Loverboy*   (Jive JS1-9284)   16, 14, 13, 20   (4)

8-10-85   *Mystery Lady*   (Jive JS1-9374)   25, 21, 18, 12, 12   (5)

5-18-85   *Suddenly*   (Jive JS1-9323)   27, 12, 9, 5, 4, 7, 12, 17, 17, 28, 28, 30   (12)

ODYSSEY

7-31-82   *Inside Out*   (RCA PB-13217)   26, 25, 16, 14, 13, 13, 20, 28   (8)

THE O'JAYS

5-19-84   *Extraordinary Girl*   (P.I. ZS4 04437)   30, 26, 18, 16, 27, 27, 30   (7)

4-03-82   *I Just Want To Satisfy*   (P.I. ZS5 02834)   26, 22, 17, 14, 12, 11, 9, 8, 8, 11, 15, 21, 28   (13)

7-17-82   *Your Body's Here With Me*   (P.I. ZS5 03009)   26, 22, 17, 15, 9, 5, 3, 3, 8, 10, 19, 23, 28   (13)

OLLIE AND JERRY

6-16-84   *Breakin' . . . There's No Stopping Us*   (Polydor 821 709-8)   30, 22, 14, 9, 7, 5, 2, 2, 1, 1, 2, 2, 3, 8, 15, 17, 22   (17)

ONE WAY

5-15-82   *Cutie Pie*   (MCA 52049)   27, 20, 13, 10, 8, 7, 6, 5, 5, 6, 3, 6, 11, 21, 30   (15)

4-14-84   *Lady You Are*   (MCA 52348)   26, 21, 17, 14, 4, 4, 3, 4, 6, 8, 12, 24, 29   (13)

7-21-84   *Mr. Groove*   (MCA 52409)   29, 18, 14, 10, 9, 15, 22   (7)

8-13-83   *Shine On Me*   (MCA 52228)   28, 25, 24, 30, 30   (5)

O'NEAL, ALEXANDER

8-10-85   *If You Were Here Tonight*   (Tabu ZS4 05418)   22, 19, 14, 23, 23   (5)

4-13-85   *Innocent*   (Tabu ZS4 04718)   20, 13, 10, 8, 8, 7, 13, 19, 24, 29   (10)

ORBIT

2-05-83   *The Beat Goes On*   (Quality 7025)   27, 19, 15, 13, 15, 14, 19, 26   (8)

OSBORNE, JEFFREY *(See also:* JOYCE KENNEDY)

12-29-84 *The Borderlines* (A&M AM 2695)   26, 26, 26, 21, 18, 17, 12, 8, 5, 5,
7, 12, 21, 21, 27   (15)

10-20-84 *Don't Stop* (A&M AM 2687)   30, 21, 21, 15, 12, 11, 7, 5, 5, 8, 17,
17, 17, 30   (14)

7-23-83 *Don't You Get So Mad* (A&M AM 2561)   26, 24, 14, 10, 9, 7, 6, 6, 4,
4, 8, 10, 10, 10, 10, 29   (16)

5-29-82 *I Really Don't Need No Light* (A&M AM 2410)   28, 23, 20, 16, 13, 9,
6, 4, 6, 4, 3, 3, 6, 10, 17, 27   (16)

10-02-82 *On The Wings Of Love* (A&M)   28, 23, 21, 18, 16, 13, 12, 10, 9, 10,
15, 17, 27, 27, 27, 30   (16)

2-11-84 *Plane Love* (A&M SP-12089)   28, 24, 22, 20, 18, 16, 16, 20   (8)

11-05-83 *Stay With Me Tonight* (A&M AM 2591)   25, 20, 11, 4, 3, 3, 3, 5, 5,
5, 5, 8, 11, 14, 19, 23, 29   (17)

5-05-84 *We're Going All The Way* (A&M AM 2618)   21, 19, 24, 29   (4)

PARKER, RAY, JR.

12-18-82 *Bad Boy* (Arista AS 1030)   28, 21, 21, 21, 9, 4, 3, 2, 8, 7, 9, 14, 20,
25   (14)

7-14-84 *Ghostbusters* (Arista AS1-9212)   30, 22, 5, 4, 2, 2, 1, 1, 1, 2, 5, 8, 11,
22   (14)

11-09-85 *Girls Are More Fun* (Arista AS1-9352)   24, 24, 17, 24, 24   (5)

12-22-84 *Jamie* (Arista AS1-9293)   26, 15, 15, 15, 15, 16, 16, 26   (8)

6-26-82 *Let Me Go* (Arista AS 0695)   29, 26, 21, 18, 15, 13, 10, 8, 4, 4, 8,
13, 14, 23, 29   (15)

3-20-82 *The Other Woman* (Arista AS 0669)   30, 23, 13, 9, 4, 2, 2, 1, 1, 2, 5,
5, 9, 9, 11, 14, 20, 25   (18)

PEACHES AND HERB

7-02-83 *Remember* (Col. 38-03872)   25, 22, 22, 23, 25   (5)

PENDERGRASS, TEDDY

11-23-85 *Never Felt Like Dancin'* (Elektra 7-69595)   26, 28, 28   (3)

5-22-82 *Nine Times Out Of Ten* (P.I. ZS5 02856)   30, 27, 26, 25, 25   (5)

10-06-84 *You're My Choice Tonight* (Asylum 7-69696)   28, 17, 15, 13, 13, 16, 25   (7)

PENDERGRASS, TEDDY, WITH WHITNEY HOUSTON

6-28-84 *Hold Me* (Asylum 7-69720)   28, 23, 18, 12, 8, 6, 6, 6, 15, 18, 15, 25   (12)

THE POINTER SISTERS

7-10-82 *American Music* (Planet JH-13254)   27, 23, 19, 15, 12, 10, 7, 6, 11, 15, 25   (11)

2-25-84 *Automatic* (Planet YB-13730)   26, 11, 6, 5, 5, 3, 7, 7, 9, 15   (10)

6-08-85 *Baby Come And Get It* (Planet YB-14041)   18, 15, 14, 24   (4)

8-24-85 *Dare Me* (RCA PB-14128)   26, 22, 22   (3)

12-10-84 *I Need You* (Planet YB-13639)   28, 25, 22, 22, 22, 22, 29   (7)

5-12-84 *Jump* (Planet YB-13780)   28, 23, 20, 13, 8, 6, 2, 3, 4, 6, 9, 14, 18, 23   (14)

2-09-85 *Neutron Dance* (Planet YB-13951)   25, 19, 16, 11, 9, 9, 19, 19, 20, 29   (10)

PRINCE (AND THE REVOLUTION)   *(See also:* ANDRE CYMONE; MORRIS DAY)

11-05-83 *Delirious* (WB 7-29503)   12, 10, 9, 17, 21, 26, 29   (7)

3-19-83 *Little Red Corvette* (WB 7-29746)   27, 21, 17, 15, 13, 10, 5, 6, 8, 9, 10, 15, 17, 23, 28   (15)

11-06-82 *1999* (WB 7-29896)   25, 10, 5, 4, 3, 3, 5, 9, 9, 9, 15, 21, 28   (13)

6-09-84 *When Doves Cry* (WB 7-29286)   27, 7, 3, 1, 1, 1, 1, 1, 1, 3, 4, 6, 4, 7, 16, 23   (16)

1-19-85   *I Would Die 4 U*   (WB 7-29121)   29, 10, 7, 6, 13, 21   (6)

8-25-84   *Let's Go Crazy*   (WB 7-29216)   27, (1), 16, 12, 6, 3, 2, 3, 7, 12, 15, 23   (11)

2-27-82   *Let's Work*   (WB)   21, 19, 15, 11, 9, 7, 15, 29   (8)

8-10-85   *Pop Life*   (Paisley Park 7-28998)   26, 22, 13, 8, 8   (5)

10-27-84   *Purple Rain*   (WB 7-29174)   15, 12, 8, 5, 4, 6, 7, 13, 16, 29, 29, 29   (12)

6-01-85   *Raspberry Beret*   (Paisley Park 7-28972)   30, 27, 22, 11, 5, 3, 3, 1, 1, 5, 17, 29   (12)

PRINCE AND THE REVOLUTION WITH APOLLONIA   (*See also:* APOLLONIA 6)

3-23-85   *Take Me With U*   (WB 7-29079)   27, 27, 22   (3)

R.J.'S LATEST ARRIVAL

6-02-84   *Shackles*   (Golden Boy PUS 7059)   26, 22, 19, 17, 16, 14, 19, 26   (8)

8-10-85   *Swing Low*   (Atl. 7-89551)   19, 18, 27   (3)

READY FOR THE WORLD

5-18-85   *Deep Inside Your Love*   (MCA 52561)   29, 21, 15, 13, 7, 3, 4, 6, 6, 15, 15, 22   (12)

11-30-85   *Digital Display*   (MCA 52734)   29, 29   (2)

8-17-85   *Oh Sheila*   (MCA 52636)   26, 17, 10, 10, (1), 20, 20,   (6)

2-02-85   *Tonight*   (MCA 52507)   28, 19, 12, 7, 6, 4, 3, 5, 5, 7, 14, 14, 20, 27   (14)

THE REDDINGS

6-12-82   *(Sittin' On) The Dock Of The Bay*   (B.I.A.D. ZS5 02836)   30, 26, 21, 18, 13, 11, 16, 28   (8)

4-20-85   *Where Did Our Love Go*   (Polydor 881 767-1)   29, 24, 22, 24, 23   (5)

RENE AND ANGELA

11-09-85   *I'll Be Good*   (Mer. 884 009-7)   11, 11, 23   (3)

2-20-82   *Imaginary Playmates*   (Cap.)   25   (1)

10-08-83   *My First Love*   (Cap. B-5272)   27, 27, 27, 27, 16, 15, 12, 8, 7, 7, 10, 15, 15, 15, 15, 24   (16)

6-15-85   *Save Your Love (For #1)*   (Mer. 880 731-7)   26, 19, 8, 5, 5, 3, 3, 3, 11, 20   (10)

RICHIE, LIONEL   *(See also:* THE COMMODORES)

10-01-83   *All Night Long*   (Motown 1698 MF)   26, 15, 15, 15, 15, 1, 1, 1, 1, 1, 1, 2, 4, 4, 4, 4, 5, 7, 10, 14, 18, 25   (22)

3-31-84   *Hello*   (Motown 1722 MF)   17, 17, 12, 7, 1, 1, 1, 2, 4, 5, 7, 12, 16, 28   (14)

4-23-83   *My Love*   (Motown 1677 MF)   25, 22, 18, 10, 10, 11, 11, 11, 12, 16, 22, 30   (12)

11-10-84   *Penny Lover*   (Motown 1762 MF)   25, 18, 8, 12, 17, 25   (6)

12-24-83   *Running With The Night*   (Motown 1710 MF)   21, 21, 21, 21, 14, 8, 5, 3, 1, 1, 7, 11, 21, 21, (1), 23, 27   (16)

11-30-85   *Say You, Say Me*   (Motown 1819 MF)   21, 21   (2)

7-28-84   *Stuck On You*   (Motown 1746 MF)   29, 24, 12, 7, 4, 9, 8, 6, 10, 12, 19, 27   (12)

10-16-82   *Truly*   (Motown 1644 MF)   24, 21, 12, 6, 3, 2, 2, 2, 1, 1, 3, 3, 3, 6, 7, 7, 15, 20, 28   (19)

1-22-83   *You Are*   (Motown 1657 MF)   23, 19, 6, 4, 2, 2, 1, 3, 6, 7, 9, 11, 14, 17, 23, 26, 29   (17)

ROBINSON, SMOKEY   *(See also:* RICK JAMES)

7-07-84   *And I Don't Love You*   (Tamla 1735 TF)   30, 25, 24, 30   (4)

1-22-83   *I've Made Love To You A Thousand Times*   (Tamla 1655 TF)   27, 23, 18, 13, 9, 6, 5, 4, 3, 4, 6, 8, 11, 18   (14)

5-29-82   *Old Fashioned Love*   (Tamla 1615 TF)   24, 22, 19, 17, 17, 16, 22, 27   (8)

2-13-82   *Tell Me Tomorrow—Part 1*   (Tamla 1601 TF)   4, 2, 16, 18, 23   (5)

ROCKWELL

6-02-84   *Obscene Phone Caller*   (Motown 1731 MF)   28, 24, 20, 18, 17, 15, 14, 13, 20, 25   (10)

2-04-84   *Somebody's Watching Me*   (Motown 1702 MF)   27, 20, 15, 10, 2, 1, 1, 1, 1, 1, 3, 5, 9, 9, 15, 22, 25   (17)

ROGER

6-02-84   *In The Mix*   (WB 7-29271)   20, 14, 11, 7, 6, 5, 8, 10, 17, 23   (10)

ROGER FEATURING THE MIGHTY CLOUDS OF JOY

9-08-84   *Midnight Hour—Part 1*   (WB 7-29231)   28, 20, 16, 19, 24   (5)

ROSS, DIANA

11-09-85   *Eaten Alive*   (RCA PB-14181)   12, 12, 10, 16, 16   (5)

2-20-82   *Mirror, Mirror*   (RCA PB-13021)   8, 6, 6, 4, 7, 17   (6)

1-19-85   *Missing You*   (RCA PB-13966)   27, 15, 11, 8, 3, 1, 1, 1, 2, 3, 3, 3, 7, 12, 17, 23   (16)

10-09-82   *Muscles*   (RCA PB-13348)   25, 20, 15, 8, 1, 4, 3, 3, 6, 10, 12, 20, 20, 20, 26   (15)

7-30-83   *Pieces Of Ice*   (RCA PB-13549)   26, 17, 13, 13, 12, 14, 14, 22, 22, 27   (10)

3-05-83   *So Close*   (RCA PB-13424)   25, 19, 16, 22, 28   (5)

9-08-84   *Swept Away*   (RCA PB-13864)   30, 26, 21, 16, 7, 6, 4, 3, 3, 7, 10, 18, 29   (13)

6-22-85   *Telephone*   (RCA PB-14032)   28, 23, 16, 16, 12, 12, 20   (7)

4-24-82   *Work That Body*   (RCA PB-13201)   30, 25, 24, 21, 17, 15, 14, 12, 10, 20, 25   (11)

RUFUS AND CHAKA KHAN   (*See also:* CHAKA KHAN)

9-03-83   *Ain't Nobody*   (WB 7-29555)   29, 29, 20, 20, 12, 9, 9, 9, 9, 3, 4, 5, 9,
          10, 12, 15, 20, 20, 20, 20, 28   (21)

2-20-82   *Better Together*   (MCA)   29, 25, 24, 24   (4)

RUN-D.M.C.

2-04-84   *Hard Times*   (Profile PRO 7036)   25, 18, 14, 12, 14, 12, 17, 17   (8)

6-22-85   *You Talk Too Much*   (Profile PRO 5069)   24, 20, 19, 19, 30, 30   (6)

RUSHEN, PATRICE

6-30-84   *Feels So Real*   (Elektra 7-69742)   21, 12, 9, 7, 9, 9, 27   (7)

3-27-82   *Forget Me Nots*   (Elektra E-47427)   30, 27, 26, 22, 18, 15, 12, 7, 4, 2,
          3, 7, 13, 15, 22, 24   (16)

S.O.S. BAND

11-13-83   *High Hopes*   (Tabu ZS4 03248)   30, 27, 23, 23, 21, 21, 29, 29,
           29   (9)

7-23-83   *Just Be Good To Me*   (Tabu ZS4 03955)   30, 22, 15, 7, 4, 3, 2, 2, 2, 2,
          3, 4, 4, 4, 4, 13, 17, 26   (18)

8-04-84   *Just The Way You Like It*   (Tabu ZS4 04523)   30, 24, 17, 13, 16, 23,
          21, 14, 10, 8, 7, 8, 14, 14, 21, 28   (16)

12-01-84   *No One's Gonna Love You*   (Tabu ZS4 04665)   24, 22, 17, 11, 5, 5, 5,
           8, 17, 24   (10)

11-05-83   *Tell Me If You Still Care*   (Tabu ZS4 04160)   22, 21, 15, 10, 9, 8, 4,
           2, 2, 2, 2, 3, 6, 8, 11, 16, 20   (17)

SADE

1-26-85   *Hang On To Your Love*   (Portrait 37-4664)   28, 21, 15, 10, 8, 8, 8, 16,
          30, 30, 25   (11)

4-06-85   *Smooth Operator*   (Portrait 37-04807)   29, 15, 8, 6, 5, 4, 3, 4, 7, 12,
          18, 29   (12)

SECRET WEAPON

3-06-82   *Must Be The Music*   (Prelude PRL 8036)   22, 17, 15, 14, 12, 10, 21, 20, 22   (9)

SHALAMAR

3-31-84   *Dancing In The Sheets*   (Col. 38-04372)   25, 22, 16, 11, 8, 6, 11, 17, 22, 30   (10)

7-09-83   *Dead Giveaway*   (Solar 7-69819)   29, 28, 25, 19, 13, 12, 6, 5, 5, 5, 8, 8, 11, 14, 14, 14, 14   (17)

3-03-84   *Deadline U.S.A.*   (MCA 52335)   27, 30   (2)

8-14-82   *I Can Make You Feel Good*   (Solar)   29, 25, 22, 18, 17, 19, 27   ((7)

3-20-82   *A Night To Remember*   (Solar S-48005)   29, 22, 16, 11, 9, 7, 6, 4, 3, 3, 11, 13, 18, 24   (14)

SHANNON

4-20-85   *Do You Wanna Get Away*   (Mirage 7-99655)   30, 26, 24, 19, 17, 14, 12, 11, 10, 9, 14, 20, 20   (13)

4-28-84   *Give Me Tonight*   (Emergency 7-99775)   25, 18, 8, 6, 7, 10, 11, 17   (8)

12-17-83   *Let The Music Play*   (Emergency 7-99810)   28, 25, 25, 25, 25, 9, 5, 1, 2, 3, 5, 5, 7, 8, 8, 8, 11, 20, 28   (19)

SHEILA E.

6-30-84   *The Glamorous Life*   (WB 7-29285)   29, 23, 18, 17, 13, 11, 7, 6, 3, 10, 19, 27   (12)

11-09-85   *A Love Bizarre*   (Paisley Park 7-28890)   16, 16, 5, 1, 1   (5)

SISTER SLEDGE

6-11-83   *B.Y.O.B. (Bring Your Own Baby)*   (Cot. 7-99885)   23, 19, 15, 15, 17, 25, 28   (7)

2-13-82   *My Guy*   (Cot.)   16, 9, 8, 9, 7, 6, 7, 23   (8)

SKIPWORTH AND TURNER

   6-29-85   *Thinking About Your Love*   (4th & B'way 414)   25, 22, 22, 16, 16   (5)

SKYY

   7-16-83   *Bad Boy*   (Salsoul S7 7057)   27, 29, 20, 19, 23   (5)

   2-13-82   *Call Me*   (Salsoul)   8   (1)

   4-03-82   *Let's Celebrate*   (Salsoul S7 7020)   28, 19, 15, 12, 10, 10, 17, 27   (8)

SLAVE

   10-08-83   *Shake It Up*   (Cot. 7-99838)   29, 29, 29, 29   (4)

SLINGSHOT

   8-27-83   *Do It Again*   (Quality QUS 044)   28, 24, 24, 26, 26   (5)

THE SPINNERS

   10-16-82   *Magic In The Moonlight*   (Atl.)   29, 27, 26, 23, 22, 20, 27, 24, 28   (9)

   4-14-84   *Right Or Wrong*   (Atl. 7-89689)   28, 23, 19, 15, 27, 25, 21, 17, 23   (9)

STARPOINT

   6-18-83   *Don't Be So Serious*   (Boardwalk NB 12-178-7)   29, 23, 19, 18, 17, 18, 23   (7)

   3-31-84   *It's All Yours*   (Elektra 7-69751)   28   (1)

STEWART, JERMAINE

   12-08-84   *The Word Is Out*   (Arista AS1-9256)   28, 27, 21, 18, 18, 18, 28   (7)

STING

   7-20-85   *If You Love Somebody Set Them Free*   (A&M AM 2738)   24, 24, 18, 12, 15   (5)

SUMMER, DONNA

7-10-82   *Love Is In Control*   (Geffen 7-29982)   26, 16, 10, 5, 2, 2, 1, 2, 5, 9, 11, 20, 25   (13)

6-18-83   *She Works Hard For The Money*   (Mer. 812 370-7)   25, 18, 12, 10, 9, 5, 2, 2, 1, 1, 1, 3, 3, 13, 13, 15, 19, 19, 19, 19   (20)

9-22-84   *There Goes My Baby*   (Geffen 7-29291)   30, 26, 23, 20, 19   (5)

11-05-83   *Unconditional Love*   (Mer. 814 008-7)   9, 14, 23, 29   (4)

SUNRIZE

9-25-82   *Who's Stickin' It?*   (Boardwalk)   28, 22, 20, 18, 16, 25   (6)

THE SYSTEM

3-10-84   *I Wanna Make You Feel Good*   (Mirage 7-99786)   27, 25, 25, 24   (4)

11-23-85   *This Is For You*   (Mirage 7-99607)   22, 15, 15   (3)

3-12-83   *You Are In My System*   (Mirage WTG 7-99937)   27, 22, 17, 14, 10, 6, 4, 4, 11, 13, 17, 24   (12)

THE T-CONNECTION

2-13-82   *A Little More Love*   (Cap.)   19, 13   (2)

TA MARA AND THE SEEN

11-09-85   *Everybody Dance*   (A&M AM 2768)   6, 6, 3, 6, 6   (5)

A TASTE OF HONEY

3-20-82   *I'll Try Something New*   (Cap. PB-5099)   22, 15, 11, 7, 5, 4, 4, 7, 16, 16, 21   (11)

TAVARES

10-01-83   *Deeper In Love*   (RCA PB-13611)   28, 23, 23, 23, 23, 27   (6)

2-12-83   *Got To Find My Way To You*   (RCA PB-13433)   30, 26, 21, 16, 13, 11, 11, 15, 22, 27, 30   (11)

8-28-82   *A Penny For Your Thoughts*   (RCA)   30, 28, 25, 21, 16, 13, 12, 11, 9,
7, 7, 6, 11, 17, 30   (15)

TAYLOR, JOHNNY

10-09-82   *What About My Love*   (Beverly Glen)   29, 26, 25, 23, 22, 20, 19, 18,
17, 26   (10)

THE TEMPTATIONS

3-26-83   *Love On My Mind Tonight*   (Gordy)   27, 20, 17, 15, 14,`9, 8, 6, 15,
20, 23   (11)

4-27-85   *My Love Is True*   (Gordy)   19, 16, 15, 30   (4)

5-05-84   *Sail Away*   (Gordy 1720 GF)   27, 18, 11, 8, 8, 9, 13, 24   (8)

11-17-84   *Treat Her Like A Lady*   (Gordy 1765 GF)   29, 21, 16, 12, 6, 4, 4, 4,
2, 2, 1, 7, 9, 17, 26   (15)

THE TEMPTATIONS FEATURING RICK JAMES   *(See also:* RICK JAMES)

5-01-82   *Standing On The Top—Part 1*   (Gordy 1616 GF)   26, 20, 15, 12, 7, 6,
5, 4, 7, 10, 14, 20, 28   (13)

THIRD WORLD

4-03-82   *Try Jah Love*   (Col. 18-02744)   30, 24, 20, 16, 14, 13, 13, 18,
25   (9)

THOMAS, LILLO

8-11-84   *Your Love's Got A Hold On Me*   (Cap. B-5357)   26, 22, 17, 17, 14, 10,
9, 9, 9, 10, 17, 27, 27   (13)

THOMAS, LILLO, WITH MELBA MOORE

12-01-84   *All Of You*   (Cap. B-5415)   30, 27, 24, 22   (4)

THOMAS, NOLAN

2-02-85   *Yo' Little Brother*   (Emergency 7-99697)   26, 22, 22   (3)

THE TIME

2-16-85   *The Bird*   (WB 7-29094)   29, 24, 22, 22, 25   (5)

7-28-84   *Ice Cream Castles*   (WB 7-29247)   25, 19, 14, 11, 9, 6, 6, 11, 26   (9)

10-13-84   *Jungle Love*   (WB 7-29181)   28, 16, 11, 8, 6, 7, 16, 27   (8)

9-11-82   *777-9311*   (WB)   26, 22, 7, 5, 4, 2, 2, 1, 5, 7, 8, 15, 27   (13)

THE TOM TOM CLUB

2-13-82   *Genius Of Love*   (Sire SRE 49682)   13, 7, 3, 8, 11, 24   (6)

TRAMAINE

11-09-85   *Fall Down*   (A&M AM 2763)   21, 21, 16, 8, 8   (5)

TURNER, TINA

10-06-84   *Better Be Good To Me*   (Cap. B-5387)   30, 26, 21, 16, 16, 12, 8, 5, 8, 9, 16, 23   (12)

2-18-84   *Let's Stay Together*   (Cap. B-5322)   25, 18, 12, 8, 7, 7, 5, 9, 13, 17, 23   (11)

11-09-85   *One Of The Living*   (Cap. B-5518)   28, 28, 27   (3)

2-16-85   *Private Dancer*   (4th & B'way 409)   30, 26, 18, 10, 5, 4, 4, 6, 12, 24   (10)

8-03-85   *We Don't Need Another Hero (Thunderdome)*   (Cap. B-5491)   27, 13, 8, 7, 5, 5   (6)

6-16-84   *What's Love Got To Do With It*   (Cap. B-29, 21, 13, 8, 5, 4, 3, 3, 5, 5, 5, 5, 5, 5, 7, 11, 14, 15, 24   (19)

TWILIGHT 22

1-28-84   *Electric Kingdom*   (Vanguard VSD 35241)   28, 22, 21   (3)

USA FOR AFRICA

4-06-85   *We Are The World*   (Col. US7-04839)   26, 10, 4, 2, 1, 1, 1, 2, 3, 6, 12, 18, 27, 29, 29   (15)

UTFO

2-16-85 *Roxanne, Roxanne* (Select 62254)   21, 15, 13, 19   (4)

VANDROSS, LUTHER

10-02-82 *Bad Boy/Having A Party* (Epic 14-03205)   24, 16, 13, 10, 4, 3, 2, 4, 5, 7, 13, 16, 24, 24, 24, 27   (16)

12-10-83 *I'll Let You Slide* (Epic 34-04321)   27, 23, 18, 18, 18, 18, 17, 14, 23   (9)

7-06-85 *It's Over Now* (Epic 34-04944)   28, 28, 18, 18, 11, 28   (6)

1-22-83 *Since I Lost My Baby* (Epic 34-03487)   22, 18, 14, 12, 11, 11, 18, 24, 28   (9)

3-31-84 *Superstar/Until You Come Back To Me* (Epic 49-04969)   29, 24, 19, 16, 13, 12, 23, 29   (8)

2-23-85 *'Til My Baby Comes Home* (Epic 34-04760)   30, 23, 18, 14, 8, 8, 4, 3, 7, 12, 15, 14, 19, 29   (14)

11-09-85 *Wait For Love* (Epic 34-05610)   10, 10, 6, 4, 4   (5)

VANITY/VANITY 6

1-19-85 *Mechanical Emotion* (Motown 1767 MF)   25, 22, 19, 29   (4)

10-23-82 *Nasty Girl* (WB 7-29908)   29, 21, 16, 14, 9, 6, 5, 6, 9, 14, 14, 14, 19, 30   (14)

10-13-84 *Pretty Mess* (Motown 1752 MF)   23, 22, 19, 19, 17, 23   (6)

WALDEN, NARADA MICHAEL, AND PATTI AUSTIN

3-16-85 *Gimme, Gimme, Gimme* (WB 7-29077)   30, 28, 28   (3)

WAR

3-27-82 *You Got The Power* (RCA PB-13061)   28, 24, 21, 18, 17, 16, 21, 30   (8)

WARWICK, DIONNE

11-20-82   *Heartbreaker*   (Arista AS 1015)   30, 26, 22, 19, 15, 11, 11, 11, 17, 28   (10)

WASHINGTON, GROVER, JR., WITH PATTI LaBELLE   *(See also:* PATTI LaBELLE)

12-11-82   *The Best Is Yet To Come*   (Elektra 7-69887)   30, 26, 19, 19, 19, 16, 11, 9, 7, 7, 14, 20, 26   (13)

THE WEATHER GIRLS

1-15-83   *It's Raining Men*   (Col. 38-03354)   28, 25, 25, 25, 25, 30   (6)

WELLS, BRANDI

2-13-82   *Watch Out*   (WMOT)   23, 22, 20   (3)

WHAM! (FEATURING GEORGE MICHAEL)

2-16-85   *Careless Whisper*   (Col. 38-04691)   28, 23, 17, 15, 13, 11, 11, 10, 27, 20   (10)

6-08-85   *Everything She Wants*   (Col. 38-04840)   28, 23, 22   (3)

THE WHISPERS

11-24-84   *Contagious*   (Solar 7-69683)   27, 19, 16, 12, 10, 9, 9, 9, 7, 7, 15, 23   (12)

5-08-82   *Emergency*   (Solar)   30, 26, 23, 20, 17, 14, 11, 9, 8, 12, 19, 27   (12)

2-13-82   *In The Raw*   (Solar S-47961)   5, 4, 2, 1, 3, 4, 4, 5, 8, 14, 19   (11)

6-11-83   *Keep On Lovin' Me*   (Solar 7-69827)   29, 24, 17, 10, 7, 6, 6, 7, 10, 19, 23   (11)

3-23-85   *Some Kinda Lover*   (Solar 7-69658)   25, 25   (2)

2-26-83   *Tonight*   (Solar 7-69842)   28, 20, 16, 14, 10, 8, 6, 3, 1, 1, 1, 3, 8, 9, 13, 20   (16)

WHITE, BARRY

8-28-82   *Change*   (Unlimited Gold)   28, 25, 21, 18, 12, 11, 10, 12, 11, 19, 29   (11)

WHITE, MAURICE   *(See also:* EARTH, WIND AND FIRE)

8-31-85   *Stand By Me*   (Col. 38-05571)   30, 30, 17, 17, 28   (5)

WHODINI

3-02-85   *Freaks Come Out At Night*   (Jive JS1-9302)   27, 26, 28   (3)

11-10-84   *Friends*   (Jive JS1-9226)   18, 11, 10, 18, 26   (5)

WILDE, EUGENE

11-09-85   *Don't Say No Tonight*   (Philly World 7-99608)   23, 23, 8, 3, 3   (5)

11-24-84   *Gotta Get You Home Tonight*   (Philly World 7-99710)   28, 25, 24, 22, 17, 8, 8, 8, 6, 4, 9, 13, 17, 25   (14)

5-04-85   *Rainbows*   (Philly World 7-99675)   28, 25, 24   (3)

WILLIAMS, DENIECE

11-17-84   *Black Butterfly*   (Col. 38-04614)   30, 24, 22, 20, 20   (5)

5-14-83   *Do What You Feel*   (Col. 38-03807)   26, 18, 15, 10, 7, 6, 5, 16, 19, 19   (10)

3-27-82   *It's Gonna Take A Miracle*   (ARC/Col. 18-02812)   26, 19, 13, 10, 6, 3, 2, 2, 1, 1, 1, 4, 8, 8, 11, 17, 22, 30   (18)

4-28-84   *Let's Hear It For The Boy*   (Col. 38-04417)   30, 24, 10, 1, 1, 1, 1, 2, 4, 5, 7, 11, 20, 28   (14)

7-24-82   *Waiting By The Hotline*   (ARC/Col. 18-03015)   24, 22, 20, 17, 16, 16, 23, 30   (8)

WITHERS, BILL   *(See also:* RALPH MacDONALD)

5-25-85   *Oh Yeah*   (Col. 38-04841)   28, 23, 20, 19   (4)

WOMACK, BOBBY (*See also:* WILTON FELDER)

8-24-85 *I Wish He Didn't Trust Me So Much* (MCA 52624) 30, 25, 25, 8, 8, 18, 28, 28 (8)

2-13-82 *If You Think You're Lonely Now* (Beverly Glen) 3 (1)

4-10-82 *Where Do We Go From Here* (Beverly Glen BG-2001) 30, 27, 26, 24, 23, 23, 22, 26, 28 (9)

WOMACK, BOBBY, AND PATTI LaBELLE (*See also:* PATTI LaBELLE)

2-25-84 *Love Has Finally Come At Last* (Beverly Glen BG-2012) 28, 22, 15, 10, 10, 4, 3, 2, 2, 7, 16, 25 (12)

WONDER, STEVIE (*See also:* CHARLENE)

6-05-82 *Do I Do* (Tamla 1612 TF) 27, 24, 18, 10, 6, 2, 1, 1, 2, 4, 13, 22 (12)

9-01-84 *I Just Called To Say I Love You* (Motown 1745 MF) 28, 18, 15, 8, 5, 3, 1, 1, 1, 2, 2, 4, 6, 10, 10, 14, 19, 30, 30, 30 (20)

12-15-84 *Love Light In Flight* (Motown 1769 MF) 29, 24, 10, 10, 10, 4, 3, 2, 2, 6, 12, 21 (12)

11-09-85 *Part-Time Lover* (Tamla 1908 TF) 2, 2, 7, 9, 9 (5)

9-11-82 *Ribbon In The Sky* (Tamla 1639 TF) 24, 17, 11, 9, 8, 7, 5, 9, 14, 21 (10)

2-13-82 *That Girl* (Tamla 1602 TF) 1, 1, 13, 15, 21, 28 (6)

WOODS, REN

2-13-82 *Take Me To Heaven* (Elektra) 29, 27 (2)

THE WORLD'S FAMOUS SUPREME TEAM

5-26-84 *Hey D.J.* (Island 7-99772) 30, 22, 19, 16, 13, 11, 10, 10, 16, 23, 27 (11)

WRIGHT, BERNARD

11-30-85   *Who Do You Love?*   (Manhattan B-50011)   25, 25   (2)

WRIGHT, BETTY

2-26-83   *She's Older Now*   (Epic 34-03523)   30, 28, 23, 21, 19, 18, 18, 23, 29, 29   (10)

XAVIER

2-20-82   *Work That Sucker To Death*   (Liberty PA-1445)   15, 7, 5, 2, 2, 1, 1, 4, 7, 8, 11, 18, 29   (13)

YARBROUGH AND PEOPLES

8-18-84   *Be A Winner*   (Total Experience TES1-2403)   26, 24, 23, 20, 18, 28   (6)

5-12-84   *Don't Waste Your Time*   (Total Experience TES1-2400)   22, 15, 11, 7, 4, 3, 6, 8, 13, 22   (10)

12-25-82   *Heartbeats*   (Total Experience TE 8204)   25, 25, 25, 21, 13, 8, 5, 3, 5, 7, 11, 22, 26, 30   (14)

ZAPP

7-31-82   *Dance Floor (Part 1)*   (WB 7-29961)   27, 26, 22, 13, 9, 2, 2, 6, 9, 14, 18, 25   (12)

10-30-82   *Do Wa Ditty*   (WB)   30, 20, 18, 14, 13, 12, 18, 29   (8)

8-13-83   *I Can Make You Dance (Part 1)*   (WB 7-29553)   26, 18, 15, 11, 11, 5, 5, 4, 6, 6, 6, 6   (12)

ZOOM

3-06-82   *Love Seasons*   (Polydor PD 2197)   25, 22, 19, 18, 17, 17, 16, 23   (8)

C. SONG-TITLE INDEX—BLACK CONTEMPORARY

Action (Evelyn "Champagne" King)
After All (Al Jarreau)
Ain't Nobody (Rufus and Chaka Khan)
All Night Long (The Mary Jane Girls)
All Night Long (All Night) (Lionel Richie)
All Of Me For All Of You (9.9)
All Of You (Lillo Thomas with Melba Moore)
All This Love (DeBarge)
American Music (The Pointer Sisters)
And I Am Telling You I'm Not Going (Jennifer Holliday)
And I Don't Love You (Smokey Robinson)
Angel (Anita Baker)
(You're My) Aphrodisiac (Dennis Edwards)
April Love (L.T.D.)
Are You Serious (Tyrone Davis)
Are You The Woman (Kashif)
At Last You're Mine (Cheryl Lynn)
Atomic Dog (George Clinton)
Attack Me With Your Love (Cameo)
Attack Of The Name Game (Stacy Lattisaw)
Automatic (The Pointer Sisters)
Axel F (Harold Faltermeyer)

B.Y.O.B. (Bring Your Own Baby) (Sister Sledge)
Baby Come And Get It (The Pointer Sisters)
Baby Come To Me (Patti Austin)
Baby Don't Break Your Baby's Heart (Kashif)
Baby I Need Your Loving (Carl Carlton)
Baby, I'm Hooked (Con Funk Shun)
Baby It's You (Stacy Lattisaw and Johnny Gill)
Back In Stride (Maze featuring Frankie Beverly)

Bad Boy (Ray Parker, Jr.)
Bad Boy (Skyy)
Bad Boy/Having A Party (Luther Vandross)
Bad Habit (Jenny Burton)
Bad Motor Scooter (The Chi-Lites)
Basketball (Kurtis Blow)
Be A Winner (Yarbrough and Peoples)
Be Your Man (Jesse Johnson)
Beat Box (Art Of Noise)
The Beat Goes On (Orbit)
Beat It (Michael Jackson)
Beat Street Breakdown (Grandmaster Melle Mel and The Furious Five)
Beep A Freak (The Gap Band)
The Best Is Yet To Come (Grover Washington, Jr., with Patti LaBelle)
Betcha She Don't Love You (Evelyn King)
Better Be Good To Me (Tina Turner)
Better Together (Rufus with Chaka Khan)
Between The Sheets (The Isley Brothers)
Big Fun (Kool and The Gang)
Billie Jean (The Time)
Black Butterfly (Deniece Williams)
Body Talk (The Deele)
Boogie Down (Jarreau)
The Borderlines (Jeffrey Osborne)
Bottom's Up (The Chi-Lites)
Breakin'. . . There's No Stopping Us (Ollie and Jerry)
Breakin' Together (O'Bryan)
Bring Back Your Love (Glenn Jones)

C.O.D. (I'll Deliver) (Mtume)
Call Me (Skyy)
Can You Help Me (Jesse Johnson's Revue)
Can You See The Light (Brass Construction)
Candy Girl (The New Edition)

Candy Man   (The Mary Jane Girls)
Can't Stop   (Rick James)
Can't Stop The Street   (*See:* Krush Groove . . .
Caravan Of Love   (Isley, Jasper, Isley)
Careless Whisper   (Wham! featuring George Michael)
Caribbean Queen (No More Love On The Run)   (Billy Ocean)
Centipede   (Rebbie Jackson)
Change   (Barry White)
Change Of Heart   (Change)
Cheating In The Next Room   (Z.Z. Hill)
Cherish   (Kool & The Gang)
Choosey Lover   (The Isley Brothers)
Circles   (Atlantic Starr)
Close (To The Edit)   (Art Of Noise)
Cold Blooded   (Rick James)
Colder Are My Nights   (The Isley Brothers)
Come Give Your Love To Me   (Janet Jackson)
Communication Breakdown   (Junior)
Contagious   (The Whispers)
Cool It Now   (The New Edition)
Coolin' Out   (Dennis Edwards)
Count Me Out   (The New Edition)
Crazy   (The Manhattans)
Crushed   (The Controllers)
Curiosity   (The Jets)
Cutie Pie   (One Way)

The Dance Electric   (Andre Cymone)
Dance Floor (Part 1)   (Zapp)
.Dance Wit' Me   (Rick James)
Dancin' In The Key Of Life (Steve Arrington)
Dancing In The Sheets   (Shalamar)
Dangerous   (Natalie Cole)
Dare Me   (The Pointer Sisters)
Dead Giveaway   (Shalamar)
Deadline U.S.A.   (Shalamar)
Deep Inside Your Love   (Ready For The World)
Deeper In Love   (Tavares)
Delirious   (Prince)
Digital Display   (Ready For The World)

Dirty Dancer   (The Bar-Kays)
Do I Do   (Stevie Wonder)
Do It (Let Me See You Shake)   (The Bar-Kays)
Do It Again (Medley With Billie Jean)   (Slingshot)
Do It To Me   (Vernon Burch)
Do Something   (Goodie)
Do Wa Ditty (Blow That Thing)   (Zapp)
Do What You Do   (Jermaine Jackson)
Do What You Feel   (Deniece Williams)
Do You Really Want To Hurt Me   (Culture Club)
Do You Wanna Get Away   (Shannon)
(Sittin' On) The Dock Of The Bay   (The Reddings)
Don't Be So Serious   (Starpoint)
Don't Go   (Dreamboy)
Don't Look Any Further   (Dennis Edwards)
Don't Say No Tonight   (Eugene Wilde)
Don't Stand Another Chance   (Janet Jackson)
Don't Stop   (Jeffrey Osborne)
Don't Throw It All Away   (Stacy Lattisaw)
Don't Waste Your Time   (Yarbrough and Peoples
Don't You Get So Mad   (Jeffrey Osborne)
Double Oh-Oh   (George Clinton)
Dynamite   (Jermaine Jackson)

Early In The Morning   (The Gap Band)
Easy Lover   (Philip Bailey with Phil Collins)
Eaten Alive   (Diana Ross)
Ebony And Ivory   (Paul McCartney and Stevie Wonder)
Ebony Eyes   (Rick James and Smokey Robinson)
8 Million Stories   (Bleeped)
Electric Avenue   (Eddy Grant)
Electric Kingdom   (Twilight 22)
Electric Lady   (Con Funk Shun)
Emergency   (Kool & The Gang)

Emergency (The Whispers)

Encore (Cheryl Lynn)

Every Girl (Wants My Guy) (Aretha Franklin)

Everybody Dance (Ta Mara and The Seen)

Everything She Wants (Wham!)

Extraordinary Girl (The O'Jays)

Fall Down (Spirit Of Love) (Tramaine)

Fall In Love With Me (Earth, Wind And Fire)

Farewell My Summer Love (Michael Jackson)

The Fat Boys Are Back (The Fat Boys)

Feel So Real (Steve Arrington)

Feels So Real (Won't Let Go) (Patrice Rushen)

Fickle (Michael Henderson)

Fidelity (Cheryl Lynn)

Fix It (Part 1) (Teena Marie)

Flamethrower (The J. Geils Band)

Flashback (Klique)

Fly Girl (The Boogie Boys)

Flashdance . . . What A Feeling (Irene Cara)

Flirt (Cameo)

Forget Me Nots (Patrice Rushen)

Fragile . . . Handle With Care (Charrelle)

Freak-A-Ristic (Atlantic Starr)

Freak-A-Zoid (Midnight Star)

Freaks Come Out At Night (Whodini)

Freakshow On The Dance Floor (The Bar-Kays)

Freaky Behavior (The Bar-Kays)

Freeway Of Love (Aretha Franklin)

Fresh (Tyrone Brunson)

Fresh (Kool & The Gang)

A Friend Of Mine (Gladys Knight & The Pips)

Friends (Whodini)

Genius Of Love (The Tom Tom Club)

Get Down On It (Kool & The Gang)

Get It Right (Aretha Franklin)

Ghostbusters (Ray Parker, Jr.)

The Gigolo (O'Bryan)

Gimme, Gimme, Gimme (Narada Michael Walden and Patti Austin)

The Girl Is Fine (So Fine) (Fatback)

The Girl Is Mine (Michael Jackson and Paul McCartney)

Girls Are More Fun (Ray Parker, Jr.)

Give Me Tonight (Shannon)

Give Me Your Love (Peabo Bryson)

The Glamorous Life (Sheila E.)

Glow (Rick James)

Go On And Cry (Bloodstone)

Got To Be There (Chaka Khan)

Got To Find My Way Back To You (Tavares)

Gotta Get You Home Tonight (Eugene Wilde)

Half Crazy (Johnny Gill)

Hang On To Your Love (Sade)

Hangin' On A String (Contemplating) (The Loose Ends)

Hard Times (Run-D.M.C.)

Hard To Get (Rick James)

Hardrock (Herbie Hancock)

Having A Party See: Bad Boy . . .

Heart Don't Lie (La Toya Jackson)

Heartbeat (The Dazz Band)

Heartbeats (Yarbrough and Peoples

Heartbreaker (Dionne Warwick)

Hello (Lionel Richie)

Hello Stranger (Carrie Lucas)

Hey D.J. (The World's Famous Supreme Team)

High Hopes (The S.O.S. Band)

High-Rise (Ashford and Simpson)

Hold Me (Teddy Pendergrass with Whitney Houston)

Honey, Honey (The Manhattans)

Hot Fun In The Summertime (Dayton)

Hot On A Thing (Called Love) (The Chi-Lites featuring Eugene Record)

Hot Spot (The Dazz Band)

How Come U Don't Call Me Anymore (Stephanie Mills)

How Do You Keep The Music Playing (James Ingram and Patti Austin)

Human Nature (Michael Jackson)

Hump To The Bump (Steve Arrington's Hall Of Fame)

I.O.U. (Freeez)

I Am Love (Jennifer Holliday)

I Can Make You Dance (Part 1) (Zapp)

I Can Make You Feel Good (Shalamar)

I Can't Believe It (Melba Moore)

I Can't Go For That (No Can Do) (Daryl Hall and John Oates)

I Didn't Mean To Turn You On (Cherrelle)

I Feel For You (Chaka Khan)

I Found My Baby (The Gap Band)

I Found Myself When I Lost You (Tyrone Davis)

I Just Called To Say I Love You (Stevie Wonder)

I Just Gotta Have You (Kashif)

I Just Wanna Hang Around (George Benson)

I Just Want To Satisfy (The O'Jays)

I Keep Forgettin' (Michael McDonald)

I Know (Philip Bailey)

I Like It (DeBarge)

I Miss You (Klymaxx)

I Need You (The Pointer Sisters)

I Never Forgot Your Eyes (Larry Graham)

I Really Don't Need No Light (Jeffrey Osborne)

I Think It's Gonna Be Alright (Carl Carlton)

I Wanna Make You Feel Good (The System)

I Want My Girl (Jesse Johnson's Revue)

I Want To Hold Your Hand (Lakeside)

I Wish He Didn't Trust Me So Much (Bobby Womack)

I Wonder If I Take You Home (Lisa Lisa and The Cult Jam with Full Force)

I Would Die 4 U (Prince and The Revolution)

I'll Be Good (Rene and Angela)

I'll Let You Slide (Luther Vandross)

I'll Try Something New (A Taste Of Honey)

I'm Freaky (O'Bryan)

I'm Leaving Baby (Con Funk Shun)

I'm Out To Catch (Leon Haywood)

I'm The One (Roberta Flack)

I've Been Watching You (Randy Hall)

I've Made Love To You A Thousand Times (Smokey Robinson)

Ice Cream Castles (The Time)

If Ever You're In My Arms Again (Peabo Bryson)

If It Ain't One Thing . . . It's Another (Richard "Dimples" Fields)

If Only You Knew (Patti LaBelle)

If This World Were Mine (Cheryl Lynn)

If You Love Somebody Set Them Free (Sting)

If You Think You're Lonely Now (Bobby Womack)

If You Were Here Tonight (Alexander O'Neal)

Imaginary Playmates (Rene And Angela)

In My House (The Mary Jane Girls)

In The Groove (Ronnie Laws)

In The Mix (Roger)

In The Name Of Love (Ralph MacDonald with Bill Withers)

In The Raw (The Whispers)

Innocent (Alexander O'Neal)

Inside Love (So Personal) (George Benson)

Inside Out (Odyssey)

Instant Love (Cheryl Lynn)

Into The Night (B.B. King)

Is This The End (The New Edition)

Itchin' For A Scratch (The Force MD's)

It's All Yours (Starpoint)

It's Gonna Be Special (Patti Austin)

It's Gonna Take A Miracle (Deniece Williams)

It's Much Deeper (Ashford and Simpson)

It's Over Now (Luther Vandross)

It's Raining Men (The Weather Girls)

Jailhouse Rap   (The Fat Boys)
Jam The Motha   (The Gap Band)
Jamie   (Ray Parker, Jr.)
Joanna   (Kool & The Gang)
Joystick   (The Dazz Band)
Juicy Fruit   (Mtume)
Jump (For My Love)   (The Pointer Sisters)
Jump To It   (Aretha Franklin)
Jungle Love   (The Time)
Just An Illusion   (Imagination)
Just Be Good To Me   (The S.O.S. Band)
Just Be Yourself   (Cameo)
Just For The Night   (Evelyn "Champagne" King)
Just The Way You Like It   (The S.O.S. Band)

Karma Chameleon   (Culture Club)
Keep Away Girls   (Stephanie Mills)
Keep It Confidential   (Nona Hendryx)
Keep It Live   (The Dazz Band)
Keep On   ("D" Train)
Keep On Lovin' Me   (The Whispers)
Keepin' My Lover Satisfied   (Melba Moore)
Knockout   (Margie Joseph)
(Krush Groove) Can't Stop The Street   (Chaka Khan)

Lady Love Me (One More Time)   (George Benson)
Lady You Are   (One Way)
Last Dance   (George Clinton)
Last Night   (Stephanie Mills)
Last Night A D.J. Saved My Life   (Indeep)
The Last Time I Made Love   (Joyce Kennedy and Jeffrey Osborne)
Let It All Blow   (The Dazz Band)
Let It Whip   (The Dazz Band)
Let Me Go   (Ray Parker, Jr.)
Let Me Tickle Your Fancy   (Jermaine Jackson)

Let The Feeling Flow   (Peabo Bryson)
Let The Music Play   (Shannon)
Let's Celebrate   (Skyy)
Let's Dance   (David Bowie)
Let's Go All The Way   (Chocolate Milk)
Let's Go Crazy   (Prince and The Revolution)
Let's Go Dancin' (Ooh La, La, La)   (Kool & The Gang)
Let's Hear It For The Boy   (Deniece Williams)
Let's Stand Together   (Melba Moore)
Let's Stay Together   (Tina Turner)
Let's Work   (Prince)
Like A Virgin   (Madonna)
A Little More Love   (T-Connection)
Little Red Corvette   (Prince)
Livin' For Your Love   (Melba Moore)
Lollipop Luv   (Bryan Loren)
Look The Other Way   (Isley, Jasper, Isley)
Loopzilla   (George Clinton)
Lost In Love   (The New Edition)
A Love Bizarre   (Sheila E.)
Love Come Down   (Evelyn King)
Love Has Finally Come At Last   (Bobby Womack and Patti LaBelle)
Love In Moderation   (Gwen Guthrie)
Love Is In Control (Finger On The Trigger)   (Donna Summer)
Love Is The Key   (Maze featuring Frankie Beverly)
Love It Away   (Ashford and Simpson)
Love Light In Flight   (Stevie Wonder)
Love Me Down   (Atlantic Starr)
Love Me In A Special Way   (DeBarge)
Love Me Right   (Melba Moore)
Love, Need And Want You   (Patti LaBelle)
Love On My Mind Tonight   (The Temptations)
Love Seasons   (Zoom)
Lovelite   (O'Bryan)
Loverboy   (Billy Ocean)
Lovergirl   (Teena Marie)
Loveride   (Nuance featuring Vikki Love)
Love's Comin' At Ya   (Melba Moore)

Magic In The Moonlight   (The Spinners)

Magnetic   (Earth, Wind and Fire)

Make It Easy On Yourself   (Ron Banks)

Making Love   (Roberta Flack)

Mama Used To Say   (Junior)

Material Thangz   (The Deele)

Mechanical Emotion   (Vanity)

The Medicine Song   (Stephanie Mills)

Meeting In The Ladies Room   (Klymaxx)

Mega-Mix   (Herbie Hancock)

The Men All Pause   (Klymaxx)

"Miami Vice" Theme   (Jan Hammer)

Midnight Hour—Part 1   (Roger featuring The Mighty Clouds Of Joy)

Million Dollar Babe   (Stacy Lattisaw)

Mind Up Tonight   (Melba Moore)

Miracles   (Stacy Lattisaw)

Mirror, Mirror   (Diana Ross)

Misled   (Kool & The Gang)

Miss Me Blind   (Culture Club)

Mr. Groove   (One Way)

Mr. Telephone Man   (The New Edition)

More, More, More   (Atlantic Starr)

Mornin'   (Al Jarreau)

Ms. Got-The-Body   (Con Funk Shun)

Murphy's Law   (Cheri)

Muscles   (Diana Ross)

Must Be The Music   (Secret Weapon)

My First Love   (Rene and Angela)

My Guy   (Sister Sledge)

My Love   (Lionel Richie)

My Love Is True   (The Temptations)

My Time   (Gladys Knight & The Pips)

Mystery Lady   (Billy Ocean)

Nasty Girl   (Vanity 6)

Neutron Dance   (The Pointer Sisters)

Never Felt Like Dancin'   (Teddy Pendergrass)

Never Gonna Let You Go   (Sergio Mendes)

Never Say I Do   (Cliff Dawson and Renee Diggs)

New Attitude   (Patti LaBelle)

New Moves   (The Crusaders)

A Night To Remember   (Shalamar)

Nights Over Egypt   (The Jones Girls)

Nightshift   (The Commodores)

Nine Times Out Of Ten   (Teddy Pendergrass)

19   (Paul Hardcastle)

1999   (Prince)

(No Matter How High I Get) I'll Still Be Lookin' Up To You   (Wilton Felder Featuring Bobby Womack introducing Alltrinna Grayson)

No One's Gonna Love You   (The S.O.S. Band)

Nobody Can Be You   (Steve Arrington's Hall Of Fame)

Nubian Nut   (George Clinton)

The Oak Tree   (Morris Day)

Obscene Phone Caller   (Rockwell)

Off And On Love   (Champagne)

Oh Sheila   (Ready For The World)

Oh Yeah   (Bill Withers)

Old Fashioned Love   (Smokey Robinson)

On The Floor   (Fatback)

On The One For Fun   (The Dazz Band)

On The Wings Of Love   (Jeffrey Osborne)

One Of The Living   (Tina Turner)

One On One   (Daryl Hall and John Oates)

The Only One   (Charles Earland)

Only You   (The Commodores)

Operator   (Midnight Star)

The Other Woman   (Ray Parker, Jr.)

Outstanding   (The Gap Band)

Outta The World   (Ashford and Simpson)

Outrageous   (Lakeside)

P.Y.T. (Pretty Young Thing)   (Michael Jackson)

Painted Picture   (The Commodores)

Part-Time Lover   (Stevie Wonder)

Party All The Time   (Eddie Murphy)

Party Time   (Kurtis Blow)

Party Train   (The Gap Band)

Pass The Dutchie   (Musical Youth)

A Penny For Your Thoughts   (Tavares)

Penny Lover   (Lionel Richie)

Perfect Combination (Stacy Lattisaw and Johnny Gill)
Pieces Of Ice (Diana Ross)
Pilot Error (Stephanie Mills)
Plane Love (Jeffrey Osborne)
Playing Hard To Get (Vernon Burch)
Pop Life (Prince and The Revolution)
Pretty Mess (Vanity)
Private Dancer (Tina Turner)
Purple Rain (Prince and The Revolution)
Put It In A Magazine (Sonny Charles)

Raid (Lakeside)
Rain Forest (Paul Hardcastle)
Rainbows (Eugene Wilde)
Raspberry Beret (Prince and The Revolution)
Read My Lips (Melba Moore)
The Real Deal (The Isley Brothers)
Remember (Peaches and Herb)
Remember What You Like (Jenny Burton)
Rhythm Of The Night (DeBarge)
Rhythm Of The Street (Patti Austin)
Ribbon In The Sky (Stevie Wonder)
Right In The Middle (Betty Lavette)
Right Or Wrong (The Spinners)
Rock Me Tonight (Freddie Jackson)
Rockit (Herbie Hancock)
Roxanne, Roxanne (UTFO)
Running With The Night (Lionel Richie)

Sad Girl (GQ)
Sail Away (The Temptations)
Sanctified Lady (Marvin Gaye)
Save The Overtime (For Me) (Gladys Knight & The Pips)
Save Your Love (For #1) (Rene and Angela)
Saving All My Love For You (Whitney Houston)
Say, Say, Say (Paul McCartney and Michael Jackson)
Say You Do (Janet Jackson)

Say You, Say Me (Lionel Richie)
The Screams Of Passion (The Family)
777-9311 (The Time)
17 (Rick James)
Sex Shooter (Apollonia 6)
Sexomatic (The Bar-Kays)
Sexual Healing (Marvin Gaye)
Sexy Ways (The Four Tops)
Shackles (R.J.'s Latest Arrival)
Shake Down (Evelyn "Champagne" King)
Shake It Up (Slave)
She Talks To Me With Her Body (The Bar-Kays)
She Works Hard For The Money (Donna Summer)
She's Just A Groupie (Bobby Nunn)
She's Older Now (Betty Wright)
She's Strange (Cameo)
Shine On (George Duke)
Shine On Me (One Way)
Shout About It (Lamont Dozier)
Show Me (Glenn Jones)
Side By Side (Earth, Wind and Fire)
Silver Shadow (Atlantic Starr)
Since I Lost My Baby (Luther Vandross)
Single Life (Cameo)
Smooth Operator (Sade)
So Close (Diana Ross)
So Fine (Howard Johnson)
Solid (Ashford and Simpson)
Some Kinda Lover (The Whispers)
Somebody Else's Guy (Jocelyn Brown)
Somebody's Watching Me (Rockwell)
Something About That Woman (Lakeside)
Something's On Your Mind ("D" Train)
Sooner Or Later (Larry Graham)
Soup For One (Chic)
Space Cowboy (The Jonzun Crew)
Spirit Of The Dancer (Evelyn King)
Stage Fright (Chic)
Stand By Me (Maurice White)
Standing On The Top—Part 1 (The Temptations featuring Rick James)
State Of Shock (The Jacksons)
Stay With Me Tonight (Jeffrey Osborne)

Steppin' Out (Kool & The Gang)
Stir It Up (Patti LaBelle)
Stone Love (Kashif)
Stop Doggin' Me Around (Klique)
Street Corner (Ashford and Simpson)
Stronger Than Before (Joyce Kennedy)
Stuck On You (Lionel Richie)
Style (Cameo)
Suddenly (Billy Ocean)
Sugar Walls (Sheena Easton)
Superstar/Until You Come Back To Me (That's What I'm Gonna Do) (Luther Vandross)
Sussudio (Phil Collins)
Swept Away (Diana Ross)
Swing Low (R.J.'s Latest Arrival)
Swing That Sexy Thang (Carl Carlton)
Swoop (I'm Yours) (The Dazz Band)

Take A Lickin' And Keep On Kickin' (William "Bootsy" Collins)
Take Me With U (Prince and The Revolution with Apollonia)
Take Me To Heaven (Ren Woods)
Talkin' Out The Side Of Your Neck (Cameo)
Taxi (J. Blackfoot)
Telephone (Diana Ross)
Tell Me If You Still Care (The S.O.S. Band)
Tell Me Tomorrow—Part 1 (Smokey Robinson)
Tenderoni (Leon Haywood)
That Girl (Stevie Wonder)
There Goes My Baby (Donna Summer)
There's No Easy Way (James Ingram)
There's No Guarantee (Peabo Bryson)
Think About You (Whitney Houston)
Thinking About Your Love (Skipworth And Turner)
This Is For You (The System)
This Is My Night (Chaka Khan)
Thriller (Michael Jackson)
Through The Fire (Chaka Khan)
'Til My Baby Comes Home (Luther Vandross)

'Til Tomorrow (Marvin Gaye)
Time Will Reveal (DeBarge)
Tonight (Kool & The Gang)
Tonight (The Whispers)
Tonight (Ready For The World)
Tonight I Celebrate My Love (Peabo Bryson and Roberta Flack)
Tonight I Give In (Angela Bofill)
Tonight I'm Gonna Love You All Over (The Four Tops)
Too Late (Junior)
Too Many Games (Maze featuring Frankie Beverly)
Too Tough (Angela Bofill)
Torture (The Jacksons)
Touch (Earth, Wind and Fire)
Touch A Four Leaf Clover (Atlantic Starr)
Treat Her Like A Lady (The Temptations)
Truly (Lionel Richie)
Try Again (Champaign)
Try Jah Love (Third World)
Try My Loving (Gimme Just Enough) (Kiddo)
20/20 (George Benson)

U Bring The Freak Out (Rick James)
Unconditional Love (Donna Summer)
Underlove (Melba Moore)
Until You Come Back To Me See: Superstar . . .
Used To Be (Charlene and Stevie Wonder)

The Very Best In You (Change)
Very Special Part (Jermaine Jackson)

Wait For Love (Luther Vandross)
Waiting By The Hotline (Deniece Williams)

Walk On By ("D" Train)

Walkin' The Line (The Brass Construction)

Wanna Be Startin' Somethin' (Michael Jackson)

Wanna Be With You (Earth, Wind and Fire)

Watch Out (Brandi Wells)

We Are The World (USA For Africa)

We Don't Have To Talk (About Love) (Peabo Bryson)

We Don't Need Another Hero (Thunderdome) (Tina Turner)

We Go A Long Way Back (Bloodstone)

We Need Love To Live (Maze)

We're Going All The Way (Jeffrey Osborne)

We've Got The Juice (Attitude)

Weak At The Knees (Steve Arrington's Hall Of Fame)

Welcome Into My Heart (The Isley Brothers)

Welcome To The Club (The Brothers Johnson)

Wet My Whistle (Midnight Star)

What About My Love (Johnny Taylor)

What's Love Got To Do With It (Tina Turner)

When Doves Cry (Prince)

When You Love Me Like This (Melba Moore)

Where Did Our Love Go (The Reddings)

Where Do We Go From Here (Bobby Womack)

White Horse (Laid Back)

Who Do You Love? (Bernard Wright)

Who's Holding Donna Now (DeBarge)

Who's Stickin' It? (Sunrize)

Who's Zoomin' Who (Aretha Franklin)

Why You Wanna Try Me (The Commodores)

Wild And Crazy Love (The Mary Jane Girls)

A Woman, A Lover, A Friend (Klique)

The Word Is Out (Jermaine Stewart)

Work That Body (Diana Ross)

Work That Sucker To Death (Xavier)

Would You Like To (Fool Around) (Mtume)

Yah Mo B There (James Ingram With Michael McDonald)

Yo' Little Brother (Nolan Thomas)

You And I (Goodie)

You And I (O'Bryan)

You Are (Lionel Richie)

You Are In My System (The System)

You Are My Lady (Freddie Jackson)

You Brought The Sunshine (Into My Life) (The Clark Sisters)

You Dropped A Bomb On Me (The Gap Band)

You Get The Best From Me (Say, Say, Say) (Alicia Myers)

You Give Good Love (Whitney Houston)

You Got The Power (War)

You Keep Me Coming Back (The Brothers Johnson)

You Look Good To Me (Cherrelle)

You, Me And He (Mtume)

You Send Me (The Manhattans)

You Talk Too Much (Run-D.M.C.)

You Used To Hold Me So Tight (Thelma Houston)

You Wear It Well (El DeBarge With DeBarge)

You're My Choice Tonight (Choose Me) (Teddy Pendergrass)

You're Number One (In My Book) (Gladys Knight & The Pips)

You're The One For Me ("D" Train)

Young Love (Janet Jackson)

Your Body's Here With Me (The O'Jays)

Your Love's Got A Hold On Me (Lillo Thomas)

Your Place Or Mine (The Bar-Kays)

Your Precious Love (Al Jarreau And Randy Crawford)

Your Wife Is Cheatin' On Us (Richard "Dimples" Fields)

D. APPENDIX: NUMBER 1 RECORDS—A CHRONOLOGICAL LISTING

1982

2-13—	2-20	*That Girl*—Stevie Wonder (2)	
2-27		*Shine On*—George Duke (1)	
3-06		*In The Raw*—The Whispers (1)	
3-13—	3-20	*Mama Used To Say*—Junior (2)	
3-27—	4-03	*Work That Sucker To Death*—Xavier (2)	
4-10—	4-17	*Get Down On It/Steppin' Out*—Kool & The Gang (2)	
4-24		*If It Ain't One Thing . . . It's Another*—Richard "Dimples" Fields (1)	
5-01		*Circles*—Atlantic Starr (1)	
5-08—	5-15	*The Other Woman*—Ray Parker, Jr. (2)	
5-22—	6-05	*It's Gonna Take A Miracle*—Deniece Williams (3)	
6-12		*Early In The Morning*—The Gap Band (1)	
6-19—	7-10	*Let It Whip*—The Dazz Band (4)	
7-17—	7-24	*Do I Do*—Stevie Wonder (2)	
7-31—	8-14	*And I Am Telling You I'm Not Going*—Jennifer Holliday (3)	
8-21		*Love Is In Control*—Donna Summer (1)	
8-28—	9-11	*Jump To It*—Aretha Franklin (3)	
9-18—	9-25	*You Dropped A Bomb On Me*—The Gap Band (2)	
10-02—	10-23	*Love Come Down*—Evelyn King (4)	
10-30		*777-9311*—The Time (1)	
11-06		*Muscles*—Diana Ross (1)	
11-13—	12-04	*Sexual Healing*—Marvin Gaye (4)	
12-11—	12-18	*Truly*—Lionel Richie (2)	
12-25		*The Girl Is Mine*—Michael Jackson and Paul McCartney (1)	

1983

1-01—	1-08	*The Girl Is Mine*—Michael Jackson and Paul McCartney (2; 3)
1-15		*Let's Go Dancin'*—Kool & The Gang (1)
1-22—	1-29	*Got To Be There*—Chaka Khan (2)
2-05		*Outstanding*—The Gap Band (1)
2-12		*Betcha She Don't Love You*—Evelyn King (1)
2-19—	2-26	*Billie Jean*—Michael Jackson (2)
3-05		*You Are*—Lionel Richie (1)
3-12—	3-19	*I Like It*—DeBarge (2)
3-26—	4-16	*Billie Jean*—Michael Jackson (4; 6)
4-23—	5-07	*Tonight*—The Whispers (3)
5-14		*Beat It*—Michael Jackson (1)
5-21		*Candy Girl*—The New Edition (1)
5-28—	6-04	*Between The Sheets*—The Isley Brothers (2)
6-11—	7-02	*Juicy Fruit*—Mtume (4)
7-09—	7-23	*Flashdance . . . What A Feeling*—Irene Cara (3)

7-30—	8-06	*Inside Love*—George Benson (2)
8-13—	8-27	*She Works Hard For The Money*—Patti LaBelle (1)
9-03—	9-10	*Freak-A-Zoid*—Midnight Star (2)
9-17—	10-01	*Cold Blooded*—Rick James (3)
10-08—	10-29	*Rockit*—Herbie Hancock (4)
11-05—	12-10	*All Night Long*—Lionel Richie (6)
12-17—	12-31	*Time Will Reveal*—DeBarge (3)

1984

1-07		*Time Will Reveal*—DeBarge (1; 4)
1-14—	2-04	*Joanna*—Kool & the Gang (4)
2-11		*If Only You Knew*—Pattie LaBelle (1)
2-18—	2-25	*Running With The Night*—Lionel Richie (2)
3-03		*If Only You Knew*—Patti LaBelle (1; 2)
3-10—	4-07	*Somebody's Watching Me*—Rockwell (5)
4-14—	4-21	*She's Strange*—Cameo (2)
4-28—	5-12	*Hello*—Lionel Richie (3)
5-19—	6-09	*Let's Hear It For The Boy*—Deniece Williams (4)
6-16		*Freakshow On The Dance Floor*—The Bar-Kays (1)
6-23		*Lovelite*—O'Bryan (1)
6-30—	8-04	*When Doves Cry*—Prince (6)
8-11—	8-18	*Breakin' . . . There's No Stopping Us*—Ollie And Jerry (2)
8-25—	9-08	*Ghostbusters*—Ray Parker, Jr. (3)
9-15		*17*—Rick James (1)
9-22		*The Last Time I Made Love*—Joyce Kennedy and Jeffrey Osborne (1)
9-29—	10-06	*Caribbean Queen*—Billy Ocean (2)
10-13—	10-27	*I Just Called To Say I Love You*—Stevie Wonder (3)
11-03—	11-17	*I Feel For You*—Chaka Khan (3)
11-24—	12-01	*Cool It Now*—The New Edition (2)
12-08—	12-22	*Solid*—Ashford and Simpson (3)
12-29		*Operator*—Midnight Star (1)

1985

1-05—	1-26	*Operator*—Midnight Star (4; 5)
2-02		*Treat Her Like A Lady*—The Temptations (1)
2-09—	2-16	*Mr. Telephone Man*—The New Edition (2)
2-23—	3-09	*Missing You*—Diana Ross (3)
3-16—	3-30	*Nightshift*—The Commodores (3)
4-06—	4-13	*(No Matter How High I Get) I'll Still Be Lookin' Up To You*—Wilton Felder/Bobby Womack/Alltrinna Grayson (2)
4-20		*Rhythm Of The Night*—DeBarge (1)
4-27		*Back In Stride*—Maze featuring Frankie Beverly (1)
5-04—	5-18	*We Are The World*—USA For Africa (3)

5-25—	6-01	*Fresh*—Kool & The Gang (2)
	6-08	*You Give Good Love*—Whitney Houston (1)
	6-15	*Sanctified Lady*—Marvin Gaye (1)
6-22—	7-13	*Rock Me Tonight*—Freddie Jackson (4)
7-20—	7-27	*Raspberry Beret*—Prince and The Revolution (2)
	8-03	*Hangin' On A String*—Loose Ends (1)
8-10—	8-17	*Freeway Of Love*—Aretha Franklin (2)
8-24—	9-07	*Saving All My Love For You*—Whitney Houston (3)
9-14—11-02		*no chart*
11-09—11-16		*The Oak Tree*—Morris Day (2)
11-23		*Who's Zoomin' Who*—Aretha Franklin (1)
11-30—12-07		*A Love Bizarre*—Sheila E. (2)

E. ARTIST INDEX—COUNTRY

ALABAMA

11-09-85   *Can't Keep A Good Man Down*   (RCA PB-14156)   1, 1, 1, 7, 7   (5)

12-11-82   *Christmas In Dixie*   (RCA PB-13358)   27, 22, 19, 19, 19, 30   (6)

9-04-82   *Close Enough To Perfect*   (RCA PB-13294)   26, 21, 18, 11, 9, 8, 6, 5, 1, 4, 10, 14, 19   (13)

5-28-83   *The Closer You Get*   (RCA PB-13524)   21, 16, 12, 11, 6, 4, 4, 1, 13, 21, 21, 27, 30   (13)

2-19-83   *Dixieland Delight*   (RCA PB-13446)   26, 20, 15, 12, 6, 3, 1, 1, 1, 11, 13, 23, 26   (13)

12-01-84   *Fire In The Night*   (RCA PB-13926)   27, 15, 12, 11, 8, 8, 6, 4, 4, 1, 6, 28   (12)

6-15-85   *Forty Hour Week*   (RCA PB-14085)   23, 19, 17, 16, 7, 4, 4, 2, 19, 23, 30   (11)

8-18-84   *If You're Gonna Play In Texas*   (RCA PB-13840)   26, 22, 16, 10, 7, 6, 6, 3, 1, 8, 8, 8   (12)

9-10-83   *Lady Down On Love*   (RCA PB-13590)   24, 16, 12, 9, 6, 5, 5, 5, 2, 2, 12, 20, 28   (13)

3-13-82   *Mountain Music*   (RCA PB-13019)   24, 15, 9, 6, 5, 2, 1, 2, 3, 4, 8, 14, 23   (13)

1-28-84   *Roll On*   (RCA PB-13648)   24, 18, 11, 5, 1, 1, 1, 1, 1, 1, 3, 7, 17, 30   (14)

5-29-82   *Take Me Down*   (RCA PB-13210)   25, 13, 10, 7, 4, 2, 1, 1, 5, 11, 19, 25   (12)

2-23-85   *There's No Way*   (RCA PB-13992)   25, 22, 21, 17, 11, 11, 11, 3, 2, 1, 2, 3, 8, 18, 18, 26   (16)

5-05-84   *When We Make Love*   (RCA PB-13763)   28, 17, 11, 6, 4, 3, 2, 1, 2, 12   (10)

ALLEN, DEBORAH

11-05-83   *Baby I Lied*   (RCA PB-13600)   24, 19, 8, 8, 6, 3, 3, 8, 8, 8, 8, 22, 26   (13)

11-24-84   *Heartache And A Half*   (RCA PB-13921)   28, 26, 21, 20   (4)

6-23-84   *I Hurt For You*   (RCA PB-13776)   28, 18, 16, 12, 11, 8, 8, 7, 7, 27   (10)

2-25-84   *I've Been Wrong Before*   (RCA PB-13692)   27, 23   (2)

ALLEN, REX, JR.

12-10-83   *The Air That I Breathe*   (Moon Shine 3017)   29, 27   (2)

ANDERSON, JOHN

12-03-83   *Black Sheep*   (WB 7-29497)   25, 20, 16, 14, 14, 14, 14, 14   (8)

1-12-85   *Eye Of A Hurricane*   (WB 7-29127)   29, 27, 27, 25, 30, 26, 24   (7)

7-23-83   *Goin' Downhill*   (WB 7-29585)   21, 17, 13, 13, 9, 9, 8, 8, 28, 29, 29   (11)

2-13-82   *I Just Came Home To Count The Memories*   (WB WBS-49860)   6   (1)

6-16-84   *I Wish I Could Write You A Love Song*   (WB 7-29276)   26, 23, 21, 19, 16, 15, 12, 12   (8)

6-01-85   *It's All Over Now*   (WB 7-29002)   25, 15, 11, 9, 8, 7, 21, 28, 28   (9)

3-03-84   *Let Somebody Else Drive*   (WB 7-29385)   26, 24, 18, 13, 9, 9, 23   (7)

10-27-84   *She Sure Got Away With My Heart*   (WB 7-29207)   20, 20, 10, 8   (4)

1-29-83   *Swingin'*   (WB 7-29788)   28, 23, 16, 14, 13, 9, 5, 1, 2, 6, 6, 4, 4, 26, 27   (15)

12-18-82   *Wild And Blue*   (WB 7-29917)   28, 22, 22, 22   (4)

5-15-82   *Would You Catch A Falling Star*   (WB WBS-50043)   30, 26, 22, 18, 17, 16, 15, 14, 10, 9, 21   (11)

ANDERSON, LYNN, AND GARY MORRIS   (*See also:* GARY MORRIS)

2-25-84   *You're Welcome To Tonight*   (Permian P-82003)   29, 27, 23, 17, 9, 16, 30   (7)

ATLANTA

8-04-84   *Pictures*   (MCA 52391)   29   (1)

7-02-83   *Atlanta Burned Again Last Night*   (MDJ A4831)   23, 15, 11, 7, 7, 7, 7, 23, 27   (9)

3-10-84   *Sweet Country Music*   (MCA 52336)   29, 25, 17, 13, 10, 8, 6, 5, 3, 3, 18   (11)

BAILEY, RAZZY

4-10-82   *Everytime You Cross My Mind*   (RCA PB-13084)   27, 23, 19, 17, 14, 12, 11, 10, 9, 8, 6, 5, 10, 28   (14)

3-31-84   *In The Midnight Hour*   (RCA PB-13718)   24, 21, 20, 19, 19, 17   (6)

9-11-82   *Love's Gonna Fall Here Tonight*   (RCA PB-13290)   29, 26, 19, 17, 15, 13, 11, 9, 9, 9, 12, 15, 21   (13)

2-13-82   *She Left Love All Over Me*   (RCA PB-13007)   24, 8, 12, 30   (4)

BANDANA

6-02-84   *Better Our Hearts Should Bend*   (WB 7—29315)   28, 28   (2)

BANDY, MOE

12-18-82   *Only If There Is Another You*   (Col. 38-03309)   29, 24, 24, 24, 28   (5)

7-17-82 *She's Not Really Cheatin'* (Col. 18-02966) 28, 24, 19, 16, 13, 12, 9, 7, 6, 16, 27 (11)

3-06-82 *Someday Soon* (Col. 18-02735) 25, 22, 18, 16, 15, 13, 9, 8, 8, 13, 26 (11)

9-15-84 *Woman Your Love* (Col. 38-04466) 25, 21, 21, 23 (4)

12-17-83 *You're Gonna Lose Her Like That* (Col. 38-04204) 29, 27, 27, 27, 27, 27 (6)

BANDY, MOE, AND JOE STAMPLEY *(See also:* JOE STAMPLEY)

6-30-84 *Where's The Dress* (Col. 38-04477) 24, 20, 17, 16, 7, 1, 1, 12, 30 (9)

BARE, BOBBY

2-13-82 *New Cut Road* (Col. 18-02690) 29, 18, 17, 16, 15, 14, 19, 26 (8)

THE BELLAMY BROTHERS

4-10-82 *For All The Wrong Reasons* (Elektra E-47431) 21, 17, 14, 12, 7, 6, 4, 3, 2, 1, 5, 10, 28 (13)

6-23-84 *Forget About Me* (MCA 52380) 27, 19, 18, 15, 14, 10, 10, 9, 5, 5, 23, 28 (12)

7-31-82 *Get Into Reggae Cowboy* (Elektra 7-29999) 27, 20, 17, 17, 16, 15, 25, 30 (8)

7-02-83 *I Love Her Mind* (WB 7-29645) 27, 20, 12, 9, 6, 5, 5, 22, 22 (9)

2-16-85 *I Need More Of Your Love* (MCA) 29, 26, 26, 26, 22, 22, 22, 22, 4, 6, 27, 28, 23, 25, 30, 30 (16)

11-09-85 *Lie To You For Your Love* (MCA 52668) 12, 12, 12, 4, 4 (5)

6-22-85 *Old Hippie* (MCA 52579) 26, 20, 18, 9, 6, 6, 3, 20, 24 (9)

10-02-82 *Redneck Girl* (WB) 28, 25, 20, 18, 14, 14, 11, 8, 6, 5, 4, 2, 29, 29, 29 (15)

2-12-83 *When I'm Away From You* (Elektra 7-69850) 26, 24, 21, 20, 15, 7, 7, 3, 5, 11, 28, 30 (12)

10-20-84   *World's Greatest Lover*   (MCA 52446)   26, 24, 24, 21, 18, 16, 13, 9, 7   (9)

BOXCAR WILLIE

3-27-82   *Bad News*   (Main Street B 951)   30, 28, 26, 25, 28   (5)

BRADY, LANE   *(See:* JOHNNY LEE)

BROOKS, KAREN   *(See:* T.G. SHEPPARD)

BRUCE, ED

1-21-84   *After All*   (MCA 52298)   29, 18, 11, 6, 6, 19   (6)

9-24-83   *If It Was Easy*   (MCA 52251)   25, 19, 19, 24, 24, 24, 29   (7)

5-29-82   *Love's Found You And Me*   (MCA 52036)   29, 28, 25, 22, 20, 18, 20, 29   (8)

3-26-83   *My First Taste Of Texas*   (MCA 52156)   27, 18, 18, 12, 12   (5)

12-08-84   *You Turn Me On*   (RCA PB-13937)   27, 25, 20, 16, 16, 14, 12, 12, 10, 8, 4, 1   (12)

2-13-82   *You're The Best Break This Old Heart Ever Had*   (MCA 51210)   3, 2   (2)

BUFFETT, JIMMY

11-30-85   *If The Phone Doesn't Ring, It's Me*   (MCA 52664)   22, 22   (2)

CAMPBELL, GLEN

7-14-84   *Faithless Love*   (Atl. America) 7-99768)   22, 20, 15, 14, 12, 11, 10, 10, 7, 26   (10)

12-29-84   *A Lady Like You*   (Atl. America 7-99691)   29, 29, 25, 23, 23, 21, 17, 14, 11, 7, 6, 4, 30, 30   (14)

6-29-85   *Letter To Home*   (Atl. America 7-99647)   29, 26, 16, 13, 13, 13, 22   (7)

CASH, JOHNNY   (*See also:* WILLIE NELSON)

2-30-82   *The Reverend Mr. Black*   (Col. 18-02669)   29   (1)

CASH, ROSANNE

6-19-82   *Ain't No Money*   (Col. 18-02937)   30, 23, 20, 18, 16, 10, 6, 5, 4, 4, 11, 29   (12)

2-13-82   *Blue Moon With Heartache*   (Col. 18-02659)   5, 3   (2)

7-13-85   *I Don't Know Why You Don't Want Me*   (Col. 38-04809)   30, 15, 15, 11, 7, 6, 4, 2, 2   (9)

12-04-82   *I Wonder*   (Col. 38-03238)   29, 25, 19, 16, 16, 16, 16, 27   (8)

4-23-83   *It Hasn't Happened Yet*   (Col. 38-03705)   26, 19, 18, 18, 26   (5)

11-30-85   *Never Be You*   (Col.)   24, 24   (2)

CHARLES, RAY

2-02-85   *Seven Spanish Angels*   (Col. 38-04715)   23, 20, 19, 16, 11, 9, 6, 1, 1, 1, 21, 29, 30   (13)

CHARLES, RAY, WITH MICKEY GILLEY   (*See also:* MICKEY GILLEY)

6-22-85   *It Ain't Gonna Worry My Mind*   (Col. 38-04860)   25, 19, 19, 11, 19, 19, 23   (7)

CHARLES, RAY, AND GEORGE JONES   (*See also:* GEORGE JONES)

1-28-84   *We Didn't See A Thing*   (Col. 38-04297)   29, 22, 17, 12, 8, 7, 6, 12, 21   (9)

CHARLES, RAY, WITH B.J. THOMAS   (*See also:* B.J. THOMAS)

9-15-84   *Rock And Roll Shoes*   (Col. 38-04531)   24, 18, 18, 30   (4)

CHARLES, RAY, WITH HANK WILLIAMS, JR.   (*See also:* HANK WILLIAMS, JR.)

11-09-85   *Two Old Cats Like Us*   (Col. 38-05575)   13, 13, 13   (3)

COE, DAVID ALLAN

4-14-84   *Mona Lisa Lost Her Smile*   (Col. 38-04396)   24, 21, 18, 16, 8, 6, 3, 1, 5, 20   (10)

4-30-83   *The Ride*   (Col. 38-03778)   16, 14, 9, 8, 7, 3, 2, 1, 12, 14, 18, 27   (12)

2-16-85   *She Used To Move Me A Lot*   (Col.)   15, 13, 10, 8, 30   (5)

CONLEE, JOHN

3-31-84   *As Long As I'm Rockin' With You*   (MCA 52351)   21, 15, 12, 9, 9, 7, 4, 4, 2, 13   (10)

8-17-85   *Blue Highway*   (MCA 52625)   26, 20, 16, 16   (4)

2-20-82   *Busted*   (MCA 52008)   25, 20, 17, 13, 11, 11, 9, 7, 7, 6, 5, 5, 9, 14, 20, 30   (16)

3-05-83   *Common Man*   (MCA 52178)   30, 23, 17, 14, 13, 13, 13, 8, 5, 4, 3, 1, 2, 11, 17, 17, 18, 22, 29, 30   (20)

10-30-82   *I Don't Remember Loving You*   (MCA 52116)   30, 27, 25, 21, 17, 15, 13, 9, 5, 5, 5, 3, 5, 8, 18, 28   (16)

7-30-83   *I'm Only In It For The Love*   (MCA 52231)   20, 16, 12, 8, 6, 2, 1, 13, 21, 25, 26, 27, 27, 27   (14)

12-03-83   *In My Eyes*   (MCA 52282) . 26, 22, 19, 12, 12, 12, 12, 8, 12, 24   (10)

7-21-84   *Way Back*   (MCA 52403)   27, 22, 20, 17, 14, 12, 7, 2, 15, 29, 29   (11)

4-13-85   *Working Man*   (MCA 52543)   27, 19, 18, 17, 13, 9, 6, 16, 24, 30   (10)

11-17-84   *Years After You*   (MCA 52470)   30, 25, 22, 17, 16, 13, 10, 10, 8, 6, 6, 11, 10   (13)

CONLEY, EARL THOMAS

2-13-82 *After The Love Slips Away* (RCA PB-13053) 26, 21, 18, 15, 12, 9, 8, 8, 15, 18 (10)

5-19-84 *Angel In Disguise* (RCA PB-13758) 26, 21, 16, 11, 7, 4, 3, 1, 9, 5, 1, 7, 29 (13)

10-06-84 *Chance Of Lovin' You* (RCA PB-13877) 24, 16, 13, 6, 6, 5, 3, 1, 2, 7 (10)

2-18-84 *Don't Make It Easy For Me* (RCA PB-13702) 26, 22, 19, 17, 8, 7, 3, 2, 1, 16 (10)

6-26-82 *Heavenly Bodies* (RCA PB-13246) 29, 23, 19, 15, 11, 9, 8, 7, 6, 6, 17, 28 (12)

10-29-83 *Holding Her And Loving You* (RCA PB-13596) 30, 20, 13, 5, 3, 1, 9, 10, 21, 21, 21, 21, 25 (13)

2-09-85 *Honor Bound* (RCA PB-13960) 24, 21, 18, 13, 11, 8, 6, 6, 5, 1, 3, 5, 8, 25 (14)

2-05-83 *I Have Loved You, Girl* (RCA PB-13414) 30, 27, 25, 22, 21, 18, 15, 13, 12, 12, 16, 30 (12)

6-15-85 *Love Don't Care* (RCA PB-14060) 22, 18, 15, 14, 6, 2, 2, 1, 18, 22 (10)

11-09-85 *Nobody Falls Like A Fool* (RCA PB-14172) 15, 15, 15, 5 5 (5)

11-06-82 *Somewhere Between Right And Wrong* (RCA PB-13320) 29, 22, 18, 16, 13, 10, 7, 11, 11, 11, 23, 30 (12)

6-04-83 *Your Love's On The Line* (RCA PB-13525) 28, 18, 16, 11, 11, 11, 7, 3, 2, 1, 14, 25, 25, 29 (14)

CROWELL, RODNEY

2-13-82 *Victim Or Fool* (WB WBS-50008) 30, 26, 26 (3)

DALTON, LACY J.

7-30-83 *Dream Baby* (Col. 38-03926) 23, 17, 17, 11, 11, 18, 27, 30 (8)

12-22-84 *If That Ain't Love* (Col. 38-04696) 30, 23, 23, 20, 19, 19, 17, 15, 13, 12, 8 (11)

11-13-82   *16th Avenue*   (Col. 18-03184)   29, 26, 25, 30   (4)

5-22-82   *Slow Down*   (Col. 18-02847)   30, 28, 24, 20, 18, 16, 13, 13, 13, 28   (10)

2-13-82   *Wild Turkey*   (Col. 18-02637)   8   (1)

DAVIES, GAIL

11-09-85   *Break Away*   (RCA PB-14184)   26, 26, 26, 14, 14   (5)

9-08-84   *It's You Alone*   (WB 7-29219)   30, 30   (2)

10-27-84   *Jagged Edge Of A Broken Heart*   (RCA PB-13912)   28, 28, 25, 22, 19, 16, 14, 13   (8)

2-20-82   *'Round The Clock Lovin'*   (WB WBS-50004)   23, 21, 18, 16, 16, 12, 11, 10, 8, 9, 14, 24   (12)

5-07-83   *Singing The Blues*   (WB 7-29726)   21, 20, 17, 15, 15, 23, 23, 25, 26   (9)

7-10-82   *You Turn Me On I'm A Radio*   (WB 7-29972)   29, 26, 23, 17, 22, 20, 20, 20, 27   (9)

DAVIS, MAC

10-09-82   *The Beer Drinkin' Song*   (Casa. 2355)   29, 26, 22, 19, 15, 13, 16, 23, 28   (9)

3-24-84   *Most Of All*   (Casa. 818 168-7)   27   (1)

DENVER, JOHN, AND EMMYLOU HARRIS   *(See also:* EMMYLOU HARRIS)

8-27-83   *Wild Montana Skies*   (RCA PB-13562)   21, 15, 11, 11, 20, 21, 28, 30, 30   (9)

DILLINGHAM, CRAIG

2-04-84   *Have You Loved Your Woman Today*   (MCA 52301)   29, 28, 28   (3)

DILLON, DEAN   *(See:* GARY STEWART)

EASTON, SHEENA   *(See:* KENNY ROGERS)

EVERETTE, LEON

3-03-84 *I Could' A Had You* (RCA PB-13717) 25, 22, 16, 11, 7, 6, 4, 4, 3, 1, 13 (11)

4-17-82 *Just Give Me What You Think Is Fair* (RCA PB-13079) 28, 23, 21, 15, 11, 1-, 12, 13, 23, 23 (10)

4-16-83 *My Lady Loves Me* (RCA PB-13466) 27, 18, 15, 15, 11, 11, 13, 25, 28, 30 (10)

2-05-83 *Shadows Of My Mind* (RCA PB-13391) 27, 22, 20, 29 (4)

8-11-84 *Shot In The Dark* (RCA PB-13834) 28, 25 (2)

10-02-82 *Soul Searchin'* (RCA PB-13282) 26, 22, 18, 16, 15, 23 (6)

EXILE

12-29-84 *Crazy For Your Love* (Epic 34-04722) 25, 25, 21, 20, 20, 16, 14, 11, 9, 5, 3, 1, 3, 3, 3 (15)

9-01-84 *Give Me One More Chance* (Epic 34-04567) 24, 15, 13, 10, 10, 9, 7, 4, 2, 2, 1, 19 (12)

11-09-85 *Hang On To Your Heart* (Epic 34-05580) 6, 6, 6, 17, 17 (5)

5-26-84 *I Don't Want To Be A Memory* (Epic 34-04421) 28, 26, 24, 17, 16, 11, 9, 6 (8)

5-18-85 *She's A Miracle* (Epic 34-04864) 28, 25, 23, 13, 9, 6, 2, 1, 18, 20, 20, 24, 25 (13)

1-28-84 *Woke Up In Love* (Epic 34-04247) 27, 20, 18, 14, 10, 8, 8, 21, 29 (9)

THE FORESTER SISTERS

7-20-85 *I Fell In Love Again Last Night* (WB 7-28988) 23, 23, 14, 9, 7, 6, 3, 3 (8)

FRICKE, JANIE

2-13-82 *Do Me With Love* (Col. 18-02644) 14 (1)

5-22-82   *Don't Worry 'Bout Me Baby*   (Col. 18-02859)   27, 24, 22, 19, 15, 12, 8, 5, 7, 15, 28   (11)

2-09-85   *The First Word In Memory Is Me*   (Col. 38-04731)   26, 25, 22, 20, 19, 15, 16, 16, 16, 20, 26, 26, 29   (13)

7-02-83   *He's A Heartache*   (Col. 38-03899)   25, 16, 8, 6, 4, 2, 1, 18, 18, 22, 22, 29, 30, 30   (14)

6-02-84   *If The Fall Don't Get You*   (Col. 38-04454)   23, 21, 15, 14, 10, 8, 7, 7, 24   (9)

9-25-82   *It Ain't Easy Bein' Easy*   (Col. 38-03214)   24, 21, 17, 15, 14, 12, 10, 8, 7, 5, 4, 2, 10, 17, 17, 17, 25   (17)

2-18-84   *Let's Stop Talking About It*   (Col. 38-04317)   25, 21, 18, 16, 6, 4, 2, 4, 13, 28   (10)

6-22-85   *She's Single Again*   (Col. 38-04896)   28, 23, 21, 12, 8, 8, 6, 4, 2, 2, 12, 12   (12)

11-09-85   *Somebody Else's Fire*   (Col. 38-05617)   21, 21, 21, 9, 9   (5)

11-05-83   *Tell Me A Lie*   (Col. 38-04091)   21, 15, 7, 5, 4, 1, 7, 18, 18, 18, 18, 24   (12)

1-29-83   *You Don't Know Love*   (Col. 38-03498)   25, 21, 10, 19, 18, 16, 14, 8, 4, 4, 3, 2, 2, 21, 20, 20   (16)

10-06-84   *Your Heart's Not In It*   (Col. 38-04578)   26, 19, 14, 13, 13, 12, 11, 2, 1, 26   (10)

FRIZZELL, DAVID

7-03-82   *I'm Gonna Hire A Wino To Decorate Our Home*   (WB WBS-50063)   29, 26, 23, 19, 14, 4, 2, 1, 1, 5, 14, 20, 29   (13)

2-02-85   *No Way Jose*   (Viva 7-29158)   19   (1)

7-09-83   *Where Are You Spending Your Nights These Days*   (WB 7-29617)   25, 20, 12, 12, 10, 10, 24, 28   (8)

FRIZZELL, DAVID, AND SHELLY WEST   *(See also:* SHELLY WEST)

2-13-82   *Another Honky-Tonk Night On Broadway*   (WB WBS-50007)   18, 12, 6, 6, 5, 5, 5, 4, 9, 16, 21   (11)

7-31-82 *I Just Came Here To Dance* (WB 7-29980) 30, 26, 22, 15, 14, 9, 7, 3, 12, 18, 24 (11)

11-10-84 *It's A Be Together Night* (Viva 7-29187) 29, 26, 23, 23 (4)

3-10-84 *Silent Partners* (Viva 7-29404) 27, 23, 19, 14, 14, 14, 30 (7)

FURMAN, MICKI

3-31-84 *I Bet You Never Thought I'd Go This Far* (MCA 52321) 26 (1)

GATLIN, LARRY, AND THE GATLIN BROTHERS BAND

4-14-84 *Denver* (Col. 38-04395) 27, 23, 22, 20, 15, 14, 12, 10, 10, 23 (10)

2-13-82 *In Like With Each Other* (Col. 18-02698) 27, 20, 22, 26, 23, 21, 20, 19, 19, 22 (10)

8-18-84 *The Lady Takes The Cowboy Every Time* (Col. 38-04533) 28, 25, 18, 17, 14, 11, 11, 10, 6, 5, 29, 29 (12)

10-30-82 *Sure Feels Like Love* (Col. 18-03159) 22, 18, 17, 15, 13, 11, 11, 23, 28, 28, 28 (11)

GAYLE, CRYSTAL (See also: EDDIE RABBITT)

8-20-83 *Baby, What About You* (WB 7-29582) 21, 15, 10, 9, 6, 2, 2, 10, 17, 17, 17, 28 (12)

3-31-84 *I Don't Wanna Lose Your Love* (WB 7-29356) 29, 24, 22, 18, 15, 13, 11, 8, 8 (9)

8-14-82 *Livin' In These Troubled Times* (Col. 18-03048) 30, 28, 27, 25, 23, 21, 17, 15, 13, 19, 25 (11)

11-09-85 *A Long And Lasting Love* (WB 7-28963) 14, 14, 14 (3)

11-17-84 *Me Against The Night* (WB 7-29203) 20, 12, 10, 6, 5, 6, 4, 4, 4, 2, 2, 2 (12)

5-04-85 *Nobody Wants To Be Alone* (WB 7-29050) 26, 21, 17, 14, 9, 6, 6, 4, 13, 13, 25 (11)

4-16-83 *Our Love Is On The Faultline* (WB 7-29719) 26, 16, 12, 12, 7, 5, 5, 4, 3, 3, 16, 16 (12)

1-15-83　*'Til I Gain Control Again*　(Elektra 7-69893)　24, 18, 11, 4, 2, 2, 6, 10, 20, 27, 30　(11)

7-28-84　*Turning Away*　(WB 7-29254)　28, 19, 16, 13, 9, 6, 3, 2, 2, 2, 7, 22　(12)

2-20-82　*You Never Gave Up On Me*　(Col. 18-02718)　19, 16, 12, 8, 6, 4, 3, 2, 1, 3, 6, 11, 17　(13)

GIBBS, TERRI

10-01-83　*Anybody Else's Heart But Mine*　(MCA 52252)　24, 24, 26, 26, 26　(5)

GILL, VINCE

8-24-85　*If It Weren't For Him*　(RCA PB-14140)　27, 22, 22　(3)

6-16-84　*Oh Carolina*　(RCA PB-13809)　27, 24, 22　(3)

3-24-84　*Victim Of Life's Circumstances*　(RCA PB-13731)　24, 22, 29　(3)

GILLEY, MICKEY　(*See also:* RAY CHARLES)

5-07-83　*Fool For Your Love*　(Epic 14-03783)　24, 19, 16, 11, 7, 7, 5, 1, 12, 17, 24, 28　(12)

4-13-85　*I'm The One Mama Warned You About*　(Epic 34-04746)　11, 10, 10, 23　(4)

2-13-82　*Lonely Nights*　(Epic 14-02578)　2　(1)

8-07-82　*Put Your Dreams Away*　(Epic 14-03056)　27, 24, 21, 17, 14, 9, 5, 3, 1, 5, 10, 17, 27　(13)

11-20-82　*Talk To Me*　(Epic 34-03326)　30, 28, 24, 19, 14, 10, 10, 10, 7, 4, 2, 3, 7, 23, 30　(15)

3-20-82　*Tears Of The Lonely*　(Epic 14-02774)　28, 22, 18, 14, 12, 10, 7, 4, 3, 2, 2, 1, 4, 9, 17, 30　(16)

10-06-84　*Too Good To Stop Now*　(Epic 34-04563)　28, 21, 18, 11, 11, 9, 9, 8, 7　(9)

11-09-85　*You've Got Something On Your Mind*　(Epic 34-05460)　23, 23, 23, 29, 29　(5)

2-18-84   *You've Really Got A Hold On Me*   (Epic 34-04269)   30, 23, 20, 18, 7, 5, 5, 20   (8)

10-08-83   *Your Love Shines Through*   (Epic 34-04018)   23, 16, 16, 16, 13, 9, 3, 2, 2, 10, 24   (11)

GILLEY, MICKEY, AND CHARLY McCLAIN   *(See also:* CHARLY McCLAIN)

3-17-84   *Candy Man*   (Epic 34-04368)   26, 18, 12, 11, 9, 8, 7, 6, 6, 24   (10)

8-20-83   *Paradise Tonight*   (Epic 34-04007)   16, 14, 11, 10, 7, 4, 3, 3, 1, 1, 1, 5, 17, 27, 28   (15)

7-14-84   *The Right Stuff*   (Epic 34-04489)   23, 22, 16, 16, 15, 15, 14   (7)

GLASER, JIM

2-25-84   *If I Could Only Dance With You*   (Noble Vision NV-104)   26, 24, 21, 11, 10, 17, 17, 30   (8)

11-09-85   *In Another Minute*   (MCA 52672)   28, 28, 28   (3)

12-15-84   *Let Me Down Easy*   (Noble Vision NV-107)   26, 19, 15, 15, 13, 11, 11, 9, 7   (9)

11-19-83   *The Man In The Mirror*   (Noble Vision NV-103)   23, 18, 14, 13, 13, 30, 30, 30, 30   (9)

7-07-84   *You're Gettin' To Me Again*   (Noble Vision NV-105)   30, 29, 29, 23, 23, 23, 23, 21, 15, 9, 6, 12, 12, 29   (14)

GOSDIN, VERN

4-28-84   *I Can Tell By The Way You Dance*   (Compleat CP-122)   27, 23, 18, 13, 11, 9, 6, 4, 2, 1, 11   (11)

1-21-84   *I Wonder Where We'd Be Tonight*   (Compleat CP-115)   17, 28   (2)

4-23-83   *If You're Gonna Do Me Wrong*   (Compleat CP-102)   22, 8, 6, 6, 19, 28   (6)

12-29-84   *Slow Burning Memory*   (Compleat CP-135)   27, 27, 23, 22, 22   (5)

7-30-83   *Way Down Deep*   (Compleat CP-108)   25, 18, 18, 12, 12, 27   (6)

8-25-84   *What Would Your Memories Do*   (Compleat CP-126)   28, 20, 19, 17, 14, 14, 13   (7)

GRAY, JAN

3-03-84   *Bad Night For Good Girls*   (Jamex 45-012)   30, 30   (2)

GRAY, MARK

11-17-84   *Diamond In The Dust*   (Col. 38-04610)   29, 26, 24, 19, 19, 14   (6)

8-20-83   *It Ain't Real*   (Col. 38-03893)   17, 17, 17, 30   (4)

3-17-84   *Left Side Of The Road*   (Col. 38-40324)   29, 26, 23, 22, 21, 20, 20   (7)

12-10-83   *Wounded Hearts*   (Col. 38-04137)   24, 23, 23, 23, 23, 23   (6)

GREENWOOD, LEE   *(See also:* BARBARA MANDRELL)

2-05-83   *Ain't No Trick*   (MCA 52150)   28, 23, 21, 19, 18, 16, 16, 21, 27, 29   (10)

6-01-85   *Dixie Road*   (MCA 52564)   27, 16, 12, 8, 4, 3, 2, 1, 1, 18, 23   (11)

9-22-84   *Fool's Gold*   (MCA 52426)   25, 25, 20, 12, 10, 5, 5, 3, 2, 10   (10)

6-09-84   *God Bless The U.S.A.*   (MCA 52386)   26, 19, 18, 14, 13, 11, 8, 5, 4, 5, 30   (11)

1-28-84   *Going, Going, Gone*   (MCA 52322)   25, 19, 15, 13, 11, 9, 9, 27   (8)

5-28-83   *I.O.U.*   (MCA 52199)   25, 24, 15, 12, 9, 8, 8, 17, 24, 29, 29   (11)

11-09-85   *I Don't Mind The Thorns*   (MCA 52656)   8, 8, 8, 1, 1   (5)

2-13-82   *It Turns Me Inside Out*   (MCA 51159)   28   (1)

5-08-82   *Ring On Her Finger, Time On Her Hands*   (MCA 52026)   29, 23, 21, 16, 14, 11, 8, 6, 5, 9, 20   (11)

9-11-82   *She's Lying*   (MCA 52087)   27, 24, 22, 22, 20, 17, 15, 24   (8)

10-01-83   *Somebody's Gonna Love You*   (MCA 52257)   23, 17, 12, 12, 12, 8, 4, 4, 7, 17, 26   (11)

1-12-85 *You've Got A Good Love Comin'* (MCA 52509)   27, 25, 25, 22, 19, 18, 15, 12, 10, 7, 5, 5, 4   (13)

HAGGARD, MERLE

5-22-82 *Are The Good Times Really Over* (Epic 14-02894)   29, 27, 25, 21, 20, 18, 15, 12, 8, 3, 3, 9, 12, 19, 29   (15)

2-13-82 *Big City* (Epic 14-02686)   21, 6, 3, 3, 2, 1, 7, 17, 23   (9)

4-17-82 *Dealing With The Devil* (MCA 52020)   30, 25, 20, 17, 15, 15, 17, 27   (8)

11-06-82 *Going Where The Lonely Go* (Epic 34-03315)   25, 19, 17, 14, 12, 9, 6, 2, 2, 2, 1, 3, 4, 8, 24   (15)

8-17-85 *Kern River* (Epic 34-05426)   28, 22, 18, 18   (4)

7-28-84 *Let's Chase Each Other Around The Room* (Epic 34-04512)   27, 18, 13, 9, 4, 3, 1, 1, 1, 1, 18   (11)

4-06-85 *Natural High* (Epic 34-04830)   28, (1), 25, 22, 21, 17, 13, 10, 3, 1, 5, 13, 24, 29   (13)

11-24-84 *A Place To Fall Apart* (Epic 34-04663)   21, 18, 13, 10, 9, 6, 6, 5, 3, 3, 3, 21   (12)

4-07-84 *Someday When Things Are Good* (Epic 34-04402)   26, 16, 12, 12, 9, 7, 5, 4, 2, 1, 10, 19   (12)

12-10-83 *That's The Way Love Goes* (Epic 34-04226)   28, 21, 16, 16, 16, 16, 12, 3, 2, 1, 2, 15, 29   (13)

8-27-83 *What Am I Gonna Do* (Epic 34-04006)   23, 16, 12, 12, 9, 5, 5, 4, 4, 4, 4, 16, 20, 23   (14)

4-23-83 *You Take Me For Granted* (Epic 34-03723)   25, 18, 16, 16, 9, 8, 8, 20, 20, 22, 30   (11)

HAGGARD, MERLE, AND GEORGE JONES *(See also:* GEORGE JONES)

8-14-82 *Yesterday's Wine* (Epic 14-03072)   28, 24, 19, 12, 8, 4, 4, 2, 1, 1, 4, 11, 16, 24   (14)

HAGGARD, MERLE, AND WILLIE NELSON   *(See also:* WILLIE NELSON)

1-15-83   *Reasons To Quit*   (Epic 34-03494)   26, 19, 15, 15, 15, 11, 11, 8, 7, 4, 8, 8, 21   (13)

HALL, TOM T.

10-13-84   *P.S. I Love You*   (Mer. 880 216-7)   27, 23, 19, 19, 18, 16, 14, 11   (8)

HALL, TOM T., AND EARL SCRUGGS

4-24-82   *There Ain't No Country Music On This Jukebox*   (Col. 18-02858)   30, 27, 26, 24, 23, 21, 20, 27   (8)

HARDIN, GUS

12-22-84   *All Tangled Up In Love*   (RCA PB-13938)   28, 20, 20, 18, 16, 16, 14, 12, 10, 8   (10)

4-14-84   *I Pass*   (RCA PB-13751)   26, 24, 24, 24   (4)

7-23-83   *If I Didn't Love You*   (RCA PB-13532)   25, 19, 19, 21, 28   (5)

HARRIS, EMMYLOU   *(See also:* JOHN DENVER)

6-26-82   *Born To Run*   (WB 7-29993)   28, 25, 21, 19, 14, 13, 12, 15, 23   (9)

4-16-83   *I'm Movin' On*   (WB 7-29729)   23, 15, 11, 8, 8, 14, 14, 29, 29, 29   (10)

4-28-84   *In My Dreams*   (WB 7-29329)   29, 27, 22, 16, 15, 12, 12, 29   (8)

9-01-84   *Pledging My Love*   (WB 7-29218)   27, 21, 19, 15, 15, 14, 29   (7)

12-22-84   *Someone Like You*   (WB 7-29138)   29, 22, 22, 19, 18, 18   (6)

2-13-82   *Tennessee Rose*   (WB WBS-49892)   15, 7, 6, 20   (4)

5-11-85   *White Line*   (WB 7-29041)   28, 19, 20, 11, 19, 25, 29   (7)

HUNLEY, CON

4-06-85   *I'd Rather Be Crazy*   (Cap. B-5457)   28   (1)

6-12-82   *Oh Girl*   (WB WBS-50058)   28, 26, 24, 24, 23, 22, 18, 24, 25   (9)

IGLESIAS, JULIO, AND WILLIE NELSON   (*See also:* WILLIE NELSON)

3-31-84   *To All The Girls I've Loved Before*   (Col. 38-04217)   19, 12, 10, 7, 6, 2, 1, 2, 16   (9)

JAMES, SONNY

2-20-82   *Innocent Lies*   (Dimension DS-1026)   28   (1)

JENNINGS, WAYLON   (*See also:* WAYLON AND WILLIE; WILLIE NELSON)

10-20-84   *America*   (RCA PB-13908)   17, 10, 10, 8, 7, 4, 4, 3, 1, 1, 7   (11)

8-13-83   *Breakin' Down*   (RCA PB-13543)   23, 15, 13, 6, 6, 21, 26, 26, 30   (9)

11-19-83   *The Conversation*   (RCA PB-13631)   22, 16, 13, 12, 8, 7, 7, 7, 7, 7, 16   (11)

8-03-85   *Drinkin' And Dreamin'*   (RCA PB-14094)   28, 16, 14, 12, 7, 7   (6)

3-31-84   *I May Be Used*   (RCA PB-13729)   25, 19, 15, 10, 8, 5, 2, 1, 14   (9)

4-09-83   *Lucille*   (RCA PB-13465)   19, 10, 6, 3, 3, 1, 3, 3, 1, 4, 18, 19, 24, 30   (14)

7-07-84   *Never Could Toe The Mark*   (RCA PB-13827)   26, 25, 24, 18, 17, 14, 10, 6, 5, 26, 28   (11)

2-13-82   *Shine*   (RCA PB-12367)   4   (1)

2-23-85   *Waltz Me To Heaven*   (RCA JK-13984)   28, 23, 22, 18, 17, 17, 17   (7)

6-26-82   *Women Do Know How To Carry On*   (RCA PB-13257)   30, 26, 22, 18, 13, 10, 7, 6, 5, 3, 3, 3, 15, 25, 29   (15)

JENNINGS, WAYLON, AND JERRY REED   (*See also:* JERRY REED)

9-10-83   *Hold On I'm Comin'*   (RCA PB-13580)   25, 19, 13, 11, 11, 18, 18, 18, 22, 28, 30   (11)

JONES, GEORGE   *(See also:* RAY CHARLES; MERLE HAGGARD)

6-18-83   *I Always Get Lucky With You*   (Epic 34-03883)   22, 13, 9, 7, 5, 2, 1, 15, 16, 19, 19, 28   (12)

2-13-82   *Same Ole Me*   (Epic 14-02696)   17, 11, 7, 5, 4, 3, 2, 2, 1, 5, 15, 22   (12)

10-13-84   *She's My Rock*   (Epic 34-04609)   24, 20, 15, 15, 13, 12, 6, 6, 5, 4, 4, 24, 24   (13)

1-22-83   *Shine On*   (Epic 34-03489)   29, 24, 19, 18, 16, 16, 11, 9, 5, 9, 20, 24, 24   (13)

10-15-83   *Tennessee Whiskey*   (Epic 34-04082)   21, 21, 21, 11, 8, 2, 1, 5, 16, 30   (10)

8-31-85   *Who's Gonna Fill Their Shoes*   (Epic 34-05443)   28, 28, 11, 11, 11   (5)

4-21-84   *You've Still Got A Place In My Heart*   (Epic 34-04413)   26, 16, 14, 12, 9, 7, 5, 4, 3, 3, 15, 25   (12)

JONES, GEORGE, AND MERLE HAGGARD   *(See also:* MERLE HAGGARD)

12-18-82   *C.C. Waterback*   (Epic 34-03405)   25, 20, 20, 20, 17, 12, 10, 9, 8, 5, 5, 23, 30   (13)

JONES, GEORGE, AND BRENDA LEE

2-02-85   *Hallelujah, I Love You So*   (Epic 34-04724)   20, 16, 12, 10, 6, 5, 3   (7)

JONES, TOM

2-04-84   *I've Been Rained On Too*   (Mer. 814 820-7)   28, 24, 19, 17, 13, 12, 30, 28   (8)

5-26-84   *This Time*   (Mer. 818 801-7)   27, 25, 23, 30   (4)

4-16-83   *Touch Me*   (Mer. 810 445-7)   20, 9, 6, 5, 5, 15, 27   (7)

11-13-82   *A Woman's Touch*   (Mer. SR 76172)   26, 22, 21, 19, 28   (5)

THE JUDDS

3-02-85　*Girls' Night Out*　(RCA PB-13991)　16, 15, 11, 9, 9, 9, 5, 4, 2, 1, 2, 7, 17, 20, 29　(15)

2-11-84　*Had A Dream*　(RCA PB-13673)　23, 17, 14, 12, 11, 14, 25, 30　(8)

11-09-85　*Have Mercy*　(RCA PB-14193)　25, 25, 25, 15, 15　(5)

6-29-85　*Love Is Alive*　(Curb PB-14093)　30, 17, 12, 12, 10, 6, 4, 3, 1, 1　(10)

5-19-84　*Mama He's Crazy*　(RCA PB-13772)　27, 22, 17, 14, 9, 7, 4, 2, 1, 12, 25, 30　(12)

10-20-84　*Why Not Me*　(RCA PB-13923)　24, 17, 17, 16, 14, 5, 5, 4, 4, 3, 2, 2　(12)

THE KENDALLS

6-12-82　*Cheater's Prayer*　(Mer. SR 76155)　30, 28, 27, 27, 24, 27　(6)

4-13-85　*Four Wheel Drive*　(Mer. 880 588-7)　28, 20, 19, 18, 16, 23, 28　(7)

11-24-84　*I'd Dance Every Dance With You*　(Mer. 880 306-7)　27, 25, 22, 22, 25　(5)

7-20-85　*If You Break My Heart*　(Mer. 880 826-7)　26, 26, 27, 15, 21　(5)

7-07-84　*My Baby's Gone*　(Mer. 822 203-7)　29, 28, 28, (2), 27, 29　(5)

7-30-83　*Precious Love*　(Mer. 812 300-7)　26, 26, 29　(3)

2-18-84　*Thank God For The Radio*　(Mer. 818 056-7)　29, 24, 22, 20, 10, 6, 4, 1, 2, 3, 17, 26　(12)

KRISTOFFERSON, KRIS　(See: WILLIE NELSON)

LANE, CRISTY

2-13-82　*Lies On Your Lips*　(Liberty PA-1443)　25, 15, 13, 11, 28　(5)

LAY, RODNEY, AND THE WILD WEST

9-25-82　*I Wish I Had A Job To Shove*　(Churchill CR 94005)　28, 25, 23, 22　(4)

LEE, BRENDA   (*See:* GEORGE JONES)

LEE, JOHNNY

  2-13-82   *Be There For Me Baby*   (Full Moon E-47301)   20, 13, 10, 22, 20, 29   (6)

11-06-82   *Cherokee Fiddle*   (Full Moon 7-69945)   30, 27, 25, 22, 20, 14, 11, 6, 6, 6, 12, 20, 27   (13)

  7-16-83   *Hey Bartender*   (Full Moon 7-29605)   23, 15, 13, 9, 9, 5, 4, 3, 2, 2, 19, 20, 27, 29, 29, 29   (16)

  2-16-85   *Rollin' Lonely*   (WB 7-29110)   30, 27, 25, 24, 20, 19, 19, 19, 18   (9)

  6-29-85   *Save The Last Chance*   (WB 7-29021)   27, 25, 27   (3)

  4-02-83   *Sounds Like Love*   (Elektra 7-69848)   22, 15, 7, 7, 27, 29   (6)

11-30-85   *They Never Had To Get Over You*   (WB 7-26901)   28, 28   (2)

10-27-84   *You Could've Heard A Heart Break*   (WB 7-29206)   27, 27, 24, 21, 7   (5)

LEE, JOHNNY, AND LANE BRADY

  3-17-84   *The Yellow Rose*   (Full Moon 7-29375)   24, 16, 11, 7, 5, 2, 2, 18   (8)

LOGGINS, DAVE   (*See:* ANNE MURRAY)

LYNN, LORETTA

  2-19-83   *Breaking It*   (MCA 52158)   29, 24, 22, 19, 19, 23, 26   (7)

  8-24-85   *Heart Don't Do This To Me*   (MCA 52621)   29   (1)

  2-13-82   *I Lie*   (MCA 51226)   19, 14, 9, 7, 6, 13, 26, 30   (8)

MANDRELL, BARBARA

11-09-85   *Angel In Your Arms*   (MCA 52645)   7, 7, 7, 25, 25   (5)

11-10-84   *Crossword Puzzle*   (MCA 52458)   28, 25, 17, 14, 10, 9, 8   (7)

3-10-84   *Happy Birthday Dear Heartache*   (MCA 52340)   26, 20, 14, 10, 8, 6, 5, 4, 4, 19   (10)

5-14-83   *In Times Like These*   (MCA 52206)   24, 23, 17, 17, 11, 7, 3, 2, 2, 16, 22, 28, 28   (13)

10-15-83   *One Of A Kind Pair Of Fools*   (MCA 52258)   11, 11, 11, 9, 5, 1, 6, 15, 23   (9)

6-30-84   *Only A Lonely Heart Knows*   (MCA 52397)   26, 22, 19, 18, 13, 13, 10, 8, 7, 4   (10)

10-30-82   *Operator, Long Distance Please*   (MCA 52111)   28, 24, 20, 19   (4)

4-13-85   *There's No Love In Tennessee*   (MCA 52537)   30, 22, 21, 20, 15, 12, 9, 4, 10, 20, 16, 16, 27   (13)

5-15-82   *'Til You're Gone*   (MCA 52038)   29, 24, 19, 15, 12, 11, 9, 6, 3, 2, 4, 8, 18, 29   (14)

MANDRELL, BARBARA, AND LEE GREENWOOD   (*See also:* LEE GREENWOOD)

3-09-85   *It Should Have Been Love By Now*   (MCA 52525)   25, 21, 14, 14, 14   (5)

8-04-84   *To Me*   (MCA 52415)   25, 19, 16, 13, 8, 4, 3, 3, 3, 6, 4, 1, 21, 21   (14)

MANDRELL, LOUISE

9-15-84   *Goodbye Heartache*   (RCA PB-13850)   29, 22, 22, 22, 17, 30   (6)

11-09-85   *I Wanna Say Yes*   (RCA PB-14151)   9, 9, 9, 27, 27   (5)

4-28-84   *I'm Not Through Loving You Yet*   (RCA PB-13752)   28, 25, 21, 15, 13, 11, 9, 6, 6, 30   (10)

5-18-85   *Maybe My Baby*   (RCA PB-14039)   30, 27, 24, 14, 10, 7, 6, 6, 20, 22, 22   (11)

11-26-83   *Runaway Heart*   (RCA PB-13469)   26, 19, 15, 12, 9, 9, 9, 9, 6, 9, 10, 15   (12)

3-12-83   *Save Me*   (RCA PB-13450)   28, 26, 20, 17, 17, 21, 21, 10, 10, 17, 20, 30   (12)

1-12-85   *This Bed's Not Big Enough*   (RCA PB-13954)   26, 24, 24   (3)

9-03-83   *Too Hot To Sleep*   (RCA PB_13567)   25, 19, 18, 15, 13, 13, 20, 20, 20, 27   (10)

MASSEY, WAYNE   (*See:* CHARLY McCLAIN)

MATTEA, KATHY

8-24-85   *He Won't Give In*   (Mer. 880 827-7)   26, 24, 24   (3)

5-11-85   *It's Your Reputation Talkin'*   (Mer. 880 595-7)   29, 29, 26   (3)

4-21-84   *Someone Is Falling In Love*   (Mer. 818 289-7)   27, 26   (2)

McCLAIN, CHARLY   (*See also:* MICKEY GILLEY)

5-12-84   *Band Of Gold*   (Epic 34-04423)   27, 19, 19   (3)

7-17-82   *Dancing Your Memory Away*   (Epic 14-02975)   30, 25, 22, 17, 14, 11, 10, 8, 5, 2, 14, 20, 30   (13)

3-23-85   *Radio Heart*   (Epic 34-04777)   29, 29, (1), 15, 15, 14, 13, 9, 3, 1, 12, 20, 26, 30   (13)

12-03-83   *Sentimental Ol' You*   (Epic 34-04172)   27, 21, 18, 13, 13, 13, 13, 9, 2, 1, 7, 23, 28   (13)

10-20-84   *Some Hearts Get All The Breaks*   (Epic 34-04586)   25, 22, 22, 19   (4)

2-13-82   *The Very Best Of You*   (Epic 14-02601)   23, 16, 11, 9, 30   (5)

12-11-82   *With You*   (Epic 34-03309)   26, 20, 18, 18, 18, 14, 10, 18, 29   (9)

McCLAIN, CHARLY, WITH WAYNE MASSEY

8-10-85   *With One Look In Your Eyes*   (Epic 34-05398)   29, 19, 16, 10, 10   (5)

McDANIEL, MEL

12-29-84   *Baby's Got Her Blue Jeans On*   (Cap. B-5418)   28, 28, 24, 21, 21, 18, 18, 17, 2, 30   (10)

7-31-82   *Big Ole Brew*   (Cap. PB-5138)   29, 24, 21, 18, 15, 13, 13, 9, 8, 13, 21, 29   (12)

12-10-83   *I Call It Love*   (Cap. PB-5298)   25, 22, 17, 17, 17, 17, 13, 4, 3, 3, 20   (11)

5-04-85   *Let It Roll*   (Cap. B-5458)   24, 18, 14, 11, 5, 3, 3, 3, 14, 12, 24   (11)

11-09-85   *Stand Up*   (Cap. B-5513)   22, 22, 22, 8, 8   (5)

3-20-82   *Take Me To The Country*   (Cap. PB-5095)   30, 25, 20, 17, 14, 12, 9, 8, 8, 9, 11, 17, 26   (13)

McDOWELL, RONNIE

3-24-84   *I Dream Of Women Like You*   (Epic 34-04367)   23, 20, 13, 11, 11, 11, 10, 9, 25   (9)

8-04-84   *I Got A Million Of 'Em*   (Epic 34-04499)   28, 24, 24, 24, 19, 14, 9, 27, 27   (9)

3-23-85   *In A New York Minute*   (Epic 34-04816)   24, 24, 24, 16, 16, 15, 14, 10, 4, 5, 15, 23, 29   (13)

8-24-85   *Love Talks*   (Epic 34-05404)   25, 20, 20   (3)

4-23-83   *Personally*   (Epic 34-03526)   24, 22, 22, 23, 24, 24, 30, 30   (8)

2-13-82   *Watching Girls Go By*   (Epic 14-02614)   11   (1)

11-12-83   *You Made A Wanted Man Out Of Me*   (Epic 34-04167)   25, 18, 14, 11, 8, 6, 4, 4, 4, 4, 2, 11, 26   (13)

7-16-83   *You're Gonna Ruin My Bad Reputation*   (Epic 34-03946)   25, 17, 15, 8, 4, 3, 1, 12, 16, 25, 28, 28   (12)

McENTIRE, REBA

12-11-82   *Can't Even Get The Blues*   (Mer. SR 76180)   29, 24, 21, 21, 21, 15, 24, 30   (8)

8-03-85   *Have I Got A Deal For You*   (MCA 52604)   26, 14, 12, 11, 6, 6   (6)

9-01-84   *He Broke Your Mem'ry Last Night*   (MCA 52404)   28, 24, 23   (3)

11-10-84   *How Blue*   (MCA 52468)   27, 24, 20, 17, 12, 11, 10, 5, 5, 3, 1,
1 (12)

7-24-82   *I'm Not That Lonely Yet*   (Mer. SR 76157)   29, 25, 21, 18, 16, 13, 10,
20, 29 (9)

4-14-84   *Just A Little Love*   (MCA 52349)   25, 22, 21, 19, 14, 10, 9, 7, 7,
22 (10)

11-30-85   *Only In My Mind*   (MCA 52691)   26, 26 (2)

3-09-85   *Somebody Should Leave*   (MCA 52527)   28, 26, 20, 20, 20, 10, 11, 9,
5, 1, 6, 16, 19, 27 (14)

2-04-84   *There Ain't No Future In This*   (Mer. 814 629-7)   23, 19, 15, 12, 10,
10 (6)

10-08-83   *Why Do We Want What We Know We Can't Have*   (Mer. 812 835-
7)   20, 15, 15, 15, 10, 10, 19, 22, 30 (9)

2-26-83   *You're The First Time I've Thought About Leaving*   (Mer. 810 338-
7)   28, 24, 21, 14, 12, 7, 7, 5, 5, 1, 20, 21, 21 (13)

McGUFFEY, LANE

6-23-84   *Day By Day*   (Atl. America 7-99778)   30, 27, 23, 21, 21 (5)

MEDLEY, BILL

6-16-84   *I Still Do*   (RCA PB-13753)   24, 21 (2)

9-08-84   *I've Always Got The Heart To Sing The Blues*   (RCA PB-13851)   25,
22, 19, 19 (4)

MILLER, ROGER, AND WILLIE NELSON WITH RAY PRICE   (*See also:* WILLIE NELSON; RAY PRICE)

7-31-82   *Old Friends*   (Col. 18-02681)   26, 23, 23, 30 (4)

MILSAP, RONNIE

5-08-82   *Any Day Now*   (RCA PB-13216)   30, 25, 17, 13, 8, 6, 3, 1, 1, 4, 5,
12, 21, 30 (14)

8-13-83 *Don't You Know How Much I Love You* (RCA PB-13564) 26, 13, 8, 7, 5, 4, 1, 1, 1, 6, 6, 6, 14, 22, 26, 30 (16)

8-28-82 *He Got You* (RCA PB-13286) 28, 23, 16, 10, 5, 3, 2, 2, 1, 3, 8, 12, 23, 29 (14)

11-27-82 *Inside* (RCA PB-13362) 26, 23, 17, 12, 7, 7, 7, 5, 2, 1, 1, 3, 8, 15, 25 (15)

8-10-85 *Lost In The Fifties Tonight* (RCA PB-14135) 28, 18, 15, 9, 9 (5)

9-22-84 *Prisoner Of The Highway* (RCA PB-13876) 20, 20, 16, 10, 7, 4, 4, 4, 4 (9)

5-11-85 *She Keeps The Homefires Burning* (RCA PB-14034) 30, 18, 15, 8, 5, 4, 2, 1, 15, 26 (10)

11-26-83 *Show Her* (RCA PB-13658) 24, 16, 14, 9, 6, 6, 6, 6, 4, 1, 6, 13, 24 (13)

6-02-84 *Still Losing You* (RCA PB-13805) 22, 20, 14, 12, 8, 6, 5, 4, 4, 3, 2, 1, 11, 30 (14)

4-30-83 *Stranger In My House* (RCA PB-13470) 20, 19, 14, 7, 4, 2, 1, 2, 15, 15, 22, 28 (12)

MORRIS, GARY *(See also:* LYNN ANDERSON)

4-03-82 *Don't Look Back* (WB WBS-50017) 27, 25, 21, 20, 19, 19, 18, 22 (8)

11-09-85 *I'll Never Stop Loving You* (WB 7-28947) 2, 2, 2, 3, 3 (5)

6-15-85 *Lasso The Moon* (WB 7-29028) 21, 17, 10, 8, 4, 17, 17, 21 (8)

6-25-83 *The Love She Found In Me* (WB 7-20682) 23, 18, 9, 9, 19, 27, 30 (7)

8-25-84 *Second Hand Heart* (WB 7-29230) 26, 22, 23, 20, 17, 17, 15, 11, 28 (9)

9-17-83 *The Wind Beneath My Wings* (WB 7-29532) 27, 24, 17, 12, 10, 10, 10, 7, 7, 25 (10)

MURPHEY, MICHAEL MARTIN

7-13-85 *Carolina In The Pines* (EMI America B-8265) 29, 14, 12, 8, 8, 8, 14, 14 (8)

6-16-84   *Disenchanted*   (Liberty B-1517)   25, 22, 20, 17, 14, 10, 9, 22   (8)

11-19-83   *Don't Count The Rainy Days*   (Liberty PB-1505)   21, 15, 12, 11, 11, 22, 22, 22, 22   (9)

11-05-83   *A Little Good News*   (Cap. PB-5264)   19, 14, 6, 4, 3, 2, 1, 5, 5, 5, 5, 20   (12)

1-13-84   *Radio Land*   (Liberty B-1523)   26, 22, 18, 18, 17   (5)

1-29-83   *Still Taking Chances*   (Liberty B-1468)   26, 20, 13, 7, 4, 6, 13, 25, 29, 30, 30, 30   (12)

1-12-85   *What She Wants*   (EMI America B-8243)   30, 28, 28, 27, 27, 23, 21, 18, 17, 13, 15, 15, 15   (13)

9-04-82   *What's Forever For*   (Liberty B-1466)   24, 18, 6, 2, 10, 16, 21, 28   (8)

MURRAY, ANNE

2-13-82   *Another Sleepless Night*   (Cap. PA-5083)   16, 10, 5, 4, 3, 2, 3, 13, 20, 29   (10)

8-21-82   *Hey! Baby!*   (Cap. B-5145)   26, 22, 18, 11, 8, 6, 5, 4, 4, 10, 16, 26   (12)

6-29-85   *I Don't Think I'm Ready For You Yet*   (Cap. B-5472)   25, 22, 13, 9, 9, 8, 21   (7)

5-19-84   *Just Another Woman In Love*   (Cap. B-5344)   28, 23, 18, 15, 11, 10, 6, 4, 2, 1, 20   (11)

11-27-82   *Somebody's Always Saying Goodbye*   (Cap. B-5183)   30, 26, 18, 15, 13, 13, 13, 10, 8, 7, 6, 5, 18, 26   (14)

2-23-85   *Time Don't Run Out On Me*   (Cap. B-5436)   29, 24, 23, 19, 18, 18, 18, 6, 5, 3, 3, 5, 20, 21, 26   (15)

MURRAY, ANNE, AND DAVE LOGGINS

10-06-84   *Nobody Loves Me Like You Do*   (Cap. PB-5401)   25, 18, 15, 12, 12, 11, 10, 9, 8, 1, 15   (11)

NELSON, WILLIE (*See also:* MERLE HAGGARD; JULIO IGLESIAS; ROGER MILLER; DOLLY PARTON; WAYLON AND WILLIE)

2-27-82 *Always On My Mind* (Col. 18-02741) 27, 19, 14, 12, 10, 7, 6, 4, 2, 1, 1, 2, 5, 8, 7, 10, 19 (17)

9-01-84 *City Of New Orleans* (Col. 38-04568) 25, 16, 12, 9, 9, 5, 5, 3, 1, 1, 22 (11)

5-18-85 *Forgiving You Was Easy* (Col. 38-04847) 27, 24, 22, 12, 8, 5, 3, 2, 1, 16, 16, 20 (12)

12-11-82 *Last Thing I Needed First Thing This Morning* (Col. 38-03385) 30, 27, 23, 23, 23, 18, 14, 9, 7, 4, 1, 1, 2, 4, 18, 22, 24, 27, 29, 29 (20)

8-21-82 *Let It Be Me* (Col. 18-03073) 29, 23, 19, 15, 12, 10, 8, 7, 5, 3, 5, 11, 18, 27 (14)

4-30-83 *Little Old-Fashioned Karma* (Col. 38-03674) 23, 11, 10, 6, 6, 14, 22, 28 (8)

11-09-85 *Me And Paul* (Col. 38-05597) 24, 24, 24, 16, 16 (5)

7-23-83 *Why Do I Have To Choose* (Col. 38-03965) 23, 18, 11, 11, 7, 5, 5, 4, 3, 3, 15, 29 (12)

2-04-84 *Without A Song* (Col. 38-04262) 25, 21, 18, 16, 14, 14, 22 (7)

NELSON, WILLIE, AND MERLE HAGGARD (*See also:* MERLE HAGGARD)

6-04-83 *Poncho And Lefty* (Epic 34-03842) 21, 14, 10, 8, 5, 5, 2, 1, 9, 20, 20, 20, 26, 30 (14)

NELSON, WILLIE, AND WAYLON JENNINGS (*See also:* WAYLON JENNINGS)

12-03-83 *Take It To The Limit* (Col. 38-04131) 22, 18, 15, 15, 15, 15, 15, 23 (8)

NELSON, WILLIE/KRIS KRISTOFFERSON/JOHNNY CASH/ WAYLON JENNINGS (*See also:* JOHNNY CASH; WAYLON JENNINGS; KRIS KRISTOFFERSON)

11-09-85   *Desperados Waiting For A Train* (Col. 38-05594) 20, 20, 20, 11, 11 (5)

6-22-85   *Highwayman* (Col. 38-04881)   27, 21, 20, 10, 7, 7, 5, 2, 1, 17, 25, 25 (12)

NELSON, WILLIE, AND WEBB PIERCE

10-16-82   *In The Jailhouse Now* (Col. 38-03231)   28, 24, 20, 19 (4)

NEWTON, JUICE

9-18-82   *Break It To Me Gently* (Cap. B-5148)   25, 15, 12, 11, 9, 8, 7, 6, 5, 9, 11, 18 (12)

5-29-82   *Love's Been A Little Bit Hard On Me* (Cap. PB-5120)   30, 21, 16, 14, 11, 9, 7, 6, 9, 18 (10)

10-06-84   *Ride 'Em Cowboy* (Cap. B-5379)   27, 20 (2)

8-24-85   *You Make Me Want To Make You Mine* (RCA PB-14139)   28, 23, 23 (3)

THE NITTY GRITTY DIRT BAND

12-03-83   *Dance Little Jean* (Liberty PB-1507)   23, 19, 17, 11, 11, 11, 11, 11, 23 (9)

2-16-85   *High Horse* (WB 7-29099)   16, 14, 9, 7, 5, 4, 4, 7, 2, 1, 4, 7, 24 (13)

11-30-85   *Home Again In My Heart* (WB 7-28897)   23, 23 (2)

10-27-84   *I Love Only You* (WB 7-29203)   26, 26, 20, 17, 15, 12, 8, 6, 5, 30, 30 (11)

6-30-84   *Long Hard Road* (WB 7-29282)   28, (5), 25, 21, 8, 29, 29 (6)

7-20-85   *Modern Day Romance* (WB 7-29027)   27, 27, 17, 12, 11, 10, 5, 5 (8)

THE OAK RIDGE BOYS

2-26-83   *American Made* (MCA 52179) 25, 19, 17, 12, 5, 5, 4, 3, 3, 24, 25, 25, 28 (13)

2-13-82   *Bobbie Sue* (MCA 51231) 10, 1, 1, 8, 17, 27 (6)

8-04-84   *Everyday* (MCA 51419) 27, 21, 19, 16, 9, 5, 4, 4, 4, 1, 14, 29 (12)

3-31-84   *I Guess It Never Hurts To Hurt Sometimes* (MCA 52342) 27, 23, 19, 15, 14, 12, 25 (7)

8-14-82   *I Wish You Could Have Turned My Head* (MCA 52095) 25, 22, 18, 16, 12, 11, 9, 6, 3, 7, 13, 21, 28 (13)

5-04-85   *Little Things* (MCA 52556) 25, 20, 16, 13, 7, 4, 2, 1, 5, 5, 19, 21, 21, 29 (14)

6-25-83   *Love Song* (MCA 52224) 24, 21, 12, 6, 5, 3, 3, 2, 1, 16, 19, 28 (12)

12-01-84   *Make My Life With You* (MCA 52488) 29, 20, 18, 15, 11, 11, 9, 7, 7, 5, 2, 1, 30 (13)

11-12-83   *Ozark Mountain Jubilee* (MCA 52288) 24, 17, 12, 10, 6, 5, 3, 3, 3, 3, 3, 15 (12)

6-05-82   *So Fine* (MCA 52065) 29, 24, 21, 19, 16, 11, 11, 22 (8)

12-04-82   *Thank God For Kids* (MCA 52145) 27, 22, 18, 15, 15, 15, 11, 7, 12, 22 (10)

8-31-85   *Touch A Hand, Make A Friend* (MCA 52646) 26, 26, 5, 5, 5, 20, 20 (7)

OSMOND, MARIE, WITH DAN SEALS   *(See also:* DAN SEALS)

8-17-85   *Meet Me In Montana* (Cap. B-5478) 29, 23, 19, 19 (4)

PARTON, DOLLY   *(See also:* KENNY ROGERS)

3-02-85   *Don't Call It Love* (RCA PB-13987) 28, 29, 27, 25, 25, 25, 9, 9, 8, 4, 6, 21, 19, 10, 7, 17, 22 (17)

10-13-84   *God Won't Get You* (RCA PB-13883) 25, 21, 16, 16, 15, 15, 13, 9 (8)

6-12-82   *Heartbreak Express*   (RCA PB-13234)   29, 24, 22, 19, 16, 14, 8, 7, 15, 26   (10)

8-28-82   *I Will Always Love You*   (RCA PB-13260)   30, 22, 17, 13, 7, 7, 6, 3, 2, 8, 13, 21   (12)

6-25-83   *Potential New Boyfriend*   (RCA PB-13514)   27, 19, 19, 26, 30   (5)

2-04-84   *Save The Last Dance For Me*   (RCA PB-13703)   27, 22, 16, 13, 11, 7, 3, 3, 15, 25   (10)

2-27-82   *Single Women*   (RCA PB-13057)   15, 10, 7, 4, 1, 1, 3, 3, 5, 15   (10)

6-30-84   *Tennessee Homesick Blues*   (RCA PB-13819)   25, 21, 18, 17, 11, 9, 6, 3, 2, 1, 6, 21, 30, 30   (14)

PARTON, DOLLY, AND WILLIE NELSON   *(See also:* **WILLIE NELSON)**

1-15-83   *Everything's Beautiful*   (Monument WS4-03408)   27, 21, 16, 10, 6, 3, 2, 1, 3, 13, 28, 28, 28   (13)

PARTON, DOLLY, WITH KENNY ROGERS   *(See also:* **KENNY ROGERS)**

6-29-85   *Real Love*   (RCA PB-14058)   26, 23, 14, 10, 10, 7, 3, 3, 1, 11, 11   (11)

PIERCE, WEBB   *(See:* **WILLIE NELSON)**

PINKARD AND BOWDEN

10-20-84   *Mama She's Lazy*   (WB 7-29205)   27, 23, 23, 23   (4)

PRESLEY, ELVIS

3-06-82   *There Goes My Everything*   (RCA PB-13058)   29   (1)

PRICE, RAY   *(See also:* **ROGER MILLER)**

4-24-82   *Forty And Fadin'*   (Dimension DS-1031)   29, 26, 22, 20, 20, 26   (6)

PRIDE, CHARLEY

11-12-83 *Ev'ry Heart Should Have One* (RCA PB-1364) 21, 15, 10, 8, 4, 2, 1, 1, 1, 1, 5, 10, 17, 29 (14)

5-01-82 *I Don't Think She's In Love Anymore* (RCA PB-13096) 28, 18, 14, 12, 7, 6, 5, 4, 3, 2, 1, 4, 7, 15, 28 (15)

2-08-84 *Missin' Mississippi* (RCA PB-13936) 28, 28, 24 (3)

3-26-83 *More And More* (RCA PB-13451) 25, 21, 10, 15, 14, 9, 9, 4, 4, 12, 19, 25, 25, 28 (14)

2-13-82 *Mountain Of Love* (RCA PB-13024) 12, 5, 2, 1, 9, 22, 29 (7)

7-23-83 *Night Games* (RCA PB-13542) 20, 16, 12, 8, 4, 3, 1, 3, 1, 18, 18, 18, 22, 22, 22 (15)

7-07-84 *The Power Of Love* (RCA PB-13821) 28, 27, 26, 21, 21, 18, 17, 17 (8)

1-15-83 *Why Baby Why* (RCA PB-13397) 29, 22, 19, 14, 11, 4, 9, 14, 26, 28 (10)

9-04-82 *You're So Good When You're Bad* (RCA PB-13293) 28, 24, 19, 13, 11, 10, 8, 6, 2, 1, 4, 6, 8, 14, 24 (15)

RABBITT, EDDIE

6-02-84 *B-B-B-Burnin' Up With Love* (WB 7-29279) 27, 25, 18, 17, 12, 10, 8, 6, 3, 5, 30 (11)

11-10-84 *The Best Year Of My Life* (WB 7-29186) 26, 18, 15, 11, 8, 7, 3, 3, 2 (9)

5-01-82 *I Don't Know Where To Start* (Elektra E-47435) 29, 25, 22, 18, 15, 12, 9, 7, 8, 12, 30 (11)

8-17-85 *She's Comin' Back To Say Goodbye* (WB 7-38976) 27, 21, 17, 17 (4)

2-13-82 *Someone Could Lose A Heart Tonight* (Elektra E-47239) 13 (1)

3-16-85 *Warning Sign* (WB 7-29089) 29, 26, 26, 29, 13, 13, 12, 11, 7, 22, 22 (11)

11-09-85 *A World Without Love* (RCA PB-14192) 30, 30, 30, 21, 21 (5)

4-30-83   *You Can't Run From Love*   (WB 7-29712)   17, 17, 12, 10, 9, 5, 5, 4, 4, 13, 17, 24, 29   (13)

10-01-83   *You Put The Beat In My Heart*   (WB 7-29512)   22, 15, 9, 9, 9, 6, 6, 24, 25   (9)

RABBITT, EDDIE, WITH CRYSTAL GAYLE   *(See also:* CRYSTAL GAYLE)

10-09-82   *You And I*   (Elektra 7-69936)   27, 23, 19, 13, 5, 3, 1, 1, 1, 3, 4, 8, 8, 8, 8, 16, 23   (17)

RAVEN, EDDY

8-04-84   *I Could Use Another You*   (RCA PB-13839)   26, 22, 20, 19, 13, 11, 8, 7, 7, 8, 30   (11)

4-07-84   *I Got Mexico*   (RCA PB-13746)   28, 18, 14, 13, 11, 10, 7, 5, 3, 2, 1, 9   (12)

8-31-85   *I Wanna Hear It From You*   (RCA PB-14164)   29, 29, 17, 17, 17   ( )

2-20-82   *A Little Bit Crazy*   (Elektra E-47413)   30, 28, 27, 26   (4)

6-08-85   *Operator, Operator*   (RCA PB-14044)   28, 15, 14, 12, 11, 23, 30, 30   (8)

12-08-84   *She's Gonna Win Your Heart*   (RCA PB-13939)   25, 24, 17, 13, 13, 11, 9, 9, 7, 5   (10)

REED, JERRY   *(See also:* WAYLON JENNINGS)

10-23-82   *The Bird*   (RCA PB-13355)   27, 17, 12, 6, 3, 2, 2, 1, 1, 9, 9, 9, 19, 28   (14)

2-12-83   *Down On The Corner*   (RCA PB-13422)   29, 22, 17, 13, 10, 10, 10, 9, 8, 8, 27, 29   (12)

7-09-83   *Good Ole Boys*   (RCA PB-13527)   28, 19, 16, 14, 14, 19, 27, 30   (8)

7-24-82   *She Got The Goldmine*   (RCA PB-13268)   27, 23, 14, 11, 8, 5, 2, 1, 1, 1, 4, 9, 16, 23   (14)

RESTLESS HEART

7-20-85 *I Want Everyone To Cry* (RCA PB-14086) 24, 24, 15, 10, 9, 9, 15, 15 (8)

3-02-85 *Let The Heartache Ride* (RCA PB-13969) 29, 30, 28, 27, 27, 30 (6)

ROBBINS, MARTY

1-22-83 *Honkytonk Man* (WB 7-29847) 26, 21, 17, 14, 13, 12, 17, 29, 29, 26, 29 (11)

10-09-82 *Tie Your Dream To Mine* (Col. 18-03236) 26, 24, 20, 18, 17, 28 (6)

ROCKIN' SIDNEY

8-03-85 *My Toot-Toot* (Epic 34-05430) 25, 13, 13, 13, 30, 30 (6)

RODRIGUEZ, JOHNNY

11-26-83 *Back On Her Mind* (Epic 34-04026) 27, 21, 17, 14, 10, 10, 10, 10, 10, 19 (10)

5-21-83 *Foolin'* (Epic 34-03598) 27, 20, 20, 24, 24, 26 (6)

9-03-83 *How Could I Love Her So Much* (Epic 34-03972) 20, 17, 10, 8, 8, 22, 25, 25, 25, 30 (10)

6-23-84 *Let's Leave The Lights On Tonight* (Epic 34-04460) 29 (1)

ROGERS, KENNY (*See also:* DOTTIE WEST)

5-28-83 *All My Life* (Liberty PB-1495) 26, 22, 16, 14, 14, 10, 10, 21, 27 (9)

2-04-84 *Buried Treasure* (RCA PB-13713) 21, 16, 11, 7, 6, 4, 2, 2, 6, 16 (10)

1-19-85 *Crazy* (RCA PB-13975) 30, 30, 29, 28, 22, 19, 15, 13, 10, 7, 7, 6, 19, 24, 25, 30 (16)

7-28-84 *Evening Star* (RCA PB-13832) 29, 24, 20, 18, 18, 12, 12, 11, 28, 28 (10)

5-12-84   *Eyes That See In The Dark*   (RCA PB-13774)   29, 21, 20   (3)

10-23-82   *A Love Song*   (Liberty PB-1485)   29, 25, 21, 16, 13, 12, 9, 6, 3, 1, 1, 1, 4, 9, 17, 25   (16)

7-17-82   *Love Will Turn You Around*   (Liberty PB-1471)   25, 17, 11, 6, 3, 2, 2, 1, 2, 14, 23, 27   (12)

11-09-85   *Morning Desire*   (RCA PB-14194)   29, 29, 29, 19, 19   (5)

9-10-83   *Scarlet Fever*   (Liberty PB-1503)   21, 15, 11, 7, 2, 2, 2, 2, 15, 30   (10)

2-13-82   *Through The Years*   (Liberty PA-1444)   7, 4, 27   (3)

1-21-84   *You Were A Good Friend*   (Liberty PB-1511)   18, 14, 14, 30   (4)

ROGERS, KENNY, AND SHEENA EASTON

2-05-83   *We've Got Tonight*   (Liberty PB-1492)   24, 17, 12, 10, 7, 6, 3, 1, 2, 2, 18, 20, 25, 26, 29   (15)

ROGERS, KENNY, AND DOLLY PARTON   (*See also:* DOLLY PARTON)

9-10-83   *Islands In The Stream*   (RCA PB-13615)   26, 20, 14, 12, 8, 3, 3, 3, 1, 1, 9, 17, 20, 30   (14)

ROGERS, KENNY, AND DOTTIE WEST   (*See also:* DOTTIE WEST)

5-05-84   *Together Again*   (Liberty PB-1516)   29, 24, 20   (3)

THE ROVERS

3-13-82   *Pain In My Past*   (Cleveland International 14-02601)   29, 25, 23   (3)

SAWYER BROWN

11-09-85   *Betty's Bein' Bad*   (Cap. B-5517)   27, 27, 27, 18, 18   (5)

12-08-84   *Leona*   (Cap. B-5403)   30, 30, 21, 21, 21   (5)

3-16-85   *Step That Step* (Cap. B-5446)   24, 21, 21, 21, 12, 12, 11, 6, 4, 1, 3, 13, 21, 27 (14)

7-20-85   *Used To Blue* (Cap. B-5477)   25, 25, 16, 11, 10, 7, 4, 4 (8)

SCHNEIDER, JOHN

2-02-85   *Country Girls* (MCA 52492)   26, 22, 20, 17, 14, 12, 9, 8, 8, 8, 22, 30 (12)

9-01-84   *I've Been Around Enough To Know* (MCA 52407)   26, 20, 18, 16, 16, 11, 8, 6, 3, 3, 2, 1 (12)

6-08-85   *It's A Short Walk From Heaven To Hell* (MCA 52567)   30, 16, 15, 11, 10, 5, 18, 18, 22 (9)

SCRUGGS, EARL (*See:* TOM T. HALL)

SEALS, DAN (*See also:* MARIE OSMOND)

4-14-84   *God Must Be A Country* (Liberty PB-1515)   28, 25, 23, 21, 20 (5)

12-22-84   *My Baby's Got Good Timing* (EMI America B-8245)   27, 19, 19, 17, 15, 15, 13, 11, 7, 5, 2, 1 (12)

5-18-85   *My Old Yellow Car* (EMI America B-8261)   26, 23, 21, 11, 7, 21, 30 (7)

8-25-84   *The Wild Side Of Me* (EMI America B-8220)   29, 21, 18, 16, 13, 13, 12, 9, 9 (9)

SHEPPARD, T.G.

11-09-85   *Doncha* (Col. 38-05591)   19, 19, 19, 10, 10 (5)

4-10-82   *Finally* (WB WBS-50041)   24, 20, 16, 13, 6, 5, 1, 1, 3, 7, 12, 21 (12)

7-13-85   *Fooled Around And Fell In Love* (Curb 38-04890)   28 (1)

12-08-84   *One Owner Heart* (WB 7-29167)   24, 23, 18, 14, 14, 12, 10, 10, 8, 4, 3, 4 (12)

2-13-82   *Only One You* (Warner WBS-49858)   9 (1)

6-30-84   *Somewhere Down The Line* (WB 7-29369)   29, 24, 24, 23, 17, 15, 11, 6, 15 (9)

9-04-82   *War Is Hell*   (WB 7-29934)   30, 26, 22, 18, 16, 14, 12, 7, 4, 3, 2, 2, 4, 7, 16, 26   (16)

5-28-83   *Without You*   (WB 7-29695)   22, 18, 13, 13, 17, 17, 26   (7)

4-13-85   *You're Going Out Of My Mind*   (WB 7-29071)   25, 17, 16, 15, 11, 5, 4, 14, 22, 28   (10)

SHEPPARD, T.G., AND KAREN BROOKS

1-15-83   *Faking Love*   (WB 7-29854)   21, 11, 5, 2, 1, 15, 23, 29   (8)

SKAGGS, RICKY

4-20-85   *Country Boy*   (Epic 34-04831)   27, 23, 22, 19, 15, 12, 6, 2, 1, 12, 22, 28   (12)

2-20-82   *Crying My Heart Out Over You*   (Epic 14-02692)   22, 19, 14, 11, 7, 6, 5, 4, 13, 18   (10)

12-17-83   *Don't Cheat In Our Hometown*   (Epic 34-04245)   25, 19, 19, 19, 19, 15, 5, 4, 2, 1, 9, 21   (12)

9-18-82   *Heartbroke*   (Epic 14-03212)   27, 21, 14, 12, 11, 9, 6, 2, 1, 4, 7, 10, 20, 30   (14)

5-21-83   *Highway 40 Blues*   (Epic 34-03812)   22, 19, 13, 10, 8, 5, 3, 1, 10, 18, 24, 24, 28   (13)

4-07-84   *Honey*   (Epic 34-04394)   27, 17, 13, 10, 8, 5, 3, 1, 6   (9)

6-26-82   *I Don't Care*   (Epic 14-02931)   25, 21, 17, 12, 6, 2, 1, 5, 10, 21   (10)

12-25-82   *I Wouldn't Change You If I Could*   (Epic 34-03482)   27, 27, 27, 22, 17, 14, 12, 10, 9, 7, 4, 1, 2, 6, 19, 22, 22   (17)

11-24-84   *Something In My Heart*   (Epic 34-04668)   29, 19, 16, 14, 12, 9, 9, 7, 5, 5, 4, 1, 6   (13)

11-09-85   *Too Much On My Heart*   (Mer. 884 016-7)   4, 4, 4, 2, 2   (5)

8-11-84   *Uncle Pen*   (Epic 34-04527)   26, 22, 20, 14, 8, 5, 5, 5, 2, 2, 16, 30, 30   (13)

11-09-85   *You Make Me Feel Like A Man*   (Epic 34-05585)   16, 16, 16, 13, 13   (5)

9-17-83   *You've Got A Lover*   (Epic 34-04044)   26, 16, 14, 9, 8, 8, 8, 3, 3, 14, 21, 29   (12)

SPACEK, SISSY

2-04-84   *If I Can Just Get Through The Night*   (Atl. America 7-99801)   30, 26, 21, 18, 15, 13, 13, 30   (8)

11-05-83   *Lonely But Only For You*   (Atl. America 7-99847)   23, 18, 13, 13, 18, 27   (6)

STAMPLEY, JOE   (*See also:* MOE BANDY)

3-17-84   *Brown-Eyed Girl*   (Epic 34-04366)   28, 22, 18, 18   (4)

1-21-84   *Double Shot*   (Epic 34-04173)   19, 8, 8, 14, 27   (5)

3-05-83   *Finding You*   (Epic 34-03558)   28, 24, 23, 24, 25, 25, 25   (7)

3-27-82   *I'm Goin' Hurtin'*   (Epic 14-02791)   28, 24, 22, 19, 17, 16, 16   (7)

THE STATLER BROTHERS/THE STATLERS

5-12-84   *Atlanta Blue*   (Mer. 818 700-7)   30, 23, 18, 14, 13, 8, 8, 5, 3, 3, 2, 14   (12)

1-28-84   *Elizabeth*   (Mer. 814 881-7)   21, 15, 10, 8, 5, 4, 2, 4, 8, 28   (10)

10-08-83   *Guilty*   (Mer. 812 988-7)   21, 13, 13, 13, 12, 12   (6)

6-01-85   *Hello Mary Lou*   (Mer. 880 685-7)   28, 17, 13, 10, 7, 4, 3, 3, 3, 19, 24   (11)

12-29-84   *My Only Love*   (Mer. 880 411-7)   26, 26, 22, 17, 17, 15, 13, 9, 6, 3, 2, 25   (12)

5-14-83   *Oh Baby Mine*   (Mer. 811 488-7)   22, 18, 18, 12, 9, 9, 7, 6, 3, 3, 14, 22, 27, 30   (14)

9-22-84   *One Takes The Blame*   (Mer. 880 130-7)   26, 26, 21, 15, 12, 14, 14, 14, 13   (9)

7-10-82   *Whatever*   (Mer. SR 76162)   27, 24, 20, 16, 13, 10, 9, 7, 6, 4, 7, 20, 24   (13)

3-27-82   *You'll Be Back*   (Mer. SR 76142)   27, 22, 18, 15, 13, 10, 9, 7, 6, 6, 11, 18, 27   (13)

STEGALL, KEITH

4-27-85   *California*   (Epic 34-04771)   29, 27, 22, 24, 29   (5)

6-16-84   *I Want To Go Somewhere*   (Epic 34-04442)   28, 25, 23   (3)

8-10-85   *Pretty Lady*   (Epic 34-04934)   30, 25   (2)

11-17-84   *Whatever Turns You On*   (Epic 34-04590)   28, 24, 21   (3)

STEVENS, RAY

1-12-85   *Mississippi Squirrel Revival*   (MCA 52492)   28, 26, 26, 24, 23   (5)

STEWART, GARY, AND DEAN DILLON

5-01-82   *Brotherly Love*   (RCA PB-13049)   30, 28, 28   (3)

STRAIT, GEORGE

3-12-83   *Amarillo By Morning*   (MCA 52162)   27, 21, 15, 14, 14, 14, 13, 7, 7, 28, 30   (11)

11-09-85   *The Chair*   (MCA 52667)   18, 18, 18, 6, 6   (5)

3-02-85   *The Cowboy Rides Away*   (MCA 52526)   27, 27, 23, 23, 23, 23, 8, 8, 7, 10, 27   (11)

10-13-84   *Does Fort Worth Ever Cross Your Mind*   (MCA 52458)   23, 19, 9, 9, 7, 5, 3, 3, 2, 2, 2, 1, 1, 1   (14)

9-06-83   *A Fire I Can't Put Out*   (MCA 52225)   23, 15, 10, 7, 4, 15, 24, 27, 27   (9)

6-29-85   *The Fireman*   (MCA 52586)   28, 24, 15, 11, 11, 9, 5, 5, 5, 13, 13   (11)

7-10-82   *Fool Hearted Memory*   (MCA 52066)   25, 21, 16, 12, 10, 8, 7, 4, 4, 22   (10)

2-27-82   *If You're Thinking You Want A Stranger*   (MCA 51228)   23, 21, 19, 19, 14, 12, 11, 10, 7, 4, 10, 13, 16, 23   (14)

6-23-84   *Let's Fall To Pieces Together*   (MCA 52392)   26, 17, 15, 10, 9, 6, 6, 4, 2, 1, 2, 22, 27   (13)

11-20-82 *Marina Del Rey* (MCA 52120) 29, 27, 25, 23, 16, 14, 14, 14, 13, 23 (10)

3-10-84 *Right Or Wrong* (MCA 52337) 25, 19, 12, 8, 5, 3, 1, 1, 15, 26 (10)

11-12-83 *You Look So Good In Love* (MCA 52279) 23, 16, 11, 9, 5, 4, 2, 2, 2, 2, 1, 7, 9, 20 (14)

SYLVIA

10-15-83 *The Boy Gets Around* (RCA PB-13589) 23, 23, 23, 16, 11, 11, 19, 24 (8)

8-17-85 *Cry Just A Little Bit* (RCA PB-14107) 30, 24, 21, 21 (4)

3-23-85 *Fallin' In Love* (RCA PB-13997) 28, 28, (1), 14, 14, 13, 12, 8, 2, 2, 1, 9, 19, 24 (13)

1-21-84 *I Never Quite Got Back* (RCA PB-13689) 28, 17, 13, 9, 7, 3, 2, 3, 5, 15 (10)

11-13-82 *Like Nothing Ever Happened* (RCA PB-13330) 30, 24, 20, 16, 12, 8, 4, 4, 4, 2, 1, 3, 5, 21, 27 (15)

6-19-82 *Nobody* (RCA PB-13223) 29, 26, 17, 14, 10, 5, 4, 2, 1, 3, 8, 20, 30 (13)

6-04-83 *Snapshot* (RCA PB-13501) 27, 19, 15, 10, 7, 6, 4, 4, 11, 22, 24, 29 (12)

5-05-84 *Victims Of Goodbye* (RCA PB-13755) 30, 23, 17, 17, 15, 16 (6)

THOMAS, B.J. *(See also:* **RAY CHARLES)**

12-15-84 *The Girl Most Likely To* (Cleveland International 38-04608) 27, 23 (2)

9-03-83 *New Looks From An Old Lover* (Cleveland International 38-03985) 21, 13, 9, 7, 4, 4, 14, 14, 14, 18, 27, 29 (12)

1-21-84 *Two Car Garage* (Col. 38-04237) 30, 20, 12, 8, 4, 4, 16 (7)

4-09-83 *Whatever Happened To Old-Fashioned Love* (Cleveland International 38-03492) 23, 17, 10, 4, 1, 2, 2, 1, 9, 21, 26, 29 (12)

5-19-84 *The Whole World's In Love When You're Lonely* (Cleveland International 38-04431) 30, 25, 20, 17, 13, 13, 13 (7)

TILLIS, MEL

6-04-83   *In The Middle Of The Night*   (MCA 52182)   26, 26, 21, 20, 20, 27, 29   (7)

3-13-82   *It's A Long Way To Daytona*   (Elektra E-47412)   27, 24, 24, 23, 30   (5)

5-19-84   *New Patches*   (MCA 52373)   29, 24, 19, 19   (4)

11-13-82   *Stay A Little Longer*   (Elektra 7-69963)   23, 20, 18, 17, 21   (5)

TOMPALL AND THE GLASERS

2-20-82   *It'll Be Her*   (Elektra E-47405)   24, 30, 28, 25, 23   (5)

TUCKER, TANYA

9-17-83   *Baby I'm Yours*   (Arista AS1-9046)   23, 23   (2)

2-12-83   *Feels Right*   (Arista AS 0677)   30, 28, 27, 26, 25, 20, 18, 15, 11, 19, 23   (11)

TWITTY, CONWAY

12-01-84   *Ain't She Somethin' Else*   (WB 7-29137)   30, 23, 21, 16, 12, 12, 10, 8, 8, 6, 3, 2   (12)

8-10-85   *Between Blue Eyes And Jeans*   (WB 7-28966)   26, 16, 14, 8, 8   (5)

2-20-82   *The Clown*   (Elektra E-47302)   9, 4, 2, 1, 10, 21, 21, 29   (8)

4-06-85   *Don't Call Him A Cowboy*   (WB 7-29057)   26, 29, 21, 20, 19, 14, 11, 8, 2, 8, 18, 23   (12)

8-18-84   *I Don't Know A Thing About Love*   (WB 7-29227)   27, 23, 17, 13, 10, 8, 8, 4, 3, 2, 25, 25   (12)

7-09-83   *Lost In The Feeling*   (WB 7-29636)   24, 14, 8, 5, 4, 3, 2, 2, 13, 29   (10)

2-13-82   *Red Neckin' Love Makin' Night*   (MCA 51199)   1   (1)

1-22-83   *The Rose*   (Elektra 7-69854)   25, 20, 16, 12, 10, 8, 5, 2, 9, 17, 23, 26, 28   (13)

4-24-82 *Slow Hand* (Elektra E-47443) 27, 24, 21, 16, 13, 9, 5, 3, 2, 2, 3, 8, 17, 30 (14)

5-26-84 *Somebody's Needin' Somebody* (WB 7-29308) 26, 24, 22, 16, 15, 9, 7, 20, 19, 30 (10)

9-18-82 *We Did But Now You Don't* (Elektra 7-69964) 28, 26, 23, 19, 14, 12, 10, 7, 7, 5, 3, 3, 8, 21, 30, 30, 30 (17)

WARINER, STEVE

6-01-85 *Heart Trouble* (MCA 52562) 29, 18, 14, 11, 9, 9, 22, 29, 29 (9)

4-03-82 *Kansas City Lights* (RCA PB-13072) 29, 28, 27, 26, 25, 27, 27, 28 (8)

1-28-84 *Lonely Women Make Good Lovers* (RCA PB-13691) 22, 16, 12, 10, 6, 5, 5, 9, 20 (9)

8-31-85 *Some Fools Never Learn* (MCA 52644) 27, 27, 3, 3, 3, 12, 12 (7)

1-19-85 *What I Didn't Do* (MCA 52506) 29, 29, 28, 29, 27, 23, 21, 20, 16, 13, 13, 13, 24 (13)

4-28-84 *Why Goodbye* (RCA PB-13768) 25, 22, 16, 12, 10, 8, 8, 5, 5 (9)

WATSON, GENE

8-03-85 *Cold Summer Day In Georgia* (Epic 34-05407) 30, 17, 15, 18 (4)

1-21-84 *Drinkin' My Way Back Home* (MCA 52309) 21, 13, 7, 5, 9, 25 (6)

5-12-84 *Forever Again* (MCA 52356) 28, 22 (2)

11-24-84 *Got No Reason Now For Goin' Home* (MCA 52457) 30, 28, 29, 29, 22, 17, 17, 15, 13, 13 (10)

9-03-83 *Sometimes I Get Lucky And Forget* (MCA 52243) 26, 20, 14, 10, 10, 14, 19, 19, 19, 26, 29 (11)

2-27-82 *Speak Softly* (MCA 52009) 29, 24, 21, 20, 15, 14, 12, 11, 11, 11, 20, 19, 25 (13)

7-24-82 *This Dream's On Me* (MCA 52074) 26, 20, 19, 16, 14, 12, 11, 10, 23, 30 (10)

11-20-82   *What She Don't Know Won't Hurt Her* (MCA 52131)   28, 24, 22, 15, 13, 12, 12, 12, 9, 6, 6, 13, 25, 30 (14)

4-23-83   *You're Out Doing What I'm Here Doing Without* (MCA 52191)   17, 14, 13, 13, 12, 10, 6, 6, 19, 21, 29 (11)

WAYLON   (*See:* WAYLON JENNINGS)

WAYLON AND WILLIE   (*See also:* WAYLON JENNINGS; WILLIE NELSON)

10-23-82   *(Sittin' On) The Dock Of The Bay* (RCA PB-13319)   30, 26, 22, 15, 11, 10, 8, 7, 5, 3, 3, 3, 6, 13, 22 (15)

3-20-82   *Just To Satisfy You* (RCA PB-13073)   26, 13, 10, 8, 6, 4, 3, 2, 1, 3, 4, 10, 15, 25 (14)

WEST, DOTTIE   (*See also:* KENNY ROGERS)

10-16-82   *She Can't Get My Love Off The Bed* (Liberty PB-1479)   27, 21, 29 (3)

2-20-82   *You're Not Easy To Forget* (Liberty PB-1451)   27, 25, 23, 18, 17, 17, 16, 16, 24 (9)

WEST, SHELLY   (*See also:* DAVID FRIZZELL)

8-13-83   *Flight 309 To Tennessee* (WB 7-29659)   33, 14, 10, 9, 7, 5, 5, 16, 16, 28, 28, 28 (12)

3-05-83   *Jose Cuervo* (WB 7-29778)   27, 22, 22, 16, 11, 10, 6, 1, 2, 2, 15, 13, 23, 23, 27, 27, 30 (17)

3-02-85   *Now There's You* (Viva 7-29106)   19, 18, 14, 12, 12, 12, 23, 28, 28 (9)

7-14-84   *Somebody Buy This Cowgirl A Beer* (Viva 7-29265)   30, 30 (2)

THE WHITES

6-09-84   *Forever You* (MCA 52381)   27, 21, 10, 16, 14, 13, 13, 26 (8)

3-19-83   *Hangin' Around* (Elektra 7-69855)   24, 19, 16, 16 (4)

8-10-85   *Hometown Gossip* (MCA 52615)   27, 17, 19 (3)

7-02-83   *I Wonder Who's Holding My Baby Tonight*   (WB 7-29659)   28, 21, 13, 10, 10, 25, 25, 26 29   (9)

4-13-85   *If It Ain't Love*   (MCA 52535)   26, 18, 17, 16, 12, 10, 7, 17, 25   (9)

9-22-84   *Pins And Needles*   (MCA 52432)   23, 23, 17, 28   (4)

10-02-82   *You Put The Blue In Me*   (Elektra 7-69982)   30, 28   (2)

WILLIAMS, DON

12-25-82   *If Hollywood Don't Need You*   (MCA 52152)   25, 25, 25, 20, 15, 13, 11, 9, 6, 3, 3, 8, 30   (13)

11-30-85   *It's Time For Love*   (MCA 52632)   30, 30   (2)

4-24-82   *Listen To The Radio*   (MCA 52037)   22, 18, 12, 10, 7, 5, 4, 2, 1, 4, 7, 15   (12)

5-21-83   *Love Is On A Roll*   (MCA 52205)   25, 16, 10, 8, 6, 2, 1, 13, 18, 26, 30   (11)

9-22-84   *Maggie's Dream*   (MCA 52448)   24, 24, 19, 13, 11, 7, 7, 6, 6, 11   (10)

8-28-82   *Mistakes*   (MCA 52097)   25, 21, 19, 17, 16, 19, 18, 25   (8)

8-27-83   *Nobody But You*   (MCA 52245)   24, 14, 14, 8, 6, 6, 7, 7, 7, 7, 17, 26, 28, 29   (14)

12-17-83   *Stay Young*   (MCA 52310)   26, 20, 20, 20, 20, 16, 6, 5, 4, 3, 2, 3, 19   (13)

6-02-84   *That's The Thing About Love*   (MCA 52389)   21, 18, 12, 11, 7, 5, 4, 3, 2, 2, 3   (11)

2-02-85   *Walkin' A Broken Heart*   (MCA 52514)   30, 25, 24, 20, 17, 16, 12, 10, 10, 10, 17, 23, 24   (13)

WILLIAMS, HANK, JR.   (*See also:* RAY CHARLES)

11-10-84   *All My Rowdy Friends Are Coming Over*   (WB 7-29184)   30, 27, 22, 20, 18, 17   (6)

10-16-82   *The American Dream*   (Elektra 7-69960)   30, 26, 23, 20, 14, 10, 9, 6, 5, 17, 26, 26, 26   (13)

7-07-84   *Attitude Adjustment*   (WB 7-29253)   27, 26, 25, 19, 11, 8, 4, 3, 11, 27   (10)

2-13-82   *A Country Boy Can Survive*   (Elektra/Curb E-47257)   22, 17, 14, 13, 10, 8, 18, 25   (8)

1-29-83   *Gonna Go Huntin' Tonight*   (Elektra 7-69846)   29, 26, 19, 17, 14, 12, 11, 11, 11, 10, 9, 9, 19, 28, 28, 27, 29, 29   (18)

6-05-82   *Honky Tonkin'*   (Elektra/Curb E-47462)   26, 22, 17, 14, 11, 6, 3, 2, 1, 3, 9, 13, 24   (13)

6-15-85   *I'm For Love*   (WB 7-29022)   24, 20, 18, 17, 8, 5, 5, 4, 1, 20   (10)

7-09-83   *Leave Them Boys Alone*   (WB 7-29633)   23, 15, 11, 8, 6, 6, 6, 20   (8)

2-16-85   *Major Moves*   (WB 7-29095)   8, 7, 4, 4, 2, 2, 2, 2, 7, 7, 6, 9, 26   (13)

11-09-85   *This Ain't Dallas*   (WB 7-28912)   10, 10, 10   (3)

WILLOUGHBY, LARRY

2-11-84   *Building Bridges*   (Atl. America 7-99801)   27, 22, 20, 17, 15, 15   (6)

WILLS, DAVID

9-03-83   *The Eyes Of A Stranger*   (RCA PB-13541)   23, 23, 22, 22   (4)

4-14-84   *Lady In Waiting*   (RCA PB-13737)   29, 29   (2)

12-17-83   *Miss Understanding*   (RCA PB-13653)   28, 26, 26, 26, 26, 26   (6)

WINSLOW, STEPHANIE

5-26-84   *Baby, Come To Me*   (MCA 52372)   30, 30, 30   (3)

2-25-84   *Dancin' With The Devil*   (MCA 52327)   30, 28, 28   (3)

11-05-83   *Kiss My Darling*   (MCA 52291)   25, 20, 10, 9, 7, 7, 20   (7)

THE WRIGHT BROTHERS

5-26-84   *Southern Women*   (Mer. 818 653-7)   29, 29, 29   (3)

WYNETTE, TAMMY

4-17-82 *Another Chance* (Epic 14-02770)   26, 24, 23, 23, 21, 19, 18, 16, 14, 13, 13, 22 (12)

THE YOUNGER BROTHERS

8-07-82 *Nothing But The Radio On* (MCA 52076)   29, 27, 27, 26 (4)

F. SONG-TITLE INDEX—COUNTRY

After All (Ed Bruce)
After The Love Slips Away (Earl Thomas Conley)
Ain't No Money (Rosanne Cash)
Ain't No Trick (Lee Greenwood)
Ain't She Somethin' Else (Conway Twitty)
The Air That I Breathe (Rex Allen, Jr.)
All My Life (Kenny Rogers)
All My Rowdy Friends Are Coming Over (Hank Williams, Jr.)
All Tangled Up In Love (Gus Hardin)
Always On My Mind (Willie Nelson)
Amarillo By Morning (George Strait)
America (Waylon Jennings)
The American Dream (Hank Williams, Jr.)
American Made (The Oak Ridge Boys)
Angel In Disguise (Earl Thomas Conley)
Angel In Your Arms (Barbara Mandrell)
Another Chance (Tammy Wynette)
Another Honky-Tonk Night On Broadway (David Frizzell and Shelly West)
Another Sleepless Night (Anne Murray)
Any Day Now (Ronnie Milsap)
Anybody Else's Heart But Mine (Terri Gibbs)
Are The Good Times Really Over (Merle Haggard)
As Long As I'm Rockin' With You (John Conlee)

Atlanta Blue (The Statlers)
Atlanta Burned Again Last Night (Atlanta)
Attitude Adjustment (Hank Williams, Jr.)

B-B-B-Burnin' Up With Love (Eddie Rabbitt)
Baby Bye Bye (Gary Morris)
Baby, Come To Me (Stephanie Winslow)
Baby I Lied (Deborah Allen)
Baby I'm Yours (Tanya Tucker)
Baby, What About You (Crystal Gayle)
Baby's Got Her Blue Jeans On (Mel McDaniel)
Back On Her Mind (Johnny Rodriguez)
Bad News (Boxcar Willie)
Bad Night For Good Girls (Jan Gray)
Band Of Gold (Charly McClain)
Be There For Me Baby (Johnny Lee)
The Beer Drinkin' Song (Mac Davis)
The Best Year Of My Life (Eddie Rabbitt)
Better Our Hearts Should Bend (Bandana)
Betty's Bein' Bad (Sawyer Brown)
Between Blue Eyes And Jeans (Conway Twitty)
Big City (Merle Haggard)
Big Ole Brew (Mel McDaniel)

The Bird (Jerry Reed)
Black Sheep (John Anderson)
Blue Highway (John Conlee)
Blue Moon With Heartache (Rosanne Cash)
Bobbie Sue (The Oak Ridge Boys)
Born To Run (Emmylou Harris)
The Boy Gets Around (Sylvia)
Break Away (Gail Davies)
Break It To Me Gently (Juice Newton)
Breakin' Down (Waylon Jennings)
Breaking It (Loretta Lynn)
Brotherly Love (Gary Stewart and Dean Dillon)
Brown-Eyed Girl (Joe Stampley)
Building Bridges (Larry Willoughby)
Buried Treasure (Kenny Rogers)
Busted (John Conlee)

C.C. Waterback (George Jones and Merle Haggard)
California (Keith Stegall)
Candy Man (Mickey Gilley and Charly McClain)
Can't Even Get The Blues (Reba McEntire)
Can't Keep A Good Man Down (Alabama)
Carolina In The Pines (Michael Martin Murphey)
The Chair (George Strait)
Chance Of Lovin' You (Earl Thomas Conley)
Cheater's Prayer (The Kendalls)
Cherokee Fiddle (Johnny Lee)
Christmas In Dixie (Alabama)
City Of New Orleans (Willie Nelson)
Close Enough To Perfect (Alabama)
The Closer You Get (Alabama)
The Clown (Conway Twitty)
Cold Summer Day In Georgia (Gene Watson)
Common Man (John Conlee)
The Conversation (Waylon Jennings)
Country Boy (Ricky Skaggs)
A Country Boy Can Survive (Hank Williams, Jr.)
Country Girls (John Schneider)

The Cowboy Rides Away (George Strait)
Crazy (Kenny Rogers)
Crazy For Your Love (Exile)
Crossword Puzzle (Barbara Mandrell)
Cry Just A Little Bit (Sylvia)
Crying My Heart Out Over You (Ricky Skaggs)

Dance Little Jean (The Nitty Gritty Dirt Band)
Dancin' With The Devil (Stephanie Winslow)
Dancing Your Memory Away (Charly McClain)
Day By Day (McGuffey Lane)
Dealing With The Devil (Merle Haggard)
Denver (Larry Gatlin and The Gatlin Brothers Band)
Desperados Waiting For A Train (Willie Nelson/Kris Kristofferson/ Johnny Cash/Waylon Jennings)
Diamond In The Dust (Mark Gray)
Disenchanted (Michael Murphey)
Dixie Road (Lee Greenwood)
Dixieland Delight (Alabama)
Do Me With Love (Janie Fricke)
(Sittin' On) The Dock Of The Bay (Waylon and Willie)
Does Fort Worth Ever Cross Your Mind (George Strait)
Don't Call Him A Cowboy (Conway Twitty)
Don't Call It Love (Dolly Parton)
Don't Cheat In Our Hometown (Ricky Skaggs)
Don't Count The Rainy Days (Michael Murphey)
Don't Look Back (Gary Morris)
Don't Make It Easy For Me (Earl Thomas Conley)
Don't Worry 'Bout Me Baby (Janie Fricke)
Don't You Know How Much I Love You (Ronnie Milsap)
Doncha (T.G. Sheppard)
Double Shot (Joe Stampley)

Down On The Corner (Jerry Reed)
Dream Baby (Lacy J. Dalton)
Drinkin' And Dreamin' (Waylon Jennings)
Drinkin' My Way Back Home (Gene Watson)

Forgiving You Was Easy (Willie Nelson)
Forty And Fadin' (Ray Price)
Forty Hour Week (For A Livin') (Alabama)
Four Wheel Drive (The Kendalls)

Elizabeth (The Statler Brothers)
Evening Star (Kenny Rogers)
Ev'ry Heart Should Have One (Charley Pride)
Everyday (The Oak Ridge Boys)
Everything's Beautiful (Dolly Parton and Willie Nelson)
Everytime You Cross My Mind (You Break My Heart) (Razzy Bailey)
Eye Of A Hurricane (John Anderson)
The Eyes Of A Stranger (David Wills)
Eyes That See In The Dark (Kenny Rogers)

Faithless Love (Glen Campbell)
Faking Love (T.G. Sheppard And Karen Brooks)
Fallin' In Love (Sylvia)
Feels Right (Tanya Tucker)
Finally (T.G. Sheppard)
Finding You (Joe Stampley)
A Fire I Can't Put Out (George Strait)
Fire In The Night (Alabama)
The Fireman (George Strait)
The First Word In Memory Is Me (Janie Fricke)
Flight 309 To Tennessee (Shelly West)
Fool For Your Love (Mickey Gilley)
Fool Hearted Memory (George Strait)
Fooled Around And Fell In Love (T.G. Sheppard)
Foolin' (Johnny Rodriguez)
Fool's Gold (Lee Greenwood)
For All The Wrong Reasons (The Bellamy Brothers)
Forever Again (Gene Watson)
Forever You (The Whites)
Forget About Me (The Bellamy Brothers)

Get Into Reggae Cowboy (The Bellamy Brothers)
The Girl Most Likely To (B.J. Thomas)
Girls' Night Out (The Judds)
Give Me One More Chance (Exile)
God Bless The U.S.A. (Lee Greenwood)
God Must Be A Cowboy (Dan Seals)
God Won't Get You (Dolly Parton)
Goin' Downhill (John Anderson)
Going, Going, Gone (Lee Greenwood)
Going Where The Lonely Go (Merle Haggard)
Gonna Go Huntin' Tonight (Hank Williams, Jr.)
Good Ole Boys (Jerry Reed)
Goodbye Heartache (Louise Mandrell)
Got No Reason Now For Goin' Home (Gene Watson)
Guilty (The Statler Brothers)

Had A Dream (The Judds)
Hallelujah, I Love You So (George Jones with Brenda Lee)
Hang On To Your Heart (Exile)
Hangin' Around (The Whites)
Happy Birthday Dear Heartache (Barbara Mandrell)
Have I Got A Deal For You (Reba McEntire)
Have Mercy (The Judds)
Have You Loved Your Woman Today (Craig Dillingham)
He Broke Your Mem'ry Last Night (Reba McEntire)
He Got You (Ronnie Milsap)
He Won't Give In (Kathy Mattea)
He's A Heartache (Janie Fricke)
Heart Don't Do This To Me (Loretta Lynn)
Heart Trouble (Steve Wariner)

Heartache And A Half   (Deborah Allen)
Heartbreak Express   (Dolly Parton)
Heartbroke   (Ricky Skaggs)
Heavenly Bodies   (Earl Thomas Conley)
Hello Mary Lou   (The Statler Brothers)
Hey! Baby!   (Anne Murray)
Hey Bartender   (Johnny Lee)
High Horse   (The Nitty Gritty Dirt
   Band)
Highway 40 Blues   (Ricky Skaggs)
Highwayman   (Willie Nelson/Kris
   Kristofferson/Johnny Cash/Waylon
   Jennings)
Hold On I'm Comin'   (Waylon Jennings
   and Jerry Reed)
Holding Her And Loving You   (Earl Tho-
   mas Conley)
Home Again In My Heart   (The Nitty
   Gritty Dirt Band)
Hometown Gossip   (The Whites)
Honey (Open That Door)   (Ricky Skaggs)
Honky Tonkin'   (Hank Williams, Jr.)
Honkytonk Man   (Marty Robbins)
Honor Bound   (Earl Thomas Conley)
How Blue   (Reba McEntire)
How Could I Love Her So Much   (Johnny
   Rodriguez)

I.O.U.   (Lee Greenwood)
I Always Get Lucky With You   (George
   Jones)
I Bet You Never Thought I'd Go This Far
   (Micki Furman)
I Call It Love   (Mel McDaniel)
*I Can Tell By The Way You
   Dance*   (Vern Gosdin)
I Could'A Had You   (Leon Everette)
I Could Use Another You   (Eddy Raven)
I Don't Care   (Ricky Skaggs)
I Don't Know A Thing About Love
   (Conway Twitty)
I Don't Know Where To Start   (Eddie
   Rabbitt)
I Don't Know Why You Don't Want Me
   (Rosanne Cash)
*I Don't Mind The Thorns (If You're The
   Rose)*   (Lee Greenwood)

I Don't Remember Loving You   (John
   Conlee)
I Don't Think I'm Ready For You Yet
   (Anne Murray)
I Don't Think She's In Love Anymore
   (Charley Pride)
I Don't Wanna Lose Your Love   (Crystal
   Gayle)
I Don't Want To Be A Memory   (Exile)
I Dream Of Women Like You   (Ronnie
   McDowell)
I Fell In Love Again Last Night   (The
   Forester Sisters)
I Got A Million Of 'Em   (Ronnie
   McDowell)
I Got Mexico   (Eddy Raven)
*I Guess It Never Hurts To Hurt Some-
   times*   (The Oak Ridge Boys)
I Have Loved You, Girl   (Earl Thomas
   Conley)
I Hurt For You   (Deborah Allen)
I Just Came Here To Dance   (David Friz-
   zell And Shelly West)
I Just Came Home To Count The Memories
   (John Anderson)
I Lie   (Loretta Lynn)
I Love Her Mind   (The Bellamy Broth-
   ers)
I Love Only You   (The Nitty Gritty Dirt
   Band)
I May Be Used   (Waylon Jennings)
I Need More Of Your Love   (The Bellamy
   Brothers)
I Never Quite Got Back   (Sylvia)
I Pass   (Gus Hardin)
I Still Do   (Bill Medley)
I Wanna Hear It From You   (Eddy Ra-
   ven)
I Wanna Say Yes   (Louise Mandrell)
I Want Everyone To Cry   (Restless
   Heart)
I Want To Go Somewhere   (Keith
   Stegall)
I Will Always Love You   (Dolly Parton)
I Wish I Could Write You A Love Song
   (John Anderson)
I Wish I Had A Job To Shove   (Rodney
   Lay and The Wild West)

I Wish You Could Have Turned My Head (The Oak Ridge Boys)

I Wonder (Rosanne Cash)

I Wonder Where We'd Be Tonight (Vern Gosdin)

I Wonder Who's Holding My Baby Tonight (The Whites)

I Wouldn't Change You If I Could (Ricky Skaggs)

I'd Dance Every Dance With You (The Kendalls)

I'd Rather Be Crazy (Con Hunley)

I'll Never Stop Loving You (Gary Morris)

I'm For Love (Hank Williams, Jr.)

I'm Goin' Hurtin' (Joe Stampley)

I'm Gonna Hire A Wino To Decorate Our Home (David Frizzell)

I'm Movin' On (Emmylou Harris)

I'm Not That Lonely Yet (Reba McEntire)

I'm Not Through Loving You Yet (Louise Mandrell)

I'm Only In It For The Love (John Conlee)

I'm The One Mama Warned You About (Mickey Gilley)

I've Always Got The Heart To Sing The Blues (Bill Medley)

I've Been Around Enough To Know (John Schneider)

I've Been Rained On Too (Tom Jones)

I've Been Wrong Before (Deborah Allen)

If Hollywood Don't Need You (Don Williams)

If I Can Just Get Through The Night (Sissy Spacek)

If I Could Only Dance With You (Jim Glaser)

If I Didn't Love You (Gus Hardin)

If It Ain't Love (Let's Leave It Alone) (The Whites)

If It Was Easy (Ed Bruce)

If It Weren't For Him (Vince Gill)

If That Ain't Love (Lacy J. Dalton)

If The Fall Don't Get You (Janie Fricke)

If The Phone Doesn't Ring, It's Me (Jimmy Buffett)

If You Break My Heart (The Kendalls)

If You're Gonna Do Me Wrong (Vern Gosdin)

If You're Gonna Play In Texas (Alabama)

If You're Thinking You Want A Stranger (There's One Coming Home) (George Strait)

In A New York Minute (Ronnie McDowell)

In Another Minute (Jim Glaser)

In Like With Each Other (Larry Gatlin and The Gatlin Brothers Band)

In My Dreams (Emmylou Harris)

In My Eyes (John Conlee)

In The Jailhouse Now (Willie Nelson and Webb Pierce)

In The Middle Of The Night (Mel Tillis)

In The Midnight Hour (Razzy Bailey)

In Times Like These (Barbara Mandrell)

Innocent Lies (Sonny James)

Inside (Ronnie Milsap)

Islands In The Stream (Kenny Rogers and Dolly Parton)

It Ain't Easy Bein' Easy (Janie Fricke)

It Ain't Gonna Worry My Mind (Ray Charles with Mickey Gilley)

It Ain't Real (Mark Gray)

It Hasn't Happened Yet (Rosanne Cash)

It Should Have Been Love By Now (Barbara Mandrell and Lee Greenwood)

It Turns Me Inside Out (Lee Greenwood)

It'll Be Her (Tompall and The Glasers)

It's A Be Together Night (David Frizzell and Shelly West)

It's A Long Way To Daytona (Mel Tillis)

It's A Short Walk From Heaven To Hell (John Schneider)

It's All Over Now (John Anderson)

It's Time For Love (Don Williams)

It's You Alone (Gail Davies)

It's Your Reputation Talkin' (Kathy Mattea)

Jagged Edge Of A Broken Heart (Gail Davies)

Jose Cuervo (Shelly West)
Just A Little Love (Reba McEntire)
Just Another Woman In Love (Anne Murray)
Just Give Me What You Think Is Fair (Leon Everette)
Just To Satisfy You (Waylon and Willie)

Kansas City Lights (Steve Wariner)
Kern River (Merle Haggard)
Kiss Me Darling (Stephanie Winslow)

Lady Down On Love (Alabama)
Lady In Waiting (David Wills)
A Lady Like You (Glen Campbell)
The Lady Takes The Cowboy Every Time (Larry Gatlin and The Gatlin Brothers)
Lasso The Moon (Gary Morris)
The Last Thing I Needed First Thing This Morning (Willie Nelson)
Leave Them Boys Alone (Hank Williams, Jr.)
Left Side Of The Bed (Mark Gray)
Leona (Sawyer Brown)
Let It Be Me (Willie Nelson)
Let It Roll (Mel McDaniel)
Let Me Down Easy (Jim Glaser)
Let Somebody Else Drive (John Anderson)
Let The Heartache Ride (Restless Heart)
Let's Chase Each Other Around The Room (Merle Haggard)
Let's Fall To Pieces Together (George Strait)
Let's Leave The Lights On Tonight (Johnny Rodriguez)
Let's Stop Talking About It (Janie Fricke)
Letter To Home (Glen Campbell)
Lie To You For Your Love (The Bellamy Brothers)
Lies On Your Lips (Cristy Lane)
Like Nothing Ever Happened (Sylvia)

Listen To The Radio (Don Williams)
A Little Bit Crazy (Eddy Raven)
A Little Good News (Anne Murray)
Little Old-Fashioned Karma (Willie Nelson)
Little Things (The Oak Ridge Boys)
Livin' In These Troubled Times (Crystal Gayle)
Lonely But Only For You (Sissy Spacek)
Lonely Nights (Mickey Gilley)
Lonely Women Make Good Lovers (Steve Wariner)
A Long And Lasting Love (Crystal Gayle)
Long Hard Road (The Nitty Gritty Dirt Band)
Lost In The Feeling (Conway Twitty)
Lost In The Fifties Tonight (Ronnie Milsap)
Love Don't Care (Earl Thomas Conley)
Love Is Alive (The Judds)
Love Is On A Roll (Don Williams)
The Love She Found In Me (Gary Morris)
Love Song (The Oak Ridge Boys)
A Love Song (Kenny Rogers)
Love Talks (Ronnie McDowell)
Love Will Turn You Around (Kenny Rogers)
Love's Been A Little Bit Hard On Me (Juice Newton)
Love's Found You And Me (Ed Bruce)
Love's Gonna Fall Here Tonight (Razzy Bailey)
Lucille (Waylon Jennings)

Maggie's Dream (Don Williams)
Major Moves (Hank Williams, Jr.)
Make My Life With You (The Oak Ridge Boys)
Mama He's Crazy (The Judds)
Mama She's Lazy (Pinkard and Bowden)
The Man In The Mirror (Jim Glaser)
Marina Del Rey (George Strait)
Maybe My Baby (Louise Mandrell)

Me And Paul (Willie Nelson)

Meet Me In Montana (Marie Osmond with Dan Seals)

Miss Understanding (David Wills)

Missin' Mississippi (Charley Pride)

Mississippi Squirrel Revival (Ray Stevens)

Mistakes (Don Williams)

Modern Day Romance (The Nitty Gritty Dirt Band)

Mona Lisa Lost Her Smile (David Allan Coe)

More And More (Charley Pride)

Morning Desire (Kenny Rogers)

Most Of All (Mac Davis)

Mountain Music (Alabama)

Mountain Of Love (Charley Pride)

My Baby's Gone (The Kendalls)

My Baby's Got Good Timing (Dan Seals)

My First Taste Of Texas (Ed Bruce)

My Lady Loves Me (Leon Everette)

My Old Yellow Car (Dan Seals)

My Only Love (The Statlers)

My Toot-Toot (Rockin' Sidney)

Natural High (Merle Haggard)

Never Be You (Rosanne Cash)

Never Could Toe The Mark (Waylon Jennings)

New Cut Road (Bobby Bare)

New Looks From An Old Lover (B.J. Thomas)

New Patches (Mel Tillis)

Night Games (Charley Pride)

No Way Jose (David Frizzell)

Nobody (Sylvia)

Nobody But You (Don Williams)

Nobody Falls Like A Fool (Earl Thomas Conley)

Nobody Loves Me Like You Do (Anne Murray And Dave Loggins)

Nobody Wants To Be Alone (Crystal Gayle)

Nothing But The Radio On (The Younger Brothers)

Now There's You (Shelly West)

Oh Baby Mine (The Statler Brothers)

Oh Carolina (Vince Gill)

Old Friends (Roger Miller and Willie Nelson With Ray Price)

Oh Girl (Con Hunley)

Old Hippie (The Bellamy Brothers)

One Of A Kind Pair Of Fools (Barbara Mandrell)

One Owner Heart (T.G. Sheppard)

One Takes The Blame (The Statlers)

Only A Lonely Heart Knows (Barbara Mandrell)

Only If There Is Another You (Moe Bandy)

Only In My Mind (Reba McEntire)

Only One You (T.G. Sheppard)

Operator, Long Distance Please (Barbara Mandrell)

Operator, Operator (Eddy Raven)

Our Love Is On The Faultline (Crystal Gayle)

Ozark Mountain Jubilee (The Oak Ridge Boys)

P.S. I Love You (Tom T. Hall)

Pain In My Past (The Rovers)

Paradise Tonight (Mickey Gilley and Charly McClain)

Personally (Ronnie McDowell)

Pictures (Atlanta)

Pins And Needles (The Whites)

A Place To Fall Apart (Merle Haggard)

Pledging My Love (Emmylou Harris)

Poncho And Lefty (Willie Nelson and Merle Haggard)

Potential New Boyfriend (Dolly Parton)

The Power Of Love (Charley Pride)

Precious Love (The Kendalls)

Pretty Lady (Keith Stegall)

Prisoner Of The Highway (Ronnie Milsap)

Put Your Dreams Away (Mickey Gilley)

Radio Heart   (Charly McClain)
Radio Land   (Michael Murphey)
Real Love   (Dolly Parton with Kenny Rogers)
Reasons To Quit   (Merle Haggard and Willie Nelson)
Red Neckin' Love Makin' Night (Conway Twitty)
Redneck Girl   (The Bellamy Brothers)
The Reverend Mr. Black   (Johnny Cash)
The Ride   (David Allan Coe)
Ride 'Em Cowboy   (Juice Newton)
Right Or Wrong   (George Strait)
The Right Stuff   (Mickey Gilley and Charly McClain)
Ring On Her Finger, Time On Her Hands (Lee Greenwood)
Rock And Roll Shoes   (Ray Charles with B.J. Thomas)
Roll On   (Alabama)
Rollin' Lonely   (Johnny Lee)
The Rose   (Conway Twitty)
'Round The Clock Lovin'   (Gail Davies)
Runaway Heart   (Louise Mandrell)

Same Ole Me   (George Jones)
Save Me   (Louise Mandrell)
Save The Last Chance   (Johnny Lee)
Save The Last Dance For Me   (Dolly Parton)
Scarlet Fever   (Kenny Rogers)
Second Hand Heart   (Gary Morris)
Sentimental Ol' You   (Charley McClain)
Seven Spanish Angels   (Ray Charles)
Shadows Of My Mind   (Leon Everette)
She Can't Get My Love Off The Bed (Dottie West)
She Got The Goldmine   (Jerry Reed)
She Keeps The Homefires Burning (Ronnie Milsap)
She Left Love All Over Me   (Razzy Bailey)
She Sure Got Away With My Heart (John Anderson)
She Used To Love Me A Lot   (David Allan Coe)
She's A Miracle   (Exile)

She's Comin' Back To Say Goodbye (Eddie Rabbitt)
She's Gonna Win Your Heart   (Eddy Raven)
She's Lying   (Lee Greenwood)
She's My Rock   (George Jones)
She's Not Really Cheatin'   (Moe Bandy)
She's Single Again   (Janie Fricke)
Shine   (Waylon Jennings)
Shine On   (George Jones)
Shot In The Dark   (Leon Everette)
Show Her   (Ronnie Milsap)
Silent Partners   (David Frizzell and Shelly West)
Singing The Blues   (Gail Davies)
Single Women   (Dolly Parton)
16th Avenue   (Lacy J. Dalton)
Slow Burning Memory   (Vern Gosdin)
Slow Down   (Lacy J. Dalton)
Slow Hand   (Conway Twitty)
Snapshot   (Sylvia)
So Fine   (The Oak Ridge Boys)
Some Fools Never Learn   (Steve Wariner)
Some Hearts Get All The Breaks (Charly McClain)
Somebody Buy This Cowgirl A Beer (Shelly West)
Somebody Else's Fire   (Janie Fricke)
Somebody Should Leave   (Reba McEntire)
Somebody's Always Saying Goodbye (Anne Murray)
Somebody's Gonna Love You   (Lee Greenwood)
Somebody's Needin' Somebody   (Conway Twitty)
Someday Soon   (Moe Bandy)
Someday When Things Are Good   (Merle Haggard)
Someone Could Lose A Heart Tonight (Eddie Rabbitt)
Someone Is Falling In Love   (Kathy Mattea)
Someone Like You   (Emmylou Harris)
Something In My Heart   (Ricky Skaggs)
Sometimes I Get Lucky And Forget (Gene Watson)
Somewhere Between Right And Wrong (Earl Thomas Conley)

Somewhere Down The Line (T.G. Sheppard)
Soul Searchin' (Leon Everette)
Sounds Like Love (Johnny Lee)
Southern Women (The Wright Brothers)
Speak Softly (You're Talking To My Heart) (Gene Watson)
Stand Up (Mel McDaniel)
Stay A Little Longer (Mel Tillis)
Stay Young (Don Williams)
Still Losing You (Ronnie Milsap)
Still Taking Chances (Michael Murphey)
Step That Step (Sawyer Brown)
Stranger In My House (Ronnie Milsap)
Sure Feels Like Love (Larry Gatlin and The Gatlin Brothers Band)
Sweet Country Music (Atlanta)
Swingin' (John Anderson)
Take It To The Limit (Willie Nelson and Waylon Jennings)
Take Me Down (Alabama)
Take Me To The Country (Mel McDaniel)
Talk To Me (Mickey Gilley)
Tears Of The Lonely (Mickey Gilley)
Tell Me A Lie (Janie Fricke)
Tennessee Homesick Blues (Dolly Parton)
Tennessee Rose (Emmylou Harris)
Tennessee Whiskey (George Jones)
Thank God For Kids (The Oak Ridge Boys)
Thank God For The Radio (The Kendalls)
That's The Thing About Love (Don Williams)
That's The Way Love Goes (Merle Haggard)
There Ain't No Country Music On This Jukebox (Tom T. Hall and Earl Scruggs)
There Ain't No Future In This (Reba McEntire)
There Goes My Everything (Elvis Presley)
There's No Love In Tennessee (Barbara Mandrell)
There's No Way (Alabama)

They Never Had To Get Over You (Johnny Lee)
This Ain't Dallas (Hank Williams, Jr.)
This Bed's Not Big Enough (Louise Mandrell)
This Dream's On Me (Gene Watson)
This Time (Tom Jones)
Through The Years (Kenny Rogers)
Tie Your Dream To Mine (Marty Robbins)
'Til I Gain Control Again (Crystal Gayle)
'Til You're Gone (Barbara Mandrell)
Time Don't Run Out On Me (Anne Murray)
To All The Girls I've Loved Before (Julio Iglesias and Willie Nelson)
To Me (Barbara Mandrell and Lee Greenwood)
Together Again (Kenny Rogers and Dottie West)
Too Good To Stop Now (Mickey Gilley)
Too Hot To Sleep (Louise Mandrell)
Too Much On My Heart (The Statler Brothers)
Touch A Hand, Make A Friend (The Oak Ridge Boys)
Touch Me (Tom Jones)
Turning Away (Crystal Gayle)
Two Car Garage (B.J. Thomas)
Two Old Cats Like Us (Ray Charles with Hank Williams, Jr.)

Uncle Pen (Ricky Skaggs)
Used To Blue (Sawyer Brown)

The Very Best Of You (Charly McClain)
Victim Of Life's Circumstances (Vince Gill)
Victim Or Fool (Rodney Crowell)
Victims Of Goodbye (Sylvia)

Walkin' A Broken Heart (Don Williams)
Waltz Me To Heaven (Waylon Jennings)

War Is Hell (T.G. Sheppard)
Warning Sign (Eddie Rabbitt)
Watching Girls Go By (Ronnie McDowell)
Way Back (John Conlee)
Way Down Deep (Vern Gosdin)
We Did But Now You Don't (Conway Twitty)
We Didn't See A Thing (Ray Charles and George Jones)
We've Got Tonight (Kenny Rogers and Sheena Easton)
What Am I Gonna Do (Merle Haggard)
What I Didn't Do (Steve Wariner)
What She Wants (Michael Martin Murphey)
What Would Your Memories Do (Vern Gosdin)
What She Don't Know Won't Hurt Her (Gene Watson)
Whatever (The Statler Brothers)
Whatever Happened To Old-Fashioned Love (B.J. Thomas)
Whatever Turns You On (Keith Stegall)
What's Forever For (Michael Martin Murphey)
When I'm Away From You (The Bellamy Brothers)
When We Make Love (Alabama)
Where Are You Spending Your Nights These Days (David Frizzell)
Where's The Dress (Moe Bandy and Joe Stampley)
White Line (Emmylou Harris)
Who Do I Have To Choose (Willie Nelson)
The Whole World's In Love When You're Lonely (B.J. Thomas)
Who's Gonna Fill Their Shoes (George Jones)
Why Baby Why (Charley Pride)
Why Do We Want What We Know We Can't Have (Reba McEntire)
Why Goodbye (Steve Wariner)
Why Not Me (The Judds)
Wild And Blue (John Anderson)
Wild Montana Skies (John Denver)
The Wild Side Of Me (Dan Seals)

Wild Turkey (Lacy J. Dalton)
The Wind Beneath My Wings (Gary Morris)
With One Look In Your Eyes (Charly McClain with Wayne Massey)
With You (Charly McClain)
Without A Song (Willie Nelson)
Without You (T.G. Sheppard)
Woke Up In Love (Exile)
Woman Your Love (Moe Bandy)
A Woman's Touch (Tom Jones)
Women Do Know How To Carry On (Waylon Jennings)
Working Man (John Conlee)
A World Without Love (Eddie Rabbitt)
World's Greatest Lover (The Bellamy Brothers)
Would You Catch A Falling Star (John Anderson)
Wounded Hearts (Mark Gray)

Years After You (John Conlee)
The Yellow Rose (Johnny Lee and Lane Brady)
Yesterday's Wine (Merle Haggard)
You And I (Eddie Rabbitt with Crystal Gayle)
You Can't Run From Love (Eddie Rabbitt)
You Could've Heard A Heart Break (Johnny Lee)
You Don't Know Love (Janie Fricke)
You Look So Good In Love (George Strait)
You Made A Wanted Man Out Of Me (Ronnie McDowell)
You Make Me Feel Like A Man (Ricky Skaggs)
You Make Me Want To Make You Mine (Juice Newton)
You Never Gave Up On Me (Crystal Gayle)
You Put The Beat In My Heart (Eddie Rabbitt)
You Put The Blue In Me (The Whites)
You Take Me For Granted (Merle Haggard)

You Turn Me On (Ed Bruce)
You Turn Me On I'm A Radio (Gail Davies)
You Were A Good Friend (Kenny Rogers)
You'll Be Back (Every Night In My Dreams) (The Statler Brothers)
You're Gettin' To Me Again (Jim Glaser)
You're Going Out Of My Mind (T.G. Sheppard)
You're Gonna Lose Her Like That (Moe Bandy)
You're Gonna Ruin My Bad Reputation (Ronnie McDowell)
You're Not Easy To Forget (Dottie West)
You're Out Doing What I'm Here Doing Without (Gene Watson)
You're So Good When You're Bad (Charley Pride)

You're The Best Break This Old Heart Ever Had (Ed Bruce)
You're The First Time I've Thought About Leaving (Reba McEntire)
You're Welcome To Tonight (Lynn Anderson And Gary Morris)
You've Got A Good Love Comin' (Lee Greenwood)
You've Got A Lover (Ricky Skaggs)
You've Got Something On Your Mind (Mickey Gilley)
You've Really Got A Hold On Me (Mickey Gilley)
You've Still Got A Place In My Heart (George Jones)
Your Heart's Not In It (Janie Fricke)
Your Love Shines Through (Mickey Gilley)
Your Love's On The Line (Earl Thomas Conley)

G. APPENDIX: NUMBER 1 RECORDS—A CHRONOLOGICAL LISTING

1982

2-13		*Red Neckin' Love Makin' Night*—Conway Twitty	(1)
2-20—	2-27	*Bobbie Sue*—The Oak Ridge Boys	(2)
3-06		*Mountain Of Love*—Charley Pride	(1)
3-13		*The Clown*—Conway Twitty	(1)
3-20		*Big City*—Merle Haggard	(1)
3-27—	4-03	*Single Women*—Dolly Parton	(2)
4-10		*Same Ole Me*—George Jones	(1)
4-17		*You Never Gave Up On Me*—Crystal Gayle	(1)
4-24		*Mountain Music*—Alabama	(1)
5-01—	5-08	*Always On My Mind*—Willie Nelson	(2)
5-15		*Just To Satisfy You*—Waylon and Willie	(1)
5-22—	5-29	*Finally*—T.G. Sheppard	(2)
6-05		*Tears Of The Lonely*—Mickey Gilley	(1)
6-12		*For All The Wrong Reasons*—The Bellamy Brothers	(1)
6-19		*Listen To The Radio*—Don Williams	(1)
6-26—	7-03	*Any Day Now*—Ronnie Milsap	(2)
7-10		*I Don't Think She's In Love Anymore*—Charley Pride	(1)
7-17—	7-24	*Take Me Down*—Alabama	(1)

7-31	*Honky Tonkin'*—Hank Williams, Jr. (1)
8-07	*I Don't Dare*—Ricky Skaggs (1)
8-14	*Nobody*—Sylvia (1)
8-21— 8-28	*I'm Gonna Hire A Wino To Decorate Our Home*—David Frizzell (2)
9-04	*Love Will Turn You Around*—Kenny Rogers (1)
9-11— 9-25	*She Got The Goldmine*—Jerry Reed (3)
10-02	*Put Your Dreams Away*—Mickey Gilley (1)
10-09—10-16	*Yesterday's Wine*—Merle Haggard and George Jones (2)
10-23	*He Got You*—Ronnie Milsap (1)
10-30	*Close Enough To Perfect*—Alabama (1)
11-06	*You're So Good When You're Bad*—Charley Pride (1)
11-13	*Heartbroke*—Ricky Skaggs (1)
11-20—12-04	*You And I*—Eddie Rabbitt with Crystal Gayle
12-11—12-18	*The Bird*—Jerry Reed
12-25	*A Love Song*—Kenny Rogers (1)

1983

1-01— 1-08	*A Love Song*—Kenny Rogers (2; 3)
1-15	*Going Where The Lonely Go*—Merle Haggard (1)
1-22	*Like Nothing Ever Happened*—Sylvia (1)
1-29— 2-05	*Inside*—Ronnie Milsap (2)
2-12	*Faking Love*—T.G. Sheppard and Karen Brooks (1)
2-19— 2-26	*Last Thing I Need First Thing This Morning*—Willie Nelson (2)
3-05	*Everything's Beautiful*—Dolly Parton and Willie Nelson (1)
3-12	*I Wouldn't Change You If I Could*—Ricky Skaggs (1)
3-19	*Swingin'*—John Anderson (1)
3-26	*We've Got Tonight*—Kenny Rogers and Sheena Easton (1)
4-02— 4-16	*Dixieland Delight*—Alabama (3)
4-23	*Jose Cuervo*—Shelly West (1)
4-30	*You're The First Time I've Thought About Leaving*—Reba McEntire (1)
5-07	*Whatever Happened To Old-Fashioned Love*—B.J. Thomas (1)
5-14	*Lucille*—Waylon Jennings (1)
5-21	*Common Man*—John Conlee (1)
5-28	*Whatever Happened To Old-Fashioned Love*—B.J. Thomas (1; 2)
6-04	*Lucille*—Waylon Jennings (1; 2)
6-11	*Stranger In My House*—Ronnie Milsap (1)
6-18	*The Ride*—David Allan Coe (1)
6-25	*Fool For Your Love*—Mickey Gilley (1)
7-02	*Love Is On A Roll*—Don Williams (1)
7-09	*Highway 40 Blues*—Ricky Skaggs (1)
7-16	*The Closer You Get*—Alabama (1)
7-23	*Poncho And Lefty*—Willie Nelson and Merle Haggard (1)
7-30	*I Always Get Lucky With You*—George Jones (1)
8-06	*Your Love's On The Line*—Earl Thomas Conley (1)
8-13	*He's A Heartache*—Janie Fricke (1)

8-20	*Love Song*—The Oak Ridge Boys (1)
8-27	*You're Gonna Ruin My Bad Reputation*—Ronnie McDowell (1)
9-03	*Night Games*—Charley Pride (1)
9-10	*I'm Only In It For The Love*—John Conlee (1)
9-17	*Night Games*—Charley Pride (1; 2)
9-24—10-08	*Don't You Know How Much I Love You*—Ronnie Milsap (3)
10-15—10-29	*Paradise Tonight*—Charley McClain and Mickey Gilley (3)
11-05—11-12	*Islands In The Stream*—Kenny Rogers and Dolly Parton (2)
11-19	*One Of A Kind Pair Of Fools*—Barbara Mandrell (1)
11-26	*Tennessee Whiskey*—George Jones (1)
12-03	*Holding Her And Loving You*—Earl Thomas Conley (1)
12-10	*Tell Me A Lie*—Janie Fricke (1)
12-17	*A Little Good News*—Anne Murray (1)
12-24—12-31	*Ev'ry Heart Should Have One*—Charley Pride (2)

1984

1-07— 1-14	*Ev'ry Heart Should Have One*—Charley Pride (2; 4)
1-21	*You Look So Good In Love*—George Strait (1)
1-28	*Show Her*—Ronnie Milsap (1)
2-04	*Sentimental Ol' You*—Charly McClain (1)
2-11	*That's The Way Love Goes*—Merle Haggard (1)
2-18	*Don't Cheat In Our Hometown*—Ricky Skaggs (1)
2-25— 3-31	*Roll On*—Alabama (6)
4-07	*Thank God For The Radio*—The Kendalls (1)
4-14	*Don't Make It Easy For Me*—Earl Thomas Conley (1)
4-21— 4-28	*Right Or Wrong*—George Strait (2)
5-05	*I Could'A Had You*—Leon Everette (1)
5-12	*To All The Girls I've Loved Before*—Julio Iglesias and Willie Nelson (1)
5-19	*I May Be Used*—Waylon Jennings (1)
5-26	*Honey*—Ricky Skaggs (1)
6-02	*Mona Lisa Lost Her Smile*—David Allan Coe (1)
6-09	*Someday When Things Are Good*—Merle Haggard (1)
6-16	*I Got Mexico*—Eddy Raven (1)
6-23	*When We Make Love*—Alabama (1)
6-30	*I Can Tell By The Way You Dance*—Vern Gosdin (1)
7-07	*Angel In Disguise*—Earl Thomas Conley (1)
7-14	*Mama He's Crazy*—The Judds (1)
7-21	*Just Another Woman In Love*—Anne Murray (1)
7-28	*Angel In Disguise*—Earl Thomas Conley (1; 2)
8-04— 8-11	*Where's The Dress*—Moe Bandy and Joe Stampley (2)
8-18	*Still Losing You*—Ronnie Milsap (1)
8-25	*Let's Fall To Pieces Together*—George Strait (1)
9-01	*Tennessee Homesick Blues*—Dolly Parton (1)
9-08— 9-29	*Let's Chase Each Other Around The Room*—Merle Haggard (4)
10-06	*Everyday*—The Oak Ridge Boys (1)

10-13	*If You're Gonna Play In Texas*—Alabama (1)
10-20	*To Me*—Barbara Mandrell and Lee Greenwood (1)
10-27—11-03	*City Of New Orleans*—Willie Nelson (2)
11-10	*Give Me One More Chance*—Exile (1)
11-17	*I've Been Around Enough To Know*—John Schneider (1)
11-24	*Chance Of Lovin' You*—Earl Thomas Conley (1)
12-01	*Your Heart's Not In It*—Janie Fricke (1)
12-08	*Nobody Loves Me Like You Do*—Anne Murray and Dave Loggins (1)
12-15—12-22	*America*—Waylon Jennings
12-29	*Does Fort Worth Ever Cross Your Mind*—George Strait (1)

1985

1-05— 1-12	*Does Fort Worth Ever Cross Your Mind*—George Strait (2; 3)
1-19— 1-26	*How Blue*—Reba McEntire (2)
2-02	*Fire In The Night*—Alabama (1)
2-09	*Something In My Heart*—Ricky Skaggs (1)
2-16	*Make My Life With You*—The Oak Ridge Boys (1)
2-23	*You Turn Me On*—Ed Bruce (1)
3-02	*Baby Bye Bye*—Gary Morris (1)
3-09	*My Baby's Got Good Timing*—Dan Seals (1)
3-16	*Crazy For Your Love*—Exile (1)
3-23— 4-06	*Seven Spanish Angels*—Ray Charles (3)
4-13	*Honor Bound*—Earl Thomas Conley (1)
4-20	*High Horse*—The Nitty Gritty Dirt Band (1)
4-27	*There's No Way*—Alabama (1)
5-04	*Girls' Night Out*—The Judds (1)
5-11	*Somebody Should Leave*—Reba McEntire (1)
5-18	*Step That Step*—Sawyer Brown (1)
5-25	*Radio Heart*—Charly McClain (1)
6-01	*Fallin' In Love*—Sylvia (1)
6-08	*Natural High*—Merle Haggard (1)
6-15	*Country Boy*—Ricky Skaggs (1)
6-22	*Little Things*—The Oak Ridge Boys (1)
6-29	*She Keeps The Homefires Burning*—Ronnie Milsap (1)
7-06	*She's A Miracle*—Exile (1)
7-13	*Forgiving You Was Easy*—Willie Nelson (1)
7-20— 7-27	*Dixie Road*—Lee Greenwood (2)
8-03	*Love Don't Care*—Earl Thomas Conley
8-10	*I'm For Love*—Hank Williams, Jr. (1)
8-17	*Highwayman*—Willie Nelson/Kris Kristofferson/Johnny Cash/Waylon Jennings (1)
8-24	*Real Love*—Dolly Parton With Kenny Rogers (1)
8-31— 9-07	*Love Is Alive*—The Judds (2)
9-14—11-02	no chart issued
11-09—11-23	*Can't Keep A Good Man Down*—Alabama (3)
11-30—12-07	*I Don't Mind The Thorns*—Lee Greenwood (2)

H. ARTIST INDEX—POP

ABC

11-09-85   *Be Near Me*   (Mer. 880 626-7)   16, 16, 13, 12, 12   (5)

12-25-82   *The Look Of Love*   (Mer. SR 76168)   20, 20, 20, 17, 19, 23   (6)

ABBA   *(See also:* FRIDA)

2-20-82   *When All Is Said And Done*   (Atl.)   22   (1)

ADAM ANT

1-15-83   *Goody Two Shoes*   (Epic 34-03367)   22, 17, 14, 9, 7, 6, 6, 12, 15, 20, 30   (11)

ADAMS, BRYAN

6-25-83   *Cuts Like A Knife*   (A&M AM 2553)   30, 25, 22, 19, 18, 13, 10, 11, 13, 15, 23, 23   (12)

5-18-85   *Heaven*   (A&M AM 2729)   27, 17, 13, 9, 4, 1, 1, 2, 2, 9, 9, 17   (12)

11-09-85   *One Night Love Affair*   (A&M AM 2770)   28, 28   (2)

11-24-84   *Run To You*   (A&M AM 2686)   27, 16, 12, 10, 6, 4, 4, 4, 2, 1, 4, 6, 10, 21   (14)

3-02-85   *Somebody*   (A&M AM 2701)   26, 21, 16, 11, 11, 9, 23   (7)

5-14-83   *Straight From The Heart*   (A&M AM 2536)   25, 19, 15, 12, 10, 9, 22   (7)

8-03-85   *Summer Of '69*   (A&M AM 2739)   21, 10, 9, 6, 5, 5   (6)

ADAMS, BRYAN, AND TINA TURNER   *(See also:* TINA TURNER)

11-30-85   *It's Only Love*   (A&M AM 2791)   28, 28   (2)

AFTER THE FIRE

3-19-83   *Der Kommissar*   (Epic 34-03559)   26, 21, 18, 17, 13, 11, 5, 4, 3, 6, 6, 10, 29   (13)

A-HA

8-31-85   *Take On Me*   (WB 7-29011)   26, 26, 8, 8, 18, 27, 27   (7)

AIR SUPPLY

7-31-82   *Even The Nights Are Better*   (Arista AS 0692)   26, 17, 15, 17, 25   (5)

9-03-83   *Making Love Out Of Nothing At All*   (Arista AS1-9056)   26, 26, 18, 18, 15, 11, 11, 11, 11, 20, 27   (11)

ALLEN, DEBORAH

1-21-84   *Baby I Lied*   (RCA PB-13600)   29, 26, 26   (3)

AMERICA

8-28-82   *You Can Do Magic*   (Cap. B-5142)   24, 17, 12, 10, 8, 5, 5, 4, 3, 8, 12, 22, 29   (13)

ANIMOTION

3-09-85   *Obsession*   (Mer. 880 266-7)   28, 24, 23, 23, 28, 9, 7, 6, 4, 10, 14, 18, 25   (13)

ANT, ADAM   *(See:* ADAM ANT)

APOLLONIA   *(See:* PRINCE AND THE REVOLUTION)

ARCADIA   *(See also:* DURAN DURAN)

11-09-85   *Election Day*   (Cap. B-5501)   22, 22, 9, 7, 7   (5)

ASHFORD AND SIMPSON

2-02-85   *Solid*   (Cap. B-5399)   27, 21, 17, 16, 25   (5)

ASIA

8-20-83   *Don't Cry*   (Geffen 7-29571)   28, 18, 9, 9, 8, 8, 11, 14, 14, 14   (10)

5-01-82   *Heat Of The Moment*   (Geffen GEF 50040)   28, 19, 14, 9, 4, 3, 2, 5, 8, 11, 19, 22   (12)

8-07-82   *Only Time Will Tell*   (Geffen 7-29970)   25, 20, 18, 13, 7, 6, 5, 5, 7, 9, 14, 23   (12)

AUSTIN, PATTI

12-11-82   *Baby, Come To Me*   (Qwest QWE 50036)   30, 26, 23, 23, 23, 13, 12, 9, 6, 3, 2, 3, 10, 13, 18, 25   (16)

AUTOGRAPH

3-16-85   *Turn Up The Radio*   (RCA PB-13953)   25, 25, 25, 20   (4)

BAILEY, PHILIP, AND PHIL COLLINS   *(See also:* PHIL COLLINS; EARTH, WIND AND FIRE)

12-15-84   *Easy Lover*   (Col. 38-04679)   29, 21, 13, 13, 13, 9, 5, 2, 2, 2, 11, 15, 25   (13)

BANANARAMA

9-08-84   *Cruel Summer*   (London 810 127-7)   28, 26, 20, 11, 8, 6, 9, 13, 13   (9)

BAND AID

12-29-84   *Do They Know It's Christmas*   (Col. 38-04749)   10, 10, 10, 7, 11, 19   (6)

BASIL, TONI

11-06-82   *Mickey*   (Chrysalis CHS 2638)   26, 20, 16, 8, 7, 5, 3, 2, 2, 2, 4, 11, 15, 22   (14)

THE BEACH BOYS

6-08-85   *Getcha Back*   (Caribou ZS4 04913)   30, 26, 23, 21, 20, 20   (6)

THE BEATLES   *(See also:* JOHN LENNON; PAUL McCARTNEY)

12-04-82   *Love Me Do*   (Cap. PB-5189)   30, 28, 27, 30, 30, 30   (6)

4-03-82   *Movie Medley*   (Cap. PB-5100)   27, 21, 15, 11, 5, 2, 3, 13, 18, 21, 28   (11)

THE BEE GEES

6-04-83   *The Woman In You*   (RSO 813 173-7)   29, 25, 23, 21, 17, 16, 18   (7)

BENATAR, PAT

8-03-85   *Invincible*   (Chrysalis VS4 42877)   29, 20, 13, 16, 10, 10   (6)

3-26-83   *Little Too Late*   (Chrysalis VS4 03536)   28, 25, 23, 27   (4)

5-28-83   *Looking For A Stranger*   (Chrysalis VS4 42688)   29, 27   (2)

10-08-83   *Love Is A Battlefield*   (Chrysalis VS4 49700)   30, 30, 30, 19, 8, 4, 4, 4, 4, 1, 1, 2, 2, 2, 2, 4, 7, 15, 23   (19)

11-06-82   *Shadows Of The Night*   (Chrysalis CHS 2647)   29, 23, 17, 15, 12, 12, 12, 16, 16, 16, 20, 28   (12)

11-10-84   *We Belong*   (Chrysalis VS4 42826)   30, 20, 17, 14, 10, 9, 8, 5, 5, 5, 10, 18, 24   (13)

BENSON, GEORGE

2-27-82   *Never Give Up On A Good Thing*   (WB WBS-50005)   26, 22, 21, 18, 16, 16, 17, 28   (8)

2-13-82   *Turn Your Love Around*   (WB WBS-49846)   16   (1)

BERLIN

5-19-84   *No More Words*   (Geffen 7-29360)   22, 20, 25   (3)

BIG COUNTRY

11-12-83   *In A Big Country*   (Mer. 814 467-7)   21, 16, 11, 8, 6, 5, 4, 4, 4, 4, 5, 12, 22   (13)

BISHOP, STEPHEN

4-23-83   *It Might Be You*   (WB 7-29792)   28, 25, 23, 24, 28   (5)

BLONDIE

6-12-82   *Island Of Lost Souls*   (Chrysalis CHS 2603)   26, 22, 16, 16, 20   (5)

BON JOVI

4-14-84   *Runaway*   (Mer. 818 309-7)   28, 25, 23, 29   (4)

BONOFF, KARLA

6-26-82   *Personally*   (Col. 18-02805)   29, 25, 22, 19, 17, 16, 16, 23, 25, 30   (10)

BOWIE, DAVID

9-29-84   *Blue Jean*   (EMI America B-8231)   28, 20, 12, 5, 4, 3, 1, 3, 5, 8, 14, 30   (12)

8-06-83   *China Girl*   (EMI America B-8165)   26, 23, 16, 11, 8, 8, 10, 10, 14, 20, 20, 20, 20   (13)

4-09-83   *Let's Dance*   (EMI America B-8158)   29, 17, 14, 6, 5, 2, 2, 2, 2, 2, 2, 2, 2, 4, 11, 13   (16)

10-01-83   *Modern Love*   (EMI America B-8177)   27, 19, 19, 19, (1), 29   (5)

BOWIE, DAVID, AND THE PAT METHENY GROUP

3-02-85   *This Is Not America*   (EMI America B-8251)   28, 26, 23, 21, 21, 19   (6)

BRANIGAN, LAURA

10-16-82   *Gloria*   (Atl.)   28, 24, 18, 13, 10, 4, 2, 3, 15, 18, 28, 28, 28   (13)

9-17-83   *How Am I Supposed To Live Without You*   (Atl. 7-89805)   25, 25, 22   (3)

8-25-84   *The Lucky One*   (Atl. 7-89636)   29, (1), 25, 22, 18, 17, 15, 15, 27   (8)

5-19-84   *Self Control*   (Atl. 7-89676)   25, 22, 19, 15, 12, 11, 7, 5, 4, 3, 5, 6, 12, 17, (1), 16   (15)

4-16-83   *Solitaire*   (Atl. 7-89868)   28, 23, 20, 18, 13, 11, 9, 8, 8, 15   (10)

BROWNE, JACKSON

7-30-83   *Lawyers In Love*   (Asylum 7-69826)   29, 20, 16, 12, 9, 6, 6, 6, 6, 10, 18, 18, 18   (13)

8-14-82   *Somebody's Baby*   (Asylum 7-69982)   27, 23, 17, 10, 8, 7, 3, 4, 8, 9, 14, 20   (12)

BRYSON, PEABO

2-20-82   *If Ever You're in My Arms Again*   18   (1)

BUCKINGHAM, LINDSEY   *(See also:* FLEETWOOD MAC)

9-22-84   *Go Insane*   (Elektra 7-69714)   27, 23, 22, 21   (4)

2-13-82   *Trouble*   (Asylum E-47223)   12   (1)

BUCKNER AND GARCIA

2-13-82   *Pac-Man Fever*   (Col. 18-02673)   25, 19, 17   (3)

CAFFERTY, JOHN, AND THE BEAVER BROWN BAND

8-31-85   *C-I-T-Y*   (Scotti Brothers ZS4 05452)   27, 27   (2)

9-29-84   *On The Dark Side*   (Scotti Brothers ZS4 04594)   30, 25, 19, 17, 14, 14, 12, 22   (8)

6-01-85   *Tough All Over*   (Scotti Brothers ZS4 04891)   30, 26, 22, 19, 17, 15, 15, 21, 21   (9)

CARA, IRENE

4-30-83   *Flashdance . . . What A Feeling*   (Casa. 811 440-7)   26, 22, 16, 3, 1, 1, 1, 1, 1, 1, 1, 2, 2, 2, 3, 3, 8, 20, 30, 30   (20)

CARNES, KIM   *(See also:* KENNY ROGERS)

5-25-85   *Crazy In The Night (Barking At Airplanes)*   (EMI America B-8267)   30, 26, 22, 21, 20, 19, 19, 19   (8)

10-29-83   *Invisible Hands*   (EMI America B-8181)   30, 19, 17, 15, 14, 14, 14, 21, 21, 21, 21, 28   (12)

8-21-82   *Voyeur*   (EMI America B-8127)   29, 26, 20, 14, 12, 12, 11, 11, 16, 22, 28   (11)

THE CARS

8-25-84 *Drive* (Elektra 7-69706)   27, 22, 16, 13, 8, 3, 2, 1, 2, 3, 4, 11, 18, 26 (14)

12-01-84 *Hello Again* (Elektra 7-69681)   26, 23, 22, 18, 17, 17, 17, 26 (8)

6-16-84 *Magic* (Elektra 7-69724)   25, 21, 20, 19, 18, 17, 17 (7)

2-13-82 *Shake It Up* (Elektra E-47250)   4 (1)

11-09-85 *Tonight She Comes* (Elektra 7-69589)   26, 26, 22, 19, 19 (5)

3-31-84 *You Might Think* (Elektra 7-69744)   29, 19, 13, 7, 4, 3, 2, 4, 5, 12, 28 (11)

CHAMPAIGN

6-18-83 *Try Again* (Col. 38-03563)   26, 24, 29 (3)

CHARLENE

4-10-82 *I've Never Been To Me* (Motown 1611 MF)   27, 20, 14, 10, 8, 6, 3, 3, 5, 10, 16 (11)

CHEAP TRICK

7-17-82 *If You Want My Love* (Epic 14-02968)   29, 26 (2)

CHICAGO

4-13-85 *Along Comes A Woman* (Full Moon 7-29082)   26, 22, 17, 16, 25 (5)

9-29-84 *Hard Habit To Break* (WB 7-29214)   27, 14, 7, 3, 2, 2, 5, 8, 10, 17, 22 (11)

7-10-82 *Hard To Say I'm Sorry* (Full Moon 7-29979)   27, 23, 19, 13, 8, 5, 4, 2, 2, 1, 4, 7, 12, 24, 29 (15)

10-09-82 *Love Me Tomorrow* (Full Moon 7-29911)   26, 23, 18, 17, 16, 15, 15, 24 (8)

12-15-84 *You're The Inspiration* (WB 7-29126)   18, 14, 9, 9, 9, 6, 4, 3, 5, 7, 14 (11)

CLAPTON, ERIC

3-23-85   *Forever Man*   (Duck 7-29081)   29, 29, 24, 18, 15, 13, 12, 15, 23   (9)

2-12-83   *I've Got A Rock 'N' Roll Heart*   (WB 7-29780)   28, 25, 22, 17, 14, 12, 10, 9, 8, 11, 19, 27   (12)

THE CLASH

11-27-82   *Rock The Casbah*   (Epic 34-03245)   28, 25, 24, 19, 19, 19, 19, 26   (8)

COCK ROBIN

8-10-85   *When Your Heart Is Weak*   (Col. 38-04875)   28, 25, 23, 19, 19   (5)

COCKER, JOE, AND JENNIFER WARNES

9-18-82   *Up Where We Belong*   (Island 7-99996)   29, 27, 25, 19, 15, 13, 4, 1, 1, 2, 4, 15, 21, 30   (14)

COLLINS, PHIL   (*See also:* GENESIS)

3-10-84   *Against All Odds*   (Atl. 7-89700)   30, 19, 19, 8, 3, 7, 2, 1, 2, 3, 5, 7, 6, 7, 14, 22, 27   (17)

8-03-85   *Don't Lose My Number*   (Atl. 7-89536)   28, 17, 11, 7, 4, 4   (6)

2-26-83   *I Don't Care Anymore*   (Atl. 7-89877)   30, 26, 22, 17, 17, 22, 28, 29, 30   (9)

2-16-85   *One More Night*   (Atl. 7-89588)   25, 15, 12, 8, 5, 2, 2, 1, 2, 4, 8, 20, 29   (13)

5-18-85   *Sussudio*   (Atl. 7-89560)   28, 23, 18, 13, 11, 4, 2, 1, 1, 2, 2, 5, 19   (13)

11-20-82   *You Can't Hurry Love*   (Atl. 7-89933)   30, 25, 21, 17, 14, 11, 11, 11, 10, 8, 7, 7, 11, 17, 23, 30   (16)

COLLINS, PHIL, AND MARILYN MARTIN   (*See also:* GENESIS)

11-09-85   *Separate Lives*   (Atl. 7-89498)   9, 9, 6, 4, 4   (5)

THE COMMODORES (*See also:* LIONEL RICHIE)

3-16-85 *Nightshift* (Motown 1773 MF)   26, 20, 20, 17, 3, 2, 2, 6, 12, 15, 24 (11)

2-20-82 *Why You Wanna Try Me* (Motown 1604 MF)   20 (1)

COUGAR, JOHN   (*See:* JOHN COUGAR MELLENCAMP)

CROSBY, STILLS AND NASH

7-03-82 *Wasted On The Way* (Atl.)   29, 25, 18, 14, 9, 6, 4, 3, 3, 6, 9, 17, 24 (13)

CROSS, CHRISTOPHER

1-29-83 *All Right* (WB 7-29843)   24, 18, 10, 7, 7, 5, 10, 15, 19, 24, 30 (11)

CULTURE CLUB

11-26-83 *Church Of The Poison Mind* (Epic 34-04144)   23, 19, 17, 16, 22, 22, 22, 22, 26 (9)

1-22-83 *Do You Really Want To Hurt Me* (Epic 34-03368)   22, 16, 11, 6, 4, 2, 1, 5, 7, 11, 14, 15, 22, 24, 28 (15)

7-30-83 *I'll Tumble 4 Ya* (Epic 34-03912)   28, 21, 20, 17, 12, 19, 19, 29, 29 (9)

5-19-84 *It's A Miracle* (Virgin 34-04457)   28, 24, 20, 16, 13, 12, 10, 14, 16, 28 (10)

12-10-83 *Karma Chameleon* (Virgin 34-04221)   30, 17, 13, 13, 13, 13, 6, 2, 2, 1, 2, 2, 1, 2, 4, 4, 7, 6, 10, 16, 28 (21)

3-03-84 *Miss Me Blind* (Virgin 34-04388)   27, 25, 25, 25, 11, 12, 9, 5, 2, 1, 6, 12, 16, 21, 26 (15)

5-07-83 *Time (Clock Of The Heart)* (Epic 34-03796)   26, 19, 16, 14, 11, 9, 3, 3, 3, 5, 4, 5, 9, 27 (14)

10-20-84 *The War Song* (Virgin 34-04638)   28, 25, 23, 16, 15, 15, 25 (7)

DANIELS, CHARLIE, BAND

4-17-82   *Still In Saigon*   (Epic AE7-1414)   21, 17, 13, 9, 7, 5, 6, 8, 12, 17   (10)

DAVIS, PAUL

3-13-82   *'65 Love Affair*   (Arista AS 0661)   30, 26, 20, 14, 12, 11, 10, 9, 10, 13, 20, 28   (12)

THE DAZZ BAND

5-29-82   *Let It Whip*   (Motown 1609 MF)   24, 22, 18, 14, 10, 8, 8, 8, 11, 23, 29   (11)

DEAD OR ALIVE

7-20-85   *You Spin Me Round (Like A Record)*   (Epic 34-04894)   23, 23, 16, 12, 10, 10, 18, 18   (8)

DeBARGE

7-16-83   *All This Love*   (Gordy 1660 GF)   26, 25, 22, 28   (4)

3-23-85   *Rhythm Of The Night*   (Gordy 1770 GF)   28, 28, 23, 4, 3, 3, 2, 4, 9, 13, 21   (11)

12-03-83   *Time Will Reveal*   (Gordy)   28, 25, 22, 20, 20, 20, 20, 18, 27   (9)

DeBURGH, CHRIS

6-18-83   *Don't Pay The Ferryman*   (A&M AM 2511)   30, 27, 24, 24, 24, 23   (6)

DEF LEPPARD

10-08-83   *Foolin'*   (Mer. 814 178-7)   26, 26, 26, 26, 9, 12, 18, 26, 29   (9)

4-02-83   *Photograph*   (Mer. 811 215-7)   27, 26, 23, 20, 17, 15, 9, 8, 7, 6, 15, 29   (12)

7-23-83   *Rock Of Ages*   (Mer. 812 370-7)   29, 26, 16, 13, 15, 16, 20, 20, 21, 21, 23   (11)

DEPECHE MODE

8-03-85   *People Are People*   (Sire 7-29221)   24, 14, 13   (3)

DEXY'S MIDNIGHT RUNNERS

3-26-83   *Come On Eileen*   (Mer. SR 76189)   23, 16, 13, 7, 3, 1, 2, 4, 7, 10, 22   (11)

DeYOUNG, DENNIS   *(See also:* **STYX)**

10-20-84   *Desert Moon*   (A&M AM 2666)   20, 18, 18, 17, 14, 24   (6)

DIAMOND, NEIL

9-25-82   *Heartlight*   (Col. 18-03219)   26, 20, 15, 13, 12, 6, 6, 3, 3, 5, 13, 19, 25   (13)

1-29-83   *I'm Alive*   (Col. 38-03503)   28, 26, 23, 19, 17, 22, 28   (7)

2-20-82   *On The Way To The Sky*   (Col. 18-02712)   26, 19, 16, 15, 13, 22   (6)

DIRE STRAITS

8-03-85   *Money For Nothing*   (WB 7-28950)   30, 18, 12, 8, 2, 2, 15, 15, 27   (9)

11-09-85   *Walk Of Life*   (WB 7-28878)   27, 27, 23, 21, 21   (5)

DR. HOOK

3-13-83   *Baby Makes Her Blue Jeans Talk*   (Casa. NB 2347)   26, 19, 13, 11, 9, 7, 6, 6, 11, 22   (10)

DOLBY, THOMAS

4-02-83   *She Blinded Me With Science*   (Cap. B-5204)   30, 25, 21, 18, 12, 7, 5, 5, 5, 5, 5, 11, 25, 30   (14)

DURAN DURAN   *(See also:* **ARCADIA; POWER STATION)**

1-29-83   *Hungry Like A Wolf*   (Cap. B-5195)   27, 20, 12, 9, 5, 3, 2, 2, 1, 2, 2, 2, 6, 16, 14, 18, 30   (17)

7-02-83   *Is There Something I Should Know*   (Cap. B-5233)   26, 23, 12, 10, 7, 5, 4, 5, 8, 11, 11, 24, 24, 29   (14)

2-11-84   *New Moon On Monday*   (Cap. B-5309)   29, 22, 19, 17, 16, 12, 12, 19, 17, 23   (10)

4-28-84   *The Reflex*   (Cap. B-5345)   25, 21, 17, 14, 12, 7, 4, 2, 2, 3, 4, 5, 8, 10, 17, 27   (16)

4-23-83   *Rio*   (Cap. B-5215)   25, 19, 16, 9, 9, 8, 7, 7, 25   (9)

2-23-85   *Save A Prayer*   (Cap. B-5438)   28, 19, 19, 18, 17, 17, 15   (7)

11-12-83   *Union Of The Snake*   (Cap. B-5290)   30, 23, 17, 13, 9, 4, 1, 1, 1, 1, 2, 3, 5, 8, 11, 16, 28   (17)

6-01-85   *A View To A Kill*   (Cap. B-5475)   27, 24, 19, 14, 11, 5, 5, 4, 4, 14   (10)

11-17-84   *The Wild Boys*   (Cap. B-5417)   30, 23, 9, 3, 1, 2, 6, 6, 6, 13, 22   (11)

EARTH, WIND AND FIRE   (*See also:* PHILIP BAILEY)

2-13-82   *Let's Groove*   (ARC/Col. 18-02536)   7   (1)

EASTON, SHEENA   (*See also:* KENNY ROGERS)

3-10-84   *Almost Over You*   (EMI America B-8186)   24, 22, 22   (3)

11-30-85   *Do It For Love*   (EMI America B-8295)   29, 29   (2)

9-15-84   *Strut*   (EMI America B-8227)   29, 24, 19, 17, 14, 12, 11, 10, 6, 4, 3, 3, 9, 13, 20   (15)

11-05-83   *Telefone*   (EMI America B-8172)   13, 16, 20, 27, 30   (5)

ELECTRIC LIGHT ORCHESTRA

7-16-83   *Rock 'N' Roll Is King*   (Jet ZS4 03964)   30, 28, 25, 19, 18, 18, 30   (7)

EURYTHMICS

2-04-84   *Here Comes The Rain*   (RCA PB-13725)   25, 20, 17, 14, 10, 8, 7, 7, 5, 16, 27   (11)

11-05-83   *Love Is A Stranger*   (RCA PB-13618)   28, 24, 22, 20, 20, 24, 30   (7)

7-09-83   *Sweet Dreams*   (RCA PB-13533)   27, 21, 19, 14, 8, 7, 2, 1, 1, 1, 3, 3, 4, 6, 6, 6, 6   (17)

8-10-85   *There Must Be An Angel*   (RCA PB-14160)   30, 27, 24, 20, 20   (5)

6-23-84   *Who's That Girl?*   (RCA PB-13900)   30, 25 30   (3)

5-11-85   *Would I Lie To You?*   (RCA PB-14078)   30, 25, 21, 16, 12, 10, 9, 5, 3, 3, 3, 3, 11   (13)

EURYTHMICS AND ARETHA FRANKLIN   (*See also:* ARETHA FRANKLIN)

11-09-85   *Sisters Are Doin' It For Themselves*   (RCA PB-14214)   24, 24, 19, 17, 17   (5)

THE EVERLY BROTHERS

10-06-84   *On The Wings Of A Nightingale*   (Mer. 880 213-7)   30, 25, 24, 24, 26   (5)

FAGEN, DONALD

10-30-82   *I.G.Y. (What A Beautiful World)*   (WB 7-29900)   29, 21, 18, 14, 13, 11, 10, 21, 29, 29, 29   (11)

FALTERMEYER, HAROLD

5-04-85   *Axel F*   (MCA 52536)   28, 21, 12, 8, 4, 2, 1, 3, 4, 12, 12   (11)

THE FIRM

3-16-85   *Radioactive*   (Atl. 7-89586)   30, 26, 26, 26, 21, 27   (6)

THE FIXX

9-08-84   *Are We Ourselves?*   (MCA 52444)   30, 28, 25, 15, 12, 10, 7, 7, 7, 13, 27   (11)

9-17-83   *One Thing Leads To Another*   (MCA 52264)   26, 26, 20, 17, 17, 17, 17, 21, 29   (9)

7-23-83   *Saved By Zero*   (MCA 52213)   30, 27, 22, 22, 20, 25, 28, 28   (8)

FLEETWOOD MAC   (*See also:* LINDSEY BUCKINGHAM; STEVIE NICKS)

9-18-82   *Gypsy*   (WB 7-29918)   26, 21, 17, 10, 8, 7, 3, 3, 6, 18, 27   (11)

6-26-82   *Hold Me*   (WB 7-29966)   28, 23, 16, 12, 8, 4, 2, 2, 6, 9, 16, 21   (12)

A FLOCK OF SEAGULLS

7-17-82   *I Ran*   (Jive VS 102)   30, 28, 24, 23, 21, 20, 19, 18, 16, 13, 10, 8, 6, 6, 9, 14   (16)

12-18-82   *Space Age Love Song*   (Jive VS 2003)   29, 27, 27, 27, 24, 23, 29   (7)

FOGELBERG, DAN

2-18-84   *The Language Of Love*   (Full Moon 34-04314)   30, 26, 19, 15, 10, 10, 13, 9, 18, 27   (10)

2-13-82   *Leader Of The Band*   (Full Moon 14-02647)   27   (1)

11-13-82   *Missing You*   (Full Moon 34-03289)   29, 23, 20, 16, 13, 17, 17, 17, 17, 23, 27   (11)

4-24-82   *Run For The Roses*   (Full Moon 14-02821)   30, 24, 21, 16, 14, 12, 9, 9, 13, 21   (10)

FOGERTY, JOHN

7-06-85   *Centerfield*   (WB 7-29053)   30, 30, 29, 29   (4)

12-29-84   *The Old Man Down The Road*   (WB 7-29100)   30, 30, 30, 21, 14, 10, 7, 6, 4, 4, 7, 12, 24, 24   (14)

4-13-85   *Rock And Roll Girls*   (WB 7-29053)   29, 25, 22, 19, 18, 29   (6)

FOREIGNER

5-29-82   *Break It Up*   (Atl.)   29, 27, 25, 23, 23, 27   (6)

12-15-84   *I Want To Know What Love Is*   (Atl. 7-89596)   25, 19, 12, 12, 12, 8, 2, 1, 1, 4, 13, 24   (12)

2-20-82   *Juke Box Hero*   (Atl.)   13, 3, 2, 2, 4, 8, 18, 22   (8)

4-13-85   *That Was Yesterday*   (Atl. 7-89571)   12, 8, 7, 14, 22   (5)

2-13-82   *Waiting For A Girl Like You*   (Atl.)   9   (1)

FOSTER, DAVID

11-09-85   *Love Theme From St. Elmo's Fire*   (Atl. 7-89528)   29, 29, 25   (3)

FRANKE AND THE KNOCKOUTS

4-24-82   *Without You*   (Millenium YB-13105)   28, 27, 24, 24, 23, 30   (6)

FRANKIE GOES TO HOLLYWOOD

3-09-85   *Relax*   (ZTT 7-99805)   24, 21, 16, 16, 16   (5)

FRANKLIN, ARETHA   (See also: EURYTHMICS)

7-20-85   *Freeway Of Love*   (Arista AS1-9354)   22, 22, 15, 5, 2, 2, 7, 7   (8)

11-09-85   *Who's Zoomin' Who*   (Arista AS1-9410)   18, 18, 15, 11, 11   (5)

FREY, GLENN

12-29-84   *The Heat Is On*   (MCA 52512)   26, 26, 26, 20, 17, 15, 14, 11, 8, 5, 4, 2, 1, 1, 4, 14, 30   (17)

7-10-82   *I Found Somebody*   (Asylum E-47466)   21, 17, 16, 19, 27   (5)

10-02-82   *The One You Love*   (Asylum 7-69974)   27, 21, 17, 15, 12, 9, 8, 13, 21, 28   (10)

7-21-84   *Sexy Girl*   (MCA 52413)   29, 27, 25, 22, 20, 19   (6)

6-25-85   *Smuggler's Blues*   (MCA 52546)   27, 22, 18, 15, 12, 10, 8, 8, 16, 16, 23   (11)

11-09-85   *You Belong To The City*   (MCA 52651)   3, 3, 1, 2, 2   (5)

FRIDA   (See also: ABBA)

3-26-83   *I Know There's Something Going On*   (Atl. 7-89984)   26, 23, 20, 14, 13, 13, 20   (7)

GAYE, MARVIN

11-13-82   *Sexual Healing*   (Col. 38-03302)   27, 24, 17, 10, 9, 8, 10, 10, 10, 18, 20, 25   (12)

GAYLE, CRYSTAL   *(See:* EDDIE RABBITT)

GEILS, J., BAND

2-13-82   *Centerfold*   (EMI America A-8012)   3   (1)

2-27-82   *Freeze Frame/Flamethrower*   (EMI America)   20, 14, 11, 7, 4, 2, 1, 1, 3, 12, 12, 19, 27   (13)

12-04-82   *I Do*   (EMI America B-8148)   27, 20, 15, 13, 13, 13, 11, 10, 13, 19   (10)

GENERAL PUBLIC

2-02-85   *Tenderness*   (I.R.S. IR-9934)   29, 25, 22   (3)

GENESIS   *(See also:* PHIL COLLINS)

12-10-83   *That's All*   (Atl. 7-89724)   28, 23, 19, 19, 19, 19, 13, 8, 6, 5, 7, 10, 15, 21, 28, 28   (16)

GIUFFRIA

1-19-85   *Call To The Heart*   (MCA 52497)   29, 23, 20, 19, 19   (5)

4-06-85   *Lonely In Love*   (Camel 52558)   28, 24, 24   (3)

THE GO-GO'S

4-07-84   *Head Over Heels*   (I.R.S. IR-9926)   26, 19, 15, 12, 11, 10, 8, 14, 18, 24, 29   (11)

7-10-82   *Vacation*   (I.R.S. IR-9907)   29, 26, 22, 14, 11, 9, 7, 4, 4, 4, 11, 17, 21   (13)

2-13-82   *We Got The Beat*   (I.R.S. IR-9903)   21, 10, 7, 6, 4, 3, 2, 1, 5, 10, 12, 16, 18, 26   (14)

GODLEY AND CREME

8-24-85   *Cry*   (Polydor 881 786-7)   27, 21, 21   (3)

GOLDEN EARRING

3-05-83   *Twilight Zone*   (21 T 1103)   27, 23, 19, 16, 13, 11, 9, 9, 10, 11   (10)

GRANT, EDDY

5-28-83   *Electric Avenue*   (Ice 37-03793)   26, 24, 19, 16, 10, 5, 2, 3, 3, 5, 23   (11)

7-14-84   *Romancing The Stone*   (Portrait 37-04433)   27, 24, 22, 20, 20   (5)

GUIDRY, GREG

4-10-82   *Goin' Down*   (Col. 18-02691)   29, 26, 26, 29   (4)

HAGAR, SAMMY   *(See also:* VAN HALEN)

2-20-82   *I'll Fall In Love Again*   (Geffen GEF 49881)   30, 29, 28   (3)

2-05-83   *Your Love Is Driving Me Crazy*   (Geffen 7-29816)   28, 26, 26, 24, 24, 30   (6)

HALL, DARYL, AND JOHN OATES

2-25-84   *Adult Education*   (RCA PB-13714)   29, 22, 18, 14, 14, 14, 11, 8, 8, 15, 20, 28   (12)

3-20-82   *Did It In A Minute*   (RCA PB-13065)   22, 18, 15, 13, 9, 5, 3, 3, 2, 2, 10, 20   (12)

5-14-83   *Family Man*   (RCA PB-13507)   26, 21, 17, 14, 11, 6, 5, 6, 7, 14, 21   (11)

2-13-82   *I Can't Go For That*   (RCA PB-12357)   2   (1)

10-23-82   *Maneater*   (RCA PB-13354)   30, 26, 19, 14, 9, 7, 5, 3, 2, 1, 1, 1, 2, 5, 8, 13, 24   (17)

1-19-85   *Method Of Modern Love*   (RCA PB-13970)   27, 15, 12, 10, 8, 7, 7, 14, 20   (9)

2-12-83   *One On One*   (RCA PB-13421)   21, 15, 11, 9, 7, 6, 3, 1, 1, 4, 5, 7, 10, 17, 24   (15)

10-06-84   *Out Of Touch*   (RCA JK-13916)   27, 18, 15, 12, 11, 7, 5, 4, 2, 1, 3, 5, 15, 15, 15, 23, 30   (17)

11-05-83   *Say It Isn't So*   (RCA PB-13654)   28, 22, 19, 12, 10, 8, 7, 3, 3, 3, 3, 3, 5, 11, 17, 27   (16)

4-20-85   *Some Things Are Better Left Unsaid*   (RCA PB-14035)   20, 19, 17, 16, 16, 22   (6)

HAMMER, JAN

11-09-85   *"Miami Vice" Theme*   (MCA 52666)   1, 1, 5, 8, 8   (5)

HART, COREY

7-06-85   *Never Surrender*   (EMI America B-8268)   28, 28, 17, 17, 13, 6, 4, 3, 11, 11   (10)

8-11-84   *Sunglasses At Night*   (EMI America B-8203)   29, 21, 10, 19, 15, 11, 19, 25   (8)

HARTMAN, DAN

7-21-84   *I Can Dream About You*   (MCA 52378)   27, 26, 24, 21, 16, 15, 14   (7)

HEAD, MURRAY

4-13-85   *One Night In Bangkok*   (RCA PB-13988)   19, 17, 14, 10, 6, 5, 9, 14, 27   (9)

HEART   (See also: MIKE RENO)

11-09-85   *Never*   (Cap. B-5512)   7, 7, 3, 3, 3   (5)

6-05-82   *This Man Is Mine*   (Epic 14-02925)   30, 27, 26, 24, 24, 24, 27   (7)

7-20-85   *What About Love?*   (Cap. B-5481)   26, 26, 22, 16, 15, 14   (6)

HENLEY, DON

3-16-85   *All She Wants To Do Is Dance*   (Geffen 7-29065)   27, 22, 22, 22, 16, 14, 11, 8, 7, 11, 16, 23   (12)

12-01-84   *The Boys Of Summer*   (Geffen 7-29141)   29, 24, 20, 17, 14, 14, 14, 11, 8, 5, 3, 3, 3, 6, 10, 29   (16)

11-06-82   *Dirty Laundry*   (Asylum 7-69894)   23, 16, 6, 3, 2, 1, 1, 4, 4, 4, 3, 3, 4, 10, 17, 24   (16)

HIGGINS, BERTIE

2-27-82   *Key Largo*   (Kat Family WS9 02524)   30, 20, 12, 8, 7, 7, 7, 14, 19, 25   (10)

HODGSON, ROGER   (*See also:* SUPERTRAMP)

12-01-84   *Had A Dream*   (A&M AM 2678)   30, 26, 23, 29   (4)

THE HONEYDRIPPERS   (*See also:* ROBERT PLANT)

2-02-85   *Rockin' At Midnight*   (Es Paranza 7-99686)   30, 26, 24, 22, 22   (5)

10-27-84   *Sea Of Love*   (Es Paranza 7-99701)   28, 28, 20, 12, 7, 6, 4, 2, 1, 2, 2, 2, 5, 13, 22   (15)

THE HOOTERS

11-09-85   *And We Danced*   (Col. 38-05568)   21, 21   (2)

HOUSTON, WHITNEY

11-09-85   *Saving All My Love For You*   (Arista AS1-9381)   11, 11, 21   (3)

6-22-85   *You Give Good Love*   (Arista AS1-9264)   28, 27, 23, 23, 14, 14, 7, 24   (8)

THE HUMAN LEAGUE

3-27-82   *Don't You Want Me*   (A&M AM 2397)   28, 26, 24, 22, 20, 18, 17, 15, 12, 9, 6, 3, 1, 1, 1, 3, 4, 3, 6, 9, 13, 15, 23   (23)

7-09-83   *Fascination*   (A&M AM 2547)   28, 25, 22, 20, 18, 14, 10, 10, 18, 18, 27, 27   (12)

HYNDE, CHRISSIE   (*See:* THE PRETENDERS; UB40)

IDOL, BILLY

6-02-84 *Eyes Without A Face* (Chrysalis VS4 42786)   22, 17, 11, 8, 5, 3, 3, 5, 6, 7, 7, 10, 21, 30   (14)

9-22-84 *Flesh For Fantasy* (Chrysalis VS4 42809)   29, 26, 23, 23, 29   (5)

2-11-84 *Rebel Yell* (Chrysalis VS4 42762)   30, 24, 20, 21, 20, 17, 17, (1), 27   (8)

IGLESIAS, JULIO, AND WILLIE NELSON   *(See also:* WILLIE NELSON)

3-31-84 *To All The Girls I've Loved Before* (Col. 38-04217)   30, 21, 16, 11, 6, 4, 1, 1, 2, 5, 9, 18, 23   (13)

IGLESIAS, JULIO, AND DIANA ROSS   *(See also:* DIANA ROSS)

8-11-84 *All Of You* (Col. 38-04507)   30, 26, 20, 25, 24, 23, 23   (7)

INGRAM, JAMES   *(See:* QUINCY JONES; KENNY ROGERS)

IRIS, DONNIE

2-13-82 *Love Is Like A Rock* (MCA 51223)   23, 21, 21   (3)

JACKSON, FREDDIE

7-20-85 *Rock Me Tonight* (Cap. B-5459)   30, 30, 25, 23, 20, 20   (6)

11-09-85 *You Are My Lady* (Cap. B-5495)   13, 13, 12, 18, 18   (5)

JACKSON, JERMAINE   *(See also:* THE JACKSONS)

12-22-84 *Do What You Do* (Arista AS1-9279)   27, 22, 22, 22, 22   (5)

JACKSON, JOE

2-12-83 *Breaking Us In Two* (A&M AM 2510)   25, 21, 18, 14, 11, 9, 6, 12, 16, 24   (10)

10-09-82 *Steppin' Out* (A&M AM 2428)   28, 26, 25, 23, 20, 13, 11, 10, 8, 8, 16, 26, 26, 26, 30   (15)

6-09-84 *You Can't Get What You Want* (A&M AM 2628) 27, 21, 19, 18, 18, 28 (6)

JACKSON, MICHAEL (*See also:* THE JACKSONS)

3-05-83 *Beat It* (Epic 34-03759) 21, 17, 11, 8, 7, 6, 5, 4, 3, 1, 1, 1, 3, 4, 4, 5, 9, 20 (18)

1-29-83 *Billie Jean* (Epic 34-03509) 30, 25, 18, 13, 12, 7, 3, 1, 4, 4, 3, 3, 8, 14, 19, 20, 26 (17)

6-02-84 *Farewell My Summer Love* (Motown 1739 MF) 29, 20, 17, 15, 13, 11, 11, 11, 30 (9)

8-13-83 *Human Nature* (Epic 34-04026) 27, 23, 22, 14, 14, 12, 12, 15, 22, 22, 22, 22 (12)

2-04-84 *Thriller* (Epic 34-04364) 29, 24, 15, 11, 8, 7, 3, 3, 4, 5, 7, 13, 27, 30 (14)

6-11-83 *Wanna Be Startin' Somethin'* (Epic 34-03914) 30, 19, 17, 13, 9, 6, 4, 4, 2, 2, 7, 13, 29, 29 (14)

JACKSON, MICHAEL, AND PAUL McCARTNEY (*See also:* THE JACKSONS; PAUL McCARTNEY)

11-13-82 *The Girl Is Mine* (Epic 34-03288) 24, 19, 11, 9, 7, 5, 3, 3, 3, 6, 6, 10, 16, 27 (14)

JACKSON, REBBIE

12-08-84 *Centipede* (Col. 38-04547) 29, 26, 23, 18, 18, 18, 16, 26, 28 (9)

THE JACKSONS (*See also:* JERMAINE JACKSON; MICHAEL JACKSON)

7-07-84 *State Of Shock* (Epic 34-04503) 22, 14, 7, 4, 3, 2, 3, 5, 3, 8, 14, 28 (12)

9-01-84 *Torture* (Epic 34-04575) 27, 23, 20, 17, 24 (5)

JAGGER, MICK (*See also:* THE ROLLING STONES)

2-16-85 *Just Another Night* (Col. 38-04743) 20, 17, 13, 9, 7, 4, 4, 3, 10, 13, 26, 29 (12)

THE JEFFERSON STARSHIP   (*See also:* THE STARSHIP)

6-09-84   *No Way Out*   (Grunt FB-13811)   29, 24, 20, 19, 17, 15, 23   (7)

JETT, JOAN, AND THE BLACKHEARTS

5-08-82   *Crimson And Clover*   (Boardwalk NB7-11-144)   23, 18, 11, 2, 1, 1, 2, 4, 7, 15, 24   (11)

9-11-82   *Do You Wanna Touch Me*   (Boardwalk NB7-11-150)   27, 23, 20, 19, 25   (5)

2-13-82   *I Love Rock 'N' Roll*   (Boardwalk NB7-11-135)   13, 3, 1, 1, 1, 1, 1, 5, 10, 17, 29   (11)

JOEL, BILLY

1-15-83   *Allentown*   (Col. 38-03413)   28, 24, 19, 15, 15, 22, 29   (7)

2-09-85   *Keeping The Faith*   (Col. 38-04681)   30, 28, 24, 20, 17, 17, 15, 15, 13   (9)

8-04-84   *Leave A Tender Moment Alone*   (Col. 38-04514)   29, 25, 23, 22   (4)

4-28-84   *The Longest Time*   (Col. 38-04400)   26, 22, 16, 13, 11, 10, 18, 26, 29   (9)

10-02-82   *Pressure*   (Col. 38-03244)   29, 27, 24, 20, 16, 14, 11, 10, 12, 17, 22   (11)

8-13-83   *Tell Her About It*   (Col. 38-04012)   29, 25, 19, 5, 5, 5, 5, 2, 1, 1, 1, 1, 15, 20, 27, 30   (16)

10-08-83   *Uptown Girl*   (Col. 38-04149)   28, 28, 28, 18, 10, 5, 2, 2, 2, 3, 6, 6, 6, 6, 9, 17, 28   (18)

8-03-85   *You're Only Human*   (Col. 38-05417)   26, 21, 17, 11, 8, 8   (6)

JOHN, ELTON

7-31-82   *Blue Eyes*   (Geffen 7-29954)   28, 26, 24, 28, 27, 23, 20, 18, 19   (9)

4-03-82   *Empty Garden*   (Geffen GEF 50049)   29, 26, 24, 22, 20, 26, 30   (7)

12-24-83   *I Guess That's Why They Call It The Blues*   (Geffen 7-29460)   25, 25, 25, 25, 15, 9, 4, 4, 4, 8, 14, 27   (12)

5-21-83 *I'm Still Standing* (Geffen ⁻-29639) 29, 25, 21, 1⁻, 12, 11, 11, 11, 13, 14, 19 (11)

6-30-84 *Sad Songs* (Geffen ⁻-29292) 28, 25, 22, 19, 16, 12, 11, 14, 28, 15, 2⁻ (11)

11-30-85 *Wrap Her Up* (Geffen ⁻-288⁻3) 26, 26 (2)

JONES, HOWARD

4-2⁻-85 *Things Can Only Get Better* (Elektra ⁻-69651) 2⁻, 24, 19, 13, 10, 6, 3, 3, 2, 3, ⁻, ⁻, 18, 18 (14)

JONES, QUINCY, FEATURING JAMES INGRAM

2-20-82 *One Hundred Ways* (A&M AM 238⁻) 1⁻, (4), 29, 28, 28 (4)

JOURNEY (See also: KENNY LOGGINS; STEVE PERRY; SANTANA)

8-06-83 *After The Fall* (Col. 38-04004) 30, 25, 21, 1⁻, 1⁻, 1⁻, 22, 22, 24 (9)

5-14-83 *Faithfully* (Col. 38-03840) 28, 23, 18, 15, 12, 8, 8, 19, 18 (9)

2-02-85 *Only The Young* (Geffen ⁻-29090) 26, 23, 21, 18, 1⁻, 16, 15, 14, 14 (9)

2-13-82 *Open Arms* (Col. 18-02687) 1, 1, 4, ⁻, 9, 12, 19, 30 (⁻)

2-12-83 *Separate Ways* (Col. 38-03513) 30, 2⁻, 21, 16, 12, 10, 9, 9, 9, 8, ⁻, 8, 17, 22 (14)

JUMP 'N' THE SADDLE

12-10-83 *The Curly Shuffle* (Atl. 7-89⁻18) 2⁻, 24, 18, 18, 18, 18, 11, 4, 3, ⁻, 9, 13 (12)

K.C.

3-03-84 *Give It Up* (Meca S-1001) 26, 23, 21, 21, 2⁻ (5)

KAJAGOOGOO

5-28-83 *Too Shy* (EMI America B-8161) 2⁻, 25, 24, 21, 19, 14, 12, 8, ⁻, 6, 24, 28 (12)

KANSAS

6-05-82   *Play The Game Tonight*   (Kirshner ZS5-02903)   25, 22, 18, 14, 12, 10, 14, 21   (8)

KATRINA AND THE WAVES

4-27-85   *Walking On Sunshine*   (Cap. B-5466)   30, 27, 24, 18, 14, 11, 7, 6, 5, 6, 22, 22, 27, 27   (14)

KHAN, CHAKA

10-06-84   *I Feel For You*   (WB 7-29195)   28, 20, 18, 16, 16, 10, 7, 6, 5, 2, 4, 9, 21, 21, 21, 30   (16)

KIHN, GREG, BAND

2-26-83   *Jeopardy*   (Beserkley 7-29848)   28, 23, 19, 16, 13, 6, 4, 1, 1, 4, 6, 6, 10, 13, 18, 26   (16)

KING, EVELYN

10-02-82   *Love Come Down*   (RCA PB-13273)   30, 23, 21, 17, 15, 15, 26   (7)

THE KINKS

6-11-83   *Come Dancing*   (Arista AS 1054)   28, 24, 20, 16, 14, 9, 8, 8, 11, 21   (10)

KOOL & THE GANG

9-25-82   *Big Fun*   (De-Lite DE 82200)   29, 26, 20, 18, 16, 25   (6)

8-24-85   *Cherish*   (De-Lite 880 869-7)   21, 14, 14   (3)

5-11-85   *Fresh*   (De-Lite 880 623-7)   28, 17, 11, 9, 6, 13, 21   (7)

3-27-82   *Get Down On It*   (De-Lite DE 818)   26, 21, 18, 16, 16, 15, 22   (7)

12-10-83   *Joanna*   (De-Lite DE 829)   23, 19, 16, 16, 16, 16, 14, 10, 9, 6, 5, 5, 18, 22   (14)

2-09-85   *Misled*   (De-Lite 880 431-7)   28, 26, 23, 23, 20, 14   (6)

LaBELLE, PATTI

  2-25-84   *If Only You Knew*   (P.I. ZS4 04248)   30, 25   (2)

  4-27-85   *New Attitude*   (MCA 52517)   24, 22, 20, 20   (4)

LAID BACK

  5-12-84   *White Horse*   (Sire 7-29346)   30, 26, 23   (3)

LAUPER, CYNDI

  11-10-84   *All Through The Night*   (Portrait 37-04639)   22, 13, 11, 11, 17, 21   (6)

  1-28-84   *Girls Just Want To Have Fun*   (Portrait 37-04120)   23, 14, 9, 6, 3, 2, 5, 9, 9, 9, 10, 15, 22   (13)

  5-25-85   *The Goonies 'R' Good Enough*   (Portrait 34-04918)   29, 24, 21, 17, 16, 15, 14, 14, 13, 13, 20   (11)

  8-04-84   *She Bop*   (Portrait 37-04516)   28, 24, 18, 13, 11, 7, 5, 3, 2, 4, 5, 8, 10, 12, 19, 29   (16)

  4-21-84   *Time After Time*   (Portrait 37-04432)   30, 22, 18, 14, 11, 9, 2, 1, 1, 4, 8, 13, 13, 20, 28   (15)

LE ROUX

  3-20-82   *Nobody Said It Was Easy (Lookin' For The Lights)*   (RCA PB-73059)   26, 25, 23, 20, 18   (5)

LENNON, JOHN   (*See also:* THE BEATLES)

  4-21-84   *I'm Stepping Out*   (Polydor 821 107-7)   26, 24, 23, 25, 30   (5)

  1-28-84   *Nobody Told Me*   (Polydor 817 254-7)   28, 17, 12, 10, 7, 7, 9, 11, 11, 12, 15, 21, 29   (13)

LENNON, JULIAN

  2-09-85   *Too Late For Goodbyes*   (Atl. 7-89589)   27, 23, 19, 14, 11, 9, 7, 7, 5, 5, 9, 23   (12)

  11-17-84   *Valotte*   (Atl. 7-89609)   26, 22, 20, 16, 12, 10, 8, 8, 8, 17, 24   (11)

LEWIS, HUEY, AND THE NEWS

3-06-82   *Do You Believe In Love*   (Chrysalis CHS 2589)   26, 25, 15, 14, 13, 14, 13, 15, 21   (9)

11-05-83   *Heart And Soul*   (Chrysalis VS4 42726)   24, 17, 14, 9, 7, 11, 13, 17, 17, 17, 17, 24   (12)

5-05-84   *The Heart Of Rock And Roll*   (Chrysalis VS4 42782)   26, 20, 18, 15, 11, 8, 6, 3, 4, 7, 9, 12, 19, 27   (14)

1-28-84   *I Want A New Drug*   (Chrysalis VS4 42766)   30, 23, 15, 12, 9, 9, 10, 5, 5, 6, 4, 4, 4, 7, 9, 15, 21, 25, 30   (19)

8-25-84   *If This Is It*   (Chrysalis VS4 42803)   26, (1), 21, 15, 9, 6, 6, 9, 11, 17, 17   (10)

7-06-85   *Power Of Love*   (Chrysalis VS4 42876)   29, 29, 19, 19, 10, 3, 1, 1, 6, 6   (10)

11-17-84   *Walking On A Thin Line*   (Chrysalis VS4 42825)   28, 25, 22, 18, 19, 26   (6)

THE LITTLE RIVER BAND

4-17-82   *Man On Your Mind*   (Cap. PB-5061)   29, 21, 17, 15, 12, 10, 16, 16, 23, 29   (10)

11-20-85   *The Other Guy*   (Cap. B-5185)   26, 23, 19, 16, 13, 12, 12, 12, 9, 7, 5, 5, 9, 14, 20, 28   (16)

6-04-83   *We Two*   (Cap. B-5231)   28, 23, 22, 18, 18, 19, 23   (7)

LOGGINS, KENNY

2-25-84   *Footloose*   (Col. 38-04310)   27, 20, 11, 8, 8, 3, 2, 1, 1, 3, 5, 8, 15, 19, 27   (15)

12-18-82   *Heart To Heart*   (Col. 38-03377)   28, 24, 24, 24, 19, 16, 11, 8, 13, 18, 25   (11)

7-07-84   *I'm Free*   (Col. 38-04452)   28, 24, 22, 20, 15, 13, 19   (7)

4-06-85   *Vox Humana*   (Col. 38-04849)   30, 25, 23, 20, 18, 17, 26, 28   (8)

4-02-83   *Welcome To Heartlight*   (Col. 38-03555)   29, 27, 25, 27, 30   (5)

LOGGINS, KENNY, WITH STEVE PERRY   (*See also:* JOURNEY; STEVE PERRY)

9-04-82   *Don't Fight It*   (Col. 18-03192)   30, 26, 22, 18, 15, 14, 12, 10, 9, 17, 28   (11)

LOS LOBOS

4-06-85   *Will The Wolf Survive?*   (Slash 7-29093)   29, 27, 28   (3)

LOVERBOY

7-16-83   *Hot Girls In Love*   (Col. 38-03941)   29, 24, 18, 13, 12, 9, 6, 12, 12, 20, 20, 25, 29, 29, 29, 29   (16)

11-09-85   *Lovin' Every Minute Of It*   (Col. 38-05569)   17, 17   (2)

5-01-82   *When It's Over*   (Col. 18-02814)   30, 25, 21, 18, 15, 13, 11, 10, 18, 26   (10)

MADNESS

6-25-83   *Our House*   (Geffen 7-29668)   26, 22, 17, 16, 12, 10, 12, 19, 19, 28   (10)

MADONNA

5-25-85   *Angel*   (Sire 7-29008)   26, 20, 15, 12, 10, 7, 6, 6, 12, 12, 27   (11)

6-30-84   *Borderline*   (Sire 7-29354)   23, 15, 20   (3)

4-13-85   *Crazy For You*   (Sire 7-29051)   6, 5, 4, 3, 1, 1, 2, 5, 8, 18, 24   (11)

8-31-85   *Dress You Up*   (Sire 7-28919)   12, 12   (2)

11-24-84   *Like A Virgin*   (Sire 7-29210)   29, 18, 13, 5, 3, 1, 1, 1, 3, 6, 9, 22   (12)

2-16-85   *Material Girl*   (Sire 7-29083)   30, 26, 21, 15, 13, 9, 9, 10   (8)

MANCHESTER, MELISSA

7-17-82   *You Should Hear How She Talks About You*   (Arista AS 0676)   25, 20, 17, 13, 11, 10, 7, 5, 3, 2, 6, 10, 18, 27   (14)

MANILOW, BARRY

4-10-82   *Let's Hang On*   (Arista AS 0675)   25, 25, 24   (3)

MARIE, TEENA

2-23-85   *Lovergirl*   (Epic 34-04619)   27, 18, 12, 10, 8, 8, 8, 11, 16, 29   (10)

MARTIN, MARILYN   (*See:* PHIL COLLINS)

THE MARY JANE GIRLS

5-11-85   *In My House*   (Motown 1741 GF)   26, 22, 15, 12, 10, 8, 8, 16   (8)

MATHIS, JOHNNY   (*See:* DIONNE WARWICK)

McCARTNEY, PAUL   (*See also:* THE BEATLES; MICHAEL JACKSON)

10-20-84   *No More Lonely Nights*   (Col. 38-04581)   30, 26, 22, 14, 9, 8, 7, 6,
           11, 15, 27, 27, 27   (13)

11-30-85   *Spies Like Us*   (Cap. B-5537)   30, 30   (2)

7-24-82   *Take It Away*   (Col. 18-03018)   27, 20, 10, 6, 5, 5, 8, 15, 19,
          28   (10)

McCARTNEY, PAUL, AND MICHAEL JACKSON   (*See also:* THE BEATLES; MICHAEL JACKSON; THE JACKSONS)

10-29-83   *Say. Say. Say*   (Col. 38-04168)   23, 12, 10, 6, 3, 3, 4, 6, 10, 10, 10,
           10, 16, 22, 30   (15)

McCARTNEY, PAUL, AND STEVIE WONDER   (*See also:* THE BEATLES; STEVIE WONDER)

4-17-82   *Ebony And Ivory*   (Col.)   23, 13, 1, 1, 1, 1, 1, 2, 4, 4, 6, 6, 12, 16, 24,
          29   (16)

McDONALD, MICHAEL

8-14-82   *I Keep Forgettin'*   (WB 7-29933)   30, 27, 22, 11, 7, 3, 2, 2, 3, 2, 2, 2,
          5, 12, 25   (15)

8-24-85   *No Lookin' Back*   (WB 7-28960)   29, 22, 22   (3)

McKENZIE, BOB AND DOUG

2-20-82   *Take Off*   (Mer. SR 76134)   23, 22, 17, 13, 10, 9, 8, 15, 19   (9)

McVIE, CHRISTINE   *(See also:* FLEETWOOD MAC)

2-18-84   *Got A Hold On Me*   (WB 7-29372)   26, 24, 23, 19, 18, 18, 15, 25   (8)

MECO

2-20-82   *Pop Goes The Movies (Part 1)*   (Arista AS 0660)   29, 27, 25, 22, 25   (5)

MEISNER, RANDY

9-18-82   *Never Been In Love*   (Epic 14-03032)   25, 23, 23   (3)

MELLENCAMP, JOHN COUGAR

4-07-84   *Authority Song*   (Riva R 216)   30, 24, 19, 16, 15, 12, 9, 6, 14, 14, 23, 27   (12)

10-29-83   *Crumblin' Down*   (Riva R 214)   28, 11, 8, 7, 6, 6, 5, 8, 12, 12, 12, 12, 19   (13)

5-15-82   *Hurts So Good*   (Riva R 209)   29, 25, 21, 17, 13, 8, 5, 4, 2, 2, 1, 2, 4, 8, 14, 18, 28   (17)

7-31-82   *Jack And Diane*   (Riva R 120)   30, 20, 17, 12, 8, 3, 2, 1, 1, 1, 1, 3, 5, 5, 7, 7, 21, 29   (18)

8-24-85   *Lonely Ol' Night*   (Riva 880 984-7)   30, 24, 24   (3)

12-17-83   *Pink Houses*   (Riva R 215)   27, 23, 23, 23, 23, 20, 15, 12, 13, 16, 22, 29   (12)

11-09-85   *Small Town*   (Riva 884 202-7)   25, 25, 20, 16, 16   (5)

MEN AT WORK

10-01-83   *Dr. Heckyll And Mr. Jive*   (Col. 38-04111)   30, 25, 25, 25, 25, 14, 18, 25, 29   (9)

11-27-82   *Down Under*   (Col. 38-03303)   26, 22, 18, 10, 8, 8, 8, 1, 1, 2, 4, 5, 10, 15, 20, 26, 29   (17)

7-09-83   *It's A Mistake*   (Col. 38-03959)   30, 27, 26, 21, 15, 9, 11, 7, 13, 13, 23, 23   (12)

4-16-83   *Overkill*   (Col. AE7-1633)   26, 21, 18, 13, 7, 4, 4, 3, 3, 4, 4, 8, 15   (13)

8-21-82   *Who Can It Be Now?*   (Col. 18-02888)   26, 21, 14, 10, 6, 4, 3, 2, 1, 1, 1, 2, 4, 5, 14, 20, 25   (17)

MEN WITHOUT HATS

9-17-83   *The Safety Dance*   (Backstreet BSR 52232)   1, 1, 1, 2, 2, 2, 2, 18, 25, 30   (10)

MENDES, SERGIO

5-28-83   *Never Gonna Let You Go*   (A&M AM 2540)   30, 26, 22, 18, 15, 15, 13, 7, 6, 3, 4, 10, 24   (13)

METHENY, PAT, GROUP   (*See:* DAVID BOWIE)

MILLER, STEVE, BAND

6-26-82   *Abracadabra*   (Cap. PRO-9785)   30, 28, 23, 20, 15, 10, 5, 3, 2, 1, 1, 5, 8, 13, 18, 29   (16)

10-27-84   *Shangri-La*   (Cap. B-5407)   30, 30, 28   (3)

MILSAP, RONNIE

5-07-83   *Stranger In My House*   (RCA PB-13470)   28, 23, 20, 21, 20, 20   (6)

MR. MISTER

11-09-85   *Broken Wings*   (RCA PB-14136)   6, 6, 2, 1, 1   (5)

MONEY, EDDIE

8-07-82   *Think I'm In Love*   (Col. 18-02964)   29, 25, 22, 20, 19, 28, 30   (7)

THE MOODY BLUES

10-01-83   *Sitting At The Wheel*   (Threshold TR 604)   28, 21, 21, 21, 21   (5)

THE MOTELS

5-22-82   *Only The Lonely*   (Cap. PB-5114)   28, 26, 23, 21, 15, 12, 10, 9, 7, 5, 3, 3, 7, 8, 12, 24   (16)

8-10-85   *Shame*   (Cap. B-5497)   27, 23, 18, 16, 16   (5)

11-05-83   *Suddenly Last Summer*   (Cap. B-5271)   19, 13, 11, 13, 18, 21, 28   (7)

9-11-82   *Take The L*   (Cap. B-5149)   29, 27, 25, 22, 30   (5)

MOTLEY CRUE

8-10-85   *Smokin' In The Boys Room*   (Elektra 7-69625)   25, 19, 17, 15, 15   (5)

MURPHEY, MICHAEL

9-11-82   *What's Forever For*   (Liberty B-1466)   25, 20, 15, 13, 13, 19, 28, 30   (8)

MURPHY, WALTER

8-28-82   *Themes From E.T.*   (MCA 52099)   29, 25, 24, 24   (4)

MURRAY, ANNE

2-13-82   *Another Sleepless Night*   (Cap. PA-5083)   26, 16, 15, 18, 20   (5)

MUSICAL YOUTH

2-05-83   *Pass The Dutchie*   (MCA 52149)   30, 20, 16, 14, 13, 18, 21   (7)

NAKED EYES

5-07-83   *Always Something There To Remind Me*   (EMI America B-8155)   29, 27, 22, 20, 19, 18, 14, 12, 12, 10, 17, 15, 16, 29   (14)

8-20-83   *Promises, Promises*   (EMI America B-8170)   29, 24, 15, 15, 13, 13, 12, 12, 12, 12, 12, 23   (12)

NELSON, WILLIE   (*See also:* JULIO IGLESIAS)

   6-19-82   *Always On My Mind*   (Col. 18-02741)   21, 13, 9, 7, 10, 13, 25, 30   (8)

NENA

   2-11-84   *99 Luftballoons*   (Epic 34-04108)   27, 21, 17, 3, 1, 1, 1, 2, 3, 5, 9, 18, 24, 29   (14)

THE NEW EDITION

   11-10-84   *Cool It Now*   (MCA 52455)   27, 19, 14, 12, 8, 7, 7, 16, 16, 16, 28   (11)

   1-26-85   *Mr. Telephone Man*   (MCA 52484)   25, 21, 13, 12, 10, 10, 18   (7)

NEWTON, JUICE

   9-04-82   *Break It To Me Gently*   (Cap. B-5148)   27, 23, 21, 16, 14, 12, 11, 11, 10, 10, 19, 27   (12)

   5-22-82   *Love's Been A Little Bit Hard On Me*   (Cap. PB-5120)   24, 17, 11, 7, 6, 3, 3, 6, 6, 18, 27   (11)

NEWTON-JOHN, OLIVIA

   10-02-82   *Heart Attack*   (MCA 52100)   24, 17, 13, 12, 6, 4, 5, 8, 16, 23   (10)

   2-13-82   *Make A Move On Me*   (MCA 52000)   29, 11, 6, 4, 5, 9, 12, 17, 19   (9)

   2-13-82   *Physical*   (MCA 51182)   11   (1)

   11-23-85   *Soul Kiss*   (MCA 52685)   26, 22, 22   (3)

   1-22-83   *Tied Up*   (MCA 52155)   29, 26, 24, 22, 21, 19   (6)

   11-26-83   *Twist Of Fate*   (MCA 52284)   25, 21, 20, 18, 15, 15, 15, 15, 8, 6, 8, 14, 20   (13)

NICKS, STEVIE   (*See also:* FLEETWOOD MAC)

   6-12-82   *After The Glitter Fades*   (Modern MR 7405)   29, 28, 27, 30   (4)

2-27-82   *Edge Of Seventeen*   (Modern MR 7401)   18, 10, 8, 6, 5, 4, 3, 5, 8, 14, 29   (11)

11-12-83   *If Anyone Falls*   (Modern 7-99832)   26, 24, 28   (3)

6-25-83   *Stand Back*   (Modern 7-99863)   28, 23, 21, 15, 11, 11, 7, 6, 4, 5, 10, 10, 17, 17, 21   (15)

11-23-85   *Talk To Me*   (Modern 7-99582)   29, 24, 24   (3)

NICKS, STEVIE, AND TOM PETTY   *(See also:* FLEETWOOD MAC; TOM PETTY AND THE HEARTBREAKERS)

2-13-82   *Leather And Lace*   (Modern MR 7341)   10   (1)

NICKS, STEVIE, WITH SANDY STEWART   *(See also:* FLEETWOOD MAC)

1-21-84   *Nightbird*   (Modern 7-99799)   27, 21, 20, 19, 25, 28   (6)

NIGHT RANGER

2-19-83   *Don't Tell Me You Love Me*   (Boardwalk NB-11-171)   29, 26, 25, 22, 27   (5)

6-08-85   *Sentimental Street*   (Camel 52591)   29, 24, 22, 20, 18, 18, 11, 11, 9, 9, 18   (11)

4-28-84   *Sister Christian*   (MCA 52350)   29, 25, 19, 17, 13, 8, 5, 3, 5, 9, 9, 12, 16, 24   (14)

9-01-84   *When You Close Your Eyes*   (MCA 55420)   29, 26, 24, 22, 20, 19   (6)

NOVA, ALDO

5-08-82   *Fantasy*   (Portrait 24-02799)   28, 25, 21, 19, 18, 16, 25   (7)

THE OAK RIDGE BOYS

2-13-82   *Bobbie Sue*   (MCA 51231)   19, 8, 12, 13, 16, 17, 23, 22, 30   (9)

OCEAN, BILLY

10-13-84   *Caribbean Queen*   (Jive JS1-9199)   17, 16, 15, 15, 9, 11, 19, 28   (8)

1-19-85   *Loverboy*   (Jive JS1-9284)   25, 19, 17, 16, 14, 5, 11, 21   (8)

6-08-85   *Suddenly*   (Jive JS1-9323)   11, 7, 7, 14, 26, 26   (6)

OLLIE AND JERRY

6-23-84   *Breakin'. . . There's No Stopping Us*   (Polydor 821 708-7)   26, 22, 20, 17, 15, 12, 11, 8, 5, 8, 10, 29   (12)

ORCHESTRAL MANOEUVRES IN THE DARK

11-09-85   *So In Love*   (A&M AM 2746)   30, 30   (2)

PARKER, RAY, JR.

1-15-83   *Bad Boy*   (Arista AS 1030)   25, 21, 18, 17, 29   (5)

7-14-84   *Ghostbusters*   (Arista AS1-9212)   21, 14, 7, 5, 1, 1, 1, 2, 3, 12, 21, 29   (12)

4-17-82   *The Other Woman*   (Arista AS 0669)   27, 23, 19, 13, 9, 7, 5, 4, 6, 9, 15, 22, 28   (13)

PARR, JOHN

2-23-85   *Naughty, Naughty*   (Atl. 7-89612)   29, 27, 27   (3)

7-20-85   *St. Elmo's Fire*   (Atl. 7-89541)   28, 28, 19, 8, 6, 4, 3, 3   (8)

PARRIS, FRED, AND THE FIVE SATINS

3-20-82   *Medley: Memories Of Days Gone By*   *(Elektra E-47411)*   *30, 27, 25*   *(3)*

PARSONS, ALAN, PROJECT

3-31-84   *Don't Answer Me*   (Arista AS1-9160)   23   (1)

8-14-82   *Eye In The Sky*   (Arista AS 0696)   22, 19, 15, 12, 11, 9, 9, 6, 4, 7, 6, 13, 30   (13)

PARTON, DOLLY *(See:* KENNY ROGERS)

PENDERGRASS, TEDDY

2-20-82   *You're My Latest, My Greatest Inspiration*   (P.I. ZS5 02619)   27   (1)

PERRY, STEVE   *(See also:* JOURNEY; KENNY LOGGINS)

12-29-84   *Foolish Heart*   (Col. 38-04693)   28, 28, 28, 24, 20, 18, 18, 18   (8)

4-14-84   *Oh Sherrie*   (Col. 38-04391)   26, 23, 17, 12, 9, 7, 4, 3, 3, 7, 10, 21   (12)

7-14-84   *She's Mine*   (Col. 38-04496)   29, 25, 10, 8, 30   (5)

PETTY, TOM, AND THE HEARTBREAKERS   *(See also:* STEVIE NICKS)

3-05-83   *Change Of Heart*   (Backstreet BSR-52181)   29, 25, 23, 20, 15, 15, 21, 30   (8)

4-13-85   *Don't Come Around Here No More*   (MCA 52496)   29, 21, 18, 15, 11, 10, 12, 17, 25   (9)

12-11-82   *You Got Lucky*   (Backstreet BSR-52144)   27, 23, 21, 21, 21, 16, 14, 12, 12, 19, 28   (11)

PLANT, ROBERT   *(See also:* THE HONEYDRIPPERS)

9-17-83   *Big Log*   (Es Paranza 7-99844)   30, 30, 26, 24, 24, 24, 24, 17, 23, 28   (10)

6-29-85   *Little By Little*   (Es Paranza 7-99644)   30, 27, 27   (3)

THE POINTER SISTERS

7-24-82   *American Music*   (Planet YB-13254)   25, 18, 15, 12, 11, 10, 21, 30   (8)

3-17-84   *Automatic*   (Planet YB-13730)   26, 26, 22, 22, 20, 17, 30   (7)

8-10-85   *Dare Me*   (RCA PB-14126)   26, 22, 19, 17, 17   (5)

5-12-84   *Jump*   (Planet YB-13780)   27, 23, 21, 16, 11, 8, 6, 6, 6, 6, 10, 15, 22   (13)

1-19-85   *Neutron Dance*   (Planet YB-13951)   18, 16, 14, 12, 9, 9, 8, 6, 8, 18, 18, 21   (12)

2-13-82   *Should I Do It*   (Planet P-47960)   15, 9, 10, 9, 10, 23   (6)

POLICE

6-11-83 *Every Breath You Take* (A&M AM 2542)   27, 20, 16, 10, 3, 1, 1, 1, 1, 1, 1, 2, 2, 2, 2, 2, 5, 8, 8, 8, 8   (21)

9-03-83 *King Of Pain* (A&M AM 2569)   27, 27, 14, 14, 9, 7, 7, 7, 7, 7, 9, 10, 16, 22, 26   (15)

2-13-82 *Spirits In The Material World* (A&M AM 2390)   6, 2, 13, 29   (4)

11-12-83 *Synchronicity II* (A&M AM 2571)   28, 21, 14, 11, 10, 9, 8, 8, 8, 8, 12, 19   (12)

2-04-84 *Wrapped Around Your Finger* (A&M AM 2614)   21, 16, 14, 12, 12, 12, 13, 13, 25, 20, 25   (11)

POST, MIKE

3-06-82 *Theme From Magnum P.I.* (Elektra E-47400)   30, 29   (2)

POWER STATION   *(See also:* DURAN DURAN)

6-29-85 *Get It On (Bang A Gong)* (Cap. B-5479)   28, 24, 24, 15, 15, 12, 4, 5, 12, 28, 28   (11)

4-13-85 *Some Like It Hot* (Cap. B-5444)   15, 11, 10, 7, 5, 4, 4, 7, 17, 25   (10)

THE PRETENDERS   *(See also:* UB40)

1-22-83 *Back On The Chain Gang* (Sire 7-29840)   26, 22, 14, 8, 5, 4, 2, 1, 4, 5, 5, 10, 19, 26   (14)

1-28-84 *Middle Of The Road* (Sire 7-29444)   16, 13, 10, 8, 6, 6, 6, 16, 16, 28   (10)

PRINCE (AND THE REVOLUTION)

11-05-83 *Delirious* (WB 7-29503)   16, 14, 13, 18, 23, 29   (6)

12-22-84 *I Would Die 4 You* (WB 7-29121)   30, 19, 19, 19, 12, 7, 6, 9, 15, 25   (10)

8-18-84 *Let's Go Crazy* (WB 7-29216)   28, 16, 18, 12, 10, 6, 4, 3, 4, 6, 6, 8, 15   (13)

3-19-83   *Little Red Corvette*   (WB 7-29746)   30, 22, 20, 19, 18, 14, 11, 9, 12, 12, 12, 16, 16, 27, 29   (15)

7-16-83   *1999*   (WB 7-29896)   28, 27, 23, 17, 17, 30   (6)

8-17-85   *Pop Life*   (Paisley Park 7-28998)   28, 15, 9, 9   (4)

10-13-84   *Purple Rain*   (WB 7-29174)   22, 13, 8, 6, 2, 2, 2, 4, 11, 17, 24   (11)

5-18-85   *Raspberry Beret*   (WB 7-28972)   30, 25, 19, 16, 14, 11, 8, 4, 4, 1, 1, 2, 15, 24   (14)

6-09-84   *When Doves Cry*   (WB 7-29286)   21, 15, 9, 2, 2, 2, 1, 1, 1, 3, 4, 3, 4, 4, 8, 15, 21   (17)

PRINCE AND THE REVOLUTION WITH APOLLONIA

3-23-85   *Take Me With U*   (WB 7-29079)   30, 30, 25   (3)

PRISM

2-20-82   *Don't Let Him Know*   (Cap. PA-5082)   28, 24, 24, 24, 29, 30   (6)

QUARTERFLASH

2-20-82   *Find Another Fool*   (Geffen GEF 50006)   24, 16, 12, 7, 5, 3, 3, 2, 6, 18, 26   (11)

2-13-82   *Harden My Heart*   (Geffen GEF 49824)   18   (1)

7-09-83   *Take Me To Heart*   (Geffen 7-29603)   29, 22, 20, 17, 14, 15, 14, 21, 22, 22   (10)

QUEEN

5-15-82   *Body Language*   (Elektra E-47452)   27, 22, 20, 19, 14, 12, 11, 19, 30   (9)

3-10-84   *Radio Ga Ga*   (Cap. B-5317)   26, 23, 23, 16, 14, 11, 10, 21, 27   (9)

QUIET RIOT

11-05-83   *Cum On Feel The Noize*   (Pasha/CBS ZS4 04005)   26, 15, 9, 7, 5, 7, 12, 14, 14, 14, 14, 21   (12)

8-04-84   *Mama Weer All Crazee Now*   (Pasha ZS4 04505)   30, 26, 24, (1), 21   (4)

RABBITT, EDDIE, AND CRYSTAL GAYLE

11-27-82   *You And I*   (Elektra 7-69936)   30, 26, 23, 20, 18, 18, 18, 27   (8)

RATT

8-10-85   *Lay It Down*   (Atl. 7-89546)   29, 26, 25   (3)

7-21-84   *Round And Round*   (Atl. 7-89693)   30, 23, 18, 15, 11, 9, 8, 6, 6, 10, 12, 13, 26   (13)

RE-FLEX

2-04-84   *The Politics Of Dancing*   (Cap. B-5301)   27, 22, 19, 18, 16, 17, 24, 24   (8)

RENO, MIKE, AND ANN WILSON   *(See also:* HEART; LOVERBOY)

6-02-84   *Almost Paradise . . . Love Theme From "Footloose"*   (Col. 38-04418)   26, 23, 19, 16, 11, 8, 7, 6, 9, 14, 23   (11)

REO SPEEDWAGON

1-26-85   *Can't Fight This Feeling*   (Epic 34-04713)   29, 25, 20, 16, 6, 3, 1, 1, 3, 3, 2, 8, 12, 16, 25   (15)

6-26-82   *Keep The Fire Burnin'*   (Epic 14-02967)   22, 17, 11, 9, 7, 5, 7, 10, 9, 16, 26   (11)

RICHARD, CLIFF

2-13-82   *Daddy's Home*   (EMI America PA-8103)   17, 7, 9, 19   (4)

RICHIE, LIONEL

10-01-83   *All Night Long*   (Motown 1698 MF)   24, 15, 15, 15, 15, 5, 1, 1, 1, 1, 3, 2, 5, 5, 5, 5, 7, 11, 18, 26   (20)

4-21-84   *Hello*   (Motown 1722 MF)   21, 10, 6, 4, 3, 3, 4, 6, 10, 17, 24   (11)

4-30-83   *My Love*   (Motown 1677 MF)   29, 25, 21, 17, 16, 13, 13, 13, 13, 28   (10)

11-10-84   *Penny Lover*   (Motown 1762 MF)   25, 23, 21, 21   (4)

12-25-83 *Running With The Night* (Motown 1710 MF)   29, 29, 29, 29, 23, 20, 19, 18, 23, 25, 30   (11)

11-23-85 *Say You, Say Me* (Motown 1819 MF)   28, 23, 23   (3)

8-25-84 *Stuck On You* (Motown 1746 MF)   6, (1), 5, 4, 7, 13, 21   (6)

10-16-82 *Truly* (Motown 1644 MF)   30, 27, 24, 8, 2, 1, 1, 1, 2, 4, 7, 7, 7, 14, 18, 21, 29   (17)

2-05-83 *You Are* (Motown 1657 MF)   21, 14, 11, 10, 8, 6, 5, 7, 11, 12, 16, 22, 23, 27, 29   (15)

ROBINSON, SMOKEY

2-20-82 *Tell Me Tomorrow—Part 1* (Tamla 1601 TF)   25, 23, 27   (3)

ROCKWELL

2-18-84 *Somebody's Watching Me* (Motown 1702 MF)   28, 23, 5, 3, 2, 2, 1, 1, 2, 3, 5, 14, 21, 27, 30   (15)

ROGERS, KENNY

7-24-82 *Love Will Turn You Around* (Liberty PB-1471)   29, 22, 18, 14, 13, 11, 15, 19, 28   (9)

2-13-82 *Through The Years* (Liberty PA-1444)   8, 6   (2)

ROGERS, KENNY, WITH KIM CARNES AND JAMES INGRAM   (*See also:* KIM CARNES)

10-06-84 *What About Me* (RCA PB-13899)   29, 24, 21, 19, 19, 18, 16, 16, 19, 25   (10)

ROGERS, KENNY, AND SHEENA EASTON   (*See also:* SHEENA EASTON)

2-05-83 *We've Got Tonight* (Liberty B-1492)   23, 16, 12, 8, 6, 4, 3, 2, 3, 5, 10, 16, 22, 24, 30   (15)

ROGERS, KENNY, AND DOLLY PARTON

10-08-83 *Islands In The Stream* (RCA PB-13615)   23, 23, 23, 14, 1, 3, 5, 8, 12, 16, 25, 28, 28, 28, 28   (15)

THE ROLLING STONES   (*See also:* MICK JAGGER)

6-26-82   *Going To A Go-Go*   (Rolling Stones RS 21301)   25, 20, 14, 11, 9, 8,
12, 16, 21, 28   (10)

3-27-82   *Hang Fire*   (Rolling Stones RS 21300)   24, 20, 16, 12, 9, 7, 7, 10,
19, 23   (10)

11-19-83   *Undercover Of The Night*   (Rolling Stones RS 45605)   26, 19, 15, 12,
11, 9, 9, 9, 9, 17, 24   (11)

2-13-82   *Waiting On A Friend*   (Rolling Stones RS 21004)   5   (1)

THE ROMANTICS

1-21-84   *Talking In Your Sleep*   (Nemperor ZS4 04135)   25, 18, 16, 21,
29   (5)

RONSTADT, LINDA

10-23-82   *Get Closer*   (Asylum 7-69948)   29, 27, 24, 21, 20, 19, 24   (7)

ROSS, DIANA   (*See also:* JULIO IGLESIAS)

2-13-82   *Mirror, Mirror*   (RCA PB-13021)   28, 14, 11, 11, 14, 28   (6)

3-09-85   *Missing You*   (RCA PB-13966)   30, 22, 19, 19, (2), 18, 12, 23   (7)

10-23-82   *Muscles*   (RCA PB-13348)   26, 22, 11, 9, 7, 6, 4, 4, 9, 14, 14, 14, 21,
25   (14)

7-30-83   *Pieces Of Ice*   (RCA PB-13549)   30, 25, 24, 26   (4)

10-20-84   *Swept Away*   (RCA PB-13864)   23, 20, 20, 23   (4)

ROTH, DAVID LEE   (*See also:* VAN HALEN)

1-26-85   *California Girls*   (WB 7-29102)   21, 13, 8, 5, 2, 2, 3, 6, 10,
10   (10)

5-04-85   *Just A Gigolo/I Ain't Got Nobody (Medley)*   (WB 7-29-040)   30, 27,
24, 20, 15, 14, 23   (7)

RUSH

9-25-82   *New World Man*   (Mer. SR 76179)   30, 28, 22, 20, 19, 19, 18, 30   (8)

SADE

4-13-85   *Smooth Operator*   (Portrait 37-04807)   22, 19, 15, 11, 8, 7, 6, 8, 20, 29   (10)

SANTANA

9-04-82   *Hold On*   (Col. 18-03160)   29, 22, 16, 11, 9, 7, 5, 4, 11, 22   (10)

12-04-82   *Nowhere To Run*   (Col. 38-03376)   29, 26, 24   (3)

SCANDAL FEATURING PATTY SMYTHE

7-28-84   *The Warrior*   (Col. 38-04424)   25, 19, 16, 12, 4, 7, 2, 1, 2, 7, 10, 16, 22, 27, 27   (15)

SCHILLING, PETER

12-03-83   *Major Tom (Coming Home)*   (Elektra 7-69811)   24, 18, 15, 11, 11, 11, 11, 10, 14, 24, 28   (11)

THE SCORPIONS

4-21-84   *Rock You Like A Hurricane*   (Mer. 818 440-7)   29, 20, 17, 13, 10, 8, 9, 13, 22, 25   (10)

SCRITTI POLITTI

11-09-85   *Perfect Way*   (WB 7-28949)   23, 23, 17, 14, 14   (5)

SEGER, BOB(, AND THE SILVER BULLET BAND)

3-12-83   *Even Now*   (Cap. B-5213)   27, 22, 18, 15, 14, 12, 10, 9, 8, 11, 15, 23   (12)

12-25-82   *Shame On The Moon*   (Cap. B-5187)   15, 15, 15, 5, 2, 1, 1, 2, 3, 9, 15, 21, 24, 27   (14)

11-24-84   *Understanding*   (Cap. B-5413)   30, 24, 20, 14, 13, 11, 11, 11, 19, 28   (10)

SEMBELLO, MICHAEL

7-30-83   *Maniac*   (Casa. 812 516-7)   24, 6, 5, 3, 4, 3, 3, 7, 7, 8, 10, 10, 10, 10, 27   (15)

SHALAMAR

5-12-84   *Dancing In The Sheets*   (Col. 38-04372)   24, 20, 18, 24, 30   (5)

SHANNON

2-11-84   *Let The Music Play*   (Emergency 7-99810)   25, 18, 15, 13, 13, 20, 20, 24   (8)

SHEILA E.

9-01-84   *The Glamorous Life*   (WB 7-29285)   24, 20, 19, 16, 10, 9, 8, 19   (8)

SIMON AND GARFUNKEL

4-17-82   *Wake Up Little Susie*   (WB WBS-50053)   30, 25, 22, 14, 11, 8, 7, 14, 17, 30   (10)

THE SIMPLE MINDS

11-09-'85   *Alive And Kicking*   (A&M AM 2738)   20, 20, 10, 9   (4)

4-13-85   *Don't You (Forget About Me)*   (A&M 2703)   13, 10, 9, 5, 3, 2, 1, 3, 5, 9, 17, 25   (12)

SISTER SLEDGE

2-20-82   *My Guy*   (Cot. 47000)   15, 14, 15, 19   (4)

SLADE

5-26-84   *Run Runaway*   (CBS Associated ZS4 04398)   28, 23, 19, 16, 14, 17, 26   (7)

SOFT CELL

6-26-82   *Tainted Love*   (Sire SRE 40655)   20, 18, 18, 13, 10, 15, 24, 29   (8)

SPANDAU BALLET

9-15-84 *Only When You Leave* (Chrysalis VS4 42792) 27, 26 (2)

9-03-83 *True* (Chrysalis VS4 42720) 25, 25, 16, 16, 13, 9, 9, 9, 9, 3, 7, 12, 22, 25 (14)

SPRINGFIELD, RICK

4-23-83 *Affair Of The Heart* (RCA PB-13497) 29, 24, 21, 14, 13, 11, 9, 6, 7, 6, 7, 26 (12)

4-27-85 *Celebrate Youth* (RCA PB-14047) 28, 26, 23, 21, 19, 29 (6)

3-13-82 *Don't Talk To Strangers* (RCA PB-13070) 28, 20, 11, 10, 6, 2, 1, 2, 4, 8, 17, 22, 29 (13)

6-23-84 *Don't Walk Away* (RCA PB-13813) 28, 26, 23, 30 (4)

8-13-83 *Human Touch* (RCA PB-13576) 30, 27, 23 (3)

2-13-82 *Love Is Alright Tonight* (RCA PB-13008) 30 (1)

3-31-84 *Love Somebody* (RCA PB-13738) 26, 28, 22, 18, 11, 8, 5, 6, 10, 15, 22, 28 (12)

SPRINGSTEEN, BRUCE

11-17-84 *Born In The U.S.A.* (Col. 38-04680) 24, 18, 13, 7, 6, 4, 3, 3, 3, 1, 3, 8, 15, 29 (14)

8-18-84 *Cover Me* (Col. 38-04561) 29, 18, 13, 9, 7, 5, 1, 1, 3, 4, 5, 5, 8, 10, 13, 23, 28 (17)

5-26-84 *Dancing In The Dark* (Col. 38-04463) 26, 17, 12, 5, 1, 1, 1, 1, 2, 2, 4, 5, 9, 17, 9, 17, 30 (17)

6-22-85 *Glory Days* (Col. 38-04924) 27, 18, 11, 11, 8, 8, 6, 13, 21 (9)

3-02-85 *I'm On Fire* (Col. 38-04772) 30, 23, 19, 13, 13, 11, 7, 6, 5, 9, 14, 19 (12)

SQUIER, BILLY

7-28-84 *Rock Me Tonight* (Cap. B-5370) 29, 23, 18, 13, 11, 12, 10, 9, 12, 16, 24 (11)

STALLONE, FRANK

8-27-83   *Far From Over*   (RSO 815 023-7)   27, 21, 21, 19, 19, 16, 16, 16, 16   (10)

STARSHIP   (*See also:* JEFFERSON STARSHIP)

11-09-85   *We Built This City*   (Grunt FB-14170)   4, 4, 4, 5, 5   (5)

STEEL BREEZE

3-12-83   *Dreamin' Is Easy*   (RCA PB-13427)   29, 25, 24, 28   (4)

STEWART, ROD

6-18-83   *Baby Jane*   (WB 7-29608)   28, 23, 21, 20   (4)

6-30-84   *Infatuation*   (WB 7-29256)   30, 27, 23, 18, 13, 9, 17, 27   (8)

10-13-84   *Some Guys Have All The Luck*   (WB 7-29215)   27, 25, 22, 24   (4)

2-13-82   *Tonight I'm Yours*   (WB WBS-49886)   14, 5, 5, 8, 17, 24   (6)

2-13-82   *Young Turks*   (WB WBS-49843)   20   (1)

STING   (*See also:* POLICE)

8-31-85   *Fortress Around Your Heart*   (A&M AM 2767)   29, 29   (2)

6-15-85   *If You Love Somebody Set Them Free*   (A&M AM 2738)   30, 26, 22, 17, 17, 10, 10, 4, 1, 7, 16   (11)

11-23-85   *Love Is The Seventh Wave*   (A&M AM 2787)   30, 25, 25   (3)

THE STRAY CATS

11-06-82   *Rock This Town*   (EMI America B-8132)   28, 25, 22, 18, 14, 11, 7, 6, 6, 6, 8, 13, 17, 27   (14)

8-27-83   *(She's) Sexy + 17*   (EMI America B-8168)   26, 16, 16, 9, 9, 6, 4, 4, 4, 4, 25   (11)

12-25-82   *Stray Cat Strut*   (EMI America B-8122)   25, 25, 25, 15, 9, 6, 3, 1, 1, 1, 4, 8, 14, 15, 21, 24, 30   (17)

STREISAND, BARBRA

2-27-82   *Memory*   (Col. 18-02717)   25, 23, 23, 21, 21, 19, 23   (7)

12-03-83   *The Way He Makes Me Feel*   (Col. 38-04177)   26, 22, 21, 27, 27, 27, 27   (7)

STYX

5-21-83   *Don't Let It End*   (A&M AM 2543)   25, 22, 17, 14, 10, 7, 4, 6, 10, 17   (10)

2-19-83   *Mr. Roboto*   (A&M AM 2525)   30, 27, 19, 16, 13, 12, 10, 8, 6, 2, 2, 3, 10, 14, 28   (15)

SUMMER, DONNA

7-17-82   *Love Is In Control*   (Geffen 7-29982)   28, 23, 21, 19, 18, 16, 14, 13, 17   (9)

7-02-83   *She Works Hard For The Money*   (Mer. 812 604-7)   27, 25, 20, 16, 12, 9, 8, 6, 3, 4, 4, 15, 15, 19, 27, 27, 27, 27   (18)

SUPERTRAMP   (*See also:* ROGER HODGSON)

6-22-85   *Cannonball*   (A&M AM 2731)   29, 26, 25, 25   (4)

11-06-82   *It's Raining Again*   (A&M AM 2502)   25, 17, 12, 9, 6, 6, 6, 5, 5, 5, 12, 15, 20   (13)

2-19-83   *My Kind Of Lady*   (A&M AM 2517)   23, 16, 11, 9, 8, 14, 17, 22   (8)

SURVIVOR

6-19-82   *Eye Of The Tiger*   (Scotti Bros. ZS5 02912)   24, 19, 13, 5, 1, 2, 1, 1, 1, 1, 6, 9, 13, 14, 22   (15)

2-23-85   *High On You*   (Scotti Bros. ZS4 04685)   30, 29, 29, 28, 27, 27   (6)

11-10-84   *I Can't Hold Back*   (Scotti Bros. ZS4 04603)   26, 25, 28, 27, 21, 16, 16, 24, 24, 24   (10)

6-15-85   *The Search Is Over*   (Scotti Bros. ZS4 04871)   28, 25, 24, 21, 21, 20, 20   (7)

SYLVIA

10-16-82 *Nobody* (RCA PB-13223) 25, 21, 21, 27 (4)

TACO

8-13-83 *Puttin' On The Ritz* (RCA PB-50727) 26, 22, 14, 7, 7, 4, 4, 3, 3, 3, 3, 3, 4, 11, 15, 24, 27 (17)

TALKING HEADS

9-17-83 *Burning Down The House* (Sire 7-29565) 28, 28, 17, 13, 13, 13, 13, 6, 6, 8, 10, 16, 19, 26, 30, 30, 30, 30 (18)

TEARS FOR FEARS

4-13-85 *Everybody Wants To Rule The World* (Mer. 880 659-7) 30, 26, 21, 13, 9, 8, 5, 1, 1, 2, 6, 9, 16, 16, 24, 24 (16)

11-09-85 *Head Over Heels* (Mer. 880 899-7) 2, 2, 8, 13, 13 (5)

6-22-85 *Shout* (Mer. 880 794-7) 30, 23, 13, 13, 7, 7, 3, 2, 3, 9, 13, 13 (12)

.38 SPECIAL

5-22-82 *Caught Up In You* (A&M AM 2412) 30, 27, 24, 20, 11, 7, 5, 4, 3, 4, 7, 14, 19, 24 (14)

12-17-83 *If I'd Been The One* (A&M AM 2594) 29, 26, 26, 26, 26, 22, 29 (7)

10-27-84 *Teacher Teacher* (Cap. B-5405) 29, 29, 24, 21, 20 (5)

THE THOMPSON TWINS

6-30-84 *Doctor! Doctor!* (Arista AS1-9209) 29, 24, 19, 13, 11, 21 (6)

4-14-84 *Hold Me Now* (Arista AS1-9164) 30, 20, 14, 10, 11, 16, 29 (7)

11-09-85 *Lay Your Hands On Me* (Arista AS1-9396) 14, 14, 11, 10, 10 (5)

'TIL TUESDAY

6-01-85 *Voices Carry* (Epic 34-04795) 28, 19, 16, 15, 12, 9, 9, 6, 6, 8, 22, 29 (12)

TOMMY TUTONE

3-13-82   *867-5309/Jenny*   (Col. 18-02646)   27, 16, 15, 12, 11, 8, 7, 8, 6, 5, 4, 8, 12, 15, 19   (15)

TOTO

11-20-82   *Africa*   (Col. 38-03335)   28, 22, 18, 14, 11, 9, 9, 9, 7, 4, 3, 2, 4, 8, 13, 18, 24, 28   (18)

3-26-83   *I Won't Hold You Back*   (Col. 38-03597)   29, 26, 21, 20, 17, 15, 12, 15, 18, 19, 20   (11)

9-04-82   *Make Believe*   (Col. 18-03143)   22, 18, 15, 14, 16, 16, 22   (7)

5-08-82   *Rosanna*   (Col. 18-02811)   27, 20, 15, 11, 7, 5, 3, 2, 2, 1, 5, 6, 11, 21, 26, 30   (16)

12-08-84   *Stranger In Town*   (Col. 38-04672)   30, 27, 28   (3)

THE TUBES

5-21-83   *She's A Beauty*   (Cap.B-5217)   27, 24, 23, 21, 17, 14, 9, 8, 5, 9, 15   (11)

TURNER, TINA   *(See also:* BRYAN ADAMS)

10-13-84   *Better Be Good To Me*   (Cap. B-5387)   29, 26, 23, 25, 21, 17, 12, 10, 15, 15, 22, 29, 29, 29   (14)

3-10-84   *Let's Stay Together*   (Cap. B-5322)   29, 27, 27, (1), 29   (4)

11-09-85   *One Of The Living*   (Cap. B-5518)   19, 19, 16, 15, 15   (5)

2-09-85   *Private Dancer*   (Cap. B-5433)   29, 27, 20, 16, 13, 11, 6, 6, 7, 20   (10)

7-20-85   *We Don't Need Another Hero (Thunderdome)*   (Cap. B-5491)   25, 25, 18, 11, 8, 5, 1, 1   (8)

7-21-84   *What's Love Got To Do With It*   (Cap. PB-5343)   26, 21, 16, 9, 2, 2, 1, 1, 2, 4, 9, 11, 28   (13)

TWILLEY, DWIGHT

3-31-84   *Girls*   (EMI America B-8196)   20, 23, 17, 14, 13, 19, 26   (7)

TWISTED SISTER

8-25-84   *We're Not Gonna Take It*   (Atl. 7-89641)   24, 23, 18, 16, 11, 14, 16, 30   (8)

TYLER, BONNIE

8-27-83   *Total Eclipse Of The Heart*   (Col. 38-03906)   29, 24, 24, 11, 11, 7, 5, 5, 5, 5, 2, 2, 3, 5, 9, 15, 20, 24, 24, 24, 24, 30   (22)

UB40 WITH CHRISSIE HYNDE   (*See also:* **THE PRETENDERS**)

8-31-85   *I Got You Babe*   (A&M AM 2758)   30, 30   (2)

USA FOR AFRICA

4-06-85   *We Are The World*   (Col. US7-04839)   12, 1, 1, 1, 1, 2, 3, 7, 10, 23, 27   (11)

ULLMAN, TRACEY

3-17-84   *They Don't Know*   (MCA 52347)   30, 30, 21, 18, 14, 12, 8, 7, 18, 24, 27   (11)

VAN HALEN   (*See also:* **SAMMY HAGAR; DAVID LEE ROTH**)

6-05-82   *Dancing In The Street*   (WB WBS 7-29986)   26, 24, 20, 17, 15, 13, 21, 30   (8)

5-05-84   *I'll Wait*   (WB 7-29307)   28, 23, 19, 17, 13, 10, 9, 13, 15, 21   (10)

1-28-84   *Jump*   (WB 7-29384)   25, 7, 2, 1, 1, 11, 14, 15, 15, 17, 24, 29   (12)

7-07-84   *Panama*   (WB)   29, 26, 21, 14, 10, 6, 7, 14, 6, 14, 25   (11)

2-13-82   *Pretty Woman*   (WB WBS-50003)   24, 12, 8, 5, 3, 2, 6, 6, 4, 3, 4, 11, 16, 23, 29   (15)

VANGELIS

2-27-82   *Main Theme From "Chariots Of Fire"*   (Polydor 2189)   28, 21, 18, 14, 10, 9, 8, 4, 2, 4, 5, 4, 6, 13, 15, 19, 27   (17)

WAGNER, JACK

12-08-84   *All I Need*   (Qwest 7-29238)   27, 24, 12, 7, 7, 7, 4, 9, 16, 24   (10)

WAITE, JOHN

8-24-85   *Every Step Of The Way*   (EMI America B-8282)   28, 23, 23   (3)

8-04-84   *Missing You*   (EMI America B-8212)   26, 19, 15, 7, 17, 13, 3, 1, 5, 7, 11, 14, 21, 21, 29   (15)

WANG CHUNG

6-02-84   *Dance Hall Days*   (Geffen 7-29310)   28, 25, 20, 18, 14, 12, 10, 9, 8, 8, 14, 22, (1), 28   (13)

WARNES, JENNIFER   (*See:* JOE COCKER)

WARWICK, DIONNE

12-11-82   *Heartbreaker*   (Arista AS 1015)   29, 22, 22, 22, 22, 29, 30   (7)

WARWICK, DIONNE, AND JOHNNY MATHIS

5-08-82   *Friends In Love*   (Arista AS 0673)   30, 28, 26, 25, 28, 30   (6)

WHAM! (FEATURING GEORGE MICHAEL)

12-29-84   *Careless Whisper*   (Col. 38-04691)   25, 25, 25, 15, 10, 7, 4, 1, 1, 1, 2, 3, 5, 5, 6, 17   (16)

4-20-85   *Everything She Wants*   (Col. 38-04840)   29, 25, 21, 13, 6, 3, 2, 4, 5, 13, 29   (11)

8-17-85   *Freedom*   (Col. 38-05409)   30, 26, 25, 25   (4)

9-22-84   *Wake Me Up Before You Go-Go*   (Col. 38-04552)   30, 22, 18, 13, 10, 9, 9, 4, 1, 1, 1, 5, 8, 11, 23, 23, 23   (17)

WILDER, MATTHEW

1-28-84   *Break My Stride*   (Private ZS4-04113)   13, 10, 11, 13, 21, 24, 28   (7)

WILLIAMS, DENIECE

4-24-82   *It's Gonna Take A Miracle*   (ARC/Col. 18-02812)   27, 23, 20, 17, 16, 14, 10, 8, 7, 9, 14, 26   (12)

4-28-84   *Let's Hear It For The Boy*   (Col. 38-04417)   19, 13, 7, 2, 1, 1, 2, 4, 7, 12, 16, 25   (12)

WILSON, ANN   (*See:* HEART; MIKE RENO)

WOLF, PETER   (*See also:* THE J. GEILS BAND)

8-11-84   *Lights Out*   (EMI America B-8208)   28, 25, 23, 20, 19, 17, 13, 18, 26   (9)

WONDER, STEVIE   (*See also:* PAUL McCARTNEY)

6-26-82   *Do I Do*   (Tamla 1612 TF)   26, 21, 17, 15, 12, 12, 22, 28   (8)

8-18-84   *I Just Called To Say I Love You*   (Motown 1745 MF)   30, 25, 26, 22, 18, 14, 8, 5, 2, 1, 1, 1, 3, 6, 9, 15, 19, 28   (18)

12-22-84   *Love Light In Flight*   (Motown 1769 MF)   25, 20, 20, 20, 14, 12, 11, 11   (8)

11-09-85   *Part-Time Lover*   (Tamla 1808 TF)   5, 5, 14, 20, 20   (5)

2-13-82   *That Girl*   (Tamla 1602 TF)   22, 4, 2, 3, 6, 11, 17, 24   (8)

YANKOVIC, WEIRD AL

3-17-84   *Eat It*   (Rock 'n' Roll ZS4 04374)   29, 29, 18, 13, 6, 6, 9, 16, 22, 29   (10)

YES

11-19-83   *Owner Of A Lonely Heart*   (Atco 7-99817)   29, 21, 17, 13, 10, 7, 7, 7, 7, 1, 1, 1, 3, 3, 4, 4, 4, 6, 6, 10, 8, 12, 24   (23)

YOUNG, PAUL

6-08-85   *Everytime You Go Away*   (Col. 38-04867)   28, 20, 18, 13, 10, 10, 5, 5, 1, 7, 14, 22   (12)

11-09-85   *I'm Gonna Tear Your Playhouse Down*   (Col. 38-05577)   12, 12, 24   (3)

ZZ TOP

6-16-84 *Legs* (WB 7-29272) 27, 24, 16, 10, 8, 4, 3, 2, 4, 6, 12, 5, 11, 21 (14)

11-09-85 *Sleeping Bag* (WB 7-28884) 10, 10, 7, 6, 6 (5)

I. SONG-TITLE INDEX—POP

Abracadabra (Steve Miller Band)
Adult Education (Daryl Hall and John Oates)
Affair Of The Heart (Rick Springfield)
Africa (Toto)
After The Fall (Journey)
After The Glitter Fades (Stevie Nicks)
Against All Odds (Take A Look At Me Now) (Phil Collins)
Alive And Kicking (Simple Minds)
All I Need (Jack Wagner)
All Night Long (All Night) (Lionel Richie)
All Of You (Julio Iglesias and Diana Ross)
All She Wants To Do Is Dance (Don Henley)
All Right (Christopher Cross)
All This Love (DeBarge)
All Through The Night (Cyndi Lauper)
Allentown (Billy Joel)
Almost Over You (Sheena Easton)
Almost Paradise . . . Love Theme From "Footloose" (Mike Reno and Ann Wilson)
Along Comes A Woman (Chicago)
Always On My Mind (Willie Nelson)
Always Something There To Remind Me (Naked Eyes)
American Music (The Pointer Sisters)
And We Danced (The Hooters)
Angel (Madonna)
Another Sleepless Night (Anne Murray)

Are We Ourselves (The Fixx)
Authority Song (John Cougar Mellencamp)
Automatic (The Pointer Sisters)
Axel F (Harold Faltermeyer)

Baby, Come To Me (Patti Austin)
Baby I Lied (Deborah Allen)
Baby Jane (Rod Stewart)
Baby Makes Her Blue Jeans Talk (Dr. Hook)
Back On The Chain Gang (The Pretenders)
Bad Boy (Ray Parker, Jr.)
Be Near Me (ABC)
Beat It (Michael Jackson)
Better Be Good To Me (Tina Turner)
Big Fun (Kool & The Gang)
Big Log (Robert Plant)
Billie Jean (Michael Jackson)
Blue Eyes (Elton John)
Blue Jean (David Bowie)
Bobbie Sue (The Oak Ridge Boys)
Body Language (Queen)
Borderline (Madonna)
Born In The U.S.A. (Bruce Springsteen)
The Boys Of Summer (After The Boys Of Summer Have Gone) (Don Henley)
Break It To Me Gently (Juice Newton)
Break It Up (Foreigner)

Break My Stride   (Matthew Wilder)
Breakin' . . . *There's No Stopping Us*   (Ollie and Jerry)
Breaking Us In Two   (Joe Jackson)
Broken Wings   (Mr. Mister)
Burning Down The House   (Talking Heads)

California Girls   (David Lee Roth)
Call To The Heart   (Giuffria)
Cannonball   (Supertramp)
Can't Fight This Feeling   (REO Speedwagon)
Careless Whisper   (Wham! featuring George Michael)
Caribbean Queen (No More Love On The Run)   (Billy Ocean)
Caught Up In You   (.38 Special)
Celebrate Youth   (Rick Springfield)
Centerfield   (John Fogerty)
Centerfold   (The J. Geils Band)
Centipede   (Rebbie Jackson)
Change Of Heart   (Tom Petty and The Heartbreakers)
Cherish   (Kool & The Gang)
China Girl   (David Bowie)
Church Of The Poison Mind   (Culture Club)
C-I-T-Y   (John Cafferty and The Beaver Brown Band)
Come Dancing   (The Kinks)
Come On Eileen   (Dexy's Midnight Runners)
Cool It Now   (The New Edition)
Cover Me   (Bruce Springsteen)
Crazy For You   (Madonna)
Crazy In The Night (Barking At Airplanes)   (Kim Carnes)
Crimson And Clover   (Joan Jett and The Blackhearts)
Cruel Summer   (Bananarama)
Crumblin' Down   (John Cougar Mellencamp)
Cry   (Godley and Creme)
Cum On Feel The Noize   (Quiet Riot)
The Curly Shuffle   (Jump 'N' The Saddle)
Cuts Like A Knife   (Bryan Adams)

Daddy's Home   (Cliff Richard)
Dance Hall Days   (Wang Chung)
Dancing In The Dark   (Bruce Springsteen)
Dancing In The Sheets   (Shalamar)
Dancing In The Street   (Van Halen)
Dare Me   (The Pointer Sisters)
Delirious   (Prince)
Desert Moon   (Styx)
Did It In A Minute   (Daryl Hall and John Oates)
Dirty Laundry   (Don Henley)
Do I Do   (Stevie Wonder)
Do It For Love   (Sheena Easton)
Do They Know It's Christmas   (Band Aid)
Do What You Do   (Jermaine Jackson)
Do You Believe In Love   (Huey Lewis And The News)
Do You Really Want To Hurt Me   (Culture Club)
Do You Wanna Touch Me (Oh Yeah)   (Joan Jett and The Blackhearts)
Doctor! Doctor!   (The Thompson Twins)
Dr. Heckyll And Mr. Jive   (Men At Work)
Don't Answer Me   (The Alan Parsons Project)
Don't Come Around Here No More   (Tom Petty and The Heartbreakers)
Don't Cry   (Asia)
Don't Fight It   (Kenny Loggins with Steve Perry)
Don't Let Him Know   (Prism)
Don't Let It End   (Styx)
Don't Lose My Number   (Phil Collins)
Don't Pay The Ferryman   (Chris DeBurgh)
Don't Talk To Strangers   (Rick Springfield)
Don't Tell Me You Love Me   (Night Ranger)
Don't Walk Away   (Rick Springfield)
Don't You (Forget About Me)   (Simple Minds)
Don't You Want Me   (The Human League)

Down Under (Men At Work)
Dreamin' Is Easy (Steel Breeze)
Dress You Up (Madonna)
Drive (The Cars)

Easy Lover (Philip Bailey and Phil Collins)
Eat It (Weird Al Yankovic)
Ebony And Ivory (Paul McCartney and Stevie Wonder)
Edge Of Seventeen (Stevie Nicks)
867-5309/Jenny (Tommy Tutone)
Election Day (Arcadia)
Electric Avenue (Eddy Grant)
Empty Garden (Hey Hey Johnny) (Elton John)
Even Now (Bob Seger)
Even The Nights Are Better (Air Supply)
Every Breath You Take (Police)
Every Step Of The Way (John Waite)
Everybody Wants To Rule The World (Tears For Fears)
Everything She Wants (Wham!)
Everytime You Go Away (Paul Young)
Eye In The Sky (The Alan Parsons Project)
Eye Of The Tiger (Survivor)
Eyes Without A Face (Billy Idol)

Faithfully (Journey)
Family Man (Daryl Hall and John Oates)
Fantasy (Aldo Nova)
Far From Over (Frank Stallone)
Farewell My Summer Love (Michael Jackson)
(Keep Feeling) Fascination (The Human League)
Find Another Fool (Quarterflash)
Flamethrower (*See:* Freeze Frame . . .)
Flashdance . . . What A Feeling (Irene Cara)
Flesh For Fantasy (Billy Idol)
Foolin' (Def Leppard)
Foolish Heart (Steve Perry)
Footloose (Kenny Loggins)

Forever Man (Eric Clapton)
Fortress Around Your Heart (Sting)
Freedom (Wham!)
Freeway Of Love (Aretha Franklin)
Freeze Frame/Flamethrower (The J. Geils Band)
Fresh (Kool & The Gang)
Friends In Love (Dionne Warwick and Johnny Mathis)

Get Closer (Linda Ronstadt)
Get Down On It (Kool & The Gang)
Get It On (Bang A Gong) (Power Station)
Getcha Back (The Beach Boys)
Ghostbusters (Ray Parker, Jr.)
The Girl Is Mine (Michael Jackson And Paul McCartney)
Girls (Dwight Twilley)
Girls Just Want To Have Fun (Cyndi Lauper)
Give It Up (K.C.)
The Glamorous Life (Sheila E.)
Gloria (Laura Branigan)
Glory Days (Bruce Springsteen)
Go Insane (Lindsey Buckingham)
Goin' Down (Greg Guidry)
Going To A Go-Go (The Rolling Stones)
Goody Two Shoes (Adam Ant)
The Goonies 'R' Good Enough (Cyndi Lauper)
Got A Hold On Me (Christine McVie)
Gypsy (Fleetwood Mac)

Had A Dream (Sleeping With The Enemy) (Roger Hodgson)
Hang Fire (The Rolling Stones)
Hard Habit To Break (Chicago)
Hard To Say I'm Sorry (Chicago)
Harden My Heart (Quarterflash)
Head Over Heels (The Go-Go's)
Head Over Heels (Tears For Fears)
Heart And Soul (Huey Lewis And The News)
Heart Attack (Olivia Newton-John)

The Heart Of Rock And Roll   (Huey
  Lewis And The News)
Heart To Heart   (Kenny Loggins)
Heartbreaker   (Dionne Warwick)
Heartlight   (Neil Diamond)
The Heat Is On   (Glenn Frey)
Heat Of The Moment   (Asia)
Heaven   (Bryan Adams)
Hello   (Lionel Richie)
Hello Again   (The Cars)
Here Comes The Rain   (Eurythmics)
High On You   (Survivor)
Hold Me   (Fleetwood Mac)
Hold Me Now   (The Thompson Twins)
Hold On   (Santana)
Hot Girls In Love   (Loverboy)
*How Am I Supposed To Live Without
  You*   (Laura Branigan)
Human Nature   (Michael Jackson)
Human Touch   (Rick Springfield)
Hungry Like A Wolf   (Duran Duran)
Hurts So Good   (John Cougar Mellen-
  camp)

*I.G.Y. (What A Beautiful
  World)*   (Donald Fagen)
I Ain't Got Nobody   (*See:* Just A Gigolo
  . . .)
I Can Dream About You   (Dan Hartman)
*I Can't Go For That (No Can
  Do)*   (Daryl Hall and John Oates)
I Can't Hold Back   (Survivor)
I Do   (The J. Geils Band)
I Don't Care Anymore   (Phil Collins)
I Feel For You   (Chaka Khan)
I Found Somebody   (Glenn Frey)
I Got You Babe   (UB40 with Chrissie
  Hynde)
*I Guess That's Why They Call It The
  Blues*   (Elton John)
I Just Called To Say I Love You   (Stevie
  Wonder)
I Keep Forgettin'   (Michael McDonald)
*I Know There's Something Going
  On*   (Frida)
I Love Rock 'N' Roll   (Joan Jett and The
  Blackhearts)

I Ran (So Far Away)   (A Flock Of
  Seagulls)
I Want A New Drug   (Huey Lewis and
  The News)
I Want To Know What Love Is   (For-
  eigner)
I Won't Hold You Back   (Toto)
I Would Die 4 U   (Prince and The
  Revolution)
I'll Fall In Love Again   (Sammy Hagar)
I'll Tumble 4 Ya   (Culture Club)
I'll Wait   (Van Halen)
I'm Alive   (Neil Diamond)
I'm Free (Heaven Helps The Man)
  (Kenny Loggins)
*I'm Gonna Tear Your Playhouse
  Down*   (Paul Young)
I'm On Fire   (Bruce Springsteen)
I'm Stepping Out   (John Lennon)
I'm Still Standing   (Elton John)
I've Got A Rock 'N' Roll Heart   (Eric
  Clapton)
I've Never Been To Me   (Charlene)
If Anyone Falls   (Stevie Nicks)
If I'd Been The One   (.38 Special)
If Only You Knew   (Patti LaBelle)
If This Is It   (Huey Lewis And The
  News)
If You Love Somebody Set Them Free
  (Sting)
If You Want My Love   (Cheap Trick)
In A Big Country   (Big Country)
In My House   (The Mary Jane Girls)
Infatuation   (Rod Stewart)
*Invincible (Theme From "The Legend Of
  Billie Jean")*   (Pat Benatar)
Invisible Hands   (Kim Carnes)
*Is There Something I Should
  Know*   (Duran Duran)
Island Of Lost Souls   (Blondie)
Islands In The Stream   (Kenny Rogers
  and Dolly Parton)
*It Might Be You (Theme From
  "Tootsie")*   (Stephen Bishop)
It's A Miracle   (Culture Club)
It's A Mistake   (Men At Work)
It's Gonna Take A Miracle   (Deniece
  Williams)

It's Only Love (Bryan Adams and Tina Turner)
It's Raining Again (Supertramp)

Jack And Diane (John Cougar Mellencamp)
Jenny (*See*: 867-5309 . . .)
Jeopardy (The Greg Kihn Band)
Joanna (Kool & The Gang)
Juke Box Hero (Foreigner)
Jump (Van Halen)
Jump (For My Love) (The Pointer Sisters)
Just A Gigolo/I Ain't Got Nobody (Medley) (David Lee Roth)
Just Another Night (Mick Jagger)

Karma Chameleon (Culture Club)
Keep The Fire Burnin' (REO Speedwagon)
Keeping The Faith (Billy Joel)
Key Largo (Bertie Higgins)
King Of Pain (Police)
Der Kommissar (After The Fire)

The Language Of Love (Dan Fogelberg)
Lawyers In Love (Jackson Browne)
Lay It Down (Ratt)
Lay Your Hands On Me (The Thompson Twins)
Leader Of The Band (Dan Fogelberg)
Leather And Lace (Stevie Nicks and Tom Petty)
Leave A Tender Moment Alone (Billy Joel)
Legs (ZZ Top)
Let It Whip (The Dazz Band)
Let The Feeling Flow (Peabo Bryson)
Let The Music Play (Shannon)
Let's Dance (David Bowie)
Let's Go Crazy (Prince and The Revolution)
Let's Groove (Earth, Wind and Fire)
Let's Hang On (Barry Manilow)
Let's Hear It For The Boy (Deniece Williams)
Let's Stay Together (Tina Turner)

Lights Out (Peter Wolf)
Like A Virgin (Madonna)
Little By Little (Robert Plant)
Lonely In Love (Giuffria)
Little Red Corvette (Prince)
Little Too Late (Pat Benatar)
Lonely Ol' Night (John Cougar Mellencamp)
The Longest Time (Billy Joel)
The Look Of Love (ABC)
Looking For A Stranger (Pat Benatar)
Love Come Down (Evelyn King)
Love Is A Battlefield (Pat Benatar)
Love Is A Stranger (Eurythmics)
Love Is Alright Tonight (Rick Springfield)
Love Is In Control (Finger On The Trigger) (Donna Summer)
Love Is Like A Rock (Donnie Iris)
Love Is The Seventh Wave (Sting)
Love Light In Flight (Stevie Wonder)
Love Me Do (The Beatles)
Love Me Tomorrow (Chicago)
Love Somebody (Rick Springfield)
Love Theme From "St. Elmo's Fire" (David Foster)
Love Will Turn You Around (Kenny Rogers)
Loverboy (Billy Ocean)
Lovergirl (Teena Marie)
Love's Been A Little Bit Hard On Me (Juice Newton)
Lovin' Every Minute Of It (Loverboy)
The Lucky One (Laura Branigan)

Magic (The Cars)
Main Theme From "Chariots Of Fire" (Vangelis)
Major Tom (Coming Home) (Peter Schilling)
Make A Move On Me (Olivia Newton-John)
Make Believe (Toto)
Making Love Out Of Nothing At All (Air Supply)
Mama Weer All Crazee Now (Quiet Riot)

Man On Your Mind (The Little River Band)
Maneater (Daryl Hall and John Oates)
Maniac (Michael Sembello)
Material Girl (Madonna)
Medley: Memories Of Days Gone By (Fred Parris and The Five Satins)
Memory (Barbra Streisand)
Method Of Modern Love (Daryl Hall and John Oates)
"Miami Vice" Theme (Jan Hammer)
Mickey (Toni Basil)
Middle Of The Road (The Pretenders)
Mirror, Mirror (Diana Ross)
Misled (Kool & The Gang)
Miss Me Blind (Culture Club)
Missing You (Dan Fogelberg)
Missing You (Diana Ross)
Missing You (John Waite)
Mr. Roboto (Styx)
Mr. Telephone Man (The New Edition)
Modern Love (David Bowie)
Money For Nothing (Dire Straits)
Movie Medley (The Beatles)
Muscles (Diana Ross)
My Guy (Sister Sledge)
My Kind Of Lady (Supertramp)
My Love (Lionel Richie)

Naughty Naughty (John Parr)
Neutron Dance (The Pointer Sisters)
Never (Heart)
Never Been In Love (Randy Meisner)
Never Give Up On A Good Thing (George Benson)
Never Gonna Let You Go (Sergio Mendes)
Never Surrender (Corey Hart)
New Attitude (Patti LaBelle)
New Moon On Monday (Duran Duran)
New World Man (Rush)
Nightbird (Stevie Nicks with Sandy Stewart)
Nightshift (The Commodores)
1999 (Prince)
99 Luftballoons (Nena)
No Lookin' Back (Michael McDonald)

No More Lonely Nights (Paul McCartney)
No More Words (Berlin)
No Way Out (The Jefferson Starship)
Nobody (Sylvia)
Nobody Said It Was Easy (Lookin' For The Lights) (Le Roux)
Nobody Told Me (John Lennon)
Nowhere To Run (Santana)

Obsession (Animotion)
Oh Sherrie (Steve Perry)
The Old Man Down The Road (John Fogerty)
On The Dark Side (John Cafferty and The Beaver Brown Band)
On The Way To The Sky (Neil Diamond)
On The Wings Of A Nightingale (The Everly Brothers)
One Hundred Ways (Quincy Jones Featuring James Ingram)
One More Night (Phil Collins)
One Night In Bangkok (Murray Head)
One Night Love Affair (Bryan Adams)
One Of The Living (Tina Turner)
One On One (Daryl Hall and John Oates)
One Thing Leads To Another (The Fixx)
The One You Love (Glenn Frey)
Only The Lonely (The Motels)
Only The Young (Journey)
Only Time Will Tell (Asia)
Only When You Leave (Spandau Ballet)
Open Arms (Journey)
The Other Guy (The Little River Band)
The Other Woman (Ray Parker, Jr.)
Our House (Madness)
Out Of Touch (Daryl Hall and John Oates)
Overkill (Men At Work)
Owner Of A Lonely Heart (Yes)

Pac-Man Fever (Buckner And Garcia)
Panama (Van Halen)

Part-Time Lover (Stevie Wonder)
Pass The Dutchie (Musical Youth)
Penny Lover (Lionel Richie)
People Are People (Depeche Mode)
Perfect Way (Scritti Politti)
Personally (Karla Bonoff)
Photograph (Def Leppard)
Physical (Olivia Newton-John)
Pieces Of Ice (Diana Ross)
Pink Houses (John Cougar Mellencamp)
Play The Game Tonight (Kansas)
The Politics Of Dancing (Re-Flex)
Pop Goes The Movies (Part 1) (Meco)
Pop Life (Prince and The Revolution)
Power Of Love (Huey Lewis And The News)
Pressure (Billy Joel)
Pretty Woman (Van Halen)
Private Dancer (Tina Turner)
Promises, Promises (Naked Eyes)
Purple Rain (Prince and The Revolution)
Puttin' On The Ritz (Taco)

Radio Ga Ga (Queen)
Radioactive (The Firm)
Raspberry Beret (Prince and The Revolution)
Rebel Yell (Billy Idol)
The Reflex (Duran Duran)
Relax (Frankie Goes To Hollywood)
Rhythm Of The Night (DeBarge)
Rio (Duran Duran)
Rock And Roll Girls (John Fogerty)
Rock 'N' Roll Is King (The Electric Light Orchestra)
Rock Me Tonight (Billy Squier)
Rock Me Tonight (For Old Times Sake) (Freddie Jackson)
Rock Of Ages (Def Leppard)
Rock The Casbah (The Clash)
Rock This Town (The Stray Cats)
Rock You Like A Hurricane (The Scorpions)
Rockin' At Midnight (The Honeydrippers)
Romancing The Stone (Eddy Grant)

Rosanna (Toto)
Round And Round (Ratt)
Run For The Roses (Dan Fogelberg)
Run Runaway (Slade)
Run To You (Bryan Adams)
Runaway (Bon Jovi)
Running With The Night (Lionel Richie)

Sad Songs (Say So Much) (Elton John)
The Safety Dance (Men Without Hats)
St. Elmo's Fire (Man In Motion) (John Parr)
Save A Prayer (Duran Duran)
Saved By Zero (The Fixx)
Saving All My Love For You (Whitney Houston)
Say, Say, Say (Paul McCartney and Michael Jackson)
Say You, Say Me (Lionel Richie)
Sea Of Love (The Honeydrippers)
The Search Is Over (Survivor)
Self Control (Laura Branigan)
Sentimental Street (Night Ranger)
Separate Lives (Love Theme From"White Nights") (Phil Collins And Marilyn Martin)
Separate Ways (Worlds Apart) (Journey)
Sexual Healing (Marvin Gaye)
(She's) Sexy + 17 (The Stray Cats)
Sexy Girl (Glenn Frey)
Shadows Of The Night (Pat Benatar)
Shake It Up (The Cars)
Shame (The Motels)
Shame On The Moon (Bob Seger and The Silver Bullet Band)
Shangri-La (The Steve Miller Band)
She Blinded Me With Science (Thomas Dolby)
She Bop (Cyndi Lauper)
She Works Hard For The Money (Donna Summer)
She's A Beauty (The Tubes)
She's Mine (Steve Perry)
Should I Do It (The Pointer Sisters)
Shout (Tears For Fears)
Sister Christian (Night Ranger)

Sisters Are Doin' It For Themselves
(Eurythmics and Aretha Franklin)
Sitting At The Wheel   (The Moody
Blues)
'65 Love Affair   (Paul Davis)
Sleeping Bag   (ZZ Top)
Small Town   (John Cougar Mellencamp)
Smokin' In The Boys Room   (Motley Crue)
Smooth Operator   (Sade)
Smuggler's Blues   (Glenn Frey)
So In Love   (Orchestral Manoeuvres In
The Dark)
Solid   (Ashford and Simpson)
Solitaire   (Laura Branigan)
Some Guys Have All The Luck   (Rod
Stewart)
Some Like It Hot   (Power Station)
Some Things Are Better Left Unsaid
(Daryl Hall and John Oates)
Somebody   (Bryan Adams)
Somebody's Baby   (Jackson Browne)
Somebody's Watching Me   (Rockwell)
Soul Kiss   (Olivia Newton-John)
Space Age Love Song   (A Flock Of Sea-
gulls)
Spies Like Us   (Paul McCartney)
Spirits In The Material World   (Police)
Stand Back   (Stevie Nicks)
State Of Shock   (The Jacksons)
Steppin' Out   (Joe Jackson)
Still In Saigon   (The Charlie Daniels
Band)
Straight From The Heart   (Bryan
Adams)
Stranger In My House   (Ronnie Milsap)
Stranger In Town   (Toto)
Stray Cat Strut   (The Stray Cats)
Strut   (Sheena Easton)
Stuck On You   (Lionel Richie)
Suddenly   (Billy Ocean)
Suddenly Last Summer   (The Motels)
Sugar Walls   (Sheena Easton)
Summer Of '69   (Bryan Adams)
Sunglasses At Night   (Corey Hart)
Sussudio   (Phil Collins)
*Sweet Dreams (Are Made Of
This)*   (Eurythmics)

Swept Away   (Diana Ross)
Synchronicity II   (Police)

Tainted Love   (Soft Cell)
Take It Away   (Paul McCartney)
Take Me To Heart   (Quarterflash)
Take Me With U   (Prince and The Rev-
olution)
Take Off   (Bob and Doug McKenzie)
Take On Me   (A-Ha)
Take The L   (The Motels)
Talk To Me   (Stevie Nicks)
Talking In Your Sleep   (The Romantics)
Teacher Teacher   (.38 Special)
*Telefone (Long Distance Love Af-
fair)*   (Sheena Easton)
Tell Her About It   (Billy Joel)
Tell Me Tomorrow—Part 1   (Smokey
Robinson)
Tenderness   (General Public)
That Girl   (Stevie Wonder)
That Was Yesterday   (Foreigner)
That's All   (Genesis)
Theme From Magnum P.I.   (Mike Post)
Themes From E.T.   (Walter Murphy)
*There Must Be An Angel (Playing With
My Heart)*   (Eurythmics)
They Don't Know   (Tracey Ullman)
Things Can Only Get Better   (Howard
Jones)
Think I'm In Love   (Eddie Money)
This Is Not America   (David Bowie and
The Pat Metheny Group)
This Man Is Mine   (Heart)
Thriller   (Michael Jackson)
Through The Years   (Kenny Rogers)
Tied Up   (Olivia Newton-John)
Time After Time   (Cyndi Lauper)
Time (Clock Of The Heart)   (Culture
Club)
Time Will Reveal   (DeBarge)
To All The Girls I've Loved Before   (Julio
Iglesias and Willie Nelson)
*Tonight I'm Yours (Don't Hurt
Me)*   (Rod Stewart)
Tonight She Comes   (The Cars)

Too Late For Goodbyes (Julian Lennon)
Too Shy (Kajagoogoo)
Torture (The Jacksons)
Total Eclipse Of The Heart (Bonnie Tyler)
Tough All Over (John Cafferty and The Beaver Brown Band)
Trouble (Lindsey Buckingham)
True (Spandau Ballet)
Truly (Lionel Richie)
Try Again (Champaign)
Turn Up The Radio (Autograph)
Turn Your Love Around (George Benson)
Twilight Zone (Golden Earring)
Twist Of Fate (Olivia Newton-John)

Undercover Of The Night (The Rolling Stones)
Understanding (Bob Seger and The Silver Bullet Band)
Union Of The Snake (Duran Duran)
Up Where We Belong (Joe Cocker and Jennifer Warnes)
Uptown Girl (Billy Joel)

Vacation. (The Go-Go's)
Valotte (Julian Lennon)
A View To A Kill (Duran Duran)
Voices Carry ('Til Tuesday)
Vox Humana (Kenny Loggins)
Voyeur (Kim Carnes)

Waiting For A Girl Like You (Foreigner)
Waiting On A Friend (The Rolling Stones)
Wake Me Up Before You Go-Go (Wham!)
Wake Up Little Susie (Simon And Garfunkel)
Walk Of Life (Dire Straits)
Walking On A Thin Line (Huey Lewis and The News)

Walking On Sunshine (Katrina and The Waves)
Wanna Be Startin' Somethin' (Michael Jackson)
The War Song (Culture Club)
The Warrior (Scandal featuring Patty Smythe)
Wasted On The Way (Crosby, Stills And Nash)
The Way He Makes Me Feel (Barbra Streisand)
We Are The World (USA For Africa)
We Belong (Pat Benatar)
We Built This City (The Starship)
We Don't Need Another Hero (Thunderdome) (Tina Turner)
We Got The Beat (The Go-Go's)
We Two (The Little River Band)
We're Not Gonna Take It (Twisted Sister)
We've Got Tonight (Kenny Rogers and Sheena Easton)
Welcome To Heartlight (Kenny Loggins)
What About Love? (Heart)
What About Me (Kenny Rogers with Kim Carnes and James Ingram)
What's Forever For (Michael Murphey)
What's Love Got To Do With It (Tina Turner)
When All Is Said And Done (Abba)
When Doves Cry (Prince)
When It's Over (Loverboy)
When You Close Your Eyes (Night Ranger)
When Your Heart Is Weak (Cock Robin)
White Horse (Laid Back)
Who Can It Be Now? (Men At Work)
Who's That Girl? (Eurythmics)
Who's Zoomin' Who (Aretha Franklin)
Why You Wanna Try Me (The Commodores)
The Wild Boys (Duran Duran)
Will The Wolf Survive? (Los Lobos)
Without You (Not Another Lonely Night) (Franke And The Knockouts)
The Woman In You (The Bee Gees)

Would I Lie To You? (Eurythmics)
Wrap Her Up (Elton John)
Wrapped Around Your Finger (Police)

You And I (Eddie Rabbitt with Crystal Gayle)
You Are (Lionel Richie)
You Are My Lady (Freddie Jackson)
You Belong To The City (Glenn Frey)
You Can Do Magic (America)
You Can't Get What You Want (Till You Know What You Want) (Joe Jackson)
You Can't Hurry Love (Phil Collins)
You Give Good Love (Whitney Houston)

You Got Lucky (Tom Petty and The Heartbreakers)
You Might Think (The Cars)
You Should Hear How She Talks About You (Melissa Manchester)
You Spin Me Round (Like A Record) (Dead Or Alive)
You're Only Human (Second Wind) (Billy Joel)
You're My Latest, My Greatest Inspiration (Teddy Pendergrass)
You're The Inspiration (Chicago)
Young Turks (Rod Stewart)
Your Love Is Driving Me Crazy (Sammy Hagar)

J. APPENDIX: NUMBER 1 POP RECORDS—A CHRONOLOGICAL LISTING

1982

2-13— 2-20	*Open Arms*—Journey (2)	
2-27— 3-27	*I Love Rock 'N' Roll*—Joan Jett and The Blackhearts (5)	
4-03	*We Got The Beat*—The Go-Go's (1)	
4-10— 4-17	*Freeze Frame*—The J. Geils Band (2)	
4-24	*Don't Talk To Strangers*—Rick Springfield (1)	
5-01— 5-29	*Ebony And Ivory*—Paul McCartney and Stevie Wonder (5)	
6-05— 6-12	*Crimson And Clover*—Joan Jett and The Blackhearts (2)	
6-19— 7-03	*Don't You Want Me*—The Human League (3)	
7-10	*Rosanna*—Toto (1)	
7-17	*Eye Of The Tiger*—Survivor (1)	
7-24	*Hurts So Good*—John Cougar (1)	
7-31— 8-21	*Eye Of The Tiger*—Survivor (4; 5)	
8-28— 9-04	*Abracadabra*—The Steve Miller Band (2)	
9-11	*Hard To Say I'm Sorry*—Chicago (1)	
9-18—10-09	*Jack And Diane*—John Cougar (4)	
10-16—10-30	*Who Can It Be Now?*—Men At Work (3)	
11-06—11-13	*Up Where We Belong*—Joe Cocker and Jennifer Warnes (2)	
11-20—12-04	*Truly*—Lionel Richie (3)	
12-11—12-18	*Dirty Laundry*—Don Henley (2)	
12-25	*Maneater*—Daryl Hall and John Oates (1)	

1983

1-01—	1-08	*Maneater*—Daryl Hall and John Oates (2; 3)
1-15—	1-22	*Down Under*—Men At Work (2)
1-29—	2-05	*Shame On The Moon*—Bob Seger and The Silver Bullet Band (2)
2-12—	2-26	*Stray Cat Strut*—The Stray Cats (3)
3-05		*Do You Really Want To Hurt Me*—Culture Club (1)
3-12		*Back On The Chain Gang*—The Pretenders (1)
3-19		*Billie Jean*—Michael Jackson (1)
3-26		*Hungry Like A Wolf*—Duran Duran (1)
4-02—	4-09	*One On One*—Daryl Hall and John Oates (2)
4-16—	4-23	*Jeopardy*—The Greg Kihn Band (2)
4-30		*Come On Eileen*—Dexy's Midnight Runners (1)
5-07—	5-21	*Beat It*—Michael Jackson (3)
5-28—	7-09	*Flashdance . . . What A Feeling*—Irene Cara (7)
7-16—	8-20	*Every Breath You Take*—Police (6)
8-27—	9-10	*Sweet Dreams*—Eurythmics (3)
9-17—	10-01	*The Safety Dance*—Men Without Hats (3)
10-08—	10-29	*Tell Her About It*—Billy Joel (4)
11-05		*Islands In The Stream*—Kenny Rogers and Dolly Parton (1)
11-12—	12-03	*All Night Long*—Lionel Richie (4)
12-10—	12-17	*Love Is A Battlefield*—Pat Benatar (2)
12-24—	12-31	*Union Of The Snake*—Duran Duran (2)

1984

1-07—	1-14	*Union Of The Snake*—Duran Duran (2; 4)
1-21—	2-04	*Owner Of A Lonely Heart*—Yes (3)
2-11		*Karma Chameleon*—Culture Club (1)
2-18—	2-25	*Jump*—Van Halen (2)
3-03		*Karma Chameleon*—Culture Club (1; 2)
3-10—	3-24	*99 Luftballons*—Nena (3)
3-31—	4-07	*Somebody's Watching Me*—Rockwell (2)
4-14—	4-21	*Footloose*—Kenny Loggins (2)
4-28		*Against All Odds*—Phil Collins (1)
5-05		*Miss Me Blind*—Culture Club (1)
5-12—	5-19	*To All The Girls I've Loved Before*—Julio Iglesias and Willie Nelson (2)
5-26—	6-02	*Let's Hear It For The Boy*—Deniece Williams (2)
6-09—	6-16	*Time After Time*—Cyndi Lauper (2)
6-23—	7-14	*Dancing In The Dark*—Bruce Springsteen (4)
7-21—	8-04	*When Doves Cry*—Prince (3)
8-11—	8-25	*Ghostbusters*—Ray Parker, Jr. (3)
9-01—	9-08	*What's Love Got To Do With It*—Tina Turner (2)
9-15		*The Warrior*—Scandal featuring Patty Smythe (1)
9-22		*Missing You*—John Waite (1)
9-29—	10-06	*Cover Me*—Bruce Springsteen (2)

10-13	*Drive*—The Cars (1)
10-20—11-03	*I Just Called To Say I Love You*—Stevie Wonder (3)
11-10	*Blue Jean*—David Bowie (1)
11-17—12-01	*Wake Me Up Before You Go-Go*—Wham! (3)
12-08	*Out Of Touch*—Daryl Hall and John Oates (1)
12-15	*The Wild Boys*—Duran Duran (1)
12-22	*Sea Of Love*—The Honeydrippers (1)
12-29	*Like A Virgin*—Madonna (1)

1985

1-05— 1-12	*Like A Virgin*—Madonna (2; 3)
1-19	*Born In The U.S.A.*—Bruce Springsteen (1)
1-26	*Run To You*—Bryan Adams (1)
2-02— 2-09	*I Want To Know What Love Is*—Foreigner (2)
2-16— 3-02	*Careless Whisper*—Wham! featuring George Michael (3)
3-09— 3-16	*Can't Fight This Feeling*—REO Speedwagon (2)
3-23— 3-30	*The Heat Is On*—Glenn Frey (2)
4-06	*One More Night*—Phil Collins (1)
4-13— 5-04	*We Are The World*—USA For Africa (4)
5-11— 5-18	*Crazy For You*—Madonna (2)
5-25	*Don't You (Forget About Me)*—Simple Minds (1)
6-01— 6-08	*Everybody Wants To Rule The World*—Tears For Fears (2)
6-15	*Axel F*—Harold Faltermeyer (1)
6-22— 6-29	*Heaven*—Bryan Adams (2)
7-06— 7-13	*Sussudio*—Phil Collins (2)
7-20— 7-27	*Raspberry Beret*—Prince (2)
8-03	*Every Time You Go Away*—Paul Young (1)
8-10	*If You Love Somebody Set Them Free*—Sting (1)
8-17— 8-24	*Power Of Love*—Huey Lewis and The News (2)
8-31— 9-07	*We Don't Need Another Hero*—Tina Turner (2)
9-14—11-02	no chart
11-09—11-16	*"Miami Vice" Theme*—Jan Hammer (2)
11-23	*You Belong To The City*—Glenn Frey (1)
11-30—12-07	*Broken Wings*—Mr. Mister (2)

MIDLINE-PRICED ALBUMS

A. INTRODUCTION

Midline-priced albums—or "midlines," as they were commonly termed—represented an attempt by the record industry to dig itself out of a recessionary vortex brought on in the late 1970s by the failure to develop new talent on a consistent, long-term basis and such extravagant practices as inflated advances for over-the-hill artists, overproduction, and expensive promotional bashes. Generally retailing for $5 or $6 apiece, midline titles were comprised of either relatively new artists striving to break through into the mainstream or classic releases whose best-selling days had long since passed. The practice of midline pricing made sound economic sense in that many of the releases required little investment other than the raw materials and labor tied into a production run.

Midlines played a key role in breaking down the monolithic pricing policies of the record companies, which had—acting in concert—almost doubled the retail list cost of the album during the 1970s. By the mid-1980s, most labels had adopted a more flexible approach to pricing, considering factors such as (1) format (*e.g.*, twelve-inch singles, ten- and twelve-inch extended play disks), (2) audience demographics, and (3) the sales potential of a given artist.

Midlines have continued to be released up to the present day. However, the renewed commercial success experienced by the industry, largely due to the public's captivation with the compact disc, had the effect of causing the major labels to pay diminishing attention to the medium.

Initial chart title/title changes: "Top 15 Midlines" (titled "Top Selling Midlines," without designated numerical positions, in the weeks prior to the institution of a chart proper)

Beginning date/termination date: December 11, 1982/September 8, 1984

Initial number of positions/changes in number of positions: 15

B. ARTIST INDEX

AC/DC

12-18-82   *Let There Be Rock*   (Atco SD-3615)   15, 15, 15, 15, 6, 7, 6, 3, 4, 7, 5, 6, 6, 8, 10, 8, 8, 6, 5, 7, 12, 15, (1), 12, 7, 6, 4, 10, 8, 15, 13, 14, 12, 14, 13, 11, 15, 14, 13, 14, 13, 15, 14, 13, 9, 8, 15, 13, 11, 7, 12, 13, 15, 15, 14, 14, 15, 12, 13   (58)

THE BEATLES

2-12-83   *Rock 'N Roll, Volume I*   (Cap. SN 16020)   6, 6, 8, 15, 15, 13, 14, 14, 13   (9)

2-04-84   *Rock 'N Roll, Volume I*   (Cap. SN 16020)   13, 12, 9, 8, 8, 6, 5, 4, 2, 3, 3, 2, 3, 6, 10, 11, 12, 13, 13, 13, 14, 13, 12, 12, 13, 14, 14, 13, 12, 12, 11, 9   (32)

2-25-84   *Rock 'N Roll, Volume II*   (Cap. SN 16021)   14, 11, 9, 6, 6, 4, 4, 5, 6, 8, 10, 11, 13, 15, 15, 14, 12, 11, 9, 8, 7, 6, 8, 10, 10, 10, 10, 9, 8   (29)

THE BLASTERS

12-11-82   *Over There; Live At The Venue, London*   (Slash 1-23735)   13   (1)

BOWIE, DAVID

7-09-83   *Diamond Dogs*   (RCA AYL1-3889)   14, 14   (2)

4-30-83   *The Rise And Fall Of Ziggy Stardust And The Spiders From Mars*   (RCA AYL1-3843)   9, 8, 6, 3, 1, 1, 2, 2, 2, 1, 1, 2, 2, 2, 2, 2, 2, 1, 1, 1, 1, 1, 1, 2, 4, 5, 3, 2, 2, 1, 3, 3, 3, 3, 3, 4, 4, 4, 4, 4, 4, 3, 3, 3, 3, 2, 2, 3, 6, 5, 4, 4, 7, 8, 7, 8, 7, 8, 7, 6, 5, 4, 4, 4, 4, 5, 7, 8, 9, 9, 10, 10   (72)

THE CARS

2-12-83   *The Cars*   (Elektra 6E-135)   9, 9, 6, 4, 4, 4, 8, 9, 11, 8, 10, 8, 6, 9, 6, 9, 11, 10, 8, 5, 5, 6, 4, 5, 4, 8, 5, 9   (28)

4-21-84   *The Cars*   (Elektra 6E-135)   8, 5, 3, 1, 1, 1, 1, 1, 1, 1, 1, 1, 1, 1, 1, 1, 1, 1, 1, 1, 1   (21)

CROSBY, STILLS, NASH AND YOUNG

12-11-82   *So Far*   (Atl. SD-19119)   2, 9, 9, 9, 13, 4, 2, 1, 5, 3, 2, 4, 5, 5, 5, 4, 3, 4, 7, 9, 12, 7, 8, 9, 14, 15, 13, 14   (28)

12-10-83   *So Far*   (Atl. SD-19119)   14, (7), 14, 14   (3)

CULTURE CLUB

12-11-82   *Kissing To Be Clever*   (Virgin/Epic ARE 38398)   15, 14, 14, 14, 14, 12   (6)

THE DOORS

12-11-82   *The Doors*   (Elektra EKS 75007)   5, 11, 11, 11, 12, 7, 3, 2, 8, 5, 3, 2, 3, 3, 1, 1, 1, 1, 3, 4, 2, 2, 3, 4, 5, 4, 3, 7, 14, 15, 12, 10, 10, 15, 13, 12, 13, 11, 10, 9, 9, 7, 7, 9, 10, 7, 5, 6, 8, 6, 5, 4, 4, 4, 4, 3, 3, 2, 2, 2, 3, 4, 4, 6, 5, 7, 13, 13, 15, 14, 15, 14, 15, 13, 12, 10, 9, 9, 12, 15, 15, 14, 13, 13, 12, 10, 9, 9, 8, 8, 6, 5   (92)

DURAN DURAN

12-11-82   *Carnival*   (Cap. ST-15006)   14, 12, 12, 12, 11, 8, 4, 5, 4   (9)

FLEETWOOD MAC

1-22-83   *Fleetwood Mac*   (Reprise MSK 2281)   15, 14, 13, 10, 11, 9, 8, 8, 6, 6, 4, 2, 5, 6, 6, 5, 4, 5, 10, 8, 7, 5, 4, 6, 5, 9, 6, 6, 5, 9   (30)

FOGELBERG, DAN

12-11-82   *Souvenirs*   (Full Moon/Epic PE 33137)   3, 3, 3, 3, 7, 5, 9, 12, 10, 8, 10, 10, 9, 9, 7, 5, 10, 7, 10, 7, 10, 10, 11, 11, 15, 13, 11, 15   (28)

11-19-83   *Souvenirs*   (Full Moon/Epic PE 33137)   14, (10), 11, 8, 6, 5, 7, 11, 10, 9, 8, 7, 6, 11, 14   (14)

GAYE, MARVIN

1-29-83   *Super Hits*   (Motown 301)   15, 15, 14, 15, 14, 12, 12   (7)

6-18-83   *Super Hits*   (Motown 301)   12, 11, 11, 9, 8, 8, 13   (7)

GENESIS

3-31-84   *Abacab*   (Atl. SD 19313)   14, 12, 11, 12, 12, 12, 13, 15, 14, 12, 10, 10, 9, 8, 7, 6, 5, 4, 3, 2, 2, 2, 3, 3   (24)

JACKSON, JANET

12-18-82   *Janet Jackson*   (A&M SP-6-4907)   13, 13, 13, 10, 13, 10, 8, 9   (8)

JACKSON, JOE

12-11-82   *Look Sharp!*   (A&M SP-6-4743)   1, 2, 2, 2, 4, 2, 5, 3, 1, 1, 1, 1, 1, 1, 1, 2, 2, 2, 5, 2, 2, 4, 4, 7, 7, 3, 3, 9, 11, 9, 10, 7, 6, 11, 14, 15, 14, 14, 12, 8, 6, 5, 4, 6, 3, 2, 4, 2, 3, 4, 4, 8, 13, 11, 7, 6, 6, 6, 10, 9, 9, 15, 11, 10, 9, 10, 12, 12, 11, 13, 11, 10, 10, 10, 9, 9, 9, 10, 10, 9, 8, 8, 7, 5, 5, 7, 6, 6, 7, 7, 7, 7, 7 ˙ (92)

JACKSON, MICHAEL, AND THE JACKSON 5

4-14-84   *Great Songs And Performances*   (Motown 5312 M)   9, 7, 6, 5, 4, 2, 2, 3, 5, 5, 4, 5, 6, 8, 8, 7, 5, 4, 3, 3, 2, 2   (22)

JOEL, BILLY

1-22-83   *Piano Man*   (Col. PC 32455)   11, 9, 6, 7, 4, 7, 7, 7, 12, 7, 12, 10, 13, 11, 14, 11, 10, 15, 11, 12, 12, 9, 6, 7, 11, (3), 10, 7, 6, 5, 2, 3, 3, 3, 3, 5, 6, 10, 12, 10, 7, 5, 4, 6, 12, 10, 13, 11, 11, 8, 13, 12, 12, 13, 13, 13, 14, 13, 11, 15   (59)

JOHN, ELTON

8-20-83   *Elton John's Greatest Hits, Volume 1*   (MCA 2128)   12, 9, 11, 15, 13, 11, 8, 8, 5, 3, 4, 4, 5, 10, 10, 5, 6, 11, 9, 8, 8, 6, 6, 5, 8, 9, 8, 7, 6, 5, 7, 10, 10, 13, 14   (35)

KING, CAROLE

12-11-82   *Tapestry*   (Epic PE 34946)   4, 4, 4, 4, 2, 1, 1, 4, 2, 2, 5, 3, 2, 2, 3, 3, 5, 9, 9, 14, 15, 14, 14, 14, 8, 9, 8, 6, 3, 3, 3, 5, 3, 9, 11, 8, 4, 6, 5, 7, 7, 12, 13, 12, 14, 15, 13, 11, 12, 13, 14, 15, (1), 12, 10, 9, 9, 9, 10, 10, 7, 10, 11, 11, 9, 8, 8, 7, 9, 10, 12, 13, 13, 15, 14, 12, 11, 11, 11, 11, 12, 15, 15, 15, 15, 13, 12, 11, 11, 11, 12, 13   (91)

LED ZEPPELIN

3-05-83   *Led Zeppelin IV*   (Atl. SD 19129)   14, 14, 11, 11, 6, 3, 1, 1, 1, 1, 1, 1, 1,
2, 2, 1, 1, 1, 2, 2, 1, 1, 1, 1, 1, 1, 2, 3, 4, 2, 2, 2, 1, 1, 1, 1, 1, 1, 3, 2, 1,
1, 2, 2, 2, 2, 3, 3, 6, 10, 15, 14, 15, 15, 14, 15, 14   (56)

2-12-83   *Presence*   (Swan Song/Atco SS 8416)   12, 8, 12   (3)

LENNON, JOHN

2-25-84   *Rock 'N Roll*   (Cap. SK-3419)   12, 12, 10, 9, 8, 7, 6, 8, 9, 9, 14, 15,
14, 13, 14, 15, 14, 13, 12, 11, 11, 10, 11, 11, 12, 13, 13, 15, 15   (29)

LOGGINS, KENNY

5-05-84   *Nightwatch*   (Col. JC 35387)   11, 8, 7, 6, 5, 4, 2, 2, 2, 2, 3, 3, 3, 4, 5,
6, 6, 8, 11   (19)

McLEAN, DON

5-07-83   *American Pie*   (U.A. LN 10337)   15, 13, 12   (3)

11-19-83   *American Pie*   (U.A. LN 10337)   15, (2), 14, 11, 13, 13, 12, 14,
15   (8)

MURRAY, ANNE

12-11-82   *Christmas Wishes*   (Cap. SN-16232)   6, 1, 1, 1, 1, 9   (6)

NELSON, WILLIE

12-11-82   *Pretty Paper*   (Col. JC 36189)   8, 7, 7, 7, 3, 11   (6)

PETTY, TOM, AND THE HEARTBREAKERS

7-23-83   *Tom Petty And The Heartbreakers*   (MCA SR 52006)   13, 10, 12   (3)

11-26-83   *Tom Petty And The Heartbreakers*   (MCA SR 52006)   15, 14   (2)

THE PRETENDERS

5-14-83   *The Pretenders*   (Sire SRK 6083)   12, 8, 6, 6, 4, 3, 7, 4, 4, 3, 4, 3, 4, 3,
3, 3, 6, 5, 11, 8, 5, 6, 7, 11, 6, 5, 3, 2, 1, 2, 2, 1, 1, 1, 1, 1, 1, 1, 1, 1, 1,
2, 2, 4, 4, 5, 3, 2, 2, 3, 2, 1, 3, 4, 5, 6, 8, 9, 10, 11, 14, 14, 14, 15, 15,
14, 15, 15, 13, 12   (70)

RIOT

1-22-83   *Riot Live*   (Elektra O-67969)   8, 7, 11   (3)

THE ROMANTICS

11-26-83   *The Romantics*   (Nemperor/CBS NJZ 36273)   11, 9, 8, 8, 8, 7, 7, 5, 5, 3, 2, 2, 2, 1, 1, 1, 1, 2, 5, 8, 13, 15   (22)

SAGA

12-11-82   *Worlds Apart*   (Portrait/CBS ARP 38246)   10, 8, 8, 8, 6, 3, 6   (7)

SCAGGS, BOZ

6-25-83   *Hits!*   (Col. FC 36841)   15, 13, 8, 7, 15   (5)

11-12-83   *Hits!*   (Col. FC 36841)   9, 8, 13, 10, 9, 9, 7, 10, 10, 11, (4), 15   (11)

SPRINGFIELD, RICK

9-17-83   *Working Class Dog*   (RCA AFL1-3697)   15, 14, 12, 15, 15, 13, 10, 7, 6, 9, 9, 8, 7, 6, 5, 5, 5, 7, 11, 11   (20)

4-28-84   *Working Class Dog*   (RCA AFL1-3697)   11, 7, 6, 5, 3, 2, 2, 4, 6, 6, 9, 10, 11, 12, 13, 15, 14, 14, 14, 14   (20)

SPYRO GYRA

4-16-83   *Morning Dance*   (MCA 9004)   14, 12   (2)

8-20-83   *Morning Dance*   (MCA 9004)   14, 13, 12, 12, 15, 14, 13, 12, 8, 11, 9, 14, (3), 15, (6), 15, 14   (15)

STEEL BREEZE

12-11-82   *Steel Breeze*   (RCA AFL1-4424)   11   (1)

STEELY DAN

7-30-83   *Aja*   (MCA 1006)   11, 9, 11, 8, 10, 9, 8, 6, 6, 4, 7, 8, 6, 9, 8, 15, (6), 15, 15, 13, 8, 7, 5, 5, 7, 10, 13, 15, 14, 12, 12, 15   (31)

STREISAND, BARBRA

12-11-82   *Christmas Album*   (Col. CS 9557)   7, 5, 5, 5, 5, 15   (6)

TOTO

8-13-83   *Toto*   (Col. FE 35317)   15, 15, 13, 12, 11   (5)

VAN HALEN

3-31-84   *Fair Warning*   (WB BSK 3540)   11, 9, 7, 5, 4, 4, 5, 6, 8, 7, 6, 7, 7, 10, 10, 9, 9, 9, 8, 6, 5, 5, 4, 4   (24)

3-19-83   *Women And Children First*   (WB 3415)   14, 12, 11, 14, 11, 15, 13, 13   (8)

2-04-84   *Women And Children First*   (WB 3415)   9, 6, 5, 4, 4, 3, 3, 1, 1, 1, 1, 1, 1, 2, 2, 3, 4, 4, 3, 3, 3, 3, 3, 2, 2, 2, 2, 3, 4, 4, 5, 6   (32)

VARIOUS ARTISTS

12-11-82   *A Country Christmas*   (RCA CPL1-4396)   9, 6, 6, 6, 8, 10   (6)

THE WAITRESSES

12-11-82   *I Could Rule The World If I Could Get The Parts*   (Ze/Polydor PX-1-507)   . 12, 10, 10, 10, 9, 14, 12, 11, 7   (9)

WASHINGTON, GROVER, JR.

2-26-83   *Winelight*   (Elektra 6E-305)   15, 13, 13, 10, 9, 7, 6, 4, 3, 3, 3, 2, 2, 4, 5, 5, 10, 8, 14   (19)

THE WHO

1-22-83   *Live At Leeds*   (MCA 3023)   14, 10, 12, 15, 14   (5)

5-21-83   *Live At Leeds*   (MCA 3023)   13, 13, 14, 15   (4)

10-29-83   *Live At Leeds*   (MCA 3023)   14, 14   (2)

2-05-83   *Meaty, Beaty, Big And Bouncy*   (MCA 37001)   14, 13, 12, 13, 11, 11, 9, 13, 15, 12, 15, 8, 5, 9, 5, 10, 7, 10, 14, 13, 12, 9, 10, 12, 9, 7, 7, 10, 10, 8, 7, 10, 8, 10, 10, 10, 9, 12   (38)

1-22-83   *Who Are You?*   (MCA 3050)   13, 13, (1), 11, 13, 11, 10, 10, 15, 15, 13, 15, 12, 13, 11, (7), 13, 12, 13, 11, 7, 5, 3, 4, 7, 7, 15, 14, 10, 9, 11, 11, 11, 14, 15, 12, 10, 12, 12, 11, 10, 13, 14   (41)

7-16-83   *Who's Next*   (MCA 3151)   15, 12, 8, 6, 6, 5, 4, 4, 2, 4, 5, 9, 4, 3, 2, 7, 13, 11, 7, 6, 7, 5, 5, 12, 12, 12, 14, 7, 8, 6, 7, 12   (32)

C. ALBUM-TITLE INDEX

Abacab   (Genesis)
Aja   (Steely Dan)
American Pie   (Don McLean)

Carnival   (Duran Duran)
The Cars   (The Cars)
Christmas Album   (Barbra Streisand)
Christmas Wishes   (Anne Murray)
A Country Christmas   (Various Artists)

Diamond Dogs   (David Bowie)
The Doors   (The Doors)

Elton John's Greatest Hits, Volume 1   (Elton John)

Fair Warning   (Van Halen)
Fleetwood Mac   (Fleetwood Mac)

Great Songs And Performances   (Michael Jackson and The Jackson 5)

Hits!   (Boz Scaggs)

I Could Rule The World If I Could Get The Parts   (The Waitresses)

Janet Jackson   (Janet Jackson)

Kissing To Be Clever   (Culture Club)

Led Zeppelin IV   (Led Zeppelin)
Let There Be Rock   (AC/DC)
Live At Leeds   (The Who)
Look Sharp!   (Joe Jackson)

Meaty, Beaty, Big And Bouncy   (The Who)
Morning Dance   (Spyro Gyra)

Over There; Live At The Venue, London   (The Blasters)

Piano Man   (Billy Joel)
Presence   (Led Zeppelin)
The Pretenders   (The Pretenders)
Pretty Paper   (Willie Nelson)

Riot Live   (Riot)
The Rise And Fall Of Ziggy Stardust And The Spiders From Mars   (David Bowie)

Rock 'N Roll (John Lennon)
Rock 'N Roll, Volume I (The Beatles)
Rock 'N Roll, Volume II (The Beatles)
The Romantics (The Romantics)

Tapestry (Carole King)
Tom Petty And The Heartbreakers (Tom Petty And The Heartbreakers)
Toto (Toto)

So Far (Crosby, Stills, Nash and Young)
Souvenirs (Dan Fogelberg)
Steel Breeze (Steel Breeze)
Super Hits (Marvin Gaye)

Who Are You? (The Who)
Who's Next (The Who)
Winelight (Grover Washington, Jr.)
Women And Children First (Van Halen)
Working Class Dog (Rick Springfield)
Worlds Apart (Saga)

D. APPENDIXES

[NUMBER 1 RECORDS—A CHRONOLOGICAL LISTING]

1982

12-11	*Look Sharp!*—Joe Jackson	(1)
12-18—12-25	*Christmas Wishes*—Anne Murray	(2)

1983

1-01— 1-08	*Christmas Wishes*—Anne Murray	(2; 4)
1-15— 1-22	*Tapestry*—Carole King	(2)
1-29	*So Far*—Crosby, Stills, Nash and Young	(1)
2-05— 3-12	*Look Sharp!*—Joe Jackson	(6; 7)
3-19— 4-09	*The Doors*—The Doors	(4)
4-16— 5-21	*Led Zeppelin IV*—Led Zeppelin	(6)
5-28— 6-04	*The Rise And Fall Of Ziggy Stardust And The Spiders From Mars*—David Bowie	(2)
6-11— 6-25	*Led Zeppelin IV*—Led Zeppelin	(3; 9)
7-02— 7-09	*The Rise And Fall Of Ziggy Stardust And The Spiders From Mars*—David Bowie	(2; 4)
7-16— 8-20	*Led Zeppelin IV*—Led Zeppelin	(6; 15)
8-27—10-01	*The Rise And Fall Of Ziggy Stardust And The Spiders From Mars*—David Bowie	(6; 10)
10-08—11-12	*Led Zeppelin IV*—Led Zeppelin	(6; 21)
11-19	*The Rise And Fall Of Ziggy Stardust And The Spiders From Mars*—David Bowie	(1; 11)
11-26	*The Pretenders*—The Pretenders	(1)
12-03—12-10	*Led Zeppelin IV*—Led Zeppelin	(2)
12-17—12-31	*The Pretenders*—The Pretenders	(3; 4)

1984

1-07—	2-18	*The Pretenders*—The Pretenders	(7; 11)
2-25—	3-17	*The Romantics*—The Romantics	(4)
3-24—	4-28	*Women And Children First*—Van Halen	(6)
5-05		*The Pretenders*—The Pretenders	(1; 12)
5-12—	9-08	*The Cars*—The Cars	(18)

[ALBUMS WITH LONGEST RUN ON CHARTS]

1. *The Doors*—The Doors.....92 weeks
1. *Look Sharp!*—Joe Jackson.....92
3. *Tapestry*—Carole King.....91
4. *The Rise And Fall Of Ziggy Stardust And The Spiders From Mars*— David Bowie.....72
5. *The Pretenders*—The Pretenders.....70
6. *Piano Man*—Billy Joel.....59
7. *Let There Be Rock*—AC/DC.....58
8. *Led Zeppelin IV*—Led Zeppelin.....56
9. *The Cars*—The Cars.....49

MUSIC VIDEOCASSETTES

A. INTRODUCTION

This format differs from videocassettes proper in that it focuses upon any of the following forms of music-based material: (1) live concerts, (2) anthologies of video clips, and (3) documentaries of musicians. Music titles also tend to differ from other videocassettes in that they carry a lower list price (typically ranging from $11 to $30) and are, accordingly, more likely to be purchased rather than rented. In addition, this material is generally able to withstand repeated viewings to a far greater extent than is the case with other videocassette genres.

Whereas most feature film releases—past and present—have found their way onto videocassettes, music-based titles have failed to exhibit any logical pattern up to the present day. Due to factors such as licensing and/or royalty disputes, artist bias, etc., acts experiencing similar success within the recording and performance sectors may reside at opposite poles with respect to the number of releases by which they are represented on videocassette. For example, whereas Elton John and Billy Joel have been featured on many releases, the Doobie Brothers and the Steve Miller Band—and even the most successful singing duo of the 1980s, Hall and Oates—have remained for the most part "missing in action."

One incongruous aspect about singling out this genre from the videocassette sector at large is that several other areas—most notably, kid vid programming and exercise videos—have sold at least as well. In short, the music industry-bias of trade publications such as *Cash Box* appears to have been a significant factor in the decision to institute the "Top 15 Music Videocassettes" chart.

Initial chart title/title changes: "Top 15 Music Videocassettes"; Subtitle: "The Cash Box Top 15 Music Videocassettes Chart Is Based

245

On Actual Pieces Rented At Retail Stores"/"The Cash Box Top 15
Music Videocassettes Chart Is Based On Actual Pieces Sold At
Retail Stores" (August 17, 1985-April 18, 1987)
Beginning date/termination date: July 13, 1985/April 18, 1987
Initial number of positions/changes in number of positions: 15

B. ARTIST INDEX

AC/DC

12-07-85   *Fly On The Wall*   (Atl. Video 50102)   14, 12, 13, 14, 14, 14, 14, 12,
11, 12, 15   (11)

ALABAMA

4-19-86   *Alabama's Greatest Hits*   (MusicVision 6-20575)   14, 12, 11, 11, 8,
7, 6, 5, 5, 5, 6, 8, 13, 13, 14, 15   (16)

THE BEACH BOYS

7-27-85   *An American Band*   (Vestron VA 4181)   13, 12, 13, 12, 12, 15   (6)

THE BEATLES

11-09-85   *The Beatles Live—Ready Steady Go!*   (Sony 97W50091)   10, 7, 6, 5,
4, 4, 5, 4, 4, 4, 3, 4, 4, 4, 5, 4, 4, 3, 3, 3, 4, 11, 14, 11, 13, 14, 14, 15,
15, 14, 13, 15, 15   (33)

10-11-86   *The Compleat Beatles*   (MGM 700166)   10, 10   (2)

BON JOVI

1-31-87   *Breakout*   (Sony Video 165)   15, 12, 9, 15, 15, 14, 9, 14, 14, 11, 14,
10   (12)

BOWIE, DAVID

7-13-85   *Jazzin' For Blue Jean*   (Sony 97W50002)   15, 15, 14   (3)

BUFFETT, JIMMY

6-14-86   *Live By The Bay*   (MCA HS 80332)   8, 7, 10   (3)

CARLISLE, BELINDA

10-04-86   *Belinda*   (MCA HS 80464)   15, 14, 9, 11, 11, 9, 9, 8, 15, 15, 15   (11)

THE CARPENTERS

7-13-85   *Yesterday Once More*   (MusicVision 6-21005)   13, 13, 12, 14, 14, 13   (6)

THE CHICAGO BEARS SHUFFLIN' CREW

2-22-86   *Super Bowl Shuffle*   (MPI MP 1302)   8, 7, 5, 5   (4)

CLARK, DICK   (*See:* VARIOUS ARTISTS)

COLLINS, PHIL   (*See also:* GENESIS)

11-16-85   *No Jacket Required*   (Atl. Video 50104)   10, 8, 7, 9, 6, 6, 6, 6, 6, 7, 5, 6, 6, 6, 5, 5, 7, 11, 8, 8, 7, 7, 5, 4, 4, 4, 4, 5, 5, 6, 7, 10, 13, 15, (2), 15, 13, 13, 13, 15, 15, 15, 14, 14, 14   (44)

3-14-87   *No Jacket Required*   (Atl. Video 50104)   10, 7, 10, 13   (4)

8-17-85   *Phil Collins Live At Perkins Palace*   (Thorn/EMI/HBO 2454)   15   (1)

COSTELLO, ELVIS, AND THE ATTRACTIONS

2-01-86   *The Best Of Elvis Costello And The Attractions*   (CBS-Fox Video 7093)   14, 10, 8, 7, 6, 6, 6, 9, 10, 9, 6, 7, 7, 8, 8, 7, 6, 7, 8, 11, 11   (21)

THE CURE

10-04-86   *Staring At The Sea*   (Elektra Entertainment 40401)   14, 13, 15, 6, 5, 3, 1, 1, 1, 3, 3, 2, 7, 7, 7, 7, 11, 10, 8, 7   (20)

DEPECHE MODE

5-17-86   *Live In Hamburg*   (Warner Music Video 38107-1)   14, 13, 13, 14   (4)

11-22-86   *Some Great Videos*   (Reprise/WB Video 3-38124)   11, 8, 11, 11, 15   (5)

DIRE STRAITS

8-09-86   *Brothers In Arms*   (Warner Music Video 38119)   14, 11, 12, 14, 12, 10, 11, 11, (1), 9, 6, 5, 6, 8, 15, (12), 13, 11, 9   (17)

THE DOORS

7-13-85   *Dance On Fire*   (MCA 80157)   4, 4, 3, 7, 7, 6, 5, 5, 6, 6, 6, 8, 8, 9, 8, 8, 10, 13, 15, 15, 15   (21)

DURAN DURAN

12-28-85   *Arena*   (Thorn/EMI/HBO Video 7085)   12, 12, 12, 10, 9, 7, 5, 4, 6, 10, 9, 8, 11, 12, 15   (15)

7-13-85   *Dancing On A Valentine*   (Sony 97W50075)   10, 10, 15, 13, 12   (5)

7-13-85   *Sing Blue Silver*   (Thorn/EMI/HBO 2852)   8, 8, 8, 6, 6, 5, 8, 8, 8, 7, 9, 10, 11, 12, 15, 15   (16)

DYLAN, BOB

10-04-86   *Don't Look Back*   (Paramount Video 2382)   12, 11, 11, 15, 12   (5)

DYLAN, BOB, AND TOM PETTY   *(See also:* TOM PETTY AND THE HEARTBREAKERS)

11-08-86   *Hard To Handle*   (CBS-Fox Music Video 3502)   10, 8, 13   (3)

FALCO

6-28-86   *Rock Me Falco*   (A&M Video 6-21015)   9, 6, 4, 5, 5, 5, 7, 9, 9, 6, 7, 8, 9, 9   (14)

THE FAT BOYS

9-20-86   *The Fat Boys On Video: Brr, Watch 'Em!*   (MCA 80382)   13, 13, 13   (3)

GTR

8-23-86   *The Making Of GTR*   (MusicVision 6-20633)   14, 13, 13, 13, 12, 12, 11   (7)

GENESIS *(See also:* PHIL COLLINS)

9-06-86   *Genesis Live—The Mama Tour*   (Atl. Video 50111-3)   9, 6, 4, 4, 4, 5, 8, 10, 10, 11, 11, 12, 10, 10, 10, 9, 8, 8, 8, 8, 5, 9, 13, 11, 8, 8, 8   (27)

HALL, DARYL, AND JOHN OATES

7-13-85   *Rock 'N Soul Live*   (MusicVision 6-20477)   14, 14   (2)

THE HOOTERS

3-29-86   *Nervous Night*   (CBS-Fox Video 7085)   13, 12, 12   (3)

HOUSTON, WHITNEY

7-12-86   *The #1 Video Hits*   (MusicVision 6-0=20631)   1, 1, 1, 1, 1, 1, 1, 1, 1, 1, 1, 1, 1, 1, 3, 3, 2, 7, 5, 4, 2, 2, 2, 2, 4, 6, 6, 6, 6, 8, 12, 14, 10, 10, 10   (33)

IRON MAIDEN

8-03-85   *Behind The Iron Curtain*   (Sony 95W50014)   10, 11, (2), 13, 13, 12, 15   (6)

1-25-86   *Live After Death*   (Song 96W50114)   13, 12, 14, 14, 12, 11, 13, 14, 14, 14, 14, 15   (12)

JACKSON, JANET

12-20-86   *Control—The Videos*   (A&M Video 61021)   13, 2, 2, 2, 2, 2, 3, 4, 3, 5, 5, 5, 6, 12, 9, 9, 12, 13   (18)

JOEL, BILLY

11-15-86   *The Video Album, Volume I*   (CBS Music Video 6198)   13, 9, 9, 7, 7, 3, 3, 3, 3, 3, 3, 2, 2, 2, 2, 4, 2, 5, 5, 6, 5, 5, 5, 8   (23)

3-07-88   *The Video Album, Volume II*   (CBS Music Video 3569)   4, 3, 3, 4, 3, 2, 2   (7)

JONES, GRACE

10-11-86   *State Of Grace*   (RCA/Col. 20500)   15, 14   (2)

JONES, HOWARD

8-17-85   *Like To Get To Know You Well*   (Warner 34070)   14, 13, 12, 15
15   (5)

JUDAS PRIEST

8-16-86   *Fuel For Life*   (CBS-Fox Music Video 7104)   15, 13, 11, 10, 11, 15,
15, (5), 12, 14, 15   (10)

10-19-85   *Judas Priest Live*   (Media M450)   14, 12, 12, 11, 11, 11   (6)

KISS

7-27-85   *Animalize Live Uncensored*   (MusicVision 6-20445)   11, 11, 10, 10,
11, 11, 11, 11, 12, 12, 13, 13, 12, 14, 15, 15   (16)

KOOL & THE GANG

9-28-85   *Tonight!*   (MusicVision 6-20368)   14, 12, 10   (3)

LaBELLE, PATTI

4-19-86   *Look To The Rainbow*   (PAZ Inc./E.J. Stewart Inc. U.S.A. Home Video
312847)   12, 11, 10, 10, 11, 12, 12, 11, 9, 8, 15, (5), 12, 8, 10, 10,
11, 12, (5), 12, 14, 15   (20)

LENNON, JOHN

6-28-86   *Imagine*   (Sony Video RO429)   7, 4, 3, 2, 2, 2, 3, 5, 5, 9, 14,
15   (12)

3-08-86   *John Lennon Live In New York*   (Sony Video LP V86060)   12, 10, 5, 3,
1, 1, 1, 1, 1, 1, 1, 1, 1, 1, 1, 1, 2, 7, 8, 9, 9, 10, 14, (6), 8, 8, 7, 7, 4,
6   (30)

LEWIS, HUEY, AND THE NEWS

11-02-85   *The Heart Of Rock 'N' Roll*   (Warner Home Video 30409)   11, 9, 8, 7,
8, 7, 9, 12, 15, 15, 15, 15   (12)

1-25-86   *Huey Lewis And The News Video Hits*   (CBS-Fox Video 6941)   14, 13,
11, 12, 14, 14   (6)

MADONNA

7-13-85   *Madonna* (WB Home Video 3-38101)   1, 1, 2, 2, 2, 2, 2, 3, 2, 2, 3, 3, 5, 6, 5, 3, 3, 3, 4, 5, 4, 5, 7, 7, 8, 8, 8, 8, 7, 8, 9, 10, 15, 15   (34)

12-07-85   *Madonna Live—The Virgin Tour*   (WB Music Video 38105)   8, 5, 3, 1, 1, 1, 1, 1, 1, 1, 1, 1, 1, 1, 1, 1, 1, 2, 2, 2, 3, 3, 3, 2, 2, 2, 2, 2, 2, 2, 3, 8, 9, 8, 7, 9, 10, 8, 5, 4, 3, 5, 5, 5, 2, 2, 8, 8, 7, 6, 10, 11, 13, 13   (54)

3-21-87   *Madonna Live—The Virgin Tour*   (WB Music Video 38105)   12, 12, 10, 14, 8, 11, 14, 11, 4   (9)

MELLENCAMP, JOHN COUGAR

7-13-85   *Ain't That America*   (MusicVision G-20455)   12, 12, 10, 15, 15   (5)

MOTLEY CRUE

12-27-86   *Uncensored*   (Elektra/Asylum 40104-3)   13, 13, 13, 13, 7, 4, 6, 14   (8)

NICKS, STEVIE

6-28-86   *I Can't Wait*   (RCA Video/MusicVision 6-20254)   3, 1, 2, 3, 4, 4, 4, 4, 3, 3, 3, 4, 6, 6, 7, (2), 9, 9, 14, 12, 14   (20)

OSBOURNE, OZZY

8-09-86   *The Ultimate Ozzy*   (CBS-Fox Music Video 6199)   5, 3, 4, 4, 5, 5, 3, 3, 2, 4, 5, 3, 1, 1, 2, 4, 4, 5, 5, 5, 12, 12, 12, 12, 14   (25)

PALMER, ROBERT

7-12-86   *Riptide*   (MusicVision 6-20635)   9, 6, 7, 8, 8, 7, 7, 7, 6, 7, 7, 7, 6, 6, 4, 4, 2, 4, 3, 6, 7, 9, 9, 7, 14, 14, 14, 14   (28)

PETTY, TOM, AND THE HEARTBREAKERS   *(See also:* BOB DYLAN)

4-05-86   *Pack Up The Plantation Live*   (MCA 80328)   13, 10, 8, 6, 5, 5, 10, 9, 8, 9, 12, 13   (12)

PINK FLOYD

4-11-87   *The Wall*   (MGM 400268)   11, 5   (2)

THE POINTER SISTERS

6-14-86   *So Excited*   (MusicVision 6-20609)   10, 9, 11, 12   (4)

POLICE

4-04-87   *Every Breath You Take—The Videos*   (A&M Video 61022)   1, 1, 1, 1,
1, 1, 1, 1, 1, 1, 3, 4, 6, 3, 1, 1, 1   (17)

PRESLEY, ELVIS

3-14-87   *Memories*   (Vestron MA 1054)   7, 13, 15   (3)

PRINCE AND THE REVOLUTION

8-17-85   *Prince And The Revolution Live!*   (WB Home Video 38102)   8, 3, 1,
1, 1, 1, 1, 1, 1, 1, 1, 1, 1, 1, 1, 2, 1, 1, 2, 2, 2, 2, 3, 3, 3, 3, 3, 3, 4, 4,
4, 5, 5, 9, 13, 14, 13, 13   (39)

RATT

9-21-85   *Ratt The Video*   (Atl. Video 50101)   10, 7, 4, 3, 4, 4, 5, 6, 5, 4, 6, 6,
8, 8, 10, 10, 10, 11, 10, 15   (20)

RICHIE, LIONEL

7-13-85   *All Night Long*   (MusicVision 6-20420)   3, 3, 6, 5, 3, 7, 7, 6, 7, 8,
11, 13, 15, 15, 13, 13, 14   (17)

1-31-87   *The Making Of Dancing On The Ceiling*   (Karl Lorimar Video
394)   13, 9, 6, 7, 13, 15, 11   (7)

ROSS, DIANA

3-21-87   *Diana Ross*   (RCA 60272)   9, 8, 7, 10   (4)

7-13-85   *Visions*   (MusicVision 6-20454)   9, 9, 9, 8, 8, 11, 14, (1), 14,
14   (9)

ROTH, DAVID LEE   (*See also:* VAN HALEN)

1-31-87   *David Lee Roth*   (WB Music Video 3-38126)   11, 10, 8, 9, 7, 7, (5),
11   (7)

RUSH

6-14-86   *Grace Under Pressure*   (MusicVision 6-20607)   14, 12, (1), 13, 12, 11,
10, 10, 15   (8)

SADE

8-24-85   *Sade: Diamond Life Video*   (CBS-Fox Video 7091)   15, 14, 12, 10, 7,
5, 6, 5, 7, 6, 6, 5, 9, 10, 10   (15)

THE SCORPIONS

9-21-85   *First Sting*   (Song Video 97W00086-7)   13, 11, 10, 8   (4)

10-19-85   *World Wide Live*   (MusicVision 6-20412)   11, 9, 7, 7, 13, 14, 13,
15   (8)

SINATRA, FRANK

4-05-86   *Portrait Of An Album*   (MGM/UA Home Video 400648)   10, 8, 15,
15, 15, 15, 12, 11, 9, 7, 4, 3, 5, 7, 10, 10, 11, 14   (18)

THE STARSHIP

9-20-86   *Video Hoopla*   (MusicVision 60278)   10, 10, 10   (3)

STREISAND, BARBRA

11-29-86   *Color Me Barbra*   (CBS-Fox Music Video 3518)   12, 8, 8, 6, 5, 5, 5, 5,
4, 6, 7, 12, 14, (3), 11, 7, 12, 9, 14   (18)

4-12-86   *The Making Of The Broadway Album*   (CBS-Fox Video 7101)   13, 9,
8, 6, 6, 5, 4, 3, 3, 3, 4, 8, 9   (13)

11-29-86   *My Name Is Barbra*   (CBS-Fox Music Video 3519)   14, 14, 14, 12,
11, 11, 11, 11, 9, 8, 11, (3), 11, 2, 1, 1, 6, 6, 3   (18)

TALKING HEADS

12-07-85   *Stop Making Sense*   (RCA/Col. Home Video 60519)   13, 11, 11, 11, 11, 11, 12   (7)

2-21-87   *Stop Making Sense*   (RCA/Col. Home Video 60519)   3, 2, 6, 8, 4, 5, 2, 8, 9   (9)

TEARS FOR FEARS

2-08-86   *Songs From The Big Chair*   (MusicVision 6-20534)   15, 13, 10, 8, 8, 7, 6, 7, 6, 5, 6, 9, 12, 12, 13, 14, 15, 15   (18)

7-13-85   *Tears For Fears*   (Sony 97W50068-9)   11, 11   (2)

TOWNSHEND, PETE

6-28-86   *Deep End*   (Atl. Video 50109)   14, 11, 15, 15   (4)

2-08-86   *White City*   (WB Music Video 50110)   13, 11, 11, 12, 10, 9, 7, 6, 4, 3, 4, 5, 7, 7, 6, 8, 10, 10, 13, 14   (20)

10-11-86   *White City*   (WB 50110)   12, 12, 14, 15   (4)

TURNER, TINA

7-13-85   *Private Dancer*   (Sony 97W50066-7)   6, 6, 4, 3, 4, 3, 6, 9, 9, 9, 8, 9, 9, 11, 9, 10, 13, 14, 12, 12, 12, 12, 15, 15   (24)

8-24-85   *Tina Live—Private Dancer Tour*   (Sony 97W50090)   9, 7, 5, 3, 2, 2, 2, 2, 2, 2, 2, 2, 2, 2, 1, 2, 2, 1, 3, 3, 5, 6, 5, 8, 9, 13, 13, 15, 15, 15, 15   (32)

U2

7-13-85   *U2 Live At Red Rock*   (Island/Music Vision 6-20613)   5, 5, 7, 9, 9, 9, 10, 10, 10, 13, 14, 15, 14, 14, 10, 11, 9, 12, 14, 13, 11   (21)

7-26-86   *U2 Live At Red Rock*   (Island/Music Vision 6-20613)   13, 11, 11, 12, 11, 12, (12), 13, 12, 12, 10, 10, 10, 10, 10, 13, 14, 15   (17)

USA FOR AFRICA

7-13-85   *We Are The World—The Video Event*   (MusicVision 6-20475)   2, 2, 1, 1, 1, 1, 1, 2, 4, 5, 5, 6, 7, 7, 6, 7, 8, 8, 6, 9, 9, 11, 14, 14, 13, 13, 13, 13, 13, 11, 10   (30)

VAN HALEN (See also: DAVID LEE ROTH)

1-24-87   *Live Without A Net*   (WB Home Video 38129)   10, 7, 5, 5, 6, 6, 13,
12, 15, 12, 10, 13, 12   (13)

VARIOUS ARTISTS

7-12-86   *Dick Clark's Best Of Bandstand*   (Vestron MA 1028)   5, 4, 3, 3, 2, 2,
2, 2, 2, 2, 2, 2, 3, 1, 1, 1, 3, 2, 5, 3, 6, 6, 6, 14, 15, 15, 15, 15, 15   (29)

6-28-86   *Hear N' Aid, The Sessions*   (Sony RO428)   12, 10, 11, 12, 12, 12   (6)

11-15-86   *MTV Closet Classics*   (Vestron 1043)   7, 5, 3, 4, 4, 11, 9, 9, 9, 9, 12,
(4), 11, 9, 13, 10, 13, 15, 15, 15   (19)

12-14-85   *Motown 25: Yesterday, Today, Forever*   (MGM/UA Home Video
300302)   13, 10, 7, 7, 7, 4, 2, 2, 2, 2, 2, 2, 2, 2, 2, 2, 3, 4, 3, 2, 2, 2,
3, 3, 4, 4, 6, 6, 4, 5, 6, 7, 6, 6, 6, 6, 6, 8, 8, 9, 8, 8, 9, 7, 13, 13, 13,
13   (48)

4-04-87   *Prince's Trust All Star Rock Concert*   (MGM MV 301089)   8, 7, 6   (3)

3-08-86   *Sun City*   (Karl Lorimar Home Video 012)   14, 12, 13   (3)

11-30-85   *Windham Hill's Water's Path*   (Paramount Home Video 2355)   14,
10, 10, 9, 9, 9, 9, 9, 15   (9)

2-14-87   *Women In Rock*   (MCA Home Video 80428)   15, 13, 14, 12, 15   (5)

WHAM!

11-01-86   *Wham! In China—Foreign Skies*   (CBS-Fox Music Video 7142)   10,
7, 5, 1, 1, 1, 4, 4, 4, 4, 6, 5, 3, 4, 4, 3, 1, 1, 2, 2, 4, 4, 7   (23)

7-13-85   *Wham! The Video*   (CBS-Fox Music Video)   7, 7, 5, 4, 5, 4, 4, 4, 3, 4,
4, 4, 3, 4, 3, 5, 4, 4, 3, 3, 3, 3, 3, 4, 5, 5, 5, 6, 8, 9, 7, 7, 9, 9, 11, 13, 10,
11, 8, 11, 10, 10, 9, 9, 9, 10, 11, 12   (48)

YOUNG, PAUL

3-22-86   *The Video Singles*   (CBS-Fox Video 7094)   12, 9   (2)

ZAPPA, FRANK

7-05-86   *Does Humor Belong In Music?*   (MPI Home Video 1304)   14, 14,
14   (3)

C. VIDEO TITLE INDEX

Memories (Elvis Presley)
Motown 25: Yesterday, Today, Forever
  (Various Artists)
My Name Is Barbra (Barbra Streisand)

Nervous Night (The Hooters)
No Jacket Required (Phil Collins)
The #1 Video Hits (Whitney Houston)

Pack Up The Plantation (Tom Petty
  and The Heartbreakers)
Phil Collins Live At Perkins Palace
  (Phil Collins)
Portrait Of An Album (Frank Sinatra)
Prince And The Revolution Live! (Prince
  and The Revolution)
Prince's Trust All Star Rock Concert
  (Various Artists)
Private Dancer (Tina Turner)

Ratt The Video (Ratt)
Riptide (Robert Palmer)
Rock Me Falco (Falco)
Rock 'N Soul Live (Daryl Hall and John
  Oates)

Sade: Diamond Life Video (Sade)
Sing Blue Silver (Duran Duran)
So Excited (The Pointer Sisters)
Some Great Videos (Depeche Mode)
Songs From The Big Chair (Tears For
  Fears)
Staring At The Sea (The Cure)
State Of Grace (Grace Jones)

Stop Making Sense (Talking Heads)
Sun City (Various Artists)
Super Bowl Shuffle (Chicago Bears
  Shufflin' Crew)

Tears For Fears (Tears For Fears)
Tina Live—Private Dancer Tour (Tina
  Turner)
Tonight! (Kool & The Gang)

U2 Live At Red Rock (U2)
The Ultimate Ozzy (Ozzy Osbourne)
Uncensored (Motley Crue)

The Video Album, Volume I (Billy Joel)
The Video Album, Volume II (Billy Joel)
Video Hoopla (The Starship)
The Video Singles (Paul Young)
Visions (Diana Ross)

The Wall (Pink Floyd)
We Are The World—The Video Event
  (USA For Africa)
Wham! In China—Foreign Skies
  (Wham!)
Wham! The Video (Wham!)
White City (Pete Townshend)
Windham Hill's Water's Path (Various
  Artists)
Women In Rock (Various Artists)
World Wide Live (The Scorpions)

Yesterday Once More (The Carpenters)

D. APPENDIXES

[NUMBER 1 MUSIC VIDEOCASSETTES—A CHRONOLOGICAL LISTING]

1985

7-13—	7-20	*Madonna*—Madonna (2)
7-27—	8-24	*We Are The World—The Video Event*—USA For Africa (5)
8-31—	11-30	*Prince and The Revolution Live!*—Prince and The Revolution (14)
12-07		*Tina Live—Private Dancer Tour*—Tina Turner (1)
12-14—	12-21	*Prince And The Revolution Live!*—Prince And The Revolution (2; 16)
12-28		*Madonna Live—The Virgin Tour*—Madonna (1)

1986

1-04—	3-29	*Madonna Live—The Virgin Tour*—Madonna (13; 14)
4-05—	6-28	*John Lennon Live In New York*—John Lennon (13)
7-05		*I Can't Wait*—Stevie Nicks (1)
7-12—	10-04	*The #1 Video Hits*—Whitney Houston (13)
10-11—	10-25	*Dick Clark's Best Of Bandstand*—Various Artists (3)
11-01—	11-08	*The Ultimate Ozzy*—Ozzy Osbourne (2)
11-15—	11-29	*Staring At The Sea*—The Cure (3)
12-06—	12-20	*Wham! In China—Foreign Skies*—Wham! (3)
12-27		*Every Breath You Take—The Videos*—Police (1)

1987

1-03—	2-28	*Every Breath You Take—The Videos*—Police (9; 10)
3-07—	3-14	*Wham! In China—Foreign Skies*—Wham! (2; 5)
3-21—	3-28	*My Name Is Barbra*—Barbra Streisand (2)
4-04—	4-18	*Every Breath You Take—The Videos*—Police (3; 13)

[MUSIC VIDEOCASSETTES WITH LONGEST RUN ON CHARTS]

1. *Madonna Live—The Virgin Tour*—Madonna.....63 weeks
2. *Motown 25: Yesterday, Today, Forever*—Various Artists.....48
2. *No Jacket Required*—Phil Collins.....48
2. *Wham! The Video*—Wham!.....48
5. *Prince and The Revolution Live!*—Prince and The Revolution.....39

6. *U2 Live At Red Rock*—U2.....38
7. *Madonna*—Madonna.....34
8. *The Beatles Live—Ready Steady Go!*—The Beatles.....33
8. *The #1 Video Hits*—Whitney Houston.....33
10. *Tina Live—Private Dancer Tour*—Tina Turner.....32
11. *John Lennon Live In New York*—John Lennon.....30
11. *We Are The World—The Video Event*—USA For Africa.....30

MUSIC VIDEOS

A. INTRODUCTION

Music videos—or "video clips"—have had a long and rich history prior to the genre's renaissance in the 1980s as a result of the round-the-clock exposure provided by MTV and a host of imitators on both network and cable television. In the early 1940s short film vignettes set to the music of the top bands and singers (*e.g.,* Cab Calloway, Fletcher Henderson, Bing Crosby) were available for public consumption in various restaurants and bars alongside the ubiquitous jukebox. Called "soundies," these shorts were divided into two major types: the concert vehicle, and storylines adapted from either the lyrics or the mood of a song. The "Silly Symphony," pioneered by Walt Disney in the 1930s, which featured animated interpretations of popular classical music pieces, proved to be a seminal influence behind the "soundies." The marvelously inventive Betty Boop cartoons, produced by the Fleischer Brothers, formed a bridge between the Silly Symphonies and soundies; for example, "I'll Be Glad When You're Dead, You Rascal You," portrayed Betty and her cohorts in a surrealistic escapade accompanied by the famous Louis Armstrong song of that title.

Visual interpretations of songs were used by rock music stars in the 1960s as a promotional device—particularly by British Invasion acts attempting to maintain a high profile in the States without the need to travel constantly back and forth across the Atlantic—to be broadcast on the rapidly proliferating television programs showcasing the genre. Given the widespread use of lipsynching (a la *American Bandstand*) at the time, many artists' were also reputed to be seeking a more imaginative—and credible—means of communicating to their fans.

Rapid technological strides in the 1970s rendered the video

medium a more economically feasible option for performing artists. In addition, the growing numbers of successful Hollywood films possessing a rock music soundtrack (*e.g., American Graffiti, Saturday Night Fever*) during that decade attracted the attention of both visually-oriented artists and record company executives. The record business recession of the late 1970s, combined with the increasingly restrictive playlists of radio stations, spurred many artists to channel a significant portion of their time and resources into the making of videos which best reflected the image they wished to project to music buyers. During the late 1970s and early 1980s they found an enthusiastic following in dance clubs and TV network programs.

The institution of MTV by Warner in Fall 1981 provided the main impetus for the use of videos as a marketing tool for the vast majority of pop music acts. Those artists whose personae didn't fit the MTV target audience demographics (*e.g.,* most black contemporary acts, country music performers, Easy Listening stars), found a countless array of substitute outlets willing to expose their videos, including Warner's companion station to MTV aimed at the thirty-something set, VH-1; the Turner Group's weekend juggernaut on WTBS, "Night Tracks"; USA's long-running program, "Nightflight"; NBC's "Friday Night Videos"; and filler slots on stations as diversified as BET, Nickelodeon, the Nashville Network, and the leading movie channels.

The music videos listing differed from the other *Cash Box* charts in one notable respect: most video clips weren't released for sale or rental to the public at large, it was impossible to employ any precise measurement standards as a means of determining the numerical positions. Rather, devices such as (1) regularity of broadcast rotation and (2) audience requests played a prominent role in the compilation of these charts. The imprecise nature of this process, however, has led *Cash Box*—and other music trade publications—to adopt such ambivalent strategies as substituting the actual playlists of various TV networks (particularly MTV) and dance venues for rung-by-rung chart breakdowns. In the meantime, the music video clip continues its role as perhaps the prime means of influencing contemporary record sales (radio having long ago receded in importance due to overspecialization in the compilation of playlists as well as the conversion of many outlets to nostalgia programming, talk shows, news, etc.).

Initial chart title/title changes: "Top 15 Music Videos"/"Top 30 Music Videos" (August 10, 1985–September 13, 1986); "Top 40 Music Videos" (September 20, 1986–June 20, 1987)

Beginning date/termination date: March 31, 1984/June 20, 1987

Initial number of positions/changes in number of positions: 15/30 (August 10, 1985–September 13, 1986); 40 (September 20, 1986–June 20, 1987)

B. ARTIST INDEX

ABC

10-05-85   *Be Near Me*   (Mer.)   24, 16, 9, 7, 6, 3, 2, 4, 6, 12, 17, 23, 23, 26, 26, 27   (16)

1-25-86   *(How To Be A) Millionaire*   (Mer.)   27, 24, 21, 21, 17, 14, 11, 12, 20, 18, 26, 26, 29, 30, 30   (15)

ABBOTT, GREGORY

5-09-87   *I've Got The Feeling (It's Over)*   (Col.)   31, 27, 24   (3)

12-06-86   *Shake You Down*   (Col.)   37, 37, 28, 24, 18, 12, 8, 8, 8, 10, 16, 26   (12)

ADAMS, BRYAN

5-25-85   *Heaven*   (A&M)   12, 8, 8, 4, 13, 11, 13, 10, 14   (9)

12-22-84   *Run To You*   (A&M)   9, 9, 9, 9, 4, 3, 2, 6, 13   (9)

3-23-85   *Somebody*   (A&M)   11, 5, 4, 14   (4)

8-10-85   *Summer Of '69*   (A&M)   18, 12, 11, 13, 12, 13, 22, 26   (8)

ADAMS, BRYAN, AND TINA TURNER   *(See also:* TINA TURNER)

11-30-85   *It's Only Love*   (A&M)   16, 10, 5, 4, 4, 3, 3, 2, 2, 3, 3, 3, 4, 13   (14)

THE ADVENTURES

8-31-85 *Send My Heart* (Chrysalis) 29, 25, 23, 26, 28, 23, 29 (7)

A-HA

2-14-87 *Cry Wolf* (WB) 35, 32, 32 (3)

1-25-86 *The Sun Always Shines On T.V.* (Reprise) 18, 15, 11, 11, 8, 8, 18, 23, 30 (9)

6-29-85 *Take On Me* (WB) 13, 8, 8, 6, 3, 2, 1, 2, 3, 4, 3, 1, 2, 2, 2, 1, 2, 2, 3, 4, 6, 6, 10, 15, 22, 25, 25 (27)

THE ALARM

11-30-85 *Strength* (I.R.S.) 22, 18, 16, 15, 15, 12, 12, 10, 10, 10, 20, 20, 23, 30 (14)

ALLEN, DONNA

2-28-87 *Serious* (21/Atco/Atl.) 28, (1), 32, 38, 19, 7, 8, 16, 16, 30 (9)

ALPERT, HERB

5-30-87 *Diamonds* (A&M) 26, 26, 6, 2 (4)

3-14-87 *Keep Your Eye On Me* (A&M) 21, 19, 23, 21, 23, 22, 22, 32 (8)

ANIMOTION

4-13-85 *Obsession* (Mer.) 4, 7, 1, 4, 3, 11, 15 (7)

ARCADIA *(See also:* DURAN DURAN)

3-22-86 *Goodbye Is Forever* (Cap.) 27, 24, 24, 24 (4)

10-11-86 *Say The Word* (Atl.) 39, 36 (2)

THE ART OF NOISE WITH MAX HEADROOM

8-23-86 *Paranoimia* (Chrysalis) 26, 22, 24, 26, 24, 22, 20, 15, 14, 19, 26, 34 (12)

ARTISTS UNITED AGAINST APARTHEID

11-23-85   *Sun City*   (Manhattan)   28, 14, 11, 9, 8, 8, 10, 10, 21   (9)

ATLANTIC STARR

5-16-87   *Always*   (WB)   28, 20, 10, 10, 11, 17   (6)

6-20-87   *One Love At A Time*   (WB)   15   (1)

3-15-86   *Secret Lovers*   (A&M)   22, 19, 14, 28, 28, 27, 27   (7)

AUSTIN, PATTI

6-16-84   *Rhythm Of The Streets*   (WB)   15, 7, 4, 9, 13   (5)

BAILEY, PHILIP, AND PHIL COLLINS   *(See also:* PHIL COLLINS)

1-19-85   *Easy Lover*   (Col.)   3, 1, 1, 1, 1, 1, 6, 12, 12, 6   (10)

BAKER, ANITA

4-25-87   *Same Ole Love (365 Days A Year)* (Elektra)   35, 30, 30, 25, 33, 39, 39   (7)

9-20-86   *Sweet Love*   (Elektra)   38, 33, 24, 22, 16, 11, 9, 9, 22, 36   (10)

BANANARAMA

9-08-84   *Cruel Summer*   (London/PolyGram)   13, 10, 8, 4, 3, 2, 1, 1, 5, 12   (10)

8-02-86   *Venus*   (London)   28, 15, 7, 1, 3, 5, 9, 18, 25, 26, 40   (11)

BAND AID

1-19-85   *Do They Know It's Christmas*   (Col.)   12, 14   (2)

THE BANGLES

3-22-86   *Manic Monday*   (Col.)   29, 15, 10, 10, 5, 3, 1, 3, 6, 22   (10)

10-25-86   *Walk Like An Egyptian*   (Col.)   35, 20, 25, 15, 13, 11, 7, 7, 7, 12, 12, 12, 21, 24, 24, 38   (16)

3-14-87 *Walking Down Your Street* (Col.) 33, 26, 25, 25, 7, 15, 19, 17, 12, 13, 12, 7, 7, 12 (14)

THE BARBUSTERS

4-04-87 *Light Of Day* (Blackheart) 36, 13, 18, 12, 11, 8, 15 (7)

BARNES, JIMMY

5-10-86 *Working Class Man* (Geffen) 27, 18, 24, 30 (4)

THE BEACH BOYS

7-06-85 *Getcha Back* (CBS) 14 (1)

THE BEASTIE BOYS

2-14-87 *(You Gotta) Fight For Your Right (To Party)* (Def Jam) 26, 23, 15, 9, 9, 16, 14, 22, 35 (9)

BEAUVOIR, JEAN

7-05-86 *Feel The Heat* (Col.) 27, 24, 24, 24, 16, 12, 15, 27 (8)

BENATAR, PAT

8-10-85 *Invincible* (Chrysalis) 15, 15, 10, 8, 5, 3, 1, 1, 5, 15, 16, 23, 29 (13)

1-25-86 *Sex As A Weapon* (Chrysalis) 20, 11, 8, 8, 6, 10, 14, 27 (8)

11-24-84 *We Belong* (Chrysalis) 8, 5, 3, 1, 2, 2, 2, 2, 8, 15 (10)

BERLIN

8-09-86 *Take My Breath Away* (Col.) 13, 9, 7, 4, 2, 3, 6, 9, 13, 12, 12, 25, 34, 40 (14)

BIG AUDIO DYNAMITE

11-29-86 *C'mon Every Beat Box* (Col.) 37, 34, 34, 34, 40, 40, 40 (7)

BIG COUNTRY

8-30-86   *Look Away*   (PolyGram)   29, 21, 21, 25, 30, 40   (6)

THE BLUE MONKEYS

7-12-86   *Digging Your Scene*   (RCA)   23, 19, 19, 12, 24, 29   (6)

BON JOVI

2-07-87   *Living On A Prayer*   (Mer./PolyGram)   28, 23, 19, 18, 19, 36   (6)

11-08-86   *You Give Love A Bad Name*   (PolyGram)   30, 25, 20, 18, 14, 14, 11, 9, 9, 18, 18, 29, 36   (13)

BOURGEOIS TAGG

5-24-86   *Mutual Surrender*   (Island)   30, 28   (2)

BOWIE, DAVID

4-18-87   *Day-In Day-Out*   (EMI America)   21, 16, 13, 9, 5, 4, 6, 6, 5, 5   (10)

BOWIE, DAVID, AND MICK JAGGER   *(See also:* MICK JAGGER)

8-31-85   *Dancing In The Streets*   (EMI America)   25, 13, 12, 8, 6, 4, 3, 3, 5, 7, 10, 15, 22   (13)

BOYS DON'T CRY

5-10-86   *I Wanna Be A Cowboy*   (Profile)   28, 24, 13, 11, 9, 9, 13, 18, 28, 30   (10)

BRANIGAN, LAURA

9-29-84   *The Lucky One*   (Atl.)   10, 8, 5, 14   (4)

6-16-84   *Self Control*   (Atl.)   14, 6, 5, 5, 3, 8, 10, 15   (8)

THE BREAKFAST CLUB

4-04-87   *Right On Track*   (MCA)   35, 11, 7, 5, 5, 2, 8, 5, 4, 4, 4, 32   (12)

BRIGHTON ROCK

5-30-87 *Can't Wait For The Night* (Atco/Atl.) 29, 29, 19, 10 (4)

BROWN, JAMES

10-11-86 *Gravity* (Scotti Bros.) 37, 33, 30, 27, 24, 24, 39 (7)

1-18-86 *Living In America* (Scotti Bros.) 29, 26, 23, 18, 18, 14, 7, 5, 3, 3, 16, 29, 29 (13)

BROWNE, JACKSON

5-03-86 *For America* (Asylum) 19, 18, 26 (3)

BUCKINGHAM, LINDSEY

9-22-84 *Go Insane* (Elektra) 14, 12, 9, 6, 5, 4, 8 (7)

BUSH, KATE *(See also:* **PETER GABRIEL)**

10-12-85 *Running Up That Hill* (EMI America) 27, 17, 15, 12, 11, 8, 8, 7, 8, 7, 7, 7, 8, 8, 12, 29 (16)

CAFFERTY, JOHN, AND THE BEAVER BROWN BAND

9-21-85 *C-I-T-Y* (CBS) 23, 17, 16, 23, 30 (5)

10-20-84 *On The Dark Side* (Epic) 15, 13, 11, 13 (4)

CAMEO

1-24-87 *Candy* (Atl. Artists) 32, 28, 20, 18, 18 (5)

3-31-84 *She's Strange* (Atl. Artists/PolyGram) 15, 13, 14, 8, 10, 10, 14, 14 (8)

9-20-86 *Word Up* (Atl. Artists) 39, 36, 33, 29, 26, 20, 16, 14, 10, 10, 10, 11, 11, 9, 8, 8, 16, 17, 18, 31, 39, 40, 38 (23)

CARDENAS, LUIS

9-06-86 *Runaway* (Allied Artists) 22, 22, 29, 10, 9, 8, 8, 7, 7, 19, 36 (11)

CARLISLE, BELINDA   (*See also:* **THE GO-GO'S**)

  6-21-86   *Mad About You*   (I.R.S.)   29, 17, 4, 2, 1, 1, 1, 1, 1, 2, 5, 18, 29,
            35   (13)

THE CARS   (*See also:* **RIC OCASEK**)

  9-08-84   *Drive*   (Elektra)   15, 12, 9, 7, 6, 9, 10, 12   (8)

  7-07-84   *Magic*   (Elektra)   12, 8, 5, 5, 11, 15   (6)

  4-07-84   *You Might Think*   (Elektra)   8, 5, 12, 9, 5, 4, 3, 1, 1, 3, 11, 15   (12)

CETERA, PETER   (*See also:* **CHICAGO**)

  7-05-86   *Glory Of Love*   (WB)   22, 18, 13, 13, 7, 5, 5, 16, 28, 30, 28, 32   (12)

CETERA, PETER, WITH AMY GRANT   (*See also:* **CHICAGO**)

  9-27-86   *The Next Time*   (WB)   38, 30, 25, 20, 17, 12, 7, 3, 3, 3, 4, 4, 4, 4, 4,
            4, 10, 19, 23, 37   (20)

CHARLES, RAY   (*See:* **BILLY JOEL**)

CHEECH AND CHONG

  9-07-85   *Born In East L.A.*   (MCA)   24, 17, 17, 15, 19, 19, 23, 28   (8)

CHERRELLE

  7-21-84   *I Didn't Mean To Turn You On*   (Tabu/CBS)   14, 9, 7, 4, 5, 8, 14   (7)

CHICAGO   (*See also:* **PETER CETERA**)

  4-27-85   *Along Comes A Woman*   (WB)   9, 13   (2)

  1-31-87   *Will You Still Love Me?*   (WB)   33, 22, 17, 15, 11, 3, 6, 4, 5, 24, 26,
            24, 34   (13)

CHINA CRISIS

  3-21-87   *Arizona Sky*   (A&M)   18, 17, 19, 21, 25, 28, 40   (7)

CHRISTOPHER, GAVIN

8-09-86 *One Step Closer To You* (Manhattan) 26, 23, 22 (3)

CLAPTON, ERIC

1-17-87 *It's In The Way That You Use It* (WB) 33, 29, 26, 25, 28, 31 (6)

8-24-85 *She's Waiting* (WB) 29, 27 (2)

CLUB NOUVEAU

3-07-87 *Lean On Me* (WB) 23, 17, 1, 1, 1, 1, 1, 2, 3, 6, 14, 19, 22, 22 (14)

COLE, NATALIE (*See:* DIONNE AND FRIENDS)

COLLINS, PHIL (*See also:* PHILIP BAILEY; GENESIS)

4-28-84 *Against All Odds* (Atl.) 8, 6, 6, 6, 15 (5)

9-07-85 *Don't Lose My Number* (Atl.) 19, 16, 14, 13, 21, 28, 29 (7)

3-30-85 *One More Night* (Atl.) 11, 6, 3, 1, 8 (5)

5-11-85 *Sussudio* (Atl.) 10, 4, 2, 2, 4, 3, 2, 1, 1, 1, 3, 12, 14, 21, 30 (15)

5-03-86 *Take Me Home* (Atl.) 28, 19, 17, 26 (4)

COLLINS, PHIL, AND MARILYN MARTIN (*See also:* GENESIS; MARILYN MARTIN)

11-02-85 *Separate Lives* (Atl.) 23, 12, 7, 5, 3, 1, 2, 2, 2, 4, 4, 5, 5, 21, 27, 27, 30 (17)

THE COMMODORES (*See also:* LIONEL RICHIE)

3-30-85 *Nightshift* (Motown) 7, 5, 6, 14 (4)

COMPANY B

5-16-87 *Fascinated* (Atl.) 32, 25, 19, 19, 8, 4 (6)

CONCRETE BLONDE

3-21-87   *Still In Hollywood*   (I.R.S.)   30, 30, 32, 39, 40   (5)

COUGAR, JOHN   (*See:* JOHN COUGAR MELLENCAMP)

THE COVER GIRLS

5-02-87   *Show Me*   (Sutra)   24, 20, 19, 35   (4)

CROWDED HOUSE

3-14-87   *Don't Dream It's Over*   (Cap.)   12, 11, 12, 11, 3, 5, 10, 10, 11, 12, 11, 11, 11, 17, 31   (15)

CRYSTAL, BILLY

9-14-85   *You Look Marvelous*   (A&M)   29, 25, 23, 22, 26   (5)

CULTURE CLUB

6-16-84   *It's A Miracle*   (Virgin/Epic)   10, 8, 7, 11, 15   (5)

4-07-84   *Miss Me Blind*   (Virgin/Epic)   10, 7, 1, 1, 2, 5, 4, 6, 6, 13   (10)

5-10-86   *Move Away*   (Epic)   16, 8, 3, 1, 2, 2, 7, 19   (8)

11-17-84   *The War Song*   (Epic)   10, 7, 6, 5, 3, 13, 13, 13, 13   (9)

THE CUTTING CREW

2-28-87   *(I Just) Died In Your Arms*   (Virgin)   22, 20, 5, 12, 10, 5, 16, 16, 20, 26, 5, 2, 6, 5, 5, 10, 16   (17)

DALTREY, ROGER

3-22-86   *Quicksilver Lightning*   (Atl.)   25, 20, 23, 23, 24, 28   (6)

DANGERFIELD, RODNEY

7-12-86   *Twist And Shout*   (MCA)   29, 25, 25, 26   (4)

DANNY WILSON

6-2087   *Mary's Prayer*   (Virgin)   27   (1)

DAVID AND DAVID

3-14-87   *Ain't So Easy*   (A&M)   16, 14, 13, 20, 34   (5)

12-06-86   *Welcome To The Boomtown*   (A&M)   38, 38, 35, 31, 31, 31, 31   (7)

DAY, MORRIS   *(See also:* PRINCE)

10-19-85   *The Oak Tree*   (WB)   26, 21, 14, 13, 12, 10, 11, 17   (8)

DEAD OR ALIVE

2-21-87   *Brand New Lover*   (Epic)   24, 20, 28, 28   (4)

6-22-85   *You Spin Me Round (Like A Record)*   (Epic)   6, 5, 9   (3)

DeBARGE   *(See also:* EL DeBARGE)

4-06-85   *Rhythm Of The Night*   (Motown)   7, 2, 3, 5, 3, 4   (6)

DeBARGE, EL   *(See also:* DeBARGE)

6-21-86   *Who's Johnny*   (Gordy)   22, 12, 8, 11, 17, 17   (6)

DeBURGH, CHRIS

5-02-87   *Lady In Red*   (A&M)   31, 29, 36, 39, 36, 36, 31, 38   (8)

DEPECHE MODE

7-13-85   *People Are People*   (Sire)   13, 12, 13, 11, 12, 11, 16, 16, 28   (9)

DEVICE

8-02-86   *Hanging On A Heart Attack*   (Chrysalis)   14, 11, 10, 17, 14, 23, 24, 30, 39   (9)

DeYOUNG, DENNIS

11-03-84   *Desert Moon*   (A&M)   10, 14   (2)

DIONNE AND FRIENDS

12-14-85   *That's What Friends Are For*   (Arista)   20, 19, 19, 17, 17, 9, 3, 1, 2, 2, 3, 12, 22, 30   (14)

DIRE STRAITS

9-14-85   *Money For Nothing*   (WB)   27, 18, 16, 12, 12, 15, 19, 22   (8)

5-03-86   *So Far Away*   (WB)   17, 13, 22   (3)

8-10-85   *Walk Of Life*   (WB)   24, 24, 30, (10), 25*, 23, 18, 30, 29, 28, (4), 16, 13, 13, 25, 25, 25   (15)   (*Second version of video released)

THE DIVINYLS

2-22-86   *Pleasure And Pain*   (Chrysalis)   28, 26, 25, 29   (4)

DOLBY, THOMAS

4-14-84   *Hyperactive*   (Cap.)   11, 13, 13, 15   (4)

DOUBLE

8-30-86   *The Captain Of Her Heart*   (A&M)   13, 6, 5, 5, 5, 7, 9, 9, 24, 33   (10)

THE DREAM ACADEMY

11-16-85   *Life In A Northern Town*   (WB)   27, 24, 19, 16, 15, 13, 13, 13, 13, 11, 9, 7, 1, 1, 1, 3, 4, 11, 22   (19)

DURAN DURAN   *(See also:* ARCADIA; POWER STATION; ANDY TAYLOR)

3-31-84   *New Moon On Monday*   (Cap.)   5, 7, 13, 15, 14   (5)

12-06-86   *Notorious*   (Cap.)   36, 36, 32, 22, 22, 22, 20, 9, 7, 5, 5, 7, 9, 15, 20, 23, 15, 6, 14, 11, 13, 14   (22)

5-12-84   *The Reflex*   (Cap.)   7, 5, 5, 7, 6, 6, 11, 13   (8)

3-23-85   *Save A Prayer*   (Cap.)   13, 13, 11, (1), 8   (4)

6-08-85   *A View To A Kill*   (Cap.)   7, 7, 10, 9, 6, 2, 2, 7, 15, 16, 23, 24, 30   (13)

12-15-84 *Wild Boys* (Cap.)   11, 5, 5, 5, 5, 9, 9, 13, 15   (9)

EASTON, SHEENA

12-21-85 *Do It For Love* (EMI America)   27, 27   (2)

11-10-84 *Strut* (EMI America)   11, 8, 5, 12   (4)

3-16-85 *Sugar Walls* (EMI America)   8, 7, 8   (3)

EDDIE, JOHN

6-28-86 *Jungle Boy* (Col.)   29, 25, 25, 26, 26, 29, 22, 25   (8)

THE ELECTRIC LIGHT ORCHESTRA

3-22-86 *Calling America* (CBS Associated)   20, 20, 20, 20, 25   (5)

EUROPE

2-21-87 *The Final Countdown* (Epic)   26, 25, 21, 15, 28, 36, 39, (1), 37, 36, 37, 18, 38, 38   (13)

5-30-87 *Rock The Night* (Epic)   25, 25, 18, 12   (4)

EURYTHMICS

3-31-84 *Here Comes The Rain* (RCA)   7, 2, 12, 11   (4)

8-30-86 *Missionary Man* (RCA)   17, 16, 15, 13, 12, 12, 21, 24, 31, 31, 37, 40   (12)

9-01-84 *Right By Your Side* (RCA)   15, 11, 9, 12, 15   (5)

11-22-86 *Thorn In My Side* (RCA)   35, 25, 23, 23, 21, 19, 19, 19, 19, 21, 31, 40   (12)

5-12-84 *Who's That Girl?* (RCA)   12, 10, 7, 8, 7, 8, 13, 15   (8)

6-29-85 *Would I Lie To You?* (RCA)   6, 3, 3, 1, 1, 5, 14, 22, 28   (9)

EURYTHMICS AMD ARETHA FRANKLIN *(See also:* ARETHA FRANKLIN)

12-14-85 *Sisters Are Doin' For Themselves* (RCA)   30   (1)

EXPOSE

3-21-87   *Come Go With Me*   (Arista)   34, 31, 37, 38   (4)

THE FABULOUS THUNDERBIRDS

4-19-86   *Tuff Enuff*   (CBS Associated)   28, 25, 22, 17, 12, 11, 9, 4, 4, 3, 3, 5, 9, 20, 20   (15)

8-23-86   *Wrap It Up*   (Epic)   20, 15, 14, 14, 12, 11, 11, 11, 25, 38   (10)

FALCO

3-15-86   *Rock Me Amadeus*   (A&M)   17, 13, 8, 8, 4, 3, 2, 6, 8, 14, 15   (11)

6-14-86   *Vienna Calling*   (A&M)   21, 9, 8, 12, 28, 29, 29   (7)

FARRENHEIT

3-14-87   *Fool In Love*   (WB)   35, 32, 32, 31, 40, 29, 37   (7)

FERRY, BRYAN   *(See also:* ROXY MUSIC)

10-26-85   *Don't Stop The Dance*   (WB)   29, 27   (2)

FERRY AID

6-13-87   *Let It Be*   (Profile)   36, 22   (2)

FIRE INC.

6-09-84   *Tonight Is What It Means To Be Young*   (MCA)   14, 5, 5, 11, 14   (5)

THE FIRM

3-29-86   *All The King's Horses*   (Atl.)   23, 22, 22, 25   (4)

A FLOCK OF SEAGULLS

9-15-84   *The More You Live*   (Jive/Arista)   13, 10, 11, 13   (4)

FOGERTY, JOHN

5-04-85   *Rock And Roll Girls*   (WB)   10, 9, 15, 15, 15, 14   (6)

10-19-85   *Vanz Kant Danz*   (WB)   24, 14, 15, 17, 28, 30   (6)

FOREIGNER

1-26-85 *I Want To Know What Love Is* (Atl.) 10, 12, 3, 3, 5, 10, 14, 14, 10, 12 (10)

4 BY FOUR

5-30-87 *Want You For My Girlfriend* (Cap.) 37, 37, 29, 29 (4)

FOX, SAMANTHA

11-22-86 *Touch Me (I Want Your Body)* (Jive/RCA) 30, 27, 25, 25, 23, 23, 23, 23, 34, (3), 33, 27 (11)

FOX, SLY

4-19-86 *Let's Go All The Way* (Cap.) 26, 21, 14, 12, 16, 28 (6)

FRANKIE GOES TO HOLLYWOOD

3-16-85 *Relax* (ZTT/Island) 10, 5, 2, 14, 8, 13, 15 (7)

10-06-84 *Two Tribes* (Island) 14, 11, 9, 6, 4, 2, 2, 4, 8, 9 (10)

FRANKLIN, ARETHA *(See also:* EURYTHMICS)

3-08-86 *Another Night* (Arista) 27, 24, 16, 21, 19, 19, 15, 23, 29 (9)

7-13-85 *Freeway Of Love* (Arista) 7, 7, 4, 3, 2, 1, 1, 2, 1, 5, 9, 22, 25 (13)

12-20-86 *Jimmy Lee* (Arista) 33, 29, 29, 29, 29, 40, (4), 37, 27, 27, 40 (10)

11-01-86 *Jumpin' Jack Flash* (Arista) 37, 22, 19, 12, 9, 8, 8, 8, 15, 15, 15, 23, 23, 38 (14)

FRANKLIN, ARETHA, AND GEORGE MICHAEL *(See also:* GEORGE MICHAEL)

3-07-87 *I Knew You Were Waiting (For Me)* (Arista) 29, 11, 9, 9, 4, 4, 4, 11, 9, 35, 40 (11)

FREHLEY, ACE

6-20-87 *Into The Night* (Atl.) 13 (1)

FREY, GLENN

8-18-84   *Sexy Girl*   (MCA)   15, 11, 12   (3)

11-02-85   *You Belong To The City*   (MCA)   17, 8, 5, 3, 1, 2, 1, 6, 6, 6, 6, 6, 6, 6, 14, 14, 22   (17)

FROZEN GHOST

5-09-87   *Should I See*   (Atl.)   28, 26, 23, 15, 15, 15, 9   (7)

GTR

7-05-86   *When The Heart Rules The Mind*   (Arista)   —, 21, 18, 18, 25   (5)

GABRIEL, PETER   *(See also:* GENESIS)

1-31-87   *Big Time*   (Geffen)   36, 30, 25, 21   (4)

6-21-86   *Sledgehammer*   (Geffen)   14, 6, 2, 1, 2, 2, 2, 4, 4, 9, 21, 25   (12)

GABRIEL, PETER, AND KATE BUSH   *(See also:* KATE BUSH; GENESIS)

5-16-87   *Don't Give Up*   (Geffen/WB)   22, 13, 14, 14, 9, 7   (6)

GEILS, J., BAND

8-10-85   *Fright Night*   (Private I)   25, 19, 21, 23   (4)

GELDOF, BOB

3-21-87   *Love Like A Rocket*   (Atl.)   21, 20, 16, 32, 36, 32   (6)

GENERAL PUBLIC

4-20-85   *Never You Done That*   (I.R.S.)   14, 14   (2)

12-15-84   *Tenderness*   (I.R.S.)   13, 10, 10, 10, 10, 10, 12, 14, (1), 10, 9, 4, 6, 6, 8, 15   (15)

GENESIS *(See also:* PHIL COLLINS; PETER GABRIEL; MIKE AND THE MECHANICS)

7-12-86 *Invisible Touch* (Atl.) 14, 10, 10, 5, 3, 3, 4, 16, 26 (9)

12-27-86 *Land Of Confusion* (Atl.) 32, 32, 32, 12, 1, 1, 2, 2, 2, 2, 1, 8, 15, 22, 30 (15)

11-15-86 *Throwing It All Away* (Atl.) 34, 22, 22, 29, 29, 37 (6)

3-07-87 *Tonight, Tonight, Tonight* (Atl.) 30, 23, 6, 6, 8, 28, 31, 40 (8)

THE GEORGIA SATELLITES

1-17-87 *Keep Your Hands To Yourself* (Elektra) 37, 26, 13, 11, 9, 4, 1, 2, 22, 22, 28 (11)

GIUFFRIA

6-28-86 *I Must Be Dreaming* (MCA) 26, 19, 20, 22, 22, 21, 30 (7)

GLASS TIGER

9-06-86 *Don't Forget Me* (Manhattan) 15, 12, 8, 7, 6, 2, 2, 4, 5, 5, 5, 18, 17, 26, 26, 38 (16)

4-11-87 *I Will Be There* (Manhattan) 25, 23, 24, 34 (4)

THE GO-GO'S *(See also:* BELINDA CARLISLE)

5-05-84 *Head Over Heels* (I.R.S./A&M) 13, 8, 8, 8 (4)

7-21-84 *Turn To You* (I.R.S./A&M) 10, 7, 4, 7, 13 (5)

GO WEST

7-13-85 *Call Me* (Chrysalis) 11, 11 (2)

3-09-85 *We Close Our Eyes* (Chrysalis) 13, 13 (2)

GRANT, AMY *(See also:* PETER CETERA)

8-10-85 *Find A Way* (A&M) 23, 25, 25 (3)

GRANT, EDDY

7-14-84   *Romancing The Stone*   (Portrait/CBS)   12, 11, 15   (3)

HAGAR, SAMMY   *(See also:* VAN HALEN)

3-21-87   *Winner Takes It All*   (Col.)   38, 37, 40   (3)

HALL, DARYL   *(See also:* DARYL HALL AND JOHN OATES)

9-13-86   *Dreamtime*   (RCA)   27, 21, 17, 15, 14, 13, 14, 15, 33   (9)

HALL, DARYL, AND JOHN OATES   *(See also:* DARYL HALL)

3-31-84   *Adult Education*   (RCA)   2, 4, 8   (3)

2-02-85   *Method Of Modern Love*   (RCA)   7, 7, 15   (3)

11-17-84   *Out Of Touch*   (RCA)   14, 10, 7, 6, 12   (5)

7-06-85   *Possession Obsession*   (RCA)   7, 6, 4, 6, 13, 19   (6)

HALL, DARYL, AND JOHN OATES, WITH DAVID RUFFIN AND EDDIE KENDRICKS

9-21-85   *The Way You Do The Things You Do*   (RCA)   20, 18, 14, 8, 7, 6, 9, 16, 17   (9)

HAMMER, JAN

12-07-85   *"Miami Vice" Theme*   (MCA)   27, 25, 30, 30   (4)

HARDCASTLE, PAUL

8-10-85   *19*   (Chrysalis)   26, 29   (2)

HARRY, DEBBIE

1-17-87   *French Kissin'*   (Geffen)   35, 25, 20, 19, 34, 28, 34   (7)

HART, COREY

11-03-84   *It Ain't Enough*   (EMI America)   13, 10, 9, 9, 4, 2, 5, 15, 15, 15, 15   (11)

7-27-85 *Never Surrender* (EMI America) 5, 4, 4, 3, 6, 5, 6, 11, 24 (9)

8-04-84 *Sunglasses At Night* (EMI America) 13, 9, 6, 5, 3, 9 (6)

HARTMAN, DAN

7-19-86 *Waiting To See You* (Epic) 28, 28, 27 (3)

12-08-84 *We Are The Young* (MCA) 13, 9, 7, 7, 7, 7 (6)

HAY, COLIN JAMES

2-21-87 *Hold Me* (Col.) 34, 31, 39 (3)

HEAD, MURRAY

5-04-85 *One Night In Bangkok* (RCA) 7, 5, 14, 13 (4)

HEADROOM, MAX *(See:* THE ART OF NOISE)

HEART

11-09-85 *Never* (Cap.) 20, 18, 26, 28, 28, 27, 29, 29, 29, 29, 30 (11)

6-07-86 *Nothin' At All* (Cap.) 18, 18, 15, 25, 30 (5)

7-20-85 *What About Love?* (Cap.) 10, 11, (1), 13, 13, 9, 12, 16, 22, 29 (9)

HEAVEN 17 *(See also:* THE HUMAN LEAGUE)

2-28-87 *Contenders* (Virgin) 35, 34, 30 (3)

5-30-87 *Trouble* (Virgin) 30, 30, 25, 23 (4)

HENLEY, DON

4-13-85 *All She Wants To Do Is Dance* (Geffen) 9, 9, 2, 1, 2, 2, 7, 15 (8)

2-02-85 *The Boys Of Summer* (Geffen) 9, 9, 6, 12, 7, 10 (6)

8-10-85 *Not Enough Love In The World* (Geffen) 28 (1)

HINES, GREGORY *(See:* LUTHER VANDROSS)

HIPSWAY

4-04-87   *Honeythief*   (Col.)   26, 22, 20, 18, 19, 16   (6)

THE HONEYDRIPPERS   *(See also:* **ROBERT PLANT**)

12-08-84   *Sea Of Love*   (Es Paranza/Atl.)   11, 6, 4, 4, 4, 4   (6)

HONEYMOON SUITE

4-26-86   *Feel It Again*   (WB)   19, 16, 14, 11, 9, 20   (6)

8-02-86   *What Does It Take*   (WB)   22, 17, 11, 10, 9, 9, 8, 17, 24, 38   (10)

THE HOOTERS

10-19-85   *And We Danced*   (Col.)   28, 27, 25, 23, 21, 29   (6)

HORNSBY, BRUCE, AND THE RANGE

2-21-87   *Mandolin Rain*   (RCA)   36, 26, 16, 40, 36, 39   (6)

11-01-86   *The Way It Is*   (RCA)   29, 17, 12, 5, 2, 1, 1, 1,   ( )

HOUSTON, WHITNEY

4-26-86   *The Greatest Love Of All*   (Arista)   15, 12, 9, 5, 4, 3, 5, 5, 18   (9)

2-01-86   *How Will I Know*   (Arista)   17, 12, 12, 9, 2, 1, 2, 2, 4, 17, 17, 23   (12)

6-20-87   *I Wanna Dance With Somebody (Who Loves Me)*   (Arista)   11   (1)

9-28-85   *Saving All My Love For You*   (Arista)   21, 11, 9, 4, 3, 1, 5, 9, 19   (9)

HOWARD, MIKI

5-16-87   *Imagination*   (Atl.)   30, 26   (2)

THE HUMAN LEAGUE   *(See also:* **HEAVEN 17**)

10-11-86   *Human*   (A&M)   33, 21, 8, 4, 1, 1, 1, 1, 3, 3, 5, 10, 10, 10, 11, 11, 12, 12, 13, 12, 24, 37   (22)

1-24-87   *I Need Your Loving*   (A&M)   28, 25, 24, 30   (4)

INXS

11-30-85   *This Time*   (Mer.)   27, 23, 19, 18, 18, 20, 20, 24   (8)

2-22-86   *What You Need*   (Atl.)   26, 20, 13, 10, 9, 3, 1, 1, 2, 7, 8, 10, 19   (13)

ICEHOUSE

10-04-86   *Cross The Border*   (Chrysalis)   34, 31, 30, 39   (4)

6-21-86   *No Promises*   (Chrysalis)   30, 27   (2)

IDOL, BILLY

6-02-84   *Eyes Without A Face*   (Chrysalis)   11, 4, 1, 1, 3, 2, 7, 13   (8)

10-06-84   *Flesh For Fantasy*   (Chrysalis)   11, 8, 6, 8, 14   (5)

3-31-84   *Rebel Yell*   (Chrysalis)   8   (1)

11-15-86   *To Be A Lover*   (Chrysalis)   27, 14, 8, 6, 6, 3, 1, 1, 1, 4, 8, 11, 13, 21, 33   (15)

JACKSON, FREDDIE

2-28-87   *Have You Ever Loved Somebody*   (Cap.)   19, 24, 38   (3)

4-18-87   *I Don't Want To Lose Your Love*   (Cap.)   30, 25, 38   (3)

11-09-85   *You Are My Lady*   (Cap.)   29, 24, 20   (3)

JACKSON, JANET

11-29-86   *Control*   (A&M)   38, 24, 24, 18, 11, 11, 11, 2, 2, 2, 4, 4, 5, 8, 4, 10, 13, 18, 23, 36, 34   (21)

6-21-86   *Nasty*   (A&M)   27, 13, 7, 4, 3, 3, 6, 8, 20   (9)

4-19-86   *What Have You Done For Me Lately*   (A&M)   17, 12, 10, 5, 4, 2, 10, 29, 29   (9)

9-13-86   *When I Think Of You*   (A&M)   16, 7, 4, 3, 1, 1, 1, 1, 4, 6, 15, 29   (12)

JACKSON, JERMAINE

    1-19-85   *Do What You Do*   (Arista)   2, 6, 6, 14   (4)

    9-01-84   *Dynamite*   (Arista)   11, 10, 7, 13   (4)

    6-15-85   *(Close To) Perfect*   (Arista)   14, 12   (2)

    5-10-86   *I Think It's Love*   (Arista)   25, 20, 20   (3)

JACKSON, REBBIE

    12-01-84   *Centipede*   (Col.)   10, 8, 4, 1, 1, 1, 1   (7)

JAGGER, MICK   *(See also:* DAVID BOWIE; THE ROLLING STONES)

    4-06-85   *Just Another Night*   (Col.)   10   (1)

THE JETS

    5-24-86   *Crush On You*   (MCA)   16, 12, 6, 6, 6, 1, 10, 22   (8)

    2-07-87   *You Got It All*   (MCA)   32, 24, 22, 17, 14, 4, 2, 4, 17, 33, 39   (11)

JOEL, BILLY

    1-19-85   *Keeping The Faith*   (Col.)   15, 13, 15, 10, 4, 4, 5, 8   (8)

    4-21-84   *The Longest Time*   (Col.)   7, 5, 4, (1), 12, 12   (5)

    9-13-86   *A Matter Of Trust*   (Col.)   6, 4, 2, 2, 5, 5, 5, 11, 12, 26, 40   (11)

JOEL, BILLY, FEATURING RAY CHARLES

    4-11-87   *Baby Grand*   (Col.)   6, 3, 8, 4, 4, 10, 9, 21, 21, 32, 39   (11)

JOHN, ELTON   *(See also:* DIONNE AND FRIENDS)

    2-22-86   *Nikita*   (Geffen)   29, 18, 12, 9   (4)

    8-18-84   *Sad Songs*   (Geffen)   12, 9, 7, 8, 14   (5)

JOHNSON, DON

1-31-87   *Heartache Away*   (Epic)   29, 27, 27   (3)

10-25-86   *Heartbeat*   (Epic)   37, 23, 16, 16, 19, 30   (6)

JOHNSON, JESSE

4-18-87   *Baby Let's Kiss*   (A&M)   33, 30, 36, 33, 39, 29, 40, 40   (8)

JONES, HOWARD

8-17-85   *Life In One Day*   (Elektra)   27, 23, 18, 15, 21, 21, 30, 28, 30   (9)

5-31-86   *No One Is To Blame*   (Elektra)   15, 7, 7, 4, 2, 1, 3, 4, 4, 10, 21   (11)

4-13-85   *Things Can Only Get Better*   (Elektra)   13, 11, 13, 15, (1), 7, 3, 6, 10, 12, 8, 8, 15   (12)

12-27-86   *You Know I Love You, Don't You*   (Elektra)   36, 36, 36, 30, 30, 30, 39   (7)

JONES, ORAN "JUICE"

10-04-86   *The Rain*   (Def Jam/Col.)   35, 32, 29, 23, 20, 15, 9, 6, 6, 9, 9, 14, 17, 17, 17, 26, 33, 40   (18)

JOURNEY   *(See also:* STEVE PERRY)

11-01-86   *Girl Can't Help It*   (Col.)   35, 20, 20, 31, 40   (5)

KANSAS

1-24-87   *All I Wanted*   (MCA)   35, 32, 31, 37   (4)

KATRINA AND THE WAVES

8-17-85   *Do You Want Crying*   (Cap.)   21, 20, 19, 10, 7, 5, 5, 6, 13, 25   (10)

6-15-85   *Walking On Sunshine*   (Cap.)   9, 9, 2, 2, 5, 13   (6)

KENDRICKS, EDDIE   *(See:* Daryl Hall And John Oates)

KHAN, CHAKA

11-10-84   *I Feel For You (Dance Mix)*   (WB)   7, 5, 1, 1, 4, 6, 14, 14, 14, 14, 1, 4, 10   (13)

KING, BEN E.

10-11-86   *Stand By Me*   (Atl.)   38, 35, 32, 28, 26, 23, 23, 31, 28, 28, 26, 26, 26, 26, 36   (15)

KLYMAXX

1-18-86   *I Miss You*   (Constellation)   23, 21, 19, 24, 24, 24, 28, 26, 28, 28   (10)

9-20-86   *Man-Sized Love*   (MCA)   34, 31, 27, 27, 40, 40   (6)

KOOL & THE GANG

9-07-85   *Cherish*   (De-Lite)   21, 15, 10, 8, 7, 6, 8, 11, 10, 18, 30   (11)

5-11-85   *Fresh*   (De-Lite)   8, 3, 8, 14   (4)

2-09-85   *Misled*   (De-Lite/PolyGram)   13, 14, 15, 15, 15, 15   (6)

4-21-84   *Tonight*   (De-Lite)   10, 7, 14, 13, 11, 10, 12, 15   (8)

1-15-86   *Victory*   (Mer.)   35, 29, 26, 20, 20, 13, 6, 6, 6, 1, 3, 4, 6, 7, 11, 13, 12, 1, 10, 11, 12, 30   (22)

L.L. COOL J.

5-30-87   *I'm Bad*   (Col.)   35, 35, 27, 24   (4)

LaBELLE, PATTI, AND MICHAEL McDONALD   *(See also: MICHAEL McDONALD)*

5-17-86   *On My Own*   (MCA)   15, 10, 2, 1, 1, 2, 9, 20   (8)

LAUPER, CYNDI

12-06-86   *Change Of Heart*   (Portrait)   35, 35, 29, 27, 27, 27, 14, 7, 5, 3, 3, 1, 4, 10, 14, 25, 33   (17)

3-31-84   *Girls Just Want To Have Fun*   (Portrait/CBS)   9   (1)

2-23-85 *Money Changes Everything* (Portrait/CBS)   13, 12   (2)

9-15-84 *She Bop* (Portrait/CBS)   11, 6, 3, 2, 1, 4, 10, 15   (8)

5-05-84 *Time After Time* (Portrait/CBS)   9, 1, 1, 3, 4, 9, 9, 11   (8)

10-18-86 *True Colors* (Portrait/CBS)   39, 33, 19, 13, 11, 11, 14, 39, 39   (9)

4-04-87 *What's Going On* (Portrait)   14, 8, 9, 7, 6, 3, 9, 10, 8, 8, 13, 14   (12)

LENNON, JULIAN

6-01-85 *Say You're Wrong* (Atl.)   10   (1)

3-02-85 *Too Late For Goodbyes* (Atl.)   8, 4, 5, 14, 14, 8, 15, 12   (8)

12-15-84 *Valotte* (Atl.)   14, 12, 12, 12, 12   (5)

LEVEL 42

4-11-87 *Lessons In Love* (Polydor)   15, 12, 14, 15, 37, (4), 37, 25   (7)

5-24-86 *Something About You* (PolyGram)   21, 18, 11, 11, 12. 23   (6)

LEWIS, HUEY, AND THE NEWS

5-05-84 *Heart Of Rock 'N' Roll* (Chrysalis)   11, 9, 7, 4, 2, 5, 3, 2, 6, 6, 11   (11)

3-31-84 *I Want A New Drug* (Chrysalis)   6, 1, 1, 6, 6   (5)

8-11-84 *If This Is It* (Chrysalis)   14, 10, 4, 1, 1, 2, 4, 9   (8)

2-28-87 *Jacob's Ladder* (Chrysalis)   29, 32   (2)

7-27-85 *Power Of Love* (Chrysalis)   14, 9, 6, 4, 2, 1, 2, 2, 3, 3, 3, 5, 11, 13, 21, 30   (16)

9-13-86 *Stuck With You* (Chrysalis)   18, 9, 6, 4, 3, 3, 3, 3, 3, 4, 4, 12, 18, 18, 24, 37, 37, 37, 40   (19)

LIMITED WARRANTY

9-27-86 *Hit You* (Atl.)   40, 39   (2)

LISA LISA AND CULT JAM

4-25-87   *Head To Toe*   (Col.)   31, 23, 17, 6, 2, 1, 1, 1, 1   (9)

LISA LISA AND CULT JAM WITH FULL FORCE

8-24-85   *I Wonder If I Take You Home*   (Col.)   18, 15, 14, 24   (4)

LOGGINS, KENNY

6-21-86   *Danger Zone*   (Col.)   17, 11, 9, 6, 5, 5, 4, 6, 22, 28   (10)

4-07-84   *Footloose*   (Col.)   6, 3, 9   (3)

LONE JUSTICE

8-31-85   *Sweet, Sweet Baby*   (Geffen)   20, 17, 20, 28   (4)

LOS LOBOS

4-04-87   *Shakin', Shakin', Shakes*   (Slash)   28, 27, 28, 27, 39   (5)

LOVERBOY

3-22-86   *This Could Be The Night*   (Col.)   21, 19, 12, 12, 12, 17, 21, 29, 29   (9)

MADONNA

5-29-84   *Borderline*   (Sire)   15, 9, 10, 11   (4)

4-27-85   *Crazy For You*   (Geffen)   11, 9, 15, 13   (4)

9-21-85   *Dress You Up*   (Sire)   27, 20, 18, 14, 18, 22, 28   (7)

5-25-85   *Into The Groove*   (Sire)   6, 4, 3, 2, 3, 4, 5, 4, 8, 15   (10)

5-23-87   *La Isla Bonita*   (Sire)   30, 23, 23, 21, 33   (5)

1-19-85   *Like A Virgin*   (Sire)   5, 5, 11, 12, 12, 11   (6)

5-24-86   *Live To Tell*   (Sire)   23, 13, 14, 14, 10, 10, 16   (7)

3-02-85   *Material Girl*   (Sire)   11, 3, 1, 1, 1, 1, 6, 15   (8)

12-27-86 *Open Your Heart* (Sire) 34, 34, 34, 17, 10, 9, 7, 6, 6, 6, 7, 13, 17, 24, 34 (15)

8-02-86 *Papa Don't Preach* (Sire) 17, 10, 8, 3, 1, 3, 13, 14, 21, 37 (10)

MARIE, TEENA

3-09-85 *Lovergirl* (Epic) 11, 7, 4, 10, 3, 12 (6)

MARTIN, MARILYN (*See also:* PHIL COLLINS)

3-08-86 *Night Moves* (Atl.) 23, 18, 15, 11, 9, 9, 13, 18, 27 (9)

MARTINEZ, NANCY

1-24-87 *For Tonight* (Atl.) 31, 21, 17, 16, 30, 39 (6)

THE MARY JANE GIRLS

6-22-85 *In My House* (Motown) 14, 15 (2)

McCARTNEY, PAUL

8-23-86 *Press* (Cap.) 24, 18, 13, 11, 11, 14, 19, 23, 38 (9)

12-14-85 *Spies Like Us* (Cap.) 26, 20, 20, 16, 16, 18, 17, 16, 13, 13, 12, 15, 28 (13)

McDONALD, MICHAEL (*See also:* PATTI LaBELLE)

8-31-85 *No Lookin' Back* (WB) 26, 20, 14, 11, 11, 13, 25 (7)

8-16-86 *Sweet Freedom* (MCA) 17, 8, 2, 1, 1, 3, 8, 8, 10, 11, 22, 32, 39 (13)

McVIE, CHRISTINE

6-02-84 *Love Will Show Us How* (WB) 13, 8, 12 (3)

MEDEIROS, GLENN

5-16-87 *Nothing's Gonna Change My Love* (Amherst) 37, 31, 28, 28, 38, 36 (6)

MELLENCAMP, JOHN COUGAR

4-07-84   *Authority Song*   (Riva/PolyGram)   12, 10, 5, 12   (4)

9-21-85   *Lonely Ol' Night*   (PolyGram)   16, 14, 17, 18, 27, 26   (6)

5-31-86   *Rain On The Scarecrow*   (Riva)   25, 19, 19, 19, 30   (5)

4-05-86   *R.O.C.K. In The U.S.A.*   (Riva)   18, 18, 16, 14, 18, 24   (6)

8-23-86   *Rumble Seat*   (Riva)   30, 24, 27   (3)

12-07-85   *Small Town*   (Riva)   20, 12, 12, 12, 14, 14, 13, 12, 9, 10, 10, 21, 29   (13)

THE MIAMI SOUND MACHINE

5-10-86   *Bad Boy*   (Epic)   21, 13, 7, 6, 17, 17   (6)

12-14-85   *Conga*   (Epic)   23, 21, 21, 21, 21, 19, 30   (7)

MICHAEL, GEORGE   (*See also:* ARETHA FRANKLIN; WHAM!)

6-07-86   *A Different Corner*   (Col.)   24, 24, 16, 15   (4)

MIKE AND THE MECHANICS   (*See also:* GENESIS)

5-17-86   *All I Need Is A Miracle*   (Atl.)   21, 17, 14, 22, 22   (5)

1-18-86   *Silent Running*   (Atl.)   26, 16, 8, 4, 4, 2, 1, 6, 16, 23, 30   (11)

8-30-86   *Taken In*   (Atl.)   20, 17, 17, 19, 26, 29   (6)

MILLER, STEVE, BAND

1-24-87   *I Want To Make The World Turn Around*   (Cap.)   38, 35, 35, 39, 40   (5)

MR. MISTER

10-05-85   *Broken Wings*   (RCA)   29, 17, 12, 10, 8, 6, 4, 2, 4, 5, 13, 14, 14, 15, 15, 22   (16)

5-17-86   *Is It Love*   (RCA)   23, 18, 17, 13, 13, 28   (6)

3-08-86 *Kyrie* (RCA) 16, 7, 5, 5, 8, 8, 21, 29 (8)

THE MODELS

5-31-86 *Out Of Mind, Out Of Sight* (Geffen) 29, 25, 25, 20, 16, 23, 26, 27, 27 (9)

MONEY, EDDIE

11-08-86 *Take Me Home Tonight* (Col.) 32, 28, 28, 39 (4)

THE MOODY BLUES

6-07-86 *Your Wildest Dreams* (Polydor) 27, 27, 21, 20, 15, 12, 9, 9, 15 (9)

THE MOTELS

8-17-85 *Shame* (Cap.) 14, 12, 11, 11, 9, 6, 4, 1, 4, 10, 12, 19, 28 (13)

MOTLEY CRUE

8-24-85 *Smokin' In The Boys Room* (Elektra) 26, 24, 23, 28, 30 (5)

MURPHY, EDDIE

11-30-85 *Party All The Time* (Col.) 29, 22, 18, 22, 22, 23, 23, 25 (8)

NENA

3-31-84 *99 Luftballoons* (Epic) 13 (1)

NEVIL, ROBBIE

12-27-86 *C'est La Vie* (Manhattan) 35, 35, 35, 15, 5, 3, 1, 1, 3, 3, 11, 19, 29, 38 (14)

3-28-87 *Dominoes* (Manhattan) 26, 18, 9, 10, 6, 7, 13, 33 (8)

THE NEW EDITION

1-19-85 *Cool It Now* (MCA) 14 (1)

2-02-85 *Mr. Telephone Man* (MCA) 8, 8, 5, 3, 2, 7, 11 (7)

NEWTON-JOHN, OLIVIA

3-31-84 *Livin' In Desperate Times* (MCA) 10 (1)

11-16-85 *Soul Kiss* (MCA) 19, 12, 8, 7, 14, 16, 16 (7)

NICKS, STEVIE

3-22-86 *I Can't Wait* (Modern) 27, 27, 22, 22, 26 (5)

NIGHT RANGER

8-10-85 *Sentimental Street* (MCA) 10, 10, 15, 22 (4)

NU SHOOZ

6-07-86 *I Can't Wait* (Atl.) 16, 16, 8, 7, 6, 13, 21, 21 (8)

9-20-86 *Point Of No Return* (Atl.) 33, 27, 22, 20, 18, 18, 22, 35 (8)

OCASEK, RIC   (*See also:* THE CARS)

11-22-86 *Emotion In Motion* (Geffen) 38, 34, 31, 31, 31, 39, 39, 39 (8)

OCEAN, BILLY

9-22-84 *Caribbean Queen* (Jive/Arista) 11, 8, 5, 3, 2, 2, 1, 3, 6, 12 (10)

8-30-86 *Love Zone* (Arista) 23, 12, 10, 15, 18, 21, 19, 15, 15, 17, 28, 38 (12)

6-01-85 *Suddenly* (Jive) 13, 12, 13 (3)

5-24-86 *There'll Be Sad Songs (To Make You Cry)* (Arista) 29, 16, 8, 8, 5, 4, 3, 5, 11, 11, 30 (11)

2-01-86 *When The Going Gets Tough, The Tough Get Going* (Arista) 22, 15, 15, 11, 5, 3, 4, 10, 22 (9)

OLLIE AND JERRY

6-30-84 *Breakin' . . . There's No Stopping Us* (Polydor/PolyGram) 14, 7, 4, 3, 8, 6, 11 (7)

ORCHESTRAL MANOEUVRES IN THE DARK

11-15-86   *(Forever) Live And Die*   (A&M)   30, 27, 23, 19, 19, 19, 21, 21, 21, 32   (10)

5-03-86   *If You Leave*   (A&M)   24, 15, 10, 5, 5, 10, 10, 23   (8)

10-12-85   *So In Love*   (A&M)   24, 20, 20, 18, 15, 11, 11, 12, 14   (9)

OSBORNE, JEFFREY

8-09-86   *You Should Be Mine*   (A&M)   23, 19, 23   (3)

OSBOURNE, OZZY

3-29-86   *Shot In The Dark*   (Epic)   25, 25, 25, 30, 26, 23, 23, 28   (8)

THE OTHER ONES

5-09-87   *We Are What We Are*   (Virgin)   36, 29, 27, 24, 24, 34, 40   (7)

THE OUTFIELD

8-09-86   *All The Love In The World*   (Col.)   20, 18, 21   (3)

4-05-86   *Your Love*   (Col.)   16, 16, 14, 11, 7, 4, 2, 1, 4, 26, 26   (11)

PALMER, ROBERT

3-01-86   *Addicted To Love*   (Island)   23, 15, 14, 12, 7, 3, 3, 1, 1, 5, 6, 7, 12, 23   (14)

9-13-86   *I Didn't Mean To Turn You On*   (Island)   23, 16, 13, 10, 6, 4, 2, 2, 2, 2, 2, 4, 5, 5, 6, 14, 14, 14, 22, 22, 37   (21)

PARKER, GRAHAM

7-13-85   *Wake Up (Next To You)*   (Elektra)   9, 9   (2)

PARKER, RAY, JR.

6-23-84   *Ghostbusters*   (Arista)   12, 9, 4, 2, 2, 1, 1, 2, 4, 6, 5, 6, 15   (13)

PARR, JOHN

7-27-85   *St. Elmo's Fire*   (Atl.)   8, 8, 5, 5, 4, 3, 4, 4, 4, 7, 10, 10, 14, 30   (14)

7-19-86   *Two Hearts*   (Atl.)   23, 23, 23, 25, 30   (5)

PERRY, STEVE   (*See also:* JOURNEY)

2-23-85   *Foolish Heart*   (Col.)   14, 13   (2)

THE PET SHOP BOYS

9-20-86   *Love Comes Quickly*   (EMI America)   40, 37, 28, 26, 23, 21, 21, 31, 39   (9)

6-28-86   *Opportunities (Let's Make Lots Of Money)*   (EMI America)   22, 17, 16, 15, 15, 8, 7, 12, 18, 30   (10)

3-29-86   *West End Girls*   (EMI America)   29, 15, 15, 9, 4, 2, 1, 3, 8, 8, 12, 12, 26   (13)

PETTY, TOM, AND THE HEARTBREAKERS

5-11-85   *Don't Come Around Here No More*   (MCA)   12, 5, 14, 12   (4)

8-10-85   *Make It Better*   (MCA)   27, 26   (2)

PLANT, ROBERT   (*See also:* THE HONEYDRIPPERS)

7-06-85   *Little By Little*   (Atl.)   12, 12   (2)

THE POINTER SISTERS

9-14-85   *Dare Me*   (RCA)   19, 13, 9, 8, 7, 5, 8, 16, 19   (9)

6-16-84   *Jump (For My Love)*   (Planet/RCA)   13, 10, 2, 3, 5, 9, 12   (7)

12-22-84   *Neutron Dance*   (Paramount Pictures)   11, 11, 11, 11, 7, 7   (6)

POISON

5-30-87   *Talk Dirty To Me*   (Cap.)   33, 33, 26, 37   (4)

POLICE   *(See also:* STING)

11-22-86   *Don't Stand So Close To Me '86*   (A&M)   37, 32, 32, 32, 40   (5)

POWER STATION   *(See also:* DURAN DURAN)

6-29-85   *Get It On (Bang A Gong)*   (Cap.)   10, 10, 15, (1), 10, 12, 11, 16, 19, 21, 29   (10)

5-18-85   *Some Like It Hot*   (Cap.)   9, 4, 5, 6, 10, 7   (6)

THE PRETENDERS

11-22-86   *Don't Get Me Wrong*   (WB)   33, 24, 16, 16, 12, 7, 7, 15, 19, 26, 32   (11)

5-26-84   *Show Me*   (Sire)   14, 14   (2)

PRINCE (AND THE REVOLUTION)

12-21-85   *America*   (WB)   24, 24   (2)

8-09-86   *Anotherloverholenyohead*   (Paisley Park)   27, 24, 25   (3)

3-29-86   *Kiss*   (Paisley Park)   27, 13, 13, 10, 5, 4, 7, 9, 19, 26   (10)

9-08-84   *Let's Go Crazy*   (WB)   12, 8, 5, 2, 1, 4, 3, 5, 7, 8, 15   (11)

6-28-86   *Mountains*   (Paisley Park)   28, 21, 17, 14, 14, 13   (6)

7-20-85   *Raspberry Beret*   (WB)   5, 2, 1, 3, 7, 14, 14, 26, 30   (9)

6-09-84   *When Doves Cry*   (WB)   10, 4, 3, 1, 1, 1, 1, 2, 2, 1, 1, 3, 10, 14   (14)

PSEUDO ECHO

6-13-87   *Funky Town*   (RCA)   35, 19   (2)

THE PSYCHEDELIC FURS

4-04-87   *Heartbreak Beat*   (Col.)   33, 31, 35, 29, 29, 22, 16, 14, 18, 18, 23   (11)

QUEEN

   3-01-86   *One Vision*   (Cap.)   25, 24, 25, 24, 26   (5)

   3-31-84   *Radio Ga Ga*   (Cap.)   14   (1)

QUIET RIOT

   9-20-86   *The Wild And The Young*   (Epic)   36, 34, 31, 30   (4)

R.E.M.

   4-11-87   *All I've Got To Do Is (Dream)*   (I.R.S.)   18, 17, 21, 27   (4)

   8-10-85   *Can't Get There From Here*   (I.R.S.)   20, 17, 13, 10, 9, 8, 12, 25   (8)

   9-20-86   *Fall On Me*   (I.R.S.)   31, 20, 18, 18, 22, 26, 38, 38   (8)

READY FOR THE WORLD

   9-07-85   *Oh Sheila*   (MCA)   27, 18, 15, 10, 9, 2, 1, 1, 5, 7, 10, 15, 15, 25   (14)

REED, LOU

   11-29-86   *The Original Wrapper*   (RCA)   33, 30, 30, 27, 25, 25, 25, 25, 27, 39   (10)

REGINA

   8-16-86   *Baby Love*   (Atl.)   28, 19, 12, 8, 7, 10, 15, 16, 16, 28, 34, 36, 36   (13)

REO SPEEDWAGON

   2-16-85   *Can't Fight This Feeling*   (Col.)   9, 6, 9, 5, 4, 3, 4, 15   (8)

RICHIE, LIONEL   (*See also:* THE COMMODORES)

   1-24-87   *Ballerina Girl*   (Motown)   34, 27, 21, 19, 17, 27, 40   (7)

   8-30-86   *Dancing On The Ceiling*   (Motown)   26, 11, 4, 2, 1, 1, 4, 6, 6, 6, 6, 18, 34   (13)

   3-31-84   *Hello*   (Motown)   4, 9, 6, 4, 2, 1, 2, 2, 2   (9)

11-15-86   *Love Will Conquer All*   (Motown)   32, 26, 20, 17, 17, 15, 13, 13, 13, 13, 13, 15, 15, 15, 25, 38   (16)

10-20-84   *Penny Lover*   (Motown)   13, 9, 6, 5, 3, 2, 2, 1, 2, 3, 3, 3, 3   (13)

11-23-85   *Say You Say Me*   (Motown)   13, 9, 6, 3, 1, 1, 1, 1, 1, 4, 4, 7, 7, 18, 24, 30   (15)

4-18-87   *Se La*   (Motown)   26, 23, 22, 38   (4)

ROBINSON, SMOKEY

5-23-87   *Just To See Her*   (Motown)   37, 34, 34, 20, 30   (5)

ROCKWELL

3-31-84   *Somebody's Watching Me*   (Motown)   1, 5, 4, 3, 3, 7, 10   (7)

THE ROLLING STONES   *(See also:* MICK JAGGER)

4-05-86   *Harlem Shuffle*   (Rolling Stones)   14, 14, 8, 6, 3, 2, 1, 6, 21, 30, 30   (11)

7-05-86   *One Hit (To The Body)*   (Rolling Stones)   14, 10, 8, 8, 9, 29   (11)

ROSS, DIANA

6-20-87   *Dirty Looks*   (RCA)   18   (1)

10-18-86   *Eat 'Em And Smile*   (WB)   37, 29, 24, 21, 17, 17, 16, 27, 27, 39   (10)

10-27-84   *Swept Away*   (RCA)   14, 12, 9, 11   (4)

ROTH, DAVID LEE   *(See also:* VAN HALEN)

2-23-85   *California Girls*   (WB)   8, 3, 1, 3, 12   (5)

4-27-85   *Just A Gigolo/I Ain't Got Nobody*   (WB)   7, 6, 7, 10, 11, 9, 13, 8, 11, 12   (10)

8-02-86   *Yankee Rose*   (WB)   19, 14, 16, 13, 7, 7, 20, 28, 35   (9)

RUFFIN, DAVID   *(See:* DARYL HALL AND JOHN OATES)

RUN-D.M.C.

3-21-87   *It's Tricky*   (Profile)   27, 19, 9, 5, 8, 1, 1, 10, 18, 34   (10)

RUN-D.M.C. WITH STEVEN TYLER

8-16-86   *Walk This Way*   (Profile)   26, 15, 8, 4, 2, 1, 3, 5, 7, 7, 9, 14, 18, 33   (14)

SADE

4-13-85   *Smooth Operator*   (Epic)   11, 10, 12, 8, 13, 12   (6)

1-25-86   *The Sweetest Taboo*   (Potrait)   28, 26, 22, 22, 19, 9, 7, 5, 6, 17   (10)

SCRITTI POLITTI

9-28-85   *Perfect Way*   (WB)   29, 26, 20, 13, 9, 4, 2, 1, 1, 2, 3, 8, 11, 11, 11, 11, 15, 19, 29, 29, 29   (21)

SEGER, BOB, AND THE SILVER BULLET BAND

5-24-86   *American Storm*   (Cap.)   27, 24, 28, 28   (4)

8-02-86   *Like A Rock*   (Cap.)   24   (1)

SEXTON, CHARLIE

2-08-86   *Beat's So Lonely*   (MCA)   19, 19, 10, 4, 2, 1, 1, 2, 7, 7, 18, 24   (12)

SHALAMAR   *(See also:* JODY WATLEY)

6-02-84   *Dancing In The Sheets*   (Col.)   9, 12   (2)

SHEILA E.

6-30-84   *The Glamorous Life*   (WB)   10, 8, 19, 7, 3, 3, 3, 3, 11, 12, 13   (10)

5-30-87   *Koo Koo*   (Paisley Park)   32, 32, 28, 34   (4)

2-01-86   *The Love Bizarre*   (Paisley Park)   27, 23, 23, 20, 19, 19, 21, 26   (8)

SIMON, PAUL

2-07-87   *Boy In The Bubble*   (WB)   23, 11, 8, 5, 5, 7, 7, 7, 13, 20, 27, 39   (12)

10-04-86   *You Can Call Me Al*   (WB)   32, 28, 19, 16, 13, 11, 7, 7, 7, 10, 10, 22, 33, 33, 33, 39   (16)

SIMPLE MINDS

11-30-85   *Alive And Kicking*   (A&M)   25, 19, 11, 10, 10, 7, 7, 3, 1, 2, 6, 6, 13, 17   (14)

5-17-86   *All The Things She Said*   (A&M)   27, 14, 7, 3, 3, 1, 14, 26   (8)

3-30-85   *Don't You (Forget About Me)*   (A&M)   9, 12, 5, 5, 10, 12, 11, 8, 5, 7, 11   (11)

3-08-86   *Sanctify Yourself*   (A&M)   17, 15, 14, 10, 6, 6, 6, 8, 9, 11, 25   (11)

SIMPLY RED

5-31-86   *Holding Back The Years*   (Elektra)   22, 15, 15, 11, 5, 11, 7, 6, 6, 18, 19, 27   (12)

9-20-86   *Money's Too Tight (To Mention)*   (Elektra)   23, 19, 17, 17, 34, 36, 39   (7)

SLEDGE, PERCY

5-09-87   *When A Man Loves A Woman*   (Atl.)   27, 20, 17   (3)

THE SMITHEREENS

2-28-87   *In A Lonely Place*   (Enigma)   23, 25, 37   (3)

SPANDAU BALLET

8-25-84   *Only When You Leave*   (Chrysalis)   13, 9, 7, 5, 7, 13, 15   (7)

SPRINGFIELD, RICK

6-08-85   *Celebrate Youth*   (RCA)   9, 11   (2)

3-31-84   *Love Somebody*   (RCA)   12, 14, (2), 11, 3, 3, 9   (6)

    8-10-85   *State Of The Heart* (RCA)   22, 18, 17, 17, 22, 26   (6)

SPRINGSTEEN, BRUCE(, AND THE E STREET BAND)

    1-19-85   *Born In The U.S.A.* (Col.)   6, 2, 3, 4, 7, 10   (6)

    8-18-84   *Dancing In The Dark* (Col.)   14, 10, 8, 5, 3, 2, 1, 4, 7, 12, 15   (11)

    2-28-87   *Fire* (Col.)   21, 18, 26   (3)

    8-10-85   *Glory Days* (Col.)   17, 20, 22, 28, 30   (5)

    4-20-85   *I'm On Fire* (Col.)   6, 4, 5, 6, 6, 9, 11, 15, 15, 15   (10)

    1-18-86   *My Hometown* (Col.)   28, 25, 25, 28, 28, 27   (6)

  12-20-86   *War* (Col.)   36, 28, 28, 28, 24, 20, 16, 16, 29, 29   (10)

SQUIER, BILLY

    7-21-84   *Rock Me Tonight* (Cap.)   12, 14, 12, 10, 9, 14   (6)

STACEY Q

  10-11-86   *Two Hearts* (Atl.)   34, 27, 27, 40   (4)

    2-21-87   *We Connect* (Atl.)   38   (1)

STARPOINT

    3-07-87   *He Wants My Body* (Elektra)   33, 32, 35, 35, 38   (5)

THE STARSHIP   *(See also:* THE JEFFERSON STARSHIP)

    3-21-87   *Nothing's Gonna Stop Us Now* (RCA)   31, 21, 15, 19, 19, 17, 16, 39   (8)

    3-01-86   *Sara* (RCA)   21, 10, 8, 7, 13, 21, 21   (7)

    5-24-86   *Tomorrow Doesn't Matter Tonight* (Grunt)   25, 19, 20, 20   (4)

  11-02-85   *We Built This City* (Grunt)   26, 21, 20, 17, 23, 26, 24, 28, 28   (9)

STEWART, JERMAINE

8-09-86 *We Don't Have To Take Our Clothes Off* (Arista) 16, 14, 6, 6, 20, 25, 26, 32, 36 (9)

STEWART, ROD

7-28-84 *Infatuation* (WB) 11, 8, 5, 2, 1, 4, 3, 6, 15 (9)

6-28-86 *Love Touch* (WB) 24, 13, 8, 7, 7, 3, 2, 2, 14, 25, 29, 30, 37 (13)

STING *(See also:* POLICE)

9-28-85 *Fortress Around Your Heart* (A&M) 24, 15, 11, 6, 4, 2, 1, 3, 9, 17, 30 (11)

8-03-85 *If You Love Somebody Set Them Free* (A&M) 10, 8, 8, 7, 6, 8, 10, 19, 19, 30 (10)

11-30-85 *Love Is The Seventh Wave* (A&M) 20, 13, 10, 9, 9, 5, 5, 7, 7, 28, 30, 30 (12)

1-25-86 *Russians* (A&M) 24, 18, 16, 16, 15, 11, 9, 6, 4, 9 (10)

STREISAND, BARBRA

12-08-84 *Left In The Dark* (Col.) 14, 10, 8, 8, 8, 8 (6)

STRYPER

2-07-87 *Calling On You* (Enigma) 33, 22, 14, 14, 17, 25, 39 (7)

SURVIVOR

1-18-86 *Burning Heart* (Scotti Bros.) 20, 14, 12, 9, 9, 7, 6, 8, 20 (9)

11-17-84 *I Can't Hold Back* (Epic) 12, 11, 14 (3)

THE SYSTEM

3-21-87 *Don't Disturb This Groove* (Atl.) 33, 29, 27, 24, 14, 15, 12, 7, 3, 1, 3, 3, 3, 6 (14)

T'PAU

5-23-87   *Heart And Soul*   (Virgin)   36, 31, 31, 39, 20   (5)

TALKING HEADS

11-16-85   *And She Was*   (Sire)   29, 27   (2)

8-10-85   *Road To Nowhere*   (Sire)   29, 28, 27   (3)

10-19-85   *Stay Up Late*   (Sire)   22, 17, 11, 9, 14, 14, 18, 21   (8)

11-08-86   *Wild Wild Life*   (WB)   27, 14, 9, 5, 2, 2, 2, 2, 2, 2, 5, 6, 10, 10, 12, 13   (16)

TAYLOR, ANDY   *(See also:* DURAN DURAN)

7-12-86   *Take It Easy*   (Atl.)   19, 16, 16, 11, 9, 6, 5, 19, 28   (9)

11-29-86   *When The Rain Comes Down*   (MCA)   36, 33, 33, 30, 30, 30, 30, 38   (8)

TEARS FOR FEARS

5-04-85   *Everybody Wants To Rule The World*   (Mer.)   2, 1, 1, 1, 1, 2, 6, 5, 14, 11, 14, 15   (12)

10-05-85   *Head Over Heels*   (Mer.)   27, 21, 19, 16, 20, 24, 26   (7)

7-27-85   *Shout*   (Mer.)   9, 6, 9, 9, 8, 9, 18, 25   (8)

TEPPER, ROBERT

3-08-86   *No Easy Way Out*   (Scotti Bros.)   20, 13, 11, 6, 5, 5, 4, 9, 13, 20   (10)

.38 SPECIAL

6-21-86   *Like No Other Night*   (A&M)   25, 21, 18, 15, 12, 12, 20, 28   (8)

9-20-86   *Somebody Like You*   (A&M)   20, 16, 14, 13, 10, 10, 18, 29, 37   (9)

11-10-84   *Teacher Teacher*   (Cap.)   15, 13, 13, 15   (4)

THE THOMPSON TWINS

7-07-84   *Doctor! Doctor!*   (Arista)   10, 6, 6, 4, 5, 12   (6)

4-14-84   *Hold Me Now*   (Arista)   9, 14, (2), 15, 13, 13, 15   (6)

3-15-86   *King For A Day*   (Arista)   —, 17, 28, 30, 30   (5)

9-20-86   *Nothing In Common*   (Arista)   27, 23, 23, 36   (4)

9-29-84   *You Take Me Up*   (Arista)   14, 12, 13   (3)

'TIL TUESDAY

6-08-85   *Voices Carry*   (Epic)   5, 5, 4, 3, 4   (5)

TIMBUK 3

11-01-86   *The Future's So Bright, I Gotta Wear Shades*   (I.R.S.)   31, 25, 19, 12,
12. 10, 5, 3, 4, 6, 9, 10, 9, 7, 13, 39, 37, 40   (18)

THE TIME

8-04-84   *Ice Cream Castles*   (WB)   10, 8, 7, 15   (4)

1-19-85   *Jungle Love*   (WB)   13   (1)

TOTO

10-18-86   *I'll Be Over You*   (Col.)   31, 12, 8, 8, 13, 16, 15, 15, 15, 17, 20, 20,
20, 28, 39   (15)

5-02-87   *Till The End*   (Col.)   33, 24, 17, 15, 38, 38   (6)

TOWNSHEND, PETE

12-07-85   *Face The Face*   (Atl.)   24, 21, 17, 17, 19, 19, 14, 8, 5, 5, 5, 5, 16,
29   (14)

TURNER, TINA   *(See also:* BRYAN ADAMS)

10-13-84   *Better Be Good To Me*   (Cap.)   12, 8, 7, 3, 4, 7, 15   (7)

6-13-87   *Better Be Good To Me*   (A&M)   33, 28   (2)

3-31-84   *Let's Stay Together*   (Cap.)   11   (1)

11-23-85   *One Of The Living*   (Cap.)   23, 21   (2)

2-09-85   *Private Dancer*   (Cap.)   11, 11, (2), 9, 9, 15, (1), 13, 7   (7)

9-27-86   *Typical Male*   (Cap.)   29, 25, 24, 17, 13, 10, 10, 8, 8, 13, 13, 13, 16, 18, 18, 18, 27, 36   (18)

8-03-85   *We Don't Need Another Hero (Thunderdome)*   (Cap.)   7, 7, 6, 5, 7, 7, 6, 7, 12, 20   (10)

7-28-84   *What's Love Got To Do With It*   (Cap.)   13, 9, 6, 3, 2, 2, 2, 4, 3, 6, 10, 15   (12)

TWILLEY, DWIGHT

4-07-84   *Girls*   (EMI America)   15, 15   (2)

TYLER, STEVEN   (*See:* RUN-D.M.C.)

U2

12-01-84   *Pride*   (Island)   11, 10, 7, 6, 6, 6, 6   (7)

4-25-87   *With Or Without You*   (Island)   33, 25, 14, 4, 3, 2, 2, 2, 8   (9)

UB40 WITH CHRISSIE HYNDE   (*See also:* THE PRETENDERS)

9-28-85   *I Got You Babe*   (A&M)   27, 23   (2)

USA FOR AFRICA

3-23-85   *We Are The World*   (Col.)   9, 6, 2, 1, 2, 3, 11   (7)

ULLMAN, TRACEY

7-14-84   *Break-A-Way*   (Stiff/MCA)   14, 15   (2)

4-28-84   *They Don't Know*   (MCA)   15, 12   (2)

THE UNFORGIVEN

7-05-86   *I Hear The Call*   (Elektra)   29, 27, 30, 30   (4)

VALENTINE, CINDY

5-02-87 *In Your Midnight Hour* (PolyGram) 21, 15, 11, 21 (4)

VAN HALEN *(See also:* SAMMY HAGAR; DAVID LEE ROTH)

1-24-87 *Best Of Both Worlds* (WB) 37, 34, 34, 38 (4)

11-24-84 *Hot For Teacher* (WB) 14, 13, 12 (3)

4-07-84 *Jump* (WB) 11 (1)

VANDROSS, LUTHER

2-21-87 *Stop To Love* (Epic) 35, 33, 31, 29 (4)

VANDROSS, LUTHER, AND GREGORY HINES

5-02-87 *There's Nothing Better Than Love* (Epic) 35, 32, 24, 22, 17, 17, 16 (7)

VEGA, SUZANNE

6-20-87 *Luka* (A&M) 21 (1)

VOICES OF AMERICA

5-31-86 *Hands Across America* (EMI America) 27, 23, 23, 24 (4)

WAGNER, JACK

5-09-87 *Weatherman Says* (Qwest/WB) 34, 31, 28, 27, 27, 40 (6)

WAITE, JOHN

10-26-85 *Every Step Of The Way* (EMI America) 18, 13, 14, 13, 16, 24 (6)

8-23-86 *If Anybody Had A Heart* (EMI America) 29, 27 (20

8-11-84 *Missing You* (EMI America) 13, 8, 7, 6, 4, 1, 1, 5, 7, 14 (10)

WALL OF VOODOO

6-20-87 *Do It Again* (I.R.S.) 26 (1)

WANG CHUNG

7-14-84   *Dance Hall Days*   (WB)   9, 4, 6, 14   (4)

11-22-86   *Everybody Have Fun Tonight*   (Geffen)   32, 28, 22, 22, 20, 16, 16, 17, 22, 36, 40   (11)

11-09-85   *To Live And Die In L.A.*   (Geffen)   27, 22, 21, 13, 9, 6, 5, 5, 9, 9, 8, 23   (12)

WARWICK, DIONNE   (*See:* DIONNE AND FRIENDS)

WATLEY, JODY   (*See also:* SHALAMAR)

3-14-87   *Looking For A New Love*   (MCA)   18, 12, 8, 3, 2, 2, 2, 3, 2, 1, 1, 7, 9, 9, 24, 35   (16)

5-23-87   *Still A Thrill*   (MCA)   32, 20, 20, 14, 3   (5)

WHAM!   (*See also:* GEORGE MICHAEL)

1-26-85   *Careless Whisper*   (Col.)   11, 5, 2, 2, 2, 1, 2, 2, 2, 3, 9   (11)

8-16-86   *The Edge Of Heaven*   (Col.)   21, 12, 11, 19   (4)

5-25-85   *Everything She Wants*   (Col.)   10, 3, 1, 1, 1, 7   (6)

10-13-84   *Wake Me Up Before You Go-Go*   (Col.)   10, 7, 3, 2, 1, 1, 3, 3, 7, 15   (10)

10-11-86   *Where Did Your Heart Go*   (Col.)   35, 32, 28, 25, 23, 21, 21, 35, 40, 40   (10)

WHAT IS THIS

11-16-85   *I'll Be Around*   (MCA)   25, 25, 26   (3)

WHITE, MAURICE

10-26-85   *Stand By Me*   (Col.)   25, 24, 26   (3)

WILDE, KIM

3-14-87   *You Keep Me Hangin' On*   (MCA)   31, 24, 27, 29, 37, 38, (2), 26, 23, 18, 13, 13, 7   (12)

WILLIAMS, DENIECE

6-02-84 *Let's Hear It For The Boy* (Col.) 5, 1, 7, 9, 12, 15 (6)

WILLIAMS, HANK, JR.

2-28-87 *My Name Is Bociphus* (WB) 30, 35 (2)

WILLIAMS, VESTA

5-02-87 *Something About You* (A&M) 28, 25, 21, 17, 12, 12, 22 (7)

WILLIS, BRUCE

2-14-87 *Respect Yourself* (Motown) 20, 16, 10, 13, 9, 8, 23, 35 (15)

4-25-87 *Young Blood* (Motown) 26, 20, 21, 34, 40 (5)

WINWOOD, STEVE

4-11-87 *The Finer Things* (Island) 10, 6, 4, 18, 40 (5)

11-15-86 *Freedom Overspill* (Island) 29, 24, 21, 21, 21, 25, 38, 38, 38 (9)

8-09-86 *Higher Love* (Island) 18, 13, 11, 10, 10, 19, 22, 28 (8)

WONDER, STEVIE (*See also:* DIONNE AND FRIENDS)

1-25-86 *Go Home* (Tamla) 22, 20, 17, 17, 16, 22 (6)

10-20-84 *I Just Called To Say I Love You* (Motown) 11, 11, 9, 6, 4, 6, 9, 15 (8)

1-19-85 *Love Light In Flight* (Motown) 11, 8, 4, 5, 8, 7, 14 (7)

4-19-86 *Overjoyed* (Tamla) 20, 16, 15, 30, 30 (5)

11-09-85 *Part-Time Lover* (Motown) 22, 16, 7, 5, 4, 4, 3, 3, 2, 2, 4, 11, 30 (13)

WORLD PARTY

2-21-87 *Ship Of Fools* (Cap.) 37, 36, 36 (3)

YANKOVIC, WEIRD AL

3-31-84   *Eat It*   (Rock 'N' Roll/CBS)   3, 3, 2, 2, 4, 8, 11   (7)

YOUNG, PAUL

8-10-85   *Everytime You Go Away*   (Col.)   30   (1)

10-12-85   *I'm Gonna Tear Your Playhouse Down*   (Col.)   22, 21, 24   (3)

ZZ TOP

5-26-84   *Legs*   (WB)   11, 3, 2, 2, 4, 8, 13   (7)

12-14-85   *Sleeping Bag*   (WB)   29, —, —, 24, 24, 17, 15, 14, 26, 26   (10)

C. MUSIC VIDEO TITLE INDEX

Addicted To Love   (Robert Palmer)
Adult Education   (Daryl Hall and John Oates)
Against All Odds (Take A Look At Me Now)   (Phil Collins)
Ain't So Easy   (David and David)
Alive And Kicking   (Simple Minds)
All I Need Is A Miracle   (Mike and The Mechanics)
All I Wanted   (Kansas)
All I've Got To Do Is (Dream)   (R.E.M.)
All She Wants To Do Is Dance   (Don Henley)
All The King's Horses   (The Firm)
All The Love In The World   (The Outfield)
All The Things She Said   (Simple Minds)
Along Comes A Woman   (Chicago)
Always   (Atlantic Starr)
America   (Prince and The Revolution)
American Storm   (Bob Seger and The Silver Bullet Band)
And She Was   (Talking Heads)
And We Danced   (The Hooters)
Another Night   (Aretha Franklin)

Anotherloverholenyohead   (Prince and The Revolution)
Arizona Sky   (China Crisis)
Authority Song   (John Cougar Mellencamp)

Baby Grand   (Billy Joel featuring Ray Charles)
Baby Let's Kiss   (Jesse Johnson)
Baby Love   (Regina)
Bad Boy   (The Miami Sound Machine)
Ballerina Girl   (Lionel Richie)
Be Near Me   (ABC)
Beat's So Lonely   (Charlie Sexton)
Best Of Both Worlds   (Van Halen)
Better Be Good To Me   (Tina Turner)
Big Time   (Peter Gabriel)
Borderline   (Madonna)
Born In East L.A.   (Cheech And Chong)
Born In The U.S.A.   (Bruce Springsteen)
Boy In The Bubble   (Paul Simon)
The Boys Of Summer   (Don Henley)
Brand New Lover   (Dead Or Alive)

Break-A-Way (Tracey Ullman)
Breakin'... There's No Stopping Us (Ollie and Jerry)
Broken Wings (Mr. Mister)
Burning Heart (Survivor)

California Girls (David Lee Roth)
Call Me (Go West)
Calling America (Electric Light Orchestra)
Calling On You (Stryper)
Candy (Cameo)
Can't Fight This Feeling (REO Speedwagon)
Can't Get There From Here (R.E.M.)
Can't Wait For The Night (Brighton Rock)
The Captain Of Her Heart (Double)
Careless Whisper (Wham!)
Caribbean Queen (Billy Ocean)
Celebrate Youth (Rick Springfield)
Centipede (Rebbie Jackson)
C'est La Vie (Robbie Nevil)
Change Of Heart (Cyndi Lauper)
Cherish (Kool & The Gang)
C-I-T-Y (John Cafferty and The Beaver Brown Band)
C'mon Every Beat Box (Big Audio Dynamite)
Come Go With Me (Expose)
Conga (The Miami Sound Machine)
Contender (Heaven 17)
Control (Janet Jackson)
Cool It Now (The New Edition)
Crazy For You (Madonna)
Cross The Border (Icehouse)
Cruel Summer (Bananarama)
Crush On You (The Jets)
Cry Wolf (A-Ha)

Dance Hall Days (Wang Chung)
Dancing In The Dark (Bruce Springsteen)
Dancing In The Sheets (Shalamar)
Dancing In The Streets (David Bowie and Mick Jagger)

Dancing On The Ceiling (Lionel Richie)
Danger Zone (Kenny Loggins)
Dare Me (The Pointer Sisters)
Day-In Day-Out (David Bowie)
Desert Moon (Dennis DeYoung)
Diamonds (Herb Alpert)
Died In Your Arms (See: {I Just} Died In Your Arms)
A Different Corner (George Michael)
Digging Your Scene (The Blow Monkeys)
Dirty Looks (Diana Ross)
Do It Again (Wall Of Voodoo)
Do It For Love (Sheena Easton)
Do They Know It's Christmas (Band Aid)
Do What You Do (Jermaine Jackson)
Do You Want Crying (Katrina and The Waves)
Doctor! Doctor! (The Thompson Twins)
Dominoes (Robbie Nevil)
Don't Come Around Here No More (Tom Petty and The Heartbreakers)
Don't Disturb This Groove (The System)
Don't Dream It's Over (Crowded House)
Don't Forget Me (Glass Tiger)
Don't Get Me Wrong (The Pretenders)
Don't Give Up (Peter Gabriel and Kate Bush)
Don't Lose My Number (Phil Collins)
Don't Stand So Close To Me '86 (Police)
Don't Stop The Music (Bryan Ferry)
Don't You (Forget About Me) (Simple Minds)
Dreamtime (Daryl Hall)
Dress You Up (Madonna)
Drive (The Cars)
Dynamite (Jermaine Jackson)

Easy Lover (Philip Bailey and Phil Collins)
Eat 'Em And Smile (David Lee Roth)
Eat It (Weird Al Yankovic)
The Edge Of Heaven (Wham!)
Emotion In Motion (Ric Ocasek)
Every Step Of The Way (John Waite)

Everybody Have Fun Tonight (Wang Chung)
Everybody Wants To Rule The World (Tears For Fears)
Everything She Wants (Wham!)
Everytime You Go Away (Paul Young)
Eyes Without A Face (Billy Idol)

Face The Face (Pete Townshend)
Fall On Me (R.E.M.)
Fascinated (Company B)
Feel It Again (Honeymoon Suite)
Feel The Heat (Jean Beauvoir)
Fight For Your Right (See: {You Gotta} Fight For Your Right)
The Final Countdown (Europe)
Find A Way (Amy Grant)
The Finer Things (Steve Winwood)
Fire (Bruce Springsteen and The E Street Band)
Flesh For Fantasy (Billy Idol)
Fool In Love (Farrenheit)
Foolish Heart (Steve Perry)
Footloose (Kenny Loggins)
For America (Jackson Browne)
For Tonight (Nancy Martinez)
(Forever) Live And Die (Orchestral Manoeuvres In The Dark)
Fortress Around Your Heart (Sting)
Freedom Overspill (Steve Winwood)
Freeway Of Love (Aretha Franklin)
French Kissin' (Debbie Harry)
Fresh (Kool & The Gang)
Fright Night (The J. Geils Band)
Funky Town (Pseudo Echo)
The Future's So Bright, I Gotta Wear Shades (Timbuk 3)

Get It On (Bang A Gong) (Power Station)
Getcha Back (The Beach Boys)
Ghostbusters (Ray Parker, Jr.)
Girl Can't Help It (Journey)
Girls (Dwight Twilley)
Girls Just Want To Have Fun (Cyndi Lauper)

The Glamorous Life (Sheila E.)
Glory Days (Bruce Springsteen)
Glory Of Love (Peter Cetera)
Go Home (Stevie Wonder)
Go Insane (Lindsey Buckingham)
Goodbye Is Forever (Arcadia)
Gravity (James Brown)
The Greatest Love Of All (Whitney Houston)

Hands Across America (Voices Of America)
Hanging On A Heart Attack (Device)
Harlem Shuffle (The Rolling Stones)
Have You Ever Loved Somebody (Freddie Jackson)
He Wants My Body (Starpoint)
Head Over Heels (The Go-Go's)
Head Over Heels (Tears For Fears)
Head To Toe (Lisa Lisa and Cult Jam)
Heart And Soul (T'Pau)
Heart Of Rock 'N' Roll (Huey Lewis and The News)
Heartache Away (Don Johnson)
Heartbeat (Don Johnson)
Heartbreak Beat (The Psychedelic Furs)
Heaven (Bryan Adams)
Hello (Lionel Richie)
Here Comes The Rain (Eurythmics)
Higher Love (Steve Winwood)
Hit You (Limited Warranty)
Hold Me (Colin James Hay)
Hold Me Now (The Thompson Twins)
Holding Back The Years (Simply Red)
Honeythief (Hipsway)
Hot For Teacher (Van Halen)
(How To Be A) Millionaire (ABC)
How Will I Know (Whitney Houston)
Human (Human League)
Hyperactive (Thomas Dolby)

I Ain't Got Nobody (See: Just A Gigolo . . .)
I Can't Hold Back (Survivor)
I Can't Wait (Stevie Nicks)
I Can't Wait (Nu Shooz)

I Didn't Mean To Turn You On (Cherrelle)

I Didn't Mean To Turn You On (Robert Palmer)

I Don't Want To Lose Your Love (Freddie Jackson)

I Feel For You (Dance Mix) (Chaka Khan)

I Got You Babe (UB40 with Chrissie Hynde)

I Hear The Call (The Unforgiven)

I Just Called To Say I Love You (Stevie Wonder)

(I Just) Died In Your Arms (The Cutting Crew)

I Knew You Were Waiting (For Me) (Aretha Franklin And George Michael)

I Miss You (Klymaxx)

I Must Be Dreaming (Giuffria)

I Need Your Loving (The Human League)

I Think It's Love (Jermaine Jackson)

I Wanna Be A Cowboy (Boys Don't Cry)

I Wanna Dance With Somebody (Who Loves Me) (Whitney Houston)

I Want A New Drug (Huey Lewis And The News)

I Want To Know What Love Is (Foreigner)

I Want To Make The World Turn Around (The Steve Miller Band)

I Will Be There (Glass Tiger)

I Wonder If I Take You Home (Lisa Lisa and The Cult Jam with Full Force)

I'll Be Around (What Is This)

I'll Be Over You (Toto)

I'm Bad (L.L. Cool J.)

I'm Gonna Tear Your Playhouse Down (Paul Young)

I'm On Fire (Bruce Springsteen)

I've Got The Feeling (It's Over) (Gregory Abbott)

Ice Cream Castles (The Time)

If Anybody Had A Heart (John Waite)

If This Is It (Huey Lewis and The News)

If You Leave (Orchestral Manoeuvres In The Dark)

If You Love Somebody Set Them Free (Sting)

Imagination (Miki Howard)

In A Lonely Place (The Smithereens)

In My House (The Mary Jane Girls)

In Your Midnight Hour (Cindy Valentine)

Infatuation (Rod Stewart)

Into The Groove (Madonna)

Into The Night (Ace Frehley)

Invincible (Theme From The Legend Of Billie Jean) (Pat Benatar)

Invisible Touch (Genesis)

Is It Love (Mr. Mister)

It Ain't Enough (Corey Hart)

It's A Miracle (Culture Club)

It's In The Way That You Use It (Eric Clapton)

It's Only Love (Bryan Adams and Tina Turner)

It's Tricky (Run-D.M.C.)

Jacob's Ladder (Huey Lewis and The News)

Jimmy Lee (Aretha Franklin)

Jump (Van Halen)

Jump (For My Love) (The Pointer Sisters)

Jumpin' Jack Flash (Aretha Franklin)

Jungle Boy (John Eddie)

Jungle Love (The Time)

Just A Gigolo/I Ain't Got Nobody (David Lee Roth)

Just Another Night (Mick Jagger)

Just To See Her (Smokey Robinson)

Keep Your Eyes On Me (Herb Alpert)

Keep Your Hands To Yourself (The Georgia Satellites)

Keeping The Faith (Billy Joel)

King For A Day (The Thompson Twins)

Kiss (Prince And The Revolution)

Koo Koo (Sheila E.)

Kyrie (Mr. Mister)

La Isla Bonita   (Madonna)
Lady In Red   (Chris DeBurgh)
Land Of Confusion   (Genesis)
Lean On Me   (Club Nouveau)
Left In The Dark   (Barbra Streisand)
Legs   (ZZ Top)
Lessons In Love   (Level 42)
Let It Be   (Ferry Aid)
Let's Go All The Way   (Sly Fox)
Let's Go Crazy   (Prince)
Let's Hear It For The Boy   (Deniece
   Williams)
Let's Stay Together   (Tina Turner)
Life In A Northern Town   (The Dream
   Academy)
Life In One Day   (Howard Jones)
Light Of Day   (The Barbusters)
Like A Rock   (Bob Seger And The Silver
   Bullet Band)
Like A Virgin   (Madonna)
Like No Other Night   (.38 Special)
Little By Little   (Robert Plant)
Live And Die   (See: {Forever} Live And
   Die)
Live To Tell   (Madonna)
Livin' In Desperate Times   (Olivia New-
   ton-John)
Living In America   (James Brown)
Living On A Prayer   (Bon Jovi)
Lonely Ol' Night   (John Cougar Mellen-
   camp)
The Longest Time   (Billy Joel)
Look Away   (Big Country)
Looking For A New Love   (Jody Watley)
The Love Bizarre   (Sheila E.)
Love Comes Quickly   (The Pet Shop Boys)
Love Is The Seventh Wave   (Sting)
Love Light In Flight   (Stevie Wonder)
Love Like A Rocket   (Bob Geldof)
Love Somebody   (Rick Springfield)
Love Touch   (Rod Stewart)
Love Will Conquer All   (Lionel Richie)
Love Will Show Us How   (Christine
   McVie)
Love Zone   (Billy Ocean)
Lovergirl   (Teena Marie)
The Lucky One   (Laura Branigan)
Luka   (Suzanne Vega)

Mad About You   (Belinda Carlisle)
Magic   (The Cars)
Make It Better (Forget About Me)   (Tom
   Petty)
Man-Sized Love   (Klymaxx)
Mandolin Rain   (Bruce Hornsby and
   The Range)
Manic Monday   (The Bangles)
Mary's Prayer   (Danny Wilson)
Material Girl   (Madonna)
A Matter Of Trust   (Billy Joel)
Method Of Modern Love   (Daryl Hall and
   John Oates)
"Miami Vice" Theme   (Jan Hammer)
Millionaire   (See: {How To Be A} Mil-
   lionaire)
Misled   (Kool & The Gang)
Miss Me Blind   (Culture Club)
Missing You   (John Waite)
Missionary Man   (Eurythmics)
Mr. Telephone Man   (The New Edition)
Money Changes Everything   (Cyndi Lau-
   per)
Money For Nothing   (Dire Straits)
Money's Too Tight   (Simply Red)
*The More You Live (The More You
   Love)*   (A Flock Of Seagulls)
Mountains   (Prince and The Revolu-
   tion)
Move Away   (Culture Club)
Mutual Surrender   (Bourgeois Tagg)
My Hometown   (Bruce Springsteen)
My Name Is Bocephus   (Hank Williams,
   Jr.)

Nasty   (Janet Jackson)
Neutron Dance   (The Pointer Sisters)
Never   (Heart)
Never Surrender   (Corey Hart)
Never You Done That   (General Public)
New Moon On Monday   (Duran Duran)
The Next Time   (Peter Cetera with Amy
   Grant)
Night Moves   (Marilyn Martin)
Nightshift   (The Commodores)
Nikita   (Elton John)
19   (Paul Hardcastle)

99 Luftballoons   (Nena)
No Easy Way Out   (Robert Tepper)
No Lookin' Back   (Michael McDonald)
No One Is To Blame   (Howard Jones)
No Promises   (Icehouse)
Not Enough Love In The World   (Don
   Henley)
Nothin' At All   (Heart)
Nothing In Common   (The Thompson
   Twins)
Nothing's Gonna Change My Love
   (Glenn Medeiros)
Nothing's Gonna Stop Us Now   (The
   Starship)
Notorious   (Duran Duran)

The Oak Tree   (Morris Day)
Obsession   (Animotion)
Oh Sheila   (Ready For The World)
On My Own   (Patti LaBelle and Michael
   McDonald)
On The Dark Side   (John Cafferty and
   The Beaver Brown Band)
One Hit (To The Body)   (The Rolling
   Stones)
One Love At A Time   (Atlantic Starr)
One More Night   (Phil Collins)
One Night In Bangkok   (Murray Head)
One Of The Living   (Tina Turner)
One Step Closer To You   (Gavin Christo-
   pher)
One Vision   (Queen)
Only When You Leave   (Spandau Ballet)
Open Your Heart   (Madonna)
*Opportunities (Let's Make Lots Of
   Money)*   (The Pet Shop Boys)
The Original Wrapper   (Lou Reed)
Out Of Mind, Out Of Sight   (The Mod-
   els)
Out Of Touch   (Daryl Hall and John
   Oates)
Overjoyed   (Stevie Wonder)

Papa Don't Preach   (Madonna)
Paranoimia   (The Art Of Noise with
   Max Headroom)

Part-Time Lover   (Stevie Wonder)
Party All The Time   (Eddie Murphy)
Penny Lover   (Lionel Richie)
People Are People   (Depeche Mode)
(Close To) Perfect   (Jermaine Jackson)
Perfect Way   (Scritti Politti)
Pleasure And Pain   (The Divinyls)
Point Of No Return   (Nu Shooz)
Possession Obsession   (Daryl Hall and
   John Oates)
Power Of Love   (Huey Lewis and The
   News)
Press   (Paul McCartney)
Pride   (U2)
Private Dancer   (Tina Turner)

Quicksilver Lightning   (Roger Daltrey)

Radio Ga Ga   (Queen)
The Rain   (Oran "Juice" Jones)
Rain On The Scarecrow   (John Cougar
   Mellencamp)
Raspberry Beret   (Prince and The Revo-
   lution)
Rebel Yell   (Billy Idol)
The Reflex   (Duran Duran)
Relax   (Frankie Goes To Hollywood)
Respect Yourself   (Bruce Willis)
Rhythm Of The Night   (DeBarge)
Rhythm Of The Streets   (Patti Austin)
Right By Your Side   (Eurythmics)
Right On Track   (The Breakfast Club)
Road To Nowhere   (Talking Heads)
Rock And Roll Girls   (John Fogerty)
R.O.C.K. In The U.S.A.   (John Cougar
   Mellencamp)
Rock Me Amadeus   (Falco)
Rock Me Tonight   (Billy Squier)
Rock The Night   (Europe)
Romancing The Stone   (Eddy Grant)
Rumble Seat   (John Cougar Mellen-
   camp)
Run To You   (Bryan Adams)
Runaway   (Luis Cardenas)
Running Up That Hill   (Kate Bush)
Russians   (Sting)

Sad Songs (Say So Much)   (Elton John)

St. Elmo's Fire (Man In Motion)   (John Parr)

Same Ole Love   (365 Days A Year)   (Anita Baker)

Sanctify Yourself   (Simple Minds)

Sara   (The Starship)

Save A Prayer   (Duran Duran)

Saving All My Love For You   (Whitney Houston)

Say The Word   (Arcadia)

Say You Say Me   (Lionel Richie)

Say You're Wrong   (Julian Lennon)

Se La   (Lionel Richie)

Sea Of Love   (The Honeydrippers)

Secret Lovers   (Atlantic Starr)

Self Control   (Laura Branigan)

Send My Heart   (The Adventures)

Sentimental Street   (Night Ranger)

Separate Lives (Love Theme From White Nights)   (Phil Collins and Marilyn Martin)

Serious   (Donna Allen)

Sex As A Weapon   (Pat Benatar)

Sexy Girl   (Glenn Frey)

Shake You Down   (Gregory Abbott)

Shakin', Shakin', Shakes   (Los Lobos)

Shame   (The Motels)

She Bop   (Cyndi Lauper)

She's Strange   (Cameo)

She's Waiting   (Eric Clapton)

Ship Of Fools   (World Party)

Shot In The Dark   (Ozzy Osbourne)

Should I See   (Frozen Ghost)

Shout   (Tears For Fears)

Show Me   (The Cover Girls)

Show Me   (The Pretenders)

Silent Running   (Mike and The Mechanics)

Sisters Are Doin' It For Themselves   (Eurythmics and Aretha Franklin)

Sledgehammer   (Peter Gabriel)

Sleeping Bag   (ZZ Top)

Small Town   (John Cougar Mellencamp)

Smokin' In The Boys Room   (Motley Crue)

Smooth Operator   (Sade)

So Far Away   (Dire Straits)

So In Love   (Orchestral Manoeuvres In The Dark)

Some Like It Hot   (Power Station)

Somebody   (Bryan Adams)

Somebody Like You   (.38 Special)

Somebody's Watching Me   (Rockwell)

Something About You   (Level 42)

Something About You   (Vesta Williams)

Soul Kiss   (Olivia Newton-John)

Spies Like Us   (Paul McCartney)

Stand By Me   (Ben E. King)

Stand By Me   (Maurice White)

State Of The Heart   (Rick Springfield)

Stay Up Late   (Talking Heads)

Still A Thrill   (Jody Watley)

Still In Hollywood   (Concrete Blonde)

Stop To Love   (Luther Vandross)

Strength   (The Alarm)

Strut   (Sheena Easton)

Stuck With You   (Huey Lewis and The News)

Suddenly   (Billy Ocean)

Sugar Walls   (Sheena Easton)

Summer Of '69   (Bryan Adams)

The Sun Always Shines On T.V.   (A-Ha)

Sun City   (Artists United Against Apartheid)

Sunglasses At Night   (Corey Hart)

Sussudio   (Phil Collins)

Sweet Freedom   (Michael McDonald)

Sweet Love   (Anita Baker)

Sweet, Sweet Baby (I'm Falling)   (Lone Justice)

The Sweetest Taboo   (Sade)

Swept Away   (Diana Ross)

Take It Easy   (Andy Taylor)

Take Me Home   (Phil Collins)

Take Me Home Tonight   (Eddie Money)

Take My Breath Away   (Berlin)

Take On Me   (A-Ha)

Taken In   (Mike and The Mechanics)

Talk Dirty To Me   (Poison)

Teacher Teacher   (.38 Special)

Tenderness   (General Public)

That's What Friends Are For   (Dionne And Friends)

When The Rain Comes Down (Andy Taylor)
Where Did Your Heart Go (Wham!)
Who's Johnny (El DeBarge)
Who's That Girl? (Eurythmics)
The Wild And The Young (Quiet Riot)
Wild Boys (Duran Duran)
Wild Wild Life (Talking Heads)
Will You Still Love Me? (Chicago)
Winner Takes It All (Sammy Hagar)
With Or Without You (U2)
Word Up (Cameo)
Working Class Man (Jimmy Barnes)
Would I Lie To You? (Eurythmics)
Wrap It Up (The Fabulous Thunderbirds)

Yankee Rose (David Lee Roth)
You Are My Lady (Freddie Jackson)

You Belong To The City (Glenn Frey)
You Can Call Me Al (Paul Simon)
You Give Love A Bad Name (Bon Jovi)
You Got It All (The Jets)
(You Gotta) Fight For Your Right (To Party) (The Beastie Boys)
You Keep Me Hangin' On (Kim Wilde)
You Know I Love You, Don't You (Howard Jones)
You Look Marvelous (Billy Crystal)
You Might Think (The Cars)
You Should Be Mine (Jeffrey Osborne)
You Spin Me Round (Like A Record) (Dead Or Alive)
You Take Me Up (The Thompson Twins)
Young Blood (Bruce Willis)
Your Love (The Outfield)
Your Wildest Dreams (The Moody Blues)

C. APPENDIXES

[NUMBER 1 VIDEOS—A CHRONOLOGICAL LISTING]

1984

3-31		*Somebody's Watching Me*—Rockwell (1)
4-07—	4-14	*I Want A New Drug*—Huey Lewis and The News (2)
4-21—	4-28	*Miss Me Blind*—Culture Club (2)
5-05		*Hello*—Lionel Richie (1)
5-12—	5-19	*Time After Time*—Cyndi Lauper (2)
5-26—	6-02	*You Might Think*—The Cars (2)
6-09		*Let's Hear It For The Boy*—Deniece Williams (1)
6-16—	6-23	*Eyes Without A Face*—Billy Idol (2)
6-30—	7-21	*When Doves Cry*—Prince (4)
7-28—	8-04	*Ghostbusters*—Ray Parker, Jr. (2)
8-11—	8-18	*When Doves Cry*—Prince (2; 6)
8-25		*Infatuation*—Rod Stewart (1)
9-01—	9-08	*If This Is It*—Huey Lewis and The News (2)
9-15—	9-22	*Missing You*—John Waite (2)
9-29		*Dancing In The Dark*—Bruce Springsteen (1)
10-06		*Let's Go Crazy*—Prince (1)
10-13		*She Bop*—Cyndi Lauper (1)

10-20—10-27	*Cruel Summer*—Bananarama (2)
11-03	*Caribbean Queen*—Billy Ocean (1)
11-10—11-17	*Wake Me Up Before You Go-Go*—Wham! (2)
11-24—12-01	*I Feel For You*—Chaka Khan (2)
12-08	*Penny Lover*—Lionel Richie (1)
12-15	*We Belong*—Pat Benatar (1)
12-22—12-29	*Centipede*—Rebbie Jackson (2)

1985

1-05— 1-12	*Centipede*—Rebbie Jackson (2; 4)
1-19	*I Feel For You*—Chaka Khan (1; 3)
1-26— 2-23	*Easy Lover*—Philip Bailey and Phil Collins (5)
3-02	*Careless Whisper*—Wham! (1)
3-09	*California Girls*—David Lee Roth (1)
3-16— 4-06	*Material Girl*—Madonna (4)
4-13	*We Are The World*—USA For Africa (1)
4-20	*One More Night*—Phil Collins (1)
4-27	*Obsession*—Animotion (1)
5-04	*All She Wants To Do Is Dance*—Don Henley (1)
5-11— 6-01	*Everybody Wants To Rule The World*—Tears For Fears (4)
6-08— 6-22	*Everything She Wants*—Wham! (3)
6-29— 7-13	*Sussudio*—Phil Collins (3)
7-20— 7-27	*Would I Lie To You?*—Eurythmics (2)
8-03	*Raspberry Beret*—Prince and The Revolution (1)
8-10	*Take On Me*—A-Ha (1)
8-17— 8-24	*Freeway Of Love*—Aretha Franklin (2)
8-31	*The Power Of Love*—Huey Lewis and The News (1)
9-07	*Freeway Of Love*—Aretha Franklin (1; 3)
9-14	*Take On Me*—A-Ha (1; 2)
9-21— 9-28	*Invincible*—Pat Benatar (3)
10-05	*Shame*—The Motels (1)
10-12	*Take On Me*—A-Ha (1; 3)
10-19—10-26	*Oh Sheila*—Ready For The World (2)
11-02	*Saving All My Love For You*—Whitney Houston (1)
11-09	*Fortress Around Your Heart*—Sting (1)
11-16—11-23	*Perfect Way*—Scritti Politti (2)
11-30	*You Belong To The City*—Glenn Frey (1)
12-07	*Separate Lives*—Phil Collins and Marilyn Martin (1)
12-14	*You Belong To The City*—Glenn Frey (1; 2)
12-21—12-28	*Say You Say Me*—Lionel Richie (2)

1986

| 1-04— 1-18 | *Say You Say Me*—Lionel Richie (3; 5) |
| 1-25 | *Alive And Kicking*—Simple Minds (1) |

2-01		*That's What Friends Are For*—Dionne And Friends (1)
2-08—	2-22	*Life In A Northern Town*—The Dream Academy (3)
3-01		*Silent Running*—Mike and The Mechanics (1)
3-08		*How Will I Know*—Whitney Houston (1)
3-15—	3-22	*Beat's So Lonely*—Charlie Sexton (2)
3-29		*Nikita*—Elton John (1)
4-05—	4-12	*What You Need*—INXS (2)
4-19—	4-26	*Addicted To Love*—Robert Palmer (2)
5-03		*Manic Monday*—The Bangles (1)
5-10		*West End Girls*—The Pet Shop Boys (1)
5-17		*Harlem Shuffle*—The Rolling Stones (1)
5-24		*Your Love*—The Outfield (1)
5-31		*Move Away*—Culture Club (1)
6-07—	6-14	*On My Own*—Patti LaBelle and Michael McDonald (2)
6-21		*All The Things She Said*—Simple Minds (1)
6-28		*Crush On You*—The Jets (1)
7-05		*No One Is To Blame*—Howard Jones (1)
7-12		*Sledgehammer*—Peter Gabriel (1)
7-19—	8-16	*Mad About You* (5)
8-23		*Venus*—Bananarama (1)
8-30		*Papa Don't Preach*—Madonna (1)
9-06—	9-13	*Sweet Freedom*—Michael McDonald (2)
9-20		*Walk This Way*—Run-D.M.C. with Steven Tyler (1)
9-27—	10-04	*Dancing On The Ceiling*—Lionel Richie (2)
10-11—	11-01	*When I Think Of You*—Janet Jackson (4)
11-08—	11-29	*Human*—The Human League (4)
12-06—	12-20	*The Way It Is*—Bruce Hornsby and The Range (3)
12-27		*To Be A Lover*—Billy Idol (1)

1987

1-03—	1-10	*To Be A Lover*—Billy Idol (2; 3)
1-17		*Victory*—Kool & The Gang (1)
1-24—	1-31	*Land Of Confusion*—Genesis (2)
2-07—	2-14	*C'est La Vie*—Robbie Nevil (2)
2-21		*Change Of Heart*—Cyndi Lauper (1)
2-28		*Keep Your Hands To Yourself*—The Georgia Satellites (1)
3-07		*Land Of Confusion*—Genesis (1; 3)
3-14		*Victory*—Kool & The Gang (1; 2)
3-21—	4-18	*Lean On Me*—Club Nouveau (5)
4-25—	5-02	*It's Tricky*—Run-D.M.C. (2)
5-09—	5-16	*Looking For A New Love*—Jody Watley (2)
5-23		*Don't Disturb This Groove*—The System (1)
5-30—	6-20	*Head To Toe*—Lisa Lisa and Cult Jam (4)

[VIDEOS WITH LONGEST RUN ON CHARTS]

1. *Take On Me*—A-Ha.....27 weeks
2. *Word Up*—Cameo.....23
3. *Human*—The Human League.....22
3. *Notorious*—Duran Duran.....22
3. *Victory*—Kool & The Gang.....22
6. *Control*—Janet Jackson.....21
6. *I Didn't Mean To Turn You On*—Robert Palmer.....21
6. *Perfect Way*—Scritti Politti.....21
9. *The Next Time*—Peter Cetera with Amy Grant.....20
10. *Life In A Northern Town*—The Dream Academy.....19
10. *Stuck With You*—Huey Lewis and The News.....19
12. *The Future's So Bright, I Gotta Wear Shades*—Timbuk 3.....18
12. *The Rain*—Oran "Juice" Jones.....18
12. *Typical Male*—Tina Turner.....18
15. *Change Of Heart*—Cyndi Lauper.....17
15. *(I Just) Died In Your Arms*—The Cutting Crew.....17
15. *You Belong To The City*—Glenn Frey.....17
18. *Be Near Me*—ABC.....16
18. *Broken Wings*—Mr. Mister.....16
18. *Don't Forget Me*—Glass Tiger.....16
18. *Looking For A New Love*—Jody Watley.....16
18. *Love Will Conquer All*—Lionel Richie.....16
18. *Power Of Love*—Huey Lewis and The News.....16
18. *Running Up That Hill*—Kate Bush.....16
18. *Say You Say Me*—Lionel Richie.....16
18. *Walk Like An Egyptian*—The Bangles.....16
18. *Wild Wild Life*—Talking Heads.....16
18. *You Can Call Me Al*—Paul Simon.....16

RAP ALBUMS/SINGLES

A. INTRODUCTION

It took nearly a decade for the record industry to recognize the importance of rap music; the appearance of the first major rap hit, the Sugar Hill Gang's "The Rapper's Delight" (Sugar Hill, 1979), predated *Cash Box*'s institution of a separate ongoing chart (in this case, two—one devoted to singles, and the other to albums) by nine years. Whereas rap existed largely as an underground phenomenon in the first half of the 1980s—spearheaded by the tough, ghetto-based commentaries of New York acts like Grandmaster Flash and Grandmaster Melle Mel—the genre has since exploded upon the mainstream. The band, Run-D.M.C. (along with the Fat Boys and the Beastie Boys), provided the main impetus for this phenomenon. These acts and others filtered up through the dance scene, followed by inroads onto the black contemporary and pop albums charts. By the time of Tone-Loc's late 1988 release, "Wild Thing," rap recordings were able to match the chart action of mainstream pop singles (based upon radio plays and retail sales). Today rap rivals other more highly visible genres such as new wave and black contemporary in popularity among youth. Given its sociocultural impact as the predominant folk poetry of the postmodern urban generation, it's not likely to disappear from the music scene for some time to come.

Initial chart title/title changes: "Cash Box Top Rap Singles"; "Cash Box Top Rap Albums"
Beginning date/termination date: May 14, 1988/December 31, 1988
Initial number of positions/changes in number of positions: 10 (albums); 15 (singles)

B. RAP ALBUMS—ARTIST INDEX

BASE, ROB, AND D.J. E-Z ROCK

10-29-88   *It Takes Two*   (Profile PRO 1267)   8, 4, 3, 2, 2, 1, 1, 1, 1, 1   (10)

BOOGIE DOWN PRODUCTIONS

5-14-88   *By All Means Necessary*   (Jive/RCA 1097-1-J)   7, 7, 7, 6, 6, 5, 6, 5, 6, 6, 7, 8, 9, 10   (14)

COLOURS

5-21-88   [Original Film Soundtrack]   (WB 1-25713)   8, 8, 2, 2, 3, 3, 4, 5   (8)

D.J. JAZZY JEFF AND THE FRESH PRINCE

5-14-88   *He's The D.J., I'm The Rapper*   (Jive/RCA 1091-1-J)   4, 2, 2, 3, 3, 2, 3, 1, 4, 3, 4, 4, 4, 4, 4, 4, 4, 6, 7, 6, 6, 5, 6, 6, 6, 7, 7, 7, 9, 10   (30)

DANE, DANA

5-14-88   *Dana Dane With Fame*   (Profile PRO 1233)   8   (1)

E.P.M.D.

6-25-88   *Strictly Business*   (Fresh/Sleeping Bag LPRE 80062)   7, 6, 4, 5, 2, 1, 1, 1, 1, 1, 1, 2, 2, 3, 2, 4, 3, 5, 5, 5, 5, 5, 6, 6, 8, 10   (26)

EAZY-E

12-10-88   *Eazy Duz It*   (Priority 57100)   9, 7, 3, 3   (4)

ERIC B. AND RAKIM

8-20-88   *Follow The Leader*   (Jive/RCA 1097-1-J)   3, 2, 3, 3, 3, 2, 4, 6, 5, 7, 7, 8, 9, 10   (14)

FAD, J.J.

8-20-88   *Supersonic—The Album*   (Ruthless 90959)   7, 7, 7, 7, 6, 8, 7, 8, 7, 9   (10)

THE FAT BOYS

7-23-88   *Coming Back Hard Again*   (Tin Pan Apple/PolyGram 835 809)   8,
10, 10, 9   (4)

FRESH, DOUG E.

6-04-88   *The World's Greatest Entertainer*   (Danya/Reality F 9658)   7, 7, 6, 4,
3, 3, 2, 3, 3, 3, 5   (11)

HAMMER, M.C.

11-26-88   *Let's Get It Started*   (Cap. 90924)   10, 9, 10, 8, 8, 8   (6)

HEAVY D. AND THE BOYZ

5-14-88   *Living Large*   (MCA MCA-5986)   3, 3, (3), 9, 10, 9, 9   (6)

ICE-T

10-22-88   *Power*   (Sire 25765)   3, 2, 2, 1, 1, 1, 2, 2, 2, 2, 2   (11)

JUST-ICE

5-14-88   *Kool And Deadly*   (Fresh LPRE-5)   5, 9, 9   (3)

KANE, BIG DADDY

7-30-88   *Long Live The Kane*   (Cold Chillin'/WB 25731)   9, 8, 6, 6, 6, 6, 4, 5,
4, 3, 2, 2, 2, 3, 3, 4, 4, 3, 3, 5, 6, 10, 10   (23)

KID N' PLAY

12-24-88   *2 Hype*   (Select 21628)   7, 7   (2)

KOOL MOE DEE

5-14-88   *How Ya Like Me Now*   (Jive/RCA 1079-1-J)   1, 1, 1, 4, 4, 4, 5, 7, 7,
4, 6, 6, 7, 7, 9   (13)

L.L. COOL J

5-14-88   *Bigger And Deffer*   (Def Jam/Col. 44042)   10   (1)

LYTE, MC

7-16-88   *Lyte As A Rock*   (First Priority/Atl. 90905)   7   (1)

M.C. SHY D

8-27-88   *Comin' Correct In '88*   (Luke Skyywalker 1005)   9, 9, 10, 9, 10, 10   (6)

MANTRONIX

5-21-88   *In Full Effect*   (Cap. C1-48336)   6, 6, 9, 9   (4)

MARKLE, BIZ

5-14-88   *Goin' Off*   (Cold Chillin'/WB 25675)   6, 5, 5, 10, 10, 7, 9, 8, 8, 8, 10   (11)

MARL, MARLEY

11-12-88   *In Control, Volume 1*   (Cold Chillin'/WB 25783)   10, 9, 8, 8, 7, 9, 9, 9   (8)

N.W.A.

10-08-88   *N.W.A. And The Posse*   (Macola 1057)   9, 8   (2)

PUBLIC ENEMY

7-23-88   *It Takes A Nation Of Millions To Hold Us Back*   (Def Jam/CBS FC 44303)   9, 7, 8, 2, 2, 3, 2, 1, 1, 1, 1, 1, 1, 1, 1, 1, 2, 3, 5, 5, 4, 5, 6, 6   (24)

5-14-88   *Yo Bum Rush The Show*   (Def Jam BFC 40658)   9, 10, 10   (3)

RUN-D.M.C.

6-04-88   *Tougher Than Leather*   (Profile PRO 1265)   1, 1, 1, 2, 1, 1, 1, 1, 2, 2, 3, 8, 8, 8, 8, 10, 9, 9, 10   (19)

SALT-N-PEPA

5-14-88 *Hot Cool And Vicious* (Next Plateau PL 1007) 2, 4, 4, 8, 8, 10 (6)

8-20-88 *A Salt With A Deadly Pepa* (Next Plateau PL 1011) 5, 5, 5, 5, 4, 5, 5, 3, 4, 4, 4, 6, 6, 6, 4, 4, 3, 3, 4, 4 (20)

SIR MIX-A-LOT

10-15-88 *Swass* (Nasty Mix 70123) 10, 10, 9, 9, 8, 8, 7, 7, 6, 4, 5, 5 (12)

STETSASONIC

7-16-88 *In Full Gear* (Tommy Boy 1017) 10, (7), 9, 8, 7, 8, 7, 9, 8, 10, 10 (10)

2 LIVE CREW

6-04-88 *Move Somethin'* (Luke Skywalker XR 102) 5, 5, 8, 8, 10, 10, 9, 5, 5, 6, 8, 10, 10, 10 (14)

C. RAP ALBUMS—TITLE INDEX

Long Live The Kane (Big Daddy Kane)

Lyte As A Rock (MC Lyte)

Move Somethin' (2 Live Crew)

N.W.A. And The Posse (N.W.A.)

Power (Ice-T)

A Salt With A Deadly Pepa (Salt-N-Pepa)

Strictly Business (E.P.M.D.)

Supersonic—The Album (J.J. Fad)

Swass (Sir Mix-A-Lot)

Tougher Than Leather (Run-D.M.C.)

2 Hype (Kid N' Play)

The World's Greatest Entertainer (Doug E. Fresh)

Yo Bum Rush The Show (Public Enemy)

D. APPENDIXES

[NUMBER 1 RAP ALBUMS—A CHRONOLOGICAL LISTING]

1988

5-14— 5-28	*How Ya Like Me Now*—Kool Moe Dee (3)
6-04— 6-18	*Tougher Than Leather*—Run-D.M.C. (3)
6-25	*He's The D.J., I'm The Rapper*—D.J. Jazzy Jeff and The Fresh Prince (1)
7-02— 7-23	*Tougher Than Leather*—Run-D.M.C. (4; 7)
7-30— 9-03	*Strictly Business*—E.P.M.D. (6)
9-10—11-05	*It Takes A Nation Of Millions To Hold Us Back*—Public Enemy (9)
11-12—11-26	*Power*—Ice-T (3)
12-03—12-31	*It Takes Two*—Rob Base and D.J. E-Z Rock (5)

[RAP ALBUMS WITH LONGEST RUN ON CHARTS]

1. *He's The D.J., I'm The Rapper*—D.J. Jazzy Jeff and The Fresh Prince.....30
2. *Strictly Business*—E.P.M.D......26
3. *It Takes A Nation Of Millions To Hold Us Back*—Public Enemy.....24
4. *Long Live The Kane*—Big Daddy Kane.....23
5. *A Salt With A Deadly Pepa*—Salt-N-Pepa.....20

E. RAP SINGLES—ARTIST INDEX

BASE, ROB, AND D.J. E-Z ROCK

12-17-88   *Get On The Dance Floor*   (Profile PRO 7239)   11, 9, 9   (3)

5-14-88   *It Takes Two*   (Profile PRO 5186)   10, 7, 7, 6, 6, 6, 7, 8, 10, 13, 15, 15, 15, 9, 9, 9, 9, 11, 11, 10, 9, 8, 7, 6, 9, 6, 9, 11, 10, 10, 11, 15   (32)

BLOW, KURTIS

7-16-88   *Back By Popular Demand*   (PolyGram 870 328-7)   11, 5, 4, 10, 10, 14   (6)

BOOGIE DOWN PRODUCTIONS

5-14-88   *My Philosophy*   (Jive/RCA 1098-7)   15, 15, 12, 12, 12, 13, 13, 15   (8)

8-27-88   *Stop The Violence*   (Jive/RCA 1120-7)   12, 10, 8, 7, 7, 7, 7, 10, 11, 11, 15   (11)

CHECKER, CHUBBY   (*See:* THE FAT BOYS)

THE CLASSICAL TWO

11-12-88   *The Classical Two Is Back*   (Jive/RCA 1153-1)   14, 13, 14   (3)

D.J. JAZZY JEFF AND THE FRESH PRINCE

12-17-88   *Brand New Funk*   (Jive/RCA 1147)   12, 10, 10   (3)

7-30-88   *Nightmare On My Street*   (Jive/RCA 1124-7)   7, 7, 5, 4, 4, 4, 4, 4, 2, 2, 1, 1, 2, 3, 7, 10, 12, 13, 15, 15   (20)

5-14-88   *Parents Just Don't Understand*   (Jive/RCA 1099-7)   2, 3, 3, 2, 3, 2, 2, 1, 2, 3, 6, 13, 13, 13, 15   (15)

DEREK B

9-24-88   *Goodgroove*   (Profile PRO 7214)   14, 13, 10, 6, 5, 7, 9, 12   (8)

E.P.M.D.

8-20-88 *Strictly Business* (Fresh/Sleeping Bag FRE-80123) 8, 6, 5, 6, 6, 5, 4, 4, 2, 1, 1, 1, 3, 3, 9, 12, 12, 13 (18)

5-14-88 *You Gots To Chill* (Fresh/Sleeping Bag FRE-80118) 5, 5, 15, 5, 5, 5, 4, 4, 5, 7, 8, 10, 11, 11, 13, 15 (16)

E.U. (*See:* SALT-N-PEPA)

EAZY-E

7-02-88 *Boys In The Hood* (Ruthless 1004) 13, 12, 8, 9, 11, 14 (6)

9-10-88 *Radio* (Priority/Restless PLS 07258) 14, 12, 11, 12, 12, 11, 10, 13 (8)

ERIC B. AND RAKIM

8-06-88 *Follow The Leader* (Uni/MCA 50003) 4, 2, 2, 2, 2, 3, 5, 6, 6, 11, 13, 15 (12)

FAD, J.J.

10-29-88 *Way Out* (Ruthless/Atl. 7-99285) 5, 4, 5, 8, 11, 14, 14 (7)

THE FAT BOYS WITH CHUBBY CHECKER

8-06-88 *The Twist* (Tin Pan Apple/PolyGram 887 571-7) 5, 7, 7, 11, 14 (5)

FRESH, DOUG E.(, AND THE GET FRESH CREW)

11-19-88 *Cut That Zero* (Reality/Danya/Fantasy 3107) 10, 8, 7, 10, 10, 11, 11 (7)

5-14-88 *Keep Rising To The Top* (Reality/Danya/Fantasy 3101) 7, 9, 9, 10, 10, 3, 4, 2, 1, 1, 2, 1, 8, 14 (14)

HAMMER, M.C.

5-14-88 *Let's Get Started* (Cap. B-44229) 9, 10, 15, 15, 15, (11), 11, 9, 8, 9, 11, 15 (11)

12-24-88 *Pump Me Up* (Cap. 44266) 12, 12 (2)

HEAVY D. AND THE BOYZ

5-14-88   *Don't You Know*   (MCA 53255)   3, 4, 6, 7, 7, 10, 10, 12, 13   (9)

ICE-T

5-14-88   *Colours*   (WB 0-20936)   8, 6, 8, 2, 3, 4, 5, 5, 8, 12, 14, 14   (12)

9-17-88   *I'm Your Pusher*   (Sire/WB 0-21026)   14, 12, 10, 9, 8, 7, 4, 3, 1, 1, 1, 1, 1, 2, 3, 3   (16)

KANE, BIG DADDY

8-27-88   *Ain't No Half-Steppin'*   (Cold Chillin'/WB 7-27834)   14, 12, 10, 9, 8, 8, 5, 4, 3, 6, 5, 8, 14, 15   (14)

KID N' PLAY

12-24-88   *Gittin' Funky*   (Select 62319)   8, 8   (2)

KOOL MOE DEE

7-09-88   *Let's Go*   (Jive/RCA 1056-7)   15, 5, 4, 3, 9, 3, 3, 3, 3, 2, 2, 3, 3, 3, 5, 8, 10, 14, 15   (19)   Titled "No Respect" 7-09/16-88.

5-14-88   *Wild, Wild West*   (Jive/RCA 1086-7)   1, 1, 1, 4, 4, 14, 14, 14   (8)

L.L. COOL J

5-14-88   *Going Back To Cali*   (Def Jam/Col. 38 07679)   14, 14   (2)

M.C. SHY D

8-13-88   *I Wanna Dance*   (Luke Skywalker GR-114)   12, 10, 7, 7, 7, 10, 13, 15, 14, 15   (10)

MARKLE, BIZ

5-14-88   *Vapors*   (Cold Chillin' PRO-5-3088)   11, 11, 8, 9, 9, 9, 9, 6, 6, 4, 3, 6, 12, 15   (14)

PUBLIC ENEMY

7-23-88   *Don't Believe The Hype*   (Def Jam 4-07934)   10, 8, 6, 8, 11, 8, 6, 5, 3, 4, 5, 6, 9, 12, 14   (15)

11-19-88   *Night Of The Living Baseheads*   (Def Jam/Col. 38-08012)   9, 6, 6, 9, 9, 7, 7   (7)

RUN-D.M.C.

10-15-88 *I'm Not Going Out Like That* (Profile PRO-5224) 14, 9, 2, 2, 2, 4, 7, 13, 13, 14 (10)

7-09-88 *Mary, Mary* (Profile PRO-5211) 4, 2, 1, 2, 3, 6, 12, 13, 15, 15, 15 (11)

5-14-88 *Run's House* (Profile PRO-5202) 4, 2, 2, 1, 1, 1, 1, 3, 3, 6, 11, 12 (12)

SALT-N-PEPA

11-05-88 *Get Up Everybody (Get Up)* (Next Plateau 50083) 8, 4, 2, 2, 2, 2, 1, 1, 1 (9)

5-14-88 *Let The Rhythm Run* (Next Plateau) 13, 13, 14, 14, 14, 12, 15 (7)

SALT-N-PEPA FEATURING E.U.

7-23-88 *Shake Your Thang* (Next Plateau KF 319) 9, 5, 1, 1, 1, 1, 1, 1, 1, 1, 1, 2, 3, 4, 8, 10, 11, 15 (18)

THE 7A3

12-03-88 *Coolin' In Cali* (Geffen 7-27695) 9, 7, 8, 15, 15 (5)

5-14-88 *Why* (Geffen 7-20898) 6, 8, 10, 11, 11, 8, 8, 9, 14, 15 (10)

SHINEHEAD

10-01-88 *Chain Gang Rap* (Elektra 0-66741) 14, 13, 12, 13, 15 (5)

SIR MIX-A-LOT

10-22-88 *Posse On Broadway* (Nasty Mix IGU 76974) 14, 12, 13, 13, 7, 5, 4, 4, 4, 6, 6 (11)

SLICK RICK

12-24-88 *Teenage Love* (Def Jam/Col. 38-08105) 13, 13 (2)

STETSASONIC

5-14-88 *Sally* (Tommy Boy TB 912) —, —, 11, 13, 13, 11, 11, 11, 11, 14, 12, 9, 2, 4, 6, 10, 13, 13 (18)

11-05-88   *Talkin' All That Jazz*   (Tommy Boy TB 918)   11, 6, 5, 3, 3, 3, 3, 2, 2   (9)

SWEET TEE

12-03-88   *On The Smooth Tip*   (Profile PRO-7230)   8, 6, 5, 4, 4   (5)

TONE-LOC

11-26-88   *Wild Thing/Loc'ed After Dark*   (Delicious Vinyl DV 102)   12, 11, 8, 6, 5, 5   (6)

TRUE MATHEMATICS

8-20-88   *For The Money*   (Select)   5, 5, 8, 12, 13, 15   (6)

2 LIVE CREW

11-05-88   *Do Wah Diddy*   (Luke Skywalker GR-106)   12, 7, 6, 4, 5, 5, 7, 14, 14   (9)

5-14-88   *Move Somethin'*   (Luke Skywalker GR-112)   12, 12, 13, 8, 8, 7, 6, 7, 7, 10, 13   (11)

YOUNG MC

6-18-88   *I Let 'Em Know*   (Delicious Vinyl DV 004)   15, 12, 10, 9, 9   (5)

F. RAP SINGLES—TITLE INDEX

Get On The Dance Floor (Rob Base and D.J. E-Z Rock)
Get Up Everybody (Get Up) (Salt-N-Pepa)
Gittin' Funky (Kid N' Play)
Going Back To Cali (L.L. Cool J)
Goodgroove (Derek B)

I Let 'Em Know (Young MC)

Keep Rising To The Top (Doug E. Fresh)

Let The Rhythm Run (Salt-N-Pepa)
Let's Get Started (M.C. Hammer)
Let's Go (Kool Moe Dee)
Loc'ed After Dark (*See: Wild Thing . . .*)

Mary, Mary (Run-D.M.C.)
Move Somethin' (2 Live Crew)
My Philosophy (Boogie Down Productions)

Night Of The Living Baseheads (Public Enemy)
Nightmare On My Street (D.J. Jazzy Jeff And The Fresh Prince)
No Respect (*See: Let's Go . . .*)

On The Smooth Tip (Sweet Tee)

Parents Just Don't Understand (D.J. Jazzy Jeff and The Fresh Prince)
Posse On Broadway (Sir Mix-A-Lot)
Pump Me Up (M.C. Hammer)

Radio (Eazy-E)
Run's House (Run-D.M.C.)

Sally (Stetsasonic)
Shake Your Thang (Salt-N-Pepa featuring E.U.)
Stop The Violence (Boogie Down Productions)
Strictly Business (E.P.M.D.)

Talkin' All That Jazz (Stetsasonic)
Teenage Love (Slick Rick)
The Twist (The Fat Boys with Chubby Checker)

Vapors (Biz Markle)

Way Out (J.J. Fad)
Why (7A3)
Wild Thing/Loc'ed After Dark (Tone-Loc)
Wild, Wild West (Kool Moe Dee)

You Gots To Chill (E.P.M.D.)

G. APPENDIXES

[NUMBER 1 RAP SINGLES—A CHRONOLOGICAL LISTING]

1988

5-14— 5-28   *Wild, Wild West*—Kool Moe Dee   (3)
6-04— 6-25   *Run's House*—Run-D.M.C.   (4)

7-02   *Parents Just Don't Understand*—D.J. Jazzy Jeff and The Fresh
                Prince   (1)
7-09— 7-16   *Keep Rising To The Top*—Doug E. Fresh   (2)
7-23   *Mary, Mary*—Run-D.M.C.   (1)
7-30   *Keep Rising To The Top*—Doug E. Fresh   (1; 3)
8-06—10-01   *Shake Your Thang*—Salt-N-Pepa   (9)
10-08—10-15   *Nightmare On My Street*—D.J. Jazzy Jeff and The Fresh
                Prince   (2)
10-22—11-05   *Strictly Business*—E.P.M.D.   (3)
11-12—12-10   *I'm Your Pusher*—Ice-T   (5)
12-17—12-31   *Get Up Everybody (Get Up)*—Salt-N-Pepa   (3)

[RAP SINGLES WITH LONGEST RUN ON CHARTS]

1. *It Takes Two*—Rob Base and D.J. E-Z Rock.....32
2. *Nightmare On My Street*—D.J. Jazzy Jeff and The Fresh Prince.....20
3. *Let's Go*—Kool Moe Dee.....19
4. *Sally*—Stetsasonic.....18
4. *Shake Your Thang*—Salt-N-Pepa featuring E.U.......18
6. *I'm Your Pusher*—Ice-T.....16
6. *You Gots To Chill*—E.P.M.D.......16

TWELVE-INCH SINGLES

A. INTRODUCTION

The twelve-inch single, generally one to three songs per side (often of extended length compared to the 45 r.p.m. format), first appeared on the domestic scene during the height of the disco era in the late 1970s. The medium was developed primarily for use in the dance clubs, where the special hot mixes possible via the widened grooves (and correspondingly shortened time span, usually five to fifteen minutes per side) contained on a standard album-sized disk functioned to heighten the rhythmic possibilities of the material. While these records were best appreciated on the large sound systems of the clubs, the individual collector was encouraged to purchase them so as to acquire the sonic ambience typifying the *Saturday Night Fever* environment. New wave tracks were often released in special extended versions geared to fans striving for completeness of a particular artist's catalog. As an added inducement, many releases were issued on colored vinyl.

The format lost a considerable degree of steam following the widespread backlash against disco music on the part of the general public in the early 1980s. However, it has made a notable comeback during the latter half of this decade, particularly with respect to black contemporary performers. In addition, a substantial wing of the new wave has mutated into electro-funk club music, ranging from the intellectual party sounds of the B-52's and Talking Heads in the States to the gloomier 4AD/Wax Trax! nexus in Europe. Bands such as Depeche Mode and Frankie Goes To Hollywood have released at least one-half dozen versions of their more popular songs (*e.g.*, "Strangelove" and "Relax," respectively). At present, the twelve-inch record represents the only vinyl format which is holding steady against the onslaught of the compact disc and cassette.

Initial chart title/title changes: "Top 30 Disco" (subtitled "compiled from audience response as reported from top disco programming artists")/"Top 40 Disco"; "Dance Top 40 Disco"; "Top 30 12-Inch Singles"; "Top 50 12-Inch Singles"; "Top 75 12-Inch Singles"; "Cash Box Top 12-Inch Dance Singles"

Beginning date/termination date: October 28, 1978/April 5, 1980; reconstituted, January 28, 1984 (as "Top 30 12-Inch Singles")/ December 31, 1988

Initial number of positions/changes in number of positions: 30/40 (May 12, 1979; further title change, January 19, 1980); 30 (January 28, 1984); 50 (September 15, 1984); 75 (March 16, 1985); 50 (October 3, 1987); 30 (July 2, 1988)

B. ARTIST INDEX

ABC

9-07-85   *Be Near Me (Munich And Ecstasy Mix)*   (Mer. 884 052-1)   45, 41, 21, 16, 12, 10, 7, 7, 11, 14, 14, 34, 42, 55, 62, 62, 61, 61   (18)

2-08-86   *How To Be A Zillionaire/Tower Of London (Extended Version)*   (Mer./ PolyGram 884 382-1)   54, 42, 42, 42, 52, 58, 59, 64, 70, 74   (10)

11-07-87   *The Night You Murdered Love*   (Mer./PolyGram 888 864-1)   42, 28, 23, 17, 13, 12, 12, 24, 24, 24, 31, 36, 47, 46, 49   (15)

8-22-87   *When Smokey Sings*   (Mer./PolyGram 888 726-1)   20, 11, 6, 6, 6, 10, 12, 13, 33, 39, 42, 47   (12)

AKB

7-21-79   *Stand Up—Sit Down*   (RSO)   38, 34, 25, 22, 20, 17, 14, 12, 11, 15, 20, 21, 40   (13)

ABBOTT, GREGORY

3-14-87   *(I Got The Feelin') It's Over*   (Col. 44-06710)   38, 35, 35, 34, 34, 39, 46, 46, 44, 64, 72   (11)

10-18-86   *Shake You Down*   (Col. 44-05959)   39, 29, 10, 5, 3, 1, 1, 1, 2, 1, 1, 1, 1, 1, 3, 3, 8, 8, 10, 11, 16, 27, 32, 51, 53, 67, 71   (27)

ABDUL, PAULA

7-23-88　*Knocked Out*　(Virgin 0-96661)　21, 7, 17, 22, 29　(5)

10-29-88　*(It's Just) The Way That You Love Me*　(Virgin 96614)　26, 22, 19, 14, 11, 11, 18, 23　(8)

ABRAMS, COLONEL

3-15-88　*I'm Not Gonna Let* (Extended Version)　(MCA 23612)　33, 20, 15, 9, 6, 6, 9, 12, 14, 15, 23, 30, 40, 54, 62, 68, 70, 75　(18)

7-28-84　*Music Is The Answer* (Dub Mix)　(Streetwise SWRL-2235)　21, 19, 20, 28　(4)

8-15-87　*Sometimes*　(MCA 23763)　63, 52, 22, 16, 16, 16, 21, 32, 44　(9)

10-25-86　*Speculation* (Remix)　(MCA 23670)　—, 46, 37, 29, 23, 23, 23, 30, 36, 52, 52, 52, 62, 66, 66, 73　(16)

8-10-85　*Trapped*　(MCA 23568)　56, 36, 33, 28, 25, 25, 22, 19, 16, 8, 6, 5, 5, 15, 15, 17, 28, 32, 47, 58, 58, 62, 62, 70, 74　(25)

12-14-85　*The Truth* (Extended Version)　(MCA 23600)　63, 55, 55, 47, 47, 44, 44, 55, 64, 66, 74　(11)

ADAMS, BRYAN

6-02-79　*Let Me Take You Dancing*　(A&M)　37, 34, 29, 28, 26, 23, 22, 22, 20, 22, 24, 25, 29, 30　(14)

AFRICAN SUITE

2-23-80　*African Suite* (all cuts)　(MCA)　37, 31, 27, 24, 22, 22, 25　(7)

AFRIKA BAMBAATAA AND JAMES BROWN

9-15-84　*Unity (Parts 1 & 5)*　(Tommy Boy TB 847)　39, 36, 36, 45　(4)

AFRIKA BAMBAATAA AND SOULSONIC FORCE

2-25-84　*Renegades Of Funk*　(Tommy Boy TB 839)　26, 18, 13, 13, 10, 10, 13, 12, 22, 29　(10)

A-HA

2-07-87   *Cry Wolf* (WB 20610-OA)   55, 50, 46, 37, 33, 28, 27, 24, 24, 51, 54, 71, 73   (13)

1-18-86   *The Sun Always Shines On T.V.* (Extended Version) (WB 0-20410)   45, 32, 20, 12, 12, 12, 14, 11, 11, 21, 43, 63, 72   (13)

ALE

10-22-88   *I Wanna Know* (Vendetta VE-7003)   15, 8, 4, 6, 6, 5, 7, 7, 7, 15, 15   (11)

ALEEM FEATURING LEROY BURGESS

3-29-86   *Love's On Fire* (Extended Version) (Atl. DMD 924)   65, 48, 40, 35, 31, 28, 28, 40, 58, 62, 73, 74   (12)

ALISHA

3-24-84   *All Night Passion* (Vanguard SPV 72-A)   22, 22, 25, 25, 20, 19, 17, 20, 24, 29   (10)

11-02-85   *Baby Talk (Special Remix)* (Vanguard SPV 89)   50, 37, 32, 22, 10, 5, 1, 2, 2, 9, 9, 18, 20, 26, 35, 43, 48, 54, 69, 74   (20)

7-11-87   *Into My Secret* (RCA 6432-1-RD)   58, 53, 47, 47, 37, 36, 40, 61, 73   (9)

1-30-88   *Let Your Heart Make Up Your Mind* (RCA 6821-1-RD)   46, 36, 36, 36, 33, 47   (6)

6-29-85   *Too Turned On* (Extended And Dub Version) (Vanguard SPV 82)   55, 45, 28, 18, 13, 8, 8, 8, 8, 9, 15, 17, 17, 23, 32, 34, 44, 54, 58, 63, 69, 74   (22)

ALLEN, DONNA

12-27-86   *Serious* (Remix) (21/Atco 0-96794)   61, 61, 61, 48, 43, 43, 32, 23, 16, 9, 11, 8, 8, 10, 14, 12, 9, 8, 7, 7, 12, 12, 21, 22, 50, 63, 63, 65, 69   (29)

ALLEN, SCOTT

1-05-80   *I Think We're Alone Now/Will You Love Me Tomorrow* (TK)   39, 39, 35, 29, 24, 22, 19, 19, 23, 25, 36, 40   (12)

ALLENTINI, GEORGIO

2-28-87 *Sexappeal* (Picture Perfect/Macola PPR-3563)   44, 36, 26, 23, 23, 43, 57, 57, 61, 61   (10)

ALMOND, MARC

12-17-88 *Tears Run Rings* (Cap. V-15418)   27, 25, 25   (3)

ALPERT, HERB

5-16-87 *Diamonds* (A&M SP-12231)   44, 41, 36, 33, 18, 4, 4, 2, 1, 2, 10, 10, 16, 28, 31, 47, 58, 66, 66, 68   (20)

3-07-87 *Keep Your Eye On Me* (A&M SP-1226)   34, 11, 9, 6, 4, 4, 4, 4, 4, 20, 28, 36, 43, 60, 69, 73   (16)

8-25-85 *Rise* (A&M)   37, 35, 32, 27, 27, 28, 35   (7)

ALPHAVILLE

12-01-84 *Big In Japan* (Atl. 0-86947)   35, 31, 27, 24, 24, 24, 23, 41, 46, 47, 46, 46, 47, 49, 49, 63, 70, 75, 75   (19)

7-19-86 *Dance With Me* (Atl. 0-86806)   62, 56, 49, 37, 37, 56, 65, 75   (8)

AMANT

12-02-78 *If There's Love* (TK)   26, 22, 19, 18, 18, 18, 17, 16, 19, 19, 23, 30   (12)

AMORETTO

5-09-87 *Clave Rocks* (Easy Street PKO-003)   55, 53, 54, 61, 61, 62, 62, 62, 68, 72   (10)

ANGELA

6-22-85 *All Hung Up* (Dub Version) (Sutra SUD 030)   58, 53, 47, 43, 39, 39, 43, 54, 56, 61, 68, 73   (12)

ANIMOTION

3-15-86 *I Engineer* (Remix Version) (Casa./PolyGram 884 433-1)   57, 41, 34, 34, 38, 43, 41, 49, 50, 70   (10)

3-09-85   *Obsession* (Special Dub & Dance Remix)   (Mer. 880 266-1)   35, 32, 25, 11, 8, 7, 6, 9, 11, 16, 18, 25, 25, 33, 33, 62, 75, 75   (18)

ANN-MARGRET

11-10-79   *Love Rush*   (Ocean)   35, 30, 23, 15, 12, 9, 9, 9, 13, 13, 14, 33, 40   (13)

3-29-80   *Midnight Message*   (MCA)   35, 29   (2)

ANNA

6-20-87   *Shy Boys*   (Parc/CBS 4Z9-06771)   55, 55, 54, 28, 15, 14, 14, 24, 30, 36, 50, 69, 72, 72   (14)

ANTHONY AND THE CAMP

5-07-88   *Suspense/Open Up Your Heart*   (Jellybean/WB 0-20817)   40, 33, 31, 31, 40, 43, 50   (7)

4-26-86   *What I Like* (Extended Dance Mix)   (WB 0-20449)   57, 45, 40, 35, 32, 26, 22, 19, 17, 15, 15, 19, 22, 35, 40, 55, 65   (17)

APOLLONIA 6

12-15-84   *Sex Shooter*   (WB 20274)   32, 30, 30, 30, 26, 26, 31, 37, 47, 48   (10)

ARCADIA   *(See also:* DURAN DURAN)

11-16-85   *Election Day* (Extended Mix)   (Cap. V-5501)   41, 26, 23, 21, 19, 19, 19, 28, 28, 31, 46, 60, 67, 70   (14)

ARMANDO('S), DON, 2ND AVENUE RHUMBA BAND

10-13-79   *Deputy Of Love*   (ZE ZEA 12-003)   36, 33, 24, 17, 10, 7, 5, 2, 2, 1, 2, 2, 4, 4, 5, 8, 15, 30, 34, 39   (20)

ARPEGGIO

12-23-78   *Let The Music Play*   (Polydor)   27, 22, 22, 16, 5, 5, 7, 7, 7, 7, 7, 11, 13, 14, 23   (15)

ARRINGTON, STEVE

8-03-85   *Dancin' In The Key Of Life* (Special Remix & Instrumental)   (Atl.
0-86874)   54, 29, 22, 22, 35, 53, 59, 62, 65, 73   (10)

5-04-85   *Feel So Real* (Instrumental & Extended Version)   (Atl. 0-86904)   47,
20, 20, 31, 46, 49, 50, 68, 67, 72   (10)

8-02-86   *Homeboy* (Remix)   (Atl. DMD 949)   58, 48, 44, 44, 56, 65, 73,
75   (8)

THE ART OF NOISE

2-11-84   *Beat Box*   (Island 0-96974)   25, 20, 15, 11, 10, 10, 4, 6, 8, 6, 5, 9,
10, 10, 12, 21, 24, 27, 30   (18)

1-04-86   *Legs* (Extended Version)   (Chrysalis 4V9-42934)   60, 60, 53, 53, 57,
65, 65, 63, 62, 66, 68, 71, 72   (13)

1-18-86   *Moments In Love* (Extended Version)   (Island/ZTT 794)   50, 26, 15,
13, 13, 13, 15, 16, 18, 19, 27, 46, 55, 71   (14)

THE ART OF NOISE FEATURING DUANE EDDY

5-17-86   *Peter Gunn* (Remix)   (Chrysalis 4V9-42992)   47, 35, 29, 25, 22, 22,
24, 31, 35, 51, 62   (11)

THE ART OF NOISE WITH MAX HEADROOM

8-16-86   *Paranoimia* (Remix)   (Chrysalis 4V9-43010)   57, 48, 31, 31, 35, 43,
42, 40, 38, 36, 34, 51, 55, 62, 69   (15)

ARTISTS UNITED AGAINST APARTHEID

12-21-85   *Sun City*   (Manhattan/Cap. 50017)   57, 57, 52, 52, 52, 57, 64, 66,
68   (9)

ASHFORD AND SIMPSON

9-27-86   *Count Your Blessings* (Long Version)   (Cap. V-15243)   63, 52, 52, 53,
63, 63, 65, 69, 75   (9)

7-14-79   *Found A Cure*   (WB)   38, 29, 25, 12, 10, 8, 6, 5, 2, 1, 2, 2, 4, 8, 13,
15, 30   (17)

2-23-85   *Outta The World* (Dub Version & LP Version)   (Cap. V-8623)   36, 24, 21, 19, 19, 30, 38, 45, 48, 59, 73   (11)

10-27-84   *Solid*   (Cap. V-8612)   31, 26, 22, 19, 14, 10, 9, 6, 5, 5, 5, 5, 5, 5, 9, 11, 17, 20, 25, 41, 61, 74   (22)

ASTLEY, RICK

10-01-88   *It Would Take A Strong Man*   (RCA 8696-1-RD)   20, 10, 10, 13, 23   (5)

12-05-87   *Never Gonna Give You Up*   (RCA 6784-1-RD)   40, 23, 17, 12, 12, 12, 4, 1, 1, 1, 1, 2, 2, 3, 10, 22, 23, 28, 44, 47   (20)

4-30-88   *Together Forever*   (RCA 8320-1-RD)   30, 27, 9, 7, 6, 4, 3, 4, 4, 4, 13, 25   (12)

ATLANTIC STARR

5-23-87   *Always*   (WB 0-20660)   43, 33, 30, 22, 21, 21, 21, 32, 45, 46, 46, 60, 68, 75   (14)

5-25-85   *Freak-A-Ristic* (Dub & Special Dance Mix)   (A&M SP-12126)   53, 47, 41, 32, 32, 32, 32, 33, 52, 66, 67, 68   (12)

10-05-85   *Silver Shadow* (Extended Version)   (A&M SP-12148)   50, 39, 34, 30, 30, 43, 57, 69, 72, 74, 75   (11)

AUSTIN, PATTI

5-10-86   *The Heat Of Heat*   (Qwest/WB 0-20462)   —, 29, 20, 17, 12, 12, 18, 20, 21, 25, 34, 45, 61, 68   (14)

10-26-85   *Honey For The Bees* (Extended Version)   (Qwest/WB 0-20361)   60, 46, 27, 23, 23, 25, 28, 30, 37, 37, 44, 44, 49, 60, 66, 71, 72   (17)

6-23-84   *Rhythm Of The Street/It's Gonna Be Special*   (Qwest QW 0-20222)   21, 19, 27, 28, 22, 20, 28   (7)

9-01-84   *Shoot The Moon/Rhythm Of The Street* (Dance Remix)   (Qwest QW 0-20235)   23, 21, 20, 50   (4)

AYERS, ROY

2-23-80   *Don't Stop The Feeling*   (Polydor)   38, 33, 33, 40   (4)

3-01-86   *Hot* (Remix)   (Col. 44-05330)   63, 49, 45, 38, 33, 33, 47, 58, 67, 73   (10)

THE B-52'S

2-16-80   *The B-52's* (all cuts)   (WB)   38, 32, 26, 26, 33, 34   (6)

8-30-86   *The Summer Of Love* (Remix)   (WB 0-20509)   —, 21, 16, 11, 9, 9, 17, 19, 30, 43, 54, 65, 71   (13)

BB&Q

9-20-86   *(I'm A) Dreamer*   (Pretty Pearl/Elektra ED 5160)   48, 43, 38, 35, 33, 33, 52, 64, 68, 74   (10)

BABYFACE

8-29-87   *I Love You Babe*   (Solar/Cap. V-71156)   58, 33, 29, 29, 24, 20, 17, 17, 23, 32, 38, 43, 47   (13)

THE BAD BOYS FEATURING K LOVE

7-20-85   *Bad Boys* (Vocal & Dub Mix)   (Starlite D-240)   54, 42, 28, 10, 5, 5, 3, 2, 2, 4, 9, 18, 27, 30, 41, 51, 56, 73   (18)

BAILEY, PHILIP   *(See also:* EARTH, WIND AND FIRE)

5-03-86   *State Of The Heart* (Dub Mix)   (Col. 44-05372)   53, 45, 41, 41, 44, 57, 63, 68, 75   (9)

BAILEY, PHILIP, AND PHIL COLLINS   *(See also:* PHIL COLLINS)

2-09-85   *Easy Lover/Woman*   (Col. 44-05160)   33, 19, 8, 4, 2, 1, 1, 4, 4, 14, 16, 22, 27, 62, 68, 74   (16)

BAKER, ANITA

4-15-87   *Same Ole Love* (365 Days A Year)   (Elektra ED 5224)   51, 47, 47, 65, 67, 74, 74   (7)

BAKER, ARTHUR

8-25-84   *Breaker's Revenge*   (Atl. DMD 768)   17, 14, 12, 17, 49   (5)

BALTIMORA

11-16-85 *Tarzan Boy* (Extended Dance Version) (Manhattan V-56011)   60, 49, 40, 36, 32, 32, 32, 37, 37, 33, 28, 28, 31, 34, 38, 47, 55, 65, 70   (19)

BANANARAMA

9-15-84 *Cruel Summer* (London 81029-1)   36, 32, 28, 25, 21, 18, 27, 39, 49   (9)

12-19-87 *I Can't Help It* (London/PolyGram 886 121-1)   39, 28, 28, 28, 21, 20, 21, 37, 39, 48   (10)

8-22-87 *I Heard A Rumour* (London/PolyGram 886 188-1)   54, 29, 21, 20, 20, 16, 11, 7, 7, 15, 30, 45, 50   (13)

4-30-88 *Love In The First Degree* (London/PolyGram 886 262-1)   41, 33, 24, 24, 37, 45   (6)

7-12-86 *Venus* (Extended Version) (London/PolyGram 886 056-1)   50, 25, 9, 3, 3, 3, 3, 3, 11, 11, 12, 16, 16, 16, 18, 18, 32, 42, 44, 49, 62, 62, 67, 73   (24)

BAND AID

1-19-85 *Do They Know It's Christmas/Feed The World* (Col. 44-05157)   31, 28, 28, 44   (4)

BAND OF GOLD

10-27-84 *Love Songs Are Back Again* (RCA JW-13867)   38, 34, 31, 31, 39, 39, 37, 36, 49, 49, 49   (11)

BANG ORCHESTRA!

9-13-86 *Sample That!* (Geffen/WB 0-20510)   52, 45, 41, 39, 61, 66, 73, 71, 75   (9)

THE BANGLES

1-16-88 *Hazy Shade Of Winter* (Def Jam/Col. 44-07540)   30, 26, 24, 21, 12, 13, 30, 50   (8)

1-24-87 *Walk Like An Egyptian* (Remix) (Col. 44-05935) 55, 55, 54, 61, 67, 74 (6)

BARDEUX

3-05-88 *Magic Carpet Ride* (Synthicide 71302-0) 21, 15, 3, 4, 11, 20, 35, 36, 49 (9)

7-18-87 *Three Time Lover* (Synthicide 71300-0) 51, 45, 45, 39, 39, 42, 63 (7)

5-28-88 *When We Kiss* (Synthicide/Restless 71306-0) 41, 35, 34, 22, 18, 15, 9, 9, 25, 30 (10)

THE BAR-KAYS

10-13-84 *Sexomatic* (Vocal & Dub) (Mer. 880 255-1) 32, 28, 23, 19, 16, 15, 12, 11, 11, 22, 39, 39, 39, 45, 48, 48, 50 (17)

BARRIER, ERIC

10-04-86 *Eric B. Is President* (Zakia 014) 44, 32, 23, 17, 9, 8, 8, 10, 10, 13, 16, 24, 24, 24, 28, 44, 44, 45, 46, 54, 65 (21)

BARRY, CLAUDIA

4-21-79 *Boogie Woogie Dancin' Shoes* (Chrysalis) 28, 22, 16, 13, 11, 9, 5, 4, 4, 4, 4, 11, 24, 28, 35 (15)

4-25-87 *Can't You Feel My Heart Beat* (Epic 49-06718) 58, 52, 46, 43, 40, 37, 51, 64, 70, 70, 75 (11)

8-23-86 *Down And Counting* (Epic 49-05926) 43, 19, 12, 8, 6, 6, 11, 13, 15, 16, 30, 44, 55, 65, 69, 69, 75 (16)

1-23-88 *Hot To The Touch* (Epic 49-07496) 35, 25, 20, 16, 16, 31, 49 (7)

8-22-87 *Secret Affair* (Epic 49-06837) 60, 27, 19, 19, 19, 9, 6, 5, 3, 17, 23, 31, 46, 50 (14)

BASE, ROB, AND D.J. E-Z ROCK

8-06-88 *It Takes Two* (Profile PRO-7186) 30, 30 (2)

THE BASEMENT BOYS

5-14-88   *Love Don't Love No More*   (Jump Street JS-1014)   38, 36, 43, 47   (4)

BASIL, TONI

1-28-84   *Over My Head*   (Chrysalis 4V9-42754)   22, 19, 26, 27, 30   (5)

THE BEASTIE BOYS

4-19-86   *Hold It, Now Hit It*   (Def Jam/Col. 44-05369)   57, 50, 46, 32, 25, 22, 19, 19, 23, 24, 25, 26, 28, 46, 59, 69, 74   (17)

11-01-86   *It's The New Style/Paul Revere*   (Def Jam/Col. 44-05958)   62, 29, 24, 13, 8, 8, 6, 3, 3, 3, 3, 3, 6, 6, 6, 13, 13, 20, 21, 53, 60, 66, 74   (23)

BEE, CELI

12-22-79   *Blow My Mind*   (TK)   33, 33, 27, 27, 24, 22, 38   (7)

2-03-79   *Fly Me On The Wings Of Love*   (APA)   29, 27, 26, 25, 25, 24, 24   (7)

BELOUIS SOME

10-12-85   *Some People* (Extended Version)   (Cap. V-8649)   54, 48, 42, 38, 38, 55, 72   (7)

BENATAR, PAT

8-31-85   *Invincible* (Remix & Instrumental)   (Chrysalis 4V9-42878)   55, 49, 45, 41, 41, 46, 58, 63, 69, 72   (10)

1-28-84   *Love Is A Battlefield*   (Chrysalis 4V9-42734)   27, 30, 29   (3)

BERLIN

4-14-84   *No More Words*   (Geffen 0-20195)   23, 24, 18, 20, 23, 20, 19, 22, 30   (9)

BEVERLY HILLS VERSION

4-13-85   *Axel F/Like Eddie Did*   (Club CL-101)   60, 54, 42, 37, 32, 24, 24, 37, 35, 42, 49, 69   (12)

BIG PIG

4-02-88 *Breakaway* (A&M SP-12259) 30, 28, 18, 13, 7, 7, 20, 25, 36, 43,
48, 49 (12)

BILLIE

7-12-86 *Ain't Nobody's Business* (Fleetwood FW 008) 57, 36, 32, 27, 27, 30,
29, 33, 49, 60, 68, 74 (12)

BILLY, TERRY

1-30-88 *Don't Lock Me Out* (Atl. 0-86623) 48, 35, 29, 26, 20, 19, 14, 13, 21,
38, 39, 43, 49 (13)

BIONIC BOOGIE

11-11-78 *Chains/Cream Always Rises* (Polydor) 25, 16, 11, 7, 7, 10, 11, 11,
11, 9, 8, 8, 12, 15, 19, 26, 27 (17)

BLACK BRITAIN

9-05-87 *Funky Nassau* (Virgin/Atl. 0-96776) 49, 36, 36, 28, 28, 32,
46 (7)

BLONDIE (*See also:* DEBBIE HARRY)

3-08-80 *Call Me* (Polydor) 34, 18, 10, 6, 4 (5)

BLOUNT, TERRY (*See:* LOUISE FREEMAN)

BLOW, KURTIS

9-15-84 *8 Million Stories* (Mer. 880 170-1) 26, 23, 21, 17, 17, 33, 45, 48,
44, 46, 50 (11)

10-04-86 *I'm Chillin'* (PolyGram) 64, 58, 50, 44, 37, 34, 31, 31, 35, 35, 57,
68, 72, 72, 72 (15)

12-07-85 *If I Ruled The World* (Extended Version) (Mer. 884 269-1) 51, 40,
36, 36, 30, 30, 30, 39, 47, 58, 60, 70 (12)

BLOW, KURTIS, AND RALPH MacDONALD

1-12-85   *Basketball/(It's) The Game*   (Polydor 881 529-1)   40, 36, 34, 38, 41, 50   (6)

BLUE MERCEDES

2-13-88   *I Want To Be Your Property*   (MCA 23817)   34, 31, 24, 14, 9, 7, 6, 13, 15, 29, 38, 43, 50   (13)

BLUE MODERNE

4-09-88   *No Use To Borrow*   (23 West/Atl. 0-86644)   41, 33, 32, 42, 49   (5)

BOB-A-RELA

6-02-79   *Spend The Night*   (Channel)   35, 28, 24, 22, 22, 19, 18, 21, 26   (9)

BOMB THE BASS

7-23-88   *Beat Dis*   (4'th & B'way/Island 462)   29, 25, 25   (3)

THE BOMBERS

2-10-79   *(Everybody) Get Dancin'*   (West End)   30, 24, 14, 9, 6, 5, 4, 4, 3, 3, 4, 13, 23, 25, 29, 40   (16)

THE BOOGIE BOYS

6-15-85   *City Life/Fly Girl* (Extended Version)   (Cap. V-8645)   57, 52, 44, 34, 29, 24, 14, 10, 6, 4, 1, 1, 3, 5, 7, 7, 8, 17, 23, 27, 35, 47, 64, 73   (24)

6-28-86   *Girl Talk* (Long Distance Version)   (Cap. V-15230)   60, 54, 49, 45, 40, 34, 30, 27, 24, 22, 22, 26, 38, 50, 66, 71   (16)

10-19-85   *You Ain't Fresh (Morning Dew Mix)*   (Cap. V-15207)   51, 40, 36, 33, 33, 44, 58, 64, 67, 70, 70, 74, 74   (13)

BOOK OF LOVE

3-09-85   *Boy/Book Of Love* (Extended & Dub Version)   (WB 20299)   39, 35, 28, 27, 27, 39, 45, 45, 59, 63, 62, 67   (12)

7-23-88 *Pretty Boys And Pretty Girls* (Sire/WB 0-20963) 24, 16, 15, 16, 25, 26, 26, 25, 26, 26 (10)

BOOM, TAKA

6-02-79 *Night Dancin'* (Ariola) 39, 36, 33, 31, 29, 28, 31, 37, 39 (9)

BOW, MICHAEL

9-17-88 *Love And Devotion* (Vendetta VE-7001) 27, 24, 18, 14, 14, 25 (6)

BOWIE, DAVID

4-19-86 *Absolute Beginners* (EMI America V-19205) 59, 53, 48, 48, 66, 68 (6)

10-06-84 *Dancing With The Big Boys* (Dance & Dub Mix)/Blue Jean (EMI America V-7838-1) 23, 18, 13, 11, 10, 12, 21, 27, 40, 44 (10)

4-25-87 *Day-In Day-Out* (EMI America V-19234) 56, 53, 48, 45, 45, 63, 63, 68, 68, 68, 74 (11)

8-02-86 *Underground* (Remix) (EMI America V-19210) 62, 56, 56, 71 (4)

BOWIE, DAVID, AND MICK JAGGER

9-21-85 *Dancing In The Street* (Extended Dance Mix & Dub) (EMI America V-19200) 16, 11, 9, 9, 20, 23, 34, 46, 61 (9)

BOY GEORGE *(See also:* CULTURE CLUB)

1-30-88 *Live My Life* (Virgin 0-96728) 42, 27, 23, 18, 12, 9, 8, 24, 39, 48 (10)

BOYER, BONNIE

8-25-85 *Got To Give In To Love* (Col.) 39, 36, 34, 32 (4)

BOYS DON'T CRY

6-07-86 *I Wanna Be A Cowboy* (Profile PRO-7084) 27, 21, 15, 13, 11, 11, 16, 29, 39, 53, 64, 70 (12)

THE BOYZ

12-10-88   *Dial My Heart*   (Motown MOT-4621)   29, 18, 12, 12   (4)

BRAINSTORM

5-12-79   *Hot For You*   (Tabu)   35, 32, 31, 38   (4)

BRANIGAN, LAURA

9-15-84   *The Lucky One*   (Atl. DMD 779)   35, 30, 29, 29, 27, 29, 43   (7)

5-19-84   *Self Control*   (Atl. 0-86954)   23, 8, 21, 21, 10, 6, 3, 4, 5, 4, 10, 11, 14, 27, 29   (15)

8-29-87   *Shattered Glass*   (Atl. 0-86675)   23, 14, 14, 14, 23, 37, 46   (7)

BRASS CONSTRUCTION

9-15-84   *Partyline* (Party Mix & Dub)   (Cap. V-8608)   42, 39, 38, 37, 43   (5)

THE BRAT PACK

11-12-88   *So Many Ways (Dot It Properly, Part II)*   (Vendetta VE-7008)   29, 25, 16, 18, 25, 24, 24, 24   (8)

BRAXTON, DHAR

5-10-86   *Jump Back (Set Me Free)*   (Sleeping Bag SLX-19)   51, 39, 18, 11, 10, 10, 10, 14, 13, 13, 10, 10, 12, 13, 20, 20, 25, 36, 46, 53, 62, 71   (22)

BREAK MACHINE

5-05-84   *Street Dance*   (Sire 0-20189)   21, 18, 14, 10, 9, 12, 13, 14, 15, 21, 30   (11)

THE BREAKFAST CLUB

10-31-87   *Never Be The Same*   (MCA 23797)   38, 30, 23, 17, 14, 9, 9, 20, 21, 21, 21, 32, 34, 44, 48   (15)

3-21-87   *Right On Track*   (MCA 23684)   28, 26, 23, 17, 12, 10, 9, 6, 4, 6, 6, 6, 5, 3, 3, 4, 7, 26, 32, 32, 35, 50, 56, 59, 71, 74, 74   (27)

BRIDGES, ALICIA

10-28-78   *I Love The Night Life*   (Polydor)   3, 2, 2, 2, 3, 4, 4, 8, 19, 27, 27   (11)

THE BRONSKI BEAT

7-05-86   *C'mon C'mon* (Remix)   (MCA 23630)   56, 44, 44, 55, 67, 70, 74   (7)

3-15-86   *Hit That Perfect Beat*   (MCA 23605)   60, 50, 28, 22, 18, 18, 20, 22, 31, 37, 62, 68, 67, 66, 75   (15)

12-15-84   *Smalltown Boy*   (London 23521)   39, 33, 33, 33, 29, 24, 21, 16, 14, 17, 17, 15, 16, 35, 61, 59, 63, 67, 69   (20)

4-20-85   *Why?/Cadillac Car* (Extended Version)   (London 23538)   47, 37, 26, 26, 40, 50, 61, 64, 65   (9)

BROOKS, PATTIE

10-28-78   *Our Ms. Brooks* (all cuts)   (Casa.)   21, 19, 17, 14, 17, 29   (6)

THE BROTHERS JOHNSON

3-08-80   *Stomp!*   (A&M)   24, 12, 6, 4, 3   (5)

7-28-84   *You Keep Me Coming Back* (Dub Version)   (A&M SP-12102)   23, 20, 16, 13, 16, 30   (6)

BROWN, BOBBY   (*See also:* THE NEW EDITION)

7-16-88   *Don't Be Cruel*   (MCA 23861)   26, 13, 8, 9, 3, 3, 5, 6, 9, 10, 11, 19, 29   (12)

11-29-86   *Girlfriend*   (MCA 23643)   51, 43, 39, 31, 25, 25, 25, 20, 16, 16, 12, 11, 11, 18, 20, 58, 64, 69, 70   (19)

10-08-88   *My Prerogative*   (MCA 23888)   21, 13, 8, 5, 3, 2, 2, 4, 8, 15, 21, 21   (13)

BROWN, JAMES

10-25-86   *Gravity*   (Scotti Bros. 4Z9-0543)   58, 47, 33, 30, 26, 26, 26, 27, 27, 41, 41, 41, 57, 62, 62, 65, 68, 75   (18)

6-11-88   *I'm Real*   (Scotti Bros./E.P.A.   4Z9-07805)   36, 30, 25, 20, 16, 15   (6)

5-31-86   *Living In America*   (R&B Dance Version)   (Scotti Bros./CBS 4Z9-0531)   75   (1)

BROWN, JOCELYN

3-07-87   *Ego Maniac*   (WB 9 20469-0)   52, 46, 43, 39, 31, 27, 25, 24, 35, 41, 62, 66, 73, 75   (14)

9-15-84   *I Wish You Would*   (Vinyl Dream VND-D03)   31, 26, 23, 20, 16, 14, 17, 20, 24, 44   (10)

12-07-85   *Love's Gonna Get You* (Dance Mix)   (WB 0-20383)   53, 38, 26, 26, 14, 14, 10, 10, 12, 9, 9, 10, 11, 24, 30, 33, 52, 65, 71   (19)

4-28-84   *Somebody Else's Guy*   (Vinyl Dream VND-D01)   20, 11, 5, 3, 2, 2, 1, 1, 1, 1, 1, 3, 3, 3, 3, 6, 8, 12, 24, 29, 30, 47   (22)

BROWN, O'CHI

4-12-86   *Whenever You Need Somebody* (Pull It Off Mix)   (Mer./PolyGram 884 572-1)   58, 40, 32, 27, 24, 21, 21, 27, 34, 46, 56, 67, 72   (13)

BROWN, PETER

6-09-79   *Crank It Up (Funk Town)*   (Drive)   40, 28, 21, 12, 5, 4, 4, 4, 10, 11, 14, 15, 18, 24, 39   (15)

11-03-84   *Love Is Just (The Game)*   (Col. 44-5102)   33, 27, 25, 23, 22, 29, 45, 46, 46, 46, 47, 50, 50   (13)

3-31-84   *They Only Come Out At Night*   (Col. 44-04957)   13, 16, 18, 17, 16, 13, 16, 19, 23, 30   (10)

3-30-85   *Zie Zie Won't Dance* (Dub & Remix)   (Col. 44-05175)   55, 50, 49, 53, 52, 53, 53, 58, 59, 67, 71, 72, 74, 72, 74, 74   (16)

BROWN, SHAWN

4-27-85   *Rappin' Duke* (Vocal & Instrumental Version)   (JWP 1456)   60, 51, 45, 40, 21, 18, 15, 12, 12, 17, 18, 19, 22, 24, 27, 46, 54, 62, 68, 71, 72, 72   (22)

BRUNSON, TYRONE

3-24-84   *Fresh* (Scratch Mix)   (B.I.A.D. 4Z9-04951)   28, 24, 24, 21, 15, 27   (6)

BURTON, JENNY

2-23-85   *Bad Habits/Let's Get Back To Love* (Long Version & LP Version)   (Atl. 0-86909)   37, 21, 19, 17, 14, 10, 10, 11, 20, 25, 25, 41, 41, 55, 66   (15)

1-28-84   *Remember What You Like*   (Atl. DMD 686)   18, 18, 15, 16, 11, 13, 16, 19, 26   (9)

BUSH, KATE

10-05-85   *Running Up That Hill* (Extended Version)   (EMI America V-7865)   53, 41, 36, 31, 31, 41, 42, 59, 66, 68, 72, 71, 71, 69, 69, 72, 72   (17)

C-BANK (FEATURING DIAMOND GIRL)

1-04-86   *Good To The Last Drop*   (Next Plateau NP 50035)   51, 51, 47, 43, 35, 28, 28, 34, 40, 44, 55, 60, 73   (14)

1-24-87   *I Won't Stop Loving You*   (Next Plateau NP 50047)   57, 57, 56, 49, 24, 15, 12, 15, 20, 22, 22, 43, 49, 63, 65, 74   (16)

8-23-86   *Nightmare Of A Broken Heart*   (Next Plateau NP 50045)   52, 36, 28, 25, 23, 23, 25, 32, 45, 68, 73   (11)

CAMEO

7-27-85   *Attack Me With Your Love* (Extended Version)   (Atlanta Artists 880 744-1)   56, 48, 42, 26, 26, 33, 39, 55, 64, 70   (10)

4-25-87   *Back And Forth*   (Atlanta Artists/PolyGram 888 385-1)   42, 34, 25, 21, 13, 10, 8, 11, 13, 13, 18, 31, 44, 44, 44, 59, 62, 68   (18)

1-17-87   *Candy*   (Atlanta Artists/PolyGram 888 193-1)   51, 26, 26, 13, 7, 6, 5, 7, 6, 5, 7, 7, 9, 10, 37, 42, 70   (17)

4-07-84   *She's Strange*   (Atlanta Artists 818 384-1)   12, 8, 2, 2, 7, 7, 16, 26, 28   (9)

9-14-85   *Single Life* (Extended Version)   (Atlanta Artists 884 010-1)   48, 36, 27, 23, 21, 10, 9, 9, 9, 11, 20, 32, 44, 48, 59, 59, 64, 64   (18)

8-30-86   *Word Up*   (Atlanta Artists/PolyGram 884 933-1)   —, 39, 27, 18, 8, 3, 2, 1, 1, 1, 1, 1, 2, 3, 3, 3, 5, 7, 7, 7, 7, 12, 12, 17, 19, 22, 30, 46, 61, 75   (30)

11-19-88   *You Make Me Work*   (Atlanta Artists/PolyGram 870 587-1)   30, 22, 14, 12, 12, 20, 20   (7)

CAMOUFLAGE

11-19-88   *The Great Commandment*   (Atl. 0-86530)   29, 18, 16, 16, 16, 11, 11   (7)

CANDIDO

7-07-79   *Jingo/Dancin' And Prancin'*   (Salsoul)   37, 33, 30, 29, 36, 40   (6)

CARA, IRENE

4-21-84   *Breakdance* (Extended Remix)   (Geffen 0-20196)   19, 13, 8, 11, 11, 20, 19, 23, 26   (9)

CARESS

9-29-79   *Catch The Rhythm*   (WB)   39, 33, 31, 40   (4)

CARLISLE, BELINDA

12-12-87   *Heaven Is A Place On Earth*   (MCA 23808)   38, 29, 26, 26, 26, 23, 37, 41, 49   (9)

6-21-86   *Mad About You* (Extended Version)   (I.R.S./MCA 23629)   60, 54, 49, 45, 41, 41, 43, 58, 58, 50, 50, 60, 64, 72   (14)

CARNE, JEAN

7-26-86   *Closer Than Close*   (Omni/Atl. 0-96816)   44, 32, 16, 16, 16, 16, 20, 23, 34, 40, 65, 69, 72   (13)

CARNES, KIM

6-01-85   *Crazy In The Night (Barking At Airplanes)* (Dance Mix)/Barking At Airplanes, Part II (Dub Mix)   (EMI America V-7857)   49, 43, 39, 36, 36, 62, 69, 69, 67, 72   (10)

CASH FLOW

3-29-86   *Party Freak* (Extended Version)   (Mer./PolyGram 884 454-1)   47, 37, 33, 29, 26, 26, 33, 38, 50   (9)

CEEJAY

6-04-88   *A Little Love*   (Next Plateau NP 50074)   32, 24, 22, 13, 13, 23, 27, 30   (8)

CERRONE

11-04-78   *Cerrone IV*   (Cot.)   28, 19, 11, 6, 3, 3, 3, 5, 7, 7, 7, 22, 27   (13)

CHAMPAIGN

10-13-84   *Off And On Love* (Dance Remix)   (Col. 44-05090)   38, 35, 33, 31, 29, 28, 36, 47, 41, 43, 45, 45, 45, 49   (14)

CHANDLER, GENE

11-25-78   *Get Down*   (20th. C.)   30, 28, 26, 26, 29   (5)

4-05-80   *A Lover's Holiday*   (WB)   34   (1)

9-15-79   *When You're #1*   (20th C.)   37, 34, 31, 26, 26, 39   (6)

CHANSON

10-28-78   *Don't Hold Back*   (Ariola)   30   (1)

5-05-79   *I Can Tell*   (Ariola)   27, 22, 21, 20, 20, 21, 27, 32   (8)

CHARLES, ELAINE

6-06-87   *Lay It On The Line*   (Atl. ADI-9539)   54, 47, 47, 47, 59, 63, 70, 74, 74   (9)

CHARLES, KELLY

10-17-87   *You're No Good*   (Next Plateau NP 50066)   42, 33, 25, 25, 45, 49   (6)

CHER

3-03-79   *Take Me Home* (Casa.)   28, 26, 23, 16, 12, 7, 5, 3, 3, 3, 4, 7, 12, 13, 16, 22, 35 (17)

CHERRELLE

7-05-86   *Artificial Heart* (Tabu/CBS 4Z9-05385)   —, 42, 29, 23, 21, 21, 29, 45, 58 (9)

9-15-84   *Fragile . . . Handle With Care* (Tabu 4Z9-05069)   44, 38, 37, 42, 48 (5)

5-26-84   *I Didn't Mean To Turn You On* (Tabu 4Z9-05003)   22, 12, 4, 4, 2, 2, 2, 4, 7, 11, 13, 11, 12, 15, 26, 30, 48 (17)

11-23-85   *You Look Good To Me* (Extended Version) (Tabu 4Z9-05279)   60, 54, 34, 31, 31, 31, 46, 46, 55, 63, 63, 67, 75 (13)

CHERRELLE WITH ALEXANDER O'NEAL *(See also:*
ALEXANDER O'NEAL)

2-01-86   *Saturday Love* (Remix) (Tabu/CBS 4Z9-05332)   48, 30, 11, 6, 2, 1, 2, 2, 4, 4, 5, 9, 10, 13, 17, 28, 43, 55, 63, 68 (20)

CHERRY, EVA

9-05-87   *Good Intentions* (Cap. V-15308)   61, 46, 46, 39, 34, 28, 28, 46, 49 (9)

2-09-80   *Ripe!!* (all cuts) (RSO)   31, 22, 15, 11, 10, 6, 3, 3, 7 (9)

CHEYNE

5-11-85   *Call Me Mr. Telephone (Answering Service)* (Dub Version) (MCA 23546)   55, 30, 27, 23, 17, 15, 15, 23, 23, 23, 33, 45, 64, 73 (14)

CHIC

6-30-79   *Good Times* (Atl.)   32, 15, 11, 9, 8, 7, 8, 9, 10, 13, 16 (11)

12-26-88   *Jack Le Freak* (Atl. 0-86634)   44, 44, 44, 22, 22, 29, 30, 41, 44 (9)

10-28-78 *Le Freak* (Atl.) 10, 6, 4, 3, 1, 1, 1, 1, 1, 5, 5, 5, 7, 13, 14, 18, 22 (17)

9-08-79 *Risque* (all cuts) (Atl.) 29, 23, 21, 23, 24 (5)

THE CHICAGO BEARS SHUFFLIN' CREW

2-08-86 *The Super Bowl Shuffle* (Extended Vocal Mix) (Red Label/Cap. V-70060) 39, 30, 27, 27, 37, 64, 65 (7)

THE CHOICE M.C.'S

11-16-85 *Beat Of The Street/Gordy's Groove* (Mayberry Mix) (Tommy Boy TB-871) 65, 54, 49, 31, 25, 21, 21, 15, 15, 15, 19, 23, 29, 38, 44, 51, 63, 73 (17)

CINDY AND ROY

8-25-79 *I Wanna Testify/Can You Feel It* (Casa.) 36, 34, 31, 31, 40 (5)

CLIFFORD, LINDA

4-07-79 *Bridge Over Troubled Waters/Don't Give It Up* (Curtom) 25, 19 (2)

4-21-79 *Let Me Be Your Woman* (all cuts) (Curtom) 17, 15, 14, 12, 12, 13, 14, 19, 21, 25, 37 (11)

CLINTON, GEORGE *(See also:* PARLIAMENT)

4-05-86 *Do Fries Go With That Shake* (Cap. V-15219) 42, 35, 31, 28, 25, 23, 23, 29, 43, 55, 62, 73 (12)

7-27-85 *Double Oh-Oh* (Mashed Mix & Mixing Parts) (Cap. V-8642) 60, 49, 45, 45, 55, 62, 68, 70, 70, 73 (10)

CLUB NOUVEAU

9-06-86 *Jealousy* (King Jay/Tommy Boy TB 884) 51, 37, 19, 10, 5, 4, 3, 2, 2, 3, 10, 12, 12, 12, 10, 9, 8, 8, 8, 11, 14, 14, 22, 22, 27, 33, 58, 69, 72 (29)

3-07-87 *Lean On Me* (Tommy Boy TB 894) 27, 10, 4, 1, 2, 2, 3, 3, 3, 3, 8, 9, 9, 15, 34, 60, 60, 66, 70 (19)

12-27-86   *Situation #9*   (Tommy Boy TB 891)   57, 57, 57, 41, 33, 33, 30, 30, 25, 22, 17, 13, 13, 18, 19, 24, 47, 55, 59, 68, 69   (21)

5-30-87   *Why You Treat Me So Bad*   (Tommy Boy TB 895)   44, 40, 32, 28, 28, 23, 17, 17, 30, 30, 32, 48, 55, 57, 67, 70, 70, 71   (18)

COGNAC

10-20-79   *How High*   (Salsoul)   36, 34, 32, 28, 38   (5)

COLDCUT

8-20-88   *Doctorin' The House*   (Col. 44-07842)   24, 21, 20, 22, 25, 30   (6)

COLE, NATALIE

5-25-85   *Dangerous* (Remix)   (Modern 0-96885)   50, 36, 22, 19, 17, 15, 15, 20, 20, 21, 30, 51, 69, 75   (14)

8-08-87   *Jump Start*   (Manhattan/EMI V-56053)   45, 41, 34, 31, 31, 34, 34, 31, 23, 22, 37, 42, 47   (13)

3-12-88   *Pink Cadillac*   (EMI-Manhattan V-56084)   39, 34, 28, 21, 11, 9, 8, 6, 4, 6, 16, 18, 23, 31, 38, 44   (16)

COLLINS, PHIL   (*See also:* PHILIP BAILEY)

8-31-85   *Don't Lose My Number* (Extended Version)   (Atl. DMD 872)   51, 34, 30, 27, 24, 24, 31, 39, 50, 68   (10)

4-27-85   *Sussudio* (Vocal & Extended Mix)   (Atl. DMD 831)   58, 29, 21, 16, 14, 12, 9, 6, 6, 6, 6, 6, 6, 8, 14, 33, 53, 63, 75   (19)

5-03-86   *Take Me Home*   (Atl. 0-86821)   59, 54, 52, 61, 63, 71, 73   (7)

COLON, WILLIE

7-19-86   *Set Fire To Me* (Remix)   (A&M SP-12181)   56, 50, 50, 63, 63, 65, 70   (7)

THE COMMODORES

11-08-86   *Goin' To The Bank*   (Polydor 885 358-1)   61, 50, 36, 30, 30, 26, 24, 22, 22, 22, 22, 22, 22, 44, 52, 57, 64, 73   (18)

3-30-85   *Nightshift* (Club Mix)   (Motown PR 166)   40, 22, 10, 8, 7, 7, 13, 13, 19, 35, 57, 64, 73   (13)

THE COMMUNARDS

2-20-88   *Never Can Say Goodbye*   (MCA 23812)   40, 19, 15, 5, 6, 20, 41, 46, 49   (9)

COMPANY B

2-07-87   *Fascinated*   (Atl. 0-86731)   39, 27, 12, 10, 6, 4, 3, 4, 5, 6, 7, 6, 5, 4, 9, 11, 13, 18, 46, 58, 58, 60, 64, 71   (24)

8-29-87   *Full Circle*   (Atl. 0-86674)   15, 9, 8, 8, 3, 3, 2, 1, 1, 6, 17, 21, 30, 41, 41, 39, 38, 45, 45, 45   (20)

2-06-88   *Perfect Lover*   (Atl. 0-86619)   40, 30, 23, 11, 6, 4, 4, 3, 1, 7, 23, 35, 39, 44, 42, 47   (16)

CON FUNK SHUN

5-18-85   *Electric Lady* (Instrumental & Extended Version)   (Mer. 880 636-1)   51, 36, 27, 27, 28, 28, 28, 29, 34, 47, 55, 70, 75   (13)

CONNIE

5-10-86   *Experience* (Extended Version)   (Sunnyview SUN 438)   —, 33, 28, 21, 18, 18, 19, 21, 23, 30, 38, 53, 66, 69, 70, 75   (16)

12-21-85   *Funky Little Beat* (Extended Version)   (Sunnyview 3028)   52, 52, 43, 43, 39, 30, 27, 24, 21, 14, 12, 12, 17, 18, 24, 25, 27, 38, 51, 60, 71   (21)

THE CONTROLLERS

12-22-79   *I Can't Turn The Boogie Loose*   (TK)   35, 35, 30, 30   (4)

COOPER, MICHAEL

1-30-88   *To Prove My Love*   (WB 0-20777)   45, 32, 27, 25, 25, 31, 33, 48   (8)

THE COVER GIRLS

10-24-87   *Because Of You*   (Fever/Sutra SF 819)   41, 26, 21, 18, 15, 11, 11, 16, 15, 23, 23, 23, 24, 21, 19, 14, 11, 11, 28, 30, 49   (21)

8-20-88   *Inside Outside* (Fever/Sutra SF 824)   26, 19, 14, 14, 15, 15, 22   (7)

2-14-87   *Show Me* (Fever/Sutra SF 814)   55, 35, 14, 3, 5, 11, 11, 11, 15, 15, 14, 12, 9, 6, 7, 18, 34, 58, 69, 69, 71, 75   (22)

7-18-87   *Spring Love* (Fever/Sutra SF 816)   60, 54, 54, 46, 45, 45, 45, 45, 49, 49, 60   (11)

THE CRIMINAL ELEMENT

9-05-87   *Put The Needle To The Record* (Criminal CR 12-014)   65, 57, 57, 44, 35, 34, 47   (7)

CRISTIE, JANICE

11-02-85   *One Love* (Extended Version) (Supertronics RY-009)   60, 54, 54, 62, 68, 72   (6)

THE CROWN HEIGHTS AFFAIR

3-29-80   *You Gave Me Love* (De-Lite)   33, 28   (2)

CRYSTAL, BILLY

8-24-85   *You Look Marvelous* (Dub & Extended Version) (A&M SP-12147)   58, 52, 47, 47, 54, 61, 69, 74, 75   (9)

CULTURAL VIBE

9-20-86   *Ma Foom Bey* (Easy Street EZS-7525)   64, 58, 57, 68, 74   (5)

CULTURE CLUB   *(See also:* BOY GEORGE)

3-31-84   *Miss Me Blind/It's A Miracle* (Epic 49-04977)   15, 7, 10, 8, 5, 4, 3, 7, 14, 20, 29   (11)

4-26-86   *Move Away* (Remix)/*Sexuality* (Virgin/Epic 49-05360)   38, 24, 20, 16, 14, 14, 23, 29, 33, 53, 61, 67   (12)

10-20-84   *The War Song* (Shriek Mix) (Epic 49-05107)   21, 15, 14, 13, 12, 17, 17, 25, 40, 48, 48, 48   (12)

THE CURE

3-26-88   *Hot Hot Hot* (Elektra 0-66783)   45, 37, 37, 37, 39, 46   (6)

11-09-85 *In Between Days* (Extended Version) (Elektra 0-66882) 60, 52, 48, 48, 62, 66, 69, 69, 70, 70, 73, 75 (12)

10-24-87 *Just Like Heaven* (Elektra 0-66793) 44, 34, 28, 27, 36, 45, 45, 45, 49 (9)

7-11-87 *Why Can't I Be You* (Elektra 0-66810) 56, 27, 24, 24, 22, 21, 19, 19, 42, 43, 43, 49 (12)

CURIOSITY KILLED THE CAT

9-19-87 *Misfit* (Mer./PolyGram 888 752-1) 42, 35, 25, 20, 20, 25, 36, 46 (8)

CYMONE, ANDRE

8-17-85 *The Dance Electric/Red Lights* (Long Version) (Col. 44-05249) 55, 48, 38, 35, 31, 25, 18, 7, 7, 18, 22, 33, 44, 51, 71, 73 (16)

CYRE

3-14-87 *Last Chance* (Fresh/Sleeping Bag FRE-008) 52, 47, 44, 39, 35, 32, 23, 20, 16, 10, 10, 11, 7, 9, 12, 12, 14, 23, 41 (19) Titled "The Rain" (Long Version) through May 9.

"D" TRAIN

1-28-84 *Something's On Your Mind* (Prelude D 670) 9, 10, 13, 10, 14, 12, 14, 25, 25 (9)

D.J. JAZZY JEFF AND FRESH PRINCE

9-06-86 *Girls Ain't Nothing But Trouble* (Ward WD 1) 45, 30, 20, 12, 10, 9, 6, 5, 5, 14, 19, 20, 21, 21, 21, 26, 37, 37, 37, 53, 58, 58, 64, 70, 74 (25)

3-07-87 *The Magnificent Jazzy Jeff* (Jive/RCA 10301 JA) 60, 48, 48, 61, 50, 30, 16, 12, 10, 10, 13, 15, 15, 19, 31, 57, 57, 63, 66, 73 (20)

10-01-88 *A Nightmare On My Street* (Jive/RCA 1125-1-JD) 13, 11, 7, 7, 14, 30 (6)

5-21-88 *Parents Just Don't Understand* (Jive/RCA 1092-1-JD) 48, 29, 25, 19, 16, 9, 8, 4, 3, 4, 13, 21, 25, 30 (14)

DADDY DEWDROP

7-21-79 *The Real Thing* (Inphasion) 40, 37, 35, 38, 40 (5)

DAILY, E.G.

9-06-86 *Love In The Shadows* (Remix) (A&M SP-12187) 59, 43, 32, 28, 23, 21, 21, 20, 29, 32, 37, 48, 65, 65, 71 (15)

8-29-87 *Mind Over Matter* (A&M SP-12246) 55, 26, 23, 23, 22, 27, 40 (7)

4-26-86 *Say It, Say It* (A&M SP-12175) 42, 32, 26, 20, 13, 10, 8, 8, 9, 11, 16, 21, 30, 39, 41, 60, 66 (17)

DANTE, STEVEN (*See:* JELLYBEAN)

DANE, DANA

1-18-86 *Nightmares* (Profile PRO-7086) 58, 51, 41, 37, 37, 36, 44, 58, 53, 38, 51, 60, 61, 66, 75 (15)

D'ARBY, TERENCE TRENT

10-29-88 *Dance Little Sister* (Col. 44-07887) 27, 14, 10, 10, 24 (5)

11-14-87 *If You Let Me Stay* (Col. 44-07450) 37, 31, 24, 19, 19, 31, 42, 42, 42, 50 (10)

2-20-88 *Wishing Well* (Col. 44-07475) 38, 29, 24, 19, 17, 14, 12, 10, 8, 6, 4, 2, 3, 13, 23, 29, 35, 46 (18)

DASH, SARA

11-25-78 *Sinner Man* (Kirshner) 24, 20, 18, 22, 28, 29, 29, 30 (8)

DAVIS, JOHN(, AND THE MONSTER ORCHESTRA)

10-28-78 *Ain't That Enough For You* (Sam) 4, 4, 3, 4, 7, 11, 12, 18, 20 (9)

5-26-79 *Love Magic/Holler* (Sam) 32, 25, 20, 17, 13, 9, 6, 6, 8, 11, 13, 14, 19, 24, 27 (15)

DAVIS, RAINY

3-28-87 *Low Down So And So* (Col. 44-05997) 53, 49, 48, 52, 54, 56, 65, 74 (8)

3-08-86 *Sweetheart* (Extended Version) (Supertronics RU 013) 60, 54, 49, 49, 49, 53, 61, 68, 71, (2), 60, 54, 46, 43, 39, 33, 30, 27, 23, 21, 17, 15, 15, 15, 23, 25, 38, 44, 57, 70 (29)

DAVY DMX

4-14-84 *One For The Treble* (Tuff City 4Z9-04955) 19, 14, 15, 28, 29 (5)

DAY, MORRIS (*See also:* THE TIME)

3-05-88 *Fishnet* (WB 0-20778) 33, 24, 14, 9, 6, 6, 5, 7, 19, 31, 47 (11)

9-28-85 *The Oak Tree* (Extended Version & Instrumental) (WB 0-20379) 42, 26, 16, 12, 4, 3, 3, 7, 8, 14, 24, 33, 44, 44, 57, 57, 71 (17)

DAYE, CORY

8-11-79 *Green Light/Pow Wow* (New York International) 34, 28, 21, 19, 11, 8, 6, 8, 10, 12, 17, 27, 37 (13)

DAYNE, TAYLOR

3-19-88 *Prove Your Love* (Arista ADI-9677) —, —, 24, 12, 11, 20, 17, 12, 10, 11, 33, 42, 44, 48 (14)

10-10-87 *Tell It To My Heart* (Arista ADI-9611) 41, 30, 26, 20, 13, 10, 8, 3, 3, 3, 4, 10, 10, 10, 11, 16, 20, 15, 15, 27, 38, 38, 46 (23)

THE DAZZ BAND

10-27-84 *Let It All Blow* (Motown 4524 MG) 20, 17, 15, 13, 11, 9, 8, 8, 11, 11, 11, 13, 16, 24, 33, 37, 43, 50, 50, (1), 70 (20)

8-30-86 *L.O.V.E. M.I.A.* (Remix) (Geffen/WB 0-20499) 54, 47, 40, 40, 51, 68, 75 (7)

6-09-84 *Swoop (I'm Yours)/Joystick* (Motown 66964-D) 20, 17, 22, 28 (4)

DEAD OR ALIVE

11-08-86 *Brand New Lover* (Epic EAS-2521) 58, 53, 41, 41, 41, 24, 22, 18, 18, 18, 12, 10, 10, 9, 9, 14, 16, 19, 25, 26, 47, 65, 72, 74 (24)

10-19-85 *Lover Come Back To Me* (Extended Remix) (Epic 49-05278) 56, 47, 43, 39, 39, 47, 63, 73 (8)

1-25-86 *My Heart Goes Bang* (Extended Mix) (Epic/CBS 49-05722) 54, 43, 27, 24, 24, 26, 36, 56, 64 (9)

5-02-87 *Something In My House* (Epic 49-06750) 37, 37, 32, 24, 20, 17, 17, 16, 16, 46, 52, 65, 70, 70, 74 (15)

5-18-85 *You Spin Me Round (Like A Record)* (Murder Mix)/Misty Circle (Extended Version) (Epic 49-05208) 54, 37, 20, 10, 8, 5, 5, 4, 4, 4, 4, 6, 7, 13, 17, 22, 28, 42, 50, 54, 65, 69, 69, 72, 74 (25)

DEAN, HAZELL

3-17-84 *Evergreen/Jealous Love* (Quality QUS 057) 24, 18, 11, 21, 30 (5)

DeBARGE *(See also:* BUNNY DeBARGE; CHICO DeBARGE; EL DeBARGE)

3-23-85 *Rhythm Of The Night/Queen Of My Heart* (Motown 4532 MG) 48, 21, 7, 1, 2, 2, 2, 2, 4, 7, 15, 32, 30, 57, 66, 70, 75 (17)

DeBARGE, BUNNY *(See also:* DeBARGE)

3-07-87 *Save The Best For Me (Best Of Your Lovin')* (Gordy/Motown 4574 MG) 54, 51, 54, 55, 59, 64, 66 (7)

DeBARGE, CHICO *(See also:* DeBARGE)

10-25-86 *Talk To Me* (Remix) (Motown 4567 MG) —, 28, 19, 14, 11, 9, 9, 8, 6, 5, 5, 5, 5, 13, 13, 14, 17, 20, 29, 55, 55, 65, 70 (23)

DeBARGE, EL, WITH DeBARGE *(See also:* DeBARGE; BUNNY DeBARGE; CHICO DeBARGE)

10-12-85 *You Wear It Well* (Club & Dùb Mix) (Gordy 4545 GG) 47, 35, 20, 17, 17, 17, 27, 36, 47, 56, 68, 68, 73, 73 (14)

DEB, DEBI

5-30-87 *I'm Searchin* (Jam Packed 2008) 52, 44, 25, 22, 22, 16, 16, 21, 41, 41, 52, 59, 66, 75 (14)

3-16-85 *Look Out Weekend* (Instrumental & Vocal) (Jam Packed JPI 103) 57, 49, 49, 61, 64, 72, 72 (7)

THE DEELE

1-28-84   *Body Talk*   (Solar 0-66981)   13, 13, 11, 17, 25, 22, 29   (7)

6-01-85   *Material Thangz* (Vocal & Instrumental Version)   (Solar ED 5051)   53, 45, 37, 34, 34, 36, 59, 61, 71   (9)

DEJA

10-10-87   *You And Me Tonight*   (Virgin 0-96755)   41, 25, 16, 10, 7, 6, 6, 16, 22, 44   (10)

DEODATO

12-08-84   *S.O.S., Fire In The Sky* (Disarmamix)   (WB 20287)   39, 33, 27, 27, 27, 25, 32, 29, 25, 25, 26, 41, 46, 50, 68, 68, 73, 73   (18)

DEPECHE MODE

5-21-88   *Behind The Wheel/Route 66*   (Sire/WB 0-20858)   20, 16, 15, 18, 20, 31   (6)

7-06-85   *People Are People* (Extended Version)   (Sire 0-20214)   60, 51, 45, 40, 40, 55, 57, 64, 73   (9)

7-18-87   *Strangelove* (Remix)   (Sire/WB 0-20696)   25, 22, 22, 13, 13, 11, 8, 11, 11, 11, 14, 19, 23, 35, 47   (15)

10-22-88   *Strangelove/Nothing*   (Sire/WB 0-21022)   23, 9, 15, 18, 19, 27   (6)

DESTINATION

9-01-79   *Move On Up/Up Up Up*   (Butterfly)   33, 20, 12, 7, 4, 2, 3, 4, 4, 5, 7, 14, 15, 37, 40   (15)

DEVO

9-10-88   *Disco Dancer*   (Enigma/Cap. V-75511)   29, 29   (2)

DEWDROP, DADDY   *(See:* DADDY DEWDROP)

DIAMOND, GREGG

10-28-78   *Starcruiser* (all cuts)   (Marlin/TK)   11, 16, 22   (3)

9-29-79 *Starcruiser/Danger* (TK)   36, 31, 28, 25, 30, 28, 39   (7)

DIRECT CURRENT

5-12-79 *Everybody Here Must Party* (TEC)   32, 30, 28, 26, 25, 31, 39   (7)

DISCO CIRCUS

8-04-79 *Over And Over* (Col.)   32, 30, 34, 38   (4)

DIVINE SOUNDS

5-12-84 *What People Do For Money* (Specific SR-243)   17, 8, 18, 8, 8, 18, 27   (7)

DR. FRESHH

5-04-85 *Roxanne's Doctor—The Real Man* (Zakia ZK 009)   52, 47, 43, 39, 39, 63   (6)

DR. JECKYLL AND MR. HYDE

1-18-86 *Yellow Panties* (Profile PRO-7092)   63, 58, 52, 48, 48, 53, 64, 67, 75, 75   (10)

DODSON, VENUS

6-30-79 *Night Rider* (RFC)   35, 25, 21, 18, 18, 18, 21, 22, 23, 24   (10)

DOLBY, THOMAS

3-24-84 *Hyperactive* (Cap. V-8576)   14, 16, 17, 24, 29   (5)

DOUBLE EXPOSURE

8-11-79 *I Got The Hots For Ya* (Salsoul)   39, 37, 35, 32, 30, 26, 26   (7)

DOUGLAS, CAROL

10-28-78 *Burnin'* (Midsong)   16, 23   (2)

6-16-79 *Love Sick* (Midsong)   40, 37, 36, 35, 39   (5)

DUKE, GEORGE

2-23-80   *I Want You For Myself* (Epic)   35, 30, 28, 25, 25, 26, 33   (7)

THE DUNCAN SISTERS

9-29-79   *The Duncan Sisters* (all cuts)   (Earmarc)   34, 27, 20, 15, 12, 10, 9, 8, 7, 9, 29, 37   (12)

DURAN DURAN

11-12-88   *I Don't Want To Be Your Love*   (Cap. V-15417)   28, 23, 15, 12, 11, 8, 8, 8   (8)

11-22-86   *Notorious*   (Cap. V-15264)   57, 46, 46, 41, 41, 42, 42, 42, 58, 64, 64, 67, 71   (13)

5-12-84   *The Reflex* (Dance Mix)   (Cap. V-8587)   25, 18, 11, 18, 14, 23, 23, 21, 19, 23, 21, 29, 29   (13)

1-28-84   *Union Of The Snake*   (Cap. SPRO-9060)   28   (1)

11-24-84   *The Wild Boys*   (Cap. V-8617)   38, 32, 28, 19, 16, 16, 16, 15, 20, 41, 41, 49   (12)

DYNASTY

10-06-79   *I Don't Want To Be A Freak*   (Solar)   39, 33, 29, 26, 25, 38   (6)

E.P.M.D.

5-28-88   *You Gots' To Chill*   (Fresh/Sleeping Bag FRE 8018)   42, 38, 32, 23, 20, 16, 15, 17, 22, 26   (10)

E.T. (aka Eddie Towns)

4-05-86   *Best Friends* (Super Mix)   (Total Experience/RCA TED1-2433)   57, 52, 47, 47, 55, 66, 75   (7)

E.U.

3-26-88   *Da' Butt*   (EMI/Manhattan V-56083)   41, 27, 21, 16, 12, 11, 9, 8, 5, 3, 7, 7, 11, 17, 23, 28   (16)

THE EARONS

5-26-84   *Land Of Hunger* (Extended Version)   (Island 0-96958)   25, 14, 13, 12, 19, 27, 29, 29   (8)

EARTH, WIND AND FIRE (*See also:* PHILIP BAILEY)

10-31-87   *System Of Survival*   (Col. 44-07475)   29, 18, 14, 2, 2, 2, 1, 1, 1, 1, 1, 1, 4, 11, 19, 32, 42   (17)

3-05-88   *Thinking Of You*   (Col. 44-07566)   39, 18, 12, 8, 3, 2, 1, 5, 10, 30, 40, 46   (12)

EARTH, WIND AND FIRE/THE EMOTIONS

6-02-79   *Boogie Wonderland*   (Col.)   40, 37, 34, 27, 25, 21, 20, 23, 27, 31, 35   (11)

THE EASTBOUND EXPRESS

2-21-87   *Knock Me Senseless*   (Vinyl Mania VMR-006)   63, 40, 30, 30, 39, 54, 62, 69, 72   (9)

EASTON, SHEENA

12-10-88   *The Lover In Me*   (MCA 23904)   19, 9, 5, 5   (4)

10-13-84   *Strut* (Dance & Dub)   (EMI America STRO-9230)   37, 32, 26, 21, 17, 14, 13, 13, 17, 16, 40, 40, 40, 42   (14)

1-26-85   *Sugar Walls* (Red & Dance Mix)   (EMI America STRO-9313)   38, 23, 9, 5, 2, 1, 1, 2, 7, 12, 20, 29, 39, 54, 64, 67   (16)

EDDY, DUANE   (*See:* THE ART OF NOISE)

EDDY "D"

5-11-85   *Backstabbin'* (Vocal, Instrumental, Dub & Freebeat)   (Philly World DMD 819)   58, 52, 52, 60, 64, 74   (6)

ELEANOR

5-07-88   *Adventure*   (Col. 44-07471)   35, 30, 30, 27, 37, 49   (6)

THE EMOTIONS (*See:* EARTH, WIND AND FIRE)

ERASURE

8-27-88 *Chains Of Love* (Sire/WB 0-20953) 20, 15, 11, 9, 9, 7, 2, 1, 1, 1, 9, 11, 16, 29 (14)

6-07-86 *Oh L'Amour* (Remix) (Sire/WB 0-20471) 62, 55, 50, 45, 45, 61, 70 (7)

6-13-87 *Sometimes* (Sire/WB 0-20614) 56, 52, 51, 50, 53, 67, 71, 71, 71, 74 (10)

9-05-87 *Victim Of Love* (Sire/WB 0-20740) 28, 26, 26, 20, 18, 25, 34, 45, 50 (9)

3-01-86 *Who Needs Love Like That/Heavenly Action* (Sire/WB 0-20404) 59, 43, 39, 34, 23, 21, 21, 28, 36, 39, 58, 60, 72 (13)

ERIC B. (AND RAKIM)

8-02-86 *Eric B. Is President/My Melody* (Zakia ZK 014) 69, 59, 54, 54, 62, 66, 70 (7)

5-16-87 *I Know You Got Soul* (Island/4th & B'way 438) 56, 55, 50, 47, 41, 37, 37, 25, 25, 43, 42, 42, 57, 64, 71 (15)

2-27-88 *Move The Crowd/Paid In Full* (4th & B'way/Island 456) 37, 29, 27, 26, 24, 31, 38, 45, 50 (9)

THE EROTIC DRUM BAND

10-28-78 *Plug Me To Death/Love Disco Style* (Prism) 22, 25, 27 (3)

3-22-80 *Pop Pop Shoo Wah* (Prism) 35, 29, 23 (3)

EROTIC EXOTIC

9-06-86 *Take Me As I Am* (Atl. DMD 966) 64, 57, 52, 48, 44, 43, 56, 69, 74 (9)

ERUPTION

10-06-79 *One Way Ticket* (Ariola) 36, 29, 24, 21, 18, 21, 26, 40 (8)

THE ESCAPE CLUB

10-29-88   *Wild Wild West*   (Atl. 0-86544)   22, 16, 14, 13, 9, 9, 15, 20   (8)

ESMERALDA, SANTA

10-27-79   *Another Cha Cha*   (Casa.)   38, 33, 32, 40   (4)

ESTEFAN, GLORIA, AND THE MIAMI SOUND MACHINE   *(See also:* THE MIAMI SOUND MACHINE

6-20-87   *Rhythm Is Gonna Get You*   (Epic 49-06772)   49, 49, 19, 12, 6, 4, 4, 4, 4, 14, 24, 55, 63, 63, 67   (15)

EURYTHMICS

2-25-84   *Here Comes The Rain*   (RCA JD-13711)   21, 17, 12, 11, 9, 8, 9, 17, 18, 26, 30   (11)

1-23-88   *I Need A Man/Beethoven*   (RCA 6820-1-RD)   46, 33, 22, 17, 9, 8, 8, 26, 36, 36, 46   (11)

8-30-86   *Missionary Man* (Remix)   (RCA PD-14409)   49, 38, 33, 30, 27, 26, 39, 41, 64, 68, 74   (11)

12-01-84   *Sexcrime (Nineteen Eighty-Four)* (Extended & Single Version)   (RCA PW-13957)   37, 34, 25, 20, 20, 20, 19, 22, 22, 24, 27, 37, 42, 45, (1), 65, 71, 74   (17)

5-18-85   *Would I Lie To You?* (Extended Mix)/Here Comes That Sinking Feeling   (RCA PW-14079)   60, 34, 31, 28, 24, 24, 21, 16, 16, 17, 20, 24, 31, 50, 65, 74   (16)

EXPOSE

1-17-87   *Come Go With Me*   (Arista ADI-9539)   54, 28, 28, 20, 10, 9, 8, 10, 9, 6, 8, 9, 8, 8, 15, 22, 36, 60, 68, 75   (20)

11-16-85   *Exposed To Love* (Extended Version)   (Arista ADI-9426)   49, 24, 20, 18, 9, 8, 8, 7, 7, 7, 11, 16, 18, 20, 21, 21, 21, 25, 37, 48, 62, 68, 68, 70, 72   (25)

9-12-87   *Let Me Be The One*   (Arista ADI-9618)   60, 60, 40, 24, 18, 11, 10, 8, 3, 3, 3, 9, 25, 42, 48   (15)

3-16-85   *Point Of No Return/Dub Of No Return*   (Arista ADI-9326)   53, 45, 37, 34, 34, 36, 38, 44, 43, 42, 41, 45, 51, 53, 53, 56, 63, 63, 66, 63, 58, 50, 46, 46, 50, 63, 69, 71   (28)

7-04-87   *Point Of No Return*   (Arista ADI-9580)   44, 41, 40, 40, 40, 51, 57, 65, 74   (9)

1-23-88   *Seasons Change*   (Arista ADI-9639)   31, 26, 23, 22, 24, 23, 34, 47   (8)

FACE TO FACE

9-15-84   *Under The Gun* (Dance And Club Mix)   (Epic 49-05033)   49, 46, 45, 43, 49, 49   (6)

FACHIN, ERIA

3-05-88   *Savin' Myself*   (Critique 0-96724)   32, 17, 15, 17, 17, 18, 24, 31, 35, 39, 49   (11)

FAD, J.J.

5-28-88   *Supersonic*   (Dream Team DTR 532)   17, 8, 5, 3, 3, 2, 1, 1, 3, 18, 22, 26   (12)

10-15-88   *Way Out*   (Ruthless/Atl.0-99285)   19, 10, 10, 11, 15, 18, 17, 30   (8)

FALCO

2-22-86   *Rock Me Amadeus/Vienna Calling*   (A&M SP-12170)   58, 29, 22, 8, 5, 2, 2, 2, 2, 6, 6, 6, 9, 9, 9, 22, 29, 44, 53, 66, 68, 73   (21)

5-24-86   *Vienna Calling* (Extended Mix)   (A&M SP-12182)   46, 38, 33, 30, 30, 32, 42, 54, 65, 72   (10)

FALTERMEYER, HAROLD   *(See:* PATTI LaBELLE)

THE FAMILY

8-17-85   *The Screams Of Passion/Yes* (Extended Version)   (Paisley Park 0-96875)   30, 19, 10, 9, 7, 6, 5, 5, 5, 5, 14, 19, 23, 29, 40, 43, 59, 65, 72, 72, 75, 75   (22)

FANTASY

3-01-86   *He's Number One*   (Spring SPR 12-418)   65, 51, 46, 42, 36, 36, 44, 55, 64, 69   (10)

THE FAT BOYS

3-16-85   *Can You Feel It* (LP & Instrumental Version)   (Sutra SUD 029)   50, 44, 44, 48, 56, 59, 64   (7)

6-13-87   *Falling In Love*   (Tin Pan Apple/Polydor 885 766-1)   53, 41, 41, 29, 29, 31, 31, 31, 33, 34, 38, 54, 57, 65, 65, 72   (16)

7-20-85   *The Fat Boys Are Back* (Extended Version & Instrumental)   (Sutra SUD 034)   37, 22, 16, 13, 11, 9, 8, 8, 10, 10, 10, 14, 24, 28, 39, 45, 61, 71   (18)

11-03-84   *Jailhouse Rap*   (Sutra SUD 027)   29, 25, 22, 22, 23, 24, 26, 38, 38, 38, 37, 30, 27, 26, 26, 32, 34, 41, 47, 62, 72   (21)

4-26-86   *Sex Machine* (Extended Version)   (Sutra SUD 045)   59, 51, 30, 22, 17, 16, 14, 14, 21, 23, 33, 43, 55, 65   (14)

8-22-87   *Wipeout*   (Tin Pan Apple/PolyGram 885 960-1)   48, 30, 17, 17, 17, 13, 13, 16, 21, 30, 44   (11)

FAT LARRY'S BAND

10-13-79   *Looking For Love*   (Fantasy)   39, 35, 33, 31, 40   (5)

FERRY, BRYAN

10-26-85   *Don't Stop The Dance/Slave To Love* (Remix Special)   (WB 0-20385)   53, 44, 40, 40, 68, 74   (6)

FESTIVAL

1-19-80   *Evita* (all cuts)   (RSO)   30, 25, 18, 12, 9, 6, 4, 3, 3, 5, 8, 9   (12)

FEVER

9-29-79   *Fever* (all cuts)   (Fantasy)   35, 25, 21, 14, 9, 7, 5, 4, 3, 8, 9, 23, 34, 34   (14)

11-04-78   *Standing In The Shadows Of Love*   (Fantasy)   30, 29, 26, 25, 24   (5)

52ND STREET

5-17-86 *Tell Me (How It Feels)* (Extended Version) (MCA 23623) 58, 49, 34, 24, 15, 13, 10, 9, 9, 13, 26, 33, 46, 45, 61, 68 (16)

FIRST CHOICE

11-18-78 *Hold Your Horses* (Salsoul) 29, 23, 18, 17, 15, 13, 12, 12, 10, 10, 10, 13, 13, 16, 21 (15)

3-10-79 *Hold Your Horses* (all cuts) (Gold Mind) 27, 21, 19, 17, 12, 9, 9, 8, 10, 14, 15, 16, 18, 31 (14)

FIVE STAR

8-17-85 *All Fall Down* (Extended Version) (RCA PW-14109) 58, 51, 31, 24, 22, 11, 6, 6, 6, 8, 19, 24, 26, 28, 39, 42, 57, 62, 74, 74 (20)

5-23-87 *Are You Man Enough* (RCA 44-05988) 59, 56, 53, 52, 66, 66, 73 (7)

10-04-86 *Can't Wait Another Minute* (RCA 5731-1-RD) 60, 50, 35, 26, 20, 13, 13, 16, 24, 24, 31, 37, 55, 55, 55, 63, 67, 67, 68, 73 (20)

1-24-87 *If I Say Yes* (RCA 5921-1-RD) 60, 60, 60, 47, 42, 36, 35, 45, 50, 63, 63, 70, 73 (13)

11-23-85 *Let Me Be The One* (Extended Version) (RCA PW 14230) 58, 52, 38, 29, 18, 18, 12, 12, 9, 5, 5, 5, 14, 15, 17, 20, 24, 24, 29, 32, 43, 51, 56, 64, 73 (25)

5-31-86 *Love Take Over* (Remix) (RCA PW 14324) 42, 35, 32, 27, 27, 27, 32, 48, 57, 72, 75, 75 (12)

FLASH AND THE PAN

4-13-85 *Midnight Man* (Extended & Instrumental Version) (Epic 49-05118) 55, 49, 49, 63 (4)

FLEETWOOD MAC

5-23-87 *Big Love* (Remix) (WB 0-20683) 57, 51, 48, 37, 26, 26, 22, 22, 35, 37, 37, 56, 61, 69 (14)

THE FLIRTS

11-17-84   *Helpless (You Took My Love)*   (Telephone TE 3)   41, 44, 45   (3)

7-19-86   *Miss You*   (CBS Associated 4Z9-05914)   58, 51, 46, 40, 40, 53, 63, 71, 72   (9)

2-22-86   *New Toy* (Extended Version)   (CBS Associated 4Z9-05334)   56, 33, 15, 10, 10, 20, 44, 50, 53, 63, 68   (11)

10-26-85   *You And Me* (Extended Version)   (CBS Associated 4Z9-05284)   51, 41, 36, 30, 30, 31, 37, 52, 54, 54, 59, 59, 69, 69, 69, 73, 75   (17)

THE FLYING LIZARDS

1-05-80   *Money*   (Virgin)   36, 36, 27, 24, 21, 21, 29, 34, 36   (9)

THE FORCE MD'S

6-22-85   *Itchin' For A Scratch* (Vocal & Instrumental Version)   (Tommy Boy TB 862)   59, 48, 48, 48, 57, 59, 61, 61, 63, 67, 71   (11)

2-01-86   *Tender Love*   (Tommy Boy TB 876)   45, 33, 26, 22, 22, 30, 37, 40, 46, 64, 70, 72   (12)

FORD, PENNYE

2-23-85   *Change Your Wicked Ways* (Special DJ Mix & Dub Version)   (Total Experience TED1-2605)   33, 31, 31, 39, 65   (5)

6-15-85   *Dangerous* (Dub Version)   (Total Experience TED1-2614)   60, 55, 50, 49, 67, 73, 73   (7)

FOWLER, FRED

9-03-88   *Times Are Changin'*   (Chrysalis 4V9-43258)   24, 20, 17, 12, 8, 4, 4, 22   (8)

FOX, SAMANTHA

3-14-87   *Do Ya Do Ya (Wanna Please Me)*   (Jive/RCA 0331-1-JD)   57, 51, 45, 46, 60, 64, 75   (7)

11-26-88   *I Wanna Have Some Fun*   (Jive/RCA 1155-1)   30, 19, 10, 6, 2, 2   (6)

2-27-88 *Naughty Girl* (Jive/RCA 1084-1) 43, 25, 23, 19, 12, 8, 8, 7, 4, 3, 3, 2, 1, 5, 14, 20, 34, 41 (18)

10-31-87 *Nothing's Gonna Stop Me Now* (Jive 1071-1-JD) 44, 34, 29, 27, 27, 40, 47, 49, 49, 49 (10)

FOX, SLY

11-30-85 *Como Tu Te Llama?* (Cap. V-8654) 62, 56, 51, 51, 51, 55, 55, 57, 62, 65, 69, 69 (12)

3-15-86 *Let's Go All The Way* (Extended Blix Mix) (Cap. V-15222) 48, 44, 37, 19, 19, 22, 22, 30, 29, 32, 31, 37, 49, 59, 67 (15)

FOX THE FOX

2-08-86 *Precious Little Diamond* (Extended Version) 53, 47, 41, 41, 41, 42, 62, 68 (8)

FRANKIE GOES TO HOLLYWOOD

10-11-86 *Rage Hard* (Island 0-46806) 57, 52, 47, 41, 41, 54, 61, 68, 68, 74 (10)

3-17-84 *Relax* (Island 0-96975) 16, 20, 29, 23, 16, 21, 25, 29 (8)

2-09-85 *Relax* (Long & Edit Version & Instrumental) (ZTT/Island DM 45796-AR) 39, 33, 28, 26, 23, 21, 18, 17, 33, 43, 56, 68, 69, 75 (15)

9-08-84 *Two Tribes* (Island DMD 760) 19, 16, 14, 13, 12, 14, 15, 19, 18, 19, 20, 16, 14, 12, 11, 10, 10, 10, 10, 10, 16, 32, 32, 41 (24)

4-13-85 *Welcome To The Pleasuredome/Get It On (Bang A Gong)/Happi Hi!/Relax* (Trevor Horn Remix) (ZTT/Island 0-96889) 57, 47, 37, 32, 28, 28, 33, 57, 66 (9)

FRANKLIN, ARETHA

2-15-86 *Another Night* (Extended Version) (Arista ADI-9454) 39, 33, 20, 14, 12, 11, 9, 14, 15, 15, 24, 31, 39, 55, 67, 66 (16)

7-06-85 *Freeway Of Love* (Rock Mix & Extended Remix) (Arista ADI-9355) 39, 24, 9, 6, 5, 5, 1, 2, 2, 7, 9, 9, 17, 27, 33, 33, 48, 55, 62, 72 (20)

10-25-86 *Jumpin' Jack Flash* (Arista ADI-9529)   45, 39, 39, 41, 42, 45, 45, 54, 66, 70, 70, 70, 74   (13)

10-12-85 *Who's Zoomin' Who* (Dance Mix) (Arista ADI-9411)   45, 25, 15, 14, 10, 6, 1, 2, 2, 4, 11, 11, 22, 22, 26, 37, 44, 56, 59, 69, 75   (21)

FRANKLIN, ARETHA, AND GEORGE MICHAEL   *(See also:* GEORGE MICHAEL)

4-25-87 *I Knew You Were Waiting* (Arista ADI-9560)   35, 31, 27, 25, 25, 29, 35, 48, 65, 65, 72   (11)

FREESTYLE

2-22-86 *Don't Stop The Rock* (Music Specialists MSI-111)   65, 56, 50, 50, 56, 70, 74   (7)

FREEEZ

1-28-84 *Pop Goes My Love* (Streetwise SWRL 2215)   16, 16, 28, 28   (4)

FREEMAN, LOUISE, AND TERRY BLOUNT

11-21-87 *Signed, Sealed, Delivered* (Suntown STLL 714)   41, 35, 30, 27, 22, 20, 20, 20, 29, 32, 34, 39, 40, 47   (14)

FREESTYLE

7-13-85 *The Party Has Just Begun* (Vocal & Instrumental) (Music Specialists MSI-108)   58, 51, 51, 56, 70   (5)

FRENCH KISS

5-05-79 *Panic* (Polydor)   30, 27, 26, 26, 36   (5)

FRESH, DOUG E., AND THE GET FRESH CREW

7-19-86 *All The Way To Heaven* (Reality/Fantasy D 264)   31, 16, 13, 10, 10, 10, 11, 15, 20, 27, 29, 29, 30, 44, 46, 59, 71, 75   (18)

5-21-88 *Keep Rising To The Top* (Reality/Danya 3101)   45, 40, 27, 26, 26, 32   (6)

8-17-85 *The Show/La-Di-Da-Di* (Extended Version) (Reality/Danya/Fantasy D 242)   24, 11, 4, 1, 1, 3, 3, 1, 1, 1, 1, 1, 1, 3, 3, 3, 4, 5, 7, 7, 11, 11, 20, 21, 29, 38, 49, 51, 66, 74   (30)

FREY, GLENN

3-23-85   *The Heat Is On* (Dance & Dub Version)   (MCA 23540)   59, 43, 35, 35, 38, 39, 57, 64, 71   (9)

THE FRONT PAGE

9-01-79   *Love Insurance*   (Panorama)   37, 27, 18, 10, 7, 7, 6, 6, 8, 11, 14, 16, 35   (13)

FULL FORCE   (*See also:* LISA LISA AND CULT JAM; U.T.F.O.)

11-16-85   *Alice, I Want You Just For Me*   (Col. 44-05282)   58, 31, 27, 20, 18, 15, 15, 13, 13, 11, 9, 9, 14, 18, 23, 24, 32, 47, 51, 63, 75   (15)

8-03-85   *Girl If You Take Me Home/Let's Dance Against The Wall* (Funky Fresh Def Mix)   (Col. 44-05232)   50, 43, 39, 36, 36, 50, 57, 61, 63, 64, 73   (11)

9-27-86   *Temporary Love Thing*   (Col. 44-05912)   61, 54, 45, 40, 37, 31, 25, 23, 21, 20, 20, 23, 25, 29, 29, 29, 33, 49, 49, 59, 69   (21)

11-29-86   *Unfaithful So Much*   (Col. 44-05955)   52, 52, 38, 35, 35, 35, 35, 52, 56, 56, 62, 66, 72   (13)

3-29-86   *Unselfish Lover*   (Col. 44-05333)   60, 43, 37, 32, 23, 20, 18, 18, 25, 28, 42, 56, 65, 70   (14)

FULL HOUSE

7-25-87   *Communicate*   (Epic 49-04632)   28, 28, 26, 25, 29, 35, 44, 47, 47, 52   (10)

FUN FUN

2-02-85   *Color My Love* (Vocal & Instrumental)   (TSR 836)   40, 31, 28, 27, 32, 42, 67, 73   (8)

FUNKADELIC   (*See also:* GEORGE CLINTON)

11-11-78   *One Nation Under A Groove*   (WB)   30, 28, 27, 27, 30, 30   (6)

GQ

2-24-79   *Disco Nights*   (Arista)   28, 23, 18, 14, 12, 10, 9, 8, 5, 5, 9, 15, 16, 18, 24, 32   (16)

G.T.

5-14-88   *I Need You*   (Atl. 0-86588)   34, 28, 25, 24, 23, 31, 42   (7)

GABRIEL, PETER   (*See also:* GENESIS)

6-07-86   *Sledgehammer* (Extended Dance Remix)   (Geffen/WB 0-20456)   53, 27, 11, 9, 8, 7, 6, 5, 5, 8, 8, 8, 14, 27, 49, 56, 68, 74   (18)

THE GAP BAND

5-19-79   *Baby Baba Boogie*   (Mer.)   40, 36, 33, 30, 35   (5)

2-16-85   *Beep A Freak* (Special Dance Mix, Instrumental & Backwards Freak Mix)   (Total Experience TED1-2405)   38, 32, 29, 25, 25, 58   (6)

11-29-86   *Big Fun*   (Total Experience 2700-1-TD)   63, 63, 55, 50, 44, 44, 44, 40, 35, 35, 34, 33, 34, 53, 63, 70   (16)

4-26-86   *Going In Circles* (Extended Version)   (Total Experience/RCA 2436-1-TD)   65, 58, 53, 53, 66, 67   (6)

GARDNER, TAANA

9-22-79   *When You Touch Me*   (West End)   31, 21, 15, 11, 9, 7, 6, 8, 15, 22, 40   (11)

3-31-79   *Work That Body*   (West End)   24, 19, 16, 12, 10, 7, 7, 8, 8, 10, 10, 14, 18, 34   (14)

GARRETT, SIEDAH

3-16-85   *Do You Want It Right Now* (Jellybean Remix)   (Qwest 0-20302)   54, 46, 41, 37, 37, 41, 41, 49, 48, 55, 65, 74, 60, 54, 54, 58, 58, 57, 62, 64, 65, 69, 70, 68, 70, 70, 75   (27)

7-16-88   *K.I.S.S.I.N.G.*   (Qwest/WB 0-20912)   21, 9, 6, 2, 1, 1, 4, 17, 18, 19, 21, 29   (12)

GARY'S GANG

12-30-78   *Keep On Dancin'*   (SAM/Col. 23-10885)   26, 26, 21, 6, 4, 3, 1, 1, 2, 3, 3, 4, 7, 9, 11, 17, 23   (17)

GAYE, MARVIN

5-11-85 *Sanctified Lady* (Instrumental) (Col. 44-05188) 33, 21, 12, 8, 7, 7, 7, 7, 8, 12, 14, 44, 69 (13)

GAYNOR, GLORIA

11-25-78 *I Will Survive* (Polydor) 29, 25, 24, 20, 16, 4, 4, 3, 1, 1, 2, 3, 3, 5, 11, 13, 15, 15, 18, 30 (20)

10-13-79 *Let Me Know* (Polydor) 38, 32, 25, 22, 22, 17, 14, 12, 11, 22, 38, 38 (12)

GENESIS (*See also:* PHIL COLLINS; PETER GABRIEL)

7-26-86 *Invisible Touch* (Atl. 0-81641) 58, 52, 47, 47, 49, 57, 73 (7)

GENUINE PARTS

2-28-87 *Did It Feel Like Love* (Remix) (Atl. 0-8744) 52, 40, 35, 33, 28, 28, 46, 50, 60, 62, 72 (11)

GEORGIO (aka Georgio Allentini)

3-26-88 *Bedrock* (Motown 4603 MG) 43, 30, 23, 12, 10, 9, 28, 44, 50 (9)

10-17-87 *Lover's Lane* (Motown 4592 MG) 36, 22, 17, 12, 11, 9, 4, 4, 4, 5, 5, 5, 5, 10, 12, 18, 38, 43, 45 (19)

7-11-87 *Tina Cherry* (Motown 4586 MG) 47, 32, 21, 21, 19, 10, 4, 4, 3, 3, 3, 12, 21, 33, 50 (15)

GIANT STEPS

10-08-88 *Another Lover* (A&M SP-12274) 26, 21, 11, 11, 26 (5)

GIBSON, DEBBIE

3-07-87 *Only In My Dreams* (Atl. 0-86744) 41, 36, 30, 29, 45, 59, 61, 62, 64, 40, 37, 34, 31, 28, 27, 42, 42, 41, 45, 59, 66, 66, 70, 70, 70 (25)

2-20-88 *Out Of The Blue* (Atl. 0-86621) 43, 34, 22, 13, 9, 7, 5, 4, 4, 3, 1, 8, 25, 37, 47 (15)

10-24-87 *Shake Your Love* (Atl. 0-86651) 40, 35, 24, 16, 14, 8, 6, 2, 2, 2, 2, 2, 5, 17, 22, 31, 45 (17)

THE GIBSON BROTHERS

5-05-79 *Cuba* (Mango) 28, 26, 22, 19, 15, 13, 9, 9, 10, 26, 35 (11)

GIGGLES

12-24-88 *Hot Spot* (Cutting/Atl. 0-86528) 26, 26 (2)

2-28-87 *Love Letter* (Cutting CR-211) 38, 32, 32, 57, 59, 57, 63, 63, 67, 69, 56, 52, 52, 67, 67, 72 (16)

GIGOLO TONY

7-05-86 *Smurf Rock* (Gold Star 100) 59, 47, 39, 36, 31, 31, 35, 62, 71, 74 (10)

GIORGIO (aka Giorgio Moroder)

2-03-79 *The Chase* (Casa.) 30, 29, 28, 30 (4)

9-29-79 *E=MC2* (all cuts) (Casa.) 30, 23, 16, 12, 10, 8, 6, 5, 4, 4, 7, 16, 21, 21, 38, 38 (16)

THE GLASS FAMILY

10-28-78 *Mr. DJ, You Know How To Make Me Dance* (JDC) 15, 12, 12, 21 (4)

GO WEST

6-15-85 *Call Me/We Close Our Eyes* (Indiscriminate Mix) (Chrysalis 4V9-42871) 59, 51, 47, 42, 38, 34, 34, 34, 44, 66 (10)

10-12-85 *Eye To Eye* (Remix) (Chrysalis 4V9-42900) 56, 38, 38, 40, 51, 60 (6)

3-16-85 *We Close Our Eyes* (Total Over-Hang Club Mix & LP Version) (Chrysalis 4V9-42853) 49, 37, 33, 30, 27, 27, 27, 22, 22, 22, 32, 54, 54, 68, 70, 73, 73, 73 (18)

GODLEY AND CREME

8-31-85 *Cry* (Polydor 881 786-1) 60, 54, 49, 56, 56, 58, 63, 70 (8)

GONZALEZ

12-30-78 *Haven't Stopped Dancin' Yet* (Cap.) 30, 30, 26, 15, 7, 6, 5, 4, 4, 6, 8, 10, 11, 13, 27 (15)

GOOD QUESTION

10-22-88 *Got A New Love* (Paisley Park/WB 0-20960) 27, 19, 13, 13, 26 (5)

GOODY GOODY

10-28-78 *#1 Dee Jay* (Atl.) 9, 11 (2)

THE GOON SQUAD

8-03-85 *Eight Arms To Hold You* (Bonus Beat & Dub) (Epic 49-05247) 39, 30, 27, 23, 18, 18, 19, 19, 31, 41, 52, 59, 66, 70 (14)

GRANDMASTER FLASH

5-25-85 *Girls Love The Way He Spins/Larry's Dance Theme* (Elektra 0-66908) 56, 41, 36, 36, 37, 39, 38, 41, 53, 54, 71, 71, 68, 69 (14)

3-16-85 *Sign Of The Times/Larry's Dance Theme* (Vocal, Edit & Instrumental Version) (Elektra ED 5024) 42, 38, 38, 57, 69 (5)

4-19-86 *Style (Peter Gunn Theme)* (Elektra ED 5134) 62, 55, 50, 46, 42, 42, 49, 60, 60, 70 (10)

3-14-87 *U Know What Time It Is* (Elektra ED 5205) 20, 15, 15, 12, 7, 6, 7, 31, 30, 35, 58, 69, 70 (13)

GRANDMASTER FLASH AND MELLE MEL (*See also:* GRANDMASTER MELLE MEL)

1-28-84 *White Lines* (Sugar Hill SH-32009) 8, 9, 10, 13, 16, 24 (6)

GRANDMASTER MELLE MEL AND THE FURIOUS FIVE WITH MR. NESS AND COWBOY (*See also:* GRANDMASTER FLASH)

6-09-84 *Beat Street* (Sugar Hill SH-32019) 18, 9, 7, 6, 5, 7, 17, 25 (8)

GRANDMIXER D.S.T.

1-28-84   *Crazy Cuts*   (Island 0-96972)   12, 12, 17, 21, 24, 23, 30   (7)

GRANT, EDDY

6-16-84   *Romancing The Stone*   (Epic AS 1853)   24, 20, 20, 18, 21, 24, 28   (7)

GREY, LAUREN

4-06-85   *Putting The Night On Hold* (Single & Coloseum Mix)   (Dice TGR 1003B)   58, 52, 52, 62, 65, 71, 72   (7)

GREY AND HANKS

1-20-79   *Dancin'*   (RCA)   29, 25, 22, 21, 18, 18, 21, 25   (8)

3-22-80   *Now I'm Fine*   (RCA)   33, 25, 20   (3)

GUTHRIE, GWEN

6-28-86   *Ain't Nothin' Goin' On But The Rent*   (Polydor 885 106-1)   62, 52, 26, 18, 8, 7, 5, 5, 4, 4, 4, 6, 7, 7, 8, 14, 14, 19, 40, 52, 59, 59, 70, 70   (24)

7-27-85   *Padlock* (Long & Short Vocal)   (Garage ITG-2001)   49, 44, 27, 25, 25, 37, 43, 56, 60, 64, 63, 72   (12)

GUY

7-30-88   *Groove Me*   (Uptown/MCA 23852)   28, 26, 24, 13, 13, 18, 21, 24, 25, 27   (10)

HALL, DARYL, AND JOHN OATES

4-14-84   *Adult Education*   (RCA JD-13715)   28, 23, 22, 26, 28, 28   (6)

1-19-85   *Method Of Modern Love/Bank On Your Love* (Vocal & Dub Version)   (RCA PW 13971)   39, 25, 17, 13, 11, 11, 15, 22, 31, 62, 66, 69   (12)

10-20-84   *Out Of Touch* (Vocal & Dub)   (RCA)   19, 13, 11, 9, 7, 4, 4, 3, 5, 6, 6, 6, 12, 13, 19, 36, 43, 45   (18)

6-29-85 *Possession Obsession/Dance On Your Knees/Everytime You Go Away* (Extended & Mixed Version) (RCA JW 14099) 57, 50, 50, 56, 57, 74 (6)

1-28-84 *Say It Isn't So* (RCA PW-13679-A) 19, 29 (2)

HAMMER, JAN

10-12-85 *"Miami Vice" Theme* (Extended Remix) (MCA 23575) 60, 50, 34, 13, 5, 4, 4, 7, 19, 24, 34, 34, 42, 42, 60, 66, 72 (15)

HANCOCK, HERBIE

1-28-84 *Autodrive* (Col. 44-04200) 20, 21, 23, 26, 28 (5)

8-18-84 *Hardrock* (Col. 44-05027) 23, 19, 15, 15, 21, 37, 48 (7)

5-05-84 *Herbie Hancock Mega Mix* (Col. 44-04960) 12, 6, 6, 5, 6, 10, 7, 8, 16 (9)

6-25-88 *Vibe Alive* (Col. 38-07718) 43 (1)

HANSON AND DAVIS

6-07-86 *I'll Take You On/Hungry For Your Love* (Fresh FRE-005X) 56, 51, 47, 42, 36, 33, 21, 18, 18, 18, 21, 18, 12, 9, 9, 10, 11, 12, 10, 10, 13, 21, 46, 47, 56, 72, 72 (27)

6-08-85 *Tonight (Love Will Make It Right)* (Vocal & Dub Version) (Fresh FRE-001X) 58, 48, 38, 38, 41, 56, 59, 61, 66, 74, 72, 72 (12)

HARDCASTLE, PAUL

6-01-85 *King Tut* (Remix) (Profile PRO-7070) 52, 31, 31, 33, 42, 65, 70, 75, 75 (9)

6-08-85 *19/The Asylum (It'z Weird)* (Extended & Destruction Mix) (Chrysalis 4V9-42875) 30, 10, 2, 2, 2, 2, 1, 1, 1, 3, 6, 7, 11, 14, 27, 39, 55, 61, 67 (19)

11-24-84 *Rain Forest* (Profile PRO-7059) 41, 38, 30, 17, 12, 12, 12, 7, 3, 1, 1, 1, 3, 3, 3, 11, 12, 17, 64, 68, 66, 65, 67, 66, 74 (25)

HARDING, CAROLYN

6-13-87 *Movin' On* (Emergency 7145) 49, 46, 46, 35, 35, 47, 59, 59, 66, 69 (10)

HARRIS, SAM

11-10-84   *Sugar Don't Bite* (New Dance Mix)   (Motown 4523 MG)   39, 36, 29, 28, 48, 47   (6)

HARRY, DEBBIE   (*See also:* BLONDIE)

11-23-85   *Feel The Spin* (Extended Dance Version)   (Manhattan V-56011)   50, 45, 40, 21, 13, 13, 4, 4, 3, 3, 7, 6, 6, 9, 16, 29, 44, 66   (18)

11-29-86   *French Kissin'*   (Geffen 0-20575)   57, 57, 52, 52, 64, 64, 64, 67, 67, 71, 74   (11)

5-23-87   *In Love With Love*   (Geffen 0-20654)   42, 39, 39, 61, 67, 67, 67, 71, 29, 20, 20, 17, 17, 23, 41, 68, 71, 71   (18)

HARTMAN, DAN

12-09-78   *Countdown/This Is It*   (Blue Sky)   28, 25, 23, 21, 21, 20, 24, 24, 26   (9)

9-08-79   *Hands Down*   (Blue Sky)   39, 35, 33, 38   (4)

6-16-84   *I Can Dream About You*   (MCA 3946)   20, 12, 11, 9, 9, 5, 4, 7, 7, 5, 9, 16, 14, 15, 15, 17, 24, 33, 45   (19)

10-28-78   *Instant Replay*   (Blue Sky)   2, 3, 6, 6, 13, 17, 25   (7)

3-16-85   *Second Nature* (Extended & Dub Version)   (MCA 23535)   59, 52, 45, 45, 50, 73   (6)

11-17-79   *Vertigo/Relight My Fire*   (Blue Sky)   34, 24, 19, 17, 10, 6, 6, 3, 3, 1, 1, 1, 1, 2, 4, 12, 13, 14, 15, 20, 21   (21)

12-01-84   *We Are The Young* (Club Version)   (MCA 23517)   24, 19, 15, 13, 13, 13, 11, 9, 9, 11, 19, 20, 29, 37, (1), 69   (15)

HAYES, ISAAC

10-13-79   *Don't Let Go*   (Polydor)   35, 30, 23, 14, 12, 11, 9, 6, 5, 4, 5, 5, 6, 6, 8, 9, 14, 15, 20, 29, 32, 40   (22)

HAYWOOD, LEON

9-16-80   *Don't Push It, Don't Force It*   (20th C.)   35, 27, 20, 14, 11, 9, 7, 6   (8)

11-03-84   *Tenderoni*   (Modern 96918)   40, 38, 38   (3)

HEAD, MURRAY

3-16-85   *One Night In Bangkok*   (RCA PW 13959)   52, 41, 34, 28, 22, 13, 11, 6, 6, 7, 15, 16, 39, 56   (14)

HEADROOM, MAX   *(See:* THE ART OF NOISE)

HEAVEN 17

3-28-87   *Contenders*   (Virgin/Atl. 0-96790)   46, 42, 39, 36, 36, 36, 42, 63, 75   (9)

HEAVY D AND THE BOYZ

8-08-87   *Chunky But Funky*   (MCA 23733)   63, 55, 50, 44, 39, 39, 39, 38, 44   (9)

12-27-86   *Mr. Big Stuff*   (MCA 23691)   58, 58, 58, 50, 39, 39, 16, 12, 8, 6, 9, 16, 16, 19, 36, 52, 58, 68, 70, 71   (20)

HENDRYX, NONA

5-30-87   *Why Should I Cry*   (EMI America V-19235)   54, 50, 45, 35, 35, 26, 26, 39, 39, 39, 49, 56, 64, 73   (14)

HENLEY, DON

4-27-85   *All She Wants To Do Is Dance* (Extended Dance & Dub Remix)   (Geffen 0-20314)   53, 46, 29, 26, 26, 26, 34, 40, 48, 61, 69, 72   (12)

HERNANDEZ, PATRICK

5-26-79   *Born To Be Alive*   (Col.)   30, 23, 17, 7, 3, 2, 2, 2, 1, 1, 2, 7, 7, 9, 12, 14, 24, 29   (18)

HEWETT, HOWARD

10-18-86   *I'm For Real*   (Elektra 69527-1)   63, 57, 49, 43, 43, 62, 73, 73   (8)

HIPSWAY

3-28-87 *The Honeythief* (Col. 44-05988) 58, 54, 42, 41, 52, 57, 66, 75 (8)

HITMAN HOWIE TEE *(See:* THE REAL ROXANNE)

HOLLIDAY, JENNIFER

10-05-85 *Hard Times For Lovers* (Extended Dance Remix) (Geffen 0-20368) 59, 46, 42, 36, 32, 32, 43, 64, 69, 69, 74 (11)

12-07-85 *No Frills Love* (Extended Dance Remix) (Geffen 0-20413) 58, 27, 25, 25, 19, 19, 17, 17, 22, 26, 36, 40, 48, 62, 67, 72 (16)

HOLLOWAY, LOLEATTA

6-16-84 *Crash Goes Love* (Dub & Blaster Mix) (Streetwise SWRL 2230) 15, 13, 10, 11, 15, 18, 17, 16, 25 (9)

10-28-78 *Queen Of The Night* (all cuts) (Gold Mind) 19, 17, 16, 27 (4)

HOTBOX

3-10-84 *Do You Wanna Lover* (Polydor 817 414-1) 25, 17, 19, 28 (4)

HOUSTON, GAIL

3-23-85 *Forever* (Club, Radio & Instrumental Mix) (Esquire HB 508) 50, 46, 42, 42, 57 (5)

HOUSTON, THELMA

11-17-84 *You Used To Hold Me So Tight* (Vocal & Dub) (MCA 23520) 26, 24, 19, 13, 10, 8, 8, 8, 8, 8, 8, 12, 21, 22, 30, 38 (16)

HOUSTON, WHITNEY

1-18-86 *How Will I Know* (Dance Remix) (Arista ADI-9449) 41, 33, 25, 16, 5, 1, 1, 3, 3, 4, 5, 8, 13, 21, 34, 38, 55, 73 (18)

5-30-87 *I Wanna Dance With Somebody (Who Loves Me)* (Arista ADI-9599) 38, 26, 7, 2, 2, 3, 3, 9, 11, 11, 10, 8, 8, 17, 40, 44, 44, 48 (18)

8-13-88 *Love Will Save The Day* (Arista ADI-9721) 29, 23, 18, 16, 12, 12, 13, 17, 28 (9)

11-21-87 *So Emotional* (Arista ADI-9641) 33, 21, 18, 14, 8, 4, 4, 4, 2, 5, 5, 13, 25, 34, 39, 48 (16)

HUDSON, AL, AND THE PARTNERS

7-07-79 *You Can Do It* (MCA) 30, 26, 24, 22, 16, 15, 13, 12, 11, 15, 19, 24, 25 (13)

THE HUMAN LEAGUE

9-27-86 *Human* (Extended Version) (A&M SP-12197) 39, 20, 11, 5, 4, 3, 2, 2, 4, 6, 6, 12, 12, 14, 14, 14, 23, 24, 24, 29, 34, 58, 66 (23)

1-24-87 *I Need Your Loving* (Remix) (A&M SP-12213) 55, 38, 38, 38, 43, 62, 68 (7)

HYDRO

11-10-79 *Stop Your Teasing* (Prism) 33, 27, 25, 24, 23, 40 (6)

HYMAN, PHYLLIS

12-22-79 *You Know How To Love Me* (Arista) 37, 37, 31, 31, 26, 23, 20, 20, 26, 33, 39 (11)

INXS

3-05-88 *Devil Inside* (Atl. 0-86622) 46, 35, 32, 26, 14, 14, 34, 45, 47 (9)

11-21-87 *Need You Tonight* (Atl. 0-86645) 37, 33, 22, 18, 15, 15, 15, 15, 13, 13, 9, 9, 14, 21, 40, 50 (16)

6-25-88 *New Sensation* (Atl. 0-86572) 39, 27 (2)

3-08-86 *What You Need* (Atl. 0-86832) 54, 31, 31, 35, 56, 62, 69, 71, 75 (9)

IAN, JANIS

2-02-80 *Fly Too High* (Col.) 37, 33, 31, 31, 35 (5)

ICE-T

6-18-88   *Colours*   (WB 0-20936)   32, 26, 18, 19, 28   (5)

11-01-86   *Dog 'N The Way*   (Techonohop 13 CRD)   64, 57, 57, 64, 67, 67, 73   (7)

10-15-88   *I'm Your Pusher*   (Sire/WB 0-21026)   24, 14, 7, 6, 9, 9, 21, 29   (8)

7-25-87   *Make It Funky*   (Sire/WB 9-20711-0)   43, 43, 31, 27, 21, 21, 29, 33, 33, 36, 41, 45, 48   (13)

IDOL, BILLY

9-15-84   *Flesh For Fantasy*   (Chrysalis AS 1901)   46, 40, 39, 36, 34, 42, 49   (7)

IMAGINATION

4-23-88   *Instinctual*   (RCA 7605-1-RD)   34, 26, 19, 16, 15, 13, 19, 40, 45, 46   (10)

INDIA

7-23-88   *Dancing On The Fire*   (WB 0-20871)   14, 14, 14, 14, 17, 28   (6)

INFORMATION SOCIETY

5-17-86   *Running*   (Tommy Boy TB-868)   63, 57, 53, 48, 48, 64, 72, 73, 74   (9)

12-24-88   *Walking Away*   (Tommy Boy TB-919)   17, 17   (2)

6-25-88   *What's On Your Mind*   (Tommy Boy TB-911)   29, 19, 14, 12, 10, 5, 5, 11, 16, 27   (10)

INNER LIFE

11-24-79   *I'm Caught Up*   (Prelude)   36, 27, 22, 17, 15, 15, 16, 16, 17, 21, 27, 34, 39   (13)

INNERCITY

10-08-88   *Big Fun*   (Virgin 0-96670)   18, 9, 5, 2, 1, 3, 4, 8, 20, 24, 29   (11)

INSTANT FUNK

12-01-79   *Body Shine/Slap, Slap, Lickedy Lap*   (Salsoul)   36, 30, 26, 23, 23, 18, 18, 21, 38   (9)

2-03-79   *I Got My Mind Made Up*   (Salsoul)   25, 22, 15, 8, 5, 4, 3, 2, 3, 4, 4, 10, 17, 22, 24, 33   (16)

THE INVISIBLE MAN'S BAND

3-01-80   *All Night Thing*   (Mango)   37, 32, 26, 17, 13, 10   (6)

THE ISLEY BROTHERS   (*See also:* ISLEY, JASPER, ISLEY)

7-25-87   *Smooth Sailin' Tonight*   (WB 0-20675)   53, 53, 48, 44, 44, 66, 66, 69, 69, 73   (10)

ISLEY, JASPER, ISLEY   (*See also:* THE ISLEY BROTHERS)

11-09-85   *Caravan Of Love*   (CBS Associated ZS9-05285)   55, 36, 25, 22, 13, 13, 14, 14, 26, 26, 29, 38, 46, 59, 61, 71   (16)

JABARA, PAUL

10-28-78   *Pleasure Island*   (Casa.)   26   (1)

JACKSON, FREDDIE   (*See also:* MELBA MOORE)

7-25-87   *Jam Tonight*   (Cap. V-15317)   65, 65, 44, 32, 32, 36, 41, 45, 45, 50   (10)

9-24-88   *Nice N' Slow*   (Cap. V-15383)   29, 26, 22, 22, 29   (5)

4-20-85   *Rock Me Tonight (For Old Times Sake)*   (Cap. V-8640)   58, 48, 42, 17, 14, 8, 7, 5, 3, 3, 3, 4, 5, 7, 7, 9, 9, 14, 21, 21, 29, 32, 46, 55, 62, 72   (25)

10-18-86   *Tasty Love*   (Cap. V-15254)   64, 40, 25, 15, 7, 6, 4, 4, 4, 10, 13, 13, 13, 21, 23, 23, 27, 32, 43, 58, 71   (21)

8-31-85   *You Are My Lady* (Special Theme Version)   (Cap. V-8650)   34, 27, 16, 14, 12, 11, 11, 21, 24, 26, 29, 37, 57, 67, 71   (15)

JACKSON, JANET

11-15-86   *Control*   (A&M SP-12209)   42, 24, 13, 13, 7, 4, 2, 2, 2, 2, 2, 2, 1, 3, 7, 13, 18, 37, 41, 57, 67, 74   (22)

9-01-84   *Don't Stand A Chance* (Remix & Dub Version) (A&M SP-12105)   22, 18, 14, 11, 10, 9, 9, 12, 16, 35, 43, 50   (12)

5-03-86   *Nasty* (Remix) (A&M SP-12178)   36, 21, 14, 10, 7, 4, 4, 4, 3, 3, 4, 4, 4, 9, 14, 11, 9, 8, 8, 12, 13, 21, 24, 27, 27, 43, 54, 69, 73   (29)

5-30-87   *The Pleasure Principle* (A&M SP-12230)   59, 55, 33, 25, 25, 9, 4, 4, 6, 6, 6, 3, 3, 12, 48, 51, 51, 58   (18)

2-15-86   *What Have You Done For Me Lately* (Extended Mix) (A&M SP-12167)   33, 20, 6, 2, 1, 1, 1, 3, 4, 3, 3, 9, 10, 13, 19, 24, 30, 29, 49, 61, 66, 70   (22)

8-23-86   *When I Think Of You* (Remix) (A&M SP-12180)   33, 15, 7, 4, 1, 1, 2, 3, 4, 6, 7, 10, 17, 25, 33, 33, 40, 61, 65, 65, 65, 69, 73, 73, 75   (25)

JACKSON, JERMAINE   *(See also:* THE JACKSONS)

8-25-84   *Dynamite* (Arista ADI-9222)   25, 20, 20, 18, 16, 15, 15, 31, 34, 42   (10)

JACKSON, MICHAEL   *(See also:* THE JACKSONS; STEVIE WONDER)

10-17-87   *Bad* (Epic OE-40600)   32, 13, 2, 1, 1, 1, 1, 1, 7, 10, 27, 27, 27, 42   (14)

9-08-79   *Don't Stop Til You Get Enough* (Epic)   25, 17, 9, 5, 3, 1, 1, 1, 3, 4, 9, 13, 33   (13)

3-19-88   *Man In The Mirror* (Epic 40-07510)   37, 34, 26, 19, 19, 22, 48   (7)

12-15-79   *Rock With You/Working Day And Night* (Epic)   29, 20, 20, 17, 17, 25   (6)

12-17-88   *Smooth Criminal* (Epic 49-07895)   26, 19, 19   (3)

2-04-84   *Thriller* (Epic AS 1805)   20, 19, 19, 13, 6, 4, 3, 5, 4, 6, 11, 16, 24   (11)

12-19-88   *The Way You Make Me Feel* (Epic 49-07487)   36, 14, 14, 14, 8, 2, 3, 3, 3, 3, 6, 20, 48   (13)

JACKSON, REBBIE

9-15-84   *Centipede* (Col. 44-05047)   34, 28, 25, 18, 12, 6, 5, 4, 4, 9, 7, 6, 5, 4, 4, 4, 4, 7, 15, 20, 23, 27, 26, 43, (1), 72   (26)

3-12-88 *Plaything* (Col. 44-07560) 41, 35, 33, 39, 42, 46 (6)

10-18-86 *Reaction* (Col. 44-05927) 59, 49, 44, 38, 36, 47, 64, 64, 69, 74 (10)

THE JACKSONS *(See also:* JERMAINE JACKSON; MICHAEL JACKSON)

12-16-78 *Blame It On The Boogie* (Epic) 28, 25, 23, 23, 27 (5)

4-21-79 *Shake Your Body (Down To The Ground)* (Epic) 30, 29, 29, 37 (4)

8-11-84 *State Of Shock* (Dance Mix) (Epic 49-05022) 19, 9, 4, 6, 10, 12, 20, 47 (8)

10-06-84 *Torture* (Dance Mix) (Epic 49-05057) 30, 26, 24, 22, 22, 26, 45 (7)

JACOBS, DEBBIE

1-19-80 *High On Your Love* (MCA) 29, 19, 11, 7, 5, 3, 2, 1, 2, 1, 1, 1 (12)

6-09-79 *Undercover Lover/Don't You Want My Love* (MCA) 38, 30, 23, 14, 10, 8, 6, 5, 5, 5, 6, 7, 8, 13, 14, 23, 26 (17)

JACQUES, PETER, BAND

2-10-79 *Fire Night Dance* (Prelude) 28, 23, 19, 14, 12, 11, 9, 7, 6, 6, 11, 18, 24, 33, 38 (15)

JAGGER, MICK *(See also:* DAVID BOWIE; THE ROLLING STONES)

2-23-85 *Just Another Night* (Album & Edited Version) (Col. AS 1991) 40, 36, 30, 28, 24, 18, 12, 12, 14, 16, 20, 61, 66, 69 (14)

JAMES, FREDDIE

7-07-79 *Get Up And Boogie* (WB) 33, 25, 16, 12, 8, 6, 5, 4, 3, 3, 4, 8, 12, 17 (14)

10-13-79 *Hollywood/Dance Little Boy Blue* (WB) 32, 26, 22, 20, 15, 12, 12, 16, 34 (9)

JAMES, JESSE

8-15-87   *I Can Do Bad By Myself* (TTED 3026-A)   60, 57, 60, 72, 75, 75, 75   (7)

JAMES, RICK

5-04-85   *Can't Stop/Oh What A Night (4 Luv)* (Long Version)   (Motown)   50, 44, 32, 29, 29, 37, 46, 61, 74   (9)

7-13-85   *Glow* (Reprise Instrumental)   (Gordy 4539 GG)   53, 32, 28, 25, 22, 20, 20, 32, 41, 58, 65, 71   (12)

1-19-80   *Love Gun*   (Motown)   38, 35, 32, 37, 40   (5)

8-18-84   *17* (Vocal & Instrumental)   (Motown 4522 MG)   16, 13, 11, 26, 40, 44, 49, 49   (8)

8-09-86   *Sweet And Sexy Thing*   (Gordy 4561 GG)   64, 59, 59, 69   (4)

JAMES, RICK, FEATURING ROXANNE SHANTE

7-23-88   *Loosey's Rap*   (Reprise/WB 0-20941)   26, 15, 13, 9, 10, 10, 19, 19, 20, 23, 30   (11)

JANICE

5-17-86   *Bye-Bye* (Extended Version)   (4th & Broadway/Island PRO-424)   50, 44, 23, 16, 16, 23, 22, 19, 16, 14, 14, 20, 25, 26, 42, 53, 62, 67, 74   (19)

JELLYBEAN

8-06-88   *Jingo*   (Chrysalis 4V9-43206)   27, 23, 22, 22, 29   (5)

4-09-88   *Just A Mirage*   (Chrysalis 4V9-43223)   34, 22, 17, 15, 15, 29, 41, 41, 49   (9)

8-18-84   *The Mexican*   (EMI America V-7831 1/2)   20, 18, 13, 9, 8, 12, 20, 32, 44, 50   (10)

3-01-86   *Sidewalk Talk* (Remix)   (EMI America V-19204)   52, 47, 36, 32, 32, 52, 59, 64, 74   (9)

7-18-87   *Who Found Who*   (Chrysalis 4V9-43089)   36, 25, 25, 23, 15, 9, 6, 4, 2, 2, 11, 15, 21, 29, 35, 41, 48   (17)

JELLYBEAN/STEVEN DANTE

9-26-87   *The Real Thing*   (Chrysalis 4V9-43171)   63, 33, 24, 14, 11, 7, 6, 5, 13, 19, 17, 20, 26, 34, 34, 34, 41, 50   (18)

JENKINS, KECHIA

3-12-88   *I Need Somebody*   (Profile PRO-7180)   43, 38, 38, 47   (4)

THE JETS

7-18-87   *Cross My Broken Heart*   (MCA 4399)   55, 50, 50, 40, 24, 18, 18, 36, 40, 40, 43, 50   (12)

3-29-86   *Crush On You* (Extended Version)   (MCA 23613)   42, 26, 16, 16, 11, 11, 11, 12, 12, 12, 20, 25, 25, 28, 29, 41, 61, 68   (17)

11-30-85   *Curiosity* (Extended Mix)   (MCA 23590)   56, 48, 44, 40, 40, 27, 27, 27, 29, 34, 44, 54, 66, 72   (14)

11-21-87   *I Do You*   (MCA 23798)   39, 34, 29, 28, 35, 43, 43, 43   (8)

8-09-86   *Private Number* (Remix)   (MCA 23637)   61, 46, 30, 30, 41, 51, 60, 66, 73   (9)

3-12-88   *Rocket 2 U*   (MCA 23822)   34, 28, 16, 10, 3, 2, 2, 2, 11, 19, 29, 46, 50   (13)

9-24-88   *Sendin' All My Love*   (MCA 23887)   28, 12, 12, 16, 19, 24   (6)

JIMMY, BOBBY, AND THE CRITTERS

11-29-86   *The New York Rapper*   (Macola 947)   56, 56, 48, 40, 36, 36, 36, 36, 51, 51, 57, 63, 70   (13)

7-12-86   *Roaches*   (Macola 924)   53, 42, 12, 4, 2, 2, 5, 7, 13, 14, 17, 18, 18, 23, 23, 39, 60, 72   (18)

JOHN, ELTON

7-30-88   *I Don't Wanna Go On With You Like That*   (MCA 23870)   22, 19, 17, 15, 11, 11, 16, 18, 19, 24   (10)

11-24-79   *Victim Of Love/Johnny B. Goode*   (MCA)   33, 29, 26, 38   (4)

JOHNNY HATES JAZZ

6-11-88   *Shattered Dreams*   (Virgin 0-96668)   29, 27, 27   (3)

JOHNSON, HOWARD

9-14-85   *Stand Up/So Tuff* (Specially Remixed Version)   (A&M SP-12137)   52, 45, 38, 28, 26, 26, 29, 37, 48, 66, 70, 75   (12)

JOHNSON, JESSE/JESSE JOHNSON'S REVUE

2-23-85   *Be Your Man/Special Love* (Specially Remixed Version)   (A&M SP-12122)   39, 33, 27, 22, 12, 7, 5, 5, 4, 4, 16, 18, 34, 38, 56, 62, 67, 75   (18)

6-01-85   *Can You Help Me/Free World* (Extended Version)   (A&M SP-12129)   43, 24, 16, 14, 14, 11, 8, 8, 12, 17, 24, 32, 43, 63, 69   (15)

10-25-86   *Crazay*   (A&M SP-2878)   —, 45, 40, 40, 44, 42, 42, 37, 29, 21, 21, 21, 17, 17, 17, 21, 21, 26, 32, 65, 73   (21)

8-17-85   *I Want My Girl* (Extended Version)   (A&M SP-12144)   52, 32, 25, 23, 20, 20, 29, 36, 36, 49, 57, 61, 69   (13)

5-21-88   *Love Struck*   (A&M SP-12265)   40, 20, 13, 13, 19, 33   (6)

1-24-87   *She (I Can't Resist)*   (A&M SP-12219)   63, 63, 46, 42, 41, 50, 61, 65, 74   (9)

JOHNSON, LORRAINE

11-25-78   *Feed The Flame*   (Prelude)   26, 22, 16, 16, 14, 13, 13, 12, 9, 9, 10, 11, 12, 15, 20, 22   (16)

JOLI, FRANCE

8-04-79   *Come To Me/Don't Stop Dancing*   (Prelude)   26, 19, 10, 8, 6, 4, 3, 1, 1, 1, 2, 2, 5, 9, 17, 18, 37   (17)

6-08-85   *Does He Dance?* (Dub Mix)   (Epic 49-05191)   48, 43, 43, 46, 53, 61, 70   (7)

JONES, BUSTA

12-08-79   *Dancing All Over The World*   (Spring)   36, 27, 24, 24, 21, 21, 16, 20, 28, 35   (10)

JONES, GRACE

11-22-86 *I'm Not Perfect (But I'm Perfect For You)* (Manhattan 56038) 55, 50, 50, 45, 39, 33, 33, 33, 30, 25, 25, 24, 24, 32, 57, 69 (16)

9-01-79 *On Your Knees* (Island) 38, 35, 34, 32, 29, 40 (6)

11-23-85 *Slave To The Rhythm* (Extended Version) (Manhattan/Island/Cap. SPRO 9533) 56, 30, 23, 8, 4, 4, 1, 1, 5, 8, 6, 15, 16, 19, 23, 39, 49, 54, 66, 73 (20)

JONES, HOWARD

8-03-85 *Life In One Day* (Vocal, Remix & LP Version) (Elektra ED 5065) 57, 47, 42, 42, 61, 67, 73, 74 (8)

1-28-84 *New Song* (Elektra 0-66977) 25, 25 (2)

3-30-85 *Things Can Only Get Better* (Elektra ED 5043) 57, 53, 44, 26, 19, 17, 14, 11, 11, 13, 13, 22, 20, 19, 17, 17, 19, 19, 37, 41, 62, 71 (22)

JONES, ORAN "JUICE"

8-16-86 *The Rain* (Long Version) (Def Jam/Col. 44-05930) 49, 40, 32, 14, 10, 4, 2, 1, 1, 2, 3, 4, 6, 12, 14, 15, 15, 17, 19, 26, 26, 26, 29, 45, 45, 47, 45, 56, 63, 75 (30)

JONES, TAMIKO

8-04-79 *Can't Live Without Your Love* (Polydor) 30, 28, 26, 26, 25, 22, 20, 20, 22, 32 (10)

THE JONES GIRLS

5-12-79 *You Gonna Make Me Love Somebody Else* (P.I.) 36, 34, 29, 28, 24, 19, 15, 13, 13, 12, 14, 15, 21, 26, 32 (15)

JUICY

3-29-86 *Sugar Free* (Super Dance Mix) (Private I/CBS 4ZP-05337) 62, 55, 48, 44, 43, 52, 61, 72 (8)

JUMP, WALLY, JUNIOR, AND THE CRIMINAL ELEMENT

3-07-87 *Turn Me Loose* (Criminal CRIM 00006) 50, 47, 46, 60, 58, 56, 56, 65, 67 (9)

JUST ICE

4-05-86 *Lataya/Put That Record Back On* (Fresh FRS-003) 54, 46, 37, 29, 19, 19, 19, 26, 35, 52, 58, 66, 74, 75 (14)

K.T.P.

5-16-87 *Certain Things Are Likely* (Magnet/Mer./PolyGram 885 722-1) 55, 53, 49, 46, 38, 32, 32, 32, 34, 48, 58, 58, 65, 71 (14)

KAH, HUBERT

12-19-88 *Military Drums* (Curb/MCA 7172) 46, 40, 40, 40, 39 (5)

KAMEN, NICK

4-25-87 *Each Time You Break My Heart* (Sire/WB 0-20632) 53, 49, 45, 41, 39, 35, 32, 20, 17, 17, 15, 15, 34, 36, 36, 47, 54, 61, 71 (19)

KANE, GENERAL

10-11-86 *Crack Killed Apple Jack* (Gordy/Motown 4568 GG) 47, 42, 38, 36, 47, 60, 60, 66, 66, 72 (10)

KANE, MADLEEN

3-17-79 *Forbidden Love* (WB) 29, 26, 19, 14, 12, 8, 6, 5, 5, 6, 6, 9, 9, 15, 19, 40 (16)

THE KANE GANG

4-09-88 *Don't Look Any Further* (Cap. V-15359) 47, 32, 26, 21, 21, 37, 44 (7)

KASHIF *(See also:* KENNY G; MELBA MOORE*)*

11-09-85 *Condition Of The Heart* (Extended Version) (Arista ADI-6416) 49, 45, 45, 61, 66, 70, 75, 75 (8)

KASHIF AND MELI'SA MORGAN *(See also:* MELI'SA MORGAN*)*

1-16-88 *Love Changes* (Arista ADI-9627) 48, 33, 30, 43, 48, 49 (6)

KEMP, JOHNNY

10-08-88   *Dancin' With Myself*   (Col. 44-07870)   23, 20, 12, 12, 18, 26   (6)

6-21-86   *Just Another Lover* (Extended Mix)   (Col. 44-05368)   57, 50, 46, 46, 57, 67   (6)

4-16-88   *Just Got Paid*   (Col. 44-07588)   41, 23, 17, 14, 14, 2, 1, 1, 1, 2, 5, 5, 11, 21, 27   (15)

KENNEDY, JOYCE

12-22-84   *Tailor Made* (Vocal & Instrumental)   (A&M SP-12117)   32, 32, 32, 31, 42, 49   (6)

KENNY G

4-21-84   *Hi, How Ya Doin'?*   (Arista AD 1-9195)   25, 30   (2)

KENNY G AND KASHIF   (*See also:* KASHIF)

6-01-85   *Love On The Rise* (Instrumental & Extended Version)   (Arista ADI-9338)   55, 50, 45, 40, 40, 52, 62, 71   (8)

KHAN, CHAKA   (*See also:* RUFUS)

10-13-84   *I Feel For You*   (WB 0-20249)   19, 8, 1, 1, 1, 1, 1, 1, 1, 2, 3, 3, 3, 3, 6, 12, 19, 24, 30, 38, 47   (21)

9-28-85   *(Krush Groove) Can't Stop The Street* (Extended Dance Mix & Instrumental)   (WB 0-20367)   47, 31, 23, 19, 16, 16, 18, 22, 34, 39, 50, 57, 65, 65, 72, 72   (16)

8-02-86   *Love Of A Lifetime* (Extended Dance Version)   (WB 0-20487)   36, 22, 14, 12, 10, 10, 13, 21, 24, 27, 53, 67, 75   (13)

2-09-85   *This Is My Night/Caught In The Act* (Extended Version)   (WB 20296)   36, 18, 13, 8, 6, 6, 9, 20, 31, 41, 46, 61, 69   (13)

KIKROKOS

10-28-78   *Jungle D.J.*   (Polydor)   24, 21, 20, 18, 28   (5)

KING

5-31-86   *Alone Without You* (Street MIX)   (Epic/CBS 49-05366)   45, 39, 39, 52, 65, 69   (6)

7-13-85   *Love And Pride* (Extended & Dub Mix)   (Epic 49-05236)   60, 50, 46, 42, 38, 38, 38, 39, 51, 53, 53, 60, 68, 75   (14)

KING, BEN E.

3-15-80   *Music Trance*   (Atl.)   34, 24, 19, 15   (4)

KING, EVELYN "CHAMPAGNE"

3-29-86   *High Horse* (Remix)   (RCA PW-14309)   58, 47, 42, 27, 25, 23, 22, 30, 34, 58, 65, 69   (12)

10-01-88   *Hold On To What You've Got*   (EMI-Manhattan V-56101)   28, 25, 25   (3)

1-27-79   *I Don't Know If It's Right*   (RCA)   29, 27, 26, 25, 29, 29   (6)

10-27-84   *Just For The Night* (Vocal & T.V. Track)/So In Love   (RCA PW-13915)   32, 30, 28, 27, 35, 42, 40, 44, 44, 44, 44, 48   (12)

11-16-85   *Your Personal Touch*   (RCA PW-14202)   56, 51, 37, 30, 26, 23, 23, 17, 17, 14, 14, 19, 23, 27, 32, 38, 48, 63, 68, 75   (20)

KING, PAUL

8-29-87   *I Know*   (Epic 49-6866)   52, 30, 30, 30, 34, 38, 48   (7)

KINNEY, FERN

8-04-79   *Groove Me*   (TK)   24, 20, 15, 13, 10, 8, 5, 5, 11, 13, 15, 18   (12)

KISSOON, KATIE

9-15-84   *I Need A Man In My Life*   (Jive JDI-9247)   41, 42, 42, 50   (4)

KITT, EARTHA

1-28-84   *Where Is My Man*   (Streetwise 2217)   11, 11, 12, 12, 17, 29   (6)

KLYMAXX

10-05-85 *I Miss You* (Extended Version & Instrumental) (Constellation 23587) 55, 49, 45, 45, 54, 70, 70 (7)

3-23-85 *Meeting In The Ladies Room/Ask Me No Questions* (Constellation 23539) 57, 47, 43, 30, 24, 15, 13, 11, 10, 10, 10, 14, 23, 25, 29, 35, 55, 65 (18)

12-15-84 *The Men All Pause* (Vocal & Dub) (Constellation) 35, 26, 26, 26, 24, 23, 17, 15, 10, 8, 7, 6, 4, 3, 3, 5, 14, 17, 22, 29, 33, 35, 44, 64, 73, 73 (26)

KNIGHT, GLADYS, & THE PIPS

11-28-87 *Love Overboard* (MCA L33-17431) 40, 23, 18, 14, 11, 11, 11, 6, 6, 4, 5, 5, 4, 5, 12, 30, 41, 46, 50 (19)

3-26-88 *Lovin' On Next To Nothin'* (MCA 23804) 47, 42, 27, 20, 18, 16, 14, 12, 12, 28, 39, 45 (12)

3-30-85 *My Time* (Extended & Instrumental Version) (Col. 44-05161) 56, 51, 51, 56, 63 (5)

KONK

8-11-84 *Your Life* (Party Mix) (Sleeping Bag SLX 009) 27, 24, 30 (3)

KOOL & THE GANG

8-03-85 *Cherish* (Remix)/*Fresh/Misled* (Special Mix) (De-Lite 880 947-1) 60, 48, 41, 37, 30, 30, 32, 42, 43, 44, 55, 61, 62, 64, 72 (15)

4-06-85 *Fresh* (Remix & Dance Mix) (De-Lite 880 623-1) 47, 33, 15, 10, 9, 4, 2, 1, 1, 3, 14, 16, 20, 22, 22, 28, 36, 63 (18)

9-22-79 *Ladies' Night* (De-Lite) 35, 27, 22, 13, 10, 6, 4, 3, 3, 6, 10, 32, 39 (13)

3-02-85 *Misled* (Remix) (De-Lite) 30, 18, 13, 13, 25, 49, 62, 66 (8)

4-11-87 *Stone Love* (Mer./PolyGram 888 292-1) 38, 23, 17, 15, 15, 15, 16, 22, 23, 59, 75 (11)

11-08-86 *Victory* (Mer./PolyGram 888 074-1) 56, 39, 33, 27, 27, 22, 17, 10, 10, 10, 8, 8, 8, 15, 18, 19, 27, 56, 68, 70, 75, 75 (22)

KOOL MOE DEE

5-30-87   *Go See The Doctor*   (Jive/Arista 1024-1-JD)   60, 57, 44, 44, 44, 55, 59   (7)

2-13-88   *How Ya Like Me Now*   (Jive/RCA 1073-1-JD)   42, 37, 35, 44   (4)

8-13-88   *Let's Go*   (Jive/RCA 1117-1-JD)   28, 20, 15, 13, 10, 8, 8, 11, 9, 23   (10)

4-16-88   *Wild, Wild West*   (Jive/RCA 1086-1-JD)   44, 30, 25, 23, 17, 10, 7, 3, 6, 8, 12, 25, 30   (13)

KRAFTWERK

11-08-86   *Musique Non Stop*   (WB 0-20549)   53, 38, 29, 25, 25, 19, 15, 12, 12, 12, 9, 7, 7, 7, 14, 15, 17, 24, 62, 66, 71, 72   (22)

5-09-87   *The Telephone Call*   (WB 0-20627)   54, 51, 49, 45, 42, 42, 59, 59, 64, 68   (10)

1-28-84   *Tour De France*   (WB 0-20146)   5, 6, 7, 7, 9, 15, 22, 21, 23, 25, 30   (11)

KRANZ, GEORGE

1-28-84   *Trommeltanz (Din Da Da)*   (Personal P-49804)   10, 8, 9, 11, 12, 14, 18, 27   (8)

THE L.A. DREAM TEAM

11-16-85   *The Dream Team Is In The House*   (Dream Team DRT-631)   59, 52, 46, 41, 35, 30, 30, 25, 25, 21, 18, 18, 21, 25, 30, 30, 25, 22, 22, 31, 35, 36, 42, 52, 61, 67, 64, 69, 65, 64, 64, 71, 73, 74   (34)

8-02-86   *Nursery Rhymes*   (MCA 23639)   42, 36, 32, 27, 24, 24, 32, 42, 53, 63, 67, 71   (12)

LAX

6-16-79   *Dancin' At The Disco*   (Prelude)   37, 34, 33, 40   (4)

L.I.F.E.

6-07-86   *All Played Out*   (Dance-Sing DS-802)   50, 50, 59, 64, 67, 72   (6)

L.L. COOL J

3-05-88   *Going Back To Cali'*   (Def Jam/Col. 44-07563)   45, 32, 29, 19, 19, 24, 30, 29, 32, 46   (10)

11-30-85   *I Can Give You More/I Can't Live Without My Radio*   (Def Jam 44-05291)   65, 43, 36, 27, 27, 24, 24, 19, 15, 13, 8, 8, 8, 9, 10, 26, 30, 44, 58, 67, 65, 73   (22)

5-30-87   *I'm Bad*   (Def Jam/Col. 44-06799)   57, 52, 35, 10, 10, 5, 5, 5, 5, 5, 5, 5, 12, 20, 32, 37, 37, 46   (18)

3-29-86   *Rock The Bells* (Original Version)   (Def Jam/Col. 44-05349)   40, 15, 9, 7, 5, 3, 3, 6, 16, 20, 28, 42, 42, 57, 63, 69, 73   (17)

6-21-86   *You'll Rock* (Remix)   (Def Jam/Col. 44-05907)   51, 47, 41, 36, 33, 28, 28, 38, 51, 63, 74   (11)

LA FLAVOUR

1-19-80   *Mandolay*   (Sweet City)   33, 26, 22, 19, 16, 13, 10, 9, 8, 8, 10, 12   (12)

12-19-87   *Mandolay*   (Sea Thru 91935)   42, 39, 39, 39, 37, 48   (6)

LABAN

12-27-86   *Love Me In Siberia*   (Critique CR 8525)   59, 59, 59, 47, 47, 47, 48, 54, 65, 72   (10)

LaBELLE, PATTI

1-28-84   *If Only You Knew*   (P.I. 44-20417)   24, 24, 22, 22, 19, 21, 20, 30   (8)

4-07-79   *Music Is My Way Of Life*   (Epic)   29, 21, 18, 16, 13, 11, 10, 7, 6, 6, 8, 8, 15, 38, 40   (15)

8-23-86   *Oh People (Remix)*   (MCA 23651)   41, 34, 30, 22, 22, 25, 34, 59, 68   (9)

3-07-87   *Something Special*   (MCA 23649)   45, 44, 61, 65, 60, 53, 53, 70, 72   (9)

7-20-85   *Stir It Up* (Extended Version & Edit)   (MCA 23567)   60, 47, 29, 18, 10, 10, 16, 16, 18, 35, 36, 45, 57, 62, 68, 71   (16)

LaBELLE, PATTI, AND HAROLD FALTERMEYER

2-16-85   *New Attitude/Axel-F* (Extended Version)   (MCA 23534)   34, 22, 14, 7, 5, 4, 1, 1, 3, 3, 3, 3, 8, 9, 9, 9, 12, 20, 22, 24, 25, 25, 40, 43, 53, 66   (26)

LaBELLE, PATTI, AND MICHAEL McDONALD   (*See also:* MICHAEL McDONALD)

4-05-86   *On My Own* (Extended Version)   (MCA 23607)   59, 45, 25, 12, 8, 4, 1, 1, 1, 2, 2, 3, 5, 5, 5, 9, 22, 29, 41, 48, 64, 64   (22)

LAIN BACK

9-21-85   *One Life/It's The Way You Do It* (Velvet Spike Mix)   (Sire 0-20358)   58, 53, 48, 48, 58, 64, 75   (7)

1-28-84   *White Horse*   (Sire 0-20178)   6, 3, 1, 4, 3, 2, 2, 2, 2, 2, 2, 1, 1, 1, 1, 8, 13, 24, 27, 28   (20)

LAKESIDE

7-07-84   *Outrageous*   (Solar 4984)   27, 19, 16, 14, 15, 15, 18, 26   (8)

LANE, SUZI

8-1879   *Ooh, La, La/Harmony*   (Elektra)   36, 33, 31, 28, 22, 16, 9, 6, 4, 3, 2, 2, 1, 1, 2, 3, 4, 5, 17, 17   (20)

THE LATIN RASCALS

10-31-87   *Disorderly Conduct/Arabian Nights*   (Tin Pan Apple 885 981-1)   37, 26, 25, 25, 36, 38, 46   (7)

5-30-87   *Macho Mozart*   (Tin Pan Apple 885 567-1)   46, 43, 36, 36, 36, 47, 49, 62, 68, 68, 72   (11)

LATTISAW, STACY

2-21-87   *Jump Into My Life*   (Motown 4574 MG)   50, 35, 29, 19, 18, 21, 21, 41, 51, 69, 71   (11)

10-04-86   *Nail It To The Wall*   (Motown 4563 MG)   47, 26, 16, 10, 6, 4, 4, 10, 16, 16, 14, 14, 16, 16, 16, 25, 32, 32, 43, 48, 60, 67   (22)

LAUPER, CYNDI

12-13-86 *Change Of Heart* (Portrait/CBS RAS 2560) 58, 49, 45, 45, 45, 45, 53, 53, 58, 65, 68, 75 (12)

3-17-84 *Girls Just Want To Have Fun (Remix)* (Portrait 4R9-04971) 12, 6, 1, 1, 2, 3, 4, 5, 12, 22, 30 (11)

8-11-84 *She Bop* (Special Dance Mix Instrumental) (Portrait 49-05011) 18, 11, 8, 5, 6, 4, 7, 5, 4, 4, 16, 30, 50 (12)

4-25-87 *What's Going On* (Portrait/Epic 4R9-06740) 40, 37, 29, 26, 22, 19, 16, 15, 15, 15, 51, 55, 68, 75, 72 (15)

LaVETTE, BETTY

11-11-78 *Doin' The Best That I Can* (West End) 28, 19, 16, 13, 10, 12, 12, 16, 16, 24, 27 (11)

LAW, BARBARA

12-01-79 *Take All Of Me* (Pavillion) 35, 31, 28, 26, 26, 24, 24, 39 (8)

LE FOXXE

6-29-85 *French Kiss* (Extended Version) (Telestar TCT 2340) 65, 54, 49, 41, 41, 47, 65, 67 (8)

LEE, TONEY

10-31-87 *My Baby Loves Me* (Jump Street JS-1011) 39, 35, 35, 43, 48 (5)

LEKAKIS, PAUL

2-21-87 *Boom Boom* (ZYX 5571) 52, 34, 23, 23, 22, 20, 17, 14, 14, 25, 40, 59, 67, 71 (14)

LEMON

1-20-79 *A-Freak-A/Chance To Dance* (Prelude) 20, 18, 16, 16, 17, 20, 22, 23, 25 (9)

LEVEL42

5-10-86 *Something About You* (Remix) (Polydor/PolyGram 883 957-1) 63, 56, 48, 39, 31, 31, 36, 51, 55, 64, 71 (11)

LEVERT

7-25-87   *Casanova*   (Atl. 0-86673)   55, 55, 34, 22, 13, 10, 8, 5, 5, 1, 1, 1, 5, 12, 19, 29, 32, 42, 47, 50   (20)

10-04-86   *Pop Pop Goes My Mind*   (Atl. 0-86780)   48, 37, 30, 27, 24, 24, 35, 46, 54, 54, 70, 75   (12)

LEWIS, HUEY, AND THE NEWS

3-31-84   *I Want A New Drug* (Dance Remix)   (Chrysalis 4V9-42779)   17, 4, 5, 9, 7, 9, 15, 29   (8)

8-10-85   *The Power Of Love* (Jellybean Remix & Instrumental)   (Chrysalis 4V9-42889)   60, 37, 29, 24, 21, 21, 28, 32, 35, 38, 52, 58, 62, 64, 74   (15)

LEWIS, SHIRLEY

11-05-88   *(You Used To Be) Romantic*   (Vendetta VE-7006)   29, 27   (2)

LIMAHL

5-11-85   *Neverending Story* (Club Mix & Instrumental)   (EMI America V-7854)   52, 47, 47, 42, 38, 38, 39, 43, 56, 68, 72   (11)

LIME

6-15-85   *Unexpected Lovers* (Extended Version)   (TSR 837)   52, 30, 13, 7, 5, 5, 5, 7, 11, 17, 31, 42, 56, 65, 66, 72   (16)

THE LIMIT

12-22-84   *Say Yeah* (Vocal & Instrumental)   (Portrait 4R9-05106)   35, 35, 35, 35, 33, 32, 35, 35, 39, 48, 48, 48, 64, 69, 70   (15)

LIPPS, INC.

2-02-80   *Funkytown*   (Casa.)   33, 23, 15, 8, 5, 2, 1, 2, 2, 2   (10)

9-22-79   *Rock It*   (Casa.)   36, 32, 28, 19, 16, 16, 15, 18, 19, 38   (10)

LIQUID GOLD

12-15-79   *Dance Yourself Dizzy*   (Parachute)   36, 30, 30, 25, 25, 40   (6)

3-31-79 *My Baby's Baby* (Parachute) 30, 26, 22, 16, 11, 8, 8, 9, 10, 11, 12, 20, 26 (13)

LISA LISA AND CULT JAM

4-26-88 *Everything Will B Fine* (Col. 44-07584) 42, 27, 24, 22, 22, 33, 45, 48 (8)

4-25-87 *Head To Toe* (Col. 44-067057) 38, 26, 22, 11, 8, 1, 1, 1, 1, 1, 1, 2, 3, 8, 8, 11, 20, 27, 43, 46, 50, 50, 57 (23)

8-22-87 *Lost In Emotion* (Col. 44-06872) 58, 39, 13, 10, 10, 5, 4, 3, 2, 2, 4, 10, 17, 21, 31, 46, 49 (17)

LISA LISA AND CULT JAM WITH FULL FORCE *(See also:* FULL FORCE)

11-23-85 *Can You Feel The Beat* (Extended Version) (Col. 44-05295) 36, 15, 8, 3, 1, 1, 2, 2, 2, 7, 8, 17, 22, 26, 34, 33, 29, 26, 26, 29, 32, 33, 33, 35, 47, 67, 75, 74 (28)

5-18-85 *I Wonder If I Take You Home* (Rap, Cult Jam Dub & Extended Version) (Col. 44-05203) 31, 16, 14, 4, 1, 4, 3, 3, 3, 2, 2, 2, 2, 2, 3, 6, 6, 6, 8, 8, 10, 20, 24, 33, 48, 68 (26)

LIVING IN A BOX

7-04-87 *Living In A Box* (Chrysalis) 52, 48, 38, 34, 34, 27, 23, 22, 16, 24, 27, 27, 30, 39, 50 (15)

LOLA

2-28-87 *Wax The Van* (Jump Street/Island JS-1007) 46, 38, 40, 36, 36, 52, 66, 69 (8)

LOOSE CHANGE

12-01-79 *Straight From The Heart* (Casa.) 34, 27, 24, 22, 22, 19, 19, 31 (8)

LOOSE ENDS

5-18-85 *Hangin' On A String (Contemplating)/A Little Spice* (Extended Dance Version) (MCA 23543) 57, 43, 33, 21, 18, 18, 18, 19, 14, 12, 11, 11, 16, 28, 40, 57, 65, 66, 73 (19)

3-14-87   *Slow Down*   (MCA 23699)   59, 55, 42, 38, 36, 30, 22, 19, 19, 27, 31, 34, 41, 63, 71   (15)

8-02-86   *Stay A Little While, Child* (Extended Version)   (MCA 23635)   55, 45, 41, 37, 37, 46, 59, 54, 47, 42, 36, 29, 25, 19, 16, 16, 17, 19, 19, 18, 20, 23, 23, 23, 26, 27, 27, 31, 36, 39, 56, 72   (32)

LOPEZ, DENISE

12-03-88   *If You Feel It*   (Vendetta VE-7013)   22, 14, 10, 6, 6   (5)

6-04-88   *Sayin' Sorry Don't Make It Right*   (Vendetta VE-7000)   26, 16, 7, 5, 3, 2, 2, 1, 2, 6, 18, 27, 30   (13)

LORBER, JEFF

3-16-85   *Step By Step* (Extended Remix & Instrumental)   (Arista ADI-9311)   51, 40, 35, 32, 32, 34, 34, 36, 46, 48, 60, 63   (12)

LORBER, JEFF, FEATURING KARYN WHITE

12-13-86   *Facts Of Love*   (WB 0-20545)   62, 46, 40, 40, 40, 34, 29, 29, 28, 28, 33, 47, 64, 72   (14)

LOREN, BRYAN

4-14-84   *Lollipop Luv*   (Philly World PWR 2015)   22, 30, 28, 24, 26   (5)

LOVE, JOESKI

12-06-86   *My Girl*   (Elektra/Asylum 66833)   55, 49, 42, 32, 32, 32, 32, 48, 48, 49, 57, 64, 70   (13)

4-12-86   *Pee-Wee's Dance*   (Vintertainment/Elektra ED 5147)   61, 26, 14, 10, 8, 8, 7, 3, 1, 5, 8, 8, 6, 6, 7, 17, 22, 28, 33, 47, 59, 69   (22)

LOVE, VIKKI

10-05-85   *Stop Playing On Me* (Extended Mix)   (4th & B'way 418)   60, 51, 46, 35, 25, 20, 18, 15, 12, 12, 17, 28, 28, 35, 35, 59, 65, 71, 75   (19)

LOVE DELUXE

6-30-79   *Here Comes That Sound Again*   (RFC)   27, 12, 9, 7, 6, 4, 3, 2, 2, 4, 6, 10, 17, 24   (14)

LOVEBUG STARSKI

3-22-86 *House Rocker* (Extended Version) (Epic/CBS 49-05328) 58, 53, 53, 60, 70 (5)

LUCAS, CARRIE

3-24-79 *Dance With You* (Solar) 29, 21, 18, 10, 6, 4, 2, 2, 2, 4, 4, 5, 6, 7, 19 (15)

9-21-85 *Hello Stranger* (Extended Version) (MCA 23589) 47, 40, 37, 37, 47, 56, 59, 74 (8)

LYNN, ABBY

8-29-87 *Play With Me* (Atl. 0-86693) 37, 18, 25, 25, 33, 40, 47 (7)

LYNN, CHERYL

1-28-84 *Encore* (Col. 44-04257) 7, 7, 4, 5, 4, 5, 7, 7, 8, 9, 15, 29 (12)

7-06-85 *Fidelity* (Extended & Special Dub Version) (Col. 44-05200) 57, 47, 43, 38, 38, 64, 74 (7)

12-23-78 *Got To Be Real/Star Love* (Col.) 26, 24, 24, 22, 17, 16, 15, 14, 14, 17, 19, 19, 20, 22 (14)

2-09-80 *In Love* (all cuts) (Col.) 32, 27, 22, 16, 12, 10, 7, 5, 5 (9)

M

9-15-79 *Pop Muzik* (Sire) 36, 28, 17, 11, 7, 5, 3, 1, 2, 6, 11, 26, 39 (13)

M & M

6-09-84 *Black Stations, White Stations* (Remix) (RCA PW-13802-A) 22, 22, 16, 12, 10, 11, 9, 8, 10, 10, 22 (11)

MC-ADE

2-22-86 *Bass Rock Express* (4 Slight 3-85-FS-9) 60, 50, 40, 35, 35, 54, 66, 66, 73 (9)

THE MAC BAND FEATURING THE McCAMPBLE BROTHERS

7-16-88   *Roses Are Red*   (MCA 53177)   13, 6, 4, 3, 6, 14, 25, 30   (8)

MACHINE

1-27-79   *There But For The Grace Of God Go I*   (RCA)   23, 21, 12, 9, 9, 8, 7, 7, 8, 8, 8, 14, 21, 21   (14)

MACHO

10-28-78   *I'm A Man*   (Prelude)   8, 10, 10, 15, 20   (5)

MADAME X

9-12-87   *Just That Type Of Girl*   (Atl. 0-86672)   61, 61, 42, 22, 15, 9, 9, 11, 19, 36, 44, 49   (12)

MADHOUSE

3-21-87   *6* (Paisley Park/WB 25545-1)   53, 43, 37, 33, 28, 28, 38, 38, 61, 70   (10)

MADONNA

6-15-85   *Angel/Into The Groove* (Extended Dance Mix)   (Sire 0-20335)   16, 4, 1, 1, 1, 1, 3, 3, 3, 1, 3, 4, 7, 11, 14, 26, 30, 38, 40, 55, 59, 63, 71   (23)

6-02-84   *Borderline* (New Mix)/Lucky Star (New Mix)   (Sire 0-20212)   15, 6, 2, 3, 4, 7, 13, 13, 15, 18, 30   (11)

10-10-87   *Causing A Commotion*   (Sire 0-20762)   —, 15, 3, 1, 2, 2, 11, 33, 47, 50   (10)

9-07-85   *Dress You Up/Shoo-Bee-Doo* (Remix & Instrumental)   (Sire 0-20369)   19, 11, 5, 4, 3, 2, 2, 2, 2, 13, 13, 13, 29, 35, 50, 63, 63, 63, 63, 75   (20)

1-28-84   *Holiday*   (Sire W9405-SOT)   23   (1)

4-18-87   *La Isla Bonita*   (Sire 0-20633)   29, 21, 17, 8, 5, 1, 2, 3, 3, 9, 9, 10, 37, 50, 61, 61, 61, 66, 73   (19)

11-24-84   *Like A Virgin*   (Sire 0-20239)   20, 15, 2, 1, 1, 1, 1, 1, 1, 2, 2, 5, 7, 12, 22, 34, 44, 61, 68, 71, 72   (21)

5-10-86   *Live To Tell* (extended Version)   (Sire 0-20461)   34, 24, 15, 13, 13, 13, 16, 16, 18, 20, 28, 37, 56, 65, 69   (15)

3-09-85   *Material Girl/Pretender* (Extended Dance Remix)   (Sire 0-20304)   17, 9, 5, 3, 2, 2, 9, 13, 19, 23, 63, 70   (12)

12-20-86   *Open Your Heart*   (Sire 0-20597)   53, 39, 39, 39, 14, 5, 5, 3, 1, 1, 2, 5, 14, 21, 25, 44, 58, 62, 74   (19)

7-26-86   *Papa Don't Preach*   (Sire 0-20492)   38, 14, 6, 4, 2, 1, 1, 2, 9, 17, 17, 18, 24, 41, 58, 70, 74   (17)

10-11-86   *True Blue*   (Sire 0-20533)   64, 49, 31, 15, 8, 5, 5, 7, 7, 9, 13, 15, 15, 15, 24, 30, 30, 42, 44, 55, 62, 74   (22)

7-11-87   *Who's That Girl*   (Sire 0-20692)   43, 33, 26, 11, 7, 3, 1, 1, 1, 6, 9, 12, 19, 21, 27, 37, 47   (17)

MAGAZINE 60

12-14-85   *Don Quichotte*   (Baja/TSR B-54)   49, 45, 45, 40, 40, 40, 36, 24, 20, 19, 17, 13, 13, 13, 17, 22, 24, 30, 41, 44, 54, 68, 74   (23)

MAGNUM FORCE

3-16-85   *Cool Out/Get In The Mix*   (Paula 1244)   60, 53, 53, 63   (4)

MAKOSSA, JACK E.

10-17-87   *Opera House*   (Minimal/Criminal)   43, 36, 24, 20, 20, 28, 38, 44, 48   (9)

MAN PARRISH

1-12-85   *Boogie Down* (Bronxe & Dub)   (Sugar Scoop SS 430)   36, 34, 40, 46, 48, 47, 49, (2), 75, 75   (9)

MANDU, KAT

8-11-79   *The Break*   (TK)   37, 24, 19, 16, 9, 7, 4, 3, 5, 5, 7, 13, 24, 27   (14)

MANHATTAN TRANSFER

3-01-80   *Twilight Zone*   (Atl.)   38, 35, 29, 21, 15, 11   (6)

MANILOW, BARRY

6-14-86   *I'm Your Man* (Club Mix)   (RCA JD-14330)   53, 48, 38, 38, 48, 59, 60, 70, 72, 71, 72, 75   (12)

MANTRONIX

6-28-86   *Bassline* (Remix)   (Sleeping Bag SLX-00018X)   58, 32, 29, 27, 27, 37, 52, 60, 60, 61, 67, 74   (12)

8-31-85   *Needle To The Groove/Jamming On The Groove* (Club & Dub Version)   (Sleeping Bag SLX-00015X)   59, 52, 29, 23, 20, 17, 15, 14, 13, 12, 12, 11, 19, 25, 39, 50, 50, 56, 56, 68, 73   (22)

4-23-88   *Simple Simon*   (Cap. V-15362)   43, 31, 29, 27, 27, 35, 41, 47   (8)

3-28-87   *Who Is It*   (Sleeping Bag SLX-00025X)   50, 47, 44, 40, 39, 43, 58, 66, 69   (9)

MANTRONIX WITH M.C. TEE

5-04-85   *Fresh Is The Word/Fresh Is The Best* (Dub, Club & Radio Mix)   (Sleeping Bag SLX-00014X)   60, 38, 38, 48, 58, 68, 73, 60, 51, 46, 42, 38, 35, 35, 59, 61, 66, 72, 74, 74, 75   (21)

MANTUS

4-14-79   *Rock It To The Top*   (S.M.I.)   28, 24, 21, 20, 18, 17, 17, 23, 25, 33   (10)

MARIE, TEENA

3-29-80   *Behind The Groove/You're All The Boogie I Need*   (Gordy)   37, 31   (2)

6-21-86   *Lips To Find You*   (Epic 49-05376)   54, 44, 39, 39, 52, 73   (6)

10-27-84   *Lovergirl* (Dance Mix & Instrumental)   (Epic 49-05100)   21, 16, 14, 11, 10, 8, 6, 3, 2, 2, 2, 2, 2, 4, 8, 8, 10, 15, 12, 10, 10, 10, 24, 39, 53, 64, 68   (27)

5-28-88   *Work It*   (Epic 34-07902)   39, 33, 28, 24, 22, 29   (6)

MARKIE, BIZ

11-01-86   *Make The Music With Your Mouth Biz*   (Prism PS 2008)   57, 49, 49, 52, 29, 29, 61, 70, 74, 74, 74   (11)

MARLEY, ZIGGY, AND THE MELODY MAKERS

11-05-88 *Tumblin' Down* (Virgin 0-96603) 25, 17, 11, 7, 6, 6, 3, 3, 3 (9)

M/A/R/R/S

12-19-88 *Pump Up The Volume* (4th & B'way/Atl. 452) 40, 16, 16, 16, 9, 3, 2, 2, 4, 5, 10, 10, 21, 27, 27, 35, 36, 41, 48 (19)

MARTINEZ, NANCY

2-20-88 *Can't Wait* (Atl. 0-86626) 33, 18, 11, 7, 8, 25, 43 (7)

8-22-87 *Crazy Love* (Atl. 0-86779) 63, 28, 22, 22, 22, 26, 31, 38, 44, 49 (10)

9-20-86 *For Tonight* (Atl. 0-86789) 51, 44, 36, 28, 25, 21, 16, 11, 9, 9, 11, 11, 16, 18, 17, 17, 17, 16, 20, 20, 25, 26, 30, 41, 43, 39, 58, 64, 69 (29)

3-21-87 *Move Out* (Atl. 0-86734) 37, 27, 18, 13, 11, 9, 8, 5, 3, 3, 4, 4, 4, 11, 11, 13, 21, 33, 35, 35, 43, 53, 62, 72 (24)

THE MARY JANE GIRLS

3-09-85 *In My House* (Extended & Instrumental Version) (Motown 4529 MG) 32, 27, 21, 14, 6, 6, 5, 5, 4, 3, 3, 2, 2, 8, 17, 19, 22, 24, 27, 42, 52, 68 (22)

8-10-85 *Wild And Crazy Love* (Remix) (Gordy 4541 MG) 49, 44, 44, 49, 59, 68 (6)

MASCARA

11-03-84 *Baja* (Dance Mix & Instrumental Dub) (Oh My OM 4005) 43, 37, 33, 33, 44, 43 (6)

MASEKELA, HUGH

6-23-84 *Don't Go Lose It Baby* (Stretch Mix) (Arista JDI-9194) 24, 17, 14, 12, 14, 19, 27 (7)

MASON

8-29-87 *Pour It On* (Elektra 0-66795) 65, 37, 32, 32, 25, 16, 9, 6, 6, 9, 15, 19, 40, 46, 49 (15)

MASON, HARVEY

6-30-79   *Groovin' You*   (Arista)   38, 34, 32, 21, 21, 19, 33, 39   (8)

MAZARATI

3-29-86   *Players' Ball* (Extended Version)   (Paisley Park/WB 0-20438)   56, 28, 28, 30, 39, 47, 62   (7)

MAZE FEATURING FRANKIE BEVERLY

3-09-85   *Back In Stride/Joy And Pain* (Extended & Single Version)   (Cap. V-8626)   38, 36, 34, 31, 25, 25, 30, 31, 31, 42, 53, 66, 72   (13)

8-30-86   *I Wanna Be With You*   (Cap. V-9750)   43, 35, 31, 31, 34, 51, 60, 65, 72, 75   (10)

THE McCAMPBLE BROTHERS   *(See:* **THE MAC BAND)**

McCARTNEY, PAUL

11-03-84   *No More Lonely Nights* (Playout Version)   (Col. 44-05077)   38, 35, 32, 32, 41   (5)

McCLAIN, JANICE

11-24-79   *Smack Dab In The Middle*   (Warner)   30, 20, 16, 12, 11, 11, 8, 8, 6, 5, 5, 10, 11, 17, 28, 38, 39   (17)

McCRAE, GEORGE

7-28-79   *Don't You Feel My Love*   (Sunshine Sound)   40, 37, 36, 35, 34   (5)

McDONALD, MICHAEL   *(See also:* **PATTI LaBELLE)**

8-16-86   *Sweet Freedom* (Remix)   (MCA 23641)   61, 39, 27, 23, 19, 14, 14, 15, 22, 43, 67, 69   (12)

McFADDEN AND WHITEHEAD

5-12-79   *Ain't No Stoppin' Us Now*   (P.I.)   28, 24, 21, 19, 14, 13, 11, 8, 8, 16, 17, 19, 38   (13)

McGILPIN, BOB

8-25-79 *Sexy Thing* (Butterfly) 32, 29, 26, 21, 18, 18, 19, 22, 28, 40 (10)

10-28-78 *Superstar* (Butterfly) 7, 7, 13, 25 (4)

McLAREN, MALCOLM

12-15-84 *Madam Butterfly* (Island DMD 797) 37, 34, 34, 34, 34, 46, 45, 48 (8)

MEL AND KIM

1-23-88 *I'm The One Who Really Loves You* (Atl. 0-86627) 47, 32, 24, 19, 19, 16, 13, 11, 25, 44, 49 (11)

5-16-87 *Respectable* (Atl. 0-86703) 49, 44, 41, 38, 28, 24, 24, 17, 10, 1, 2, 2, 3, 19, 26, 46, 60, 68, 68, 70 (20)

12-13-86 *Showing Out* (Atl. 0-86755) 65, 54, 49, 49, 49, 38, 31, 31, 19, 6, 3, 1, 1, 2, 2, 3, 8, 11, 26, 41, 45, 60, 68, 74 (24)

MEN WITHOUT HATS

11-28-87 *Pop Goes The World* (Mer. 888 859-1) 42, 37, 29, 25, 25, 25, 25, 28, 28, 31, 47 (11)

MENAGE

5-09-87 *At This Moment* (Profile PRO-7134) 53, 50, 50, 68, 69, 74 (6)

MENDES, SERGIO

10-06-79 *I'll Tell You* (Elektra) 37, 30, 21, 17, 13, 11, 10, 8, 7, 6, 7, 14, 14, 23, 23 (15)

MERGE FEATURING DEBBIE A.

523-87 Let's Have Some Fun (Atl. 0-86717) 61, 58, 56, 54, 64, 64, 69, 73 (8)

METROPOLIS

10-28-78 *Greatest Show On Earth* (Salsoul) 27, 27 (2)

MEYERS, ALICIA

8-25-84   *You Get The Best From Me*   (MCA 23511)   21, 19, 13, 9, 8, 6, 3, 2, 2,
8, 27, 41   (12)

THE MIAMI SOUND MACHINE

4-05-86   *Bad Boy* (Remix)   (Epic/CBS 49-05338)   31, 26, 20, 18, 15, 13, 11,
11, 9, 9, 20, 28, 41, 58, 66   (15)

9-07-85   *Conga* (Extended Version & Instrumental)   (Epic 49-05253)   42, 35,
18, 14, 13, 13, 13, 21, 21, 19, 16, 12, 9, 9, 20, 33, 33, 39, 39, 43, 52,
62, 62, 64, 73   (30)

7-21-84   *Dr. Beat*   (Epic 49-05023)   25, 22, 21, 21, 29, 27, 29   (7)

MICHAEL, GEORGE   *(See also:* **ARETHA FRANKLIN**)

12-19-88   *Faith*   (Col. 44-07478)   37, 22, 22, 22, 18, 9, 8, 18, 35, 41, 41,
43   (12)

3-05-88   *Father Figure*   (Col. 44-07574)   37, 16, 10, 5, 2, 1, 6, 11, 33, 36,
46   (11)

10-24-87   *Hard Day*   (Col. 44-07466)   38, 21, 14, 12, 10, 6, 5, 5, 19, 31, 31,
31, 36, 43, 50   (15)

7-04-87   *I Want Your Sex*   (Col. 44-06814)   31, 13, 7, 3, 3, 2, 2, 1, 1, 7, 12,
12, 27, 47   (14)

8-06-88   *Monkey*   (Col. 44-07849)   28, 19, 11, 3, 1, 1, 2, 1, 2, 5, 6, 30   (12)

MIDNEY, BORIS

10-28-78   *Beautiful Bend* (all cuts)   (Marlin/TK)   5, 8, 9, 20   (4)

MIDNIGHT RHYTHM

2-24-79   *Climb/Rushin' To Meet You*   (Atl.)   27, 24, 21, 18, 17, 16, 16   (7)

10-28-78   *Workin' And Slavin'*   (Atl.)   25, 20, 15, 8, 8, 12, 19, 24, 30   (9)

MIDNIGHT STAR

6-08-85   *Body Snatchers* (Vocal & Remix)   (Solar ED 5056)   56, 51, 46, 41, 37,
37, 48, 62   (8)

10-29-88   *Don't Rock The Boat*   (Solar/Cap. V-71166)   21, 8, 7, 5, 4, 2, 2, 1, 1, 1   (10)

2-21-87   *Engine No. 9*   (Solar/Elektra 7-69501)   45, 31, 28, 31, 31, 49, 56, 61, 65, 73, 75   (11)

5-31-86   *Headlines* (Extended Mix)   (Solar/Elektra ED 51337)   32, 21, 9, 5, 4, 4, 3, 3, 3, 15, 17, 19, 26, 41, 52, 62, 69, 72   (18)

9-06-86   *The Midas Touch*   (Solar/Elektra ED 51338)   53, 45, 37, 31, 30, 15, 12, 11, 11, 17, 26, 32, 32, 32, 34, 57, 64, 64, 64, 68, 72, 72   (22)

11-24-84   *Operator*   (Solar ED 5018)   25, 21, 16, 12, 7, 7, 7, 6, 4, 3, 3, 6, 9, 14, 19, 36, 41, 66   (18)

3-02-85   *Scientific Love*   (Solar ED 5035)   39, 28, 23, 23, 42, 55, 61, 62, 66   (9)

MIDWAY

9-15-84   *Set It Out* (Vocal & Funky Breakdown Mix)   (Personnel P 49811)   32, 34, 43, 39, 35, 31, 28, 28, 42, 47, 49   (11)

MILLS, ELEANOR

5-09-87   *Mr. Right*   (Vinylmania VMR 007)   43, 40, 32, 28, 25, 24, 33, 33, 61, 65, 72   (11)

MILLS, STEPHANIE

7-20-85   *Bit By Bit (Theme From "Fletch")*   (MCA 23564)   58, 50, 45, 36, 33, 30, 26, 26, 28, 48, 58, 71   (12)

7-18-87   *I Feel Good All Over*   (MCA 23740)   20, 17, 17, 15, 14, 15, 26, 50, 54, 54, 54   (11)

9-08-84   *The Medicine Song* (Vocal & Dub)   (Casa. 880 180-1)   17, 13, 9, 8, 5, 1, 1, 6, 7, 8, 16, 26, 31, 50, 48   (15)

6-23-79   *Put Your Body In It/You Can Get Over*   (20th C.)   40, 31, 29, 27, 25, 23, 14, 12, 12, 11, 9, 7, 9, 13, 14, 16, 17   (17)

7-26-86   *Rising Desire/I Have Learned To Respect The Power Of Love*   (MCA 23644)   52, 47, 34, 31, 28, 28, 43, 56, 66, 70   (10)

1-18-86   *Stand Back* (Extended Version)   (MCA 23598)   61, 56, 49, 43, 35, 31, 31, 38, 61, 67   (10)

10-27-79 *You Can Get Over* (20th C.)   37, 35, 25, 22, 16, 14, 14, 25, 39, 39   (10)

8-29-87 *(You're Puttin') A Rush On Me* (MCA 23740)   34, 20, 18, 18, 7, 8, 8, 16, 19, 22, 27, 41, 45, 50   (14)

MINOGUE, KYLIE

6-04-88 *I Should Be So Lucky* (Geffen 0-20914)   34, 27, 25, 35   (4)

10-08-88 *The Loco-Motion* (Geffen 0-21043)   20, 12, 6, 6, 5, 5, 7, 12, 21, 30   (10)

MISS THANG

10-04-86 *Thunder And Lightning* (TB 889)   45, 29, 17, 14, 12, 12, 20, 30, 31, 31, 32, 48, 60, 60, 60, 65, 69, 69, 70, 74   (20)

MITCHELL, LISA

2-06-88 *Rescue Me* (Jump Street JS-1013)   41, 28, 21, 17, 26, 42, 46, 49   (8)

MONET

5-23-87 *My Heart Gets All The Breaks* (Ligosa LIG 501)   62, 53, 49, 40, 34, 34, 34, 43, 56, 63, 63, 68, 75   (13)

MOORE, JACKIE

1-26-80 *How's Your Love Life Baby* (Col.)   36, 31, 27, 23, 20, 17, 19, 31, 32, 39   (10)

6-23-79 *This Time Baby* (Col.)   38, 28, 17, 14, 10, 7, 3, 2, 1, 1, 2, 5, 6, 11, 13, 14, 18   (17)

MOORE, MELBA

1-28-84 *Keepin' My Lover Satisfied* (Cap. V-8569)   30   (1)

3-24-79 *Pick Me Up, I'll Dance* (Epic)   28, 25, 23, 23, 22, 20, 20, 23, 25, 38   (10)

5-11-85 *Read My Lips* (Extended Remix & Instrumental) (Cap. V-8627)   59, 49, 44, 44, 53, 62, 64, 64, 71   (9)

10-28-78   *You Stepped Into My Life*   (Col.)   20, 18, 14, 12, 10, 10, 14, 14, 15, 25, 25, 29   (12)

MOORE, MELBA, AND KASHIF   (*See also:* KASHIF)

7-12-86   *Love The One I'm With (A Lot Of Love)*   (Cap. V-15236)   55, 49, 49, 68, 73, 73   (6)

MOORE, MELBA, AND FREDDIE JACKSON   (*See also:* FREDDIE JACKSON)

10-25-86   *A Little Bit More*   (Cap. V-15256)   48, 38, 31, 27, 27, 29, 29, 29, 34, 38, 38, 38, 56, 59, 59, 63, 67, 73   (18)

MORE, BILLY

11-24-79   *Go Dance*   (Emergency)   34, 31, 28, 32, 40, 40   (6)

MORGAN, MELI'SA   (*See also:* KASHIF)

12-14-85   *Do Me Baby* (Interlude)   (Cap. V-15211)   60, 43, 43, 32, 32, 32, 22, 10, 7, 4, 3, 3, 4, 4, 15, 18, 23, 25, 56, 66, 70   (21)

1-23-88   *If You Can Do It*   (Cap. V-15345)   30, 17, 16, 24, 20, 26, 27, 37, 49   (9)

MORODER, GIORGIO   (*See:* GIORGIO; PHILIP OAKEY)

MTUME

6-21-86   *Breathless*   (Epic 49-05385)   63, 56, 48, 40, 40, 42, 51, 51, 55, 69   (10)

8-04-84   *You, Me And He*   (Epic 49-05024)   26, 22, 15, 11, 8, 8, 7, 6, 7, 10, 10, 27, 44   (13)

MURDOCK, SHIRLEY

3-22-86   *No More* (Extended Version)   (Elektra 0-66865)   55, 45, 41, 41, 46, 54, 62, 72   (8)

MURPHY, EDDIE

9-28-85   *Party All The Time* (Instrumental Version)   (Col. 44-05280)   45, 33, 12, 11, 11, 20, 25, 24, 19, 6, 1, 2, 3, 3, 3, 3, 6, 12, 17, 19, 23, 29, 36, 61, 70   (25)

MUSIQUE

10-28-78   *Keep On Jumpin' In The Bush*   (Prelude)   6, 5, 5, 7, 14, 19   (6)

11-10-79   *Love Massage/Good And Plenty Lover*   (Prelude)   30, 25, 17, 13, 10, 8, 7, 7, 10, 10, 11, 12, 16, 24, 33, 40   (16)

NARADA   *(See also:* NARADA MICHAEL WALDEN)

5-07-88   *Divine Emotions*   (Reprise/WB 0-20874)   34, 26, 22, 12, 11, 8, 6, 8, 14, 25, 30   (11)

NAUGHTON, DAVID

3-17-79   *Makin' It*   (RSO)   30, 25, 20, 15, 13, 13, 12, 18, 19, 20, 24, 29, 35   (13)

NAYOBE

3-23-85   *Please Don't Go* (Dub & Extended Version)   (Sutra/Fever SF 802A)   55, 48, 40, 31, 28, 23, 23, 31, 35, 45, 59, 67, 71, 72   (14)

5-09-87   *Second Chance For Love*   (Sutra/Fever SF 815)   57, 54, 51, 47, 45, 39, 39, 39, 56, 60, 75   (11)

NELSON, PHYLLIS

11-09-85   *I Like You* (Extended Version)   (Carrere 4Z9-05268)   53, 48, 29, 16, 10, 6, 6, 6, 6, 6, 1, 2, 3, 4, 10, 16, 18, 27, 32, 45, 59, 67, 69, 66, 72   (25)

NENA

3-03-84   *99 Luftballoons*   (Epic 49-04109)   20, 15, 18, 13, 21, 29   (6)

NEVIL, ROBBIE

12-13-86   *C'est La Vie*   (Manhattan/EMI V-56036)   59, 45, 28, 28, 28, 10, 1, 1, 2, 5, 5, 7, 4, 7, 10, 9, 13, 16, 44, 49, 63, 73   (22)

THE NEW EDITION

9-29-84   *Cool It Now* (Vocal & Dub)   (MCA 23515)   18, 13, 11, 9, 7, 6, 5, 4, 9, 16, 18, 31, 41, 41, 41, 44, 44, 44, 45, 45   (20)

11-16-85   *Count Me Out* (Extended Version)   (MCA 23595)   50, 35, 24, 15, 12, 9, 9, 8, 8, 8, 16, 21, 25, 32, 37, 46, 56, 69, 74   (19)

9-06-86   *Earth Angel*   (MCA 23669)   56, 50, 46, 35, 31, 24, 22, 22, 27, 30, 32, 37, 36, 36, 46, 63, 67, 67, 67, 71, 75, 75   (22)

7-16-88   *If It Isn't Love*   (MCA 23830)   16, 12, 9, 9, 7, 7, 7, 8, 15, 16, 18, 23   (12)

3-08-86   *A Little Bit Of Love (Is All It Takes)*   (MCA 23608)   46, 20, 16, 11, 11, 14, 14, 19, 29, 37, 48, 65, 70   (13)

12-20-86   *Once In A Lifetime Groove* (Remix)   (MCA 23692)   60, 53, 53, 53, 43, 37, 37, 37, 40, 51, 60, 68, 60, 68, 73, 68, 75   (17)

11-05-88   *You're Not My Kind Of Girl*   (MCA 23903)   23, 20, 20, 19, 24, 28   (6)

THE NEW JERSEY MASS CHOIR

3-16-85   *I Want To Know What Love Is/Jesus Is Right On Time*   (Savoy SCS 0004)   43, 22, 16, 16, 19, 32, 35, 56, 65   (9)

NEW ORDER

2-14-87   *Bizarre Love Triangle*   (Qwest/WB)   56, 37, 28, 26, 29, 49, 62, 61, 68, 70   (10)

5-14-88   *Blue Monday*   (Qwest/WB 0-20869)   43, 35, 15, 10, 10, 18, 19, 30   (8)

6-15-85   *The Perfect Kiss/The Kiss Of Death/Perfect Pit* (Original & Dub Version)   (Qwest 0-20330)   34, 23, 16, 13, 11, 10, 10, 13, 17, 19, 34, 45, 58, 61, 63, 68, 75   (17)

4-19-86   *Shell Shock*   (A&M SP-12174)   50, 45, 40, 36, 36, 36, 57, 66, 67, 74   (10)

11-23-85   *Sub Culture/Sub Vulture* (Remix)   (Qwest 0-20390)   43, 38, 33, 23, 20, 20, 20, 20, 24, 24, 30, 40, 50, 55, 67, 72   (16)

9-12-87   *True Faith* (Remix)   (Qwest/WB 0-20733)   28, 28, 19, 14, 11, 8, 8, 18, 32, 42, 46   (11)

NEWCLEUS

9-01-84   *Computer Age (Push The Button)* (Vocal & Instrumental)   (Sunnyview SUN 416)   25, 22, 23, 22, 30, 34, 39, 46, 47, 45, 50   (11)

4-07-84   *Jam On It* (Instrumental)   (Sunnyview SUN 411B)   14, 14, 7, 6, 2, 1, 2, 3, 3, 5, 6, 5, 7, 15, 16, 19, 27   (17)

NEWTON-JOHN, OLIVIA

11-23-85   *Soul Kiss* (Extended Dance Mix)   (MCA 23593)   61, 55, 55, 61, 67, 67, 68, 68   (8)

NICE AND WILD

9-06-86   *Diamond Girl*   (Top Hits TH-106)   61, 54, 49, 45, 41, 40, 38, 36, 34, 28, 24, 22, 17, 17, 15, 11, 11, 11, 11, 19, 21, 21, 26, 29, 31, 42, 62, 71   (28)

NICHOLS, BILLY

7-14-79   *Give Your Body Up To The Music*   (West End)   36, 34, 32, 27, 27, 30, 31, 40   (8)

NICOLE

3-08-86   *Don't You Want My Love*   (Portrait/CBS 4R9-05331)   42, 28, 25, 25, 27, 31, 36, 40, 43, 64, 71, 74, 72, 75, 75   (15)

NIGHTLIFE UNLIMITED

6-16-79   *Disco Choo Choo*   (Casa.)   32, 29, 24, 18, 17, 20, 21, 23, 25, 27, 30   (11)

NINE, SADIE

5-02-87   *Let's Work It Out*   (Omni/Atl. 0-96774)   39, 31, 29, 26, 23, 20, 19, 20, 20, 45, 51, 64, 64, 64, 69, 72   (16)

9.9

9-07-85   *All Of You For All Of Me*   (Remix Version)   57, 33, 30, 25, 21, 19, 17, 17, 29, 35, 44, 66, 71, 75   (14)

NOCERA

11-14-87 *Let's Go* (Sleeping Bag SLX-29) 39, 35, 28, 24, 21, 11, 8, 8, 8, 7, 8, 10, 11, 20, 32 (15)

9-13-86 *Summertime, Summertime* (Sleeping Bag SLX-22) 47, 41, 36, 33, 25, 20, 17, 9, 7, 6, 3, 2, 2, 1, 2, 6, 6, 6, 6, 9, 9, 10, 16, 21, 25, 44, 64, 73 (28)

NOEL

4-09-88 *Like A Child* (4th & B'way 458) 40, 26, 24, 12, 6, 5, 6, 9, 16, 25, 36, 38 (12)

10-29-88 *Out Of Time* (4th & B'way/Island 469) 28, 19, 16, 12, 10, 10, 9, 13, 28, 28 (10)

8-08-87 *Silent Morning* (4th & B'way 439) 50, 40, 28, 13, 23, 15, 15, 8, 7, 14, 24, 29, 45 (13)

NOHO

7-18-87 *Touch* (Epic 49-06817) 57, 48, 48, 38, 37, 41, 62, 74 (8)

NORA

6-23-84 *I'm Falling In Love With You* (New York Music NYM 9) 29, 29 (2)

NORTH END

2-02-80 *Kind Of Life* (West End) 38, 32, 28, 25, 23, 21, 27, 28, 38 (9)

NOVELLE, JAY

7-14-84 *If This Ain't Love* (Emergency EMDS 6544) 22, 23, 26, 25, 26, 25, 28 (7)

NU SHOOZ

10-01-88 *Are You Looking For Somebody Nu* (Atl. 0-86531) 25, 15, 15, 21, 30 (5)

2-22-86 *I Can't Wait* (Extended Version) (Atl. 0-86828) 46, 39, 18, 6, 3, 3, 1, 3, 4, 4, 4, 6, 3, 2, 2, 6, 7, 7, 7, 10, 15, 17, 25, 30, 42, 43, 58, 72 (28)

7-19-86   *Point Of No Return* (Remix)   (Atl. 0-86829)   37, 20, 8, 7, 7, 6, 5, 5, 7, 8, 19, 19, 12, 9, 8, 8, 21, 25, 28, 34, 34, 42, 62, 66, 66, 66, 70, 74, 74   (29)

5-07-88   *Should I Say Yes?*   (Atl. 0-86599)   43, 35, 42, 26, 20, 14, 9, 10, 11, 21, 29   (11)

NUANCE (FEATURING VIKKI LOVE)

12-08-86   *Loveride*   (4th & Broadway 409)   36, 28, 22, 22, 22, 22, 29, 43, 43, 42, 44, 44, 44, 45, 55, 64, 72   (17)

7-21-84   *Take A Chance*   (4th & Broadway 403)   27, 24, 22, 29, 26, 23, 28   (7)

OAKEY, PHILIP, AND GIORGIO MORODER   *(See also:* GIORGIO)

8-31-85   *Good-Bye Bad Times* (Extended Version & Instrumental)   (A&M SP-12141)   56, 48, 43, 38, 37, 40, 43, 57, 63, 69   (10)

O'BRYAN

4-28-84   *Lovelite*   (Cap. V-9085)   23, 14, 13, 10, 7, 7, 9, 19, 15, 14, 12, 10, 11, 18, 23, 28, 30   (17)

OCEAN, BILLY

7-14-84   *Caribbean Queen* (Special Mix)   (Jive/Arista JDI-9199)   25, 20, 13, 6, 5, 3, 5, 4, 5, 5, 4, 3, 1, 3, 5, 4, 5, 6, 6, 8, 12, 15, 18, 36, 36, 36, 41, 47, 47, 49   (30)

4-02-88   *Get Outta' My Dreams, Get Into My Car*   (Jive/Arista JDI-9679)   34, 29, 25, 23, 20, 20, 39, 43, 50   (9)

8-23-86   *Love Zone* (Remix)   (Jive/Arista JDI-9509)   55, 38, 32, 28, 24, 22, 22, 46, 58, 71   (10)

11-17-84   *Loverboy* (Extended Club Remix)   (Jive/Arista JDI-9280)   40, 37, 34, 27, 24, 23, 23, 23, 20, 14, 1o, 4, 2, 2, 6, 11, 14, 15, 33   (19)

1-18-86   *When The Going Gets Tough, The Tough Get Going* (Extended Version)   (Jive/Arista JDI-9431)   34, 23, 14, 10, 7, 4, 4, 5, 5, 6, 8, 20, 24, 48, 60, 67   (16)

O'CONNOR, SINEAD

9-03-88 *I Want Your (Hands On Me)* (Chrysalis 4V9-43256) 27, 23, 23, 27 (4)

OINGO BOINGO

9-14-85 *Weird Science* (Extended Dance Version) (MCA 23574) 60, 43, 39, 39, 44, 54, 61, 66, 75 (9)

OLLIE AND JERRY

6-30-84 *Breakin' . . . There's No Stopping Us* (Polydor PRO-284-1) 13, 3, 2, 2, 2, 2, 3, 6, 6, 9, 16, 24, 48 (13)

ONE WAY

12-20-86 *Don't Think About It* (Remix) (MCA 23659) 56, 48, 48, 48, 46, 54, 54, 61, 64, 69, 71 (11)

4-18-87 *You Better Quit* (MCA 23716) 42, 31, 28, 28, 31, 37, 55, 59, 67 (9)

O'NEAL, ALEXANDER *(See also:* CHERRELLE)

11-14-87 *Criticize* (Tabu 4Z9-07469) 33, 27, 20, 14, 11, 9, 9, 9, 9, 20, 41, 49 (12)

7-04-87 *Fake* (Tabu/Epic 4Z9-06788) 36, 14, 8, 1, 1, 1, 1, 2, 2, 2, 7, 7, 18, 26, 29, 45, 50 (17)

3-16-85 *Innocent* (LP & Instrumental Version) (Tabu 4Z9-05140) 45, 31, 28, 26, 23, 21, 17, 15, 15, 17, 22, 22, 40, 58, 63, 63, 68 (17)

5-17-86 *What's Missing* (Remix) (Tabu/CBS 4Z9-05361) 65, 59, 59, 69, 71 (5)

ORCHESTRAL MANOEUVRES IN THE DARK/O.M.D.

5-28-88 *Dreaming* (A&M SP-12258) 30, 21, 17, 17, 28 (5)

5-10-86 *If You Leave* (Extended Version) (A&M SP-12176) 56, 51, 51 (3)

OSBORNE, JEFFREY

1-19-85   *The Borderlines* (Special Remix Dub)   (A&M SP-12116)   35, 30, 21, 17, 13, 9, 9, 12, 29, 54, 71, 74, 75, 75   (14)

2-04-84   *Plane Love* (Remix)   (A&M SP-12089)   23, 16, 9, 7, 9, 11, 15, 16, 23, 26   (10)

9-17-88   *She's On The Left*   (A&M SP-12280)   28, 20, 16, 13, 11, 18, 25   (7)

7-19-86   *Soweto*   (A&M SP-12190)   50, 34, 23, 19, 17, 17, 18, 19, 29, 39, 49, 59, 65, 70   (14)

6-28-86   *You Should Be Mine (The Woo Woo Song)*   (A&M SP-12169)   46, 34, 34, 43, 46, 45, 50, 52, 51, 55, 63, 69   (12)

PAGAN, BRUNI

8-18-79   *Fantasy*   (Elektra)   31, 25, 22, 18, 15, 12, 10, 9, 9, 11, 14, 27   (12)

PAIGE, SHARON

2-16-80   *Tonight's The Night*   (Source)   37, 30, 24, 22, 22, 28, 30, 37   (8)

PALMER, ROBERT

10-25-86   *I Didn't Mean To Turn You On*   (Island DMD 969)   52, 35, 23, 11, 7, 5, 5, 5, 8, 9, 9, 9, 13, 15, 15, 23, 25, 38, 54, 66, 74   (21)

THE PARADISE EXPRESS

12-16-78   *Dance*   (Fantasy)   29, 24, 19, 19, 18, 12, 11, 11, 10, 11, 13, 15, 16, 17, 18   (15)

PARKER, PAUL

3-14-87   *One Look (One Look Was Enough)*   (Dice TGR 1011)   50, 45, 41, 40, 54, 59, 72, 74   (8)

PARTON, DOLLY

12-20-78   *Baby I'm Burnin'*   (RCA PD-11425)   17, 17, 15, 13, 17, 18, 19, 21, 24, 26   (10)

PASSION

3-22-80   *Don't Bring Back Memories/In New York*   (Prelude)   37, 32, 30   (3)

PEACHES AND HERB

12-08-79   *Roller Skatin' Mate*   (Polydor)   33, 30, 27, 27, 33, 33   (6)

11-04-78   *Shake Your Groove Thing*   (Polydor)   26, 18, 10, 4, 2, 2, 2, 2, 3, 3, 4,
4, 6, 9, 9, 10, 16, 18, 20, 22   (20)

PEBBLES

12-05-88   *Girlfriend*   (MCA 23794)   39, 30, 24, 19, 19, 19, 17, 29, 38, 34, 31,
22, 15, 4, 3, 2, 1, 4, 9, 10, 21, 36, 38, 50   (24)

9-26-87   *Love/Hate*   (MCA 23780)   62, 45, 43, 49   (4)

4-30-88   *Mercedes Boy*   (MCA 23838)   34, 26, 15, 9, 4, 2, 2, 2, 1, 1, 3, 5, 20,
29   (14)

PEEPLES, NIA

5-07-88   *Trouble*   (Mer./PolyGram 870 154-1)   41, 31, 26, 19, 17, 12, 10, 7,
7, 7, 7, 18, 24, 24, 27   (15)

PENDERGRASS, TEDDY

6-11-88   *Joy*   (Asylum/Elektra 0-66766)   33, 29, 23, 22, 26   (5)

PEPSI AND SHIRLEY

7-18-87   *Heartache*   (Polydor/PolyGram 885 929-1)   42, 27, 27, 20, 12, 10, 7,
12, 24, 24, 32, 42, 49   (13)

PERRY, TODD, PROJECT

4-30-66   *Bango/Back To The Beat*   (Fresh/Sleeping Bag FRE-80117)   28, 25,
23, 23, 34, 36, 42, 47, 49   (9)

11-19-88   *Just Wanna Dance/Weekend*   (Fresh/Sleeping Bag FRE-80125)   27,
14, 8, 5, 4, 4, 4   (7)

THE PET SHOP BOYS

4-09-88   *Always On My Mind*   (EMI/Manhattan V-56089)   43, 27, 25, 18, 13, 13, 14, 24, 31, 39, 43, 50   (12)

11-12-88   *Domino Dancing*   (EMI/Manhattan V-56116)   25, 21, 20, 17, 17, 30, 30, 30   (8)

9-20-86   *Love Comes Quickly* (Remix)   (EMI America V-19218)   59, 54, 49, 49, 61, 70, 72   (7)

6-21-86   *Opportunities (Let's Make Lots Of Money)*   (EMI America V-19206)   46, 29, 24, 17, 15, 13, 11, 11, 18, 19, 26, 40, 48, 55, 64, 72   (16)

3-15-86   *West End Girls* (Dance Mix)   (EMI America V-19206)   62, 53, 21, 12, 8, 5, 2, 1, 2, 5, 5, 18, 26, 26, 26, 30, 37, 58, 68, 74   (20)

12-12-88   *What Have I Done To Deserve This*   (EMI/Manhattan V-56080)   36, 30, 29, 29, 29, 25, 14, 7, 6, 7, 10, 13, 16, 28, 30, 37, 40, 48, 50   (19)

PHILLY CREAM

11-22-86   *Love Can't Turn Around*   (Cot./Atl. 0-96805)   54, 48, 48, 44, 44, 56, 56, 56, 64, 68, 68, 69, 72   (13)

PIECES OF A DREAM

9-20-86   *Joyride*   (Manhattan V-56034)   65, 59, 58, 66, 73   (5)

THE PLAYERS ASSOCIATION

3-29-80   *Get Down Mellow Sound/We Got The Groove*   (Vanguard)   34, 26   (2)

POINDEXTER, BUSTER, AND HIS BANSHEES OF BLUE

12-26-88   *Hot Hot Hot*   (RCA 6737-1-RD)   48, 48, 48, 35, 19, 15, 10, 10, 8, 7, 7, 31, 47   (13)

POINTER, BONNIE   (*See also:* THE POINTER SISTERS)

5-12-79   *Heaven Must Have Sent You*   (Motown)   40, 37, 34, 31, 29, 23, 20, 18, 16, 13, 13, 14, 15, 16, 18, 22, 23   (17)

1-05-80   *I Can't Help Myself*   (Motown)   34, 34, 19, 10, 7, 5, 4, 2, 1, 4, 5, 13, 23, 27   (14)

9-15-84   *Your Touch* (Club Version & Dub)   (Private I 4Z9-04996)   33, 31, 35, 48   (4)

THE POINTER SISTERS   *(See also:* BONNIE POINTER)

2-04-84   *Automatic* (Remix)   (Planet JD-13721)   28, 21, 23, 10, 8, 6, 5, 7, 7, 10, 9, 10, 8, 19, 27   (15)

4-27-85   *Baby Come And Get It* (Dance Mix)   (Planet YD-14042)   50, 30, 26, 23, 23, 24, 26, 29, 35, 60, 67, 71   (12)

8-03-85   *Dare Me/I'll Be There* (Extended & Instrumental Version)   (RCA PD-14127)   52, 26, 15, 13, 13, 13, 13, 15, 15, 25, 29, 29, 37, 42, 52, 63   (16)

11-22-86   *Goldmine* (Remix)/Sexual Power   (RCA 5774-1-RD)   53, 47, 47, 43, 43, 47, 47, 47, 60, 61, 61, 66, 75   (13)

5-12-79   *Happiness*   (Planet)   39, 36, 35, 34, 33, 38   (6)

5-05-84   *Jump (For My Love)*   (Planet JW-13781)   18, 9, 5, 4, 4, 3, 5, 10, 9, 6, 6, 8, 7, 9, 9, 17, 24   (17)

12-22-84   *Neutron Dance*   (Planet JR-13952)   25, 25, 25, 21, 21, 20, 18, 15, 15, 18, 16, 16, 18, 39, 63, 66, 73   (17)

POUSSEZ

4-28-79   *Poussez* (all cuts)   (Vanguard)   28, 25, 18, 17, 14, 12, 11, 11, 14, 17, 39   (11)

POWER STATION   *(See also:* DURAN DURAN)

6-22-85   *Get It On/Go To Zero* (45 Mix & Extended Mix)   (Cap. V-8646)   47, 37, 33, 30, 30, 37, 62, 72, 75, 73   (10)

3-30-85   *Some Like It Hot And The Heat Is On* (Extended Version)/Some Like It Hot (7" Mix)/The Heat Is On (Instrumental)   (Cap. V-8631)   60, 41, 26, 19, 14, 12, 12, 15, 20, 21, 23, 35, 45, 59, 66   (15)

PRETTY POISON

8-15-87   *(Catch Me) I'm Falling*   (Virgin/Atl. 0-96752)   38, 25, 14, 10, 9, 9, 4, 5, 10, 10, 5, 3, 4, 13, 18, 25, 31, 33, 43, 47, 47, 47, 49   (23)

9-15-84   *Nightime* (Dance Mix & Dub)   (Svengali SR 8403 B)   45, 43, 41, 41, 50   (5)

4-09-88   *Nightime*   (Virgin 0-96710)   33, 15, 9, 5, 1, 1, 3, 10, 22, 38, 42, 48   (12)

8-20-88   *When I Look Into Your Eyes*   (Virgin 0-96642)   19, 14, 9, 8, 6, 5, 4, 7, 27   (9)

PRINCE (AND THE REVOLUTION)   *(See also:* ANDRE CYMONE; SHEILA E.)

5-21-88   *Alphabet St.*   (Paisley Park/WB 0-20990)   38, 11, 9, 4, 5, 6, 6, 12, 23, 28   (10)

11-09-85   *America* (Remix)/*Girl*   (Paisley Park 0-20389)   45, 38, 33, 33, 39, 53, 53, 53, 58, 58   (10)

9-06-86   *Anotherloverholenyohead/Girls And Boys*   (Paisley Park/WB 0-20516)   37, 24, 16, 13, 13, 19, 34, 59, 67, 73   (10)

12-26-87   *I Could Never Take The Place Of Your Man*   (Paisley Park/WB 0-20728)   35, 35, 35, 26, 25, 14, 8, 8, 12, 22, 42, 45, 50   (13)

11-17-79   *I Wanna Be Your Lover*   (WB)   37, 32, 23, 19, 15, 8, 8, 5, 5, 4, 3, 3, 3, 3, 5, 13, 17, 32   (18)

1-19-85   *I Would Die 4 U/Another Lonely Christmas* (Extended Version)   (WB 0-20291)   37, 26, 22, 22, 21, 21, 23, 44   (8)

6-13-87   *If I Was Your Girlfriend*   (Paisley Park/WB 0-20697)   43, 30, 30, 30, 30, 30, 26, 26, 25, 31, 37, 53, 56, 64, 64, 69   (16)

3-22-86   *Kiss* (Remix)/*Love Or Money*   (Paisley Park/WB 0-20442)   39, 14, 5, 1, 1, 1, 2, 1, 2, 3, 6, 17, 24, 31, 36, 50, 63, 72, 75   (19)

9-22-84   *Let's Go Crazy/Erotic City*   (WB 0-20246)   17, 14, 8, 6, 3, 2, 2, 2, 2, 2, 3, 10, 13, 17, 17, 17, 17, 15, 14, 13, 20, 24, 35, 42, 46, 48, 63, 65, 65, 65, 68, 71, 71, 75   (34)

1-28-84   *Let's Pretend We're Married/Irresistible Bitch*   (WB 0-20170)   26, 26, 30, 29   (4)

6-21-86   *Mountains* (Remix)   (Paisley Park/WB 0-20478)   41, 31, 25, 10, 5, 2, 2, 4, 6, 14, 20, 33, 44, 58, 67   (15)

8-24-85   *Pop Life/Hello* (Fresh Dance Mix)   (Paisley Park/WB 0-20357)   39, 15, 4, 3, 2, 2, 4, 4, 4, 6, 15, 16, 25, 37, 47, 61, 64, 66, 66, 67, 67   (21)

10-20-84   *Purple Rain*   ((WB 0-20267)   36, 29, 23, 20, 18, 18, 29, 35, 50   (9)

7-13-85   *Raspberry Beret/She's Always In My Heart* (New Mix)   (Paisley Park/WB 0-20355)   32, 16, 7, 4, 4, 9, 12, 17, 20, 23, 31, 34, 51, 64, 66, 73, 73   (17)

3-21-87   *Sign "O" The Times*   (Paisley Park/WB 0-20648)   24, 5, 1, 1, 2, 2, 2, 1, 1, 2, 7, 10, 21, 23, 23, 53, 57, 69, 73, 73   (20)

8-29-87   *U Got The Look*   (Paisley Park/WB 0-20727)   25, 15, 13, 13, 15, 17, 19, 22, 28, 33, 39, 49   (12)

7-07-84   *When Doves Cry*   (WB 0-20228)   13, 1, 1, 1, 1, 1, 1, 2, 2, 3, 10, 10, 9, 14, 22, 26, 48   (17)

PRINCESS

1-25-86   *After The Love Has Gone* (Extended Version)   (Next Plateau NP 50037)   47, 37, 22, 15, 11, 10, 9, 9, 9, 19, 40, 57, 63, 69, 74   (15)

8-08-87   *Red Hot*   (Polydor/PolyGram 885 885-1)   58, 52, 47, 42, 35, 35, 35, 37, 43   (9)

10-05-85   *Say I'm Your Number One* (Extended Version)   (Next Plateau NP 50035)   57, 50, 40, 32, 27, 24, 20, 18, 18, 27, 42, 38, 38, 38, 38, 37, 41, 53, 60, 62, 64, 71, 75   (23)

PROMISE CIRCLE

2-13-88   *Easy To Touch*   (Atl. 0-86618)   33, 30, 27, 23, 20, 21, 42, 45, 50   (9)

PROPAGANDA

2-01-86   *P Machinery* (Extended Version)   (ZZT/Island 0-96835)   56, 51, 45, 45, 49, 59, 59, 61, 69   (9)

PSEUDO ECHO

6-13-87   *Funky Town*   (RCA 6431-1-RD)   51, 45, 45, 38, 20, 10, 7, 7, 7, 7, 16, 32, 59, 67, 67, 74   (16)

THE PSYCHEDELIC FURS

6-23-84   *The Ghost In You/Heart Beat*   (Col. BFC 39278)   26, 25   (2)

3-28-87   *Heartbreak Beat*   (Col. 44-05969)   38, 33, 31, 33, 48, 55, 64, 73   (8)

PUBLIC ENEMY

9-03-88   *Don't Believe The Hype*   (Def Jam 4W9-7846)   28, 26   (2)

7-25-87   *You're Gonna Get Yours*   (Def Jam/Col. 44-06861)   60, 60, 55, 49, 49, 51, 51, 52, 52, 59   (10)

QUEEN SAMANTHA

9-29-79   *Take A Chance*   (TK)   37, 29, 24, 22, 20, 19, 23   (7)

R.J.'S LATEST ARRIVAL

6-16-84   *Shackles*   (Quality QUS 059)   14, 17, 26   (3)

6-29-85   *Swing Low* (Long Version & Dub Mix)   (Atl. DMD 847)   49, 44, 39, 29, 27, 23, 23, 35, 41, 58, 61, 64, 69, 75   (14)

THE RAES

10-28-78   *A Little Lovin'*   (A&M)   28, 24, 21, 17, 12, 8, 8, 5, 4, 6, 6, 6, 19, 20, 24   (15)

RALPH, SHERYL LEE

9-15-84   *In The Evening*   (New York Music Co. NYM-11A)   37, 33, 31, 31, 42, 48, 46, 44, 45, 49   (10)

RAWW

10-11-86   *Don't You Try It*   (Emergency EMDS 6567)   63, 57, 56, 56, 67, 71   (6)

RAZE

10-08-88   *Break 4 Love*   (Col. 44-07890)   27, 18, 9, 4, 2, 1, 1, 1, 3, 3, 14, 16, 16   (13)

READY FOR THE WORLD

6-01-85   *Deep Inside Your Love/I'm The One Who Loves You*   (MCA 23541)   38, 25, 21, 21, 27, 27, 54, 63, 72   (9)

12-21-85   *Digital Display* (Extended Mix)   (MCA)   42, 42, 29, 29, 13, 4, 1, 3, 3, 5, 7, 7, 21, 29, 41, 61   (16)

11-08-86   *Love You Down*   (MCA 23680)   38, 22, 19, 14, 14, 11, 7, 4, 4, 4, 4, 4, 4, 11, 15, 18, 23, 53, 54, 62, 67   (21)

11-12-88   *My Girly*   (MCA 23865)   21, 17, 13, 13, 20   (5)

8-10-85   *Oh Sheila* (Extended Version & Dubstrumental)   (MCA 23572)   34, 31, 24, 14, 10, 4, 1, 1, 2, 3, 3, 3, 4, 7, 9, 10, 21, 29, 46, 56, 56, 71, 71   (23)

3-02-85   *Tonight*   (MCA 23527)   35, 29, 20, 15, 13, 13, 16, 23, 30, 41, 56, 64, 68, 69, 72, 75   (16)

THE REAL ROXANNE WITH HITMAN HOWIE TEE

6-07-86   *Bang Zoom Let's Go-go!*   (Select FMS 62269)   54, 45, 29, 18, 14, 12, 11, 11, 19, 23, 22, 31, 46, 57, 63, 62, 60, 67, 73, 75   (20)

8-24-85   *Romeo (Parts I & II)/Roxanne's Groove*   (Select FMS 62260)   60, 48, 44, 40, 40, 46, 47, 59, 64, 70   (10)

REGINA

5-31-86   *Baby Love* (Extended Version)   (Atl. DMD 939)   51, 41, 38, 32, 26, 22, 14, 8, 6, 6, 12, 13, 13, 13, 16, 15, 25, 26, 28, 42, 48, 61, 61, 63, 67, 73   (26)

11-22-86   *Best Of Love* (Remix)   (Atl. 0-86772)   58, 51, 51, 50, 64, 68, 68, 68, 72   (9)

7-09-88   *Extraordinary Love*   (Atl. 0-86583)   27, 24, 23   (3)

REIMY

4-23-88   *Speed Of Light*   (A&M SP-12268)   37, 27, 24, 18, 18, 43, 44, 50   (8)

RENE AND ANGELA

9-07-85   *I'll Be Good* (Special Mix And Instrumental)   (Mer. 884 009-1)   55, 39, 32, 28, 20, 18, 15, 12, 7, 6, 5, 5, 5, 16, 22, 29, 29, 34, 34, 56, 63, 67, 72, 74   (24)

5-25-85   *Save Your Love (For #1)* (Club Mix & Instrumental)   (Mer. 880 731-1)   46, 28, 19, 13, 13, 11, 10, 10, 13, 17, 18, 20, 23, 35, 47, 62, 71   (17)

7-05-86   *You Don't Have To Cry*   (Mer./PolyGram 884 587-1)   62, 59, 53, 48, 44, 44, 53, 68, 73   (9)

1-25-86   *Your Smile*   (Mer./PolyGram 884 271-1)   61, 54, 49, 41, 35, 32, 17, 14, 12, 12, 17, 23, 24, 30, 34, 35, 46, 64, 71   (19)

REVANCHE

9-08-79   *Revenge/Music Man*   (Atl.)   37, 28, 22, 19, 20, 23, 27, 39   (8)

RICHIE, LIONEL

1-28-84   *All Night Long*   (Motown 4514 MG)   29   (1)

9-13-86   *Dancing On The Ceiling* (Remix)   (Motown 4564 MG)   36, 33, 33, 35, 54, 62, 74   (7)

RILEY, CHERYL "PEPSI"

12-03-88   *Thanks For My Child*   (Col. 44-07871)   25, 23, 17, 14, 14   (5)

THE RING

7-07-79   *Savage Lover*   (Vanguard)   32, 28, 26, 24, 19, 17, 16, 16, 17, 19, 40   (11)

THE RITCHIE FAMILY

9-01-79   *Put Your Feet To The Beat*   (Casa.)   39, 36, 25, 19, 15, 12, 10, 8, 11, 12, 20, 28   (12)

ROBEY

3-16-85   *One Night In Bangkok*   (Silver Blue 429-5145)   46, 36, 36, 46, 58, 61, 65, 72, 72, 74   (10)

ROBINSON, VICKI SUE

3-31-79   *Nightime Fantasy*   (RCA)   26, 24, 20, 20, 30   (5)

ROCCA, JOHN

5-12-84   *I Want It To Be Real*   (Streetwise SWRL 2225)   21, 17, 15, 10, 7, 21, 28, 30   (8)

11-10-84   *Once Upon A Time* (Vocal & Dub)   (Streetwise SWRL 2236)   40, 39, 45, 46, 46   (5)

ROCHELLE

1-04-86   *My Magic Man* (Extended Version)   (WB 0-20376)   53, 53, 48, 49, 59, 61, 63, 72   (8)

ROCK MASTER SCOTT AND THE DYNAMIC 3

12-08-84   *Request Line*   (Reality D 230)   38, 34, 31, 31, 31, 27, 17, 6, 5, 4, 4, 4, 10, 13, 14, 30, 58, 60, 71, 74, 74, 74, 73, 73, 71, 70, 70, 70, 69, 68   (30)

7-06-85   *The Roof's On Fire (Scratchin' & Jivin')*   (Reality D 239)   59, 35, 26, 18, 15, 12, 12, 16, 19, 22, 24, 29, 35, 42, 53, 60, 67, 67, 67, 67, 75   (21)

ROCKWELL

1-28-84   *Somebody's Watching Me*   (Motown 4515 MG)   17, 17, 8, 1, 1, 1, 1, 1, 1, 3, 5, 4, 6, 12, 23   (15)

ROGER   *(See also:* SCRITTI POLITTI)

11-21-87   *I Want To Be Your Man*   (Reprise/WB 0-20771)   38, 23, 16, 13, 7, 7, 7, 7, 19, 23, 28, 33, 47, 50   (14)

ROLLE, RALPH

5-04-85   *Roxanne's A Man (The Untold Story)* (Dub Version)   (Streetwise 2239)   45, 24, 19, 17, 17, 44, 61, 67   (8)

THE ROLLING STONES

4-05-86   *Harlem Shuffle* (Remix)   (Rolling Stones/Col. ZSS 17945)   39, 22, 13, 13, 14, 15, 26, 33, 46, 59, 65   (11)

THE ROMANTICS

1-28-84   *Talking In Your Sleep* (Nemperor AS 1767) 14, 14, 18, 15, 22, 27, 26, 23, 27, 30 (10)

ROMEO VOID

11-03-84 *A Girl In Trouble (Is A Temporary Thing)* (Col. 44-05103) 36, 33, 30, 30, 50 (5)

THE ROSE BROTHERS

5-03-86 *I Got Off On You/Freaky Lover* (Extended Mix) (Muscle Shoals Records 3001) 63, 57, 57, 56, 61, 68, 70 (7)

ROSEBUD

5-05-79 *Have A Cigar* (WB) 26, 21, 14, 11, 8, 7, 5, 5, 6, 7, 10, 15, 16, 39 (14)

ROSS, DIANA

7-07-79 *The Boss/No One Gets The Prize* (Motown) 24, 15, 11, 9, 6, 4, 4, 3, 1, 1, 2, 3, 6, 8, 14, 19, 35, 39 (18)

2-08-86 *Chain Reaction* (Remix) (RCA PD-14267) 57, 52, 52, 60, 70, 71, 73 (7)

6-20-87 *Dirty Looks* (RCA 6416-1-RD) 50, 50, 49, 46, 61, 67, 67, 75 (8)

9-28-85 *Eaten Alive* (Hot Extended Dance Mix) (RCA PD-14183-A) 50, 34, 25, 22, 18, 18, 22, 27, 38, 53, 63, 69 (12)

9-22-84 *Swept Away* (Vocal & Dub) (RCA) 18, 12, 6, 5, 4, 3, 3, 3, 3, 5, 7, 14, 42, 43, 43, 43, 43, 49 (18)

ROSS, DIANA, AND THE SUPREMES

4-05-80 *Medley Of Hits* (Motown) 32 (1)

ROXANNE WITH U.T.F.O. *(See also:* U.T.F.O.)

2-09-85 *The Real Roxanne/Roxanne's Backside (Scratchit)* (Bleeped & Uncensored Version) (Select FMS 62256) 40, 29, 19, 13, 9, 8, 6, 6, 19, 38, 42, 55, 61, 60, 59, 58, 61, 74 (18)

ROY, BARBARA

4-11-87   *Gonna Put Up A Fight*   (RCA 5943-1-RD)   26, 21, 18, 18, 17, 17, 28, 40, 58, 65, 72   (11)

8-23-86   *Gotta See You Tonight*   (RCA PW-14405)   57, 47, 34, 34, 35, 37, 37, 34, 31, 28, 26, 18, 15, 15, 22, 22, 28, 33, 51, 51, 51, 61, 65, 65, 72   (25)

ROYAL HOUSE

3-05-88   *Party People*   (Idler/Warlock WAR-015)   35, 29, 23, 18, 18, 26, 31, 33, 38, 42, 45, 49   (12)

RUFUS AND CHAKA KHAN   *(See also:* CHAKA KHAN)

12-01-79   *Do You Love What You Feel*   (MCA)   28, 24, 20, 16, 16, 12, 12, 9, 6, 4, 4, 6, 14, 22, 31, 38   (16)

RUN-D.M.C.

12-07-85   *Can You Rock It Like This/Together Forever*   (Profile PRO-7088)   49, 34, 24, 24, 18, 18, 16, 13, 11, 11, 17, 18, 19, 26, 40, 46, 61, 71   (18)

1-28-84   *Hard Times*   (Profile PRO-7036)   3, 5, 6, 6, 5, 10, 9, 9, 15, 18, 22, 27, 28   (13)

3-21-87   *It's Tricky*   (Profile PRO-5131)   59, 30, 25, 21, 19, 19, 23, 21, 19, 19, 25, 37, 60   (13)

5-24-86   *My Adidas/Peter Piper*   (Profile PRO-7102)   30, 15, 7, 1, 1, 2, 2, 2, 2, 7, 16, 20, 23, 22, 39, 50, 61, 71, 75   (19)

5-26-84   *Rock Box*   (Profile PRO-7045)   17, 11, 17, 16, 11, 22   (6)

5-21-88   *Run's House*   (Profile PRO-7202)   17, 14, 12, 11, 13, 14, 26, 29   (8)

9-01-84   *30 Days*   (Profile PRO-7051A)   27, 23, 19, 19, 46   (5)

11-15-86   *You Be Illin'*   (Profile PRO-7119)   52, 35, 28, 28, 25, 23, 20, 20, 20, 18, 18, 18, 18, 20, 23, 24, 25, 56, 63, 68, 73   (21)

5-25-85   *You Talk Too Much/Daryll And Joe (Krush Groove 3)*   (Profile PRO-7069)   42, 34, 29, 27, 27, 30, 30, 44, 55, 65, 73   (11)

RUN-D.M.C. WITH STEVEN TYLER

8-09-86   *Walk This Way*   (Profile PRO-7112)   26, 12, 7, 6, 3, 3, 3, 4, 7, 6, 13, 15, 23, 50, 58, 66, 75, 75   (18)

RUSHEN, PATRICE

6-02-84   *Feels So Real (Won't Let Go)*   (Elektra ED 4961)   16, 16, 8, 9, 5, 8, 8, 6, 9, 12, 24   (11)

1-05-80   *Haven't You Heard*   (Elektra)   35, 35, 22, 15, 10, 8, 7, 7, 11, 15, 16, 21, 22   (14)

S-EXPRESS

11-05-88   *Superfly Guy*   (Cap. V-15409)   28, 22, 22, 26   (4)

6-25-88   *Theme From S-Express*   (Cap. V-15377)   37, 12, 10, 6, 5, 3, 11, 15, 21, 24, 23, 30   (12)

THE S.O.S. BAND

8-02-86   *Borrowed Love* (Remix)   (Tabu/Epic 4Z9-05920)   60, 39, 25, 23, 21, 18, 18, 26, 38, 55, 70   (11)

4-05-86   *The Finest* (Special Dance Mix)   (Tabu/CBS 4Z9-05364)   51, 29, 17, 8, 5, 5, 4, 4, 4, 3, 3, 6, 6, 7, 8, 12, 19, 25, 33, 39, 38, 52   (22)

8-04-84   *Just The Way You Like It*   (Tabu 4Z9-05031)   24, 17, 7, 3, 3, 4, 3, 2, 2, 7, 8, 20, 39, 49   (14)

3-07-87   *No Lies* (Remix)   (Tabu/Epic 4Z9-06030)   48, 41, 38, 31, 29, 23, 20, 20, 24, 33, 58, 64, 71, 73   (14)

11-17-84   *No One's Gonna Love You*   (Tabu 4Z9-05121)   37, 31, 26, 22, 20, 19, 19, 19, 32, 43   (10)

SABU

1-19-80   *Sabu* (all cuts)   (Ocean)   37, 31, 25, 18, 14, 11, 9, 7, 7, 11, 12, 19   (12)

SADE

5-10-86   *Never As Good As The First Time*   (Portrait/CBS 4R9-05375)   59, 54, 54, 52, 61, 61, 72   (7)

12-01-84 *Hang On To Your Love* (Portrait 4R9-05122) 27, 20, 14, 9, 9, 9, 9, 12, 11, 10, 7, 6, 5, 5, 8, 11, 27, 54, 64, 74 (20)

SA-FIRE

8-27-88 *Boy I've Been Told* (Cutting/Mer. 870 519-1) 29, 25, 17, 11, 7, 5, 3, 2, 2, 3, 10, 12, 15, 25 (14)

10-25-86 *Don't Break My Heart* (Cutting CR-209) 62, 50, 45, 45, 50, 61, 61, 66, 72 (9)

6-20-87 *Let Me Be The One* (Cutting CR-212) 53, 53, 40, 40, 52, 52, 52, 36, 35, 39, 56, 70, 73, 73 (14)

ST. TROPEZ

4-14-79 *Belle De Jour* (all cuts) (Butterfly) 26, 24, 23, 17, 16, 19, 22, 27, 39 (9)

SALT-N-PEPA (FEATURING E.U.)

12-10-88 *Get Up Everybody* (Next Plateau NP 50083) 27, 19, 9, 9 (4)

9-13-86 *I'll Take Your Man* (Next Plateau NP 50002) 55, 50, 46, 43, 33, 28, 24, 22, 20, 18, 18, 18, 18, 20, 21, 27, 27, 27, 31, 46, 46, 50, 62, 71 (24)

4-04-87 *My Mike Sounds Nice* (Next Plateau NP 50055) 26, 22, 22, 45, 48, 61, 70, 73 (8)

8-06-88 *Shake Your Thang* (Next Plateau NP 50077) 18, 12, 6, 1, 2, 4, 5, 10, 14, 16, 30 (11)

11-07-87 *Tramp/Push It* (Next Plateau NP 50063) 43, 38, 34, 30, 28, 35, 41, 46, 46, 46, 40, 27, 23, 17, 13, 7, 3, 2, 1, 1, 2, 7, 13, 28, 42, 45, 48 (27)

SANDEE

5-16-87 *You're The One* (Atl. 0-86711) 30, 27, 24, 21, 14, 14, 14, 12, 11, 11, 29, 29, 30, 47, 53, 69 (16)

SANTANA

4-27-85 *Say It Again/Instrumental* (Jellybean Remix) (Col. 44-05168) 46, 40, 36, 36, 49, 75 (6)

SCARLET AND BLACK

5-07-88   *You Don't Know*   (Virgin 0-96737)   37, 32, 32, 44, 49   (5)

SCOTT, MILLIE

4-11-87   *Every Little Bit*   (4th & B'way/Island 432)   45, 34, 30, 30, 34, 59, 65, 72, 72   (9)

SCRITTI POLITTI

11-02-85   *Perfect Way* (Way Perfect Mix)   (WB 0-20363)   47, 30, 26, 21, 17, 14, 14, 17, 17, 25, 25, 25, 25, 33, 42, 53, 57, 68, 71   (19)

9-08-85   *Wood Beez (Pray Like Aretha Franklin)/Absolute*   (WB 0-20225)   24, 22, 29, 27, 26, 25, 25, 24, 25, 30, 42, 46   (12)

SCRITTI POLITTI FEATURING ROGER   (*See also:* ROGER)

7-30-88   *Boom! There She Was*   (WB 0-20870)   23, 20, 20, 28   (4)

SECRET TIES

7-19-86   *Dancin' In My Sleep*   (Nightwave NWDS-2001)   60, 54, 54, 66, 67, 67, 67, 70, 71   (9)

SEQUAL

4-30-88   *I'm Over You*   (Cap. V-15347)   37, 32, 21, 21, 38, 46, 46   (7)

6-29-85   *It's Not Too Late/Not Too Late To* (Dub & Extended Version)   (Joey Boy JD 5003)   62, 51, 45, 35, 32, 21, 19, 18, 18, 21, 31, 36, 44, 52, 56, 66, 73   (17)

SHALAMAR   (*See also:* JODY WATLEY)

3-10-84   *Dancing In The Sheets*   (Col. 44-04949)   19, 14, 21, 20, 19, 13, 13, 17, 16, 19, 26, 27, 29   (13)

3-16-85   *My Girl Loves Me*   (Solar ED 5034)   47, 42, 39, 36, 36, 40, 51, 62, 66, 69, 75   (11)

4-05-80   *Right In The Socket*   (Solar)   35   (1)

11-10-79 *The Second Time Around/Right In The Socket* (Solar) 36, 29, 19, 11, 8, 6, 3, 3, 1, 1, 2, 2, 2, 6, 8, 12, 14, 16, 17, 19, 24 (21)

SHAN, M.C.

6-14-86 *The Bridge/Beat Biter* (Bridge 001) 47, 43, 43 (3)

5-31-86 *Feed The World* (MCA 23603) 56, 51 (2)

SHANNON

4-13-85 *Do You Wanna Get Away* (Long Dub Version & Vocal) (Mirage DMD 826) 46, 29, 20, 10, 9, 5, 5, 4, 2, 2, 8, 8, 14, 15, 21, 26, 36, 63 (18)

3-31-84 *Give Me Tonight* (Emergency EMDS-6542) 12, 11, 7, 4, 3, 6, 4, 4, 6, 13, 15, 25, 30 (13)

1-28-84 *Let The Music Play* (Emergency EMDS-6549) 1, 1, 2, 3, 2, 3, 3, 6, 11, 26, 27 (11)

8-10-85 *Stronger Together* (Long & Dub Mix) (Mirage DMD 859) 57, 49, 45, 41, 37, 34, 34, 33, 49, 61, 67, 74 (12)

SHANTE, ROXANNE   (*See also:* RICK JAMES; ROXANNE)

7-25-87 *Have A Nice Day* (Cold Chillin' CC 32105) 57, 57, 53, 46, 46, 67 (6)

4-06-85 *Queen Of Rox* (Pop Art PA 1408) 56, 48, 35, 28, 28, 25, 25, 28, 30, 47, 63, 65, 70 (13)

1-26-85 *Roxanne's Revenge* (Vocal Mix) (Pop Art PA 1406) 39, 27, 15, 16, 10, 7, 5, 2, 2, 2, 3, 13, 17, 18, 24, 27, 37, 54, 65 (19)

SHEILA E.   (*See also:* PRINCE)

1-19-85 *The Belle Of St. Mark/Too Sexy* (Dance Remix & Instrumental) (WB 0-20285) 38, 33, 29, 29, 35, 46, (2), 71 (7)

8-25-84 *The Glamorous Life* (WB 0-20251) 14, 10, 2, 1, 1, 1, 2, 7, 7, 12, 15, 21, 24, 43, 49, 47, 46, 50, 50, 50 (20)

2-14-87 *Hold Me* (Paisley Park/WB 20579-1) 60, 49, 43, 39, 34, 34, 32, 41, 55, 60, 66, 68, 75 (13)

8-24-85   *Sister Fate/Save The People* (Extended Version) (Paisley Park 0-20359)   56, 40, 29, 26, 24, 22, 22, 30, 37, 49, 56, 65, 75   (13)

SHY, JEANNE

11-03-79   *Nightdancer* (RSO)   38, 29, 24, 20, 17, 15, 13, 13, 13, 14, 14, 15, 18, 34   (14)

SIGLER, BUNNY

3-24-79   *By The Way You Dance* (Gold Mind)   30, 28, 28, 27, 25, (2), 30, 28, 39   (8)

SILK, J.M.

11-15-86   *I Can't Turn Around* (Remix) (RCA 5702-1-RD)   51, 43, 39, 39, 35, 32, 31, 31, 31, 37, 52, 52, 53, 53, 61, 69   (16)

2-21-87   *Let The Music Take Control* (RCA 5958-1-RD)   40, 26, 22, 18, 14, 13, 10, 10, 24, 43, 50, 62, 71   (13)

5-10-86   *Shadows Of Your Love* (D.J. International DJ 777)   65, 59, 53, 48, 43, 40, 40, 55, 64, 62, 63, 71, 73   (13)

SILVER, KAREN

9-22-79   *Hold On I'm Comin'* (Arista)   37, 33, 30, 27, 23, 19, 40   (7)

SIMFONIA (FEATURING CARMEN BROWN)

7-11-87   *It Ain't Right* (Atl. 0-86700)   54, 49, 49, 49, 64, 67, 74   (7)

8-02-86   *You And Me* (Atl./Cot. 0-96811)   63, 57, 50, 46, 42, 42, 53, 63, 69   (9)

THE SIMON ORCHESTRA

10-06-79   *Mr. Big Shot* (all cuts) (Polydor)   34, 25, 20, 18, 16, 19, 20, 39   (8)

SIMPLE MINDS

3-23-85   *Don't You (Forget About Me)* (A&M SP-12125)   47, 32, 15, 8, 7, 6, 5, 5, 12, 18, 19, 20, 26, 29, 31, 43, 66, 74, 74   (19)

3-08-86   *Sanctify Yourself* (Extended Version) (A&M SP-12172)   57, 52, 52, 67, 72, 73   (6)

SIMS, JOYCE

12-12-88   *Come Into My Life* (Sleeping Bag)   34, 28, 18, 18, 18, 12, 10, 9, 12, 14, 29, 36, 36, 44, 39, 48 (15)

6-20-87   *Lifetime Love* (Sleeping Bag SLX-00026X)   40, 40, 28, 27, 14, 12, 12, 12, 26, 30, 48, 54, 62, 62, 64 (15)

3-01-86   *(You Are My) All And All* (Sleeping Bag SLX-00017X)   61, 53, 38, 23, 17, 13, 11, 8, 7, 7, 7, 7, 6, 5, 5, 11, 12, 19, 20, 23, 24, 33, 35, 35, 36, 36, 48, 55, 66, 73 (30)

SINITTA

2-28-87   *Feels Like The First Time* (Omni/Atl. 0-96784)   45, 31, 33, 56, 56, 51, 28, 17, 13, 13, 13, 16, 23, 26, 31, 57, 61, 61, 70, 74 (20)

SIOUXSIE AND THE BANSHEES

10-15-88   *Peek-A-Boo* (Geffen 0-20977)   28, 28 (2)

SIR MIX-A-LOT

12-03-88   *Posse On Broaadway* (Nastymix IGU 76974)   27, 22, 22, 27, 27 (5)

SIREN

7-28-79   *Open Up For Love* (Midsong International)   38, 34, 31, 29, 28, 26, 23, 16, 14, 16, 18, 37 (12)

SISTER POWER

9-08-79   *Gimme Back My Love Affair* (Ocean)   38, 33, 30, 40 (4)

10-20-79   *Sister Power/Love Potion* (Ocean)   38, 36, 34, 31, 39 (5)

SISTER SLEDGE

1-26-80   *Got To Love Somebody* (Cot.)   37, 30, 25, 21, 18, 15, 15, 16, 30, 40 (10)

2-10-79   *He's The Greatest Dancer/We Are Family* (Cot.)   25, 20, 10, 4, 1, 1, 1, 1, 2, 2, 2, 2, 6, 10, 13, 15, 16, 22 (18)

THE SKATT BROTHERS

3-08-80   *Walk The Night*   (Casa.)   36, 27, 20, 17, 16   (5)

THE SKINNY BOYS

4-26-86   *Jock Box (America Loves The Skinny Boys)*   (Warlock WAR-002)   62, 56, 49, 44, 40, 40, 44, 52, 61, 69   (10)

SKIPWORTH AND TURNER

5-04-85   *Thinking About Your Love* (Extended Version & Instrumental)   (4th And B'way 414)   58, 37, 27, 13, 11, 11, 11, 11, 11, 9, 9, 9, 11, 16, 22, 28, 51, 59, 67, 72   (19)

SKYY

3-22-80   *High/Skyy Zoo*   (Salsoul)   38, 31, 24   (3)

SLAVE

2-02-80   *Just A Touch Of Love*   (Atl.)   35, 28, 25, 21, 18, 18, 19, 31, 38, 40   (10)

THE SMITHS

11-09-85   *The Boy With The Thorn In His Side*   (Sire 0-20392)   57, 47, 41, 41, 52, 59, 64, 64, 66, 66   (10)

3-23-85   *How Soon Is Now?*   (Sire 0-20284)   60, 52, 52, 67, 71, 73, 75   (7)

SOCCIO, GINO

2-24-79   *Dancer/Dance To Dance*   (RFC)   23, 16, 9, 6, 3, 2, 1, 1, 1, 1, 1, 3, 5, 5, 7, 8, 10, 17, 21   (19)

SOFONDA C.

3-14-87   *Pick It Up*   (Klub KR 511)   22, 17, 16, 16, 20, 38, 47, 51, 63, 72   (10)

SPAGNA

3-19-88   *Call Me*   (Epic 49 07573)   45, 40, 29, 22, 13, 15, 29, 45, 48   (9)

SPARKS

7-26-86 *Music That You Can Dance To* (Curb/MCA 23640) 61, 53, 32, 28, 21, 17, 17, 21, 29, 30, 53, 62, 69 (13)

SPARKY D

3-16-85 *Sparky's Turn* (Roxanne You're Through) (Instrumental & Dub Version) (Nia NI 1245) 40, 16, 15, 21, 28, 33, 33, 38, 54, 61, 62, 62, 69 (13)

THE SPINNERS

11-17-79 *Body Language* (Atl.) 35, 29, 22, 20, 19, 19, 19, 26, 26 (9)

1-19-80 *Working My Way Back To You/Forgive Me, Girl* (Atl.) 36, 27, 19, 16, 13, 10, 8, 8, 13, 14, 16, 18 (12)

SPYDER-D (FEATURING D.J. DOC)

5-24-86 *I Can't Wait (To Rock The Mike)* (Profile PRO-7103) 55, 50, 45, 41, 38, 35, 35, 37, 54, 63 (10)

SPRINGSTEEN, BRUCE

1-19-85 *Born In The U.S.A.* (Dub, Radio & Freedom Mix) (Col. 44-05147) 40, 35, 30, 30, 36, 45, (2), 73 (7)

10-20-84 *Cover Me* (Undercover Mix) (Col. 44-05087) 30, 25, 24, 23, 29, 42, 48 (7)

7-07-84 *Dancing In The Dark* (Blaster & Dub Mix) (Col. 44-05028) 24, 17, 12, 6, 5, 4, 4, 7, 12, 25, 28, 28, 34, 47 (14)

STACEY Q

3-05-88 *Don't Make A Fool Of Yourself* (Atl. 0-86616) 41, 25, 16, 10, 9, 5, 3, 1, 8, 16, 28, 39, 48 (13)

6-13-87 *Insecurity* (Atl. 0-86716) 54, 51, 49, 43, 43, 12, 9, 9, 9, 9, 17, 33, 43, 48, 48, 51 (16)

10-17-87 *Music Out Of Bounds* (Atl. 0-86669) 41, 31, 31, 36, 49 (5)

6-21-86 *Two Of Hearts* (Dance Mix) (Atl. 0-86797) 55, 37, 28, 24, 20, 15,

10, 9, 9, 11, 9, 6, 1, 2, 3, 4, 5, 11, 12, 18, 27, 34, 38, 44, 44, 64, 71, 75, 75, 75   (30)

11-29-86   *We Connect*   (Atl. DMD 990)   53, 53, 36, 28, 19, 19, 19, 15, 11, 11, 5, 4, 4, 3, 14, 21, 25, 33, 48, 65, 68   (21)

STANLEY, CHUCK

4-25-87   *Day By Day*   (Def Jam/Col. 44-46021)   44, 41, 39, 39, 60, 70, 71   (7)

STANLEY, PAMELA

3-24-84   *Coming Out Of Hiding*   (TSR 830)   17, 14, 18, 20, 26, 21, 25, 30, 30   (9)

4-20-85   *If Looks Could Kill* (Local & Long Dub Version)   (Mirage DMD 821)   50, 43, 39, 39, 46, 57, 71   (7)

10-06-79   *This Is Hot*   (EMI America)   38, 34, 31, 29, 26, 24, 23, 21, 38   (9)

THE STAPLE SINGERS

9-15-84   *Slippery People*   (Private I 4Z9-05078)   38, 35, 33, 28, 23, 17, 14, 13, 18, 17, 19, 33, 49   (13)

STARGARD

10-20-79   *Wear It Out*   (WB)   34, 28, 23, 16, 13, 10, 5, 3, 3, 1, 1, 2, 2, 3, 4, 12, 14, 28, 36, 40   (20)

STARPOINT

3-07-87   *He Wants My Body*   (Elektra 0-66824)   57, 49, 44, 40, 30, 25, 18, 16, 16, 18, 20, 21, 17, 14, 13, 31, 31, 58, 62   (19)

8-31-85   *Object Of My Desire (Extended Version)*   (Elektra 0-66891)   44, 40, 37, 33, 26, 15, 14, 9, 8, 6, 2, 2, 7, 11, 22, 28, 39, 39, 49, 49, 64, 70, 73   (23)

3-29-86   *Restless* (Extended Version)   (Elektra ED 5127)   51, 45, 39, 39, 37, 37, 42, 62, 73   (9)

1-18-86   *What You've Been Missin'*   (Elektra ED 5101)   51, 45, 39, 34, 29, 25, 25, 35, 43, 63, 71   (11)

STARR, BRENDA K.

11-28-87 *Breakfast In Bed* (MCA 23796) 44, 42, 37, 44, 36, 36, 36, 33, 38, 43, 42, 46 (12)

8-03-85 *Pickin' Up The Pieces* (Extended Version & Dub Mix) (Mirage 0-96873) 55, 37, 34, 28, 20, 17, 15, 13, 13, 19, 28, 31, 44, 52, 59, 68 (16)

2-07-87 *What You See Is What You Get* (MCA 23704) 51, 41, 28, 21, 15, 12, 12, 12, 15, 19, 45, 57, 60, 69 (14)

STARR, EDWIN

11-18-78 *Contact* (20th C.) 30, 21, 14, 9, 4, 3, 1, 1, 1, 3, 3, 4, 8, 8, 11, 13, 17, 19, 23 (19)

6-16-79 *H.A.P.P.Y. Radio* (20th C.) 39, 36, 30, 27, 23, 19, 17, 17, 18, 23, 27, 28 (12)

STATON, CANDI

10-28-78 *Victim* (WB) 23 (1)

5-26-79 *When You Wake Up In The Morning* (WB) 37, 32, 26, 16, 10, 5, 3, 3, 5, 10, 11, 13, 17, 18, 21, 40 (16)

12-13-86 *You Got The Love* (Source SR 9001) 68 (1)

STETSASONIC

12-03-88 *Talkin' All That Jazz* (Tommy Boy TB-918) 23, 21, 21, 23, 23 (5)

STEVIE B

3-19-88 *Dreamin' Of Love* (LMR 4001) 40, 29, 23, 16, 17, 14, 13, 10, 11, 19, 21, 30, 37, 40, 47 (15)

9-05-87 *Party Your Body* (LMR 4000) 25, 21, 21, 17, 10, 6, 4, 4, 15, 23, 44, 48 (12)

7-30-88 *Spring Love* (LMR 4002) 17, 16, 13, 8, 9, 5, 2, 1, 3, 3, 6, 8, 26 (13)

STEWART, AMII

2-17-79 *Knock On Wood* (Ariola) 27, 22, 17, 14, 8, 6, 5, 5, 7, 15, 19 (11)

STEWART, JERMAINE

4-12-86 *We Don't Have To Take Our Clothes Off* (Dance Remix) (Arista ADI-0423) 54, 49, 49, 57, 69, 68, 70, 69, 72, 72, 69, 71, 71, 68, 66, 66, 57, 49, 42, 32, 29, 29, 42, 47, 56, 69, 74 (27)

1-12-85 *The Word Is Out* (Dub Short & Extended) (Arista) 38, 28, 18, 14, 12, 12, 16, 18, 26, 33, 56, 67, 70, 70, 70, 70, 70, 70, 70, 73 (20)

STEWART, ROD

1-20-79 *Do Ya Think I'm Sexy* (WB) 26, 15, 5, 2, 2, 1, 1, 2, 2, 5, 6, 10, 18 (13)

STICKY FINGERS

3-10-79 *Sticky Fingers* (all cuts) (Prelude) 29, 26, 24, 22, 22, 29 (6)

STING

8-10-85 *If You Love Somebody Set Them Free/Another Day* (Jellybean Remix) (A&M SP-12132) 25, 16, 15, 12, 12, 12, 37, 51, 54, 65, 72 (11)

11-28-87 *We'll Be Together* (A&M SP-12251) 39, 34, 25, 21, 17, 17, 17, 16, 24, 36, 50 (11)

STOCK, AITKEN, WATERMAN

11-14-87 *Roadblock* (A&M SP-12250) 40, 37, 32, 26, 26, 32, 38, 38, 38, 44 (10)

STREISAND, BARBRA (*See also:* DONNA SUMMER)

7-21-79 *The Main Event/Fight* (Col.) 35, 30, 28, 23, 21, 20, 20, 21, 38 (9)

SUAVE

6-18-88 *My Girl* (Cap. V-15366) 44, 40 (2)

THE SUGAR HILL GANG

11-03-79   *The Rappers Delight*   (Sugar Hill)   36, 34, 31, 28, 25, 21, 18, 29, 29, 40, 40   (11)

SUMMER, DONNA

5-12-79   *Bad Girls* (all cuts)   (Casa.)   6, 3, 1, 2, 2, 1, 1, 1, 1, 1, 2, 3, 9, 9, 11, 14, 15, 17, 29, 38   (20)   (*See also: Hot Stuff*)

10-17-87   *Dinner With Gershwin*   (Geffen 0-20635)   40, 24, 16, 16, 22, 32, 43, 48   (8)

4-28-79   *Hot Stuff*   (Casa.)   25, 11   (2)   (*See also: Bad Girls*)

10-28-78   *MacArthur Park Suite*   (Casa.)   1, 1, 1, 1, 2, 5, 5, 6, 10, 14, 14, 19, 28   (13)

12-01-79   *On The Radio*   (Casa.)   32, 25, 21, 18, 18, 15, 15, 20, 39   (9)

11-24-84   *Supernatural Love* (Extended Dance Remix)   (Geffen 0-20273)   40, 36, 33, 30, 29, 29, 29, 39   (8)

SUMMER, DONNA, AND BARBRA STREISAND   (*See also:* BARBRA STREISAND)

10-27-79   *No More Tears*   (Casa.)   31, 21, 13, 2, 1, 1, 1, 2, 4, 4, 7, 7, 10, 13, 26, 39   (16)

SUPERNATURE

11-02-85   *The Show Stoppa (Is Stupid Fresh)*   (Pop Art PA 1613)   53, 28, 19, 16, 13, 11, 11, 12, 12, 16, 16, 23, 27, 31, 41, 57, 68, 74   (18)

SUPERTRAMP

7-27-85   *Cannonball* (Extended & Instrumental Version)   (A&M SP-12130)   58, 46, 40, 40, 40, 65   (6)

1-23-88   *I'm Beggin' You*   (A&M SP-12254)   42, 40, 45, 50   (4)

THE SUPREMES   (*See:* DIANA ROSS)

SURE!, AL B.

4-02-88   *Nite And Day*   (WB 0-20782)   36, 31, 21, 19, 14, 5, 4, 2, 1, 5, 9, 12, 16, 21, 24   (15)

7-16-88   *Off On Your Own* (Girl)   (WB 0-20952)   22, 15, 11, 8, 5, 5, 6, 7, 13, 14, 14, 21, 30   (13)

11-26-88   *Rescue Me*   (WB 0-21038)   28, 26   (2)

SURFACE

4-11-87   *Happy*   (Col. 44-06739)   47, 37, 27, 14, 11, 7, 5, 3, 2, 2, 6, 6, 16, 16, 16, 28, 42, 43, 64, 75   (20)

SUZY

9-20-86   *Can't Live Without Your Love*   (Atl. 0-86791)   57, 52, 46, 41, 35, 26, 33, 35, 46, 63, 74, 74   (12)

SWEAT, KEITH

12-05-87   *I Want Her*   (Vintertainment/Elektra 80-66788)   35, 24, 13, 13, 13, 13, 13, 15, 12, 7, 6, 6, 4, 5, 6, 20, 22, 20, 30, 36, 46   (21)

SWEET SENSATION

10-04-86   *Hooked On You*   (Next Plateau NP 50046)   62, 56, 51, 50, 55, 62, 66, 72, 58, 58, 51, 51, 62, 62, 62, 66, 70, 70, 71, 58, 53, 51, 51, 67, 71   (25)

8-27-88   *Never Let You Go*   (Atco/Atl. 0-96636)   23, 12, 6, 4, 2, 1, 1, 3, 3, 13, 20, 30   (12)

4-23-88   *Take It While It's Hot*   (Next Plateau NP 50072)   28, 22, 18, 7, 8, 8, 6, 22, 33, 36   (10)

SWING OUT SISTER

10-17-87   *Breakout*   (Mer. 888 836-1)   38, 20, 14, 8, 8, 16, 29, 43, 43, 45, 50, 50, 50   (13)

1-23-88   *Twilight World*   (Mer./PolyGram 870 015-1)   39, 37, 28, 18, 17, 14, 18, 40, 44 50   (10)

SYBIL

9-26-87 *My Love Is Guaranteed* (Next Plateau NP 50067) 65, 46, 30, 18, 14, 13, 11, 9, 5, 5, 8, 17, 27, 32, 32, 32, 38, 44 (18)

SYLVESTER

11-17-79 *Can't Stop Dancing* (Fantasy) 32, 27, 21, 18, 14, 12, 12, 9, 9, 7, 7, 8, 11, 18, 26, 34 (16)

3-31-79 *I (Who Have Nothing)* (Fantasy) 29, 21, 15, 14, 14, 19, 31, 39 (8)

5-09-87 *Mutual Attraction* (WB PRO 2734) 52, 48, 48, 64, 68, 75 (6)

11-29-86 *Someone Like You* (WB 0-20548) 60, 60, 47, 38, 34, 34, 34, 27, 19, 19, 4, 2, 2, 4, 2, 3, 7, 14, 20, 49, 55, 64, 66 (23)

5-12-79 *Stars* (all cuts) (Fantasy) 29, 27, 23, 22, 18, 18, 16, 16, 31, 37 (10)

3-03-84 *Trouble In Paradise* (Remix) (Megatone MT-126) 25, 24, 26, 30 (4)

10-28-78 *You Make Me Feel (Mighty Real)/Dance* (Disco Heat) (Fantasy) 12, 15, 23 (3)

SYMBOLIC THREE FEATURING DR. SHOCK

12-21-85 *No Show* (Reality/Danya/Fantasy D 250) 47, 47, 41, 41, 38, 35, 32, 32, 40, 47, 53, 68 (12)

THE SYSTEM

4-18-87 *Don't Disturb This Groove* (Atl. 0-86741) 48, 33, 33, 26, 24, 17, 12, 9, 8, 8, 8, 8, 9, 13, 13, 13, 19, 29, 35, 49, 53, 55, 55, 61 (24)

8-03-85 *The Pleasure Seekers* (Mirage 0-96875) 41, 32, 29, 27, 27, 36, 51, 59, 66, 74 (10)

T-CONNECTION

1-13-79 *At Midnight* (TK) 25, 14, 12, 8, 6, 5, 3, 2, 5, 9, 10, 11, 17, 25 (14)

THP

12-08-79 *THP* (all cuts) (Atl.)   35, 31, 25, 25, 22, 22, 18, 28, 36, 40   (10)

12-02-78 *Tender Is The Night* (Butterfly)   23, 20, 17, 17, 15, 15, 13, 11, 14, 17, 20, 29   (12)

TJM

11-10-79 *TJM* (all cuts) (Casa.)   37, 33, 31, 30, 38   (5)

TKA

12-20-86 *Come Get My Love* (Tommy Boy TB-887)   58, 50, 50, 50, 44, 40, 40, 40, 38, 48, 61, 70   (12)

4-19-86 *One Way Love* (Tommy Boy TB-866)   54, 46, 41, 38, 27, 27, 33, 38, 37, 37, 39, 60, 60, 69, 70, 75   (16)

1-30-88 *Tears May Fall* (Tommy Boy TB-901)   39, 26, 21, 15, 9, 17, 12, 11, 13, 16, 25, 39, 47   (13)

TLA ROCK

8-30-86 *Breaking Bells* (Fresh FRE 6Y)   45, 26, 17, 15, 15, 21, 20, 26, 32, 53, 60, 63, 70   (13)

TA MARA AND THE SEEN

10-26-85 *Everybody Dance/Lonely Heart* (Extended Version) (A&M SP-12149)   46, 22, 11, 8, 6, 1, 3, 15, 16, 16, 31, 31, 35, 50, 61, 68, 71   (17)

TAFFY

5-17-86 *I Love My Radio (Midnight Radio)* (Emergency EMDS 6561)   61, 45, 41, 37, 34, 34, 34, 47, 52, 64, 64, 71, 71   (13)

TALK TALK

5-19-84 *It's My Life* (EMI America V 7821-1)   25, 13, 25   (3)

3-22-86 *Life's What You Make It* (Remix) (EMI America V-19203)   57, 50, 50, 56, 67, 75   (6)

TALKING HEADS

11-30-85 *And She Was/Television Man* (Extended Mix) (Sire 0-20378) 60, 54, 54, 61, 61, 65, 65, 74 (8)

2-09-80 *I Zimbra/Life During Wartime* (Sire) 36, 30, 25, 21, 20, 20, 26, 27, 36 (9)

THE TASTE-T-UPS

3-19-88 *Hypnotize* (Mer. 870 169-1) 43, 35, 25, 17, 14, 16, 44 (7)

TAURUS BOYZ

9-05-87 *Looking For A Lover* (Cooltempo/Chrysalis 4V9-4312) 63, 58, 58, 55, 49, 35, 27, 27, 46 (9)

TAYLOR, LAURA

10-28-78 *Dancin' In My Feet* (TK) 14, 9, 7, 13, 15 (5)

TEARS FOR FEARS

4-20-85 *Everybody Wants To Rule The World* (Extended Version) (Mer. 880 659-1) 60, 36, 14, 10, 8, 4, 3, 1, 5, 9, 10, 21, 21, 27, 30, 31, 62, 64, 74 (19)

10-12-85 *Head Over Heels* (Extended Version) (Mer. 880 929-1) 42, 32, 28, 28, 31, 31, 42, 57, 65, 71 (10)

7-20-85 *Shout* (U.S. & U.K. Remix) (Mer. 880 929-1) 49, 25, 12, 9, 7, 6, 5, 5, 8, 12, 21, 29, 32, 41, 52, 57, 66 (17)

TEASE

5-24-86 *Firestarter* (Extended Version) (Epic/CBS 49-05339) 52, 47, 47, 49, 58, 63, 57, 51, 47, 47, 59, 62, 72, 74 (14)

THE TEE VEE TOONS MASTER MIX

5-10-86 *Jane, Get Me Off This Crazy Thing* (Late Night Dance Mix)/The Jetsons (Tee Vee Tunes TVT 5005) 60, 49, 39, 36, 36, 35, 35, 48, 53, 65, 74 (11)

TELEX

1-05-80   *Moskow Diskow*   (Sire)   37, 37, 32, 30, 39   (5)

TEMPER

8-04-84   *No Favors* (Dub Version)   (MCA 25306)   17, 13, 10, 10, 7, 11, 11, 13, 11, 16, 29, 40, 41, 46, 47   (15)

THE TEMPEST TRIO

12-08-79   *The Tempest Trio* (all cuts)   (Marlin)   37, 34, 31, 31   (4)

THE TEMPTATIONS

1-18-86   *Do You Really Love Your Baby*   (Gordy 4550 GG)   65, 59, 50, 46, 46, 50, 58, 65, 72   (9)

2-13-88   *Look What You Started*   (Motown 4598 MG)   38, 35, 32, 28, 22, 18, 15, 15, 32, 40, 44, 50   (12)

1-26-85   *Treat Her Like A Lady* (Club Mix & Dub)   (Motown PR 163)   37, 31, 28, 25, 25, 27, 43, 58, 67, 69, 72   (11)

TEN CITY

6-18-88   *Right Back To You*   (Atl. 0-86574)   35, 24, 17, 11, 8, 8, 20, 23   (8)

THE THE

2-28-87   *Infected*   (Epic 49-05982)   48, 42, 42, 52, 52, 56, 62, 67   (8)

THEODORE, MIKE, ORCHESTRA

5-12-79   *High On Mad Mountain*   (Westbound)   34, 31, 27, 21, 15, 12, 12, 11, 14, 19, 27, 28   (12)

THIRD WORLD

5-04-85   *Sense Of Purpose* (Extended Club Mix)   (Col. 44-05146)   54, 49, 45, 40, 40, 61, 69   (7)

THOMAS, EVELYN

8-11-84   *High Energy*   (TSR 833)   23, 19, 20, 17, 27, 25, 21, 19, 19, 30, 47   (11)

THOMAS, LILLO

7-18-87   *I'm In Love*   (Cap. V-15293)   63, 51, 51, 42, 33, 33, 38, 38, 41, 41, 47   (11)

11-07-87   *I'm In Love*   (Cap. V-15331)   34, 26, 22, 22, 36, 47   (6)

THOMAS, NOLAN

6-01-85   *One Bad Apple* (Vocal & Dub Mix)   (Emergency EMDS 6550)   50, 46, 41, 41, 52, 61, 65, 67, 69   (9)

12-08-84   *Yo' Little Brother* (Dub Mix)   (Emergency EMDS 6546)   32, 29, 28, 28, 28, 28, 27, 42, 44, 38, 31, 24, 20, 20, 26, 20, 19, 29, 40, 44, 57, 67, 68   (23)

THOMAS, TASHA

11-18-78   *Shoot Me With Your Love*   (Atl.)   22, 18, 15, 11, 11, 9, 9, 9, 11, 21, 22, 28   (12)

THE THOMPSON TWINS

5-05-84   *Hold Me Now*   (Arista ADP-9158)   15, 14, 27, 28   (4)

THE THREE DEGREES

11-18-78   *New Dimensions*   (Ariola)   24, 19, 16, 13, 21, 22, 28, 28, 28, 30   (10)

THURSTON, BOBBY

3-08-80   *You Got What It Takes*   (Prelude)   37, 30, 23, 18, 14   (5)

TIA

12-20-86   *Boy Toy*   (RCA 5769-1-RD)   59, 54, 54, 54, 49, 42, 42, 35, 31, 17, 12, 13, 17, 29, 48, 66, 73   (17)

TIFFANY

10-24-87 *I Think We're Alone Now* (MCA 23793) 43, 28, 22, 15, 12, 12, 20, 32, 34, 41, 41, 41, 47 (13)

THE TIME

3-09-85 *The Bird/My Drawers* (Remix & LP Version) (WB 20315) 37, 34, 29, 23, 23, 24, 31, 32, 43, 57, 67 (11)

THE TIME BANDITS

8-17-85 *I'm Only Shooting Love* (Extended & Dub Version) (Col. 44-05229) 60, 52, 46, 46, 50, 57, 67, 70 (8)

THE TIMELORDS

12-03-88 *Doctorin' The Tardis* (TVT 4020) 28, 26, 25, 29, 29 (5)

THE TIMEX SOCIAL CLUB

5-17-86 *Rumors/Vicious Rumors* (Extended Version) (Jay 001) 45, 37, 25, 11, 6, 2, 1, 1, 1, 1, 1, 1, 1, 1, 1, 2, 2, 5, 5, 5, 6, 7, 7, 7, 13, 26, 28, 39, 49, 49, 56, 67, 71, 71, 71, 75 (36)

TINA B

5-09-87 *January February* (Criminal 00009) ·49, 46, 46, 65, 65, 73 (6)

9-10-88 *Bodyguard* (Vendetta VE-7004) 27, 22, 17, 10, 8, 5, 4, 29 (8)

9-15-84 *Honey To A Bee* (Vocal & Dub) (Elektra ED 5005) 47, 45, 50, 46, 41, 39, 34, 32, 32, 43, 47 (11)

3-12-88 *Miracles Explode* (Criminal CR 12-019) 38, 33, 30, 33, 45, 48 (6)

TODAY

12-17-88 *Him Or Me* (Motown MOT-4619) 28, 18, 18 (3)

TODD, PAM

12-02-78 *Baise Moi* (Channel) 30, 29, 27 (3)

TOLGA

3-12-88   *Leave It All Behind*   (Cutting CR-216)   36, 31, 31, 44, 49   (5)

11-05-88   *Lovin' Fool*   (Cutting CR-222)   27, 24, 24   (3)

TONE LOC

12-24-88   *Wild Thing*   (Delicious/Island DV 1002)   22, 22   (2)

TONY! TONI! TONE!

6-04-88   *Little Walter*   (Wing/PolyGram 887 385-1)   28, 21, 15, 11, 10, 7, 10, 27   (8)

TORCH SONG

2-18-84   *Prepare To Energize*   (I.R.S. SP-70412)   25, 18, 16, 23, 29   (5)

TORRES, JUDY

1-16-88   *Come Into My Life*   (Profile PRO-7165)   46, 40, 35, 29, 26, 28   (6)

TORRES, LIZ

5-16-87   *Can't Get Enough*   (State Street SSR 1002)   34, 30, 27, 24, 23, 29, 29, 33, 42, 54, 62, 62, 67, 73   (14)

TOTAL CONTRAST

3-01-86   *The River/Sunshine*   (London/PolyGram 886 032-1)   57, 45, 41, 36, 30, 30, 34, 45, 58, 65, 74   (11)

11-23-85   *Takes A Little Time* (Dub Version)   (London 886 004-1)   65, 51, 46, 41, 41, 41, 45, 45, 62, 68, 75   (11)

TOUCH

4-11-87   *Without You*   (Supertronics RY-017)   40, 35, 32, 32, 23, 23, 20, 16, 13, 12, 18, 18, 37, 44, 58, 69, 69, 73   (18)

TOWNES, CAROL LYNN

3-30-85   *Believe In The Beat* (Special Dance Remix & Instrumental Version)   (Polydor)   59, 54, 54, 63   (4)

7-14-84   *99 1/2* (Dub & Club Mix) (Polydor 881 009-1)   20, 15, 12, 8, 8, 14, 22, 21, 28, 50 (10)

T'PAU

6-20-87   *Heart And Soul* (Virgin 0-96779)   43, 43, 39, 39, 24, 19, 19, 18, 18, 24, 40, 52, 53, 53, 56 (15)

TRACY, JEANIE

9-15-84   *Sing Your Own Song/Time Bomb* (Megatone MT 125)   43, 41, 44, 44, 47 (5)

TRAMAINE

9-21-85   *Fall Down (Spirit Of Love)* (A&M SP-12146)   51, 44, 30, 22, 16, 10, 8, 8, 10, 9, 8, 7, 7, 10, 10, 21, 21, 28, 31, 36, 45, 55, 59, 70 (24)

2-01-86   *In The Morning Time* (Shout Mix) (A&M SP-12166)   58, 50, 44, 39, 35, 31, 27, 27, 39, 60, 65, 75 (12)

TRANCE DANCE

3-07-87   *Do The Dance* (Epic 49-06022)   49, 43, 40, 37, 35, 29, 27, 26, 25, 32, 33, 38, 62, 62, 66, 74 (16)

TRANS-X

6-14-86   *Living On Video* (Remix) (Atco/Atl. DMD 941)   57, 44, 40, 40, 56, 67, 71, 73 (8)

TRICKY TEE

12-14-85   *Johnny The Fox* (Bonus Beats) (Sleeping Bag SLX-00016X)   58, 49, 49, 36, 36, 36, 40, 51, 55, 58, 61, 69, 73 (13)

TRINERE

6-08-85   *All Night* (Extended & Dub Mix) (Jam Packed JPI-104)   52, 44, 31, 25, 20, 18, 15, 15, 20, 21, 48, 57, 69, 75 (14)

8-02-86   *How Can We Be Wrong* (Jam Packed JPI-2003)   48, 43, 38, 35, 35, 44, 58, 67, 71, 75, 72 (11)

2-22-86   *I'll Be All You Ever Need* (Jam Packed JPI-2001)   54, 43, 23, 16, 14, 10, 7, 7, 10, 15, 16, 16, 17, 24, 31, 32, 33, 45, 59, 65, 71, 75 (22)

4-04-87   *They're Playing Our Song*   (Jam Packed JPI-2007)   27, 18, 13, 11, 11, 14, 18, 29, 42, 64, 70   (11)

TROOP

8-06-88   *Mamacita*   (Atl. 0-86565)   29, 21, 18, 17, 21, 28   (6)

TRUSSEL

12-22-79   *Love Injection*   (Elektra)   36, 36, 28, 28, 23, 17, 13, 13, 17, 23, 29, 30, 37, 39   (14)

TURNER, TINA

11-07-87   *Afterglow*   (Cap. V-16349)   41, 29, 24, 18, 15, 8, 6, 6, 6, 6, 14, 18, 27, 44, 44, 46   (16)

9-29-84   *Better Be Good To Me*   (Cap. V-8609)   26, 22, 13, 10, 9, 8, 11, 10, 15, 18, 21, 38, 42, 42, 42, 46   (16)

2-04-84   *Let's Stay Together*   (Cap. V-8579)   27, 14, 8, 6, 4, 5, 4, 3, 5, 3, 3, 11, 11, 27   (14)

11-09-85   *One Of The Living* (Extended Version)   (Cap. V-15205)   49, 46, 46, 59, 67   (5)

3-09-85   *Private Dancer/City Limits*   (Cap. V-8620)   40, 38, 32, 26, 24, 18, 18, 24, 55   (9)

9-13-86   *Typical Male* (Remix)   (Cap. V-51249)   39, 28, 20, 14, 8, 8, 9, 14, 22, 33, 34, 37, 37, 60, 69, 73, 73, 73   (18)

8-10-85   *We Don't Need Another Hero (Thunderdome)*   (Cap. V-8655)   52, 47, 47, 53, 64, 63, 67, 69, 67, 70, 74   (11)

7-07-84   *What's Love Got To Do With It*   (Cap. V-8597)   16, 14, 10, 5, 4, 2, 2, 1, 1, 1, 2, 3, 4, 11, 20, 41, 50   (17)

TWILIGHT 22

1-28-84   *Electric Kingdom*   (Vanguard SPV-68A)   4, 4, 5, 14, 23, 28, 27, 28   (8)

6-02-84   *Siberian Night*   (Vanguard SPV-73A)   23, 26, 29   (3)

2 LIVE CREW

6-28-86 *Trow The D. And Ghetto Base* (Luke Skywalker 100) 52, 44, 31, 26, 24, 24, 49, 34, 34, 51, 58, 68 (12)

2 PUERTO RICANS, A BLACK MAN AND A DOMINICAN

9-05-87 *Do It Properly* (Grooveline GRL 5001) 34, 31, 31, 29, 29, 37, 39, 48 (8)

TWO SISTERS

2-11-84 *Destiny* (Sugar Scoop SS4 26B) 27, 30, 29 (3)

TWO TONS O' FUN

3-08-80 *Got The Feeling* (Fantasy) 39, 28, 18, 11, 8 (5)

TYLER, STEVEN *(See:* RUN-D.M.C.)

U.N.

1-05-80 *U.N.* (all cuts) (Prelude) 32, 32, 28, 40 (4)

USA FOR AFRICA

3-30-85 *We Are The World* (Col. VS 205179) 29, 11, 4, 1, 1, 1, 1, 1, 3, 5, 18, 25, 26, 26, 26, 52, 64, 70, 75 (19)

U.T.F.O. *(See also:* ROXANNE)

7-06-85 *Leader Of The Pack* (Special Instrumental Mix & Extended Version) (Select FMS 62259) 55, 36, 31, 31, 32, 35, 43, 50, 64, 66, 67 (11)

12-22-84 *Roxanne, Roxanne* (Select FMS 62254) 37, 37, 37, 33, 25, 13, 6, 3, 1, 1, 2, 3, 7, 8, 8, 17, 20, 25, 47, 48, 50, 56, 63, 68, 75 (25)

10-04-86 *Split Personality* (Select FMS 62276) 61, 51, 46, 42, 42, 51, 64, 68 (8)

6-28-86 *We Work Hard* (Select SEL 21616) 49, 43, 38, 35, 30, 26, 24, 24, 25, 44, 54, 65, 70, 73 (14)

U.T.F.O. WITH FULL FORCE   (*See also:* FULL FORCE)

9-14-85   *Bite It* (Extended & Dub Version)   (Select FMS 62263)   54, 49, 48,
        52, 62, 65, 65, 65, 73   (9)

ULLANDA

6-30-79   *Want Ads*   (Ocean)   39, 36, 34, 33, 33, 40   (6)

THE ULTIMATE

1-27-79   *The Ultimate* (all cuts)   (Casa.)   26, 20, 17, 13, 12, 10, 10, 12, 13, 14,
        20   (11)

UNYQUE

10-20-79   *Keep On Making Me High/Party Down*   (DJM)   37, 32, 29, 26, 21, 18,
        39   (7)

VANDROSS, LUTHER

8-17-85   *It's Over Now* (Remix)   (Epic 49-05228)   59, 54, 54, 60, 62, 68,
        74   (7)

1-17-87   *Stop To Love* (Remix)   (Epic 34-06523)   59, 41, 41, 41, 39, 47, 59,
        59, 63, 67, 72, 64, 71, 75   (14)

3-02-85   *'Til My Baby Comes Home* (Dance & Album Version)   (Epic 49-
        051059)   40, 33, 30, 26, 22, 18, 15, 12, 12, 18, 19, 33, 35, 48, 59,
        66, 71   (17)

VANESS, THEO

4-14-79   *Bad Bad Boy*   (Prelude)   24, 19, 9, 4, 1, 1, 3, 3, 3, 3, 6, 7, 22, 30,
        36   (15)

12-15-79   *Thank God There's Music/I Can't Dance Without You*   (Prelude)   33,
        28, 28, 20, 20, 13, 11, 9, 9, 10, 16, 19, 21, 23, 29, 36, 39   (17)

VANITY

11-17-84   *Pretty Mess/Mechanical Emotion*   (Motown 4526 MG)   35, 28, 25, 23,
        21, 18, 18, 18, 16, 19, 36, 42, 50, 49   (14)

4-12-86   *Under The Influence* (Remix)   (Motown 4558 MG)   63, 52, 48, 44,
        44, 43, 63, 64, 74   (9)

VANNELLI, GINO

6-15-85   *Black Cars* (Special Dance Mix & Instrumental Dub Mix)   (HME 4W9-05205)   47, 42, 35, 31, 31, 44, 53, 59, 67   (9)

VARIOUS ARTISTS

7-13-85   *Fuzz Dance (EP)*   (Sire 1-25273)   46, 36, 33, 19, 15, 14, 14, 23, 33, 44, 52, 59, 62, 68, 68, 75   (16)

VEGA, TATA

5-12-79   *I Just Keep Thinking About You Baby*   (Motown)   38, 35, 33, 30, 27, 26, 24, 20, 20, 29, 32   (11)

VIDAL, MARIA

10-27-84   *Body Rock* (Dance & Dub Mix)   (EMI America V-7836-1)   40, 37, 34, 23, 21, 20, 42, 49   (8)

THE VILLAGE PEOPLE

10-28-78   *Cruisin'*   (Casa.)   18, 14, 11, 9, 9, 9, 23   (7)

4-14-79   *In The Navy*   (Casa.)   30, 27, 27   (3)

12-15-79   *Ready For The 80's/Sleazy*   (Casa.)   35, 32, 32, 29, 29   (5)

12-09-78   *Y.M.C.A.*   (Casa.)   15, 9, 6, 8, 8, 8, 18, 21, 23, 24   (10)

VITAMIN Z

6-15-85   *Burning Flame* (Extended Dance Mix & Dub Version)   (Geffen 0-20325)   55, 44, 33, 28, 26, 23, 23, 26, 39, 65   (10)

THE VOICE IN FASHION

4-11-87   *Only In The Night*   (Atl. 0-86719)   50, 43, 34, 27, 24, 22, 18, 14, 12, 10, 5, 5, 7, 8, 23, 33, 33, 41, 51, 59, 70   (21)

VOYAGE

12-09-78   *Fly Away* (all cuts)   (Marlin/TK)   21, 13, 7, 2, 2, 2, 2, 2, 1, 4, 6, 6, 12, 15, 16, 20   (16)

WA-WA-NEE

11-07-87 *Sugar Free* (Epic 49-06864) 33, 24, 19, 15, 10, 10, 23, 37, 37, 37, 45 (11)

WAITE, JOHN

9-29-84 *Missing You* (Extended Version) (EMI America V-7833-1) 32, 27, 24, 22, 37, 47 (6)

WALDEN, NARADA MICHAEL (*See also:* NARADA)

1-26-80 *Dance Of Life* (all cuts) (Atl.) 32, 23, 17, 12, 9, 6, 5, 4, 4, 9, 13 (11)

WANG CHUNG

5-19-84 *Dance Hall Days/Don't Let Go* (Geffen 20194-OA) 21, 16, 26, 24, 27, 25, 24, 25, 28, 30 (10)

11-01-86 *Everybody Have Fun Tonight* (Geffen 0-20589) 59, 48, 45, 38, 38, 33, 30, 30, 30, 30, 35, 50, 50, 52, 59, 66, 73 (17)

3-21-87 *Let's Go!* (Geffen 0-20602) 42, 34, 33, 32, 46, 50, 58, 67 (8)

WARD, ANITA

4-21-79 *Ring My Bell* (TK) 29, 26, 12, 9, 4, 2, 1, 1, 2, 2, 3, 4, 7, 12, 13, 20, 29, 33 (18)

WAS (NOT WAS)

10-22-88 *Spy In The House Of Love* (Chrysalis 4V9-43262) 20, 15, 12, 8, 8, 6, 5, 4, 5, 13, 13 (11)

WASHINGTON, DEBORAH/DEBRA WASHINGTON

11-17-79 *Rock It* (Ariola) 36, 26, 18, 13, 11, 10, 10, 11, 11, 12, 14, 17, 29, 36 (14)

10-28-78 *Standing In The Shadows Of Love* (Ariola) 13, 22, 24 (3)

WATERS, RUTH

9-08-79 *Never Gonna Be The Same* (Millennium) 33, 30, 39 (3)

WATLEY, JODY   *(See also:* SHALAMAR)

9-26-87   *Don't You Want Me*   (MCA 23785)   66, 48, 27, 12, 7, 5, 5, 4, 4, 13, 12, 15, 16, 30, 30, 30, 34, 45   (18)

2-14-87   *Looking For A New Love*   (MCA 23689)   51, 29, 19, 8, 1, 1, 2, 3, 3, 1, 1, 1, 2, 2, 4, 5, 11, 16, 19, 19, 27, 33, 46, 56, 56, 62, 65, 72   (28)

5-14-88   *Most Of All*   (MCA 23825)   36, 34   (2)

1-16-88   *Some Kind Of Lover*   (MCA 23816)   27, 11, 6, 4, 2, 1, 1, 1, 2, 5, 11, 22, 35, 38, 40, 40, 47   (17)

6-20-87   *Still A Thrill*   (MCA 23747)   38, 38, 20, 18, 18, 23, 23, 29, 43, 51, 68   (11)

WELLS, JAMES

10-28-78   *My Claim To Fame/True Love Is My Destiny*   (AVI)   17, 13, 8, 5, 5, 6, 6, 7, 8, 10, 10, 14, 23, 28   (14)

WELLS, TERRI

6-30-84   *I'll Be Around*   (Philly World 0-96944)   23, 22, 24, 26   (4)

9-29-84   *I'm Givin' All My Love*   (Vocal & Instrumental)   (Philly World 0-96924)   40, 38, 36, 37, 36, 42, 48, 48, 48   (9)

WHAM! (FEATURING GEORGE MICHAEL)   *(See also:* GEORGE MICHAEL)

3-16-85   *Careless Whisper* (Extended & Instrumental Version)   (Col. 44-05170)   37, 11, 9, 9, 9, 11, 21, 21, 51, 65, 72   (11)

3-30-85   *Everything She Wants* (Remix)/Like A Baby   (Col. 44-05180)   50, 44, 21, 10, 8, 8, 7, 6, 6, 6, 6, 9, 10, 12, 12, 13, 25, 29, 33, 53, 73   (21)

8-24-85   *Freedom/Heartbeat* (Long Mix & Instrumental)   (Col. 44-05238)   49, 43, 38, 38, 46, 57, 66, 71, 71, 71   (10)

12-21-85   *I'm Your Man* (Extended Simulation)   (Col. 44-05322)   60, 60, 48, 48, 42, 42, 42, 52, 51, 49, 55, 64, 66, 69, 74   (15)

10-06-84   *Wake Me Up Before You Go-Go* (Vocal & Instrumental)   (Col. 44-05049)   35, 28, 23, 18, 12, 10, 8, 6, 5, 4, 9, 15, 15, 15, 30, 45   (16)

WHEN IN ROME

6-11-88   *The Promise*   (Virgin 0-96642)   30, 28, 30   (3)

10-15-88   *The Promise*   (Virgin 0-96642)   26, 16, 16, 24   (4)

THE WHISPERS

1-19-80   *And The Beat Goes On*   (Solar)   34, 16, 6, 2, 1, 1, 3, 6, 9, 12, 14, 17   (12)

5-16-87   *Rock Steady*   (Solar/Cap. V-71153)   57, 56, 48, 36, 30, 27, 27, 24, 24, 19, 15, 15, 8, 6, 6, 9, 27, 38, 38, 45   (20)

WHISTLE

2-22-86   *Just Buggin'*   (Select FMS 62267)   62, 45   (2)

10-18-86   *Just For Fun*   (Select FMS 62274)   60, 54, 48, 48, 61, 67, 71, 71   (8)

WHITE, BARRY

10-28-78   *Your Sweetness Is My Weakness*   (20th C.)   29, 29, 26, 23, 22, 21   (6)

WHITE, KARYN   (*See also:* JEFF LORBER)

10-29-88   *The Way You Love Me*   (WB 0-21025)   20, 7, 4, 3, 3, 1, 1, 2, 7, 7   (10)

WHITE, MAURICE   (*See also:* EARTH, WIND AND FIRE)

10-19-85   *Stand By Me* (Extended Version)   (Col. 44-05262)   53, 43, 39, 34, 34, 67, 70   (7)

WHODINI

11-07-87   *Be Yourself*   (Jive JDI-9628)   40, 30, 26, 26, 32, 41, 50   (7)

4-13-85   *Big Mouth* (Beat Box Mix)   (Jive JDI-9332)   59, 51, 40, 35, 30, 29, 30, 32, 42, 49, 50, 54, 64, 64, 68, 68   (16)

2-16-85   *Freaks Come Out At Night* (Instrumental)   (Jive JDI-9303)   40, 31, 28, 24, 24, 43, 62, 67, 68, 69, 75   (11)

9-15-84   *Friends/Five Minutes Of Funk*   (Jive JDI-9227)   27, 24, 22, 21, 15, 11, 10, 9, 7, 5, 3, 2, 7, 7, 14, 14, 14, 14, 11, 7, 7, 16, 23, 23, 34   (25)

4-12-86   *Funky Beat* (Extended Version)   (Jive/Arista JDI-9462)   49, 34, 21, 17, 12, 10, 8, 8, 15, 17, 14, 12, 12, 18, 19, 31, 38, 54, 62, 66, 66, 72, 75   (23)

9-06-86   *One Love* (Remix)   (Jive/Arista JDI-9506)   48, 41, 36, 32, 32, 31, 47, 55, 66, 68, 72   (11)

THE WILD MARYS

5-16-87   *No One Knows*   (Atl. 0-86736)   38, 35, 32, 29, 29, 56, 56, 62, 67, 74   (10)

WILDE, EUGENE

11-23-85   *Don't Say No Tonight* (Extended Version)   (Philly World/Atl. DMD 885)   63, 50, 45, 45, 46, 46, 50, 50, 66, 67, 68, 70, 73   (13)

12-01-84   *Gotta Get You Home Tonight*   (Philly World 0-96919)   30, 26, 23, 21, 21, 21, 18, 18, 23, 34, 34, 42, 43, (2), 74   (14)

WILDE, KIM

3-16-85   *Go For It* (Extended Dance Mix & Dub Version)   (MCA 23533)   56, 51, 51, 62   (4)

10-22-88   *You Came*   (MCA 23884)   24, 18, 17, 23, 28   (5)

2-21-87   *You Keep Me Hanging On*   (MCA 23717)   59, 49, 37, 24, 19, 17, 6, 5, 5, 5, 6, 12, 14, 14, 8, 5, 6, 7, 7, 11, 19, 37, 38, 38, 54, 59, 67   (27)

WILDER, MATTHEW

1-28-84   *Break My Stride*   (Private I 4Z9-04312)   15, 15, 24, 24, 27, 30, 28   (7)

WILL TO POWER

7-04-87   *Dreamin'*   (Epic XS9-06830)   42, 36, 22, 18, 18, 14, 11, 5, 5, 5, 4, 4, 2, 2, 4, 13, 32, 40, 50   (19)

7-09-88   *Say It's Gonna Rain*   (Epic 49-07589)   20, 18, 11, 10, 10, 8, 12, 12, 10, 7, 7, 6, 9, 17, 29   (15)

WILLIAMS, DENIECE

6-16-79   *I've Got The Next Dance*   (ARC)   36, 30, 23, 9, 5, 3, 2, 1, 1, 3, 5, 7, 10, 13, 25   (15)

4-28-84   *Let's Hear It For The Boy*   (Col. 44-04988)   14, 3, 2, 1, 1, 1, 2, 3, 4, 8, 20, 27, 29   (13)

9-15-84   *Next Love*   (Col. 44-05043)   29, 25, 24, 40, 45, 43   (6)

WILLIAMS, JAMES (D-TRAIN)

12-20-86   *Misunderstanding*   (Col. 44-05967)   55, 46, 46, 46, 42, 34, 34, 33, 35, 44, 55, 67, 75   (13)

9-20-86   *You Are Everything*   (Col. 44-05941)   61, 55, 50, 48, 54, 66, 70   (7)

WILLIAMS, JESSICA

1-26-80   *Queen Of Fools*   (Polydor)   34, 29, 26, 24, 24, 27, 29, 35, 36   (9)

WILLIAMS, VANESSA

6-18-88   *The Right Stuff*   (Wing/PolyGram 887 386-1)   39, 21, 9, 6, 4, 2, 1, 1, 24, 16, 22, 24, 30   (14)

WILLIAMS, VESTA

6-20-87   *Don't Blow A Good Thing*   (A&M SP-12229)   48, 48, 48, 50, 66, 72, 72   (7)

12-13-86   *Once Bitten Twice Shy*   (A&M SP-12206)   63, 47, 43, 43, 43, 39, 36, 36, 36, 37, 36, 39, 47, 66, 69, 74, 71   (17)

WILSON, PRECIOUS

6-07-86   *I'll Be Your Friend*   (Jive/Arista JDI-9457)   58, 36, 20, 17, 17, 22, 32, 43, 64, 67, 68, 73   (12)

WILSON, SHANICE

10-10-87   *(Baby Tell Me) Can You Dance*   (A&M SP-12235)   39, 23, 18, 12, 9, 7, 7, 7, 21, 31, 33, 33, 33, 33, 43, 49   (16)

WINWOOD, STEVE

11-15-86   *Freedom Overspill/Higher Love* (Remix) (Island/WB Island 7-28710)   56, 40, 40, 40, 53, 65, 69, 69, 69, 73   (10)

7-16-88   *Roll With It*   (Virgin 0-96648)   19, 16, 12, 7, 4, 2, 2, 3, 5, 13, 22   (11)

WISH FEATURING FONDA RAE

11-10-84   *Touch Me (All Night Long)* (Vocal & Dub)   (KN/Personal KN 1001)   36, 34, 34, 43, 45, 41, 47, 47, 47, 50   (10)

WITCH QUEEN

3-10-79   *Bang A Gong*   (Roadshow)   30, 27, 21, 15, 13, 11, 7, 7, 15, 17, 23, 25   (12)

WOLF, PETER

9-01-84   *Lights Out* (Extended Dance Mix & Dub Mix)   (EMI America V-7834-1)   18, 7, 6, 5, 16, 33, 46, 44   (8)

WONDER, STEVIE

12-14-85   *Go Home* (Remix)   (Tamla 4553 TG)   43, 35, 35, 10, 10, 4, 1, 2, 2, 2, 7, 8, 8, 23, 43, 55, 69, 75   (18)

2-02-85   *Lovelight In Flight* (Vocal & Instrumental)   (Motown 67410-D)   39   (1)

10-19-85   *Part-Time Lover* (Special Remix)   (Tamla 4548 TG)   43, 26, 10, 4, 1, 2, 4, 6, 16, 22, 22, 33, 33, 54, 64, 70, 74   (17)

11-14-87   *Skeletons*   (Motown 4593 MG)   31, 20, 10, 7, 6, 3, 3, 3, 3, 3, 3, 7, 16, 25, 37, 39   (15)

WONDER, STEVIE, AND MICHAEL JACKSON   *(See also:* MICHAEL JACKSON)

6-11-88   *Get It*   (Motown 4604 MG)   41, 41, 45   (3)

THE WONDER BAND

3-03-79   *Stairway To Love/Whole Lotta Love*   (Atl.)   30, 28, 28, 27, 27   (5)

WOODS, ROZALIN

7-21-79 *Whatcha' Gonna Do About It* (A&M) 39, 36, 33, 32, 38, 40 (6)

WORLD PREMIERE

3-03-84 *Share The Night* (Easy Street EZS 7506-A) 26, 21, 22, 29 (4)

THE WORLD'S FAMOUS SUPREME TEAM

5-12-84 *Hey D.J.* (Island 0-96956) 22, 9, 9, 5, 11, 11, 18, 18, 26, 26, 28, 30, 30 (13)

WRIGHT, BERNARD

11-23-85 *Who Do You Love?* (Extended Version) (Manhattan/Cap. V-56007) 55, 35, 17, 10, 5, 5, 5, 5, 12, 34, 38, 47, 56, 67, 73 (15)

WRIGHT, BETTY

4-20-85 *Sinderella* (Extended Version) (Jamaica TR 9004) 55, 44, 34, 34, 39, 51, 51, 55, 65, 66, 71 (11)

WRIGHT, JANET

10-13-84 *I Can't Take It* (Atl. 0-96922) 40, 37, 35, 41, 46 (5)

WYLIE, PETE

9-05-87 *Sinful* (Virgin/Atl. 0-96776) 64, 59, 59, 53, 36, 31, 31, 37, 43, 49 (10)

XENA

1-28-84 *On The Upside* (Emergency EMDS 6451) 21, 22, 20, 18, 20, 19, 17, 20, 24, 27 (10)

YARBROUGH AND PEOPLES

4-07-84 *Don't Waste Your Time* (Total Experience TED1-2601) 20, 15, 12, 10, 22, 24, 15, 12, 17, 19, 28 (11)

1-18-86 *Guilty* (Total Experience/RCA TED1-2425) 55, 48, 40, 36, 31, 28, 28, 28, 34, 47, 57, 68, 64, 74 (14)

YAZZ AND THE PLASTIC POPULATION

11-26-88   *The Only Way Is Up*   (Elektra 0-66732)   23, 15, 13, 11, 10, 10   (6)

YELLO

9-27-86   *Oh Yeah (Dance Mix)*   (Mer. 8NV 930-1)   65, 56, 55, 55, 65, 65, 66, 70   (8)

YES

1-28-84   *Owner Of A Lonely Heart*   (Atco/Atl. 0-96976)   2, 2, 3, 2, 8, 7, 8, 8, 12, 19, 28, 26, 27   (13)

YOUNG, KAREN

12-09-78   *Bring On The Boys/Baby You Ain't Nothing Without Me*   (West End)   27, 23, 21, 20, 20, 23, 25, 30   (8)

YOUNG, PAUL

6-22-85   *Everytime You Go Away* (Extended Version)/*This Means Anything*   (Col. 44-05196)   56, 45, 40, 40, 46, 48, 51, 58, 71, 70   (10)

9-28-85   *I'm Gonna Tear Your Playhouse Down* (Special Ya Ya Mix)   (Col. XSM 174580)   49, 43, 35, 27, 25, 23, 21, 21, 32, 44, 60, 68, 73, 73   (14)

YOUNG, VAL

2-22-86   *If You Should Ever Be Lonely* (Remix)   (Gordy 4557 GG)   43, 37, 19, 15, 13, 13, 16, 17, 19, 27, 33, 52, 69, 71, 73   (15)

10-26-85   *Seduction* (Extended Mix)   (Gordy 4544 GG)   55, 49, 42, 35, 28, 26, 26, 37, 48, 48, 54, 54, 67, 71, 74   (15)

ZZ TOP

7-28-84   *Legs* (Special Dance Mix)   (WB 0-20207)   16, 14, 12, 21   (4)

ZAPP

3-15-86   *Computer Love* (Extended Version)   (WB 0-20442)   51, 28, 16, 10, 10, 12, 16, 18, 25, 31, 47, 60, 70   (13)

ZEE

4-25-87 *Madness* (Warlock WAR 009) 59, 54, 50, 47, 47, 66, 66, 71 (8)

ZEVON, WARREN

9-05-87 *Leave My Monkey Alone* (Virgin/Atl.) 62, 56, 56, 41, 30, 26, 26, 34,
48 (9)

C. SONG-TITLE INDEX

A-Freak-A/Chance To Dance (Lemon)
Absolute (See: *Wood Beez . . .*)
Absolute Beginners (David Bowie)
Adult Education (Hall & Oates)
Adventure (Eleanor)
African Suite (African Suite)
After The Love Has Gone (Princess)
Afterglow (Tina Turner)
Ain't No Stoppin' Us Now (McFadden
And Whitehead)
Ain't Nobody's Business (Billie)
Ain't Nothin' Goin' On But The Rent
(Gwen Guthrie)
Ain't That Enough For You (John Davis
and The Monster Orchestra)
Alice, I Want You Just For Me (Full
Force)
All And All (See: *{You Are My} All
And All . . .*)
All Fall Down (Five Star)
All Hung Up (Angela)
All Night Long (Lionel Richie)
All Night Passion (Alisha)
All Night Thing (The Invisible Man's
Band)
All Of You For All Of Me (9.9)
All Played Out (L.I.F.E.)
All She Wants To Do Is Dance (Don
Henley)
All The Way To Heaven (Doug E. Fresh
and The Get Fresh Crew)
Alone Without You (King)

Alphabet Street (Prince)
Always (Atlantic Starr)
Always On My Mind (The Pet Shop
Boys)
America/Girl (Prince)
And She Was/Television Man (Talking
Heads)
And The Beat Goes On (The Whispers)
Angel/Into The Groove (Madonna)
Another Cha Cha (Santa Esmeralda)
Another Day (See: *If You Love Somebody
Set Them Free . . .*)
Another Lonely Christmas (See: *I Would
Die 4 U . . .*)
Another Lover (Giant Steps)
Another Night (Aretha Franklin)
*Anotherloverholenyohead/Girls And
Boys* (Prince and The Revolution)
Arabian Knights (See: *Disorderly Con-
duct . . .*)
Are You Looking For Somebody Nu (Nu
Shooz)
Are You Man Enough (Five Star)
Artificial Heart (Cherrelle)
Ask Me No Questions (See: *Meeting In
The Ladies Room . . .*)
The Asylum (See: *19 . . .*)
At Midnight (T-Connection)
At This Moment (Menage)
Attack Me With Your Love (Cameo)
Autodrive (Herbie Hancock)
Automatic (The Pointer Sisters)

Axel-F   (*See: New Attitude . . .*)
Axel F/Like Eddie Did   (Beverly Hills
   Version)

The B-52's   (The B-52's)
Baby Baba Boogie   (The Gap Band)
Baby Come And Get It   (The Pointer
   Sisters)
Baby I'm Burnin'   (Dolly Parton)
Baby Love   (Regina)
Baby Talk   (Alisha)
(Baby Tell Me) Can You Dance   (*See:
   Can You Dance . . .*)
Baby You Ain't Nothing Without Me
   (*See: Bring On The Boys . . .*)
Back And Forth   (Cameo)
Back In Stride/Joy And Pain   (Maze fea-
   turing Frankie Beverly)
Back To The Beat   (*See: Bango . . .*)
Backstabbin'   (Eddy "D")
Bad   (Michael Jackson)
Bad Bad Boy   (Theo Vaness)
Bad Boy   (The Miami Sound Machine)
Bad Boys   (Bad Boys featuring K Love)
Bad Girls   (Donna Summer)
*Bad Habits/Let's Get Back To
   Love*   (Jenny Burton)
Baise Moi (Kiss Me)   (Pam Todd)
Baja   (Mascara)
Bang A Gong   (Witch Queen)
Bang Zoom Let's Go-Go!   (The Real
   Roxanne with Hitman Howie Tee)
Bango/Back To The Beat   (The Todd
   Perry Project)
Bank On Your Love   (*See: Method Of
   Modern Love . . .*)
Barking At Airplanes, Part II   (*See:
   Crazy In The Night . . .*)
Basketball/(It's) The Game   (Kurtis
   Blow and Ralph MacDonald)
Bass Rock Express   (MC-Ade)
Bassline   (Mantronix)
Be Near Me   (ABC)
Be Your Man/Special Love   (Jesse
   Johnson's Revue)
Be Yourself   (Whodini)
Beat Biter   (*See: The Bridge . . .*)

Beat Box   (The Art Of Noise)
Beat Dis   (Bomb The Bass)
Beat Of The Street/Gordy's Groove   (The
   Choice M.C.'s)
Beat Street   (Grandmaster Melle Mel
   and The Furious Five with Mr. Ness
   and Cowboy)
Beautiful Bend   (Boris Midney)
Because Of You   (The Cover Girls)
Bedrock   (Georgio)
Beep A Freak   (The Gap Band)
Beethoven   (*See: I Need A Man . . .*)
*Behind The Groove/You're All The Boogie I
   Need*   (Teena Marie)
Behind The Wheel/Route 66   (Depeche
   Mode)
Believe In The Beat   (Carol Lynn
   Townes)
Belle De Jour   (St. Tropez)
The Belle Of St. Mark/Too Sexy   (Sheila
   E.)
Best Friends   (ET)
Best Of Love   (Regina)
Better Be Good To Me   (Tina Turner)
Big Fun   (The Gap Band)
Big Fun   (Innercity)
Big In Japan   (Alphaville)
Big Love   (Fleetwood Mac)
Bit By Bit (Theme From "Fletch")
   (Stephanie Mills)
Big Mouth   (Whodini)
Bite It   (U.T.F.O. With Full Force)
Bizarre Love Triangle   (New Order)
Black Cars   (Gino Vannelli)
Black Stations, White Stations   (M & M)
Blame It On The Boogie   (The Jacksons)
Blow My Mind   (Celi Bee)
Blue Jean   (*See: Dancing With The Big
   Boys . . .*)
Blue Monday   (New Order)
Body Language   (Spinners)
Body Rock   (Maria Vidal)
Body Shine/Slap, Slap, Lickedy Lap
   (Instant Funk)
Body Snatchers   (Midnight Star)
Body Talk   (Deele)
Bodyguard   (Tina B)
Boogie Down   (Man Parrish)

Boogie Wonderland (Earth, Wind and Fire/The Emotions)
Boogie Woogie Dancin' Shoes (Claudja Barry)
Book Of Love (See: *Boy . . .*)
Boom Boom (Paul Lekakis)
Boom! There She Was (Scritti Politti featuring Roger)
Borderline/Lucky Star (Madonna)
The Borderlines (Jeffrey Osborne)
Born In The U.S.A. (Bruce Springsteen)
Born To Be Alive (Patrick Hernandez)
Borrowed Love (The S.O.S. Band)
The Boss/No One Gets The Prize (Diana Ross)
Boy/Book Of Love (Book Of Love)
Boy I've Been Told (Sa-Fire)
Boy Toy (Tia)
The Boy With The Thorn In His Side (The Smiths)
Brand New Lover (Dead Or Alive)
The Break (Kat Mandu)
Break 4 Love (Raze)
Break My Stride (Matthew Wilder)
Breakaway (Big Pig)
Breakdance (Irene Cara)
Breaker's Revenge (Arthur Baker)
Breakfast In Bed (Brenda K. Starr)
Breakin' . . . There's No Stopping Us (Ollie and Jerry)
Breaking Bells (TLA Rock)
Breakout (Swing Out Sister)
Breathless (Mtume)
The Bridge/Beat Biter (M.C. Shan)
Bridge Over Troubled Waters/Don't Give It Up (Linda Clifford)
Bring On The Boys/Baby You Ain't Nothing Without Me (Karen Young)
Burnin' (Carol Douglas)
Burning Flame (Vitamin Z)
By The Way You Dance (Bunny Sigler)
Bye-Bye (Janice)

Cadillac Car (See: *Why? . . .*)
Call Me (Blondie)

Call Me (Spagna)
Call Me/We Close Our Eyes (Go West)
Call Me Mr. Telephone (Answering Service) (Cheyne)
(Baby Tell Me) Can You Dance (Shanice Wilson)
Can You Feel It (See: *I Wanna Testify . . .*)
Can You Feel It (The Fat Boys)
Can You Feel The Beat (Lisa Lisa and Cult Jam with Full Force)
Can You Help Me/Free World (Jesse Johnson's Revue)
Can You Rock It Like This/Together Forever (Run-D.M.C.)
Candy (Cameo)
Cannonball (Supertramp)
Can't Get Enough (Liz Torres)
Can't Live Without Your Love (Tamiko Jones)
Can't Live Without Your Love (Suzy)
Can't Stop Dancing (Sylvester)
Can't Stop/Oh What A Night (4 Luv) (Rick James)
(Krush Groove) Can't Stop The Street (Chaka Khan)
Can't Wait (Nancy Martinez)
Can't You Feel My Heart Beat (Claudja Barry)
Caravan Of Love (Isley, Jasper, Isley)
Careless Whisper (Wham! featuring George Michael)
Caribbean Queen (Billy Ocean)
Casanova (Levert)
(Catch Me) I'm Falling (See: *I'm Falling . . .*)
Catch The Rhythm (Caress)
Caught In The Act (See: *This Is My Night . . .*)
Causing A Commotion (Madonna)
Centipede (Rebbie Jackson)
Cerrone IV (Cerrone)
Certain Things Are Likely (K.T.P.)
C'est La Vie (Robbie Nevil)
Chain Reaction (Diana Ross)
Chains/Cream Always Rises (Bionic Boogie)
Chance To Dance (See: *A-Freak-A . . .*)

Change Your Wicked Ways (Pennye Ford)

The Chase (Giorgio)

Cherish/Fresh/Misled (Kool and The Gang)

Chunky But Funky (Heavy D and The Boyz)

City Life/Fly Girl (The Boogie Boys)

City Limits (*See: Private Dancer . . .*)

Clave Rocks (Amoretto)

Climb/Rushin' To Meet You (Midnight Rhythm)

Closer Than Close (Jean Carne)

C'mon C'mon (The Bronski Beat)

Color My Love (Fun Fun)

Colours (Ice-T)

Come Get My Love (TKA)

Come Go With Me (Expose)

Come Into My Life (Joyce Sims)

Come Into My Life (Judy Torres)

Come To Me/Don't Stop Dancing (France Joli)

Coming Out Of Hiding (Pamela Stanley)

Communicate (Full House)

Como Tu Te Llama? (Sly Fox)

Computer Age (Push The Button) (Newcleus)

Computer Love (Zapp)

Condition Of The Heart (Kashif)

Conga (The Miami Sound Machine)

Contact (Edwin Starr)

Contenders (Heaven 17)

Control (Janet Jackson)

Cool It Now (The New Edition)

Cool Out/Get In The Mix (Magnum Force)

Count Me Out (The New Edition)

Count Your Blessings (Ashford and Simpson)

Countdown/This Is It (Dan Hartman)

Cover Me (Bruce Springsteen)

Crack Killed Apple Jack (General Kane)

Crank It Up (Funk Town) (Peter Brown)

Crash Goes Love (Loleatta Holloway)

Crazay (Jesse Johnson)

Crazy Cuts (Grandmixer D.S.T.)

Crazy In The Night (Barking At Airplanes)/Barking At Airplanes, Part II (Kim Carnes)

Crazy Love (Nancy Martinez)

Cream Always Rises (*See: Chains . . .*)

Criticize (Alexander O'Neal)

Cross My Broken Heart (The Jets)

Cruel Summer (Bananarama)

Cruisin' (Village People)

Crush On You (The Jets)

Cry (Godley and Creme)

Cry Wolf (A-Ha)

Cuba (The Gibson Brothers)

Curiosity (The Jets)

Da' Butt (E.U.)

Dance (Disco Heat) (*See: You Make Me Feel . . .*)

Dance (Paradise Express)

The Dance Electric/Red Lights (Andre Cymone)

Dance Hall Days/Don't Let Go (Wang Chung)

Dance Little Boy Blue (*See: Hollywood . . .*)

Dance Little Sister (Terence Trent D'Arby)

Dance Of Life (*Narada Michael Walden*)

Dance On Your Knees (*See: Possession Obsession . . .*)

Dance To Dance (*See: Dancer . . .*)

Dance With Me (Alphaville)

Dance With You (Carrie Lucas)

Dance Yourself Dizzy (Liquid Gold)

Dancer/Dance To Dance (Gino Soccio)

Dancin' (Grey And Hanks)

Dancin' And Prancin' (*See: Jingo . . .*)

Dancin' At The Disco (LAX)

Dancin' In My Feet (Laura Taylor)

Dancin' In My Sleep (Secret Ties)

Dancin' In The Key Of Life (Steve Holloway)

Dancin' With Myself (Johnny Kemp)

Dancing All Over The World (Busta Jones)

Dancing In The Dark (Bruce Springsteen)

Dancing In The Sheets (Shalamar)

Dancing In The Street (David Bowie and Mick Jagger)

Dancing On The Ceiling (Lionel Richie)

Dancing On The Fire (India)

Dancing With The Big Boys/Blue Jean (David Bowie)

Danger (Gregg Diamond/Starcruiser)

Dangerous (Natalie Cole)

Dangerous (Pennye Ford)

Dare Me/I'll Be There (The Pointer Sisters)

Daryll And Joe (See: You Talk Too Much . . .)

Day By Day (Chuck Stanley)

Day-In Day-Out (David Bowie)

Deep Inside Your Love/I'm The One Who Loves You (Ready For The World)

Deputy Of Love (Don Armando's 2nd Avenue Rhumba Band)

Destiny (Two Sisters)

Devil Inside (INXS)

Dial My Heart (The Boys)

Diamond Girl (Nice And Wild)

Diamonds (Herb Alpert)

Did It Feel Like Love (Genuine Parts)

Digital Display (Ready For The World)

Dinner With Gershwin (Donna Summer)

Dirty Looks (Diana Ross)

Disco Choo Choo (Nightlife Unlimited)

Disco Dancer (Devo)

Disco Nights (GQ)

Disorderly Conduct/Arabian Knights (The Latin Rascals)

Divine Emotions (Narada)

Do Fries Go With That Shake (George Clinton)

Do It Properly (2 Puerto Ricans, A Black Man and A Dominican)

Do Me Baby (Interlude) (Meli'sa Morgan)

Do The Dance (Trance Dance)

Do They Know It's Christmas/Feed The World (Band Aid)

Do Ya Do Ya (Wanna Please Me) (Samantha Fox)

Do Ya Think I'm Sexy (Rod Stewart)

Do You Love What You Feel (Rufus And Chaka Khan)

Do You Really Love Your Baby (The Temptations)

Do You Wanna Get Away (Shannon)

Do You Wanna Lover (Hotbox)

Do You Want It Right Now (Siedah Garrett)

Dr. Beat (The Miami Sound Machine)

Doctorin' The House (Coldcut)

Doctorin' The Tardis (The Timelords)

Does He Dance (France Joli)

Dog 'N The Way (Ice-T)

Doin' The Best That I Can (Betty LaVette)

Domino Dancing (The Pet Shop Boys)

Don Quichotte (Magazine 60)

Don't Be Cruel (Bobby Brown)

Don't Believe The Hype (Public Enemy)

Don't Blow A Good Thing (Vesta Williams)

Don't Break My Heart (The Sa-Fires)

Don't Bring Back Memories/In New York (Passion)

Don't Disturb This Groove (The System)

Don't Give It Up (See: Bridge Over Troubled Waters . . .)

Don't Go Lose It Baby (Hugh Masekela)

Don't Hold Back (Chanson)

Don't Let Go (See: Dance Hall Days . . .)

Don't Let Go (Isaac Hayes)

Don't Lock Me Out (Terry Billy)

Don't Look Any Further (The Kane Gang)

Don't Lose My Number (Phil Collins)

Don't Make A Fool Of Yourself (Stacey Q)

Don't Push It, Don't Force It (Leon Haywood)

Don't Rock The Boat (Midnight Star)

Don't Say No Tonight (Eugene Wilde)

Don't Stand A Chance (Janet Jackson)

Don't Stop Dancing (See: Come To Me . . .)

Don't Stop The Dance/Slave To Love (Bryan Ferry)

Don't Stop The Feeling (Roy Ayers)

Don't Stop The Rock (Freestyle)

Don't Stop Til You Get Enough (Michael Jackson)

Don't Think About It (One Way)

Don't Waste Your Time (Yarbrough and Peoples)

Don't You Feel My Love (George McCrae)

Don't You (Forget About Me) (Simple Minds)

Don't You Try It (Raww)

Don't You Want Me (Jody Watley)

Don't You Want My Love (See: *Undercover Lover . . .*)

Don't You Want My Love (Nicole)

Double Oh-Oh (George Clinton)

Down And Counting (Claudja Barry)

The Dream Team Is In The House (L.A. Dream Team)

Dreamer (See: *{I'm A} Dreamer*)

Dreamin' (Will To Power)

Dreamin' Of Love (Stevie B)

Dreaming (Orchestral Manoeuvres In The Dark)

Dress You Up/Shoo-Bee-Doo (Madonna)

Dub Of No Return (See: *Point Of No Return . . .*)

The Duncan Sisters (The Duncan Sisters)

Dynamite (Jermaine Jackson)

E=MC2 (Giorgio)

Each Time You Break My Heart (Nick Kamen)

Easy Lover/Woman (Philip Bailey and Phil Collins)

Easy To Touch (Promise Circle)

Eaten Alive (Diana Ross)

Ego Maniac (Jocelyn Brown)

Eight Arms To Hold You (The Goon Squad)

8 Million Stories (Kurtis Blow)

Election Day (Arcadia)

Electric Kingdom (Twilight 22)

Electric Lady (Con Funk Shun)

Encore (Cheryl Lynn)

Engine No. 9 (Midnight Star)

Eric B. Is President (Eric Barrier)

Eric B. Is President/My Melody (Eric B. featuring Rakim)

Erotic City (See: *Let's Go Crazy . . .*)

Evergreen/Jealous Love (Hazell Dean)

Every Little Bit (Millie Scott)

Everybody Dance/Lonely Heart (Ta Mara and The Seen)

Everybody Have Fun Tonight (Wang Chung)

Everybody Here Must Party (Direct Current)

Everybody Wants To Rule The World (Tears For Fears)

Everything She Wants/Like A Baby (Wham!)

Everything Will B Fine (Lisa Lisa and Cult Jam)

Everytime You Go Away (See: *Possession Obsession . . .*)

Everytime You Go Away/This Means Anything (Paul Young)

Evita (Festival)

Experience (Connie)

Exposed To Love (Expose)

Extraordinary Love (Regina)

Eye To Eye (Go West)

Facts Of Love (Jeff Lorber featuring Karyn White)

Faith (George Michael)

Fake (Alexander O'Neal)

Fall Down (Spirit Of Love) (Tramaine)

Falling In Love (The Fat Boys)

Fantasy (Bruni Pagan)

Fascinated (Company B)

The Fat Boys Are Back (The Fat Boys)

Father Figure (George Michael)

Feed The Flame (Lorraine Johnson)

Feed The World (See: *Do They Know It's Christmas . . .*)

Feed The World (M.C. Shan)

Feel So Real (Steve Arrington)

Feel The Spin (Debbie Harry)

Feels Like The First Time (Sinitta)

Feels So Real (Won't Let Go) (Patrice Rushen)
Fever (Fever)
Fidelity (Cheryl Lynn)
Fight (See: The Main Event . . .)
The Finest (The S.O.S. Band)
Fire Night Dance (The Peter Jacques Band)
Firestarter (Tease)
Fishnet (Morris Day)
Five Minutes Of Funk (See: Friends . . .)
Flesh For Fantasy (Billy Idol)
Fly Away (Voyage)
Fly Girl (See: City Life . . .)
Fly Me On The Wings Of Love (Celi Bee)
Fly Too High (Janis Ian)
Follow The Leader (Eric B. and Rakim)
For Tonight (Nancy Martinez)
Forbidden Love (Madleen Kane)
Forever (Gail Houston)
Forgive Me, Girl (See: Working My Way Back To You . . .)
Found A Cure (Ashford and Simpson)
Fragile . . . Handle With Care (Cherrelle)
Freak-A-Ristic (Atlantic Starr)
Freaks Come Out At Night (Whodini)
Freaky Lover (See: I Get Off On You . . .)
Free World (See: Can You Help Me . . .)
Freedom/Heartbeat (Wham!)
Freedom Overspill/Higher Love (Steve Winwood)
Freeway Of Love (Aretha Franklin)
French Kiss (Le Foxxe)
French Kissin' (Debbie Harry)
Fresh (See: Cherish . . .)
Fresh (Kool & The Gang)
Fresh (Tyrone Brunson)
Fresh Is The Beat (See: Fresh Is The Word . . .)
Fresh Is The Word/Fresh Is The Beat (Mantronix with M.C. Tee)
Friends/Five Minutes Of Funk (Whodini)
Full Circle (Company B)
Funky Beat (Whodini)
Funky Little Beat (Connie)
Funky Nassau (Black Britain)

Funkytown (Lipps, Inc.)
Funkytown (Pseudo Echo)
Fuzz Dance (Various Artists)

(It's) The Game (See: Basketball . . .)
(Everybody) Get Dancin' (The Bombers)
Get Down (Gene Chandler)
Get Down Mellow Sound/We Got The Groove (The Players' Association)
Get In The Mix (See: Cool Out . . .)
Get It (Stevie Wonder and Michael Jackson)
Get It On (See: Welcome To The Pleasuredome . . .)
Get It On/Go To Zero (Power Station)
Get Outta' My Dreams, Get Into My Car (Billy Ocean)
Get Up And Boogie (Freddie James)
Get Up Everybody (Salt-N-Pepa)
The Ghost In You/Heart Beat (The Psychedelic Furs)
Gimme Back My Love Affair (Sister Power)
Girl (See: America)
Girl If You Take Me Home/Let's Dance Against The Wall (Full Force)
A Girl In Trouble (Is A Temporary Thing) (Romeo Void)
Girl Talk (The Boogie Boys)
Girlfriend (Bobby Brown)
Girlfriend (Pebbles)
Girls Ain't Nothing But Trouble (D.J. Jazzy Jeff and The Fresh Prince)
Girls And Boys (See: Anotherloverholenyohead . . .)
Girls Just Want To Have Fun (Cyndi Lauper)
Girls Love The Way He Spins/Larry's Dance Theme (Grandmaster Flash)
Give Me Tonight (Shannon)
Give Your Body Up To The Music (Billy Nichols)
The Glamorous Life (Sheila E.)
Glow (Rick James)
Go Dance (Billy More)
Go For It (Kim Wilde)
Go Home (Stevie Wonder)

Go See The Doctor (Kool Moe Dee)
Go To Zero (See: Get It On . . .)
Goin' To The Bank (The Commodores)
Going Back To Cali' (L.L. Cool J)
Going In Circles (The Gap Band)
Goldmine/Sexual Power (The Pointer Sisters)
Gonna Put Up A Fight (Barbara Roy)
Good And Plenty Lover (See: Love Massage . . .)
Good Intentions (Eva Cherry)
Good Times (Chic)
Good To The Last Drop (C-Bank)
Good-Bye Bad Times (Philip Oakey and Giorgio Moroder)
Gordy's Groove (See: Beat Of The Street. . .)
Got A New Love (Good Question)
Got The Feeling (Two Tons O' Fun)
Got To Be Real/Star Love (Cheryl Lynn)
Got To Give In To Love (Bonnie Boyer)
Got To Love Somebody (Sister Sledge)
Gotta Get You Home Tonight (Eugene Wilde)
Gotta See You Tonight (Barbara Roy)
The Great Commandment (Camouflage)
Greatest Show On Earth (Metropolis)
Green Light/Pow Wow (Cory Daye)
Groove Me (Guy)
Groove Me (Fern Kinney)
Groovin' You (Harvey Mason)
Guilty (Yarbrough And Peoples)

H.A.P.P.Y. Radio (Edwin Starr)
Hands Down (Dan Hartman)
Hang On To Your Love (Sade)
Hangin' On A String (Contemplating)/A Little Spice (Loose Ends)
Happi Hi! (See: Welcome To The Pleasuredome . . .)
Happiness (The Pointer Sisters)
Happy (Surface)
Hard Day (George Michael)
Hard Times (Run-D.M.C.)
Hard Times For Lovers (Jennifer Holliday)
Hardrock (Herbie Hancock)

Harlem Shuffle (The Rolling Stones)
Harmony (See: Ooh, La, La . . .)
Have A Cigar (Rosebud)
Have A Nice Day (Roxanne Shante)
Haven't Stopped Dancin' Yet (Gonzalez)
Haven't You Heard (Patrice Rushen)
Hazy Shade Of Winter (The Bangles)
He Wants My Body (Starpoint)
He's Number One (Fantasy)
He's The Greatest Dancer/We Are Family (Sister Sledge)
Head Over Heels (Tears For Fears)
Head To Toe (Lisa Lisa and Cult Jam)
Headlines (Midnight Star)
Heart And Soul (T'Pau)
Heart Beat (See: The Ghost In You . . .)
Heartache (Pepsi And Shirley)
Heartbeat (See: Freedom . . .)
Heartbreak Beat (The Psychedelic Furs)
The Heat Is On (See: Some Like It Hot And The Heat Is On . . .)
The Heat Is On (Glenn Frey)
The Heat Of Heat (Patti Austin)
Heaven Is A Place On Earth (Belinda Carlisle)
Heaven Must Have Sent You (Bonnie Pointer)
Heavenly Action (See: Who Needs Love Like That . . .)
Hello (See: Pop Life . . .)
Hello Stranger (Carrie Lucas)
Helpless (You Took My Love) (The Flirts)
Herbie Hancock Mega Mix (Herbie Hancock)
Here Comes That Sinking Feeling (See: Would I Lie To You? . . .)
Here Comes That Sound Again (Love Deluxe)
Here Comes The Rain (Eurythmics)
Hey D.J. (The World's Famous Supreme Team)
Hi, How Ya Doin'? (Kenny G)
High Energy (Evelyn Thomas)
High Horse (Evelyn "Champagne" King)
High/Skyy Zoo (Skyy)
High On Mad Mountain (Mike Theodore Orchestra)

High On Your Love (Debbie Jacobs)
Higher Lover (*See: Freedom Overspill . . .*)
Him Or Me (Today)
Hit That Perfect Beat (The Bronski Beat)
Hold It, Now Hit It (The Beastie Boys)
Hold Me (Sheila E.)
Hold Me Now (The Thompson Twins)
Hold On I'm Comin' (Karen Silver)
Hold On To What You've Got (Evelyn "Champagne" King)
Hold Your Horses (First Choice)
Holiday (Madonna)
Holler (*See: Love Magic . . .*)
Hollywood/Dance Little Boy Blue (Freddie James)
Homeboy (Steve Arrington)
Honey For The Bees (Patti Austin)
Honey To A Bee (Tina B)
The Honeythief (Hipsway)
Hooked On You (Sweet Sensation)
Hot (Roy Ayers)
Hot For You (Brainstorm)
Hot Hot Hot (The Cure)
Hot Hot Hot (Buster Poindexter and His Banshees Of Blue)
Hot Spot (Giggles)
Hot Stuff (Donna Summer)
Hot To The Touch (Claudja Barry)
House Rocker (Lovebug Starski)
How Can We Be Wrong (Trinere)
How High (Cognac)
How Soon Is Now? (The Smiths)
How To Be A Zillionaire/Tower Of London (ABC)
How Will I Know (Whitney Houston)
How Ya Like Me Now (Kool Moe Dee)
How's Your Love Life Baby (Jackie Moore)
Human (The Human League)
Hungry For Your Love (*See: I'll Take You On . . .*)
Hyperactive (Thomas Dolby)
Hypnotize (Taste-T-Ups)

I Can Do Bad By Myself (Jesse James)
I Can Dream About You (Dan Hartman)

I Can Give You More/I Can't Live Without My Radio (L.L. Cool J)
I Can Tell (Chanson)
I Can't Dance Without You (*See: Thank God There's Music . . .*)
I Can't Help It (Bananarama)
I Can't Help Myself (Bonnie Pointer)
I Can't Live Without My Radio (*See: I Can Give You More . . .*)
I Can't Take It (Janet Wright)
I Can't Turn Around (J.M. Silk)
I Can't Turn The Boogie Loose (The Controllers)
I Can't Wait (Nu Shooz)
I Can't Wait (To Rock The Mike) (Spyder-D Featuring D.J. Doc)
I Could Never Take The Place Of Your Man (Prince)
I Didn't Mean To Turn You On (Cherrelle)
I Didn't Mean To Turn You On (Robert Palmer)
I Do You (The Jets)
I Don't Know If It's Right (Evelyn "Champagne" King)
I Don't Wanna Go On With You Like That (Elton John)
I Don't Want To Be A Freak (Dynasty)
I Don't Want To Be Your Love (Duran Duran)
I Engineer (Animotion)
I Feel For You (Chaka Khan)
I Feel Good All Over (Stephanie Mills)
I Get Off On You/Freaky Lover (The Rose Brothers)
I Got My Mind Made Up (Instant Funk)
(I Got The Feelin') It's Over (Gregory Abbott)
I Got The Hots For Ya (Double Exposure)
I Have Learned To Respect The Power Of Love (*See: Rising Desire . . .*)
I Heard A Rumour (Bananarama)
I Just Keep Thinking About You Baby (Tata Vega)
I Knew You Were Waiting (Aretha Franklin and George Michael)

I Know (Paul King)
I Know You Got Soul (Eric B.)
I Like You (Phyllis Nelson)
I Love My Radio (Midnight Radio) (Taffy)
I Love The Night Life (Disco Round) (Alicia Bridges)
I Love You Babe (Babyface)
I Miss You (Klymaxx)
I Need A Man/Beethoven (Eurythmics)
I Need A Man In My Life (Katie Kissoon)
I Need Somebody (Kechia Jenkins)
I Need You (G.T.)
I Need Your Loving (The Human League)
I Should Be So Lucky (Kylie Minogue)
I Think We're Alone Now (Tiffany)
I Think We're Alone Now/Will You Love Me Tomorrow (Scott Allen)
I Wanna Be A Cowboy (Boys Don't Cry)
I Wanna Be With You (Maze featuring Frankie Beverly)
I Wanna Be Your Lover (Prince)
I Wanna Dance With Somebody (Who Loves Me) (Whitney Houston)
I Wanna Have Some Fun (Samantha Fox)
I Wanna Know (Ale)
I Wanna Testify/Can You Feel It (Cindy And Roy)
I Want A New Drug (Huey Lewis and The News)
I Want It To Be Real (John Rocca)
I Want My Girl (Jesse Johnson's Revue)
I Want To Be Your Man (Roger)
I Want To Be Your Property (Blue Mercedes)
I Want To Know What Love Is/Jesus Is Right On Time (The New Jersey Mass Choir)
I Want You For Myself (George Duke)
I Want Your (Hands On Me) (Sinead O'Connor)
I Want Your Sex (George Michael)

I (Who Have Nothing) (Sylvester)
I Will Survive (Gloria Gaynor)
I Wish You Would (Jocelyn Brown)
I Wonder If I Take You Home (Lisa Lisa and The Cult Jam with Full Force)
I Won't Stop Loving You (C-Bank featuring Diamond Girl)
I Would Die 4 U/Another Lonely Christmas (Prince and The Revolution)
I Zimbra/Life During Wartime (Talking Heads)
I'll Be All You Ever Need (Trinere)
I'll Be Around (Terri Wells)
I'll Be Good (Rene and Angela)
I'll Be There (See: Dare Me . . .)
I'll Be Your Friend (Precious Wilson)
I'll Take You On/Hungry For Your Love (Hanson and Davis)
I'll Take Your Man (Salt-N-Pepa)
I'll Tell You (Sergio Mendes)
(I'm A) Dreamer (B B & Q)
I'm A Man (Macho)
I'm Bad (L.L. Cool J)
I'm Beggin' You (Supertramp)
I'm Caught Up (Inner Life)
I'm Chillin' (Kurtis Blow)
(Catch Me) I'm Falling (Pretty Poison)
I'm Falling In Love With You (Nora)
I'm For Real (Howard Hewett)
I'm Givin' All My Love (Terri Wells)
I'm Gonna Tear Your Playhouse Down (Paul Young)
I'm In Love (Lillo Thomas)
I'm Not Gonna Let (Colonel Abrams)
I'm Not Perfect (But I'm Perfect For You) (Grace Jones)
I'm Only Shooting Love (The Time Bandits)
I'm Over You (Sequal)
I'm Real (James Brown)
I'm Searchin' (Debi Deb)
I'm The One Who Loves You (See: Deep Inside Your Love . . .)
I'm The One Who Really Loves You (Mel And Kim)
I'm Your Man (Barry Manilow)
I'm Your Man (Wham!)

I'm Your Pusher (Ice-T)
I've Got The Next Dance (Deniece Williams)
If I Ruled The World (Kurtis Blow)
If I Say Yes (Five Star)
If I Was Your Girlfriend (Prince)
If It Isn't Love (The New Edition)
If Looks Can Kill (Pamela Stanley)
If Only You Knew (Patti LaBelle)
If There's Love (Amant)
If This Ain't Love (Jay Novelle)
If You Can Do It, I Can Too (Meli'sa Morgan)
If You Feel It (Denise Lopez)
If You Leave (Orchestral Manoeuvres In The Dark)
If You Let Me Stay (Terence Trent D'Arby)
If You Love Somebody Set Them Free/ Another Day (Sting)
If You Should Ever Be Lonely (Val Young)
In Between Days (Cure)
In Love (Cheryl Lynn)
In Love With Love (Debbie Harry)
In My House (The Mary Jane Girls)
In New York (See: Don't Bring Back Memories . . .)
In The Evening (Sheryl Lee Ralph)
In The Morning Time (Tramaine)
In The Navy (Village People)
Infected (The The)
Innocent (Alexander O'Neal)
Insecurity (Stacey Q)
Inside Outside (The Cover Girls)
Instant Replay (Dan Hartman)
Instinctual (Imagination)
Into My Secret (Alisha)
Into The Groove (See: Angel . . .)
Invincible (Pat Benatar)
Invisible Touch (Genesis)
Irresistible Bitch (See: Let's Pretend We're Married . . .)
It Ain't Right (Simphonia featuring Carmen Brown)
It Takes Two (Rob Base and D.J. E-Z Rock)

It Would Take A Strong Man (Rick Astley)
It's A Miracle (See: Miss Me Blind . . .)
It's Gonna Be Special (See: Rhythm Of The Street . . .)
(It's Just) The Way You Love Me (Paula Abdul)
It's My Life (Talk Talk)
It's Not Too Late/Not Too Late To (Sequal)
It's Over (See: {I Got The Feelin'} It's Over . . .)
It's Over Now (Luther Vandross)
It's The New Style/Paul Revere (The Beastie Boys)
It's The Way You Do It (See: One Life . . .)
It's Tricky (Run-D.M.C.)
Itchin' For A Scratch (The Force MD's)

Jack Le Freak (Chic)
Jailhouse Rap (The Fat Boys)
Jam On It (Newcleus)
Jam Tonight (Freddie Jackson)
Jamming On The Groove (See: Needle To The Groove . . .)
Jane, Get Me Off This Crazy Thing/The Jetsons (The Tee Vee Toons Master Mix)
January February (Tina B)
Jealousy (Club Nouveau)
Jesus Is Right On Time (See: I Want To Know What Love Is . . .)
The Jetsons (See: Jane, Get Me Off This Crazy Thing . . .)
Jingo (Jellybean)
Jingo/Dancin' And Prancin' (Candido)
Jock Box (America Loves The Skinny Boys) (The Skinny Boys)
Johnny B. Goode (See: Victim Of Love . . .)
Johnny The Fox (Bonus Beats) (Tricky Tee)
Joy (Teddy Pendergrass)
Joy And Pain (See: Back In Stride . . .)
Joyride (Pieces Of A Dream)
Joystick (See: Swoop . . .)

Jump Back (Set Me Free) (Dhar Braxton)

Jump (For My Love) (The Pointer Sisters)

Jump Into My Life (Stacy Lattisaw)

Jump Start (Natalie Cole)

Jungle D.J. (Kikrokos)

Just A Mirage (Jellybean)

Just A Touch Of Love (Slave)

Just Another Lover (Johnny Kemp)

Just Another Night (Mick Jagger)

Just Buggin' (Whistle)

Just For Fun (Whistle)

Just For The Night/So In Love (Evelyn "Champagne" King)

Just Got Paid (Johnny Kemp)

Just Like Heaven (The Cure)

Just That Type Of Girl (Madame X)

Just The Way You Like It (The S.O.S. Band)

Just Wanna Dance/Weekend (The Todd Perry Project)

Keep On Dancin' (Gary's Gang)

Keep On Jumpin' In The Bush (Musique)

Keep On Making Me High/Party Down (Unyque)

Keep Rising To The Top (Doug E. Fresh and The Get Fresh Crew)

Keep Your Eyes On Me (Herb Alpert)

Keepin' My Lover Satisfied (Melba Moore)

Kind Of Life (Kind Of Love) (The North End)

King Tut (Paul Hardcastle)

Kiss/Love Or Money (Prince And The Revolution)

The Kiss Of Death (See: *The Perfect Kiss* . . .)

K.I.S.S.I.N.G. (Siedah Garrett)

Knock Me Senseless (The Eastbound Express)

Knock On Wood (Amii Stewart)

Knocked Out (Paula Abdul)

Krush Groove (See: *Can't Stop The Street*)

La-Di-Da-Di (See: *The Show* . . .)

La Isla Bonita (Madonna)

Ladies' Night (Kool & The Gang)

Land Of Hunger (The Earons)

Larry's Dance Theme (See: *Girls Love The Way He Spins* . . .)

Larry's Dance Theme (See: *Sign Of The Times* . . .)

Last Chance (Cyre)

Latoya/Put That Record Back On (Just Ice)

Lay It On The Line (Elaine Charles)

Le Freak (Chic)

Leader Of The Pack (U.T.F.O.)

Lean On Me (Club Nouveau)

Leave It All Behind (Tolga)

Leave My Monkey Alone (Warren Zevon)

Legs (The Art Of Noise)

Legs (ZZ Top)

Let It All Blow (The Dazz Band)

Let Me Be The One (Expose)

Let Me Be The One (Five Star)

Let Me Be The One (Sa-Fire)

Let Me Be Your Woman (Linda Clifford)

Let Me Know (I Have A Right) (Gloria Gaynor)

Let Me Take You Dancing (Bryan Adams)

Let The Music Play (Arpeggio)

Let The Music Play (Shannon)

Let The Music Take Control (J.M. Silk)

Let Your Heart Make Up Your Mind (Alisha)

Let's Dance Against The Wall (See: *Girl If You Take Me Home* . . .)

Let's Get Back To Love (See: *Bad Habit* . . .)

Let's Go (Kool Moe Dee)

Let's Go (Nocera)

Let's Go! (Wang Chung)

Let's Go All The Way (Sly Fox)

Let's Go Crazy/Erotic City (Prince and The Revolution)

Let's Have Some Fun (Merge featuring Debbie A.)

Let's Hear It For The Boy (Deniece Williams)

Let's Pretend We're Married/Irresistible Bitch (Prince)

Let's Stay Together (Tina Turner)

Let's Work It Out (Sadie Nine)

Life During Wartime (See: I Zimbra . . .)

Life In One Day (Howard Jones)

Life's What You Make It (Talk Talk)

Lifetime Love (Joyce Sims)

Lights Out (Peter Wolf)

Like A Baby (See: Everything She Wants . . .)

Like A Child (Noel)

Like A Virgin (Madonna)

Like Eddie Did (See: Axel F . . .)

Lips To Find You (Teena Marie)

A Little Bit More (Melba Moore and Freddie Jackson)

A Little Bit Of Love (Is All It Takes) (The New Edition)

A Little Love (Ceejay)

A Little Lovin' (Keeps The Doctor Away) (The Raes)

A Little Spice (See: Hangin' On A String . . .)

Little Walter (Tony! Toni! Tone!)

Live My Life (Boy George)

Live To Tell (Madonna)

Living In A Box (Living In A Box)

Living In America (James Brown)

Living On Video (Trans-X)

The Loco-Motion (Kylie Minogue)

Lollipop Luv (Bryan Loren)

Lonely Heart (See: Everybody Dance . . .)

Look Out Weekend (Debbie Deb)

Look What You Started (The Temptations)

Looking For A Lover (The Taurus Boys)

Looking For A New Love (Jody Watley)

Looking For Love (Fat Larry's Band)

Loosey's Rap (Rick James featuring Roxanne Shante)

Lost In Emotion (Lisa Lisa and Cult Jam)

Love And Devotion (Michael Bow)

Love And Pride (King)

Love Can't Turn Around (Philly Cream)

Love Changes (Kashif and Meli'sa Morgan)

Love Comes Quickly (The Pet Shop Boys)

Love Disco Style (See: Plug Me To Death . . .)

Love Don't Live No More (The Basement Boys)

Love Gun (Rick James)

Love/Hate (Pebbles)

Love In The First Degree (Bananarama)

Love In The Shadows (E.G. Daily)

Love Injection (Trussel)

Love Insurance (The Front Page)

Love Is A Battlefield (Pat Benatar)

Love Is Just (The Game) (Peter Brown)

Love Letter (Giggles)

L.O.V.E. M.I.A. (The Dazz Band)

Love Magic/Holler (John Davis)

Love Massage/Good And Plenty Lover (Musique)

Love Me In Siberia (Laban)

Love Of A Lifetime (Chaka Khan)

Love On The Rise (Kenny G and Kashif)

Love Or Money (See: Kiss . . .)

Love Overboard (Gladys Knight & The Pips)

Love Potion (See: Sister Power . . .)

Love Rush (Ann-Margret)

Love Sick (Carol Douglas)

Love Songs Are Back Again (Band Of Gold)

Love Struck (Jessie Johnson)

Love Take Over (Fire Star)

Love The One I'm With (A Lot Of Love) (Melba Moore and Kashif)

Love Will Save The Day (Whitney Houston)

Love You Down (Ready For The World)

Love Zone (Billy Ocean)

Lovelight In Flight (Stevie Wonder)

Lovelite (O'Bryan)

Lover Come Back To Me (Dead Or Alive)

The Lover In Me   (Sheena Easton)
Loverboy   (Billy Ocean)
Lovergirl   (Teena Marie)
Loveride   (Nuance featuring Vikki Love)
A Lover's Holiday   (Change)
Lovers' Lane   (Georgio)
Love's Gonna Get You   (Jocelyn Brown)
Love's On Fire   (Aleem featuring Leroy Burgess)
Lovin' Fool   (Tolga)
Lovin' On Next To Nothin'   (Gladys Knight & The Pips)
Low Down So And So   (Rainy Davis)
The Lucky One   (Laura Branigan)
Lucky Star   (*See: Borderline . . .*)

Ma Foom Bey   (Cultural Vibe)
MacArthur Park Suite   (Donna Summer)
Macho Mozart   (The Latin Rascals)
Mad About You   (Belinda Carlisle)
Madame Buttlerfly   (Malcolm McLaren)
Madness   (Zee)
Magic Carpet Ride   (Bardeux)
The Magnificent Jazzy Jeff   (DJ Jazzy Jeff and The Fresh Prince)
The Main Event/Fight   (Barbra Streisand)
Make It Funky   (Ice-T)
Make The Music With Your Mouth Biz   (Biz Markie)
Makin' It   (David Naughton)
Mamacita   (Troop)
Man In The Mirror   (Michael Jackson)
Mandolay   (La Flavour)
Material Girl/Pretender   (Madonna)
Material Thangz   (The Deele)
Mechanical Emotion   (*See: Pretty Mess . . .*)
The Medicine Song   (Stephanie Mills)
Medley Of Hits   (Diana Ross And The Supremes)
Meeting In The Ladies Room/Ask Me No Questions   (Klymaxx)
The Men All Pause   (Klymaxx)
Mercedes Boy   (Pebbles)

Method Of Modern Love/Bank On Your Love   (Daryl Hall And John Oates)
The Mexican   (Jellybean)
Miami Vice Theme   (Jan Hammer)
Midnight Man   (Flash and The Pan)
Midnight Message   (Ann-Margret)
Military Drums   (Hubert Kah)
Mind Over Matter   (E.G. Daily)
Miracles Explode   (Tina B)
Misfit   (Curiosity Killed The Cat)
Misled   (*See: Cherish . . .*)
Misled   (Kool & The Gang)
Miss Me Blind/It's A Miracle   (Culture Club)
Miss You   (The Flirts)
Missing You   (John Waite)
Missionary Man   (Eurythmics)
Mr. Big Shot   (The Simon Orchestra)
Mr. Big Stuff   (Heavy D and The Boyz)
Mr. DJ You Know How To Make Me Dance   (The Glass Family)
Mr. Right   (Eleanor Mills)
Misty Circle   (*See: You Spin Me Round . . .*)
Misunderstanding   (James "D-Train" Williams)
Moments In Love   (The Art Of Noise)
Money   (The Flying Lizards)
Monkey   (George Michael)
Moskow Diskow   (Telex)
Most Of All   (Jody Watley)
Mountains   (Prince and The Revolution)
Move Away/Sexuality   (Culture Club)
Move On Up/Up Up Up   (Destination)
Move Out   (Nancy Martinez)
Move The Crowd/Paid In Full   (Eric B. & Rakim)
Movin' On   (Carolyn Harding)
Music Is My Way Of Life   (Patti La-Belle)
Music Is The Answer   (Colonel Abrams)
Music Man   (*See: Revenge . . .*)
Music Out Of Bounds   (Stacey Q)
Music That You Can Dance To   (Sparks)
Music Trance   (Ben E. King)
Musique Non Stop   (Kraftwerk)
Mutual Attraction   (Sylvester)

My Addidas/Peter Piper (Run-D.M.C.)
My Baby Loves Me (Toney Lee)
My Baby's Baby (Liquid Gold)
My Bird/My Drawers (The Time)
My Claim To Fame/True Love Is My Destiny (James Wells)
My Drawers (See: My Bird . . .)
My Girl (Suave)
My Girl Loves Me (Shalamar)
My Girly (Ready For The World)
My Heart Gets All The Breaks (Monet)
My Heart Goes Bang (Dead Or Alive)
My Love Is Guaranteed (Sybil)
My Magic Man (Rochelle)
My Melody (See: Eric B. Is President . . .)
My Mike Sounds Nice (Salt-N-Pepa)
My Prerogative (Bobby Brown)
My Time (Gladys Knight & The Pips)

Nasty (Janet Jackson)
Naughty Girl (Samantha Fox)
Need You Tonight (INXS)
Needle To The Groove/Jamming On The Groove (Mantronix)
Neutron Dance (The Pointer Sisters)
Never As Good As The First Time (Sade)
Never Be The Same (The Breakfast Club)
Never Can Say Goodbye (The Communards)
Never Gonna Be The Same (Ruth Waters)
Never Gonna Give You Up (Rick Astley)
Never Let You Go (Sweet Sensation)
Neverending Story (Limahl)
New Attitude/Axel-F (Patti LaBelle and Harold Faltermeyer)
New Dimensions (The Three Degrees)
New Sensation (INXS)
New Song (Howard Jones)
New Toy (The Flirts)
The New York Rapper (Bobby Jimmy and The Critters)
Next Love (Deniece Williams)
Nice N' Slow (Freddie Jackson)
Night Dancin' (Taka Boom)

Night Rider (Venus Dodson)
The Night You Murdered Love (ABC)
Nightdancer (Jeanne Shy)
Nightime (Pretty Poison)
Nightime Fantasy (Vicki Sue Robinson)
Nightmare Of A Broken Heart (C-Bank)
A Nightmare On My Street (D.J. Jazzy Jeff and The Fresh Prince)
Nightmares (Dana Dane)
Nightshift (The Commodores)
19/The Asylum (It'z Weird) (Paul Hardcastle)
99 1/2 (Carol Lynn Townes)
99 Luftballons (Nena)
Nite And Day (Al B. Sure!)
No Favors (Temper)
No Frills Love (Jennifer Holliday)
No Lies (The S.O.S. Band)
No More (Shirley Murdock)
No More Lonely Nights (Paul McCartney)
No More Tears (Enough Is Enough) (Donna Summer and Barbra Streisand)
No More Words (Berlin)
No One Gets The Prize (See: The Boss . . .)
No One Knows (The Wild Marys)
No One's Gonna Love You (The S.O.S. Band)
No Show (The Symbolic Three featuring Dr. Shock)
No Use To Borrow (Blue Moderne)
Not Too Late To (See: It's Not Too Late . . .)
Nothing (See: Strangelove . . .)
Nothing's Gonna Stop Me Now (Samantha Fox)
Now I'm Fine (Grey and Hanks)
#1 Dee Jay (Goody Goody)
Nursery Rhymes (The L.A. Dream Team)

The Oak Tree (Morris Day)
Object Of My Desire (Starpoint)
Obsession (Animotion)

Off On Your Own (Al B. Sure!)
Oh L'Amour (Erasure)
Oh People (Patti LaBelle)
Oh Sheila (Ready For The World)
Oh What A Night (4 Luv) (*See: Can't Stop . . .*)
Oh Yeah (Yello)
On And Off Love (Champaign)
On My Own (Patti LaBelle and Michael McDonald)
On The Radio (Donna Summer)
On The Upside (Xena)
On Your Knees (Grace Jones)
Once Bitten Twice Shy (Vesta Williams)
Once In A Lifetime Groove (The New Edition)
Once Upon A Time (John Rocca)
One Bad Apple (Nolan Thomas)
One For The Treble (Davy DMX)
One Life/It's The Way You Do It (Laid Back)
One Look (One Look Was Enough) (Paul Parker)
One Love (Janice Cristie)
One Love (Whodini)
One Nation Under A Groove (Funkadelic)
One Night In Bangkok (Murray Head)
One Night In Bangkok (Robey)
One Of The Living (Tina Turner)
One Way Love (TKA)
One Way Ticket (Eruption)
Only In My Dreams (Debbie Gibson)
Only In The Night (The Voice In Fashion)
The Only Way Is Up (Yazz and The Plastic Population)
Ooh, La, La/Harmony (Suzi Lane)
Open Up For Love (Siren)
Open Up Your Heart (*See: Suspense*)
Open Your Heart (Madonna)
Opera House (Jack E. Makossa)
Operator (Midnight Star)
Opportunities (Let's Make Lots Of Money) (The Pet Shop Boys)
Our Ms. Brooks (Patti Brooks)
Out Of The Blue (Debbie Gibson)
Out Of Time (Noel)

Out Of Touch (Daryl Hall and John Oates)
Outrageous (Lakeside)
Outta The World (Ashford and Simpson)
Over And Over (Disco Circus)
Over My Head (Toni Basil)
Owner Of A Lonely Heart (Yes)

P Machinery (Propaganda)
Padlock (Gwen Guthrie)
Paid In Full (*See: Move The Crowd . . .*)
Panic (French Kiss)
Papa Don't Preach (Madonna)
Paranoimia (The Art Of Noise With Max Headroom)
Parents Just Don't Understand (D.J. Jazzy Jeff and The Fresh Prince)
Part-Time Lover (Stevie Wonder)
Party All The Time (Eddie Murphy)
Party Down (*See: Keep On Making Me High . . .*)
Party Freak (Cash Flow)
The Party Has Just Begun (Freestyle)
Party People (Royal House)
Party Your Body (Stevie B)
Partyline (Brass Construction)
Paul Revere (*See: It's The New Style . . .*)
Pee-Wee's Dance (Joeski Love)
Peek-A-Boo (Siouxsie and The Banshees)
People Are People (Depeche Mode)
The Perfect Kiss/The Kiss Of Death/Perfect Pit (New Order)
Perfect Lover (Company B)
Perfect Pit (*See: The Perfect Kiss . . .*)
Perfect Way (Scritti Politti)
Peter Gunn (The Art Of Noise featuring Duane Eddy)
Peter Piper (*See: My Adidas*)
Pick It Up (Sofonda C.)
Pick Me Up, I'll Dance (Melba Moore)
Pickin' Up The Pieces (Brenda K. Starr)
Pink Cadillac (Natalie Cole)
Plane Love (Jeffrey Osborne)
Play Me To Death/Love Disco Style (The Erotic Drum Band)

Play With Me (Abby Lynn)
Players Ball (Mazarati)
Plaything (Rebbie Jackson)
Please Don't Go (Nayobe)
Pleasure Island (Paul Jabara)
The Pleasure Principle (Janet Jackson)
The Pleasure Seekers (The System)
Point Of No Return (Expose)
Point Of No Return (Nu Shooz)
Pop Goes My Love (Freeez)
Pop Goes The World (Men Without Hats)
Pop Life/Hello (Prince and The Revolution)
Pop Muzik (M)
Pop Pop Goes My Mind (Levert)
Pop Pop Shoo Wah (The Erotic Drum Band)
Posse On Broadway (Sir Mix-A-Lot)
Possession Obsession/Dance On Your Knees/ Everytime You Go Away (Daryl Hall and John Oates)
Pour It On (Mason)
Poussez (Poussez)
Pow Wow (See: Green Light . . .)
The Power Of Love (Huey Lewis and The News)
Precious Little Diamond (Fox The Fox)
Prepare To Energize (Torch Song)
Pretender (See: Material Girl . . .)
Pretty Boys And Pretty Girls (Book Of Love)
Pretty Mess/Mechanical Emotion (Vanity)
Private Dancer/City Limits (Tina Turner)
Private Number (The Jets)
The Promise (When In Rome)
Prove Your Love (Taylor Dayne)
Pump Up The Volume (M/A/R/R/S)
Purple Rain (Prince and The Revolution)
Push It (See: Tramp . . .)
Put That Record Back On (See: Latoya . . .)
Put The Needle To The Record (Criminal Element)
Put Your Body In It/You Can Get Over (Stephanie Mills)

Put Your Feet To The Beat (The Ritchie Family)
Putting The Night On Hold (Lauren Grey)

Queen Of Fools (Jessica Williams)
Queen Of My Heart (See: Rhythm Of The Night . . .)
Queen Of Rox (Roxanne Shante)
Queen Of The Night (Loleatta Holloway)

Rage Hard (Frankie Goes To Hollywood)
The Rain (Cyre)
The Rain (Oran "Juice" Jones)
Rain Forest (Paul Hardcastle)
The Rappers Delight (The Sugar Hill Gang)
Rappin' Duke (Shawn Brown)
Raspberry Beret/She's Always In My Heart (Prince and The Revolution)
Reaction (Rebbie Jackson)
Read My Lips (Melba Moore)
Ready For The 80's/Sleazy (The Village People)
The Real Roxanne/Roxanne's Backside (Scratchit) (Roxanne With U.T.F.O.)
The Real Thing (Daddy Dewdrop)
The Real Thing (Jellybean/Steven Dante)
Red Hot (Princess)
Red Lights (See: The Dance Electric . . .)
The Reflex (Duran Duran)
Relax (See: Welcome To The Pleasuredome . . .)
Relax (Frankie Goes To Hollywood)
Relight My Fire (See: Vertigo)
Remember What You Like (Jenny Burton)
Renegades Of Funk (Afrika Bambaataa and Soulsonic Force)
Request Line (Rock Master Scott and The Dynamic 3)

Rescue Me (Lisa Mitchell)
Rescue Me (Al B. Sure!)
Respectable (Mel And Kim)
Restless (Starpoint)
Revenge/Music Man (Revanche)
Rhythm Is Gonna Get You (Gloria Estefan and The Miami Sound Machine)
Rhythm Of The Night/Queen Of My Heart (DeBarge)
Rhythm Of The Street (*See: Shoot The Moon . . .*)
Rhythm Of The Street/It's Gonna Be Special (Patti Austin)
Right Back To You (Ten City)
Right In The Socket (*See: The Second Time Around . . .*)
Right In The Socket (Shalamar)
Right On Track (The Breakfast Club)
The Right Stuff (Vanessa Williams)
Ring My Bell (Anita Ward)
Ripe!!! (Ava Cherry)
Rise (Herb Alpert)
Rising Desire/I Have Learned To Respect The Power Of Love (Stephanie Mills)
Risque (Chic)
The River/Sunshine (Total Contrast)
Roaches (Bobby Jimmy and The Critters)
Roadblock (Stock, Aitken, Waterman)
Rock Box (Run-D.M.C.)
Rock It (Lipps, Inc.)
Rock It (Deborah Washington)
Rock It To The Top (Mantus)
Rock Me Amadeus/Vienna Calling (Falco)
Rock Me Tonight (For Old Times Sake) (Freddie Jackson)
Rock Steady (The Whispers)
Rock The Bells (Original Version) (L.L. Cool J)
Rock With You/Working Day And Night (Michael Jackson)
Rocket 2 U (The Jets)
Roll With It (Steve Winwood)
Roller Skatin' Mate (Peaches and Herb)
Romancin' The Stone (Eddy Grant)

(You Used To Be) Romantic (Shirley Lewis)
Romeo (Parts I & II)/Roxanne's Groove (The Real Roxanne With Howie Tee)
The Roof's On Fire (Scratchin' & Jivin') (Rock Master Scott and The Dynamic 3)
Roses Are Red (The Mac Band featuring The McCampble Brothers)
Route 66 (*See: Behind The Wheel . . .*)
Roxanne, Roxanne (U.T.F.O.)
Roxanne's A Man (The Untold Story) (Ralph Rolle)
Roxanne's Backside (*See: The Real Roxanne . . .*)
Roxanne's Doctor—The Real Man (Dr. Freshh)
Roxanne's Groove (*See: Romeo . . .*)
Roxanne's Revenge (Roxanne Shante)
Rumors/Vicious Rumors (The Timex Social Club)
Running (The Information Society)
Running Up That Hill (Kate Bush)
Run's House (Run-D.M.C.)
(You're Puttin') A Rush On Me (Stephanie Mills)
Rushin' To Meet You (*See: Climb . . .*)

S.O.S., Fire In The Sky (Deodato)
Sabu (Sabu)
Same Ole Love (365 Days A Year) (Anita Baker)
Sample That! (The Bang Orchestra!)
Sanctified Lady (Marvin Gaye)
Sanctify Yourself (Simple Minds)
Saturday Love (Cherrelle With Alexander O'Neal)
Savage Lover (The Ring)
Save The Best For Me (The Best Of Your Lovin') (Bunny DeBarge)
Save The People (*See: Sister Fate . . .*)
Save Your Love (For #1) (Rene and Angela)
Savin' Myself (Eria Fachin)
Say I'm Your Number One (Princess)

Say It Again/Instrumental (Santana)
Say It Isn't So (Daryl Hall and John Oates)
Say It, Say It (E.G. Daily)
Say It's Gonna Rain (Will To Power)
Say Yeah (The Limit)
Sayin' Sorry Don't Make It Right (Denise Lopez)
Scientific Love (Midnight Star)
The Screams Of Passion/Yes (The Family)
Seasons Change (Expose)
Second Chance For Love (Nayobe)
Second Nature (Dan Hartman)
The Second Time Around/Right In The Socket (Shalamar)
Secret Affair (Claudja Barry)
Seduction (Val Young)
Self Control (Laura Branigan)
Sendin' All My Love (The Jets)
Sense Of Purpose (Third World)
Serious (Donna Allen)
Set Fire To Me (Willie Colon)
Set It Out (Midway)
17 (Rick James)
Sex Machine (The Fat Boys)
Sex Shooter (Apollonia 6)
Sexappeal (Georgio Allentini)
Sexcrime (Nineteen Eighty-Four) (Eurythmics)
Sexomatic (The Bar-Kays)
Sexual Power (See: Goldmine . . .)
Sexuality (See: Move Away . . .)
Sexy Thing (Bob McGilpin)
Shackles (R.J.'s Latest Arrival)
Shadows Of Your Love (J.M. Silk)
Shake You Down (Gregory Abbott)
Shake Your Body (Down To The Ground) (The Jacksons)
Shake Your Groove Thing (Peaches and Herb)
Shake Your Love (Debbie Gibson)
Shake Your Thang (Salt-N-Pepa [featuring E.U.])
Share The Night (World Premiere)
Shattered Dreams (Johnny Hates Jazz)
Shattered Glass (Laura Branigan)

She Bop (Cyndi Lauper)
She (I Can't Resist) (Jesse Johnson)
She's Always In My Hair (See: Raspberry Beret . . .)
She's On The Left (Jeffrey Osborne)
She's Strange (Cameo)
Shell Shock (New Order)
Shoo-Bee-Doo (See: Dress You Up . . .)
Shoot Me With Your Love (Tasha Thomas)
Shoot The Moon/Rhythm Of The Street (Patti Austin)
Should I Say Yes? (Nu Shooz)
Shout (Tears For Fears)
The Show/La-Di-Da-Di (Doug E. Fresh and Get Fresh Crew)
Show Me (The Cover Girls)
The Show Stoppa (Is Stupid Fresh) (Supernature)
Showing Out (Mel and Kim)
Shy Boys (Anna)
Siberian Night (Twilight 22)
Sidewalk Talk (Jellybean)
Sign "O" The Times (Prince)
Sign Of The Times/Larry's Dance Theme (Grandmaster Flash)
Signed, Sealed, Delivered (Louise Freeman and Terry Blount)
Silent Morning (Noel)
Silver Shadow (Atlantic Starr)
Simple Simon (Mantronix)
Sinderella (Betty Wright)
Sinful (Pete Wylie)
Sing Your Own Song/Time Bomb (Jeanie Tracy)
Single Life (Cameo)
Sinner Man (Sara Dash)
Sister Fate/Save The People (Sheila E.)
Sister Power/Love Potion (Sister Power)
Situation #9 (Club Nouveau)
6 (Madhouse)
Skeletons (Stevie Wonder)
Skyy Zoo (See: High . . .)
Slap, Slap, Lickedy Lap (See: Body Shine . . .)
Slave To Love (See: Don't Stop The Dance . . .)

Slave To The Rhythm   (Grace Jones)
Sleazy   (*See: Ready For The 80's* . . .)
Sledgehammer   (Peter Gabriel)
Slippery People   (The Staple Singers)
Slow Down   (Loose Ends)
Smack Dab In The Middle   (Janice McClain)
Smalltown Boy   (The Bronski Beat)
Smooth Criminal   (Michael Jackson)
Smooth Sailin' Tonight   (The Isley Brothers)
Smurf Rock   (Gigolo Tony)
So Emotional   (Whitney Houston)
So In Love   (*See: Just For The Night* . . .)
So Many Ways (Do It Properly, Part II) (The Brat Pack)
So Tuff   (*See: Stand Up* . . .)
Solid   (Ashford and Simpson)
Some Kind Of Lover   (Jody Watley)
Some Like It Hot And The Heat Is On/Some Like It Hot/The Heat Is On   (Power Station)
Some People   (Belouis Some)
Somebody Else's Guy   (Jocelyn Brown)
Somebody's Watching Me   (Rockwell)
Someone Like You   (Sylvester)
Something About You   (Level 42)
Something In My House   (Dead Or Alive)
Something Special   (Patti LaBelle)
Something's On Your Mind   ("D" Train)
Sometimes   (Colonel Abrams)
Sometimes   (Erasure)
Soul Kiss   (Olivia Newton-John)
Soweto   (Jeffrey Osborne)
Sparky's Turn (Roxanne You're Through)   (Sparky D)
Special Love   (*See: Be Your Man* . . .)
Speculation   (Colonel Abrams)
Speed Of Light   (Reimy)
Spend The Night   (Bob-A-Rela)
Split Personality   (U.T.F.O.)
Spring Love   (The Cover Girls)
Spring Love   (Stevie B)
Spy In The House Of Love   (Was [Not Was])
Stairway To Love/Whole Lotta Love   (The Wonder Band)
Stand Back   (Stephanie Mills)

Stand By Me   (Maurice White)
Stand Up—Sit Down   (AKB)
Stand Up/So Tuff   (Howard Johnson)
Standing In The Shadows Of Love   (Fever)
Standing In The Shadows Of Love   (Debra Washington)
Star Love   (*See: Got To Be Real* . . .)
Starcruiser   (Gregg Diamond)
Stars   (Sylvester)
State Of Shock   (The Jacksons)
State Of The Heart   (Philip Bailey)
Stay A Little While, Child   (Loose Ends)
Step By Step   (Jeff Lorber)
Sticky Fingers   (Sticky Fingers)
Still A Thrill   (Jody Watley)
Stir It Up   (Patti LaBelle)
Stomp!   (The Brothers Johnson)
Stone Love   (Kool & The Gang)
Stop Playing On Me   (Vikki Love)
Stop To Love   (Luther Vandross)
Stop Your Teasing   (Hydro)
Straight From The Heart   (Loose Change)
Strangelove   (Depeche Mode)
Strangelove/Nothing   (Depeche Mode)
Stranger Together   (Shannon)
Street Dance   (Break Machine)
Strut   (Sheena Easton)
Style (Peter Gunn Theme)   (Grandmaster Flash)
Sub Culture/Sub Vulture   (New Order)
Sub Vulture   (*See: Sub Culture*)
Sugar Don't Bite   (Sam Harris)
Sugar Free   (Juicy)
Sugar Free   (Wa-Wa-Nee)
Sugar Walls   (Sheena Easton)
The Summer Of Love   (The B-52's)
Summertime, Summertime   (Nocera)
The Sun Always Shines On T.V.   (A-Ha)
Sun City   (Artists United Against Apartheid)
Sunshine   (*See: The River* . . .)
The Super Bowl Shuffle   (The Chicago Bears Shufflin' Crew)
Superfly Guy   (The S-Express)
Supernatural Love   (Donna Summer)
Supersonic   (J.J. Fad)
Superstar   (Bob McGilpin)

Suspense/Open Up Your Heart (Anthony and The Camp)
Sussudio (Phil Collins)
Sweet And Sexy Thing (Rick James)
Sweet Freedom (Michael McDonald)
Sweetheart (Rainy Davis)
Swept Away (Diana Ross)
Swing Low (R.J.'s Latest Arrival)
Swoop (I'm Yours)/Joystick (The Dazz Band)
System Of Survival (Earth, Wind and Fire)

THP (THP)
TJM (TJM)
Tailor Made (Joyce Kennedy)
Take A Chance (Nuance)
Take A Chance (Queen Samantha)
Take A Little Time (Total Contrast)
Take All Of Me (Barbara Law)
Take It While It's Hot (Sweet Sensation)
Take Me As I Am (Erotic Exotic)
Take Me Home (Cher)
Take Me Home (Phil Collins)
Talk To Me (Chico DeBarge)
Talkin' All That Jazz (Stetsasonic)
Talking In Your Sleep (The Romantics)
Tarzan Boy (Baltimora)
Tasty Love (Freddie Jackson)
Tears May Fall (T.K.A.)
Tears Run Rings (Marc Almond)
The Telephone Call (Kraftwerk)
Television Man (See: And She Was . . .)
Tell It To My Heart (Taylor Dayne)
Tell Me (How It Feels) (52nd Street)
Tempest Trio (Tempest Trio)
Tender Is The Night (THP Orchestra)
Tender Love (The Force MD's)
Tenderoni (Leon Haywood)
Thank God There's Music/I Can't Dance Without You (Theo Vaness)
Thanks For My Child (Cheryl "Pepsi" Riley)
Theme From S-Express (S-Express)
There But For The Grace Of God Go I (Machine)

They Only Come Out At Night (Peter Brown)
They're Playing Our Song (Trinere)
Things Can Only Get Better (Howard Jones)
Thinking About Your Love (Skipworth And Turner)
Thinking Of You (Earth, Wind and Fire)
30 Days (Run-D.M.C.)
This Is Hot (Pamela Stanley)
This Is It (See: Countdown . . .)
This Is My Night/Caught In The Act (Chaka Khan)
This Means Anything (See: Everytime You Go Away . . .)
This Time Baby (Jackie Moore)
Three Time Lover (Bardeux)
Thriller (Michael Jackson)
Thunder And Lightning (Miss Thang)
'Til My Baby Comes Home (Luther Vandross)
Time Bomb (See: Sing Your Own Song . . .)
Times Are Changin' (Fred Fowler)
Tina Cherry (Georgio)
To Prove My Love (Michael Cooper)
Together Forever (See: Can You Rock It Like This . . .)
Together Forever (Rick Astley)
Tonight (Love Will Make It Right) (Hanson And Davis)
Tonight (Ready For The World)
Tonight's The Night (Sharon Paige)
Too Sexy (See: The Belle Of St. Mark . . .)
Too Turned On (Alisha)
Torture (The Jacksons)
Touch (Noho)
Touch Me (All Night Long) (Wish featuring Fonda Rae)
Tour De France (Kraftwerk)
Tower Of London (See: How To Be A Zillionaire . . .)
Tramp/Push It (Salt-N-Pepa)
Trapped (Colonel Abrams)
Treat Her Like A Lady (The Temptations)
Trommeltanz (Din Da Da) (George Kranz)

Trouble (Nia Peeples)

Trouble In Paradise (Sylvester)

Trow The D. And Ghetto Base (2 Live Crew [Ghetto Style])

True Blue (Madonna)

True Faith (New Order)

True Love Is My Destiny (See: My Claim To Fame . . .)

The Truth (Colonel Abrams)

Tumblin' Down (Ziggy Marley and The Melody Makers)

Turn Me Loose (Wally Jump Junior and The Criminal Element)

Twilight World (Swing Out Sister)

Twilight Zone (Manhattan Transfer)

Two Of Hearts (Stacey Q)

Two Tribes (Frankie Goes To Hollywood)

Typical Male (Tina Turner)

U Got The Look (Prince)

U Know What Time It Is (Grandmaster Flash)

U.N. (U.N.)

Ultimate (Ultimate)

Under The Gun (Face To Face)

Under The Influence (Vanity)

Undercover Lover/Don't You Want My Love (Debbie Jacobs)

Underground (David Bowie)

Unexpected Lovers (Lime)

Unfaithful So Much (Full Force)

Union Of The Snake (Duran Duran)

Unity (Parts 1 & 5) (Afrika Bambaataa and James Brown)

Unselfish Lover (Full Force)

Up Up Up (See: Move On Up . . .)

Venus (Bananarama)

Vertigo/Relight My Fire (Dan Hartman)

Vibe Alive (Herbie Hancock)

Vicious Rumors (See: Rumors . . .)

Victim (Candi Staton)

Victim Of Love (Erasure)

Victim Of Love/Johnny B. Goode (Elton John)

Victory (Kool & The Gang)

Vienna Calling (See also: Rock Me Amadeus . . .)

Vienna Calling (Falco)

Wake Me Up Before You Go-Go (Wham!)

Walk Like An Egyptian (The Bangles)

Walk The Night (The Skatt Brothers)

Walk This Way (Run-D.M.C. With Steven Tyler)

Walking Away (The Information Society)

Want Ads (Ullanda)

The War Song (Culture Club)

Wax The Van (Lola)

Way Out (J.J. Fad)

(It's Just) The Way You Love Me (Paula Abdul)

The Way You Love Me (Karyn White)

The Way You Make Me Feel (Michael Jackson)

We Are Family (See: He's The Greatest Dancer . . .)

We Are The World (USA For Africa)

We Are The Young (Dan Hartman)

We Close Our Eyes (See: Call Me . . .)

We Close Our Eyes (Go West)

We Connect (Stacey Q)

We Don't Have To Take Our Clothes Off (Jermaine Stewart)

We Don't Need Another Hero (Thunderdome) (Tina Turner)

We Got The Groove (See: Get Down Mellow Sound . . .)

We Work Hard (U.T.F.O.)

We'll Be Together (Sting)

Wear It Out (Stargard)

Weekend (See: Just Wanna Dance . . .)

Weird Science (Oingo Boingo)

Welcome To The Pleasuredome/Get It On (Bang A Gong)/Happi Hi!/Relax (Frankie Goes To Hollywood)

West End Girls (The Pet Shop Boys)

What Have I Done To Deserve This (The Pet Shop Boys)

What Have You Done For Me Lately (Janet Jackson)

What I Like (Anthony and The Camp)

What People Do For Money (Divine Sounds)

What You Need (INXS)

What You See Is What You Get (Brenda K. Starr)

What You've Been Missin' (Starpoint)

Whatcha' Gonna Do About It (Rozalin Woods)

What's Going On (Cyndi Lauper)

What's Love Got To Do With It (Tina Turner)

What's Missing (Alexander O'Neal)

What's On Your Mind (The Information Society)

When Doves Cry (Prince)

When I Look Into Your Eyes (Pretty Poison)

When I Think Of You (Janet Jackson)

When Smokey Sings (ABC)

When The Going Gets Tough, The Tough Get Going (Billy Ocean)

When We Kiss (Bardeux)

When You Touch Me (Taana Gardner)

When You Wake Up In The Morning (Candi Staton)

When You're #1 (Gene Chandler)

Whenever You Need Somebody (O'chi Brown)

Where Is My Man (Eartha Kitt)

White Horse (Laid Back)

White Lines (Grandmaster Flash and Melle Mel)

Who Do You Love? (Bernard Wright)

Who Found Who (Jellybean)

Who Is It (Mantronix)

Who Needs Love Like That/Heavenly Action (Erasure)

Whole Lotta Love (See: Stairway To Love . . .)

Who's That Girl (Madonna)

Who's Zoomin' Who (Aretha Franklin)

Why?/Cadillac Car (The Bronski Beat)

Why Can't I Be You (The Cure)

Why Should I Cry (Nona Hendryx)

Why You Treat Me So Bad (Club Nouveau)

Wild And Crazy Love (The Mary Jane Girls)

The Wild Boys (Duran Duran)

Wild Thing (Tone Loc)

Wild Wild West (The Escape Club)

Wild, Wild West (Kool Moe Dee)

Will You Love Me Tomorrow (See: I Think We're Alone Now . . .)

Wipeout (The Fat Boys)

Wishing Well (Terence Trent D'Arby)

Without You (Touch)

Woman (See: Easy Lover . . .)

Wood Beez (Pray Like Aretha Franklin)/ Absolute (Scritti Politti)

The Word Is Out (Jermaine Stewart)

Word Up (Cameo)

Work It (Teena Marie)

Work That Body (Taana Gardner)

Workin' And Slavin' (The Midnight Rhythm)

Working Day And Night (See: Rock With You . . .)

Working My Way Back To You/Forgive Me, Girl (The Spinners)

Would I Lie To You?/Here Comes That Sinking Feeling (Eurythmics)

Y.M.C.A. (The Village People)

Yellow Panties (Dr. Jeckyll and Mr. Hyde)

Yes (See: The Screams Of Passion . . .)

Yo' Little Brother (Nolan Thomas)

You Ain't Fresh (The Boogie Boys)

You And Me (The Flirts)

You And Me (Simfonia)

You And Me Tonight (Deja)

You Are Everything (James "D Train" Williams)

(You Are My) All And All (Joyce Sims)

You Are My Lady (Freddie Jackson)

You Be Illin' (Run-D.M.C.)
You Better Quit (One Way)
You Came (Kim Wilde)
You Can Do It (Al Hudson and The Partners)
You Can Get Over (See: Put Your Body In It . . .)
You Can Get Over (Stephanie Mills)
You Don't Have To Cry (Rene and Angela)
You Don't Know (Scarlet and Black)
You Gave Me Love (The Crown Heights Affair)
You Get The Best From Me (Alicia Meyers)
You Gonna Make Me Love Somebody Else (The Jones Girls)
You Got The Love (Candi Staton)
You Got What It Takes (Bobby Thurston)
You Gots' To Chill (E.P.M.D.)
You Keep Me Coming Back (The Brothers Johnson)
You Keep Me Hanging On (Kim Wilde)
You Know How To Love Me (Phyllis Hyman)
You Look Good To Me (Cherrelle)
You Look Marvelous (Billy Crystal)
You Make Me Feel (Mighty Real)/Dance (Disco Heat) (Sylvester)
You Make Me Work (Cameo)
You, Me And He (Mtume)
You Should Be Mine (The Woo Woo Song) (Jeffrey Osborne)

You Spin Me Round (Like A Record)/Misty Circle (Dead Or Alive)
You Stepped Into My Life (Melba Moore)
You Talk Too Much/Daryll And Joe (Run-D.M.C.)
(You Used To Be) Romantic (Shirley Lewis)
You Used To Hold Me So Tight (Thelma Houston)
You Wear It Well (El DeBarge With DeBarge)
You'll Rock (L.L. Cool J)
You're All The Boogie I Need (See: Behind The Groove . . .)
You're Gonna Get Yours (Public Enemy)
You're No Good (Kelly Charles)
You're Not My Kind Of Girl (The New Edition)
(You're Puttin') A Rush On Me (See: A Rush On Me)
You're The One (Sandee)
Your Life (Konk)
Your Personal Touch (Evelyn "Champagne" King)
Your Smile (Rene And Angela)
Your Sweetness Is My Weakness (Barry White)
Your Touch (Bonnie Pointer)

Zie Zie Won't Dance (Peter Brown)

D. APPENDIXES

(NUMBER 1 RECORDS—A CHRONOLOGICAL LISTING)

1978

10-28—11-18   *MacArthur Park Suite*—Donna Summer   (4)
11-25—12-23   *Le Freak*—Chic   (5)
12-30   *Contact*—Edwin Starr   (1)

1979

1-06—	1-13	*Contact*—Edwin Starr (2; 3)
1-20—	1-27	*I Will Survive*—Gloria Gaynor (2)
2-03		*Fly Away*—Voyage (1)
2-10—	2-17	*Keep On Dancin'*—Gary's Gang (2)
2-24—	3-03	*Do Ya Think I'm Sexy*—Rod Stewart (2)
3-10—	3-31	*He's The Greatest Dancer/We Are Family*—Sister Sledge (4)
4-07—	5-05	*Dancer/Dance To Dance*—Gino Soccio (5)
5-12—	5-19	*Bad Bad Boy (LP)*—Theo Vaness (2)
5-26		*Bad Girls (LP)*—Donna Summer (1)
6-02—	6-09	*Ring My Bell*—Anita Ward (2)
6-16—	7-14	*Bad Girls (LP)*—Donna Summer (5; 6)
7-21—	7-28	*Born To Be Alive*—Patrick Hernandez (2)
8-04—	8-11	*I've Got The Next Dance*—Deniece Williams (2)
8-18—	8-25	*This Time Baby*—Jackie Moore (2)
9-01—	9-08	*The Bass/No One Gets The Prize*—Diana Ross (2)
9-15		*Found A Cure*—Ashford and Simpson (1)
9-22—10-06		*Come To Me/Don't Stop Dancing*—France Joli (3)
10-13—10-27		*Don't Stop Til You Get Enough*—Michael Jackson (3)
11-03		*Pop Muzik*—M (1)
11-10—11-17		*Ooh, La La/Harmony*—Suzi Lane (2)
11-24—12-08		*No More Tears*—Donna Summer/Barbra Streisand (3)
12-15		*Deputy Of Love*—Don Armando's 2nd Avenue Rhumba Band (1)
12-22—12-29		*Wear It Out*—Stargard (2)

1980

1-05—	1-12	*The Second Time Around/Right In The Socket*—Shalamar (2)
1-19—	2-09	*Vertigo/Relight My Fire*—Dan Hartman (4)
2-16—	2-23	*And The Beat Goes On*—The Whispers (2)
3-01		*I Can't Help Myself*—Bonnie Pointer (1)
3-08		*High On Your Love*—Debbie Jacobs (1)
3-15		*Funkytown*—Lipps, Inc. (1)
3-22—	4-05	*High On Your Love*—Debbie Jacobs (3; 4)

1984

1-28—	2-04	*Let The Music Play*—Shannon (2)
2-11		*White Horse*—Laid Back (1)
2-18—	3-24	*Somebody's Watching Me*—Rockwell (6)
3-31—	4-07	*Girls Just Want To Have Fun*—Cyndi Lauper (2)
4-14—	5-05	*White Horse*—Laid Back (4; 5)
5-12		*Jam On It*—Newcleus (1)
5-19—	6-02	*Let's Hear It For The Boy*—Deniece Williams (3)
6-09—	7-07	*Somebody Else's Guy*—Jocelyn Brown (5)

7-14—	8-18	*When Doves Cry*—Prince (6)
8-25—	9-08	*What's Love Got To Do With It*—Tina Turner (3)
9-15—	9-29	*The Glamorous Life*—Sheila E. (3)
10-06		*Caribbean Queen*—Billy Ocean (1)
10-13—	10-20	*The Medicine Song*—Stephanie Mills (2)
10-27—	12-08	*I Feel For You*—Chaka Khan (7)
12-15—	12-29	*Like A Virgin*—Madonna (3)

1985

1-05—	1-19	*Like A Virgin*—Madonna (3; 6)
1-26—	2-09	*Rain Forest*—Paul Hardcastle (3)
2-16—	2-23	*Roxanne, Roxanne*—U.T.F.O. (2)
3-02—	3-09	*Sugar Walls*—Sheena Easton (2)
3-16—	3-23	*Easy Lover/Woman*—Philip Bailey and Phil Collins (2)
3-30—	4-06	*New Attitude/Axel-F*—Patti LaBelle and Harold Faltermeyer (2)
4-13		*Rhythm Of The Night/Queen Of My Heart*—DeBarge (1)
4-20—	5-18	*We Are The World*—U.S.A. For Africa (5)
5-25—	6-01	*Fresh*—Kool & The Gang (2)
6-08		*Everybody Wants To Rule The World*—Tears For Fears (1)
6-15		*I Wonder If I Take You Home*—Lisa Lisa and Cult Jam With Full Force (1)
6-22—	7-13	*Angel/Into The Groove*—Madonna (4)
7-20—	8-03	*19/The Asylum (It'z Weird)*—Paul Hardcastle (3)
8-10		*Angel/Into The Groove*—Madonna (1; 5)
8-17		*Freeway Of Love*—Aretha Franklin (1)
8-24—	8-31	*Fly Girl/City Life*—The Boogie Boys (2)
9-07—	9-14	*The Show/La-Di-Da-Di*—Doug E. Fresh and The Get Fresh Crew (2)
9-21—	9-28	*Oh Sheila*—Ready For The World (2)
10-05—	11-09	*The Show/La-Di-Da-Di*—Doug E. Fresh and The Get Fresh Crew (6; 8)
11-16		*Part-Time Lover*—Stevie Wonder (1)
11-23		*Who's Zoomin' Who*—Aretha Franklin (1)
11-30		*Everybody Dance/Lonely Heart*—Ta Mara and The Seen (1)
12-07		*Party All The Time*—Eddie Murphy (1)
12-14		*Baby Talk*—Alisha (1)
12-21—	12-28	*Can You Feel The Beat*—Lisa Lisa and Cult Jam With Full Force (2)

1986

1-04—	1-11	*Slave To The Rhythm*—Grace Jones (2)
1-18		*Like You*—Phyllis Nelson (1)
1-25		*Go Home*—Stevie Wonder (1)

2-01		*Digital Display*—Ready For The World (1)
2-08—	2-15	*Living In America*—James Brown (2)
2-22—	3-01	*How Will I Know*—Whitney Houston (2)
3-08		*Saturday Love*—Cherrelle
3-15—	3-29	*What Have You Done For Me Lately*—Janet Jackson (3)
4-05		*I Can't Wait*—Nu Shooz (1)
4-12—	4-26	*Kiss*—Prince and The Revolution (3)
5-03		*West End Girls*—The Pet Shop Boys (1)
5-10		*Kiss*—Prince and The Revolution (1; 4)
5-17—	5-31	*On My Own*—Patti LaBelle and Michael McDonald (3)
6-07		*Pee-Wee's Dance*—Joeski Love
6-14—	6-21	*My Adidas/Peter Piper*—Run-D.M.C. (2)
6-28—	8-23	*Rumors/Vicious Rumors*—The Timex Social Club (9)
8-30—	9-06	*Papa Don't Preach*—Madonna (2)
9-13		*Two Hearts*—Stacey Q (1)
9-20—	9-27	*When I Think Of You*—Janet Jackson (2)
10-04—	10-11	*The Rain*—Oran "Juice" Jones (2)
10-18—	11-15	*Word Up*—Cameo (5)
11-22—	12-06	*Shake You Down*—Gregory Abbott (3)
12-13		*Summertime, Summertime*—Nocera (1)
12-20—	12-27	*Shake You Down*—Gregory Abbott (2; 5)

1987

1-03—	1-17	*Shake You Down*—Gregory Abbott (3; 8)
1-24—	1-31	*C'est La Vie*—Robbie Nevil (2)
2-07		*Control*—Janet Jackson (1)
2-14—	2-21	*Open Your Heart*—Madonna (2)
2-28—	3-07	*Showing Out*—Mel and Kim (2)
3-14—	3-21	*Looking For A New Love*—Jody Watley (2)
3-28		*Lean On Me*—Club Nouveau (1)
4-04—	4-11	*Sign "O" The Times*—Prince (2)
4-18—	5-02	*Looking For A New Love*—Jody Watley (3; 5)
5-09—	5-16	*Sign "O" The Times*—Prince (2; 4)
5-23		*La Isla Bonita*—Madonna (1)
5-30—	7-04	*Head To Toe*—Lisa Lisa and Cult Jam (6)
7-11		*Diamonds*—Herb Alpert (1)
7-18		*Respectable*—Mel and Kim (1)
7-25—	8-15	*Fake*—Alexander O'Neal (4)
8-22—	8-29	*I Want Your Sex*—George Michael (2)
9-05—	9-19	*Who's That Girl*—Madonna (3)
9-26—	10-10	*Casanova*—Levert (3)
10-17—	10-24	*Full Circle*—Company B (2)
10-31		*Causing A Commotion*—Madonna (1)
11-07—	12-05	*Bad*—Michael Jackson (5)
12-12—	12-26	*System Of Survival*—Earth, Wind and Fire (3)

1988

1-02—	1-16	*System Of Survival*—Earth, Wind and Fire (3; 6)
1-23—	2-13	*Never Gonna Give You Up*—Rick Astley (4)
2-20—	3-05	*Some Kind Of Lover*—Jody Watley (3)
3-12—	3-19	*Tramp/Push It*—Salt-N-Pepa (2)
3-26		*Girlfriend*—Pebbles (1)
4-02		*Perfect Lover*—Company B (1)
4-09		*Father Figure*—George Michael (1)
4-16		*Thinking Of You*—Earth, Wind and Fire (1)
4-23		*Don't Make A Fool Of Yourself*—Stacey Q (1)
4-30		*Out Of The Blue*—Debbie Gibson (1)
5-07—	5-14	*Nightime*—Pretty Poison (2)
5-21		*Naughty Girl*—Samantha Fox (1)
5-28		*Nite And Day*—Al B. Sure! (1)
6-04—	6-18	*Just Got Paid*—Johnny Kemp (3)
6-25—	7-02	*Mercedes Boy*—Pebbles (2)
7-09—	7-16	*Supersonic*—J.J. Fad (2)
7-23		*Sayin' Sorry Don't Make It Right*—Denise Lopez (1)
7-30—	8-06	*The Right*—Vanessa Williams (2)
8-13—	8-20	*K.I.S.S.I.N.G.*—Siedah Garrett (2)
8-27		*Shake Your Thang*—Salt-N-Pepa (1)
9-03—	9-10	*Monkey*—George Michael (2)
9-17		*Spring Love*—Stevie B (1)
9-24		*Monkey*—George Michael (1; 3)
10-01—	10-08	*Never Let You Go*—Sweet Sensation (2)
10-15—	10-29	*Chains Of Love*—Erasure (3)
11-05		*Big Fun*—Innercity (1)
11-12—	11-26	*Break 4 Love*—Raze (1) (3)
12-03—	12-10	*The Way You Love Me*—Karyn White (2)
12-17—	12-31	*Don't Rock The Boat*—Midnight Star (3)

[RECORDS WITH LONGEST RUN ON CHARTS]

1. *Rumors/Vicious Rumors*—The Timex Social Club.....36
2. *The Dream Team Is In The House*—The L.A. Dream Team.....34
2. *Let's Go Crazy/Erotic City*—Prince and The Revolution . . . 34
4. *Fresh*—Kool & The Gang.....33
5. *Relax*—Frankie Goes To Hollywood.....32
5. *Stay A Little While, Child*—Loose Ends.....32
7. *Caribbean Queen*—Billy Ocean.....30
7. *The Rain*—Oran "Juice" Jones.....30
7. *Request Line*—Rock Master Scott and The Dynamic 3.....30
7. *The Show/La-Di-Da-Di*—Doug E. Fresh and The Get Fresh Crew.....30
7. *Two Of Hearts*—Stacey Q.....30

7. *Word Up*—Cameo.....30
7. *(You Are My) All And All*—Joyce Sims.....30
14. *For Tonight*—Nancy Martinez.....29
14. *Point Of No Return*—Nu Shooz.....29
14. *Serious*—Donna Allen.....29

[MOST CHART HITS PER ARTIST*]

1. Prince and The Revolution.....17
2. Madonna.....13
3. Run-D.M.C......10
4. Michael Jackson.....8
4. Stephanie Mills.....8
4. Tina Turner.....8
7. Cameo.....7
7. Full Force.....7
7. The Jets.....7
7. Patti LaBelle.....7
7. Midnight Star.....7
7. The New Edition.....7
7. The Pointer Sisters.....7
7. Donna Summer.....7

*Includes collaborations with other artists

VIDEO GAMES

A. INTRODUCTION

By 1982 it was clear that video games were a national obsession. National tournaments sponsored by the manufacturers attracted many participants, and books and magazines devoted to the games were thriving. New arcades were everywhere, and unless they were banned, machines could be found squeezed into delicatessens, pizza parlors, cinema lobbies, bars, diners, laundries, and even colleges and churches.

It was estimated that twenty billion quarters were devoured by arcade machines in 1981; in addition, consumers paid an estimated one billion dollars that year for video-game consoles that connected to home TV sets and for cassettes containing the various game programs. For purposes of comparison, that figure represented about twice the take in 1981 of all the casinos in Nevada. It was almost twice the $2.9-billion box-office gross of the U.S. film industry for that period.

While the medium possessed a long lineage reaching back far before the twentieth century (including many variants of pinball), *Space Invaders,* designed in Japan and marketed in the U.S. by Bally, launched the craze in 1979. While the arcade machines provided the original impetus for the rapid growth of the industry in the early 1980s, a second arm appeared in short order: the home video game system. Atari, a major player in the arcade division as well, dominated the home market, with Mattel's Intellivision and Magnavox's Odyssey 2 providing the primary competition.

In the wake of Pac-Man's incredible success in 1981 came a wide variety of industry-based spinoffs. Coleco Industries produced a battery-run, table-top model to complement Atari's home video version, while Milton Bradley offered a puzzle, a card game, and a nonelectric board game. In addition to toys, pajamas, lunch boxes, and bumper stickers, there were Hallmark cards and gift wrapping, Dan River sheets and pillowcases, and J.C. Penney children's clothing. A Columbia Records single, Buckner and Garcia's "Pac-Man Fever," reached the nationwide Top Ten charts in March 1982, and book publishers weighed in with titles such as *How To Win At Pac-Man* (Pocket Books) and *Mastering Pac-Man* (Signet), the latter of which made the *New York Times* bestseller list.

By 1983 the industry had undergone a perceptible drop in popularity, primarily due to the loss of novelty and the onslaught of newer, more attractive media (*e.g.,* home computers, videocassettes, compact discs). While video games have found a new lease on life via home computer software, which allowed for a more subtle form of visual graphics than had been previously possible, the medium's popularity has lacked sufficient intensity, according to *Cash Box,* to merit week-by-week chart documentation.

Initial chart title/title changes: "Top Selling Video Games"/"Top 15 Video Games" (December 11, 1982)
Beginning date/termination date: November 13, 1982/April 7, 1984
Initial number of positions/changes in number of positions: 15 (weeks prior to November 13, 1982 did not designate chart positions)

B. TITLE INDEX

ATLANTIS

12-25-82   (Imagic 3203)   12, 12, 12, 11, 11, 15, 14   (7)

BATTLE ZONE

10-29-83   (Atari AX 2681)   13, 11, 12, 15   (4)

BERZERK

11-13-82   (Atari CX 2640)   5, 5, 4, 6, 4, 8, 8, 8, 7, 5, 5, 6, 7, 11   (14)

BIG BUG

   2-11-84   (Atari CX 2677)   15, 12, 9, 9, 7, 4, 5, 5, 5   (9)

BURGER TIME

   7-30-83   (Intellivision 4549)   12, 12, 11, 7, 8, 9, 9, 5, 5, 6, 5, 5, 5, 3, 4, 4, 6, 8,
               9, 9, 12, 12, 13, 13, 12, 12, 14, 13, 12, 11, 11, 11, 15   (33)

CARNIVAL

   11-27-82   (Coleco 2468)   11, 14, 13, 14   (4)

CENTIPEDE

   3-26-83   (Atari CX 2676)   8, 5, 4, 3, 3, 3, 2, 2, 1, 1, 1, 1, 1, 1, 1, 3, 2, 2, 2, 2,
               2, 2, 2, 2, 2, 2, 3, 3, 3, 3, 6, 9, 12, 10, 9, 9, 8, 8, 7, 7, 7, 7, 7, 6, 5, 4, 5,
               6, 5, 5, 6, 8, 8, 10, 10   (55)

CONGO BONGO

   3-17-84   (Sega 006)   15, 11, 11   (3)

CRACK POTS

   9-17-83   (Activision AX 029)   14, 13, 13, 15, 15, 15   (6)

DECATHLON

   9-03-83   (Atari CX 2673)   14, 13, 13, 12, 12, 9, 8, 8, 7, 9, 11, 11, 14, 14, 14,
               15, 15, 15, 15, 13, 14, 15, 15, 14, 15, 15, 15, 13, 14   (29)

DEFENDER

   11-13-82   (Atari CX 2609)   7, 10, 13   (3)

DEMON ATTACK

   11-27-82   (Imagic 3200)   12, 15, 14, 12, 12, 12, 11, 13, 15, 13, 12, 12, 14, 12,
               10, 12, 13, 11, 11, 13, 14, 14, 15, 13, 11, 12, 12, 13, 15, 13   (30)

DOLPHIN

   6-25-83   (Activision AX 024)   15, 12, 11, 12, 13, 15   (6)

DONKEY KONG

11-13-82 (Coleco 2451) 3, 3, 3, 3, 6, 4, 4, 4, 3, 3, 3, 4, 5, 4, 4, 5, 6, 9, 8, 7, 7, 6, 8, 10, 11 (25)

DONKEY KONG JR.

4-02-83 (Coleco 2601) 13, 11, 8, 4, 2, 3, 3, 5, 6, 6, 6, 7, 8, 8, 6, 9, 8, 7, 8, 10, 10, 14 (22)

DRAGONFIRE

2-19-83 (Imagic IA 3611) 12, 10, 9, 10, 9, 14 (6)

DUNGEONS AND DRAGONS

11-13-82 (Mattel 3410) 9, 14 (2)

E.T.

12-04-82 (Atari CX 2674) 8, 7, 5, 5, 5, 4, 4, 7, 10, 13 (10)

EARTHWORLD

11-20-82 (Atari (CX 2656) 12, 8 (2)

THE EMPIRE STRIKES BACK

11-13-82 (Parker Brothers 5050) 6, 8, 9, 10, 12, 15, 15, 15, 15 (9)

ENDURO

6-18-83 (Activision AX 026) 15, 4, 3, 1, 1, 1, 1, 1, 1, 1, 1, 1, 1, 1, 1, 1, 2, 2, 2, 2, 5, 6, 8, 8, 7, 7, 7, 6, 5, 5, 5, 6, 9, 11, 14, (5)15, 14, 12, 12 (38)

FROGGER

11-13-82 (Parker Brothers 5300) 2, 2, 2, 2, 2, 2, 2, 2, 2, 2, 2, 3, 3, 3, 3, 3, 3, 3, 2, 2, 4, 5, 5, 6, 7, 5, 5, 4, 4, 4, 3, 4, 5, 5, 7, 5, 6, 5, 6, 6, 6, 9, 12, 14, 15, 15, 14 (47)

GORF

7-02-83 (Coleco 2449) 15, 15, 15, 14 (4)

JOUST

12-03-83   (Atari CX 2691)   15, 15, 13, 12, 12, 12, 14, 15, 13, 12, 9, 7, 6, 6, 5, 5, 4, 4, 4   (18)

JUNGLE HUNT

8-06-83   (Atari CX 2688)   13, 12, 8, 7, 7, 6, 6, 6, 5, 4, 4, 4, 4, 3, 2, 2, 2, 2, 2, 4, 8, 8, 8, 10, 11, 10, 9, 8, 8, 8, 8, 10, 10, 11, 14, 14   (36)

KANGAROO

11-26-83   (Atari CX 2689)   12, 11, 11, 11, 11, 11, 11, 8, 7, 6, 6, 6, 5, 7, 7, 9, 11, 13, 15, 15   (20)

KEYSTONE KAPERS

5-14-83   (Activision AX 025)   13, 11, 5, 3, 5, 3, 3, 4, 4, 4, 4, 4, 4, 4, 4, 4, 4, 5, 10, 10, 9, 12, 13, 12, 12   (25)

LOCK 'N CHASE

11-13-82   (Mattel 5663)   12, 9, 10, 13   (4)

MEGAMANIA

11-13-82   (Activision AX 017)   4, 4, 6, 4, 3, 3, 3, 3, 5, 6, 8, 7, 6, 6, 7, 9, 12, 15, 15   (19)

MR. DO!

10-08-83   (Coleco 2622)   13, 11, 9, 8, 7, 5, 4, 3, 6, 6, 8, 10, 10, 10, 11, 10, 9, 7, 7, 9, 10, 10, 8, 7, 7, 6, 6   (27)

MOUSE TRAP

11-13-82   (Coleco 2419)   14, 15, 15, 13, 15, 14, 11, 10, 10, 10, 8, 10, 15, 14, 14   (15)

MS. PAC-MAN

3-05-83   (Atari CX 2675)   13, 4, 1, 1, 1, 1, 1, 1, 1, 1, 1, 1, 2, 2, 2, 2, 2, 2, 2, 2, 3, 3, 3, 3, 3, 3, 3, 3, 3, 4, 4, 4, 6, 7, 7, 6, 5, 6, 5, 5, 3, 3, 3, 3, 3, 3, 2, 2, 3, 3, 3, 3, 3, 3, 3, 3, 3, 3   (58)

Video Games

OINK!

5-07-83 (Activision AX 023) 15, 12, 10, 10, 9, 12, 10, 13, 14, 14, 13, 12, 11, 15, 15, 15, 12 (17)

PAC-MAN

11-13-82 (Atari CX 2646) 8, 6, 5, 7, 10, 11, 11, 11, 10, 14, 12, 11, 15, 14, 15, 14 (16)

PHOENIX

3-19-83 (Atari CX 2673) 14, 12, 9, 10, 9, 8, 6, 8, 9, 9, 11, 10, 9, 9, 11, 11, 12, 11, 10, 9, 9, 13, 13, 13, 15, 15 (26)

PITFALL!

11-13-82 (Activision AX 018) 1, 1, 1, 1, 1, 1, 1, 1, 1, 1, 1, 1, 1, 1, 1, 1, 1, 2, 2, 4, 3, 2, 2, 2, 2, 4, 4, 4, 3, 3, 5, 4, 6, 7, 6, 5, 6, 5, 6, 5, 5, 5, 5, 6, 10, 11, 14, 15, 14, 14, 13, 14, 13, 14, 12, 10, 10, 10, 10, 9, 9, 9, 9, 8, 8, 8, 10, 10, 12, 12, 11, 9, 9, 9, 9 (74)

POLE POSITION

9-03-83 (Atari CX 2694) 13, 11, 9, 7, 7, 7, 6, 3, 2, 2, 3, 3, 4, 4, 4, 2, 2, 2, 2, 3, 3, 1, 1, 1, 2, 2, 2, 2, 2, 2, 2, 2 (32)

POPEYE

12-03-83 (Parker Brothers 5370) 13, 13, 9, 6, 6, 6, 5, 4, 4, 5, 4, 4, 4, 4, 4, 6, 6, 7, 7 (19)

PRO FOOTBALL

11-13-82 (Mattel 5658) 15 (1)

Q-BERT

9-03-83 (Parker Brothers 5360) 5, 4, 3, 2, 1, 1, 1, 1, 1, 1, 1, 1, 1, 1, 1, 1, 1, 1, 1, 1, 1, 2, 2, 2, 1, 1, 1, 1, 1, 1, 1, 1 (32)

RAIDERS OF THE LOST ARK

12-04-82 (Atari CX 2659) 12, 9, 7, 7, 7, 6, 9, 9, 8, 10, 9, 11, 13, 15 (14)

REAL SPORTS: BASEBALL

11-27-82   (Atari CX 2640)   14, 11, 11, 10, 10, 10, 13, 12, 10, 9, 9, 8, 8, 11, 11, 14   (16)

REAL SPORTS: FOOTBALL

2-05-83   (Atari CX 2668)   11, 10, 9, 7, 8, 8, 11, 15   (8)

RIVER RAID

1-15-83   (Activision AX 020)   8, 4, 2, 2, 2, 2, 2, 1, 1, 3, 4, 3, 3, 4, 5, 5, 6, 6, 7, 7, 7, 7, 5, 6, 7, 8, 8, 11, 13, 10, 9, 12, 11, 10, 8, 8, 8, 8, 8, 10, 10, 10, 8, 7, 7, 6, 5, 5, 5, 4, 4, 4, 4, 5, 7, 10, 13, 14, 14, 14, 14, 13, 12, 13, 13   (65)

ROBOT TANK

7-23-83   (Activision AX 028)   15, 14, 11, 8, 9, 6, 8, 7, 7, 9, 11, 11, 12, 11, 11, 10, 9, 10, 15   (19)

SEA QUEST

4-02-83   (Activision AX 022)   15, 14, 12, 11, 10, 10, 10, 13   (8)

SPACE DUNGEONS

3-31-84   (Atari CX 5232)   15, 13   (2)

SPACE SHUTTLE

1-21-84   (Activision AX 033)   13, 12, 11, 11, 13, 13, 13, 12, 12, 10, 8, 8   (12)

SPIDER FIGHTER

2-12-83   (Activision AX 021)   13, 10, 8, 7, 6, 5, 9, 12, 12, 11, 9, 12, 11, 14, 14, 13, 12, 14   (18)

STAR RAIDERS

11-13-82   (Atari CX 2660)   13, 13   (2)

STRAWBERRY SHORTCAKE MUSICAL MATCH UP

   4-23-83   (Parker Brothers 5910)   12, 9, 9, 8, 8, 9, 11, 10, 14, 14   (10)

SWORD QUEST: EARTHWORLD

   12-04-82   (Atari CX 2656)   5, 5, 6, 8, 9, 6, 6, 9, 10, 13   (10)

TIME PILOT

   11-05-83   (Coleco 2679)   14, 13, 13, 11, 12, 12, 14, 14, 14, 14, 15   (11)

TRON: DEADLY DISCS

   3-12-83   (M Network 5662)   13, 12, 13, 14   (4)

TURBO

   12-11-82   (Coleco 2473)   15, 13, 13, 13, 14, 15, 14, 14   (8)

VANGUARD

   1-29-83   (Atari 2669)   12, 8, 7, 6, 4, 4, 5, 7, 6, 8, 9, 13, (5), 15, 14, 11, 12, 12,
            13, 13, 14   (20)

VENTURE

   11-13-82   (Coleco 2457)   10, 11, 15, 15, 15, 13, 13, 12, 15, 15, 14, 15, 13, 11,
            10, 10, 10, 10, 9, 10, 14, 14, 14, 15   (24)

ZAXXON

   11-13-82   (Coleco 2435)   11, 7, 7, 9, 9, 9, 8, 7, 6, 5, 4, 5, 5, 6, 5, 7, 6, 5, 6, 7, 6,
            7, 8, 7, 7, 6, 8, 8, 8, 8, 9, 9, 9, 7, 7, 8, 7, 7, 11, 10, 11, 12, 12, 11, 10,
            10, 9, 14, 15, 15   (50)

C. APPENDIX: NUMBER 1 VIDEO GAMES—A
CHRONOLOGICAL LISTING

1982

11-13—12-25   *Pitfall!*   (7)

1983

1-01—	2-26	*Pitfall!*	(9; 16)
3-05—	3-12	*River Raid*	(2)
3-19—	5-14	*Ms. Pac-Man*	(9)
5-21—	7-02	*Centipede*	(7)
7-09—	9-24	*Enduro*	(12)
10-01—	12-31	*Q-Bert*	(14)

1984

1-07—	1-21	*Q-Bert*	(3; 17)
1-28—	2-11	*Pole Position*	(3)
2-18—	4-07	*Q-Bert*	(8; 25)

VIDEOCASSETTES

A. INTRODUCTION

The home video revolution had its genesis in the American experiments of the 1950s and 1960s by companies such as Ampex and RCA. Sony made a quantum leap forward with the introduction, first, of its U-Matic recorder and, ultimately, its Betamax machine. By the late 1970s Sony's chief Japanese competitors had agreed to commit their resources to the VHS format, and the race for public favor was on. While Sony's Beta line has continued to lose ground during the 1980s, the success of the videotape medium has represented the most significant development in the consumer electronics field since the rise of television. By the latter part of the decade, the majority of households owned a VCR.

Various research studies have indicated that the primary use of the VCR during its early years on the home market was for "time-shifting"; *i.e.,* taping programs broadcast on TV for viewing at a later time. However, by the early 1980s a substantial number of VCR owners had begun renting tapes from the many rental outlets (*e.g.,* specialty outlets, supermarkets, drugstores, department stores) which were springing up at this time. The purchase of tapes remained a marginal practice until the mid-1980s, at which point many of the video arms of the major film studios began offering popular movie titles (always the backbone of the video software catalog) at competitive prices ($15 to $40).

Gradually a pricing strategy somewhat akin to the hardcover-paperback sequence employed by the book publishing world emerged within the video software industry: *i.e.,* films appeared on video approximately one year after their theatrical release, usually retailing for $80-to-$90; within another year or so the list price of these titles would be lowered to the $15 to $30 range.

503

Accordingly, the chart compilation process was modified to factor in video software unit sales as well as rental figures. In 1988, it was decided to split the videocassette chart off into separate rental and retail sale entities in order to reflect the differences between them:

(1) The bestselling videocassettes tended to be economically priced and/or include programming other than Hollywood features; and

(2) The top performing rental tapes were generally recently released films, most of which had also been theatrical smashes.

In addition, music videocassettes and video clips, respectively, were provided with separate chart status. Despite the growing sophistication of its treatment of the video phenomenon, *Cash Box* has thus far chosen to ignore certain sectors of the field, most notably laser discs (and, until its demise in 1984, RCA's competing CED format) and compact disc-video (CD-Vs).

Initial chart title/title changes: "Top 30 Videocassettes"/"Top 40 Videocassettes"; "Cash Box Top Rental Video Cassettes" and "Cash Box Top Retail Video Cassettes"; Subtitles—"Top 30 Videocassettes is a compilation of the fastest moving titles in both Beta and VHS formats, based primarily on rental activity, as reported by various accounts around the country" (July 3, 1982); "Top 30 Videocassettes is a compilation of the fastest moving titles in both Beta and VHS formats, based on sales and rental activity, as reported by various accounts around the country" (December 11, 1982); "The Cash Box Top 40 Videocassettes Chart Is Based Solely On Rentals At Various Retail Outlets" (July 13, 1985); "Cash Box Top 40 Video Cassettes is based solely on actual pieces sold at retail stores" (July 11, 1987)

Beginning date/termination date: April 3, 1982/September 19, 1987; March 5, 1988/June 18, 1988 ("Cash Box Top Rental Video Cassettes" and "Cash Box Top Retail Video Cassettes")

Initial number of positions/changes in number of positions: 30/40 (June 29, 1985); 30 ("Cash Box Top Rental Video Cassettes" and "Cash Box Top Retail Video Cassettes")

B. TITLE INDEX

ABOUT LAST NIGHT

3-14-87   (RCA 20735)   10, 2, 2, 5, 3, 4, 5, 7, 6, 8, 13, 20, 21, 17, 19, 19, 19,
29, 29, 29, 29, 29, 29, 36, 36, 36, 36, 36   (28)

ABSENCE OF MALICE

7-10-82   (Col. 10005)   21, 8, 6, 4, 3, 3, 4, 5, 5, 5, 7, 10, 9, 10, 10, 16, 17, 19,
27, 29   (20)

THE ADVENTURES OF BUCKAROO BANZAI

3-09-85   (Vestron VB 5056)   16, 16, 10, 10, 13, 13, 14, 14, 20, 20, 28,
28   (12)

AFTER HOURS

9-13-86   (Warner 11528)   20, 18, 18, 18, 14, 17, 21, 33   (8)

AGAINST ALL ODDS

10-13-84   (RCA/Col. 60077)   10, 10, 4, 4, 4, 4, 3, 3, 5, 5, 9, 9, 9, 16, 16, 15, 15,
14, 14, 21, 21   (21)

AGNES OF GOD

5-31-86   (RCA/Col. 6-20563)   16, 14, 7, 6, 6, 7, 7, 8, 7, 9, 10, 12, 13, 17, 21,
25, 33, 33, 34, 36   (20)

AIRPLANE

4-10-82   (Paramount 1305)   29   (1)

AIRPLANE II

5-14-83   (Paramount 1489)   24, 15, 4, 4, 4, 4, 8, 9, 11, 18, 18, 17, 17, 14, 13,
15, 17, 19, 25, 30   (20)

ALIEN

  9-06-86   (CBS/Fox 1090)   36, 30, 26, 26, 27, 22, 24, 20, 17, 14, 14, 22, 31, 31, 31, 21, 23, 23, 23, 23, 27, 27, 28, 31, 30, 39, (4), 14, 12, 11, 14, 9, 16, 10, 6   (34)

ALIENS

  4-11-87   (CBS/Fox 1504)   7, 5, 4, 4, 3, 2, 2, 2, 6, 11, 13, 13, 13, 26, 26, 27, 27, 27, 27, 28, 28, 28, 28, 28   (24)

ALL OF ME

  2-23-85   (Thorn/EMI 2715)   10, 10, 3, 3, 2, 2, 2, 2, 5, 5, 8, 8, 9, 9, 13, 13, 23, 23, 27, 27, 31, 31, 39   (23)

ALL THE MARBLES

  5-22-82   (MGM/UA 00112)   22, 16, 15, 25, 23, 23, 25, 26, 27   (9)

ALL THE RIGHT MOVES

  6-23-84   (CBS/Fox 1299)   21, 16, 10, 7, 5, 8, 6, 8, 8, 12, 12, 16, 15, 15, 23, 23, 25, 25   (18)

ALPHABET CITY

  10-27-84   (CBS/Fox 6741)   26, 26, 23, 23, 26, 26   (6)

ALTERED STATES

  4-10-82   (Warner 61076)   25, 24, 25, 26   (4)

AMADEUS

  10-12-85   (Thorn/EMI/HBO TVA 2997)   15, 7, 3, 2, 2, 2, 4, 3, 3, 3, 4, 11, 11, 11, 14, 13, 14, 13, 18, 23, 23, 24, 23, 25, 23, 26, 27, 25, 33, 33, 33, 39   (32)

  10-11-86   (HBO/Cannon TVA 2997)   28, 14, 10, 3, 6, 7, 5, 16, 16, 16, 23, 27, 27, 27, 27, 25, 22, 17, 23, 16, 20, 17, 35   (20)

THE AMATEUR

11-06-82 (20th Century Fox 1147) 30, 24, 16, 16, 13, 15, 15, 26, 26, 26, 26, 26, 30 (13)

AMERICAN DREAMER

9-14-85 (CBS/Fox 7082) 35, 31, 26, 23, 30 (5)

AMERICAN FLYERS

5-17-86 (Warner 11475) 29, 20, 18, 15, 15, 20, 21, 24, 23, 32, 38, 40 (12)

AMERICAN NINJA

1-04-86 (MGM/UA 800705) 28, 28, 26, 26 (4)

AN AMERICAN WEREWOLF IN LONDON

4-03-82 (MCA 77004) 4, 1, 3, 4, 6, 5, 8, 7, 10, 9, 14, 15, 13, 23, 24, 23, 21, 25, 27, 30 (20)

AMITYVILLE II: THE POSSESSION

4-16-83 (Embassy 1709) 25, 23, 22, 24, 23, 21, 22 (7)

ANGEL

6-09-84 (HBO TVA 2372) 19, 21, 18, 15, 11, 17, 19, 17, 21, 24, 23, 24, 27, 27, 27, 27 (16)

ANNIE

12-18-82 (RCA/Col. 10008) 27, 14, 14, 14, 8, 6, 7, 5, 5, 6, 7, 8, 8, 10, 10, 12, 13, 15, 17, 16, 20, 20, 23, 25, 25, 28, 28 (27)

APOCALYPSE NOW

4-03-82 (Paramount 2306) 19 (1)

ARMED AND DANGEROUS

3-14-87 (RCA 20724) 24, 18, 20, 15, 11, 10, 8, 6, 10, 14, 18, 14, 20, 27, 27, 27, 27 (17)

ARTHUR

5-08-82   (Warner 72020)   25, 11, 3, 2, 1, 4, 3, 3, 3, 4, 4, 3, 5, 4, 5, 6, 7, 6, 7,
          6, 6, 5, 6, 6, 7, 5, 9, 9, 15, 15, 17, 23, 20, 29, 29, 29, 27, 25, 27,
          29   (40)

ASSASSINATION

7-25-87   (Media M 928)   23, 23, 23, 23, 20, 20, 20, 20, 20   (9)

ATLANTIC CITY

4-03-82   (Paramount 1460)   3, 7, 5, 6, 7, 7, 9, 13, 12, 21, 27, 30, 29, 28, 27,
          29, 29   (17)

AUTHOR AUTHOR

11-20-82   (CBS/Fox 1181)   25, 17, 12, 9, 7, 10, 10, 10, 14, 14, 16, 24, 22, 24,
           27   (15)

AUTOMATIC GOLF

2-14-87   (Video Reel VA 39)   35, 33, 34, 38   (4)

AVENGING ANGEL

7-13-85   (New World 8506)   34, 34, 27, 21, 24, 26, 25, 29, 33   (9)

BABY, SECRET OF THE LOST LEGEND

11-09-85   (Touchstone 269)   27, 21, 18, 15, 14, 14, 18, 22, 22, 22, 26, 25, 36,
           39, 40   (15)

BACHELOR PARTY

3-23-85   (CBS/Fox 1440)   16, 16, 10, 10, 7, 7, 4, 4, 4, 4, 9, 9, 11, 11, 20, 20,
          21, 21, 22, 35, 36   (21)

BACK TO SCHOOL

2-14-87   (HBO/Cannon TVA 2988)   12, 9, 4, 2, 2, 5, 7, 4, 5, 6, 6, 11, 18, 30,
          37, 24, 22, 16, 17, 17, 17, 28, 28, 28, 28, 28, 28, 33, 33, 33, 33,
          33   (32)

BACK TO THE FUTURE

6-07-86   (MCA 80196)   20, 10, 1, 1, 1, 1, 1, 1, 1, 1, 1, 1, 1, 2, 2, 1, 2, 2, 3, 4, 4,
3, 9, 12, 12, 7, 3, 10, 10, 12, 20, 20, 20, 20, 22, 26, 26, 28, 26, 26, 30,
29, 32, 33, 38, 32   (45)

BAD BOYS

9-17-83   (Thorn/EMI 1633)   7, 8, 5, 4, 5, 5, 9, 10, 10, 16, 19, 27, 27, 26   (14)

BARBAROSSA

2-12-83   (CBS/Fox 9048)   29, 23, 21, 20, 27, 30   (6)

THE BEASTMASTER

8-20-83   (MGM/UA 00226)   24, 18, 13, 11, 9, 9, 11, 12, 18, 16, 24   (11)

BERRY GORDY'S THE LAST DRAGON

2-01-86   (CBS/Fox 6294)   29, 20, 17, 16, 16, 21, 29, 33, 31, 33, 36   (11)

BEST DEFENSE

2-09-85   (Paramount 1587)   20, 20, 9, 9, 12, 12, 13, 13, 17, 17, 20, 20, 24,
24   (14)

BEST FRIENDS

6-04-83   (Warner 11265)   7, 2, 2, 4, 4, 6, 6, 6, 7, 8, 8, 12, 13, 12, 12, 19, 19,
28, 27, 27   (20)

THE BEST LITTLE WHOREHOUSE IN TEXAS

12-25-82   (MCA 77014)   15, 15, 15, 10, 5, 4, 3, 4, 4, 6, 6, 6, 8, 7, 9, 10, 12, 12,
12, 12, 11, 13, 17, 26, 26, 29, 30   (27)

THE BEST OF JOHN BELUSHI

12-28-85   (Warner 34078)   23, 23, 23, 17, 15, 13, 12, 22, 24, 24, 27, 36, 37,
38, 39, 39   (16)

THE BEST OF TIMES

7-19-86 (Embassy 1307)   28, 22, 15, 11, 11, 11, 11, 14, 19, 22, 22, 22, 25, 35 (14)

BETTER OFF DEAD

4-12-86 (Key Video 7083)   26, 25, 23, 26, 28, 31, 36   (7)

BEVERLY HILLS COP

11-16-85 (Paramount 1134)   10, 2, 1, 1, 2, 1, 1, 1, 1, 1, 1, 1, 1, 2, 2, 4, 5, 6, 7, 8, 10, 15, 18, 23, 31, 31, 30, 35, 36, 33, 32, 31, 28, 31, 33, 36, 34, 33, 33, 31, 31, 33, 38, 38, 40, (9), 31, 25, 19, 19, 16, 13, 13, 13, 13, 18, 20, 21, 24, 20, 19, 16, 11, 19, 21, 33   (61)

THE BIG CHILL

8-11-84 (RCA/Col. 10021)   21, 10, 4, 1, 1, 1, 1, 1, 1, 1, 2, 2, 5, 5, 6, 6, 7, 7, 16, 16, 21, 21, 21, 23, 23, 22, 22, 24, 24   (28)

BIG TROUBLE IN LITTLE CHINA

2-28-87 (CBS/Fox 1502)   33, 28, 37, (10), 26, 26   (5)

BILL COSBY HIMSELF

5-18-85 (CBS/Fox 1350)   27, 27, 20, 20, 27, 27, 33, 33, 40, 40   (10)

BIRDY

7-27-85 (RCA/Col. 60457)   34, 24, 22, 25, 27, 36, 38, 40, 38, 38   (10)

BLACK MOON RISING

6-21-86 (New World 8503)   35, 29, 21, 13, 11, 14, 14, 12, 13, 12, 15, 19, 21, 23, 23, 31, 40   (17)

THE BLACK STALLION RETURNS

10-22-83 (CBS/Fox 4712)   17, 15, 14, 14, 17, 26, 29, 29   (8)

BLADE RUNNER

3-12-83   (Embassy 1380)   14, 3, 2, 2, 2, 2, 2, 2, 2, 2, 5, 6, 6, 10, 12, 14, 14, 15, 15, 21, 22, 21, 21, 27, 28, 30, 30   (27)

BLAME IT ON RIO

7-28-84   (Vestron 5040)   18, 11, 6, 4, 3, 2, 5, 3, 3, 2, 2, 5, 5, 8, 8, 12, 12, 22, 22, 26, 26   (21)

BLOOD SIMPLE

8-31-85   (MCA 80190)   26, 25, 20, 15, 11, 11, 16, 19, 21, 24, 24, 29, 34, 37, 39   (15)

BLUE THUNDER

11-12-83   (RCA/Col. 10026)   24, 3, 1, 1, 1, 2, 2, 2, 2, 2, 7, 7, 7, 7, 7, 10, 11, 11, 11, 16, 19, 21, 22, 29   (24)

BLUE VELVET

5-09-87   (Lorimar 399)   37, 26, 24, 11, 12, 9, 8, 8, 8, 12, 12, 14, 14, 14, 14, 17, 17, 17, 17, 17   (20)

THE BOAT (DAS BOOT)

2-05-83   (RCA/Col, 10149)   22, 11, 5, 5, 5, 7, 7, 8, 7, 6, 5, 6, 7, 7, 5, 6, 7, 8, 15, 15, 18, 18, 23, 26, 29, 30   (26)

BODY DOUBLE

5-18-85   (RCA/Col. 6-20411)   15, 15, 4, 4, 4, 4, 9, 9, 9, 9, 13, 18, 18, 18, 18, 19, 20, 24, 25, 31, 33, 36   (22)

BODY HEAT

4-10-82   (Warner LD-70005)   17, 7, 3, 3, 6, 4, 5, 6, 6, 8, 10, 9, 13, 15, 17, 16, 15, 24, 28,   (12), 19, 18, 20, 23, 25, 29   (25)

11-15-86   (Warner 20005)   34, 33, 33, 37, 37, 39, 40, 40, 40, 40   (10)

BOLERO

1-12-85   (USA 217-468)   25, 25, 21, 21, 25, 25, 28, 28   (8)

THE BORDER

7-31-82   (MCA 71007)   26, 18, 10, 7, 6, 8, 12, 12, 18, 22, 28, 28, 30   (13)

THE BOSTONIANS

5-04-85   (Vestron 5067)   25, 25   (2)

THE BOUNTY

11-10-84   (Vestron 5044)   18, 18, 14, 14, 9, 9, 19, 19, 19,   (9)

THE BOY WHO COULD FLY

5-30-87   (Lorimar 351)   32, 28, 32, 30, 30, 30, 37, 37, 37, 37, 37, 37   (12)

THE BOYS IN COMPANY C

10-16-82   (Col. 10065)   30, 26, 24   (3)

BRAINSTORM

2-04-84   (MGM/UA 800314)   22, 10, 6, 6, 7, 7, 7, 8, 9, 13, 14, 18, 17, 21, 27, 27, 24, 25, 27   (19)

BRAZIL

8-16-86   (MCA 80171)   17, 15, 14, 17, 17, 17, 17, 19, 29, 39   (10)

BREAKER MORANT

4-03-82   (Col. 8300E)   28   (1)

THE BREAKFAST CLUB

10-05-85   (MCA 80167)   32, 14, 4, 1, 1, 1, 1, 3, 4, 4, 4, 6, 8, 8, 8, 12, 12, 11, 17, 20, 19, 19, 25, 32, 30, 29, 29, 25, 22, 24, 25, 25, 31, 32, 37, 39, 40   (36)

BREAKIN'

11-10-84 (MGM/UA 800440) 20, 20, 16, 16, 11, 11, 18, 18, 18, 20, 20, 19, 19, 17, 17, 30, 30 (17)

BREAKIN' 2—ELECTRIC BOOGALOO

8-03-85 (MGM/UA 800580) 27, 27, 28, 29 (4)

BREATHLESS

12-17-83 (Vestron 5017) 8, 9, 9, 9, 9, 10, 11, 18, 17, 17, 16, 18, 21 (13)

BREWSTER'S MILLIONS

11-30-85 (MCA 80194) 29, 17, 16, 12, 6, 6, 6, 5, 7, 8, 8, 10, 13, 17, 22, 28, 32, 32, 32, 31, 28, 35, 35, 38 (24)

THE BRIDE

4-12-86 (RCA/Col. 60569) 34, 18, 14, 17, 15, 17, 22, 33 (8)

BUTTERFLY

9-04-82 (Vestron V 6007) 29, 27, 25, 20, 18, 16, 17, 17, 20, 22, 28, 30 (12)

THE CAGE

11-22-86 (Paramount 60040-01) 29, 20, 24, 24, 24, 28, 28, 28, 28, 24, 21, 22, 27, 36 (14)

CALIGULA (UNRATED)

5-12-84 (Penthouse 5032) 24, 16, 13, 8, 8, 19, 25, 28, 30 (9)

CALLANETICS

3-07-87 (MCA 80429) 35, 25, 27, 29 (4)

CANNERY ROW

8-21-82 (MGM/UA 00143) 29, 24, 17, 14, 13, 13, 12, 17, 20, 19, 18, 18, 25 (13)

CANNONBALL RUN

4-03-82   (Vestron VA 6001)   13, 19, 28, 28, 29, 30   (6)

CANNONBALL RUN II

11-24-84   (Warner 11377)   25, 25, 19, 19, 16, 16, 16, 21, 21, 26, 26   (11)

THE CARE BEARS MOVIE

8-10-85   (Vestron VA 5082)   25, 20, 23, 25, 27, 26, 32, 34, 36, 37   (10)

CAT PEOPLE

8-28-82   (MCA 77008)   26, 12, 6, 4, 3, 3, 2, 3, 5, 9, 8, 11, 13, 14, 19, 28   (16)

CAT'S EYE

11-23-85   (Key Video 4731)   24, 19, 13, 11, 9, 9, 9, 9, 21, 21, 32, 35   (12)

CHARIOTS OF FIRE

8-28-82   (Warner 70004)   20, 4, 2, 1, 1, 1, 1, 1, 1, 1, 5, 5, 7, 9, 14, 18, 24, 30, 30, 30   (20)

CHILDREN OF A LESSER GOD

6-13-87   (Paramount 1839)   19, 6, 6, 6, 1, 1, 1, 1, 1, 1, 7, 7, 7, 7, 7   (15)

CHILDREN OF THE CORN

7-21-84   (Embassy 4039)   16, 12, 7, 3, 3, 9, 9, 12, 16, 16, 19, 19, 24, 24, 30, 30   (16)

CHOOSE ME

6-29-85   (Media M 787)   30, 30, 29, 29, 36, 39, 40, 40, 40   (9)

A CHORUS LINE

5-24-86   (Embassy 2183)   33, 35, 31, 19, 12, 14, 15, 17, 21, 25, 26, 25, 28, 35, 40   (15)

3-14-87 (Embassy 2183) 26, 24, 31 (3)

CHRISTINE

6-16-84 (RCA/Col. 10141) 16, 12, 3, 4, 4, 6, 6, 9, 9, 11, 13, 14, 17, 21, 21, 25, 25, 29, 29 (19)

CITY HEAT

6-01-85 (Warner 11433) 21, 21, 10, 10, 6, 6, 6, 6, 9, 12, 16, 17, 17, 17, 17, 23, 23, 28, 29, 32, 36, 37, 40 (23)

CLAN OF THE CAVE BEAR

10-11-86 (CBS/Fox 6795) 24, 23, 27, 38, 38 (5)

CLASH OF THE TITANS

4-03-82 (MGM/UA 700074) 8, 10, 10, 10, 9, 8, 10, 11, 11, 11, 13, 12, 17, 22, 22, 21, 22, 24, 22, 29, 28 (21)

CLASS

2-18-84 (Vestron 5026) 18, 14, 12, 14, 12, 11, 13, 15, 19, 19, 21 (11)

CLASS OF '84

7-16-83 (Vestron 5022) 23, 23 (2)

CLOAK AND DAGGER

2-09-85 (MCA 80124) 18, 18, 7, 7, 6, 6, 9, 9, 15, 15, 24, 24 (12)

CLUB PARADISE

2-28-87 (Warner 11600) 29, 26, 38, 38, 37, 28, 22, 28, 31, (4), 37, 35, 40 (12)

CLUE

9-13-86 (Paramount 1840) 18, 8, 8, 8, 23, 34, 34, 23, 17, 16, 27, 39, 39, 39 (14)

COBRA

12-20-86 (Warner 11594) 35, 26, 26, 26, 26, 19, 13, 10, 8, 5, 5, 3, 13, 14, 16, 25, 36, 40 (18)

THE COCA-COLA KID

3-15-86 (Vestron 5099) 20, 19, 20, 19, 19, 21 (6)

COCOON

5-17-86 (CBS/Fox 1476) 19, 12, 4, 2, 2, 2, 2, 3, 3, 3, 3, 2, 3, 6, 7, 8, 8, 14, 16, 16, 15, 13, 32, 33 (24)

CODE OF SILENCE

12-14-85 (Thorn/EMI/HBO TVA 2985) 29, 21, 13, 13, 13, 7, 9, 9, 9, 12, 17, 20, 19, 19, 26, 28, 30, 35, 38 (19)

THE COLOR OF MONEY

6-13-87 (Touchstone 513) 8, 3, 3, 3, 3, 3, 9, 9, 9, 9, 6, 6, 6, 6, 6 (15)

THE COLOR PURPLE

8-22-87 (Warner) 1, 1, 1, 1, 1 (5)

COMMANDO

4-12-86 (CBS/Fox 1484) 32, 19, 8, 4, 1, 2, 2, 3, 4, 5, 5, 8, 9, 10, 10, 13, 13, 16, 15, 14, 21, 23, 24, 29, 29, 35 (26)

THE COMPANY OF WOLVES

11-09-85 (Vestron 5092) 25, 17, 16, 16, 25, 28, 28, 31, 31, 31, 36 (11)

THE COMPLEAT BEATLES

11-06-82 (MGM/UA 00166) 26, 18, 11, 10, 10, 11, 10, 18, 18, 18, 18, 23, 21, 28, 27, 26, 30 (17)

COMPROMISING POSITIONS

4-26-86 (Paramount 1829) 30, 27, 19, 18, 22, 28, 36, 37 (8)

CONAN THE BARBARIAN

9-25-82   (MCA 77010)   25, 13, 4, 2, 2, 2, 1, 1, 1, 1, 3, 3, 8, 13, 13, 13, 17, 17,
19, 25, 24, 28   (22)

CONAN THE DESTROYER

12-08-84   (MCA 80079)   24, 24, 17, 17, 17, 9, 9, 8, 8, 10, 10, 14, 14, 28,
28   (15)

CONTINENTAL DIVIDE

4-03-82   (MCA 71001)   2, 8, 13, 16, 15, 20, 22, 23, 28, 27, 30, 29   (12)

COSBY, BILL (See: BILL COSBY HIMSELF)

THE COTTON CLUB

5-18-85   (Embassy 1714)   17, 17, 3, 3, 3, 3, 5, 5, 5, 5, 10, 19, 19, 24, 24, 27,
28, 32, 35, 36, 39, 40, 39, 39, 38, 40   (26)

COUNTRY

4-20-85   (Touchstone 241)   22, 22, 13, 13, 7, 7, 6, 6, 5, 5, 13, 13, 22, 22, 28,
26, 30, 30, 33, 39, 39, 36, 36, 37   (24)

CREATOR

3-08-86   (Thorn/EMI/HBO TVA 2999)   23, 22, 18, 22, 20, 17, 18, 32,
37   (9)

CREEP SHOW

4-02-83   (Warner 11306)   25, 16, 11, 7, 4, 4, 4, 4, 5, 5, 14, 13, 16, 16, 22, 22,
22, 23, 22, 25   (20)

CRIMES OF PASSION

3-23-85   (New World 8418)   24, 24, 14, 14, 16, 16, 15, 15, 23, 23   (10)

CRIMES OF THE HEART

8-22-87   (Lorimar 421)   8, 8, 8, 8, 8   (5)

CRITTERS

10-25-86 (RCA 62666) —, 24, 25, 24, 23, 19, 27, 27, 34, 36, 36, 36, 36, 39, 39, 40 (16)

CROSSROADS

10-25-86 (RCA 60665) 35, 22, 10, 6, 10, 14, 15, 15, 22, 24, 24, 24, 24, 28, 31, 32, 40 (17)

CUJO

1-28-84 (Warner 11331) 24, 11, 9, 9, 9, 8, 9, 10, 9, 11, 12, 13, 20, 23, 28, 28 (16)

CUTTER'S WAY

10-23-82 (MGM/UA 700164) 28, 26, 23, 22, 28 (5)

D.A.R.Y.L.

2-01-86 (Paramount 1810) 27, 16, 14, 12, 11, 13, 21, 29, 30, 31, 29, 37 (12)

D.C. CAB

5-05-84 (MCA 80061) 19, 14, 10, 5, 10, 11, 15, 19, 30, 30, 27, 29 (12)

THE DARK CRYSTAL

12-03-83 (Thorn/EMI 1966) 11, 11, 9, 10, 10, 10, 14, 14, 14, 14, 15, 16, 20, 22, 29 (15)

DAWN OF THE DEAD

1-21-84 (Thorn/EMI 1977) 22, 17, 16, 19, 28 (5)

DAY OF THE DEAD

6-21-86 (Media M 839) 19, 22, 20, 27, 38, 37, 39, 40 (8)

DEAD MEN DON'T WEAR PLAID

11-06-82 (MCA 77011) 20, 14, 12, 11, 7, 13, 17, 27, 27, 27, 29 (11)

DEAD ZONE

4-21-84 (Paramount 1646)   16, 7, 5, 3, 2, 2, 4, 3, 6, 9, 12, 13, 18, 20, 22, 22, 25, 27, 28   (19)

DEADLY FRIEND

5-30-87 (Warner 11601)   30, 31, 35, 40, 40, 40   (6)

DEAL OF THE CENTURY

3-17-84 (Warner 11339)   20, 14, 16, 14, 6, 13, 15, 15, 22, 24   (10)

DEATH WISH 3

5-31-86 (MGM/UA 800821)   29, 26, 14, 8, 7, 6, 9, 9, 10, 11, 15, 19, 23, 30, 37, 40, 40   (18)

DEATH WISH II

10-09-82 (Warner 26032)   25, 19, 15, 7, 3, 3, 3, 8, 11, 12, 14, 23, 23, 23, 23, 28   (16)

DEATHTRAP

10-09-82 (Warner 11256)   23, 16, 12, 10, 4, 4, 4, 4, 5, 5, 12, 20, 20, 20, 25, 29   (16)

DEF-CON 4

1-18-86 (New World 8424)   30, 30, 26, 26, 27, 27, 32   (7)

DELTA FORCE

8-23-86 (Media M 841)   21, 13, 9, 8, 13, 13, 14, 10, 22, 32, 40   (11)

DESPERATELY SEEKING SUSAN

9-14-85 (Thorn/EMI/HBO TVA 2991)   17, 6, 1, 1, 2, 2, 5, 5, 4, 7, 8, 9, 9, 13, 20, 21, 21, 21, 25, 28, 28, 31, 34, 39, 39, 40   (26)

DIAMONDS ARE FOREVER

8-28-82 (20th Century-Fox 4605)   25, 20, 19, 19, 16, 16, 19, 22, 21, 21, 25   (11)

DINER

12-04-82   (MGM/UA 00164)   26, 16, 9, 7, 7, 7, 11, 11, 12, 12, 13, 16, 20, 21, 21, 24, 22, 21, 21, 21, 25, 25, 25, 28, 28, 28   (26)

DIVA

2-19-83   (MGM/UA 00183)   21, 16, 14, 17, 17, 23, 23, 28   (8)

DOCTOR DETROIT

10-01-83   (MCA 8001)   23, 9, 7, 6, 5, 5, 4, 10, 11, 10, 10, 11, 16, 26, 26, 26, 30   (17)

DOCTOR NO

4-03-82   (20th Century-Fox 4525)   23   (1)

DOWN AND OUT IN BEVERLY HILLS

10-18-86   (Touchstone 473V)   25, 19, 4, 2, 2, 3, 6, 5, 5, 3, 5, 5, 5, 5, 6, 7, 4, 4, 3, 3, 7, 14, 9, 11, 21, 33   (26)

DRAGONSLAYER

6-12-82   (Paramount 1367)   17, 6, 5, 4, 5, 7, 7, 7, 8, 11, 10, 13, 13, 17, 21, 24, 21, 21, 23, 25, 29, 29   (22)

DREAMSCAPE

1-12-85   (Thorn/EMI 2722)   18, 18, 7, 7, 6, 6, 4, 4, 9, 9, 21, 21, 23, 23   (14)

THE DRESSER

9-29-84   (RCA/Col. 10184)   27, 27, 18, 18, 12, 12, 19, 19, 29, 29   (10)

DUMBO

4-03-82   (Disney 24)   25, 27   (2)

DUNE

6-01-85   (MCA 80161)   24, 24, 6, 6, 3, 3, 4, 4, 12, 17, 21, 23, 22, 22, 22, 27, 27, 32, 34, 35, 38, 38, 39   (23)

EASY MONEY

3-17-84   (Vestron 5029)   18, 12, 10, 11, 12, 8, 9, 10, 13, 18, 21, 22, 29, 30   (14)

EATING RAOUL

10-29-83   (CBS/Fox 1291)   25, 23, 19, 18, 20, 23, 23   (7)

EDDIE AND THE CRUISERS

2-11-84   (Embassy 2066)   18, 14, 13, 16, 15, 15, 18, 23, 24, 25, 30   (11)

EDDIE MURPHY DELIRIOUS

12-03-83   (Paramount 2323)   21, 21, 17, 14, 17, 17, 17, 17, 18, 20, 23, 21, 25, 25, 25, 27, 27, 26, 29   (19)

EDUCATING RITA

7-14-84   (RCA/Col. 10189)   22, 12, 7, 4, 7, 5, 5, 6, 6, 7, 7, 11, 11, 17, 17, 22, 22   (17)

8 MILLION WAYS TO DIE

11-08-86   (CBS/Fox 6118)   34, 30, 28, 26, 21, 21, 29, 31, 31, 31, 31, 33, 36, 39, 33, 37   (16)

ELECTRIC DREAMS

2-23-85   (MGM/UA 800487)   25, 25, 18, 18, 28, 28   (6)

ELENI

6-14-86   (Embassy 7609)   34, 31, 30, 34, 35   (5)

THE EMERALD FOREST

11-30-85   (Embassy 2179)   32, 16, 9, 3, 4, 4, 4, 4, 5, 5, 6, 8, 10, 12, 14, 17, 23, 25, 27, 28, 27, 34, 34, 35   (24)

THE EMPIRE STRIKES BACK

12-08-84   (CBS/Fox 1425)   20, 20, 2, 2, 2, 1, 1, 1, 1, 3, 3, 11, 11, 19, 19, 15, 15, 20, 20, 26, 26, 29, 29   (23)

ENEMY MINE

8-30-86   (CBS/Fox 1492)   18, 11, 10, 9, 9, 11, 9, 20, 18, 32, 37   (11)

THE ENTITY

10-22-83   (CBS/Fox 1234)   19, 11, 11, 16, 19, 21, 22, 22, 22   (9)

ESCAPE FROM NEW YORK

11-20-82   (Embassy 1601)   21, 13, 9, 6, 6, 8, 8, 8, 15, 20, 28, 30   (12)

EVIL THAT MEN DO

2-23-85   (RCA/Col. 620407)   17, 17, 10, 10, 7, 7, 11, 11, 18, 18, 22, 22   (12)

EXCALIBUR

4-10-82   (Warner 72018)   13, 8, 8, 11, 13, 13, 12, 17, 17, 19, 19, 19, 26, 29, 28   (15)

EXPLORERS

2-01-86   (Paramount 1676)   22, 11, 11, 18, 27, 29, 33, 35, 35, 37   (11)

EXTERMINATOR 2

4-06-85   (MGM/Col. 20404)   24, 24, 19, 19, 26, 26   (6)

EXTREMITIES

2-21-87   (Atl./Paramount 12511)   28, 22, 34, 36, 33, 39, 34, 26, 32, 33, (4), 33, 37, 39   (13)

EYE OF THE NEEDLE

4-03-82   (20th Century-Fox 4581)   16, 15, 21, 19, 17, 17, 21, 25, 25, 24, 28, 27   (12)

EYEWITNESS

4-03-82   (20th Century-Fox 1116)   30   (1)

F/X

10-11-86 (EMI/HBO 3769) 29, 15, 12, 14, 5, 5, 8, 13, 11, 11, 8, 11, 11, 11, 11, 14, 17, 20, 20, 19, 15, 19, 16, 21, 24 (22)

FALCON AND THE SNOWMAN

8-03-85 (Vestron VA 5073) 16, 8, 6, 3, 1, 4, 3, 4, 6, 8, 8, 16, 18, 23, 29, 35, 35, 38, 37, 40, 40, 40, 40, 40, 40, 40 (26)

FALLING IN LOVE

6-15-85 (Paramount 1628) 18, 18, 18, 18, 21, 23, 28, 29, 26, 23, 26, 30 (12)

FANNY AND ALEXANDER

5-19-84 (Embassy 2067) 26, 28, 24, 21, 28 (5)

FAST TIMES AT RIDGEMONT HIGH

1-29-83 (MCA 77015) 26, 13, 10, 9, 8, 7, 9, 9, 9, 8, 8, 7, 9, 9, 9, 10, 11, 15, 16, 27, 26, 27, 29 (23)

FERRIS BUELLER'S DAY OFF

5-09-87 (Paramount 1890) 32, 22, 17, 3, 2, 2, 1, 1, 1, 2, 2, 7, 7, 7, 7, 11, 11, 11, 11, 11 (20)

52 PICK-UP

4-11-87 (Cannon M 892) 27, 22, 18, 16, 11, 16, 15, 34, 38, 34, 32, 32, 32, 38, 38, 38, 38, 38, 38 (19)

FINAL COUNTDOWN

8-20-83 (Vestron 4047) 28, 20, 19, 18, 21, 20, 18, 25, 21, 29, 27 (11)

A FINE MESS

3-14-87 (RCA 60723) 18, 34, 3, 9, 9, 7, 12, 7, 9, 11, 36, 32, 38 (14)

FIRE STARTER

11-10-84   (MCA 80075)   15, 15, 10, 10, 6, 6, 7, 7, 7, 11, 11, 17, 17, 28, 28   (15)

FIREFOX

11-27-82   (Warner 11219)   28, 22, 4, 3, 3, 3, 3, 3, 7, 6, 8, 7, 10, 11, 10, 10, 12, 11, 10, 12, 14, 14, 13, 19, 21, 27   (26)

FIREWALKER

5-02-87   (Cannon/Media M 895)   28, 28, 28, 21, 21, 21, 21, 21, 21, 31, 31, 31, 31, 31   (14)

FIRST BLOOD

5-14-83   (Thorn/EMI 1573)   26, 2, 1, 1, 1, 1, 1, 1, 1, 2, 3, 5, 5, 6, 5, 6, 5, 5, 5, 8, 7, 8, 11, 10, 15, 21, 22, 26   (27)

8-17-85   (Thorn/EMI 1573)   37, 36, 32, 37   (4)

FIRST BORN

5-18-85   (Paramount 1744)   25, 25, 17, 17, 15, 15, 22, 22, 37, 37   (10)

FIRST MONDAY IN OCTOBER

4-03-82   (Paramount 1408)   24, 24   (2)

THE FLAMINGO KID

7-27-85   (Vestron VA 5072)   15, 7, 4, 3, 5, 7, 9, 9, 8, 9, 12, 13, 18, 20, 21, 22, 28, 30, 36, 38   (20)

FLASHDANCE

9-24-83   (Paramount 1454)   21, 1, 1, 1, 1, 1, 1, 1, 1, 2, 2, 2, 3, 3, 8, 8, 8, 8, 8, 8, 8, 8, 8, 10, 13, 17, 21, 20, 19, 20, 23, 28   (32)

FLASHPOINT

4-06-85   (Thorn/EMI 2880)   19, 19, 10, 10, 12, 12, 21, 21, 28, 28   (10)

FLETCH

1-18-86 (MCA 80190) 13, 8, 6, 5, 7, 7, 10, 11, 16, 27, 24, 22, 23, 35, 39, 40, 40 (17)

FLIGHT OF THE NAVIGATOR

4-04-87 (Walt Disney 499) 23, 17, 21, 27, 32, 36, 27, 31, 18, 16, 29, 29, 29, 29, 36, 36, 36, 36, 36, 36 (20)

THE FLY

6-02-87 (CBS/Fox 1503) 24, 21, 6, 8, 12, 11, 7, 10, 10, 10, 17, 17, 19, 19, 19, 19, 29, 29, 29, 29, 29 (21)

FONDA, JANE (See: JANE . . .)

FOOTLOOSE

9-29-84 (Paramount 1589) 9, 9, 4, 4, 3, 3, 3, 3, 8, 8, 21, 21, 24, 24, 24, 22, 22, 23, 23, 26, 26 (21)

FOR YOUR EYES ONLY

4-03-82 (20th Century-Fox 1128) 11, 4, 2, 2, 5, 4, 3, 8, 8, 12, 10, 13, 16, 16, 19, 20, 18, 23, 21, 19, 19, 21, 26, 29 (24)

FORCE TEN FROM NAVARONE

5-14-83 (Warner 26034) 29, 29, 29 (3)

FORT APACHE, THE BRONX

4-03-82 (Vestron 6000) 1, 2, 14, 18, 16, 16, 18, 18, 20, 20, 26, 24, 28, 29 (14)

48 HOURS

7-02-83 (Paramount 1139) 25, 1, 1, 1, 1, 1, 1, 1, 1, 2, 2, 2, 2, 3, 3, 3, 3, 3, 3, 3, 4, 4, 4, 4, 6, 11, 13, 13, 13, 11, 12, 17, 21, 20, 21, 23, 23, 21, 22, 24, 23, 27 (42)

FOUR SEASONS

4-10-82   (Universal City Studios 77003)   28, 29, 30   (3)

FRANCES

6-25-83   (Thorn/EMI 1621)   15, 8, 10, 10, 15, 13, 11, 11, 10, 10, 9, 13, 14, 14, 16, 19, 26   (17)

FRATERNITY VACATION

11-23-85   (New World 8509)   37, 33, 32, 34, 34   (5)

THE FRENCH LIEUTENANT'S WOMAN

4-17-82   (20th Century-Fox 4868)   19, 9, 1, 1, 1, 1, 3, 4, 6, 5, 7, 11, 11, 16, 20, 17, 26, 25, 27, 30   (20)

FRIDAY THE 13TH, PART V—A NEW BEGINNING

10-19-85   (Paramount 1823)   13, 9, 8, 6, 8, 11, 12, 20, 26, 27, 36, 36, 36, 39   (14)

FRIDAY THE 13TH, PART III

2-26-83   (Paramount 1539)   26, 22, 20, 20, 21, 20, 23, 28, 28, 28, 28   (11)

FRIDAY THE 13TH, THE FINAL CHAPTER

11-10-84   (Paramount 1756)   21, 21, 17, 17, 13, 13, 23, 23, 23   (9)

FRIGHT NIGHT

4-26-86   (RCA/Col. 20562)   10, 7, 8, 10, 10, 11, 10, 12, 15, 18, 22, 21, 27, 30, 34, 34, 35, 38   (18)

FROM BEYOND

5-30-87   (Empire/Vestron 5182)   19, 17, 21, 24, 24, 24, 34, 34, 33, 33, 33, 33, 38, 38, 38, 38, 38   (17)

FROM RUSSIA WITH LOVE

4-24-82   (20th Century-Fox 4566)   27, 27, 26, 28   (4)

FUN HOUSE

4-03-82   (MCA 55051)   27   (1)

GALLIPOLI

5-01-82   (Paramount 1504)   30, 28, 27, 24, 24   (5)

GANDHI

10-22-83   (RCA/Col. 10237)   26, 2, 2, 2, 2, 3, 3, 3, 4, 5, 6, 6, 6, 9, 9, 9, 11, 12, 15, 17, 18, 19, 30, 29   (24)

GHOST STORY

5-29-82   (MCA 77006)   27, 22, 16, 14, 10, 8, 8, 10, 13, 12, 12, 16, 24, 29   (14)

GHOSTBUSTERS

11-09-85   (RCA/Col. 60413)   12, 3, 1, 2, 2, 1, 2, 3, 3, 3, 2, 3, 4, 4, 4, 8, 9, 12, 14, 20, 21, 24, 22, 33, 36, 38, 37   (27)

11-22-86   (RCA/Col. 60413)   34, 27, 26, 26, 32, 35, 35, 35, 35, 37, 37, 37   (12)

GHOULIES

6-29-85   (Vestron VA 5081)   23, 23, 10, 10, 14, 10, 15, 19, 19, 21, 21, 25, 29, 33, 38, 38, 40, 40   (18)

GIVE MY REGARDS TO BROAD STREET

5-04-85   (CBS/Fox 1448)   27, 27, 29, 29   (4)

THE GODS MUST BE CRAZY

3-07-87   (Playhouse 1450)   33, 22, 29, 32, 27, 23, 29, 32   (8)

GODZILLA 1985

2-01-86   (New World 8522)   34, 33, 32, 32, 31, 30   (6)

THE GOLDEN CHILD

8-22-87   (Paramount)   2, 2, 2, 2, 2   (5)

GOLDFINGER

7-24-82   (20th Century-Fox 4595)   30, 20, 13, 8, 13, 15, 21, 23, 23, 26, 29   (11)

GONE WITH THE WIND

3-23-85   (MGM/UA MB 900284)   20, 20, 12, 12, 6, 6, 6, 6, 11, 11, 25, 25   (12)

8-31-85   (MGM/UA MB 900284)   35, 34, 33, 39, 39, 40   (6)

2-14-87   (MGM/UA MB 900284)   26, 25, 30, 23, 31   (5)

THE GOOD, THE BAD AND THE UGLY

3-21-87   (CBS/Fox 4545)   37, 26, 29, 39, 39, 40, 40   (7)

THE GOONIES

4-19-86   (Warner 11474)   20, 9, 5, 5, 6, 6, 8, 8, 11, 14, 17, 19, 20, 23, 24, 31, 33, 38, 40   (19)

GORKY PARK

5-26-84   (Vestron 5053)   15, 11, 6, 3, 4, 5, 6, 5, 8, 9, 13, 14, 17, 16, 15, 21, 22, 22, 26, 26   (20)

GOTCHA!

11-02-85   (MCA 80188)   29, 26, 22, 13, 11, 18, 19, 15, 18, 18, 18, 24, 23, 31, 34, 36   (16)

GREASE 2

11-27-82   (Paramount 1193)   26, 20, 20, 22   (4)

THE GREAT ESCAPE

4-03-82   (20th Century-Fox 4558)   29   (1)

GREMLINS

12-14-85 (Warner 11388) 23, 10, 2, 2, 2, 3, 2, 2, 3, 3, 6, 7, 9, 12, 16, 17, 18, 21, 31, 37, 36, 39, 38, 39 (24)

GREY FOX

12-31-83 (Media 258) 24, 24, 22, 21, 21, 21, 24, 23, 28, 28, 26, 24, 29, 28, 28 (15)

GREYSTOKE: THE LEGEND OF TARZAN, THE LORD OF THE APES

10-27-84 (Warner 11375) 14, 14, 9, 9, 5, 5, 4, 4, 6, 6, 6, 6, 6, 11, 11, 15, 15, 24, 24, 25, 25, 30, 30 (23)

GUNG HO

10-11-86 (Paramount 1751) 19, 6, 5, 2, 4, 4, 4, 12, 13, 13, 13, 14, 14, 14, 14, 20, 23, 23, 34, 40 (20)

HALLOWEEN III: SEASON OF THE WITCH

4-16-83 (MCA 71011) 27, 21, 20, 22, 22 (5)

HALLOWEEN II

5-01-82 (MCA 77005) 18, 9, 6, 6, 7, 7, 9, 16, 22, 21, 25, 26, 28, 29 (14)

HANNAH AND HER SISTERS

7-11-87 (HBO/Cannon 3897) 24, 24, 4, 4, 4, 4, 4, 4, 4, 4, 4 (11)

HARD TO HOLD

9-01-84 (MCA 80073) 21, 19, 20, 20, 28, 28 (6)

HARRY AND SON

8-25-84 (Vestron 5037) 23, 16, 14, 13, 13, 21, 21, 13, 19, 19, 27, 27 (13)

HAUNTED HONEYMOON

5-30-87 (HBO/Cannon TVA 3911) 29, 29, 33, 36, 36, 36 (6)

HEARTBREAK

3-21-87 (Paramount 1688)   25, 10, 9, 10, 12, 11, 13, 12, 17, 28   (10)

HEARTBREAK RIDGE

6-13-87 (Warner 11701)   26, 22, 22, 22, 6, 6, 6, 6, 6, 6, 10, 10, 10, 10, 10   (15)

HEAVEN HELP US

.6-15-85 (Thorn/EMI TVA 2986)   24, 24, 29, 29, 27, 27, 30, 36   (8)

HEAVENLY BODIES

11-02-85 (Key 6844)   34, 33, 32, 33   (4)

THE HEAVENLY KID

1-25-86 (Thorn/EMI/HBO TVA 3261)   22, 15, 23, 23, 30, 29, 28, 37, 38, 37, 38, 40   (12)

HELP

3-14-87 (MPI 342)   28, 20, 27, 37, 38, 31, 30, 29, 31, 25, 23   (11)

HER MAJESTY'S SECRET SERVICE

1-28-84 (CBS/Fox 4604)   26, 25, 28   (3)

HIGH ROAD TO CHINA

7-02-83 (Warner 11309)   21, 5, 5, 3, 3, 3, 3, 3, 4, 4, 4, 4, 4, 7, 7, 9, 14, 16, 18, 18, 30, 30   (22)

THE HINDENBERG

9-25-82 (MCA 55056)   28, 24, 24, 23, 22   (5)

HISTORY OF THE WORLD, PART I

4-10-82 (20th Century-Fox 1114)   30   (1)

THE HITCHER

8-23-86 (Thorn/EMI/HBO TVA 3756)   24, 20, 15, 12, 10, 10, 9, 8, 11, 15, 29, 29, 36, 40, 38   (15)

HONKY TONK MAN

4-09-83 (Warner 11305)   26, 22, 18, 17, 17, 17, 16, 20, 28   (9)

HOTEL NEW HAMPSHIRE

9-08-84 (Vestron 5042)   20, 17, 17, 16, 16, 21, 21, 23, 23   (9)

HOUSE

8-30-86 (New World 8525)   34, 16, 9, 6, 6, 6, 7, 10, 13, 16, 22, 38   (12)

HOWARD THE DUCK

2-14-87 (MCA 80511)   14, 12, 11, 6, 9, 15, 17, 16, 24, 38, 39   (11)

THE HOWLING

4-03-82 (20th Century-Fox 4075)   10, 3, 4, 7, 10, 11, 12, 17, 21, 25, 29   (11)

HOWLING II

6-07-86 (Thorn/EMI/HBO TVA 3004)   25, 23, 25, 32, 37, 40   (6)

THE HUNGER

12-17-84 (MGM/UA 800281)   23, 21, 16, 16, 19, 15, 15, 13, 14   (9)

I, THE JURY

7-09-83 (CBS/Fox 1186)   28, 20, 20, 21, 26   (5)

ICE MAN

9-29-84 (MCA 80074)   15, 15, 11, 11, 6, 6, 7, 7, 6, 6, 7, 7, 14, 14, 14, 19, 19, 30, 30   (19)

ICE PIRATES

10-27-84   (MGM 800427)   21, 21, 16, 16, 11, 11, 12, 12, 22, 22, 22, 28,
           28   (13)

IDOLMAKER

6-23-84   (MGM 600370)   27, 22, 24, 20   (4)

INDIANA JONES AND THE TEMPLE OF DOOM

11-15-86   (Paramount 1643)   35, 13, 1, 1, 1, 1, 1, 1, 1, 1, 1, 1, 1, 2, 1, 2, 4, 12,
           6, 8, 11, 14, 13, 19, 25, 19, 13, 9   (28)

INTO THE NIGHT

8-03-85   (MCA 80170)   25, 20, 16, 15, 13, 11, 10, 10, 13, 15, 20, 21, 28, 28,
           34, 39   (16)

INVASION U.S.A.

5-03-86   (MGM/UA MB 800764)   28, 23, 12, 8, 6, 5, 4, 4, 9, 12, 12, 15, 19,
           23, 26, 29, 34, 39, 40   (19)

IRON EAGLE

8-30-86   (CBS/Fox 6160)   12, 10, 6, 4, 4, 1, 1, 2, 4, 8, 11, 21, 37, 34, 34, 34,
           36, 37, 37, 37, 37, 40, 40   (23)

IRRECONCILABLE DIFFERENCES

4-20-85   (Vestron VA 5057)   13, 13, 9, 9, 5, 5, 2, 2, 13, 13, 14, 14, 23, 23, 26,
           30, 39, 39, 39   (19)

JACKSON, MICHAEL (See: MICHAEL . . .)

JAGGED EDGE

6-21-86   (RCA/Col. 60591)   23, 13, 8, 6, 4, 5, 4, 2, 2, 3, 5, 6, 7, 12, 12, 12, 15,
           16, 14, 11, 16, 32, 39, 37, 38, 38, 40   (27)

JANE FONDA'S LOW IMPACT WORKOUT

11-08-86   (KVC-RCA Video Production/Karl Lorimar 070)   31, 23, 11, 10, 8,
           8, 5, 3, 3, 3, 3, 2, 2, 2, 1, 2, 1, 1, 3, 4, 6, 7, 6, 3, 3, 2, 2, 3, 3   (29)

JANE FONDA'S NEW WORKOUT

10-18-86 (KVC-RCA Video Productions/Karl Lorimar 069) 30, 26, 37, 24, 18, 12, 11, 9, 9, 7, 4, 4, 4, 4, 4, 4, 5, 5, 7, 9, 10, 7, 7, 9, 13, 16, 16, 12, 8, 5, 4, 4 (32)

JANE FONDA'S PRIME TIME WORKOUT

10-11-86 (KVC-RCA Video Productions/Karl Lorimar 058) 34, 31, 30 (3)

JANE FONDA'S WORKOUT

7-03-82 (KVC-RCA Video Productions/Karl Lorimar 042) 20, 16, 12, 12, 18, 25, 20, 17, 16, 15, 15, 14, 9, 8, 9, 9, 8, 13, 13, 12, 14, 18, 21, 24, 23, 25, 25, 25, 21, 18, 17, 16, 16, 15, 14, 16, 19, 18, 17, 16, 15, 16, 19, 23, 23, 27, 24, 21, 21, 23, 22, 23, 27, 26, 25, 26, 27, 28, 28, 26, 21, 20, 21, 26, 25, 24, 24, 25, 25, 23, 26, 29, 25, 28, 28, 28, 30, 29, 30, 30, 27, 27, 29, 26, 27, 25, 23, 24, 24, 22, 25, 27, 30, 29, 28, 27, 27, 25, 28, 25, 27, 28 (102)

JAWS 3

12-24-83 (MCA 80044) 22, 15, 15, 12, 12, 10, 10, 13, 13, 17, 19, 20, 29 (13)

THE JEWEL OF THE NILE

7-19-86 (CBS/Fox 1491) 17, 9, 3, 6, 3, 2, 1, 1, 4, 3, 3, 5, 5, 8, 8, 13, 20, 20, 36, 36 (20)

JO JO DANCER: YOUR LIFE IS CALLING

12-20-86 (RCA/Col. 21878) 33, 25, 25, 25, 25, 29, 29, 27 (8)

JOHNNY DANGEROUSLY

7-27-85 (CBS/Fox 1456) 19, 11, 9, 9, 11, 10, 12, 13, 18, 22, 26, 28 (12)

JOLSON STORY

10-18-86 (RCA/Col. 60686) 28, 24, 19, 21, 33, 38 (6)

THE JOURNEY OF NATTY GANN

   5-17-86   (Walt Disney 400)   32, 26, 23, 21, 18, 18, 23, 29, 31, 30, 31, 36,
             39   (13)

JUMPIN' JACK FLASH

   7-11-87   (CBS/Fox 1508)   23, 22, 13, 13, 13, 13, 12, 12, 12, 12, 12   (11)

JUST ONE OF THE GUYS

   12-28-85   (RCA/Col. 20493)   28, 28, 28, 20, 18, 17, 21, 21, 22, 25, 31, 31, 34,
              36, 34, 33   (16)

THE KARATE KID

   6-01-85   (RCA/Col. 60406)   15, 15, 1, 1, 1, 1, 1, 1, 1, 2, 1, 1, 2, 2, 1, 1, 1, 3,
             3, 4, 6, 8, 9, 13, 14, 14, 17, 21, 18, 22, 24, 24, 24, 27, 31, 30, 32, 35,
             38, 37, 37   (41)

THE KARATE KID II

   2-28-87   (RCA/Col. 6-2071719)   25, 20, 17, 35, 35, 20, 20, 14, 15, 18, 14, 19,
             29, 15, 18, 22, 26, 26, 26, 40, 40, 40, 40, 40, 40   (25)

KATHY SMITH'S BODY BASICS

   11-01-86   (JCI 8111)   34, 33, 27, 26, 22, 18, 18, 15, 10, 10, 10, 10, 13, 12, 12,
              18, 15, 16, 29, (7), 28, 22, 34, 35, 39   (24)

KELLY'S HEROES

   9-03-83   (MGM/UA 700168)   29   (1)

THE KILLING FIELDS

   9-14-85   (Warner 11419)   28, 14, 15, 6, 1, 1, 2, 3, 3, 4, 7, 8, 8, 8, 11, 15, 15,
             15, 22, 20, 21, 27, 30, 35, 35, 39, 39   (27)

KING DAVID

   9-14-85   (Paramount 1284)   31, 26, 21, 20, 26, 29, 33   (7)

THE KING OF COMEDY

10-01-83   (RCA/Col. 191200)   20, 16, 17, 12, 12, 25   (6)

KING SOLOMON'S MINES

6-28-86   (MGM/UA 800876)   35, 32, 25, 19, 18, 17, 17, 16, 18, 27, 27, 31, 37, 37, 38   (15)

KISS ME GOODBYE

7-02-83   (CBS/Fox 1217)   24, 18, 11, 12, 12, 13, 13, 17, 17, 18, 24, 22   (13)

KISS OF THE SPIDER WOMAN

4-19-86   (Charter 90001)   29, 12, 9, 6, 5, 4, 2, 3, 3, 9, 10, 11, 11, 12, 15, 18, 14, 18, 22, 24, 30, 34, 39, 39, 40   (25)

KRULL

3-17-84   (RCA/Col. 10364)   23, 24, 18, 17, 18, 15, 20, 22, 21, 30, 26, 30   (12)

KRUSH GROOVE

5-24-86   (Warner 11529)   30, 26, 23, 21, 27, 39   (6)

LABYRINTH

2-28-87   (Tri Star/Embassy 8553)   27, 24, 21, 16, 18, 10, 13, 15, 13, 17, 23, 33   (12)

LADY CHATTERLY'S LOVER

3-19-83   (MGM/UA 00184)   29, 28   (2)

LADYHAWKE

11-16-85   (Warner 11464)   16, 9, 7, 5, 5, 7, 7, 7, 7, 8, 11, 12, 18, 26, 33, 33, 34, 35, 39, 39, 40, 40   (22)

LASSITER

8-11-84   (Warner 11372)   23, 15, 10, 5, 3, 2, 2, 5, 5, 9, 9, 13, 13, 14, 14, 23, 23, 27, 27, 29, 29, 29, 30, 30   (24)

THE LAST DRAGON (See: BERRY GORDY'S THE LAST DRAGON)

THE LAST STARFIGHTER

   12-22-84   (MCA 88087)   13, 13, 13, 8, 8, 5, 5, 5, 5, 13, 13, 13, 13, 29, 29, 26,
          26   (17)

THE LAST UNICORN

   5-07-83   (CBS/Fox 9054)   26, 25, 22, 23   (4)

LEGAL EAGLES

   5-09-87   (MCA 80479)   14, 11, 7, 6, 3, 4, 4, 4, 4, 8, 8, 12, 12, 12, 12, 19, 19,
          19, 19, 19   (20)

THE LEGEND OF BILLIE JEAN

   3-08-86   (Key Video 6925)   32, 30, 28, 26, 28, 39   (6)

LET'S SPEND THE NIGHT TOGETHER

   6-11-83   (Embassy 2056)   29, 27, 28, 30, 30, 30   (6)

LIFEFORCE

   2-01-86   (Vestron VA 5107)   24, 19, 16, 15, 15, 16, 24, 24, 27, 25, 24,
          39   (10)

LITTLE DRUMMER GIRL

   5-04-85   (Warner 11416)   21, 21, 12, 12, 19, 19   (6)

LITTLE SHOP OF HORRORS

   3-28-87   (Warner 11702)   36, 31, 37, 36, 37, 36, (9), 15, 15, 3, 3, 3, 3, 3, 5, 5, 5,
          5, 5   (17)

LIVE AND LET DIE

   11-19-83   (CBS/Fox 4633)   26, 25, 25, 25   (4)

LONE WOLF McQUADE

11-12-83   (Vestron 6008)   22, 21, 14, 15, 15   (5)

THE LONELY GUY

6-30-84   (MCA 80014)   23, 22, 19, 13, 15, 15, 15, 20, 26, 29, 28, 29, 29   (13)

THE LORDS OF DISCIPLINE

6-11-83   (Paramount 1433)   8, 7, 7, 7, 9, 8, 7, 9, 9, 9, 9, 9, 14, 17, 18, 18   (16)

LOST HORIZON

4-18-87   (RCA/Col. 6-20763)   26, 23, 33, 40, (1), 30, 38, 34   (7)

LOST IN AMERICA

12-07-85   (Warner 11460)   26, 20, 17, 12, 12, 12, 11, 17, 18, 24, 25, 31, 30, 36, 40, 40, 40   (17)

LOVESICK

6-04-83   (Warner 20011)   9, 7, 6, 9, 10, 12, 12, 14, 14, 18, 19, 23   (12)

LUCAS

12-06-86   (CBS/Fox 1495)   32, 32, 26, 19, 19, 19, 19, 21, 25, 25, 32, 31, 40   (13)

MAD MAX

7-23-83   (Vestron 4030)   11, 8, 7, 7, 8, 8, 7, 7, 10, 10, 13, 14, 23, 28   (14)

MAD MAX—BEYOND THUNDERDOME

2-08-86   (Warner 11519)   22, 15, 9, 4, 3, 3, 4, 9, 13, 13, 16, 21, 24, 28, 34, 38, 40   (17)

MAKING LOVE

7-24-82   (20th Century-Fox 1146)   23, 19, 14, 12, 12, 10, 16, 16, 15, 15, 19, 27, 26, 29, 30   (15)

THE MAN FROM SNOWY RIVER

9-24-83   (CBS/Fox 1233)   27, 10, 8, 8, 8, 8, 8, 8, 8, 8, 12, 12, 15, 18, 19, 19, 20, 24, 25, 24, 26, 29   (22)

THE MAN WHO LOVED WOMEN

5-19-84   (Col. 10369)   22, 19, 18, 14, 14, 11, 17, 15, 13, 17, 21, 24   (12)

THE MAN WITH ONE RED SHOE

2-22-86   (CBS/Fox 1477)   26, 21, 15, 11, 12, 13, 14, 20, 30, 38, 39   (11)

THE MAN WITH THE GOLDEN GUN

3-26-83   (CBS/Fox 4606)   26, 24, 24, 26, 30   (5)

THE MAN WITH TWO BRAINS

11-05-83   (Warner 11319)   24, 21, 14, 13, 17, 17, 14, 23, 23, 23, 24, 25, 28, 28   (14)

MAN, WOMAN AND CHILD

8-27-83   (Paramount 1652)   27, 24, 27   (3)

MANHUNTER

4-04-87   (Lorimar 411)   26, 21, 20, 17, 14, 13, 28, 35, 21, 25, 31, 38, 38, 38   (14)

MARIE

8-23-86   (MGM/UA 800926)   32, 31, 31, 28, 27, 27, 30   (7)

MASK

1-25-86   (MCA 80173)   26, 16, 10, 5, 3, 2, 4, 6, 6, 5, 6, 9, 10, 16, 20, 21, 21, 23, 25, 34, 33, 36, 34, 35, 38, 36, 34, 37, 37, 36   (30)

MASS APPEAL

8-31-85   (MCA 80168)   34, 31, 39   (3)

MAX DUGAN RETURNS

11-19-83 (CBS/Fox 1236) 20, 16, 13, 13, 13, 15, 14, 14, 16, 16, 19, 19, 22, 22, 30, 29 (16)

MAXIE

8-02-86 (Thorn/EMI/HBO TVA 3672) 24, 21, 32, 31 (4)

MAXIMUM OVERDRIVE

2-14-87 (Karl Lorimar 395) 21, 18, 17, 21, 33 (5)

THE MEAN SEASON

8-10-85 (Thorn/EMI/HBO TVA 2981) 29, 22, 20, 18, 18, 16, 19, 25, 27, 22, 22, 30, 30, 35, 40 (15)

MEGAFORCE

12-04-82 (CBS/Fox 1182) 29, 22, 19, 24, 24, 24, 28 (7)

MERRY CHRISTMAS, MR. LAWRENCE

4-07-84 (MCA 80049) 26, 23, 26, 26 (4)

METAL STORM

4-14-84 (MCA 80045) 24, 25, 29, 26 (4)

MIAMI VICE II—THE PRODIGAL SON

9-20-86 (MCA 80349) 30, 30, 28, 33, 37, 40 (6)

MICHAEL JACKSON: MAKING THE THRILLER VIDEO

12-31-83 (Vestron 1000) 21, 21, 10, 3, 3, 3, 3, 3, 4, 4, 4, 6, 6, 7, 9, 8, 11, 13, 16, 18, 19, 20, 19, 20, 24, 28, 27, 29, 30 (29)

MICKI AND MAUDE

6-29-85 (RCA/Col. 20456) 36, 36, 15, 15, 11, 9, 7, 13, 13, 11, 10, 11, 13, 16, 21, 27, 34, 34, 35, 38 (20)

A MIDSUMMER NIGHT'S SEX COMEDY

1-22-83   (Warner 22025)   22, 20, 20, 25   (4)

MIKE'S MURDER

2-09-85   (Warner 20015)   23, 23, 15, 15, 20, 20, 18, 18, 18, 18, 30, 30   (12)

MISSING

12-25-82   (MCA 71009)   19, 19, 19, 13, 10, 9, 9, 8, 7, 9, 13, 12, 13, 15, 17, 17, 19, 20, 18, 15, 13, 17, 18, 27, 30, 30   (26)

MISSING IN ACTION

6-15-85   (MGM/UA MB 800557)   14, 14, 10, 10, 7, 7, 5, 6, 13, 14, 16, 15, 15, 19, 22, 30, 31, 34, 30, 23, 22, 21, 19, 20, 20, 23, 27, 29, 37, 37, 37   (31)

MISSING IN ACTION 2—THE BEGINNING

10-19-85   (MGM/UA MB 800591)   33, 25, 11, 8, 6, 6, 6, 7, 10, 13, 16, 16, 16, 23, 24, 35, 38, 39   (18)

MODERN PROBLEMS

5-22-82   (20th Century-Fox 1129)   29, 18, 14, 12, 9, 8, 7, 12, 15, 19, 21, 20, 23, 21, 27, 28, 30, 29   (18)

MOMMIE DEAREST

4-03-82   (Paramount 1263)   5, 12, 12, 21, 21, 19, 23, 26, 29, 30   (10)

MONA LISA

6-13-87   (HBO TVA 9955)   25, 21, 21, 21, 25, 25, 24, 24, 24, 24, 25, 25, 25, 25, 25   (15)

THE MONEY PIT

11-15-86   (MCA 80387)   29, 15, 8, 7, 7, 6, 7, 7, 7, 7, 10, 10, 13, 13, 6, 8, 11, 27, 31, 28, 39   (21)

MONSIGNOR

3-26-83 (CBS/Fox 1108) 16, 13, 11, 8, 5, 5, 6, 6, 7, 8, 10, 19, 19, 20, 23, 25, 29 (17)

MONTY PYTHON AND THE HOLY GRAIL

12-04-82 (RCA/Col. 10127) 30, 27, 26, 28, 28, 28, 30 (7)

MONTY PYTHON'S THE MEANING OF LIFE

11-05-83 (MCA 71016) 21, 12, 11, 10, 9, 9, 24 (7)

MOONRAKER

3-05-83 (CBS/Fox 4636) 25, 22, 19, 19, 22, 22, 24, 29, 30, 30 (10)

THE MORNING AFTER

7-11-87 (Tri-Star/CBS/Fox 3800) 5, 5, 2, 2, 2, 2, 3, 3, 3, 3, 3 (11)

MOSCOW ON THE HUDSON

11-10-84 (RCA/Col. 60309) 24, 24, 15, 15, 10, 10, 4, 4, 4, 5, 5, 10, 10, 12, 12, 18, 18, 26, 26 (19)

MOSQUITO COAST

6-20-87 (Warner 11711) 31, 31, 31, 7, 7, 5, 5, 5, 5, 9, 9, 9, 9, 9 (14)

MOVING VIOLATIONS

12-14-85 (CBS/Fox 1462) 33, 31, 30, 30, 30, 31 (6)

MR. MOM

2-25-84 (Vestron 5025) 24, 14, 8, 4, 3, 2, 2, 2, 2, 4, 8, 7, 7, 6, 16, 16, 18, 26, 25, 25, 28, 27, 26, 26, 26, 25, 30, 30 (28)

MRS. SOFFEL

9-07-85 (MGM/UA MV800600) 30, 21, 16, 12, 9, 7, 8, 10, 18, 20, 20, 21, 23, 22, 22, 26, 33, 33, 33, 37, 39 (21)

THE MUPPETS TAKE MANHATTAN

2-23-85   (CBS/Fox 6731)   22, 22, 14, 14, 22, 22, 30, 30   (8)

MURPHY'S LAW

11-29-86   (Cannon/Media M 849)   35, 20, 20, 17, 22, 22, 22, 22, 26, 30, 30, 37, 39   (13)

MURPHY'S ROMANCE

8-23-86   (RCA/Col. 20649)   17, 7, 5, 3, 5, 5, 4, 3, 1, 2, 7, 9, 8, 18, 18, 23, 23, 27, 29, 29, 29, 29, 31, 32, 31, 39, 34, 32, 37   (29)

THE MUSIC MAN

10-18-86   (Warner 11473)   27, 23, 35, 19, 17, 20, 24, 35, 35, 37, 38, 38, 38, 38, 38, 38, 38   (17)

MY CHAUFFEUR

5-31-86   (Vestron 5135)   34, 28, 24, 32, 33, 31, 32, 40   (8)

MY FAIR LADY

2-07-87   (CBS/Fox 7038)   36, 30, 38, 36   (4)

MY FAVORITE YEAR

6-11-83   (MGM/UA 00188)   5, 5, 6, 6, 8, 9, 9, 10, 12, 12, 14, 14, 15, 15, 20, 24, 30, 29   (18)

MY NAME IS BARBRA

12-06-86   (CBS/Fox 3519)   33, 33, 25, 18, 18, 18, 18, 11, 8, 7, 6, 14, 31, 36   (14)

MY SCIENCE PROJECT

2-08-86   (Touchstone 360)   30, 24, 20, 18, 10, 9, 11, 15, 16, 14, 15, 28, 32, 34, 40   (15)

MY TUTOR

8-27-83 (MCA 80022) 24, 21, 16, 17, 17 (5)

NAME OF THE ROSE

5-30-87 (20th Century-Fox/Embassy 1342) 10, 9, 15, 25, 25, 25, 35, 35, 34, 34, 34, 34 (12)

NATIONAL LAMPOON'S CLASS REUNION

8-20-83 (Vestron 5021) 30, 29, 28, 29, 30 (5)

NATIONAL LAMPOON'S EUROPEAN VACATION

3-15-86 (Warner 11521) 18, 15, 12, 9, 6, 7, 6, 12, 20, 25, 28, 31, 37, 36, 39, 40, 40 (17)

NATIONAL LAMPOON'S VACATION

12-03-83 (Warner 11315) 26, 26, 5, 4, 4, 4, 4, 4, 4, 4, 4, 4, 5, 5, 5, 8, 10, 12, 16, 17, 22, 25, 30 (23)

THE NATURAL

12-22-84 (Col./RCA 60380) 15, 15, 15, 7, 7, 4, 4, 2, 2, 3, 3, 4, 4, 5, 5, 9, 9, 12, 12, 17, 17, 26, 26 (23)

NEIGHBORS

6-19-82 (Col. 10445) 22, 14, 9, 7, 5, 9, 11, 16, 17, 18, 17, 23, 26, 30 (14)

NEVER CRY WOLF

11-24-84 (Disney 182) 19, 19, 14, 14, 11, 11, 11, 15, 15, 20, 20, 19, 19, 26, 26, 24 24 (17)

NEVER SAY NEVER

3-10-84 (Warner 11337) 17, 9, 7, 3, 3, 3, 1, 1, 4, 5, 6, 7, 5, 10, 5, 6, 8, 7, 15, 18, 20, 23, 30, 30 (24)

THE NEVERENDING STORY

    1-26-85   (Warner 11399)   18, 18, 9, 9, 6, 6, 7, 7, 8, 8, 16, 16, 21, 21, 28, 28 (16)

NEWTON-JOHN, OLIVIA (See: TWIST OF FATE)

NICE DREAMS

    10-09-82   (Col. 10456)   20, 12, 9, 6, 6, 10, 9, 19, 25 (9)

'NIGHT, MOTHER

    7-11-87   (MCA 80542)   31, 31, 31, 31, 31, 31, 39, 39, 39, 39, 39 (11)

NIGHT OF THE COMET

    8-17-85   (CBS/Fox 6743)   35, 35, 33 (3)

NIGHT PATROL

    6-15-85   (New World 8425)   20, 20, 21, 21, 38, 38, 31, 40 (8)

NIGHT SHIFT

    1-29-83   (Warner 20006)   29, 17, 14, 12, 12, 9, 11, 14, 12, 11, 9, 9, 11, 10, 10, 9, 12, 13, 18, 24, 24, 29 (22)

A NIGHTMARE ON ELM STREET

    7-27-85   (Media M 790)   25, 13, 10, 8, 8, 9, 7, 7, 9, 10, 14, 17, 20, 27, 32, 31, 37, 36, 28, 24, 24, 24, 27, 27, 27, 28, 32, 33, 37, 38, 37, 38, 38 (33)

A NIGHTMARE ON ELM STREET 2; FREDDY'S REVENGE

    7-12-86   (Media M 838)   30, 24, 8, 6, 4, 5, 5, 6, 7, 11, 14, 14, 17, 18, 21, 31, 39, 39 (18)

NIGHTMARES

    2-18-84   (MCA 80037)   24, 22, 20, 22, 26 (5)

9 1/2 WEEKS

11-08-86 (MGM/UA 800973) 28, 13, 6, 4, 4, 4, 9, 12, 12, 12, 17, 15, 19, 22, 24, 24, (2), 26, 22, 19, 15, 18, 22, 34, 38 (24)

1984

6-29-85 (USA 217-547) 38, 38, 30, 30, 24, 34, 35, 36, 37 (9)

NINJA III—THE DOMINATION

6-01-85 (MGM/UA 800546) 27, 27, 21, 21, 31, 31, 28, 28, 37, 37 (10)

NO MERCY

8-22-87 (RCA/Col. 6-20791) 15, 15, 15, 15, 15 (5)

NO SMALL AFFAIR

4-20-85 (RCA/Col. 60429) 25, 25, 16, 16, 16, 16 (6)

NORTH BY NORTHWEST

3-07-87 (MGM/UA 660104) 27, 20, 17, 19, 18, 26, 33, 34, 39 (9)

NOTHING IN COMMON

5-30-87 (HBO/Cannon TVA 9960) 23, 14, 6, 9, 9, 9, 13, 13, 16, 16, 16, 16, 18, 18, 18, 18, 18 (17)

OCTOPUSSY

4-14-84 (CBS/Fox 4715) 21, 10, 8, 6, 8, 5, 11, 7, 7, 9, 13, 18, 20, 25, 25, 27 (16)

OFFBEAT

9-20-86 (HBO/Cannon TVA 3676) 20, 20, 16, 11, 12, 16, 31, 40 (8)

AN OFFICER AND A GENTLEMAN

2-26-83 (Paramount 1467) 1, 1, 1, 1, 1, 1, 1, 1, 1, 1, 1, 1, 1, 1, 2, 2, 3, 3, 5, 5, 7, 7, 10, 11, 10, 10, 11, 11, 11, 10, 13, 13, 14, 15, 15, 23, 30, 20, 30, 28, 29, 30, 30, 28 (43)

OH GOD, YOU DEVIL

5-18-85   (Warner 7470)   22, 22, 23, 23, 12, 12, 12, 12, 20, 20, 23   (11)

ON GOLDEN POND

6-05-82   (20th Century Fox 9037-80)   29, 2, 2, 2, 2, 2, 2, 2, 2, 2, 2, 2, 2, 1, 1, 2, 2, 2, 3, 5, 4, 3, 7, 6, 5, 6, 8, 17, 21, 21, 21, 21, 20, 19, 18, 26, 28, 27, 29, 29, 30   (41)

ONCE BITTEN

5-17-86   (Vestron 5115)   23, 16, 15, 13, 16, 21, 24, 30, 33   (9)

ONCE UPON A TIME IN AMERICA

3-09-85   (Warner 20019)   27, 27, 12, 12, 7, 7, 4, 4, 7, 7, 13, 13, 26, 26   (14)

ONE CRAZY SUMMER

5-30-87   (Warner 11602)   17, 19, 23, 23, 23, 23, 27, 27, 26, 26, 26, 26, 35, 35, 35, 35, 35   (17)

ONE FROM THE HEART

7-23-83   (RCA/Col. 10463)   30, 24, 25, 30   (4)

ONE HALF MOON STREET

5-30-87   (Twentieth Century-Fox/Embassy 1328)   22, 23, 28, 34, 34, 34   (6)

ONLY WHEN I LAUGH

4-03-82   (Col. 10462)   24, 14, 6, 5, 4, 3, 5, 9, 9, 8, 15, 20, 20, 19, 18, 22, 26, 30   (18)

OSTERMAN WEEKEND

4-28-84   (Thorn/EMI 1981)   16, 13, 11, 11, 9, 9, 9, 10, 15, 19, 19, 23, 24, 24, 28, 27, 26, 29   (18)

OUT OF AFRICA

10-04-86   (MCA 80350)   26, 17, 3, 1, 1, 1, 1, 1, 7, 6, 6, 10, 9, 9, 9, 9, 12, 14, 18, 17, 13, 14, 15, 15, 12, 14, 8, 8, 8, 10, 15, 28, 37   (33)

OUT OF BOUNDS

2-14-87 (RCA/Col. 620722) 38, 32, 28, 25 (4)

OUTLAND

4-17-82 (Warner 70002) 17, 17, 20, 18, 17, 19, 23 (7)

THE OUTSIDERS

9-17-83 (Warner 11310) 5, 5, 6, 5, 4, 4, 6, 6, 7, 12, 17, 19, 19, 19, 20, 20, 20, 21, 23, 22, 30 (21)

OXFORD BLUES

6-01-85 (CBS/Fox 4725) 22, 22, 19, 19, 28, 28, 32, 32, 40 (9)

PALE RIDER

12-28-85 (Warner 11475) 25, 25, 25, 10, 4, 3, 1, 1, 5, 8, 8, 8, 14, 19, 17, 16, 17, 27, 30, 36, 37, 37 (22)

PARADISE

12-18-82 (Embassy 1603) 25 (1)

PARIS, TEXAS

10-05-85 (CBS/Fox 1457) 35, 31, 27, 24, 25, 28, 33, 40 (8)

PARTNERS

9-18-82 (Paramount 1446) 27, 21, 17, 15, 14, 13, 12, 14, 17, 20, 24 (11)

A PASSAGE TO INDIA

9-28-85 (RCA/Col. 60485) 18, 13, 10, 9, 7, 6, 9, 11, 17, 18, 19, 25, 25, 32, 32, 32, 33, 35, 38 (19)

PATERNITY

4-03-82 (Paramount 1401) 6, 16, 23, 23, 22, 21, 26, 27, 30, 28 (10)

PEE-WEE'S BIG ADVENTURE

3-15-86   (Warner 11523)   15, 10, 8, 5, 4, 4, 5, 8, 11, 11, 15, 17, 17, 25, 26, 26, 27, 26, 25, 26, 27, 29, 30, 30, 33, 37, 39   (27)

PEGGY SUE GOT MARRIED

5-30-87   (Tri-Star/CBS-Fox 3380)   8, 7, 1, 2, 2, 2, 4, 4, 8, 8, 8, 8, 13, 13, 13, 13, 13   (17)

PENNIES FROM HEAVEN

9-04-82   (MGM/UA 00147)   24, 22, 18, 17, 23, 29   (6)

PERFECT

12-14-85   (RCA/Col. 20494)   21, 16, 17, 17, 17, 16, 16, 20, 25, 29, 34, 34, 35, 38   (14)

PERSONAL BEST

8-07-82   (Warner 61242)   28, 14, 11, 11, 18, 18, 24, 23, 28   (9)

PHILADELPHIA EXPERIMENT

11-24-84   (Thorn/EMI 2547)   20, 20, 15, 15, 12, 12, 12, 17, 17, 12, 12, 13, 13, 19, 19, 30, 30, 26, 26   (19)

PHYSICAL

4-03-82   (MCA 55050)   22   (1)

PINK FLOYD'S THE WALL

12-17-83   (MGM/UA 400268)   25, 19, 18, 18, 18, 19, 23, 23, 25, 27, 29, 30   (12)

PINOCCHIO

8-10-85   (Walt Disney 239V)   23, 15, 14, 12, 16, 14, 14, 17, 24, 23, 25, 26, 26, 32, 34, 31, 31, 30, 32, 33, 29, 29, 29, 29, 33   (25)

10-11-86   (Walt Disney 239V)   31, 29, 29, 27, 30, 22, 21, 28, 22, 22, 18, 15, 15, 15, 15, 8, 11, 9, 9, 10, 12, 12, 4, 22, 23, 40, (4), 30, 24, 21   (26)

PLACES IN THE HEART

6-15-85 (CBS/Fox 6836) 28, 28, 7, 7, 3, 3, 4, 5, 6, 5, 7, 6, 8, 8, 12, 14, 17, 21, 23, 32, 27, 30, 36, 39 (24)

PLAYBOY, THE MAGAZINE, VOL. I

12-04-82 (CBS/Fox 6201) 24, 19, 13, 11, 11, 11, 12, 16, 15, 19, 21, 19, 25, 28, 29 (15)

PLAYBOY VIDEO CALENDAR

1-24-87 (Karl Lorimar 510) 30, 24, 24, 25, 35, 35, 39, 39, 40, 34, 32, 40, 35, 36, 37, 39, 40, 38 (18)

PLAYBOY VIDEO CENTERFOLD IV

12-27-86 (Karl Lorimar 513) 33, 33, 33, 33, 16, 18, 15, 16, 23, 21, 32, 23, 30, 30, 36, (3), 30, 25, 21, 22, 39, 39 (21)

PLAYBOY VIDEO CENTERFOLD III

10-25-86 (Karl Lorimar 509) 36, 26, 26, 25, 24, 17, 14, 14, 11, 8, 8, 8, 8, 5, 5, 8, 10, 17, 13, 13, 30, 38, 38, 35, 25, 30, 26, 31, 35, 39, 36 (31)

PLAYBOY VIDEO, VOLUME II

4-30-83 (CBS/Fox 6202) 24, 21, 15, 14, 14, 19, 21, 25, 26 (9)

PLAYBOY'S PLAYMATE REVIEW

8-06-83 (CBS/Fox 6355) 27, 24 (2)

PLENTY

4-26-86 (Thorn/EMI/HBO TVA 3394) 15, 13, 12, 14, 13, 13, 18, 27, 37, 37, 39 (11)

POLICE ACADEMY

1-12-85 (Warner 20016) 12, 12, 6, 6, 1, 1, 2, 2, 2, 2, 4, 4, 6, 6, 11, 11, 10, 10, 8, 8, 8, 8, 25, 25, 17, 17, 25, 25, 33, 33, 37, 38, 38, 40, 40 (35)

POLICE ACADEMY 2, THEIR FIRST ASSIGNMENT

10-19-85   (Warner 20020)   26, 16, 7, 5, 5, 5, 5, 6, 6, 8, 10, 10, 10, 15, 14, 19, 28, 31, 36, 36   (20)

POLICE AROUND THE WORLD

11-12-83   (I.R.S. 001)   27, 27, 23, 24, 24, 29, 27   (7)

POLTERGEIST

12-25-82   (MGM/UA 00164)   12, 12, 12, 6, 2, 1, 1, 1, 1, 2, 3, 3, 5, 4, 4, 4, 4, 4, 6, 5, 7, 10, 11, 11, 18, 21, 24, 26, 27, 28   (30)

POLTERGEIST II/THE OTHER SIDE

3-07-87   (MGM/UA 800940)   31, 32   (2)

THE POPE OF GREENWICH VILLAGE

5-18-85   (MGM/UA 800490)   20, 20, 7, 7, 7, 7, 11, 11, 19, 19, 18, 32, 34, 34, 23, 31, 29, 37   (18)

PORKY'S

8-13-83   (CBS/Fox 1149)   26, 5, 2, 1, 1, 1, 1, 2, 2, 2, 2, 4, 4, 5, 7, 7, 7, 7, 10, 24, 25, 25, 25, 26   (24)

PORKY'S REVENGE!

10-19-85   (CBS/Fox 1463)   31, 22, 16, 10, 9, 10, 10, 15, 17, 23, 26, 26, 26, 32, 37   (15)

PORKY'S II

2-18-84   (CBS/Fox 1294)   26, 19, 15, 12, 13, 15, 17, 20, 16, 14, 22, 24, 29, 29, 29, 28   (16)

POWER

6-21-86   (Karl Lorimar 401)   33, 16, 10, 15, 13, 12, 16, 18, 22, 26, 32   (11)

PRAY FOR DEATH

9-06-86 (U.S.A. 938) 35, 32, 31, 31, 32 (5)

PRETTY IN PINK

10-25-86 (Paramount 1858) 39, 21, 7, 3, 2, 2, 3, 3, 4, 6, 6, 6, 6, 7, 6, 11, 11, 11, 10, 8, 8, 13, 15, 24, 35, 37, 38 (27)

PRINCE OF THE CITY

4-10-82 (Warner 72021) 21, 15, 13, 13, 15, 15, 16, 15, 16, 21, 26, 24, 27, 30 (14)

PRIVATE BENJAMIN

4-17-82 (Warner 61075) 20, 20, 24 (3)

PRIVATE LESSONS

6-26-82 (MCA 71008) 27, 18, 9, 6, 5, 6, 5, 6, 8, 9, 10, 11, 10, 14, 15, 14, 21, 20, 19, 21, 23, 23, 30 (23)

PRIZZI'S HONOR

1-25-86 (Vestron VA 5106) 29, 23, 15, 6, 2, 3, 2, 2, 2, 4, 4, 5, 5, 2, 2, 4, 8, 14, 14, 16, 22, 24, 27, 26, 29, 39, 39, 35, 35, 34, 36, 35, 34, 38 (34)

PROTOCOL

6-29-85 (Warner 11434) 25, 25, 14, 14, 7, 8, 12, 12, 12, 14, 13, 18, 21, 29, 30, 33, 32, 31, 33, 37 (20)

PRYOR, RICHARD (See: RICHARD ...)

PSYCHO II

11-05-83 (MCA 80008) 12, 9, 5, 5, 5, 5, 7, 7, 12, 12, 15, 18, 20, 27, 29, 30 (16)

PURPLE HEART

9-29-84 (Warner 20018) 22, 22, 14, 14, 7, 7, 8, 8, 12, 12, 25, 25, 28, 28, 28, 24, 24, 29, 29 (19)

PURPLE RAIN

12-08-84   (Warner 11398)   17, 17, 5, 5, 5, 2, 2, 2, 2, 4, 4, 5, 5, 8, 8, 19, 19, 21, 21   (19)

THE PURPLE ROSE OF CAIRO

9-21-85   (Vestron VA 5068)   30, 23, 18, 18, 15, 12, 12, 14, 15, 22, 26, 34, 38, 38   (14)

QUEST FOR FIRE

10-30-82   (20th Century-Fox 1148)   16, 2, 2, 2, 3, 4, 7, 11, 16, 16, 16, 19, 21, 22, 27, 30, 29   (17)

QUICKSILVER

9-20-86   (RCA/Col. 60644)   15, 15, 7, 6, 9, 7, 12, 32, 40   (9)

RACING WITH THE MOON

10-13-84   (Paramount 1668)   15, 15, 11, 11, 13, 13, 18, 18, 23, 23, 26, 26, 26   (13)

RAGGEDY MAN

4-03-82   (MCA 71003)   18, 26   (2)

RAGTIME

7-17-82   (Paramount 1486)   18, 11, 8, 6, 4, 5, 4, 7, 8, 11, 11, 14, 13, 11, 14, 15, 16, 16, 22, 27   (20)

RAIDERS OF THE LOST ARK

12-17-83   (Paramount 1376)   1, 1, 1, 1, 1, 1, 1, 1, 1, 1, 2, 2, 2, 2, 2, 4, 7, 9, 9, 14, 14, 17, 20, 22, 21, 25, 17, 16, 14, 14, 12, 15, 16, 17, 20, 19, 18, 25, 25, 26, 26, 30, 30   (43)

RAMBO: FIRST BLOOD, PART II

2-15-86   (Thorn/EMI/HBO TVA 3002) 19, 1, 1, 1, 1, 1, 1, 2, 2, 3, 4, 6, 9, 13, 18, 19, 19, 26, 30, 28, 28, 28, 26, 28, 28, 27, 33, 37, 36, 36, 36   (31)

THE RAZOR'S EDGE

4-20-85 (RCA/Col. 60410) 17, 17, 11, 11, 18, 18, 29, 29, 29, 29, 35, 35, 35, 35 (14)

REAL GENIUS

4-05-86 (RCA/Col. 6-20568) 21, 15, 13, 26, 29, 31, 36, 40 (8)

RE-ANIMATOR

4-26-86 (Vestron 5114) 19, 15, 14, 24, 24, 27, 35, 35 (8)

REAR WINDOW

6-09-84 (MCA 80081) 22, 23, 20, 21, 16, 11, 10, 11, 10, 12, 13, 19, 19, 23, 23, 23 (16)

RECKLESS

9-08-84 (MGM/UA 800421) 22, 18, 18, 17, 17, 23, 23, 29, 29 (9)

RED DAWN

3-09-85 (MGM/UA 800499) 11, 11, 6, 6, 3, 3, 1, 1, 2, 2, 6, 6, 12, 12, 17, 17, 32, 32, 26, 26, 29, 31, 33, 33, 34 (25)

RED SONJA

2-22-86 (CBS/Fox 4733) 29, 22, 18, 10, 9, 18, 23, 26, 36, 40 (10)

REDS

1-15-83 (Paramount 1180) 22, 12, 10, 10, 9, 8, 10, 11, 15, 16, 24, 26, 27, 30 (14)

REMO WILLIAMS: THE ADVENTURE BEGINS

7-05-86 (Thorn/EMI/HBO TVA 3676) 16, 8, 7, 11, 12, 13, 14, 16, 23, 29, 33, 38, 38, 37, 39 (15)

RETURN OF THE JEDI

3-22-86 (CBS/Fox 1478) 13, 3, 1, 1, 1, 1, 1, 2, 3, 3, 5, 6, 6, 10, 11, 13, 14, 16, 20, 20, 22, 25, 27, 25, 24, 23, 28, 28, 33, 35 (30)

RETURN OF THE LIVING DEAD

   8-09-86   (Thorn/EMI/HBO TVA 3395)   32, 21, 20, 19, 22, 26, 35, 35, 36 (9)

REVENGE OF THE NERDS

   3-23-85   (CBS/Fox 1439)   14, 14, 8, 8, 3, 3, 1, 1, 3, 3, 5, 5, 16, 16, 15, 15, 16, 16, 17, 28, 32, 32, 31, 30, 32, 38, 40 (27)

REVENGE OF THE NINJA

   6-09-84   (MGM/UA 800312)   23, 29, 30 (3)

REVOLUTION

   7-19-86   (Warner 11532)   37, 29, 22, 23, 24 (5)

RHINESTONE

   2-23-85   (CBS/Fox 1438)   20, 20, 15, 15, 25, 25, 28, 28, 28, 28 (10)

RICH AND FAMOUS

   4-17-82   (MGM/UA 00111)   22, 12, 8, 10, 14, 14, 14, 13, 20, 25, 26, 30, 28, 30 (14)

RICHARD PRYOR LIVE IN CONCERT

   4-03-82   (Vestron 4000)   9, 6, 16, 14, 14, 12, 16, 15, 19, 18, 22, 21, 21, 24, 23, 24, 24, 27, 29 (19)

RICHARD PRYOR LIVE ON SUNSET STRIP

   12-04-82   (RCA/Col. 10469)   18, 8, 5, 4, 4, 4, 4, 13, 13, 18, 20, 25, 28 (13)

THE RIGHT STUFF

   7-07-84   (Warner 20024)   23, 14, 4, 2, 2, 2, 2, 1, 3, 2, 4, 4, 4, 4, 6, 6, 9, 9, 11, 11, 13, 13, 22, 22, 27, 27, 27, 29, 29, 28, 28 (31)

RISKY BUSINESS

   12-24-83   (Warner 11323)   6, 3, 3, 3, 2, 2, 2, 2, 2, 3, 3, 3, 3, 4, 5, 4, 5, 6, 11, 12, 16, 17, 18, 20, 24, 26, 29, 29 (28)

THE RIVER

6-29-85 (MCA 80160) 16, 16, 8, 8, 8, 15, 17, 21, 21, 20, 23, 29, 33, 35, 37, 39, 37, 35, 37 (19)

ROAD WARRIOR

2-26-83 (Warner 11181) 24, 15, 4, 2, 3, 3, 3, 3, 3, 3, 3, 3, 3, 3, 3, 3, 9, 9, 11, 12, 13, 13, 17, 18, 16, 16, 16, 12, 16, 14, 16, 15, 15, 18, 30 (34)

ROBIN HOOD

1-26-85 (Disney 228) 24, 24, 22, 22, 23, 23, 21, 21 (8)

ROCKY IV

6-21-86 (CBS/Fox 4735) 17, 4, 2, 2, 2, 2, 5, 5, 7, 8, 9, 12, 15, 19, 19, 21, 26, 40 (18)

ROCKY III

12-25-82 (CBS/Fox 4708) 5, 5, 5, 2, 1, 2, 2, 2, 3, 4, 4, 5, 6, 6, 5, 5, 6, 8, 8, 11, 18, 18, 16, 17, 17, 17, 19, 20, 21, 21, 25, 28, 30, 27, 29, 30 (36)

ROCKY II

6-12-82 (20th Century-Fox 4565) 23, 18, 15, 14, 17, 19, 17, 16, 15, 26, 30 (11)

ROLLOVER

8-14-82 (Warner 72022) 27, 25, 22, 22, 20, 20, 22, 26, 30, 29 (10)

ROMANCING THE STONE

9-29-84 (CBS/Fox 1358) 8, 8, 1, 1, 1, 1, 1, 1, 1, 1, 1, 1, 1, 1, 1, 1, 3, 3, 3, 3, 7, 7, 8, 8, 17, 17, 27, 27, 22, 22, 23, 23, 30, 30, 30, 30 (33)

ROMANTIC COMEDY

8-25-84 (CBS/Fox 4722) 25, 18, 13, 9, 9, 20, 20, 22, 22, 24, 24, 29, 29 (13)

A ROOM WITH A VIEW

5-02-87   (CBS/Fox 6915)   26, 20, 20, 20, 7, 8, 13, 12, 12, 12, 16, 16, 17, 17,
17, 17, 21, 21, 21, 21, 21   (17)

RUMBLEFISH

4-07-84   (MCA 80056)   18, 15, 21, 24, 20, 30   (6)

RUNAWAY

8-03-85   (RCA/Col. 60469)   20, 14, 11, 9, 8, 6, 5, 5, 5, 7, 11, 11, 13, 13, 15,
25, 29, 35, 36   (19)

RUNAWAY TRAIN

10-25-86   (MGM 800867)   37, 25, 13, 10, 17, 15, 12, 12, 14, 21, 21, 21, 21,
23, 28, 29, 36   (17)

RUNNING BRAVE

5-05-84   (Walt Disney 183VS)   25, 23, 23, 23, 23, 30   (6)

RUNNING SCARED

3-07-87   (MGM/UA 801-0083)   14, 1, 1, 3, 6, 4, 7, 9, 5, 9, 12, 12, 13, 15, 18,
20, 20, 20, 30, 30, 32, 32, 32, 32, 34, 34, 34, 34, 34   (17)

RUTHLESS PEOPLE

3-21-87   (Touchstone 485)   8, 5, 2, 2, 2, 2, 3, 4, 5, 5, 4, 4, 12, 14, 27, 27, 27,
27, 27   (17)

S.O.B.

4-03-82   (MGM/CBS CR 001100)   12, 9, 11, 11, 12, 14, 20, 21, 26, 26, 24,
28, 30   (13)

ST. ELMO'S FIRE

2-22-86   (RCA/Col. 6-20559)   14, 6, 5, 4, 3, 2, 3, 8, 8, 7, 11, 18, 17, 21, 21,
22, 29, 34, 36, 36, 39, 35, 36, 38, 38, 40   (26)

SANTA CLAUS—THE MOVIE

11-15-86 (Media 846) 31, 30, 30, 30, 30, 28, 30, 30, 30, 30, 32, 33, 35 (13)

SAVANNAH SMILES

7-23-83 (Embassy 2058) 27, 25, 23, 23, 22, 25, 25, 28, 28, 28, 22, 21, 24, 24 (14)

SCANNERS

4-03-82 (20th Century-Fox 4073) 7, 5, 9, 15, 19, 29, 29 (7)

SCARFACE

6-16-84 (MCA 80047) 12, 1, 1, 1, 2, 3, 3, 3, 4, 6, 6, 7, 7, 8, 8, 14, 14, 28, 28, 27, 27, (9), 26, 26, 25, 25, 30, 30 (27)

SCARFACE

5-16-87 (RCA/Col.) 23, 19 (2)

SECRET ADMIRER

11-16-85 (Thorn/EMI/HBO TVA 2990) 24, 15, 13, 12, 12, 14, 14, 14, 14, 18, 27, 37, 36, 37 (14)

THE SECRET OF NIMH

4-23-83 (MGM/UA 800211) 26, 21, 16, 12, 9, 10, 15, 20, 20, 22, 22, 24, 27 (13)

SECRETS OF THE TITANIC

1-24-87 (National Geographic/Vestron 1063) 36, 19, 16, 19, 29, 37, 40, 40, 39, 40, 30, 31, 23, 21, 19, 17, 15, 14 (18)

THE SEDUCTION

10-02-82 (Media 196) 24, 18, 13, 11, 8, 10, 13, 19, 23, 28, 29, 30 (12)

SHARKY'S MACHINE

8-07-82   (Warner 72024)   23, 9, 3, 3, 3, 3, 3, 5, 6, 7, 8, 10, 14, 12, 15, 17, 21, 27, 26 (19)

SHE'S GOTTA HAVE IT

5-30-87   (Island/Key 3860)   28, 30, 36, 35, 35, 35 (6)

SHEENA

4-06-85   (RCA/Col. 20404)   25, 25, 15, 15, 23, 23 (6)

THE SHINING

4-17-82   (Warner 61079)   30, 29 (2)

SHOOT THE MOON

7-24-82   (MGM/UA 00141)   27, 22, 17, 15, 15, 18, 25, 24, 22, 27, 30 (11)

SHORT CIRCUIT

5-30-87   (CBS/Fox 3724)   25, 27, 30, 33, 33, 33, 39, 39, 39, 39, 39, 39 (12)

SID AND NANCY

5-30-87   (Zenith/Intial/Embassy 1309)   27, 24, 20, 18, 18, 18, 20, 20, 22, 22, 22, 22, 30, 30, 30, 30, 30 (17)

SILKWOOD

6-16-84   (Embassy 1377)   13, 3, 2, 2, 3, 2, 4, 5, 5, 7, 8, 8, 10, 14, 14, 13, 13, 19, 19, 28, 28 (21)

SILVER BULLET

4-19-86   (Paramount 1827)   32, 29, 21, 15, 9, 9, 10, 12, 13, 16, 20, 23, 22, 31, 40 (15)

SILVERADO

3-15-86   (RCA/Col. 60567)   25, 17, 11, 8, 3, 2, 3, 3, 3, 4, 5, 7, 7, 9, 13, 12, 17, 19, 18, 17, 21, 19, 23, 29, 37, 39 (26)

SIX WEEKS

8-20-83 (RCA/Col. 91001) 25, 16, 10, 9, 12, 12, 17, 26, 29 (9)

SIXTEEN CANDLES

10-27-84 (MCA 80076) 17, 17, 10, 10, 9, 9, 8, 8, 10, 10, 10, 13, 13, 14, 14, 21, 21, 29, 29 (19)

SLEEPING BEAUTY

11-15-86 (Walt Disney 476) 28, 14, 5, 2, 2, 2, 2, 2, 2, 2, 3, 3, 3, 3, 4, 7, 5, 5, 11, 13, 12, 18, 19, 24, 23, 22, 31, 33 (28)

THE SLUGGER'S WIFE

10-05-85 (RCA/Col. 60486) 28, 25, 24, 19, 17, 17, 18, 23, 22, 28, 31, 32 (12)

SOLAR BABIES

7-11-87 (MGM/UA 801027) 33, 33, 30, 30, 30, 30, 37, 37, 37, 37, 37 (11)

A SOLDIER'S STORY

8-03-85 (RCA/Col. 60408) 14, 11, 7, 6, 5, 5, 4, 3, 2, 2, 3, 3, 6, 10, 11, 13, 19, 21, 27, 30, 30, 38, 38, 38, 38, 38, 40, 40 (28)

SMOKEY AND THE BANDIT III

2-25-84 (MCA 80013) 26, 27, 28, 30 (4)

SO FINE

5-29-82 (Warner 11143) 22, 19, 18, 17, 18, 17, 20, 25, 25, 28, 30 (11)

SOME KIND OF HERO

8-21-82 (Paramount 1118) 23, 14, 11, 10, 8, 7, 11, 12, 18, 22, 28, 27, 26, 26, 29 (15)

SOMETHING WICKED THIS WAY COMES

10-29-83 (Walt Disney 116) 22, 16, 11, 9, 9, 8, 8, 12, 26, 27, 27 (11)

SOMETHING WILD

8-22-87   (HBO 001)   22, 22, 22, 22, 22   (5)

SONGWRITER

6-29-85   (RCA/Col. 60437)   26, 26, 24, 24, 32, 38, 38   (7)

SOPHIE'S CHOICE

6-25-83   (CBS/Fox 9076)   2, 2, 3, 2, 2, 2, 4, 4, 4, 6, 6, 6, 6, 6, 9, 10, 11, 11, 19, 29, 23   (21)

SOUL MAN

5-23-87   (New World 1736)   27, 16, 13, 10, 7, 7, 7, 9, 9, 20, 20, 20, 20, 24, 24, 24, 24, 24   (17)

SOUND OF MUSIC

10-18-86   (CBS/Fox 1051)   33, 28, 20, 36   (4)

SOUTHERN COMFORT

10-01-83   (Thorn/EMI 3015)   27, 23, 20, 30   (4)

SPACE CAMP

2-21-87   (ABC 5174)   21, 18, 18, 34   (4)

SPACEHUNTER: ADVENTURES IN THE FORBIDDEN ZONE

11-26-83   (RCA/Col. 10512)   18, 16, 16, 18, 17, 22, 22, 30   (8)

SPIES LIKE US

8-16-86   (Warner 11533)   10, 6, 3, 3, 2, 1, 1, 2, 2, 5, 6, 10, 15, 15, 25, 32, 36, 36, 38, 39, 39, 39, 39   (23)

SPLASH

9-29-84   (Touchstone 213)   10, 10, 3, 3, 2, 2, 2, 2, 2, 2, 2, 2, 3, 3, 3, 4, 4, 9, 9, 11, 11, 16, 16, 22, 22, 23, 23, 29, 29, 29, 29   (31)

SPRING BREAK

10-15-83 (RCA/Col. 10513) 28, 27, 18, 15, 25, 23, 27 (7)

STAND BY ME

4-18-87 (RCA/Col. 20736) 24, 16, 10, 8, 7, 10, 5, 5, 5, 5, 5, 5, 10, 10, 11, 11, 11, 11, 16, 16, 16, 16, 16 (23)

STAR CHAMBER

3-17-84 (CBS/Fox 1295) 25, 20, 15, 10, 11, 7, 10, 11, 10, 12, 16, 14, 15, 20, 17, 24, 26, 26, 26, 28, 29, 29, 28 (23)

STAR 80

4-21-84 (Warner 20013) 24, 12, 9, 9, 9, 8, 12, 13, 11, 14, 13, 18, 21, 23, 25, 27 (16)

STAR TREK III—THE SEARCH FOR SPOCK

3-23-85 (Paramount 1621) 11, 11, 1, 1, 2, 2, 3, 3, 2, 2, 16, 16, 26, 26, 24, 24, 33, 33 (18)

6-16-87 (RCA/Col.) 29, 25 (2)

STAR TREK II: THE WRATH OF KHAN

11-27-82 (Paramount 1180) 7, 1, 1, 1, 1, 1, 1, 1, 1, 3, 3, 6, 6, 11, 13, 12, 13, 11, 13, 14, 20, 20, 22, 26, 27, 30, 30, 30, 30 (28)

11-22-86 (Paramount 1180) 32, 29, 29, 29, 19, 16, 16, 16, 16, 9, 9, 6, 7, 8, 6, 9, 6, 10, 12, 17, 30, 25, 25, 20, 15, 18, 16 (27)

STAR WARS

6-12-82 (20th Century-Fox 1130) 1, 1, 1, 1, 1, 1, 1, 1, 1, 1, 1, 1, 1, 2, 4, 5, 4, 4, 5, 4, 3, 4, 11, 8, 8, 12, 16, 21, 18, 17, 17, 17, 16, 15, 14, 15, 18, 18, 18, 24, 25, 25, 30, 28, 29, 29, 27, 27, 29 (48)

4-11-87 (CBS/Fox 1130) 19, 17, 20, 21, 33, 34, 32, 40, 40 (9)

STARMAN

6-29-85 (RCA/Col. 20412) 37, 37, 11, 11, 2, 1, 2, 2, 1, 3, 2, 2, 2, 4, 4, 5, 12, 14, 14, 16, 31, 28, 27, 31, 36, 37, 39, 39, 39 (29)

STAYING ALIVE

2-25-84   (Paramount 1302)   11, 6, 6, 5, 5, 8, 8, 10, 12, 19, 18, 19, 21, 27,
26   (15)

STICK

8-31-85   (MCA 80139)   24, 19, 15, 11, 7, 5, 6, 10, 11, 19, 19, 27, 27, 34, 35,
39, 39   (17)

THE STILL OF THE NIGHT

6-04-83   (CBS/Fox 4711)   12, 12, 11, 12, 11, 16, 16, 16, 16, 15, 18, 19, 23,
27, 20, 23   (16)

STILL SMOKIN'

9-03-83   (Paramount 2315)   26, 25, 15, 16, 19, 20, 14, 22, 26   (9)

STING II

7-02-83   (MCA 71015)   19, 19, 14, 13, 15, 14, 15, 15, 22, 22, 22, 27, 26, 29,
28   (15)

STIR CRAZY

4-03-82   (Col. 10248E)   17, 20, 26, 26, 25, 22, 24, 30   (8)

STRANGE BREW

4-21-84   (MGM/UA 800322)   27, 30, 29, 26, 25, 30, 29   (7)

STRAWBERRY SHORTCAKE IN BIG APPLE CITY

3-05-83   (MGM/UA 00338)   30, 28, 28   (3)

STREETS OF FIRE

12-22-84   (MCA 80085)   20, 20, 20, 10, 10, 13, 13, 16, 16, 27, 27, 29,
29   (13)

STRIPES

5-08-82   (Col. 10600)   23, 7, 2, 1, 2, 3, 4, 4, 5, 3, 3, 4, 3, 7, 7, 9, 8, 14, 13, 16,
19, 20, 22, 27, 27, 27   (26)

STROKER ACE

11-05-83   (Warner 11322)   28, 13, 13, 12, 14, 14, 20, 30, 29, 29, 28, 29   (12)

SUDDEN IMPACT

4-21-84   (Warner 11341)   17, 6, 3, 1, 1, 1, 1, 1, 1, 2, 4, 5, 6, 7, 5, 8, 11, 12, 14,
17, 18, 19, 19, 24, 24, 27, 27   (27)

SUMMER LOVERS

1-22-83   (Embassy 1704)   24, 23, 23, 23, 30   (5)

SUMMER RENTAL

3-15-86   (Paramount 1785)   26, 22, 14, 10, 7, 6, 13, 17, 22, 22, 27, 30, 29, 28,
40   (15)

SUPERGIRL

5-04-85   (U.S.A. 217-515)   18, 18, 10, 10, 10, 10, 22, 22, 19, 19, 39, 39,
38   (13)

SUPERMAN II

4-10-82   (Warner 61120)   11, 1, 1, 2, 2, 2, 4, 5, 5, 7, 8, 12, 12, 10, 13, 10, 10,
9, 13, 16, 23, 27, 25, 28, 30, 27, 26, 25, 24, 23, 28   (31)

SUPERMAN III

12-24-83   (Warner 11320)   12, 7, 7, 7, 6, 6, 6, 6, 10, 12, 13, 16, 16, 21, 21, 22,
28   (17)

THE SURE THING

9-21-85   (Embassy 278)   34, 27, 16, 9, 5, 4, 4, 7, 12, 12, 14, 11, 15, 19, 19, 19,
19, 19, 19, 25, 29, 33, 40, 40   (24)

THE SURVIVORS

12-17-83   (RCA/Col. 10521)   16, 13, 11, 11, 11, 13, 13, 12, 12, 15, 18, 21, 19,
28, 28, 30   (16)

SWAMP THING

12-11-82   (Embassy 1605)   30, 28   (2)

SWEET DREAMS

5-10-86   (MCA 80172)   32, 16, 11, 9, 9, 8, 11, 15, 14, 18, 22, 27, 29, 30, 37, 39   (16)

SWING SHIFT

9-01-84   (Warner 11376)   23, 15, 11, 11, 12, 12, 16, 16, 20, 20, 28, 28, 30, 30   (14)

THE SWORD AND THE SORCERER

11-06-82   (MCA 71010)   17, 7, 6, 5, 6, 14, 16, 22, 22, 23, 24, 30   (12)

THE SWORD IN THE STONE

4-12-86   (Disney 229)   34, 24, 20, 16, 13, 26, 25, 24, 24, 30   (10)

TABLE FOR FIVE

9-24-83   (CBS/Fox 2043)   29, 21, 17, 13, 13, 13   (6)

TAI PAN

6-13-87   (DEG/Vestron 5180)   14, 16, 16, 16, 32, 32, 35, 35, 35, 35, 40, 40, 40, 40, 40   (15)

TANK

8-04-84   (MCA 80072)   14, 10, 9, 7, 11, 9, 10, 10, 7, 7, 12, 12, 16, 16, 17, 17, 24, 24, 28, 28, 30, 30, 30   (23)

TAPS

6-18-82   (20th Century-Fox 1128)   20, 13, 12, 11, 11, 11, 10, 13, 11, 15, 13, 11, 22, 22, 28, 30   (16)

TARGET

9-20-86   (CBS/Fox 1092)   34, 34, 20, 12, 7, 9, 5, 8, 19, 35, 40, 40, 40   (13)

TARZAN, THE APEMAN

4-03-82   (MGM/UA 00109)   14, 23, 18, 22, 23, 27, 25, 28   (8)

TATTOO

4-03-82   (20th Century-Fox 1123)   20   (1)

TAXI DRIVER

9-11-82   (Col. 10542)   28, 17, 12, 10, 8, 7, 6, 11, 15, 20, 24   (11)

TEACHERS

6-01-85   (CBS/Fox 4728)   18, 18, 9, 9, 4, 4, 12, 12, 16, 22, 26, 27, 28, 37   (14)

TEEN WOLF

2-22-86   (Paramount 2350)   25, 13, 7, 5, 5, 6, 12, 11, 11, 14, 18, 24, 30, 34, 38, 40, 39   (17)

10 TO MIDNIGHT

1-14-84   (MGM/UA 800 243)   23, 20, 16, 15, 16, 19, 27, 26, 27   (9)

TENDER MERCIES

10-15-83   (Thorn/EMI 1640)   19, 10, 10, 9, 15, 15, 15, 18, 18, 27, 25   (11)

THE TERMINATOR

5-04-85   (Thorn/EMI TVA 2535)   14, 14, 1, 1, 1, 1, 2, 2, 2, 2, 2, 2, 3, 3, 3, 4, 4, 4, 3, 6, 7, 10, 12, 14, 17, 20, 23, 26, 30, 33, 35, 35, 34, 34, 34, 34, 36, 39   (39)

TERMS OF ENDEARMENT

6-23-84   (Paramount 1407)   24, 7, 3, 1, 1, 1, 1, 1, 1, 2, 4, 4, 5, 5, 6, 6, 7, 7, 18, 18, 26, 26, 28, 28, 30, 30   (26)

TESTAMENT

6-09-84   (Paramount 1739)   26, 25, 23, 20, 21, 24, 30, 29   (8)

TEX

5-21-83 (Walt Disney 142) 26, 12, 13, 13, 14, 17, 17, 20, 24 (9)

TEXAS CHAINSAW MASSACRE

4-03-82 (Wizard 034) 15, 18, 27 (3)

THAT CHAMPIONSHIP SEASON

7-23-83 (MGM/UA 00221) 28, 20, 20, 20, 20, 26 (6)

THAT WAS THEN . . . THIS IS NOW

7-12-86 (Paramount 1954) 34, 29, 23, 25, 20, 20, 19, 22, 28, 27, 25, 25, 24,
37 (14)

THIEF OF HEARTS

5-18-85 (Paramount 1660) 19, 19, 11, 11, 8, 8, 8, 8, 17, 17, 17, 17, 20, 29,
31, 31, 30, 38 (16)

THE THING

11-27-82 (MCA 77009) 22, 15, 10, 4, 6, 6, 6, 9, 9, 11, 14, 17, 17, 23, 23, 26,
27, 27, 30, 30 (20)

THINGS ARE TOUGH ALL OVER

2-12-83 (RCA/Col. 10546) 26, 20, 19, 18, 23, 23, 29, 29 (8)

THIS IS SPINAL TAP

11-10-84 (Embassy 2081) 25, 25, 21, 21, 18, 18, 25, 25, 25, 27, 27, 27, 27,
29, 29 (15)

THUNDERBALL

6-04-83 (CBS/Fox 4611) 24, 22, 23, 25, 28, 29 (6)

TIGHTROPE

2-09-85 (Warner 11400) 8, 8, 1, 1, 1, 1, 3, 3, 5, 5, 9, 9, 19, 19, 24, 24, 30,
30, (2), 39, 39 (20)

TIME BANDITS

5-15-82 (Paramount 2310) 19, 10, 4, 3, 5, 7, 6, 6, 6, 9, 8, 9, 10, 24, 20, 19, 19, 21, 26, 29 (20)

TIMERIDER

6-04-83 (Pacific Arts PAVR 528) 23, 11, 10, 13, 13, 14, 17, 19, 19, 19, 17, 18, 19, 23, 24, 29 (16)

TO BE OR NOT TO BE

7-21-84 (CBS/Fox 1336) 22, 19, 18, 17, 21, 22, 24, 30, 30, 30 (10)

TO LIVE AND DIE IN L.A.

6-07-86 (Vestron 5123) 30, 17, 7, 5, 5, 5, 6, 6, 8, 9, 9, 10, 16, 20, 22, 24, 24, 25, 32, 36 (20)

TOOTSIE

2-11-84 (RCA/Col. 10535) 20, 11, 1, 1, 1, 1, 1, 1, 1, 1, 3, 5, 7, 6, 8, 12, 17, 18, 22, 22, 26, 28, 29, 29, 30, 30 (26)

TOP GUN

3-21-87 (Paramount 1692) 28, 1, 1, 1, 1, 1, 1, 1, 1, 1, 1, 1, 3, 11, 11, 11, 14, 14, 15, 15, 15, 15, 26, 26, 26, 26, 26 (17)

TOUGH GUYS

5-02-87 (Touchstone 6915) 28, 26, 38, 40, 9, 10, 14, 15, 15, 15, 23, 23, 25, 25, 25, 25, 32, 32, 32, 32, 32 (17)

THE TOY

6-18-83 (RCA/Col. 10538) 18, 3, 3, 4, 4, 4, 4, 5, 6, 7, 7, 8, 8, 11, 11, 12, 13, 12, 18, 29, 30 (21)

TRADING PLACES

3-24-84 (Paramount 1551) 23, 14, 6, 7, 4, 3, 1, 2, 3, 3, 3, 3, 4, 4, 10, 10, 12, 10, 14, 14, 19, 22, 22, 21, 26 (24)

TRANSYLVANIA 6-5000

   4-26-86   (New World 8515)   23, 19, 16, 20, 19, 20, 27, 32   (8)

TRENCHCOAT

   7-30-83   (Walt Disney 163)   26, 24, 22, 21   (4)

TROLL

   7-26-86   (Vestron VA 5121)   35, 30, 28, 26, 25, 29, 32, 35   (8)

TRON

   12-25-82   (Walt Disney 122)   9, 9, 9, 5, 4, 5, 11, 15, 14, 17, 17, 16, 15, 14, 18, 19, 18, 15, 14, 13, 19, 25, 26, 29   (24)

TROUBLE IN MIND

   9-20-86   (Charter 90109)   32, 32, 29, 38, 38   (5)

TRUE CONFESSIONS

   8-14-82   (MGM/UA 00145)   21, 14, 12, 9, 9, 9, 8, 7, 11, 15, 18, 25, 24, 30   (14)

TRUE STORIES

   5-30-87   (Warner 11654)   31, 33, (1), 37, 37, 37   (5)

TUFF TURF

   8-31-85   (New World 8501)   28, 24, 22, 20, 20, 19, 24, 28, 29, 31, 36   (11)

TURK 182

   9-21-85   (CBS/Fox 7082)   28, 24, 22, 19, 17, 15, 15, 18, 26, 32, 39, 40, 37, 36   (14)

TWICE IN A LIFETIME

   6-21-86   (Vestron VA 5119)   29, 19, 18, 16, 14, 16, 19, 24, 27, 28, 26, 25, 29, 36, 36, 39   (16)

TWILIGHT ZONE—THE MOVIE

12-24-83   (Warner 11314)   8, 5, 5, 5, 5, 5, 5, 5, 5, 7, 9, 10, 14, 17, 22, 25, 26   (17)

TWIST OF FATE

3-24-84   (MCA 80066)   26, 25, 27, 30   (4)

TWO OF A KIND

8-04-84   (CBS/Fox 1339)   20, 18, 18, 20, 22, 26, 25, 25   (8)

2010

6-29-85   (MGM/UA MB 800 591)   34, 34, 13, 13, 6, 4, 5, 10, 10, 16, 14, 12, 17, 19, 25, 29, 35, 36, 36, 39, 38, 38, 40   (23)

UNCOMMON VALOR

5-12-84   (Paramount 1657)   20, 13, 4, 2, 2, 2, 5, 6, 9, 8, 9, 10, 12, 13, 16, 15, 20, 24, 24, 24, 29, 29, 26, 26, 25, 25, 30, 30   (28)

UNDER FIRE

5-05-84   (Vestron 5033) —, —, —, 14, 13, 12, 8, 8, 9, 8, 9, 11, 13, 16, 19, 24, 27, 28, 29, 28, 28   (21)

UNFAITHFULLY YOURS

8-25-84   (CBS/Fox 1340)   17, 13, 8, 6, 6, 3, 3, 8, 8, 15, 15, 22, 22, 27, 27, 29, 29   (17)

UP THE ACADEMY

11-16-85   (Warner 11313)   30, 25, 24, 29   (4)

VACATION (See: NATIONAL LAMPOON'S VACATION)

VALLEY GIRL

10-01-83   (Vestron 5016)   25, 22, 22, 20, 20, 19, 28, 22   (8)

VERDICT

7-23-83 (CBS/Fox 1188)   8, 6, 2, 2, 2, 3, 3, 3, 3, 3, 4, 6, 6, 9, 14, 13, 20, 24, 22, 20, 20   (21)

VERTIGO

8-11-84 (MCA 80082)   16, 14, 11, 10, 11, 12, 12, 18, 18, 30, 30   (11)

VICE SQUAD

4-02-83 (Embassy 2002)   27, 25, 23, 24, 29   (5)

VICTOR VICTORIA

11-13-82 (MGM/UA 00151)   21, 10, 2, 2, 2, 2, 2, 2, 2, 7, 8, 8, 7, 12, 13, 15, 19, 18, 22, 20, 19, 18, 17, 16, 19, 18, 16, 19, 19, 20, 25   (31)

VICTORY

4-03-82 (MGM/CBS 600108)   26   (1)

VIDEODROME

5-28-83 (MCA 71013)   24, 22, 6, 8, 10, 15, 17, 19, 24, 29, 29, 29   (12)

A VIEW TO A KILL

12-28-85 (CBS/Fox 4730)   20, 20, 20, 9, 6, 7, 7, 9, 11, 14, 17, 27, 31, 33, 36, 38, 40   (17)

VISION QUEST

11-30-85 (Warner 11459)   25, 10, 7, 5, 5, 5, 5, 6, 10, 10, 14, 13, 21, 28, 33, 34, 36, 34, 37, 37   (20)

VOLUNTEERS

3-22-86 (Thorn/EMI/HBO TVA 2983)   21, 16, 11, 10, 9, 22, 26, 29, 33, 35, 39   (11)

THE WALL (See: PINK FLOYD . . .)

WANTED DEAD OR ALIVE

7-11-87   (New World 86230)   11, 11, 10, 10, 10, 10, 14, 14, 14, 14, 14   (11)

WAR GAMES

3-24-84   (CBS/Fox 4714)   13, 6, 5, 4, 5, 2, 2, 4, 4, 10, 6, 5, 7, 7, 11, 17, 16, 21, 23, 25, 28, 29   (22)

A WEEK WITH RAQUEL

5-02-87   (HBO TVA 9965)   35, 29, 32, 26   (4)

WEIRD SCIENCE

3-08-86   (MCA 80200)   20, 13, 7, 7, 7, 12, 12, 17, 22, 27, 27, 29, 32, 38, 38, 38, 38, 38, 37   (19)

WHITE CHRISTMAS

12-28-85   (Paramount 6104)   35, 35, 35, 35, 34   (5)

WHITE NIGHTS

7-23-86   (RCA/Col. 6061)   20, 21, 10, 7, 4, 4, 4, 5, 7, 7, 10, 21, 18, 22, 18, 35, 37   (17)

WHOSE LIFE IS IT ANYWAY?

6-26-82   (MGM/UA 00140)   25, 15, 14, 14, 14, 14, 19, 18, 26   (9)

WILDCATS

11-01-86   (Warner 11583)   30, 18, 11, 9, 9, 17, 17, 30, 32, 32, 32, 34, 34, 34   (15)

WILDLIFE

3-09-85   (MCA BTA 80145)   23, 23, 17, 17, 27, 27, 27, 27   (8)

WINDWALKER

10-29-83   (CBS/Fox 6345)   28, 27,   (2)

WISDOM

8-22-87   (Warner 37081)   23, 23, 23, 23, 23   (5)

WISE BOYS

3-07-87   (CBS-Fox 4739)   22, 19, 23, 25, 22, 34, 34, 35, 38   (9)

WISE GUYS

5-30-87   (CBS/Fox 4739)   35, 36, 37, 39, 39, 39   (6)

WITHOUT A TRACE

10-22-83   (CBS/Fox 1235)   21, 17, 17, 17, 29, 24   (6)

WITNESS

5-10-86   (Paramount 1736)   1, 1, 1, 1, 1, 3, 3, 4, 4, 5, 4, 7, 8, 8, 9, 10, 13, 16, 21, 21, 23, 20, 26, 25, 36   (26)

4-11-87   (Paramount 1736)   29, 27, 29, 27, 27, 36, 34   (7)

WOLFEN

4-17-82   (Warner 72019)   25, 24   (2)

WOMAN IN RED

2-23-85   (Orion 5055)   12, 12, 5, 5, 1, 1, 4, 4, 8, 8, 5, 5, 14, 14, 14, 14, 30, 30, 40, 40, 36, 36, 35   (23)

THE WORLD ACCORDING TO GARP

1-29-83   (Warner 11261)   24, 4, 3, 2, 3, 2, 2, 4, 5, 6, 7, 10, 10, 11, 8, 8, 8, 9, 14, 16, 16, 21   (22)

WRESTLEMANIA

9-07-85   (Coliseum WF 004)   36, 34, 37, 40   (4)

WRONG IS RIGHT

11-13-82   (Col. 10565)   29, 27, 25   (3)

THE YEAR OF LIVING DANGEROUSLY

10-15-83   (MGM/UA 00243)   16, 7, 7, 7, 6, 6, 6, 6, 6, 21, 28, 28, 28, 29, 28, 27, 29, 30   (18)

YEAR OF THE DRAGON

4-12-86   (MGM/UA 800713)   30, 14, 11, 10, 7, 7, 7, 12, 11, 20, 22, 25, 25, 24, 33, 32, 32, 36, 39   (19)

YENTL

1013084   (CBS/Fox 4724)   20, 20, 11, 10, 5, 5, 4, 4, 3, 3, 8, 8, 8, 14, 14, 16, 16, 27, 27   (19)

YES, GIORGIO

3-19-83   (MGM/UA 00192)   26, 25   (2)

YOU ONLY LIVE TWICE

9-10-83   (CBS/Fox 4526)   26, 22, 23, 26, 30   (5)

YOUNG DOCTORS IN LOVE

3-05-83   (Vestron 5012)   27, 24, 21, 18, 15, 14, 13, 13, 15, 14, 14, 20, 27   (13)

YOUNG SHERLOCK HOLMES

10-11-86   (Amblin/Paramount 1670)   30, 13, 11, 6, 3, 9, 19, 23, 25, 25, 31, 34, 34, 34, 34, 35, 35, 33, 29, 27, 38   (21)

YOUNGBLOOD

9-06-86   (MGM/UA 800966)   18, 13, 11, 11, 13, 16, 19, 17, 15, 23, 39   (11)

ZAPPED

1-22-83   (Embassy 1604)   27, 25, 21, 19, 22, 22, 26   (7)

ZELIG

4-28-84   (Warner 22027)   18, 17, 12, 15, 17, 15, 17, 27   (8)

ZORRO, THE GAY BLADE

5-01-82   (20th Century-Fox 1124)   28, 24, 30   (3)

C. APPENDIXES

[NUMER 1 VIDEOCASSETTES—A CHRONOLOGICAL LISTING]

1982

4-03		*Fort Apache, The Bronx* (1)
4-10		*An American Werewolf In London* (1)
4-17—	4-24	*Superman II* (2)
5-01—	5-22	*The French Lieutenant's Woman* (4)
5-29		*Stripes* (1)
6-05		*Arthur* (1)
6-12—	8-28	*Star Wars* (12)
9-04—	9-11	*On Golden Pond* (2)
9-18—	10-30	*Chariots Of Fire* (7)
11-06—	11-27	*Conan The Barbarian* (4)
12-04—	12-25	*Star Trek II* (4)

1983

1-01—	1-15	*Star Trek II* (3; 7)
1-22		*Rocky III* (1)
1-29—	2-19	*Poltergeist* (4)
2-26—	5-21	*An Officer And A Gentleman* (13)
5-28—	7-02	*First Blood* (6)
7-09—	8-27	*48 Hours* (8)
9-03—	9-24	*Porky's* (4)
10-01—	11-19	*Flashdance* (8)
11-26—	12-10	*Blue Thunder* (3)
12-17—	12-31	*Raiders Of The Lost·Ark* (3)

1984

1-07—	2-18	*Raiders Of The Lost Ark* (7; 10)
2-25—	4-14	*Tootsie* (8)
4-21—	4-28	*Never Say Never* (2)
5-05		*Trading Places* (1)
5-12—	6-16	*Sudden Impact* (6)
6-23—	7-07	*Scarface* (3)

7-14—	8-18	*Terms Of Endearment*	(6)
8-25		*The Right Stuff*	(1)
9-01—	10-06	*The Big Chill*	(6)
10-13—	12-29	*Romancing The Stone*	(12)

1985

1-05		*Romancing The Stone*	(1; 13)
1-12—	2-02	*The Empire Strikes Back*	(4)
2-09—	2-16	*Police Academy*	(2)
2-23—	3-16	*Tightrope*	(4)
3-23—	3-30	*Woman In Red*	(2)
4-06—	4-13	*Star Trek III—The Search For Spock*	(2)
4-20—	4-27	*Red Dawn*	(2)
5-04—	5-11	*Revenge Of The Nerds*	(2)
5-18—	6-08	*The Terminator*	(4)
6-15—	7-27	*The Karate Kid*	(7)
8-03		*Starman*	(1)
8-10—	8-17	*The Karate Kid*	(2; 9)
8-24		*Starman*	(1; 2)
8-31		*Falcon And The Snowman*	(1)
9-07—	9-21	*The Karate Kid*	(3; 12)
9-28—	10-05	*Desperately Seeking Susan*	(2)
10-12—	10-19	*The Killing Fields*	(2)
10-26—	11-16	*The Breakfast Club*	(4)
11-23		*Ghostbusters*	(1)
11-30—	12-07	*Beverly Hills Cop*	(2)
12-14		*Ghostbusters*	(1; 2)
12-21—	12-28	*Beverly Hills Cop*	(2; 4)

1986

1-04—	2-01	*Beverly Hills Cop*	(5; 9)
2-08—	2-15	*Pale Rider*	(2)
2-22—	3-29	*Rambo: First Blood, Part II*	(6)
4-05—	5-03	*Return Of The Jedi*	(5)
5-10		*Commando*	(1)
5-17—	6-14	*Witness*	(5)
6-21—	8-23	*Back To The Future*	(10)
8-30—	9-06	*The Jewel Of The Nile*	(2)
9-13		*Back To The Future*	(1; 11)
9-20—	9-27	*Spies Like Us*	(2)
10-04—	10-11	*Iron Eagle*	(2)
10-18		*Murphy's Romance*	(1)
10-25—	11-22	*Out Of Africa*	(5)
11-29—	12-27	*Indiana Jones And The Temple Of Doom*	(5)

1987

1-03—	2-07	*Indiana Jones And The Temple Of Doom*	(6; 11)
2-14		*Jane Fonda's Low Impact Workout*	(1)
2-21		*Indiana Jones And The Temple Of Doom*	(1; 12)
2-28—	3-07	*Jane Fonda's Low Impact Workout*	(2; 3)
3-14—	3-21	*Running Scared*	(2)
3-28—	6-06	*Top Gun*	(11)
6-13		*Peggy Sue Got Married*	(1)
6-20—	7-04	*Ferris Bueller's Day Off*	(3)
7-11—	8-15	*Children Of A Lesser God*	(6)
8-22—	9-19	*The Color Purple*	(5)

[VIDEOCASSETTES WITH LONGEST RUN ON CHARTS]

1. *Jane Fonda's Workout*.....102
2. *Beverly Hills Cop*.....61
3. *Star Wars*.....57
4. *Star Trek II: The Wrath Of Khan*.....55
5. *Amadeus*.....52

D. RENTAL VIDEOCASSETTES—TITLE INDEX

ADVENTURES IN BABYSITTING

5-14-88   (Touchstone 595)   6, 6, 3, 3, 3, 2   (6)

AMAZON WOMEN OF THE MOON

4-23-88   (MCA 80684)   26, 27   (2)

ANGEL HEART

3-05-88   (IVE 60460)   26, 23, 27, 27, 29   (5)

BABY BOOM

6-11-88   (CBS/Fox 4744)   14, 6   (2)

BACK TO THE BEACH

3-05-88   (Paramount)   15, 17, 25   (3)

THE BELIEVERS

3-05-88   (HBO 0034)   16, 21, 23, 23, 20, 23, 26, 27, 28   (9)

BEVERLY HILLS COP II

4-02-88   (Paramount 1860)   17, 5, 1, 1, 1, 2, 2, 5, 6, 7, 8, 10   (12)

THE BIG EASY

3-19-88   (HBO 0052)   12, 9, 5, 7, 7, 8, 8, 9, 12, 12, 21, 19, 22, 20   (14)

BLIND DATE

3-05-88   (RCA/Col. 6-20822)   23, 30   (2)

BORN IN EAST L.A.

6-04-88   (MCA 80727)   18, 15, 15   (3)

THE BUDDY HOLLY STORY

3-05-88   (RCA/Col. 6-2080)   19, 24, 28, 30   (4)

CAN'T BUY ME LOVE

6-18-88   (Touchstone 597)   13   (1)

DATE WITH AN ANGEL

5-28-88   (HBO 0060)   29, 21, 29   (3)

DEATH WISH 4: THE CRACKDOWN

5-14-88   (Media M 941)   28, 24, 18, 24, 24, 23   (6)

DIRTY DANCING

3-05-88   (Vestron 6013)   1, 1, 2, 3, 1, 1, 2, 4, 4, 4, 7, 7, 9, 10, 10, 11   (16)

DISORDERLIES

3-12-88   (Warner 11752)   15, 14, 21, 26, 27   (5)

DRAGNET

3-05-88   (MCA 45030)   9, 11, 9, 11, 12, 11, 13, 18, 18, 25, 30   (11)

EXTREME PREJUDICE

3-05-88   (IVE 62178)   18, 28   (2)

FLOWERS IN THE ATTIC

5-14-88   (New World 85160)   29, 15, 14, 16, 19, 18   (6)

THE FOURTH PROTOCOL

3-05-88   (Lorimar 320)   14, 16, 20, 22, 23, 25, 30   (7)

GARDEN OF STONE

3-05-88   (CBS/Fox 3731-80)   29   (1)

HAMBURGER HILL

4-02-88   (Vestron 6015)   9, 9, 9, 11, 11, 12, 19, 19, 25, 30   (10)

HARRY AND THE HENDERSONS

3-05-88   (MCA 80677)   17, 22, 16, 17, 22, 29   (6)

HELLRAISER

4-16-88   (New World A 87007)   25, 24, 25, 16, 14   (5)

THE HIDDEN

5-07-88   (Media M 940)   15, 10, 17, 16, 20, 30   (6)

HIDING OUT

6-11-88   (HBO 0042)   20, 24   (2)

HOLLYWOOD SHUFFLE

3-05-88   (Virgin Vision 70032)   20, 27, 29, 29, (3), 28, 29   (6)

HOOSIERS

3-12-88   (HBO 0041)   22, 25, 30   (3)

IN THE MOOD

3-05-88   (Lorimar 475)   24, 19, 26, 26   (4)

INNERSPACE

5-07-88   (Warner 11754)   10, 4, 3, 5, 6, 5, 7   (7)

JAWS; THE REVENGE

3-05-88   (MCA 80723)   30, 20, 19, 18, 18, 21, 22, 21, 21   (9)

LA BAMBA

3-05-88   (RCA/Col. 6-20854)   6, 4, 5, 5, 10, 12, 12, 16, 16, 17, 22, 30   (12)

LADY AND THE TRAMP

3-05-88   (Walt Disney 582)   28, 29   (2)

LADY BEWARE

3-05-88   (IVE 63753)   21   (1)

LESS THAN ZERO

5-14-88   (CBS/Fox 1649)   21, 10, 8, 8, 11, 14   (6)

LETHAL WEAPON

3-05-88   (Warner 11709)   12, 10, 10, 10, 11, 15, 18, 17, 17, 20, 25   (11)

THE LIVING DAYLIGHTS

4-16-88   (CBS/Fox 4745)   14, 7, 7, 6, 5, 8, 10, 12, 16, 21   (10)

LOST BOYS

   3-26-88   (Warner 11748)   14, 7, 4, 4, 2, 2, 5, 8, 9, 11, 11, 18, 19   (13)

MADE IN HEAVEN

   5-07-88   (Lorimar 423)   21, 15, 18, 23, 26   (5)

MAID TO ORDER

   4-09-88   (IVE 64311)   18, 15, 13, 13, 13, 13, 20, 22, 27   (9)

MASTERS OF THE UNIVERSE

   3-05-88   (Warner 37073)   27   (1)

THE MONSTER SQUAD

   3-12-88   (Vestron 6014)   18, 24, 24, 27, 26, 29   (6)

MY LIFE AS A DOG

   5-21-88   (Paramount 12651)   26, 19, 25, 26, 29   (5)

NADINE

   3-19-88   (CBS/Fox 3841)   15, 12, 15, 16, 20, 20, 20, 27   (8)

NO MAN'S LAND

   5-07-88   (Orion 8710)   22, 18, 21, 24, 28, 23, 28   (7)

NO WAY OUT

   3-05-88   (HBO 0051)   5, 8, 8, 4, 4, 6, 5, 6, 6, 7, 11, 11, 12, 13, 13, 16   (16)

OUTRAGEOUS FORTUNE

   3-05-88   (Touchstone 569)   10, 12, 13, 15, 24, 24, 27, 29, 30   (9)

THE PICK-UP ARTIST

   5-21-88   (CBS/Fox 1529)   22, 13, 9, 12, 12   (5)

PLATOON

3-05-88　(HBO 0040)　2, 2, 1, 1, 3, 3, 6, 9, 9, 11, 17, 16, 17, 23　(14)

A PRAYER BEFORE DYING

3-26-88　(Samuel Goldwyn/Virgin Vision 70050)　28, 21, 20, 23, 22, 23, 23　(7)

PREDATOR

3-05-88　(CBS/Fox 1526)　3, 6, 6, 6, 6, 8, 8, 10, 10, 18, 20, 25, 27　(13)

THE PRINCESS BRIDE

4-30-88　(Nelson 7709)　22, 3, 3, 2, 7, 5, 4, 5　(8)

RAISING ARIZONA

3-05-88　(CBS/Fox 5191)　25, 26, 21, 20, 25, 28　(6)

REAL MEN

6-18-88　(CBS/Fox 4743)　25　(1)

REVENGE OF THE NERDS II: NERDS IN PARADISE

3-19-88　(CBS/Fox 1514)　17, 16, 14, 13, 16, 14, 14, 28　(8)

ROBOCOP

3-05-88　(Orion 8610)　4, 3, 3, 2, 2, 2, 3, 5, 5, 8, 9, 14, 15, 15, 17, 27　(16)

THE ROSARY MURDERS

5-07-88　(Virgin Vision 70064)　26, 24, 27, 30, 22　(5)

ROXANNE

3-05-88　(RCA/Col. 6-20853)　7, 7, 7, 8, 13, 14, 17, 15, 15, 29　(10)

THE RUNNING MAN

6-11-88　(Vestron 6021)　9, 4　(2)

RUSSKIES

5-21-88   (Lorimar 761)   29, 26, 29, 21, 26   (5)

THE SECRET OF MY SUCCESS

3-05-88   (MCA 80637)   8, 9, 11, 13, 16, 19, 21, 23, 24   (9)

THE SICILIAN

5-14-88   (Vestron 6024)   27, 13, 20, 17, 28, 30   (6)

SLAM DANCE

4-16-88   (Key 3856)   24, 25, 26, 24, 26   (5)

SOMEONE TO WATCH OVER ME

6-04-88   (RCA/Col. 6-20877)   14, 7, 9   (3)

SPACEBALLS

3-12-88   (MGM/UA 90179)   5, 4, 7, 8, 10, 11, 12, 12, 14, 23, 28, 28   (12)

THE SQUEEZE

4-02-88   (HBO 0053)   28, 17, 19, 19, 19, 30   (6)

STAKEOUT

4-16-88   (Touchstone 599)   10, 3, 3, 1, 1, 1, 2, 4, 6, 8   (10)

STEEL DAWN

6-11-88   (Vestron 6017)   25, 22   (2)

SUMMER SCHOOL

3-05-88   (Paramount 1518)   11, 13, 18, 19, 19, 22, 28, 30   (8)

SURRENDER

5-07-88   (Warner 37077)   19, 16, 23   (3)

TIN MEN

3-05-88   (Touchstone 571)   13, 14, 22, 25, 30, 30   (6)

THE UNTOUCHABLES

5-21-88   (Paramount 1886)   4, 1, 2, 2, 3   (5)

WEEDS

6-11-88   (HBO 0062)   27, 17   (2)

THE WITCHES OF EASTWICK

5-28-88   (Warner 11741)   4, 1, 1, 1   (4)

E. APPENDIX: NUMBER 1 RENTAL
VIDEOCASSETTES—A CHRONOLOGICAL LISTING

1988

3-05—	3-12	*Dirty Dancing*	(2)
3-19—	3-26	*Platoon*	(2)
4-02—	4-09	*Dirty Dancing*	(2; 4)
4-16—	4-30	*Beverly Hills Cop II*	(3)
5-07—	5-21	*Stakeout*	(3)
5-28		*The Untouchables*	(1)
6-04—	6-18	*The Witches Of Eastwick*	(3)

F. RETAIL VIDEOCASSETTES—TITLE INDEX

ADVENTURES IN BABYSITTING

5-14-88   (Touchstone 595)   17, 15, 19, 24, 30   (5)

ALICE IN WONDERLAND

3-19-88   (Walt Disney 36)   24, 22, 24, 20, 18, 17, 18, 30, 30   (9)

AN AMERICAN TAIL

   3-05-88   (MCA 80536)   4, 3, 4, 6, 4, 7, 9, 10, 10, 6, 7, 8, 12, 18, 8, 11   (16)

ANIMAL HOUSE

   5-21-88   (MCA 66000)   17, 13, 7, 15, 22   (5)

BABY BOOM

   6-11-88   (CBS/Fox 36)   27, 28   (2)

BEVERLY HILLS COP

   4-16-88   (Paramount 1134)   10, 9, 9, 8, 9, 14, 14, 15, 16, 18   (10)

BEVERLY HILLS COP II

   4-09-88   (Paramount 1860)   6, 5, 6, 6, 10, 12, 21, 27, 29   (9)

BORN IN EAST L.A.

   6-04-88   (MCA 80727)   28   (1)

CALLANETICS

   3-05-88   (MCA)   9, 5, 3, 3, 3, 3, 3, 3, 3, 3, 3, 4, 2, 1, 2, 4   (16)

CHINA GIRL

   4-23-88   (Vestron 5238)   29, 29   (2)

CROCODILE DUNDEE

   3-05-88   (Paramount 32029)   21, 14, 20, 19, 21, 28   (6)

THE CURE IN ORANGE

   4-09-88   (Elektra 40107-3)   13, 16, 14, 14, 14, 20   (6)

DEATH WISH 4: THE CRACKDOWN

   5-07-88   (Media M 941)   17, 10, 12, 15, 27   (5)

DIRTY DANCING

3-05-88   (Vestron 6013)   3, 9, 6, 4, 5, 10, 11, 11, 11, 11, 11, 11, 16, 14, 22, 23   (16)

DORF ON GOLF

3-05-88   (J2 Communications J2-0009)   22, 29, 26, 24, 27, 29   (6)

DRAGNET

3-05-88   (MCA 45030)   27, 28, 30   (3)

ELVIS '56

3-26-88   (Media M 470)   18, 10, 16, 22, 22, 23, 23, 27   (8)

FLOWERS IN THE ATTIC

5-07-88   (New World 85160)   27, 18, 22, 30   (4)

FONDA, JANE (See: JANE FONDA'S LOW IMPACT AEROBIC WORKOUT; JANE FONDA'S NEW WORKOUT; START UP WITH JANE FONDA)

THE GODFATHER

3-05-88   (Paramount 8049)   7, 12, 7, 10, 14, 12, 12, 18, 19, 18, 16, 27, 21, 17, 17, 25   (16)

THE GRATEFUL DEAD SO FAR

3-05-88   (6 West SW-5701)   28, 19, 23, 20, 18, 24, 24, 24, 25, 28   (10)

HAMBURGER HILL

4-02-88   (Vestron 6015)   29, 22, 23, 20, 21, 29   (6)

INDIANA JONES AND THE TEMPLE OF DOOM

6-18-88   (Paramount 60040-64)   21   (1)

JANE FONDA'S LOW IMPACT AEROBIC WORKOUT

     3-05-88   (Lorimar 070)   2, 2, 2, 2, 2, 2, 4, 4, 4, 4, 5, 5, 7, 4, 4, 2   (16)

JANE FONDA'S NEW WORKOUT

     3-05-88   (Lorimar 069)   5, 4, 5, 5, 6, 5, 6, 5, 5, 5, 4, 2, 3, 5, 7, 6   (16)

KATHY SMITH'S BODY BASICS

     3-05-88   (JCI 8111)   15, 26, 19, 12, 19, 14, 20, 16, 16, 15, 28   (11)

KATHY SMITH'S STARTING WORKOUT

     3-05-88   (JCI 8103)   8, 7, 11, 15, 26, 26, 28, 30, (3), 23, 20, 19, 19, 17   (13)

KATHY SMITH'S ULTIMATE VIDEO WORKOUT

     3-05-88   (JCI 8100)   29,   (10), 19, 18, 16, 21, 13   (6)

KATHY SMITH'S WINNING WORKOUT

     3-05-88   (Fox Hills FH 1012)   19, 23, 29,   (7), 15, 20, 26, 26, 13, 15   (9)

LA BAMBA

     3-05-88   (RCA/Col. 6-20854)   11, 20, 28   (3)

LADY AND THE TRAMP

     3-05-88   (Walt Disney 582)   1, 1, 1, 1, 1, 1, 1, 1, 1, 1, 2, 3, 4, 2, 3, 3   (16)

LESS THAN ZERO

     5-21-88   (CBS/Fox 1649)   28, 25, 20, 25, 26   (5)

LOST BOYS

     3-26-88   (WB 11748)   29, 25, 30   (3)

MARY POPPINS

     3-05-88   (Walt Disney 23)   17, 15, 15, 14, 17, 21, 29, 27, 28, 25, 23, 29, 29, 30, 29, 29   (16)

THE MONSTER SQUAD

3-12-88 (Tri-Star/Vestron 6014) 25, 29 (2)

NO WAY OUT

3-26-88 (HBO 0051) 27, 22 (2)

ONE VOICE

3-26-88 (CBS/Fox 5150) 26m30 (2)

PINK FLOYD'S THE WALL

3-05-88 (MGM/UA 400268) 12, 10, 14, 9, 9, 8, 8, 8, 8, 7, 6, 7, 6, 8, 10, 9 (16)

PINOCCHIO

3-05-88 (Walt Disney) 23, 27, 25, 30 (4)

PLATOON

3-05-88 (HBO 0040) 13, 13, 10, 11, 13, 25, 26, 28, 30, 36, 29 (11)

PLAYBOY 1988 PLAYMATE VIDEO CALENDAR

3-05-88 (Lorimar 524) 25, 18, 22, 23, 28, 23, 30 (7)

PLAYBOY'S 1988 PLAYMATE OF THE YEAR

6-11-88 (HBO 0078) 28, 12 (2)

PREDATOR

3-05-88 (CBS/Fox 1526) 20, 22, 21, 28 (4)

PRINCE (See: SIGN "O" THE TIMES)

THE PRINCESS BRIDE

4-30-88 (Nelson 7709) 17, 16, 21, 26, 28 (5)

RAIDERS OF THE LOST ARK

3-05-88   (Paramount 1376)   26, 30   (2)

ROBOCOP

3-05-88   (Orion 8610)   6, 6, 9, 8, 12, 17, 21, 21, 22, 21, 24, 24, 22, 21, 24, 30   (16)

SCARFACE

3-05-88   (MCA 80047)   24, 17, 18, 21, 23, 19, 25, 23, 24, 22, 22, 18, 23, 22, 26, 27   (16)

SIGN "O" THE TIMES

6-04-88   (MCA 80797)   12, 9, 7,   (3)

SLEEPING BEAUTY

3-05-88   (Walt Disney 476)   14, 16, 16, 16, 15, 18, 19, 19, 20, 12, 13, 9, 9, 11, 20, 20   (16)

SMITH, KATHY (*See: KATHY SMITH'S BODY BASICS; KATHY SMITH'S STARTING WORKOUT; KATHY SMITH'S ULTIMATE VIDEO WORKOUT; KATHY SMITH'S WINNING WORKOUT*)

THE SOUND OF MUSIC

3-05-88   (CBS/Fox 1051)   18, 11, 13, 13, 16, 11, 15, 12, 12, 13, 14, 13, 11, 9, 17, 19   (16)

STAKEOUT

4-16-88   (Touchstone 599)   13, 15, 15, 19, 25, 30   (6)

STAR TREK IV—THE VOYAGE HOME

3-05-88   (Paramount 1797)   10, 8, 8, 7, 8, 9, 7, 7, 7, 9, 8, 10, 10, 10, 5, 5   (16)

START UP WITH JANE FONDA

4-02-88   (Lorimar 077)   7, 4, 2, 2, 2, 2, 1, 1, 1, 3, 1, 1   (12)

SUPER BOWL XXII; NFL CHAMPIONS WASHINGTON REDSKINS

4-16-88   (Fox Hills)   14, 25, 26   (3)

TOP GUN

3-05-88   (Paramount 1629)   16, 24, 12, 25, 20, 27, 27, 26, 27, 24, 26, 25, 24, 23, 11, 8   (16)

THE UNTOUCHABLES

5-21-88   (Paramount 1886)   6, 5, 6, 6, 10   (5)

THE WALL (See: **PINK FLOYD . . .**)

THE WITCHES OF EASTWICK

5-28-88   (Warner 11741)   8, 13, 12, 16   (4)

THE WIZARD OF OZ

3-05-88   (MGM/UA 60001)   30, 21, 17, 17, 11, 15, 17, 13, 13, 20, 19, 16, 17, 25, 23, 24   (16)

WRESTLEMANIA IV

6-11-88   (JCI 8110)   18, 14   (2)

G. APPENDIX: NUMBER 1 RETAIL VIDEOCASSETTES—A CHRONOLOGICAL LISTING

1988

3-05— 5-07   *Lady And The Tramp*   (10)
5-14— 5-28   *Start Up With Jane Fonda*   (3)
6-04   *Callanetics*   (1)
6-11— 6-18   *Start Up With Jane Fonda*   (2; 5)

ABOUT THE AUTHORS

FRANK W. HOFFMANN (B.A., M.L.S., Indiana University; Ph.D., University of Pittsburgh) is Associate Professor of Library Science at Sam Houston State University and has taught at the Graduate Library School of Louisiana State University. He has been a library practitioner at close to a dozen public, academic, and special libraries. He currently serves on the Board of Trustees for the Montgomery County (Texas) Library System and as a Voting Representative for the Houston Area Libraries System. In addition to serving on many national and regional professional committees, he regularly evaluates federal grant applications, speaks to libraries and educational groups on various popular culture topics, and edits a quarterly academic journal, *Popular Culture in Libraries* (Haworth Press). He has published numerous articles (including five entries in the recently published *Encyclopedia of Recorded Sound,* Garland Press) and approximately 20 books, most notably the multivolume sets, *The Encyclopedia of Fads,* the *Cash Box* chart series (Scarecrow Press) and the *Literature of Rock* series (Scarecrow Press).

GEORGE ALBERT has become a legendary figure in the music business. A songwriter in the heyday of Tin Pan Alley, he writes a syndicated newspaper column and is founder and president of *Cash Box,* whose scope and distribution are international.